Worshipp

Scholar, author, former editor and minister, Arun Shourie is one of the most prominent voices in our country's public life and discourse.

By the same author:

We Must Have No Price
Are We Deceiving Ourselves Again?
Where Will All This Take Us?
The Parliamentary System
Falling Over Backwards
Will the Iron Fence Save a Tree Hollowed by Termites?
Governance, and the Sclerosis That Has Set In
Courts and Their Judgments
Harvesting Our Souls
Eminent Historians
The World of Fatwas
Missionaries in India
A Secular Agenda
Indian Controversies
'The Only Fatherland'
The State as Charade
These Lethal, Inexorable Laws
Individuals, Institutions, Processes
Religion in Politics
Mrs. Gandhi's Second Reign
Institutions in the Janata Phase
Symptoms of Fascism
Hinduism: Essence and Consequence
Does He know a mother's heart?: How Suffering Refutes Religion

Worshipping False Gods

Ambedkar, and the facts which have been erased

ARUN SHOURIE

HarperCollins *Publishers* India

First published by ASA Publications in 1997

This edition published in India in 2012 by
HarperCollins *Publishers* India

P-ISBN: 978-93-5029-343-0
E-ISBN: 978-93-5029-539-7

6 8 10 9 7

HarperCollins *Publishers*
A-75, Sector 57, Noida, Uttar Pradesh 201301, India
1 London Bridge Street, London, SE1 9GF, United Kingdom
Hazelton Lanes, 55 Avenue Road, Suite 2900, Toronto, Ontario M5R 3L2
and 1995 Markham Road, Scarborough, Ontario M1B 5M8, Canada
25 Ryde Road, Pymble, Sydney, NSW 2073, Australia
195 Broadway, New York, NY 10007, USA

Typeset in Palatino Linotype 11/14
InoSoft Systems Noida

Printed and bound in India by
Replika Press Pvt. Ltd.

For those few
who speak the truth
to the people also…

Contents

Introduction

A nation forges deities in its imaginings, in its sacred literature, in wood and stone. The forms it gives them, the forces it has them embody, the virtues with which it endows them reflect the accumulated experience of the nation, the insights of its seers; they answer to its needs. When the nation is overpowered physically, when it is vanquished spiritually and intellectually, it is made to shift, and per force it actually shifts those representations from public places and cabines them within private dwellings. Next, within those dwellings it herds them into almirahs. Soon enough it is made to feel ashamed of, and it actually becomes ashamed of those deities and representations. Eventually it repudiates its own gods, its own tradition, its own history and experience, and starts worshipping the gods of the conquerors.

This sequence was in full swing in northern India by the fourteenth–fifteenth century, and would have proceeded to completion had the country not been saved by the bhakti movement. By the late nineteenth century again the process was gathering momentum—the Christian missionaries, Macaulay were all set to succeed. The country was rescued from drowning by Swami Dayananda, Ramakrishna Paramahamsa, Swami Vivekananda, by Sri Aurobindo, by Narayan Guru, by Bankim Chandra Chatterjee and a handful of others. They reminded us of our heritage, they restored our faith in our traditions, our gods and goddesses, in our forms of worship, in a word in ourselves. They showed us that far from being ashamed of our past, our nation and country had gleaned and then, in spite of the vicissitudes of centuries, preserved for the world the pearl of great price.

The net result of the last fifty years is that once again in India today that same sequence is afoot. The Lokmanya is as good as forgotten. Few outside Kerala know of Narayan Guru. Apart from a narrow circle of devotees no one remembers what Swami Dayananda, Ramakrishna Paramahamsa, Sri Aurobindo, Ramana Maharshi, the Paramacharya at Kanchi did to stand us on our feet. Swami Vivekananda is dusted up and taken out on occasion—dressed up exactly as the secularist he would have berated. Gandhiji is in the dock every day—one day for having been a throwback, the next for having pushed the Muslim leaders into insisting on Pakistan. And persons like Ambedkar are deified.

Indeed, no one is idolized these days the way he is. His statue is one of the largest in the Parliament complex. His portrait in the Central Hall of Parliament is larger than life. The Bharat Ratna has been conferred on him posthumously, a national holiday has been decreed in his honour. Postage stamps have been issued in his honour. Universities have been named after him. His statues—dressed in garish blue, holding a copy of the Constitution—have been put up in city after city: it is a fair guess that by now they far outnumber those of Gandhiji. Politicians, activists and other notables flock to these on several anniversaries of his—on the anniversary of his birth, on the anniversary of the day on which he converted to Buddhism, on the anniversary of his *parinirvana,* the term which must compulsorily be used now for his death. He is hailed as the one who gave us the Constitution we now have—the fourteen volumes of his speeches and writings which have been published in his honour officially by the Government of Maharashtra include the *Draft Constitution* among his writings. He is hailed as the one who strove to lift the lower castes, indeed the dispossessed in general. Not just that, while Gandhiji and other Congress leaders—provided of course that they were Hindus, at least by birth—are held to have been responsible for the Partition of the country, because of the propaganda surrounding his name Ambedkar is assumed to have been, and shown to have been one of the fighters for the country's freedom—in the television spots which were put out by government to mark the fiftieth anniversary of the country's Independence, Ambedkar's photograph has been shown between those of Bhagat Singh and Subhash Chandra Bose!

Several factors account for this inversion. During the last fifty years the history of the country's struggle for freedom has been reduced to a few paragraphs in high school textbooks. Indeed, nationalism has been made a dirty word. Moreover, with less and less to commend themselves, politicians have lunged for casteist politics—and so they have made icons of persons like Ambedkar.

But in addition there is a factor for which our intellectuals are directly responsible. Discourse today consists of 'slogan-cum-stampede'. Some slogan is floated—*Garibi Hatao* one day, 'Social Justice' the next. No one goes into the details of it. Instead, there is a stampede in its wake. In the case of persons like Ambedkar and their deification there is in addition verbal terrorism, and, increasingly, actual, physical assault: once the slogan has been put out, and the stampede with it as the banner has begun, anyone who draws attention to the facts, even to the things which the man himself said and did, things which he flaunted, that person, as I can testify from personal experience, is set upon.

Soon what started as the convenience of some politician becomes myth, and myth becomes fact. And the country adopts as its deities the very ones who had striven for decades and decades with its enemies to keep it in subjugation.

Disorientation, and from that disarray, and thence disintegration are the certain outcome.

The Freedom Fighter

1

The freedom fighter

Ambedkar's public life begins in a sense from a public meeting held at the Damodar Hall in Bombay on 9 March 1924. The struggle for freeing the country from the British was by then in full swing. Swami Vivekananda's work, Sri Aurobindo's work, the Lokmanya's work had already stirred the country. Lokmanya Tilak had passed away in 1920. The leadership of the national movement had fallen to Gandhiji. He had already led the country in the Champaran satyagraha, the Khilafat movement, in the satyagraha against the Rowlatt Act, against the killings in Jallianwala Bagh and the merciless repression in Punjab. This national movement culminated in the country's Independence in 1947. In a word, a quarter-century of Ambedkar's public career overlapped with this struggle of the country to free itself from British rule. There is not one instance, not one single, solitary instance in which Ambedkar participated in any activity connected with that struggle to free the country. Quite the contrary—at every possible turn he opposed the campaigns of the national movement, at every setback to the movement he was among those cheering the failure.

Thus, while the years culminated in the country's Independence, in Ambedkar's case they culminated in his becoming a member of the Viceroy's Council, that is—to use the current terms—a minister in the British Cabinet in India.

The writings of Ambedkar follow the same pattern. The Maharashtra government has by now published fourteen volumes of the speeches and writings of Ambedkar. These cover 9,996 pages. Volumes up to the twelfth contain his speeches and writings up to 1946. These extend to 7,371 pages. You would be hard put to find one article, one speech, one passage in which Ambedkar can be seen even by inference to be arguing for India's Independence. Quite the contrary.

Pause for a minute and read the following:

> Allow me to say that the British have a moral responsibility towards the Scheduled Castes. They may have moral responsibilities towards all minorities. But it can never transcend the moral responsibility which rests on them in respect of the Untouchables. It is a pity how few Britishers are aware of it and how fewer are prepared to discharge it. British Rule in India owes its very existence to the help rendered by the Untouchables. Many Britishers think that India was conquered by the Clives, Hastings, Cootes and so on. Nothing can be a greater mistake. India was conquered by an army of Indians and the Indians who formed the army were all Untouchables. British Rule in India would have been impossible if the Untouchables had not helped the British to conquer India. Take the Battle of Plassey which laid the beginning of British Rule or the battle of Kirkee which completed the conquest *of* India. In both these fateful battles the soldiers who fought for the British were all Untouchables...

Who is pleading thus to whom? It is B.R. Ambedkar writing on 14 May 1946 to a member of the (British) Cabinet Mission, A.V. Alexander.[1]

Nor was this a one-off slip, an argument crafted just for the occasion. Indeed, so long as the British were ruling over India, far from trying to hide such views, Ambedkar would

---

1 The letter is reproduced in *Dr. Babasaheb Ambedkar, Writings and Speeches,* Vol. X, pp. 492–99. Unless otherwise indicated, wherever words appear in italics, they have been italicized by me, A.S., as have explanatory words enclosed in square parenthesis.

lose no opportunity to advertise them, and to advertise what he had been doing to ensure that they came to prevail in practice. Among the faithful, his book *What Congress and Gandhi Have Done to the Untouchables* is among the most admired and emulated of his writings. It was published in 1945, that is, just two years or so before India became independent. As we shall see when we turn to Ambedkar's views on how Harijans may be raised, it is an out and out regurgitation of the things that the British rulers and the missionaries wanted to be said, of the allegations and worse that they had been hurling at our civilization and people. The book has been published officially by the Department of Education, Government of Maharashtra, and is sold at a subsidized price! It constitutes Volume IX of the set *Dr. Babasaheb Ambedkar, Writings and Speeches.* It reproduces the speech Ambedkar made at the Round Table Conference—a speech which served the designs of the British rulers to the dot, and for which, as we shall soon see, they were ever so grateful to Ambedkar, for it became one of the principal devices for thwarting Gandhiji. In the speech Ambedkar addresses the prime minister and says, 'Prime Minister, permit me to make one thing clear. *The Depressed Classes are not anxious, they are not clamorous, they have not started any movement for claiming that there shall he an immediate transfer of power from the British to the Indian people... Their position, to put it plainly, is that we are not anxious for transfer of political power...'* But if the British were no longer strong enough to resist the forces which were clamouring for such transfer, Ambedkar declared, then his demand was that they make certain arrangements—arrangements which we shall encounter repeatedly in his speeches and writings—the essential point about which was to tie clown the new government of independent India.[2]

---

2 *Dr. Babasaheb Ambedkar, Writings and Speeches,* Vol. IX, pp. 63–67.

Ambedkar and his patrons were dealt a humiliating blow by the elections of 1937. There were a total of 1,585 seats in the eleven Assemblies in 'British India'. Of these 777 were 'tied'—in the sense that they were to be filled by communal or special representation from chambers of commerce, plantations, labour, etc. Of the 808 'general' seats, the Congress, which Ambedkar, Jinnah and others denounced from the housetops, won 456. It secured absolute majorities in five Assemblies—those of Madras, the United Provinces, the Central Provinces, Bihar and Orissa. And it was the largest single party in four others—Bombay, Bengal, Assam and the NWFP. From the point of view of Ambedkar and the British—who had been holding him up to counter the Congress claim that it represented the Harijans as much as any other section of Indian society—worse was the fact that the Congress did extremely well in the seats which had been reserved for Harijans. Thirty seats were reserved for Harijans in Madras Presidency, the Congress contested twenty-six and won twenty-six. In Bihar, there were twenty-four reserved seats—in nine of these Congress candidates were returned unopposed; of the remaining fifteen reserved seats, it contested fourteen, and won fourteen. In Bombay, of the fifteen reserved seats, it secured one unopposed, contested eight and won five. In the United Provinces, there were twenty reserved seats; two of its candidates were returned unopposed; it contested seventeen seats and won sixteen. In Bengal, of the thirty reserved seats, it contested seventeen and won six. In the Central Provinces, of the nineteen reserved seats, it contested nine and won five.[3]

The lesson was there for all to see. Reporting to the viceroy on the results in the Bombay Presidency, the governor, Lord Brabourne, wrote, 'Dr. Ambedkar's boast of winning, not only the 15 seats which are reserved for

3 Mitra's *Annual Register, 1937*, Vol. I, pp. 168a–p.

the Harijans, but also a good many more—looks like being completely falsified, as I feared it would be.'[4]

The electorate, including the Harijans may have punctured his claims but there was always the possibility of reviving one's fortunes through politicking and manoeuvres. Efforts of all these elements were focused on the objective of installing non-Congress ministries in Bombay and wherever else this was a possibility. Brabourne reported to the viceroy that Jamnadas Mehta, the finance minister 'who is Chief Minister in all but name', was telling him that the ministry in Bombay would survive motions on the budget and may even get through the motion of no confidence: 'His calculations are based on the fact that he expects to get the support of the bulk of the Muhammadans, the whole of Ambedkar's Scheduled Castes Party, and of half a dozen or so of those individuals who stood as Congressmen merely to get elected,' he reported. But added, 'I gather that he is in touch with Ambedkar, who is carrying on negotiations for him, but, as you will find from the next succeeding paragraph, it rather looks to me as if Ambedkar is playing a thoroughly double game, in which case Jamnadas Mehta's hopes are likely to be rudely shattered.'

The governor went on to report that he had also had a long conversation with Jinnah, and that Jinnah had told him that, in the event of the ministry being defeated, the Muslim League would be prepared to form a ministry provided they could secure a majority of even two or three in the Assembly. 'He [that is, Jinnah] went on to say that Ambedkar and his party were prepared to back him in this,' Brabourne reported, 'and that he expected to get the support of ten or a dozen of the so-called Congress M.L.As. mentioned above. He made it quite clear to me that they

---

4 L/P.O./6/99Q in *Towards Freedom, 1937–47*, Vol. I, *Experiments with provincial autonomy, 1 January 1937 to 31 December 1937*, P.N. Chopra (ed.), Indian Council of Historical Research, New Delhi, 1985, pp. 123–25.

would not support the present Ministry.' The governor was sceptical about the claims and assurances of all of them. He wrote, 'It is, of course, quite impossible to rely on anything that Jinnah tells me, and the only thing for me to do is to listen and keep silent. I obviously cannot tell Jamnadas Mehta what Jinnah told me, or *vice versa,* as both of them are hopelessly indiscreet. The only thing that is clear is that a vast amount of intrigue is going on behind the scenes, but, in the long run, I cannot see anything coming out of it at all, as none of these people trust each other round the corner. Were I to hazard a guess, it would still be that the present Ministry will be defeated on the budget proposals and the alternative will then lie between Congress or Section 93'—the equivalent of our present-day governor's rule.[5]

Congress ministries were formed. And in 1939 they resigned in view of the British government's refusal to state what it intended to do about Indian Independence after the war. Jinnah announced that the Muslim League would celebrate the resignations as 'Deliverance Day'. Guess who was at his side in these 'celebrations', addressing meetings from the same platforms? Ambedkar, of course.

Nationalist leaders were neither surprised that Ambedkar was on the platforms with Jinnah, nor had they any doubts about the inspiration behind these celebrations. Addressing the Congress Legislature Party in Bombay on 27 December 1939, Sadar Patel noted, 'We cannot forget how Sir Samuel Hoare set the Muslims against the Hindus when the unity conference was held at Allahabad. The British statesmen in order to win the sympathy of the world, now go on repeating that they are willing to give freedom to India, were India

---

5 Brabourne to Linlithgow, 5 June 1937, in *Towards Freedom, 1937–47,* Vol. I, *Experiments with provincial autonomy, 1 January 1937 to 31 December 1937,* P.N. Chopra (ed.), Indian Council of Historical Research, New Delhi, 1985, pp. 623–26.

united. The "Day of Deliverance" was evidentlycalculated to make the world and particularly the British public believe that India was not united and that the Hindus and Muslims were against each other. But when several sections of Muslims were found to oppose the "Day of Deliverance", the proposed anti-Hindu demonstrations were converted into a Jinnah-Ambedkar-Byramji protest against the Congress Ministries and the Congress High Command....'[6]

That rout in the election remained a thorn in the heart of Ambedkar for long. A large part of *What Congress and Gandhi Have Done to the Untouchables* which Ambedkar published in 1945 is a tortuous effort to explain that actually the Congress had not done well in the election, that in fact, while groups such as his which had opposed Congress had been mauled even in reserved constituencies, they had triumphed, and the Congress, in spite of the seats having gone to it, had actually been dealt a drubbing! Though this is his central thesis, Ambedkar gives reasons upon reasons to explain why he and his kind have lost and why the Congress has won! One of the reasons he says is that the people in general believe that the Congress is fighting for the freedom of the country. This fight for freedom, Ambedkar says, 'has been carried on mostly by Hindus'. It is only once that the Mussalmans took part in it and that was during the short-lived Khilafat agitation. They soon got out of it, he says. The other communities, particularly the Untouchables, never took part in it. A few stray individuals may have joined it—and they did so, Ambedkar declares, for personal gain. But the community as such has stood out. This is particularly noticeable in the last campaign of the 'Fight For Freedom', which followed the 'Quit India' resolution passed by the Congress in August 1942, Ambedkar says. And this too has not been just an oversight;

---

6 *The Collected Works of Sardar Patel,* Vol. VIII, P.N. Chopra (ed.), Konark, New Delhi, 1996, pp. 194–97.

in Ambedkar's reckoning it was a considered boycott. The Untouchables have stayed out of the freedom movement for good and strong reasons, he says again and again.

The freedom struggle, in his words

For one thing the movement is unnecessary, for another it is a sham, a hoax to fool the people of India.

The movement which Gandhi is leading is unjustified, it is unnecessary, Ambedkar declares, for the simple reason that the British do not want to stay, they do not want to rule India in any case, indeed they are anxious to leave. They are being compelled to stay by the fact that Indians are not able to come to an agreement among themselves about the form that the new country, the new constitution should take.

It is true, he allows, that in the mid-nineteenth century the then British rulers did want to rule India. But since then the character and objectives of British rule have changed completely, Ambedkar certifies. 'There was a time when the British Government held the view which was a complete negation of India's claim for freedom. It was proclaimed by Lawrence whose statue in Calcutta has the motto, "The British conquered India by the sword and they will hold it by the sword." This attitude is dead and buried and it is no exaggeration to say that every Englishman today is ashamed of it,' Ambedkar writes. Do recall these certificates when we deal with the views of the British viceroy and prime minister of whose administration Ambedkar was a part at the time this book was published. 'This stage was followed by another,' Ambedkar acknowledges, 'in which the argument of the British Government against India's freedom was the alleged incapacity of Indians for Parliamentary institutions... We have now entered the third or the present stage. British Government is now ashamed to say that they will hold India by the sword. It no longer says that Indians have no capacity to run Parliamentary institutions. The British Government admits India's right to freedom, even to independence, if Indians so desire. The British Government admits the right of Indians to frame their own constitution. There can be no greater proof of this new angle of vision than the Cripps Proposals. The condition precedent laid down by the British Government for India's freedom is that Indians must produce a constitution which has the concurrence of the important elements in the national life of the country. Such is the stage we have reached. The Untouchables cannot therefore understand why the Congress instead of trying to achieve agreement among Indians, should keep on talking in terms of a "Fight for Freedom" and maligning the Untouchables in not joining it.'[7]

The so-called fight for freedom is nothing but a 'dishonest agitation', Ambedkar declares, and it is therefore no wonder that the Untouchables, by which, as we shall see, he always meant himself and his band of associates, have refused to take part in it.[8] The British have been continuously transferring power to Indians, Ambedkar declares, and 'If from 1939 there has been a halt, it is mainly because Indians are not agreed on the sort of constitution they want for their country.'[9] 'India's Freedom,' Ambedkar declares, 'is like property held by a Receiver. The British Government has placed itself in the position of a Receiver. As soon as the dispute is over and the right kind of constitution is settled, it has bound itself to hand over the property to its rightful owners, namely, Indians...'[10] Exactly, but exactly the British line, in fact more

---

7 *Dr. Babasaheb Ambedkar, Writings and Speeches,* Vol. IX, p. 177.

8 *Dr. Babasaheb Ambedkar, Writings and Speeches,* Vol. IX, p. 178.

9 *Dr. Babasaheb Ambedkar, Writings and Speeches,* Vol. IX, p. 179.

10 *Dr. Babasaheb Ambedkar, Writings and Speeches,* Vol. IX, pp. 179-80.

than just their line: for even the British were not as fulsome in giving themselves certificates in such terms. But then such passages surprise us today only because we do not remember where Ambedkar was when the book was written and published in 1945.

Congress talk of nationalism is nothing but a ruse, it is just a device to fool the people, Ambedkar proclaims. And for good reason do the Congress and Gandhi keep harping on 'nationalism', he declares. 'To put it briefly the governing class [and by that Ambedkar did not mean the British but, as we shall see, an altogether different group] is aware that a political campaign based on class ideology, class interests, class issues and class conflicts will toll its death knell. It knows that the most effective way of side-tracking the servile classes and fooling them is to play upon the sentiment of nationalism and national unity, and realizes that the Congress platform is the only platform that can effectively safeguard the interests of the governing class. For if there is any platform from which all talk of conflict between rich and poor, Brahmin and Non-Brahmin, landlord and tenant, creditor and debtor which does not suit the governing class, can be effectually banned it is the Congress platform which is not only bound to preach nationalism and national unity which is what the governing classes want and on which their safety entirely depends, but which prohibits any other ideology inconsistent with nationalism being preached from its platform.'[11] If we are surprised at the fact that all this sounds so much like the stuff which the communists were spewing forth to denounce Gandhiji at the time—the time when they had come to a secret understanding with the British to sabotage the 'Quit India' movement—that is so only because we do not today

---

11 *Dr. Babasaheb Ambedkar, Writings and Speeches,* Vol. IX, pp. 233–34.

remember that each of the two was the friend of a friend. Though there was a slight difference, a sort of formal one: while the communists were supporting the British only from the outside, to use the current phrase, Ambedkar was doing much more.

And it cannot be otherwise, Ambedkar insists, to the great approval of the British. 'The Hindu Communal Majority is the backbone of the Congress,' he proclaims. 'It [the Congress] is made up of the Hindus and is fed by the Hindus. It is this majority which constitutes the clientele of the Congress and the Congress, therefore, is bound to protect the rights of its clients.'[12] The Congress 'is deceiving the world by using nationalism as a cloak for a free field for rank communalism'.[13] Congress and Gandhi are not fighting for the freedom of the people of the country, they are just fighting to get the ruling classes whom they represent and embody the freedom to enslave the classes they have kept servile all these centuries, Ambedkar insists in the chapter entitled, 'Let Not Tyranny Have Freedom to Enslave'. 'Society', 'Nation', 'Country', are just words, Ambedkar declares—exactly what the Christian Missionaries had been preaching to Indians for a hundred years. They are just 'amorphous, ambiguous terms', he declares. Freedom to be real must be thought of in terms of the classes which constitute the reality behind these terms, in particular the servile classes, he maintains. Gandhi and the Congress are not fighting for the freedom of these classes, they are merely trying to secure freedom for the governing classes to perpetuate their tyranny.

Even if the Congress wants to change its objectives, which of course it does not in any way plan to do, it will not

---

12 *Dr. Babasaheb Ambedkar, Writings and Speeches,* Vol. IX, p. 172.

13 *Dr. Babasaheb Ambedkar, Writings and Speeches,* Vol. IX, p. 172.

be able to do so, Ambedkar pronounces, for the governing classes in whose grip it is and whose instrument and agent it is, will not let it do so.

And who constitute these 'governing classes'? The Brahmin and the Bania, declares Ambedkar. As for the former, 'There is a real gulf between him and the lower classes of Shudras and Untouchables. He is not only alien to them, he is hostile to them. In relationship with them, there is no room for conscience and there is no call for justice,' Ambedkar declares, and draws a picture of Brahmins as a group that demands and extracts, among other privileges, the right to sleep with the wives of others. As for the second constituent of the 'governing classes', 'The Bania,' declares Ambedkar, 'is the worst parasitic class known to history. In him the vice of money-making is unredeemed by culture or conscience. He is like an undertaker who prospers when there is an epidemic. The only difference between the undertaker and the Bania is that the undertaker does not create an epidemic while the Bania does... With no conscience, there is no fraud, and no chicanery that he will not commit. His grip over the nation is complete. The whole of poor, starving, illiterate India is mortgaged to the Bania.'

'To sum up,' Ambedkar concludes, 'the Brahmin enslaves the mind and the Bania enslaves the body. Between them they divide the spoils which belong to the governing classes. Can anyone who realizes what the outlook, tradition and social philosophy of the governing class in India is believe that under the Congress regime, a sovereign and independent India will be different from the India we have today?'[14] Where can there be the question then of any right-thinking man joining this 'Fight for Freedom' which Gandhi and his Congress are waging? That is Ambedkar's argument.

---

14 *Dr. Babasaheb Ambedkar, Writings and Speeches,* Vol. IX, pp. 216–17.

Nor is it just a question of political domination, Ambedkar contends. With the Hindu, the one who is the be-all-and-end-all of the Congress and of this so-called 'Fight for Freedom', keeping the servile classes suppressed is a matter of faith, it is of the very essence of his religion. By this doctrine and religion the Hindu has discarded all conscience. Even if by some miracle he is led to do the ethical thing, the Hindu will never give up Untouchability because for him it is 'a gold mine'—the economic and social advantages it confers are so great that the Hindu, Ambedkar asserts, the one who controls the Congress and through that this so-called 'Fight for Freedom', the one on whose behalf Gandhi labours to fool and 'kill with kindness' the Untouchables, will never, but never give up this particular evil.[15]

'In the light of what has been said,' Ambedkar declares in a typical passage of conclusions, 'it will be found that the Fight for Freedom led by the governing class is, from the point of view of the servile classes, a selfish, if not a sham, struggle. The freedom which the governing class in India is struggling for is freedom to rule the servile classes. What it wants is the freedom for the master race to rule the subject race which is nothing but the Nazi or Nietchian [sic.] doctrine of freedom for the superman to rule the common man.'[16]

Writing as he is when Nazism is at its height and the West is engaged in a mighty war against it, Ambedkar takes great care to characterize the Indian social system as being nothing but another version of the Nazism of Hitler with which the West had perforce become familiar, and of characterizing those who were fighting for freedom from the British as those who were fighting for the perpetuation

---

15 For instance, *Dr. Babasaheb Ambedkar, Writings and Speeches,* Vol. IX, pp. 192–97.

16 *Dr. Babasaheb Ambedkar, Writings and Speeches,* Vol. IX, p. 231.

of this brand of Nazism at home. In the companion volume written specially for the American audience, *Mr. Gandhi and the Emancipation of the Untouchables,* Ambedkar writes, 'What my fear is that the problem of the Untouchables may be forgotten as it has been so far. That would indeed be a calamity. For the ills which the Untouchables are suffering, if they are not as much advertised as those of the Jews, are not less real. Nor are the means and methods of suppression used by the Hindus against the Untouchables less effective because they are less bloody than the ways which the Nazis have adopted against the Jews. The Anti-Semitism of the Nazis against the Jews is in no way different in ideology and in effect from the Sanatanism of the Hindus against the Untouchables...'[17]

Writing about the foreigners who he maintained had been misled by Congress propaganda into supporting the demands of this so-called fight for freedom, Ambedkar says that 'It is a pity that they do not seem to distinguish the case of the tyrant who is held down and who pleads for liberty because he wants to regain his right to oppress and the case of an oppressed class seeking to be free from the oppression of the tyrant. In their hurry to bring freedom to India they have no time to realize that by siding with the Congress what they are doing is not to make India safe for democracy but to free the tyrant to practice his tyrannies. Is it necessary to tell them that to support the Congress is to let tyranny have freedom to enslave?'[18]

It is because the Untouchables see this truth that they are not and have never been part of this sham 'Fight for Freedom', Ambedkar claims. The reason they have not joined this sham 'Fight', Ambedkar maintains, 'is not because they

---

17 *Dr. Babasaheb Ambedkar, Writings and Speeches,* Vol. IX, pp. 397–98.

18 *Dr. Babasaheb Ambedkar, Writings and Speeches,* Vol. IX, p. 238.

are the tools of British Imperialism but because they fear that freedom of India will establish Hindu domination which is sure to close to them and forever all prospect of life, liberty and pursuit of happiness and that they will be made the hewers of wood and drawers of water.'[19] And they have from the beginning been the loyal supporters of and the beneficiaries of British rule in India, he says. 'Until the advent of the British, the Untouchables were content to remain Untouchables,' Ambedkar writes. 'It was a destiny pre-ordained by the Hindu God and enforced by the Hindu State. As such there was no escape from it. Fortunately or unfortunately, the East India Company needed soldiers for their army in India and it could find none but the Untouchables. The East India Company's army consisted, at any rate in the early part of its history, of the Untouchables and although the Untouchables are now included among the non-martial classes and are therefore excluded from the Army, it is with the help of an army composed of Untouchables that the British conquered India....' The Untouchables too gained, he adds: among the things that were done to the recruits was to give them education. This awakened them both to their condition, and to the fact that there was no justification for it...[20]

Notice first that were this claptrap to be written by anyone today—unless, of course, he is a champion of 'Social Justice'—he would be hauled up and prosecuted, for not only is it full of conjured up falsehood about groups and classes, it is nothing but incitement and is calculated to sow enmity between groups. But as it has been written by Ambedkar, and Ambedkar has been anointed the Redeemer,

---

19 *Dr. Babasaheb Ambedkar, Writings and Speeches,* Vol. IX, p. 168.

20 *Dr. Babasaheb Ambedkar, Writings and Speeches,* Vol. IX, p. 189.

it is sold all over the country at a subsidized price. Second, were these assertions actually rationalizations for what Ambedkar was himself doing at this time, or were they genuinely representative of the opinion of the depressed classes? Notice also that there was no obfuscation at that time: Ambedkar repeatedly and explicitly declares that neither he nor the Untouchables on whose behalf he always claims the sole authority to speak have or have ever had anything to do with the freedom struggle. His whole effort is to manufacture reasons to justify opposing that movement and for the pejoratives which he has continually hurled at Gandhiji for twenty years. Far from trying to hide his working for and with the British, those days Ambedkar used to recall these 'facts' at every opportunity to convince the British of his loyalty and his continuing usefulness. To take one example from a completely different context, on 5 April 1946 Ambedkar called on the cabinet delegation and the new viceroy, Field Marshal Viscount Wavell. Wavell recorded a *'Secret'* memorandum about the discussion. Here too Ambedkar urged his case in the same words: 'The Scheduled Castes had been the earliest source of man-power for the East India Company's army, and so it was with their help that the British had conquered India,' the viceroy recorded Ambedkar as arguing. 'They had been the friends of the British ever since. Yet the British had never consciously and deliberately helped them, though since 1892 they had given enormous help to the Muslims.'

'He (Ambedkar) thought that if India became independent it would be one of the greatest disasters that could happen,' Wavell recorded. 'Before they left, the British must ensure that the new Constitution guaranteed to the Scheduled Castes the elementary human rights of life, liberty and the pursuit of happiness, and that it restored their separate electorates and gave them

the other safeguards which they demanded. At present disillusionment was driving his followers towards terrorism and Communism. He was on trial with them for the efficacy of constitutional methods....'

He had no faith in Indians being able to ensure justice, Ambedkar told the delegation and the viceroy—those in the proposed Constituent Assembly who did not belong to the Scheduled Castes were determined to do them in, he maintained, and the members of the Assembly who did belong to the Scheduled Castes 'would be bought over to vote against the interests of their communities'.

Therefore, recorded Wavell, 'Dr. Ambedkar said he did not want a Constituent Assembly at all.' Instead he wanted the tasks which were being thought of for the Constituent Assembly to be divided into two classes of questions. The first set were constitutional questions properly so-called—relations between the executive and the legislature, composition and functions of the executive, etc. 'To deal with them was beyond the mental capacity of the type of men whom Provincial Assemblies might be expected to send up, and was a job for experts,' Ambedkar told the viceroy. Accordingly, Ambedkar said, such questions 'should be referred to a Commission presided over by an eminent constitutional lawyer from Great Britain or the U.S.A. The other members should be two Indian experts and one representative each of the Hindu and Muslim communities...'

The second set of questions, according to Ambedkar, were 'communal questions', that is the rights of and safeguards for 'communities'. In regard to these also Ambedkar wanted the ultimate say to be that of the British. These questions 'should be referred to a conference of the leaders of the different communities', he maintained. 'If the conference failed to arrive at an agreed solution, His Majesty's Government would have to make an award. This would no doubt be accepted if it were reasonable.....'[21]

These being articles of faith with him, at every juncture Ambedkar was arrayed on the side opposed to the national struggle for freedom—on the side of the British at the Round Table Conference, on the side of Jinnah in celebrating the 'deliverance' of the country from the Congress.

A typical instance

The Congress had done well in the 1937 elections. As a result along with its allies it controlled governments in nine of the eleven provinces. But much had happened in thirty months.

The Congress ministries had continued. Jinnah had launched his fusillade of calumnies and concoctions: allegations of 'atrocities' were the order of the day, 'evidence' was fabricated—the notorious Pirpur Report was the final result. The British were alert to the danger that a consolidation of Congress rule would spell for them. They had been casting around for allies, and gauging the issues on which each could be ignited. On 31 January 1939, in a secret communication the viceroy, Lord Linlithgow, apprised the Secretary of State, Lord Zetland, of one enthusiastic supporter in Bombay Presidency who looked promising:

> I had a talk with Ambedkar whom I found very interesting. He appears to be emerging as a sort of rival, though at the present stage of not too important a type, to the Congress ministry and told me bluntly that he believed they would lose the next election and that he would be in. Lumley tells me that he thinks Ambedkar is, in fact, beginning to emerge to a degree which his ministry find slightly embarrassing, and [E.G.] Kher [prime minister of Bombay] has, it appears, instructed the police to keep a very close watch on

---

21 *Transfer of Power,* Vol. VII, pp. 142–47.

> his speeches, which have been of a somewhat violent character. With me he was cynical and amusing, and I should have said, realist. On the [Princely] States side, he did not conceal that he was in no way concerned with that problem, save to the extent that it directly reacted on his own, and that if it suited his own politics, the obligations of the Crown Representative to the States would carry very little weight with him. He is perhaps a little of a swashbuckler, but I should have said he was of good quality, and would be a useful colleague if he could be harnessed. Incidentally, he vouchsafed the view that Congress will suffer a sharp setback in the elections for the Bombay municipality which are due to take place about February 7. Ministers, on the other hand, assured me that Congress will for the first time achieve an independent majority in the Council, or at least go very near *to* securing a majority. By the time you read this we will know who has been right in their estimate.[22]

The situation in Europe too descended precipitously. By August 1939 England was at the abyss of a full-scale war.

Gandhiji met the viceroy within the week. He told the viceroy that the Congress was with Britain in this struggle, and that personally he was for extending unconditional support to Britain. The Congress Working Committee declared its opposition to fascism, its support for the ideals for which the Allies had declared they were fighting. It said that to enable India to participate fully in the war effort Britain should declare what it intended to do about India's constitutional future once the war was over. The British ignored the Congress and unilaterally committed India to the war.

The viceroy, Lord Linlithgow, addressed the Central Legislative Assembly in Simla on 11 September 1939. Much was expected. Many hoped that he would announce Britain's war aims, among them a commitment to apply to India the principles for which Britain was saying it was fighting Hitler. He said nothing of the kind. Quite the

---

22 MSS.EUR.F/125/7, p. 48.

contrary. He read out a message from the King Emperor. In it the king said that 'the widespread attachment of India to the cause in which we have taken arms has been a source of deep satisfaction to me. I also value most highly the many and generous offers of assistance made to me by the Princes and people of India.' The king said that he was confident that 'we can count on the sympathy and support from every quarter of the Indian continent' in the struggle. 'Britain is fighting for no selfish ends,' he declared, 'but for the maintenance of a principle vital to the future of mankind—the principle that relations between civilised states must be regulated not by force but by reason and law so that men live free from terror of war, to pursue happiness and well-being which should be the destiny of mankind.' 'The message is signed by His Majesty's own hand,' the viceroy told the House.

In a word, the government already had the assurances of support it needed. And while the principle for which the war was being waged was that relations between civilized states must not be regulated by force but by reason and law, the manner in which India was being held did not fall within the ambit of that principle. The viceroy announced that further efforts to implement the federation part of the 1935 Act were being suspended for the time being.

The Secretary of State for India, Lord Zetland sprinkled salt on the wound. Speaking in the House of Lords on 26 September 1939 he said that while it was natural for the Congress to demand that Britain declare what it intended to do about India after the war, he could not but say that they had chosen the wrong moment to urge this demand. 'I think the British people are very susceptible to a treatment which they regard as honourable and appropriate to a particular occasion,' Zetland told the Lords. 'I think that they will be very much more willing, when the time comes, to listen to the claims made to them than if they are animated by a spirit of resentment at the choosing of such an occasion for taking action which may be calculated to be embarrassing to them in a life and death struggle.' This of course was true to form—in the reckoning of the rulers it never is the right time to make such demands: when things are quiet there is no reason to make the demand for everyone seems at peace with the way things are; when difficulties arise it isn't right to ask for such things for it can only put people's back up; and making such demands at such a time is morally wrong to boot for it amounts to taking advantage of the bind in which the other has been put.

The Secretary of State knew what the Congress was contemplating, that it was moving towards asking its ministries in the provinces to resign. He said—we shall soon have occasion to recall the words when we see the allegations which Jinnah and Ambedkar were soon to put out—'I am sorry for a further reason [about the step the Congress ministries are contemplating]. I agree... that it was a tremendous advantage to India that there are now a tremendous number of ardent Indian nationalists who have had the advantage of experience in the actual work of administration. It will be a calamity if such men, at this time, were to withdraw from Government in the Provinces. They have shown that they are capable of dealing with problems which face them in their country and they have co-operated in an admirable spirit with the Governors with whom they have been associated. I have nothing but praise for the manner in which up to now they have co-operated in carrying through measures which have been necessitated by the outbreak of the War....' Having lauded the work the ministries had done, he turned on the party to which they belonged, and insinuated that the Congress did not represent the country, that it was actually just a Hindu body.

Gandhiji, Pandit Nehru and others reacted sharply. Congress ministries moved resolutions in the provincial Assemblies urging the British government to declare its aims for the war and the subsequent peace. The resolutions were duly passed. Gandhiji and the other leaders went over for meetings with the viceroy.

The viceroy and the governors were meeting potential counters to the Congress also. On 7 October 1939, as the crisis hurtled towards a break the viceroy gave the Secretary of State an account of his meeting with Ambedkar. There was a convergence of views, to put it at the minimum. The viceroy wrote:

> He [Ambedkar] and I had seen something of one another in 1934–35; but he had had time to think since then, and the general conclusion which he had in the result reached was that the parliamentary system would not do in India. I asked him whether he would say that in public, to which he replied that he would be perfectly ready to do so, with the utmost emphasis. *He was 100 per cent opposed to self-government at the Centre and would resist it in any possible way.* As to self-government at the Centre he favoured a consultative group but he was strongly opposed to an All Parties meeting on the ground that there would be no hope whatever of our being able to do business at one, owing to the dissensions that would arise. He was equally opposed to an expanded Executive Council which he thought would never work together and he begged that no responsibility should be given at the Centre but that whatever organizations we might devise should be consultative in character only.[23]

On 17 October the viceroy issued an exceptionally long statement. War aims could not be spelled out at this stage, he declared. They could not after all be the aims of just one of the Allies. Moreover, the war was at too early a stage and it was not possible to contemplate what changes might

23 MSS.EUR.F/125/8, pp. 168–69.

follow in its wake. All that could be said for the time being, the viceroy declared, was that 'we are fighting to resist aggression whether directed against ourselves or others.' The Viceroy said that beyond this nothing could, indeed nothing need be said.

He too was full of praise for the way the scheme of governance established under the Government of India Act of 1935, and under which the Congress ministries had been constituted, had been working. 'For nearly two and a half years now the Provinces have been conducting their own affairs under the scheme of the Act,' the Viceroy said. 'That they have done so, on the whole, with great success, even if now and then difficulties have arisen, no one can question. Whatever the political party in power in those Provinces, all can look with satisfaction on a distinguished record of public achievement during the last two and a half years.'

The viceroy slammed the door on all proposals for constitutional advance. He declared that the scheme of the 1935 Act had been working well, that the experience of the preceding thirty months demonstrated that the scheme was 'essentially sound'. All that could be said was that 'when the time comes to resume consideration of the plan for the future Federal Government of India'—after the war, naturally—government would enter into consultations to assess 'the extent to which the details of the Act of 1935 remain appropriate'.

Whereas nationalist opinion had been demanding that the future constitution be settled by a Constituent Assembly consisting of Indians, the procedure that the viceroy specified was the one procedure which had served the British so well for decades and decades—the procedure which had enabled them to decide who would have a say, the procedure which by giving equal weight to the ones they chose to listen to gave the groups and persons they picked a veto, the procedure which induced leaders to insist on what they could use to differentiate themselves rather than to see how these edges could be harmonized. The viceroy declared, 'And I am authorised by His Majesty's Government now to say that at the end of the War they will be very willing to enter into consultation with representatives of the several communities, parties and interests in India, and with the Indian Princes, with a view to securing their aid and co-operation in the framing of such modifications as may seem desirable.'

Not just that, the process of consultation was to have a special feature, one that had proved its worth all these years to the rulers. Representatives of minorities who had met him, the viceroy said, had expressed the apprehension that they might not get an adequate hearing in the process of consultations. 'On that I need say no more than that over more than a decade at the Round Table Conferences, and at the Joint Select Committee, His Majesty's Government consulted with and had the assistance or advice of representatives of all parties and all interests in this country,' the viceroy said. 'It is unthinkable that we should now proceed to plan afresh or to modify in any respect any important part of India's future constitution without again taking counsel with those who have in the recent past been so closely associated in a like task with His Majesty's Government and with Parliament.'

In a word, all that would be aimed at would be to review whether the details of the Government of India Act of 1935 needed to be revised. This would be done by consultations with those the government thought ought to be consulted; and the spokesmen of 'minorities' would have in effect a veto on the outcome.

The viceroy said that he was of course aware that certain quarters in the country desired 'some even more extensive scheme than I have mentioned, some even more widely phrased indication of the intentions of His Majesty's Government'. For these quarters, that is for the Congress leaders he had nothing but a snub. Given the state of world politics and of political realities in India itself, the viceroy said, given the fact of differences over constitutional questions among the parties and interests here 'there is nothing to be gained by phrases which widely and generally expressed, contemplate a state of things which is unlikely to stand at the present point of political development the test of practical application, or to result in that unified effort by all parties and all communities in India on the basis of which alone India can hope to go forward as one and to occupy the place to which her history and destiny entitle her...'

As a sop the viceroy announced that he was going to set up 'a consultative group, representative of all major political parties in British India and of the Indian Princes, over which the Governor General would himself preside, which would be summoned at his invitation, and which would have as its object the association of public opinion in India with the conduct of the War and with questions relating to War activities'. In other words, a group which would have nothing to do with constitutional issues, a group the object of which would be solely to mobilize public opinion for the policies of the British government for the war whose aims in regard to India the government was not prepared to spell, a group that would meet only as and when the viceroy thought it should, a transient group whose status would be only consultative.

The next day the Secretary of State, Lord Zetland, made a statement in the House of Lords which not only reiterated these features of the proposed group but also specified that from among the members of the consultative group the viceroy would invite those persons 'to attend particular meetings at which, according to the business to be taken into consideration, their presence was desirable'.

As for the future, Lord Zetland held out no greater hope for the nationalists. He said that of course the British government continued to be committed to seeing India evolve towards the status of a Dominion in the Empire. He reiterated that experience had shown the scheme of the 1935 Act to be sound, 'but if, at the end of the upheaval caused by the War, when the circumstances may well differ from what they are today, there is a desire on the part of those concerned for modifications of particular features of the plan, then His Majesty's Government declare now that they will in such circumstances be very willing to enter into consultation with representatives of the several communities, parties and interests in India and with Indian Princes with a view to securing their aid and co-operation in the framing of such modifications as may then seem desirable.' Thus, once again: only modifications in the scheme by which India was being governed as a colony; and for that not a Constituent Assembly but 'consultations' with such persons as the British decided ought to have a say.

As the viceroy had done, Zetland also commended the decision to set up a 'consultative group'. That sort of a group would not only help mobilize public opinion for the war effort, the Secretary of State said, it would have a salutary educational effect also. By bringing them together to work for a common objective such a group would 'tend to lessen the differences and emphasise the extent of the common interest of all those taking part in it and of those whom they represent'.[24]

That is what the viceroy and the Secretary of State were

24 For the texts of the viceroy's statement in the Central Assembly, his statement of 17 October 1939 and Lord Zetland's statements in the House of Lords referred to above, see Mitra's *Annual Register,* 1939, Vol. II, pp. 97–100, 381–82, 384–89, 389–93.

saying about this morsel in public—that it would open up the opportunities for Indian parties and groups to play an effective part in aspects of the war effort, that it would bring them together. In *Secret and Personal* communications, on the other hand, the Secretary of State and the viceroy had already determined that the consultative group would have no powers at all, they had agreed upon methods of summoning its meetings which would ensure that it would be nothing but the creature and instrument of the viceroy. The viceroy felt that some sort of statement ought to be made on the question of constitutional advance, but he was just as sure that it could be made in terms which would ensure that in the end nothing would come of it: as usual progress could be promised on the condition that the major Indian communities should come to an agreement among themselves—and naturally which these communities were that had to agree, and who was to represent each of them was to be decided by government. The viceroy had assured the War Cabinet through the Secretary of State that he would himself preside over the meetings of the consultative group, that there would be no permanent membership of the group save the Governor General himself, that only those persons would attend a meeting whom the viceroy personally invited to do so. 'I am entirely clear,' he told the Secretary of State in his telegram of 28 September 1939, 'that if Committee showed signs of getting out of hand, immediate adjournment, and if need be a decision not again to assemble it (whatever the consequences of that decision might be) would be called for.'

Similarly, all those protestations about the consultative group being useful from another point of view—in that it would accustom Indians to working together for common objectives—was also so much humbug. As were those sanctimonious—but always contingent—statements about the government being ever so ready to make progress on the constitutional question if only the sections that constituted India could agree among themselves. Even as they were mouthing those homilies in public about the consultative group bringing the Hindu and Muslim leaders together, the viceroy and the Secretary of State were reassuring each other that actually the divisions between the two communities would mean that the group would never be able to acquire the cohesion that could make it a problem for the government. In his cable of 27 September 1939 the Secretary of State had conveyed the apprehensions which had been expressed at the Cabinet meeting. 'War Cabinet were critical of our proposed approach to Congress, chief criticism being directed to consultative committee,' the Secretary of State had said. 'There was a fear that it might entrench itself too deeply in the machinery of Government and that in due course great pressure would be brought to bear on us to give it some measure of control...' 'I have of course in considering the constitution and procedure of any committee, but particularly of a consultative committee, had throughout in mind the risk that it might impinge on field of responsibility of, or even usurp the function of the Government of India or my Executive Council, or for that matter trench upon the province of legislature,' the viceroy had cabled in response. 'My own judgement is that this risk would be largely minimised by the existence within committee of communal differences and by avoidance of decisions taken by vote, but principal security would be by an effective chairmanship...'

The viceroy was just as alert to the contribution that the tensions between the principal communities would make towards neutralizing the main demand for constitutional advance. His point only was that the Congress had a substantial 'nuisance value'. For this reason and 'because of the extreme importance of setting ourselves right with public opinion abroad as well as in India, and in the event of a break, giving Congress something to chew on the basis of which they can, on more mature reflection, if necessary, eat their words,' he wanted some sort of wording which would allay the Congress leaders for the time being. The demand for Independence had been made, he said, but there were the intense communal feelings, the claims of the minorities, those of the princely states. 'The Princes and the minorities alike will of course pay lip service to freedom and independence,' the viceroy said, 'and I shall not be in the least surprised if the Muslim League stress this by way of asserting their patriotism in any manifesto they may issue. But it is, I am certain, essential to safeguard their interests and the type of safeguards which both Muslims and Princes want is quite incompatible with any relinquishment of our control or interest in the country.'[25]

Later when it was again proposed that some sort of advance ought to be made on the constitutional question, if only by a statement of long term intent, Churchill told the Cabinet that he was opposed to any concession being made to the Congress leaders, and that he wanted this question of Hindu-Muslim tensions to be seen for the significance it had for the Empire. The record of the Cabinet discussion states:

> *The First Lord of the Admiralty* said that in November 1939 alarming prospects had been held out of what would happen if the Provincial Ministries resigned. The War Cabinet had been prepared to go very far to avoid the anticipated results, but not far enough to satisfy the Congress Party.
>
> The War Cabinet had taken a firm stand against the immoderate demands of the Congress, and had given their full support to the Viceroy and to the Provincial Governors in taking the necessary measures for the maintenance of law and order. What had been

25 For the exchange of telegrams between the Secretary of State and the viceroy, CAB 67/1 VPG(39)24, pp. 169–76.

the result? India had enjoyed a period of perfect tranquillity. For the first time for several years the Congress Provinces had been properly administered.

We were now being told that we are again being faced with danger, and that to avoid that danger it was of the utmost importance that the Viceroy should reach agreement with Mr. Gandhi. The Memoranda before the War Cabinet, and the telegrams which had been exchanged with the Viceroy, recommended far-reaching constitutional proposals. Was it fair that Parliament and the War Cabinet should have to involve themselves in these complications in the midst of a great war? No doubt the Viceroy must see Mr. Gandhi, but he should make it clear that he had nothing to add to his previous statements. He should point out once again that a standing offer was already open to the Congress ex-Ministries, and that they could return to office at any moment, if they chose.

The First Lord said that he did not share the anxiety to encourage and promote unity between the Hindu and Muslim communities. Such unity was, in fact, almost out of the realm of practical politics, while, if it were to be brought about, the immediate result would be that the united communities would join in showing us the door. He regarded the Hindu-Muslim feud as a bulwark of British rule in India.[26]

Gandhiji said in a statement to the press that the declaration of the viceroy was 'profoundly disappointing'. He said that 'the long statement made by the Viceroy simply shows that the old policy of divide and rule is to continue,' that it 'shows clearly that there is to be no democracy for India if Britain can prevent it'. 'Another Round Table is promised at the end of the War,' he remarked with his usual precision. 'Like its predecessor it is bound to fail. The Congress asked for bread, and it has got a stone.' Maulana Azad and Pandit Nehru in a joint statement said that they had read the viceroy's declaration 'with deep regret'. 'The whole statement is a complete repudiation of all that India stands

26 CAB 65/5 WM 30(40)4, pp. 236–41, at pp. 237–38.

for nationally and internationally,' they pointed out. 'It is a statement which would have been out of date twenty years ago; today it has absolutely no relation to reality. There is no mention in it of freedom, democracy or self-determination.'[27]

The Working Committee of the Muslim League expressed satisfaction at the viceroy's statement. It was particularly gratified it said by the British government's recognition that the League alone could speak for the Muslims, and for the assurance that the rights of minorities would be secured in any future consultations about the future constitution. And Ambedkar also, as usual, endorsed the viceroy's statement. 'What else could the Viceroy have done in the circumstances of the case?', he asked in the course of a press interview.[28]

On 22 October the Congress Working Committee met at Wardha and passed a resolution directing all Congress ministries to resign. And between 27 October and 8 November all of them, including the government in the NWFP did so. The resignations shook the country. They were also a considerable setback to the British.

A meeting was agreed to between Jinnah and Pandit Nehru to search out ways for resolving the communal deadlock. As the date came around, Jinnah out of the blue issued a statement on 6 December—that is, more than a month after the Congress ministries had demitted office—asking Muslims all over the country to observe Friday, 22 December as the 'Day of Deliverance'. He asked all units of the Muslim League to hold meetings to give thanks to God for the Muslims having been delivered from the Congress. He also released a resolution which he directed all units to have adopted at the meetings. The resolution read as follows:

---

27 Mitra's *Annual Register,* 1939, Vol. II, p. 33.

28 Mitra's *Annual Register,* 1939, Vol. II, pp. 33, 34.

This public meeting of the Mussalmans of (name of the place) records its opinion that the Congress Ministry has conclusively demonstrated and proved the falsehood of the Congress claim that it represents all interests, justly and fairly, by its decidedly anti-Muslim policy.

It is the considered opinion of this meeting that the Congress Ministry has failed to safeguard the rights and interests of the Mussalmans and other minorities and interests.

That the Congress Ministry both in the discharge of its duties of the administration and in the Legislature has done its best to flout the Muslim opinion and destroy Muslim culture, and has interfered with their religious and social life, and trampled upon their economic and political rights.

That in matters of difference and disputes, the Congress Ministry invariably has sided with, supported and advanced the cause of Hindus in total disregard and to the prejudice of the Muslim interests.

The Congress Government constantly interfered with the legitimate and routine duties of the district officers, even in petty matters, to the serious detriment of the Mussalmans, and thereby created an atmosphere which spread the belief amongst the Hindu public that there was established a Hindu *raj*, and emboldened the Hindus, mostly Congressmen, to ill-treat Muslims at various places and interfere with their elementary rights of freedom.

This meeting, therefore, expresses its deep sense of relief at the termination of the Congress regime in various provinces and rejoices in observing this day as the day of deliverance from tyranny, oppression and injustice during the last two and a half years, and prays to God to grant such strength, discipline and organisation to Muslim India as successfully to prevent the advent of such a Ministry again and to establish a truly popular Ministry which would do even justice to all communities and interests.

This meeting urges upon His Excellency the Governor of (name of the place) and his Council of Advisers to inquire into the legitimate grievances of the Mussalmans and the wrongs done to them by the outgoing Congress Ministry, and redress the same at the earliest moment in accordance with the announcements that have been made by the Governors in taking over the Government

> of various provinces under Section 93 of the Government of India Act of 1935 and thus assure the people that the new regime stands for even justice to all communities and interests concerned.

Gandhiji appealed to Jinnah to desist from the 'celebrations'. He said he heartily endorsed requests to the governors to examine Jinnah's charges against the Congress ministries. He requested the viceroy to pronounce on the charges. He said that Jinnah had taken upon himself 'the tremendous responsibility' of being simultaneously the accuser and the judge, that on the one hand Jinnah had appealed to the governors to have his charges examined and on the other he had exhorted Muslims to thank God as if those charges were already proven facts. Gandhiji and other leaders also criticized the rejection by Jinnah of the proposal for a Constituent Assembly. Jinnah—who, like Sir Syed Ahmed, had always opposed any and every move towards democratization on the charge that it would consign Muslims to the mercy of the 'permanent majority', the Hindus—shot back: in the existing conditions a Constituent Assembly will only mean 'a second and larger edition of the Congress'.

M.C. Chagla who had worked with Jinnah as his secretary denounced Jinnah's appeal as an 'insult to the principles and tenets of Islam'. 'Every decent minded Muslim who loves his country,' Chagla said, 'will be shocked and horrified at the statement issued by Mr. Jinnah, calling upon the Muslims of India to observe Friday, December 22 as a day of deliverance.' He pointed out that 'the creed of the League is still independence, not of a community, but of the whole country,' and asked, 'How can members of the League put up with a statement from their accredited leader who gloats over the failure of democracy and the triumph of autocratic rule? How can they sit quiet and see the country, which they are pledged to liberate, torn into pieces by tactics which Mr. Jinnah proposes in the statement?' He declared that as he was not one of Jinnah's followers, 'if his *appeal* had been made to them, perhaps I would have said nothing, but when he chooses to issue this appeal to the Muslims of India, I think it is my duty to protest against this insult to the principles and tenets of Islam.'

Leaders who had headed the Congress ministries—C. Rajagopalachari in Madras, E.G. Kher in Bombay, and others—refuted Jinnah's charges. If Congress and its ministries had been unjust to Muslims, if there had been any of the atrocities on them which Jinnah had alleged, they asked, how come the British governors—who, after all, were no friends of the ministries and even less of the Congress—had kept silent? They had all the power to take up the issue with the ministries. They had the power to remove them. And then there had been the certificates of the Secretary of State, of the viceroy.

Maulana Azad was more cutting. 'For the last two years, I have persistently tried to have the mutual differences between the Congress and the Muslim League removed,' he testified. 'In this endeavor I have left no stone unturned,' he continued. 'I firmly believe that in order to attain the national objective, all attempts of this nature should be persisted in, with the fullest honesty of purpose and sincerity of action.' 'But,' he said, 'I have to say with the deepest regret that whenever the Congress opens the door for negotiations and mutual understanding, another hand appears all of a sudden from the opposite direction, which wants to close it at the crucial moment. This hand is that of none else than the President of the Muslim League—Mr. Mohammed Ali Jinnah.'

Mr Jinnah's statement, the Maulana said, contains an appeal to Muslims 'which no Muslim having an iota of self-respecting consciousness of his political existence could ever give to his co-religionists'.

He pointed out that by being asked to thank God for being delivered from the Congress when the latter had resigned in defence of India's freedom and the rights of all subject peoples, the Muslims were being put in the position of opposing both the country's freedom and also the rights of subject peoples everywhere.

Turning to Jinnah's charges about atrocities against Muslims, the Maulana said, 'If we admit for the time being that the picture which Mr. Jinnah has presented is correct, let us consider what conclusion can be derived from it. The conclusion is patently obvious. The Governments of eight provinces have been decidedly anti-Muslim. They have been interfering in the religious and social life of Muslims. They continued to destroy their culture. They trampled down their economic and political rights; and all this havoc was caused not only for a few days; it continued for two and a half years.'

'What action then did the 80,000,000 Muslims of India take under such impossible circumstances?,' the Maulana asked. 'Only this, that they waited for 30 long months in the hope of the resignations of the Congress Ministries by their own choice and free will. And when this dream of theirs came true, they began to pour out their hearts to the Almighty in a spirit of thanksgiving, and began to proclaim to the world, like the children of Israel, that, after all, their day of deliverance had come.' 'What an honorable picture of the Muslims of India Mr. Jinnah wants to paint before the world!,' Maulana Azad lamented. 'It is impossible for me, as a Muslim, to tolerate for a moment such a degrading picture.'

The Maulana concluded by affirming, 'I have often declared before, and I do the same again, with all possible sense of responsibility, that all these accusations against the Congress Ministries are absolutely baseless. It is a mountain of falsehood to say that the policy of the Congress Ministries was "decidedly anti-Muslim", and that they have been "trampling down the religious, political and economic rights of the Mussalmans". It is the duty of Mr. Jinnah, or anyone who chooses to advance such allegations, to prove them by any method commonly prevailing in the world. And if he is unable to do so, every sensible man would expect him at least to keep a restraint on his language and pen.'

Even those who habitually supported Jinnah, even those who stood by British rule felt that Jinnah had been intemperate—both in his words and his decision. *The Times of India* urged him to reconsider his call. Its lead article on 13 December reported, 'An impartial observer, who has been watching the country's reactions is compelled to say that few actions or utterances of Mr. Jinnah in the recent past have met with such severe criticism as his call for the "Deliverance Day" celebration.' Citing strictures from papers across the country it noted that 'the entire daily press (published in English) with the solitary exception of a Muslim daily of Calcutta, has made a more or less bitter attack on Mr. Jinnah.' *The Hindu* of Madras, the article recalled, has described Jinnah's appeal as 'a hymn of hate that Mr. Jinnah wants to be chanted from a thousand lay pulpits, though like the Hebrew prophets he prefers to call it thanksgiving for deliverance... It is high time that the Viceroy and the Governors told the world plainly what they think of Mr. Jinnah's organised grouse which the longer it is left unquestioned by those in authority the more malignant it becomes, gathering a specious authority and a sinister momentum from mere iteration.'

The *Hindustan Times,* the columnist noted, had written, 'Mr. Jinnah's policy is a thinly-veiled, but a complete negation of Indian national aspirations.' 'We wonder why Mr. Jinnah should fight shy of a duly elected body of representatives,' it asked. 'Is it because it would replace self-appointed leadership?' It was not the fault of the Congress if a Constituent Assembly was not going to be different from the Congress, it said. 'The fact of the matter is probably that Mr. Jinnah apprehends that the Muslim section of the Constituent Assembly would not be a "second and larger edition" of the League.'

The Amrita Bazar Patrika wrote, 'Mr. Jinnah with his men has appeared on the Indian stage at a psychological moment to play a part which has been carefully prepared for them by the enemies of India's freedom'—that is, the British.

The Tribune, then published from Lahore, lamented, 'This once valiant champion of nationalism and liberty now actually prefers non-Indian to Indian, autocratic to autonomous, government, simply because in the latter his own community, though adequately represented, is not represented by a nominee of the League, that is his own nominee.' *The Indian Express,* castigating Jinnah, wrote, 'He asks the members of the Muslim League to be at prayer rendering thanks to Providence that Government by Indians has been displaced by a foreign regime in full once more. Let the son die, if only for enjoyment at the sight of the daughter-in-law's weeping.' And so on.

Jinnah tried to backtrack a bit. The celebrations were not going to be anti-Hindu, he said, they were only aimed at conveying thanks to God for delivering the Muslims from the Congress. He also demanded that a royal commission be set up to examine his charge of atrocities.

Sir Stafford Cripps was in India exploring possibilities for securing cooperation of all for the war effort through some constitutional advance. On 18 December *The Times of India* reported that in his opinion no royal commission was called for. Reporting his remarks at a press conference the paper wrote, 'Sir Stafford thought that the fact the Governors to whom the allegations were referred by the minorities about the oppression by the Congress did nothing about them was complete proof that in their view there was no substance in the allegations.'

But sure as death, Ambedkar supported Jinnah's call. He had only one regret, Ambedkar told *The Times of India:* 'When I read Mr. Jinnah's statement, I felt ashamed to have allowed him to steal a march over me and rob me of the language and the sentiments which I, more than Mr. Jinnah, was entitled to use.'

'Whatever anyone may say with regard to the tyranny alleged to have been practiced by the Hindus over the Muslims during the Congress regime,' Ambedkar declared, 'no one can entertain any doubt as to the position of millions of "Untouchables" who had the misfortune to be ruled by the Congress Government in this province, in common with some others. If Mr. Jinnah and the Muslims can prove five out of 100 cases of oppression, I am prepared to place 100 out of 100 cases before any impartial tribunal. I, therefore, am anxious, more than Mr. Jinnah can ever be, for the appointment of a Royal Commission to investigate the cases of tyranny and oppression by the Congress Government.' He added the sort of logic which, as we shall see as we proceed, was typical of him. He said, 'Although the oppressors, so far as the "Untouchables" are concerned, are Hindus, I can assure my Hindu friends that this is not an anti-Hindu move; it is anti-Congress, and therefore, purely political. If attack on the Congress is interpreted by the Hindus as an attack on them, they have to thank themselves then for the consequences. It proves two things: that the Congress is a Hindu body and that the Hindus are attached to the Congress and are not prepared to put that organisation on its trial.'

Ambedkar declared that he would join Jinnah's celebrations.

The Congress president endorsed the demand for an impartial inquiry, and said that in fact there was no need to wait for the Government to set up a Royal Commission. Let the charges be submitted to and examined by the Chief Justice, Sir Maurice Gwyer.

The tone of the pro-British sections shifted. Mr Jinnah had clarified that the celebrations were not anti-Hindu, they now stressed. And as evidence they cited what they said was a significant fact—that Dr Ambedkar was joining the celebrations.

'"Deliverance Day" scenes, Great enthusiasm in Bombay, Prayers and sermons in mosques, Non-Congress groups join celebrations' ran the headlines in *The Times of India.* The meetings had been attended by large numbers, it reported. 'The occasion was unique, in political history,' it said, 'for, though the celebrations were not anti-Hindu in spirit, it is doubtful whether on any previous occasion the relinquishment of office of any one party has been celebrated with prayer by its political opponents.' It gave the text of the prayer which had been read at each of the meetings. The prayer was:

> Oh Creator of heaven and earth—God Almighty, Oh Protector of the weak and the oppressed, we have foregathered at Thine altar of bounty and mercy to express our heartfelt gratitude and thanks for Thy boundless mercy in having relieved us from the oppression and injustice of the Congress regime which sought to trample upon the Muslim rights and would have ultimately enslaved us. That Government had become so intoxicated with power that it disregarded all appeals of the Mussalmans.
>
> Oh Lord of the two worlds !, we pray to Thee with utmost humility and beseech Thee to bring about unity and discipline amongst us Mussalmans of India and collect us to prevent dominance of any oppressive rule which disregards the rights of the weak and the minorities.
>
> Oh King of Kings, the all powerful and source of all power and greatness, who makes and unmakes kings and kingdoms, who bestows power and takes it away at will; oh great and all powerful God raise the Muslims of India and make them united and powerful to enable them to hold the Islamic flag aloft.

Oh king and merciful God, endow us Mussalmans with light and understanding.

Oh God bestow long life and strength to our illustrious leader Mohammed Ali Jinnah so that he may be able to guide us from position to position of solidarity and greatness.

The resolution—which, as we have seen, Jinnah had circulated earlier—'was passed amidst scenes of unbounded enthusiasm', *The Times of India* reported. 'Dr. B.R. Ambedkar, Leader of the Independent Labour Party,' it reported, 'was given a huge ovation as he rose to second the resolution.' 'After the resolution had been carried with acclamation,' it reported, 'Mr. Jinnah addressed the gathering. He was given a thunderous ovation....'[29]

The British were pleased as punch. So long as there had been some prospect that the Congress ministries might hold on, that the Congress might agree to support the war effort without asking for any commitment about the post-war future of India, till then praise for what the ministries had been doing during the thirty months they had been in office was in order. But as the ministries had resigned, everyone who was prepared to denounce it was an ally, every occasion on which it was denounced was a celebration. Jinnah had brought over an entire community for them. And Ambedkar had made it possible for it to be said that the celebrations had been non-religious....

So many coincidences?

For India the latter part of the nineteenth and the first half of the twentieth centuries have one great theme: the leaders

29 For the preceding accounts *The Times of India*, 6–25 December 1939.

of the movement for national revival—Swami Dayanand, Ramakrishna Paramahamsa, Swami Vivekananda, Sri Aurobindo, Lokmanya Tilak, Gandhiji, Ramana Maharshi—were engaged in a mighty effort to roll back the debilitating effects of the calumnies about our culture and religion which Christian missionaries and British rulers had implanted in our minds. While they were exerting with their very lives to restore in us a sense of self-worth and thereby stand us on our feet, every single thing that Ambedkar wrote was a continuation of the calumnies—it was as if a painter's assistant had been put to adding some even more garish colours to the caricature that the missionaries and rulers had put out.

And as during the years in which Ambedkar was politically active, Gandhiji was the highest and most vivid symbol of our culture, our religious traditions, as he was the leader of the movement to rid the country of the British, as Gandhiji was the one who was doing everything possible to raise the ones in whose name Ambedkar claimed to speak, Ambedkar, we shall soon see, heaped the worst possible denunciations on this one man. In saying that he felt for the Harijans, that he was one of them Gandhi was just a hypocrite, declared Ambedkar. His work on their behalf was nothing but a ruse to lull them into the belief that something was being done for them, it was just fraud, declared Ambedkar. Gandhi was doing all this only to keep them from discerning his real purpose of perpetuating their exploitation, declared Ambedkar.

Finally, the basic political thesis which Ambedkar articulated throughout his political career during the British rule was a verbatim copy of the thesis which Muslim separatists and collaborators of the British—from Sir Syed Ahmed to Jinnah—advocated. With just two changes. The word 'Muslim' was replaced by 'Scheduled Castes'. And as the 'Scheduled Castes' were neither concentrated in one geographical area nor in a majority in any particular area, the 'solution' that Ambedkar advocated was not just 'Partition' but 'Partition *Plus*'—the country ought to be partitioned as the Muslim League is demanding because the Hindus and Muslims cannot live together, he said; but in addition as the departure of the British will result in the tyranny of high-caste Hindus, for as long as possible the British should *not* leave: 'Granting independence to India will be the greatest disaster,' we have just seen Ambedkar telling the viceroy, Lord Wavell as late as in April 1946, that is just about fifteen months before the country became independent.

Second, if the British decide that they just cannot hold on any longer, they must tie the governments of post-Independence India down in two ways. They must make the new government enter into a treaty with Great Britain which would give the latter a handle to intervene in Indian affairs after Independence; and through this treaty they must tie India down into not just making specific concessions to the 'Scheduled Castes', these concessions must in particular include two points: separate autonomous tracts of territory for 'Scheduled Castes' all over the country; and separate electorates for them; in addition, the British must have the new government accept provisions in the treaty which would give some external agency the right and authority to intervene in Indian affairs on the ground that it is duty-bound to ensure that the concessions are enforced.

The Secretary of State for India, L.S. Amery, was naturally quite enthusiastic that such demands were being made. Unlike the Muslims who had a majority in some areas, he and Sir D. Monteath had noted in their minutes on 2 March 1942, the Scheduled Castes were dispersed all over the country. Therefore, they recorded, 'Their only hope lies in the proviso that the constitution-making body shall negotiate a Treaty with the British Government in all matters affected by the transfer of control from British to Indian hands. But the influence that the depressed classes are likely to exercise in a constituent body composed on the basis proposed is not likely to be very effective for the 'depressed classes' have not a long purse to draw on.' [Recall the words Ambedkar was to use later to Lord Wavell, and which have been reproduced above, and see how well they correspond to this formulation of Amery and Monteath.] And to buttress their proposal whom should they cite but the person who had once again made the helpful statement—Ambedkar! 'Mr. Ambedkar's statement in tele(gram)....of 27th Feb. is very relevant. [In this statement Ambedkar had criticized the appeal Chiang Kai-shek had made in support of the position of the Congress, an appeal the British had found so distasteful.] The transition from the conception of agreements between elements to agreements between units will hit him and his community hard.'[30]

Initially, even Sir Stafford Cripps—whom Ambedkar was to accuse of not giving him, that is Ambedkar, and his people the importance he had given the Congress and its leaders and the Muslim League and its leaders—was quite enthusiastic about this idea of engaging the successor government in a treaty. In his meeting with Cripps on 30 March 1942, Ambedkar urged that the 'Scheduled Castes' be recognized as a racial and religious minority. When Cripps agreed that this was in order they pressed him on the provisions that would be made in the treaty. 'I stated that these would probably be along the lines of the League of Nations minority treaties,' Cripps recorded in his note about the meeting as well in his subsequent report to the War Cabinet, 'And if already there were special provisions in

30 *Transfer of Power*, Vol. I, p. 287.

the constitution these would probably be repeated in the Treaty, and there would be some obligation to refer the matter to some outside authority in cases of dispute, the government of the Indian union undertaking to abide by the decision so given, and that if they did not do so it would constitute a breach of Treaty, whereupon the British Government could take such steps as it considered wise in the particular circumstances.' That Ambedkar did not consider even this to be enough is evident from what Cripps added: 'I stated that though this form of protection might no doubt seem to them inadequate, once granted the idea of self-government and self-determination for India, there was no other possible way by which we could intervene to protect any minority in India.'[31]

Eventually even Cripps thought better of this proposal and dropped it. Amery, the Secretary of State, and Linlithgow, the viceroy, both had their own reasons for resenting the way Cripps had gone about his task, and they were forever writing to each other about how they were having to pick up the pieces after Cripps's tour. Amery returned to this proposal in his communication to the viceroy of 8 February 1943 about tying the new government in a treaty which would give a ground for the British to continue their influence in Indian affairs. As one would expect of the interlocutors, the point was put only in the interest of the Scheduled Castes, it just so happened that the operational result would have been to furnish Britain the right to intervene in the conduct of Indian affairs even after conceding Independence to the country!

'I was greatly interested to read Ambedkar's further

31 *Transfer of Power,* Vol. I, pp. 552–53; and *Transfer of Power,* Vol. II, pp. 336–37. In this meeting Amhedkar was accompanied by the other important leader of the Scheduled Castes, M.C. Rajah, whom also, as we shall soon see, Ambedkar was to denounce as one of the Scheduled Caste types who had sold their soul to the Hindu Congress.

memorandum on the Cripps proposals,' Amery wrote to Linlithgow. 'Logically his criticism is, I fear, unanswerable.' It is true that at first glance treaties cannot protect minorities, Amery conceded, but there are ways around that. 'The protection given to a minority by Treaty may be a very illusory thing,' he wrote. 'Not only the Irish Treaty, but even more the Minority Treaties in the Peace Settlement, bear witness to that. On the other hand, there may be conditions in which a Treaty may contain within itself effective leverage for the enforcement of its provisions. This is particularly the case where the party which has pledged itself to good behaviour is very much dependent on the other party for financial or military help. The Egyptian and Iraq Treaties, for instance, have not been without value in enabling us to have a say in the conduct of the governments concerned and so of course have our treaties with the Indian states.'

Cripps had undermined the case by focusing on the minorities too much, Amery implied, the Indians would have been more receptive if the proposal had been put in the context of military and other forms of assistance. 'What I regretted about Cripps's handling about the treaty business,' Amery wrote, 'was that he seemed simply to imply that it was concerned entirely with minorities, whereas of course the main object of the treaty conception as discussed at this end was to cover such matters as the continuance of our military assistance, the position of the services, the position of the Crown Representative, &c., all of which Cripps I fear slurred over. Also it was always the idea at this end that the treaty protection of minorities should only come in if the constitution itself failed to afford them effective protection. That means, of course, not only that the constitution in its first form should afford that protection, but also that the possibility of changing the constitution should be so hedged round with safeguards as to make the abrogation of such protection practically impossible.'[32] Store these formulations, and recall them when we turn to the constitutional proposals which Ambedkar was to advance soon, and you will see their exact isomorph.

But to resume, the idea was: the new constitution should contain provisions which the British thought afforded the protection which they thought would be required to groups which they thought needed such protection; in addition the constitution must contain provisions which would make it impossible for those protective provisions to be altered subsequently; and if all this was not done, the new government must enter into a treaty with Britain which would, to recall the words Amery had used to describe the virtues of the treaties with Iraq and Egypt 'enable us to have a say in the conduct of the Government concerned'. As I said, the proposal was being urged and considered only because of the great concern of the British for the Scheduled Castes! It just so happened that the operational result was to give the British a hand in determining the new constitution, and, if that turned out to be short of their expectations, a Treaty that would give them a more direct avenue for having a say in the conduct of affairs in the country to which they had just had to concede Independence. It was Bernard Shaw's Englishman all over again. The proposal was being urged and contemplated only out of principle, the principle in this case of protecting the interests of the poor wretches whose care Providence had placed in the hands of the British, and only because the one and only representative of these poor wretches, Ambedkar that is, was urging that the new government be tied into such a treaty! Alas, Cripps had botched it all up. So, Amery and Linlithgow didn't get much farther with these contemplations.

---

32 *Transfer of Power,* Vol. III, p. 633.

But who do you think continued to peddle this proposal, namely that the new government of independent India be tied down by a treaty which would give Britain the right to intervene in Indian affairs even after leaving the rulership of the country? Meeting in Bombay on 4 June 1946—as late as that—the Working Committee of Ambedkar's All-India Scheduled Castes Federation demanded that before granting Independence the British must get the new (Indian) government to sign a treaty with Britain which should provide inter alia, that the Scheduled Castes shall constitute a separate electorate, and that such constitution as the country may adopt 'shall contain a provision making it obligatory on the Government to undertake the formation of separate settlements for the Scheduled Castes'.[33]

Everyone else is ungrateful

By now Ambedkar was thoroughly discredited as the person who had always been opposing the national movement, as the one who had always been opposing its leaders—in particular Gandhiji—exactly in terms that best served the British purpose, as one in a word who had for a quarter of a century been the handmaiden of the British. As we shall see, he remonstrated with the British: there is no need to agree to the nationalists' demand for a Constituent Assembly, giving Independence to India will be the greatest disaster you can inflict. The British could not resist the demand any longer. In early 1946 therefore, elections were held for the Assemblies.

Ambedkar reached Sholapur during his campaign. 'Addressing a public meeting at the place,' records his adoring

33 *Dr. Babasaheb Ambedkar, Writings and Speeches,* Vol. X, pp. 503–08.

biographer, 'Ambedkar declared vehemently that if the Scheduled Castes Federation candidates were not returned, he would surrender to the Congress, wear a white cap and work under the Congress!'[34]

Given what he had been doing on behalf of the British to thwart them, the nationalists were not idle either. Sardar Patel who was handling the organization of the Congress campaign wrote to the president of the Vidarbha Provincial Congress Committee, 'The question of Scheduled Castes candidates in your province and in Nagpur requires careful consideration. The Mahar community is largely found in these areas and hence we must particularly [take] care to see that no one of the followers of Dr. Ambedkar succeeds...'[35] Ambedkar was dealt an even worse blow than he had been in 1937. The total number of seats was 1,585. The Congress won 923. Ambedkar's Scheduled Castes Federation won *one.* And that too only in the Central Provinces and Berar. In the Bombay Presidency there were a total of 175 seats. The Congress won 125. Ambedkar's party won *none.* Worse, the Scheduled Castes voters rejected Ambedkar and his party as decisively as every other section: of the total 151 constituencies reserved for Scheduled Castes, the Congress walked off with 141.[36]

'It was all over with Ambedkar's Scheduled Castes Federation,' writes his biographer. 'His party was utterly routed. Absence of and indifference to the co-operation of caste Hindu votes and lack of organization made Ambedkar eat his words which he had uttered at Sholapur. This was a stunning blow to his prestige as a leader, which drove him to

---

34 Dhananjay Keer, *Dr. Ambedkar, Life and Mission,* Popular Prakashan, 1990, pp. 376–77.

35 *Sardar Patel's Correspondence,* Durga Das (ed.), Vol. II, pp. 344–45.

36 Mitra's *Annual Register,* 1946, Vol. I, pp. 229–30.

desperation and his bitter mind began to think of drastic methods....'[37]

So, what did Ambedkar do? Now he pleaded and remonstrated with the British not just to tie India in a treaty which would give them the right to intervene in India's affairs. He pleaded and remonstrated with them to assure his organization—by now a thoroughly discredited body—positions in the new government and in the committees, etc., which were being set up to determine what the future set-up would be. Even the British were embarrassed, it would seem that they were almost put out. Things had gone too far. The Ambedkars were now of no use. Following a single sequence will bring home the denouement of Ambedkar as well as the pleadings he continued to address right up to the end. And his characteristic conclusion—namely, that those demurring at his demands were an ungrateful lot!

When the interim government was to be formed, Ambedkar pleaded with Clement Atlee, by then the British prime minister, that Atlee ensure that Scheduled Castes get two (later, three) seats in it, and that these positions be filled by nominees of his own Federation—'which', Ambedkar told Atlee in his telegram, '[the British Cabinet] Mission knows alone represents Scheduled Castes'. Ambedkar felt it necessary to add that 'to avoid misunderstanding of my motive, I like to state that I have no desire to be in Interim Government and will stand out.' When the Minorities Advisory Committee—of which we shall see a good deal subsequently—was to be formed, again Ambedkar was appealing to the British prime minister to see that his organization was on it. It was British rectitude, coupled with their assessment that in fact most Harijans were with the Congress, which kept them from

37 Dhananjay Keer, *Dr. Ambedkar, Life and Mission,* Popular Prakashan, 1990, p. 378.

acting on his pleadings.[38] But to their evident annoyance, Ambedkar wouldn't let go!

'Representation to Scheduled Castes Congressmen is no representation to Scheduled Castes,' he cabled Clement Atlee on 1 July 1946. 'It is representation to Congress. Cabinet Mission heaping upon Scheduled Castes one wrong after another, bent on sacrificing them with view to appease Congress and destroying their independent position in public life of country. Please intervene and redress wrong by directing Mission to give Scheduled Castes two seats to be filled by nominees of Federation which Mission knows alone represents Scheduled Castes...'

Atlee was gentle, but firm. '...We appreciate that there are grounds for the view that the present electoral system does not do justice to those Scheduled Castes candidates who are opposed to Congress,' he wrote to Ambedkar on 1 August 1946. 'On the other hand, I do not find that figures substantiate what you say about the achievements of candidates belonging to your Federation at the primary elections. While I do not propose to go into the matter in detail here, the facts are that primary elections were held in only 43 of the 151 seats reserved for the Scheduled Castes. Of these 43 primary elections, the Scheduled Castes Federation contested 22 and topped the poll in only 13.'

Ambedkar was touched to the quick. His reply gives us a glimpse of the kind of reasoning on which he equated the Scheduled Castes with himself.

'With regard to the analysis you have given of the result of the achievements of the Federation in the Primary Elections,' he wrote to Atlee on 12 August 1946, 'all I can say is that you have misunderstood the situation and I am afraid no outsider who does not know the significance of the facts

---

38 See *Dr. Babasaheb Ambedkar, Writings and Speeches,* Vol. X, pp. 509–19.

or the method of the election will be able to understand what they mean without proper explanation... That the Mission was grossly misinformed is proved by my election to the Constituent Assembly from Bengal. The Cabinet Mission stated in the House of Commons that my influence was confined to Bombay and C.P. How is it then that I was elected from Bengal? In connection with my election, I would like to impress upon you three facts: One is that I did not merely scrape through but I came up at the top of the poll beating even Mr. Sarat Chandra Bose, the Bengalee leader of the Congress Party. Secondly, I am in no way connected by communal ties with the Scheduled Castes community of Bengal. They are of different caste (than the one) to which I belong. In fact the people of my caste do not exist in Bengal at all and yet the Bengalee Scheduled Castes supported me, so strongly that I was able to come first. Thirdly, though the Scheduled Castes in Bengal had been returned on the Congress ticket yet they broke the rule of their Party not to vote for any body [sic] except for Congressmen and voted for me. Does this prove that I have no following in Bengal? I am sure if the Cabinet Mission are honest in their conclusion, they ought to revise the erroneous opinion which they have expressed in the House of Commons and revise the view and give proper recognition to the Federation...'

Pethick-Lawrence, now the Secretary of State, took Ambedkar's 'evidence' apart. In a minute to the prime minister, he wrote, 'Shortly, the facts are that in the primary elections which were contested, Congress polled more votes than Ambedkar's organization, while a still larger proportion were polled by Independent candidates who may or may not be supporters of Ambedkar. But apart from this, two-third [sic] of the seats were won by Congress unopposed.' Turning to Ambedkar's claims about Bengal he pointed out, 'I have made inquiries as to what happened in the Bengal Election to the Constituent Assembly which is, of course, by proportional representation. Ambedkar got five first preference votes. Sarat Chandra Bose also received five first preference votes. The quota for election in Bengal was four votes. Naturally the Congress would organize their voters to secure as nearly as possible four first preferences for each of their candidates. The phrase 'top of the poll' has really no meaning in a proportional election. No one denies that Ambedkar has influence among some of the depressed classes in Bengal. There are twenty five Scheduled Caste members of the Bengal Assembly, four of whom were returned as Independents and one as an Ambedkar candidate. I do not know whether all the Independents voted for Ambedkar in the Constituent Assembly election or whether he got some Anglo-Indian votes.'

As regards Ambedkar's plea that the British ensure that two nominees of his Federation were included in the Minorities Advisory Committee, Pethick-Lawrence pointed out that 'we have left the composition of the Advisory Committee to be decided by the Constituent Assembly and we cannot now prescribe it ourselves...'[39] That sort of reasoning could only have confirmed Ambedkar in his charge that, like everyone else, the British were an ungrateful lot.

In any event, Ambedkar and his party had not the seats in the Bombay Assembly to return him to the Constituent Assembly. And so it was from Bengal that he sought to be elected to the Constituent Assembly—he got through either with the help, as Pethick-Lawrence surmised, of the Anglo-Indian members and 'Independents' or, as his biographer says, with the help of the Muslim League.[40]

---

39 On these exchanges, see *Dr. Babasaheb Ambedkar, Writings and Speeches,* Vol. X, pp. 510–19.

40 Dhananjay Keer, *Dr. Ambedkar, Life and Mission,* Popular Prakashan, 1990, p. 382.

But soon enough Partition came. Bengal was to be split in two. Accordingly, Ambedkar stood to lose his seat. With no leg to stand on in the Bombay Assembly, Ambedkar was set to be out of the reckoning all together. But by now the Congress leadership had decided to proceed on the basis, to recall Sardar Patel's phrase, of 'forget and forgive'. On 30 June 1947 Dr Rajendra Prasad, then president of the Constituent Assembly, wrote to the chief minister of Bombay, B.C. Kher, to ensure that Ambedkar was elected to the Assembly. Sardar Patel spoke to Kher that day to the same effect, and the next day wrote to him, 'Confirming my conversation with you last night, you have to make arrangements for Dr. Ambedkar's election, if possible before the 14th. If the date for nomination is the 4th, then there would be no difficulty, but if the nomination date is changed to the llth, then the only way to finish the work before the 14th is to persuade other candidates to withdraw. Anyway, you will do your best.'[41] And that is how Ambedkar continued in the Constituent Assembly.

The Congress had complete control over the Constituent Assembly. Of the 296 seats, the Congress had won 205. The Muslim League had won 73. But the latter had boycotted the Assembly, demanding instead a separate Assembly for an independent Pakistan. Therefore, the Congress had 205 of 223 seats. But in accordance with the decision of the leadership to 'forget and forgive', in constituting the seven-member 'Drafting Committee' the party decided that only one of the seven members should be a Congressman. And, as was to be acknowledged by the Scheduled Caste members of the Assembly themselves, it was because of the large-heartedness of the Congress leaders and their decision that all must be joined in completing the national task that Ambedkar was 'elected' the chairman of this Committee.

41 *Sardar Patel's Correspondence*, Durga Das (ed.), Vol. V, p. 149.

A minister again

Independence came. For all the venom which he had poured at Gandhiji and the Congress, Ambedkar was back in the Cabinet, this time Pandit Nehru's Cabinet of independent India. How did he get there?

Ambedkar's own explanation was typical of the man: he had done nothing to seek a position in the new government, Ambedkar asserted later, it was the new prime minister, Jawaharlal Nehru, who had urged him to join the new government; the offer had come to him, as a surprise, he said, he had been full of doubts, but in the end he had yielded to the call of duty and to the plea that he make his talents available to the new government—that is how things had gone according to Ambedkar. Recall the pleas to Atlee, and set them against Ambedkar's reconstruction of the sequence in the speech he made in the Lok Sabha. It was 10 October 1951 and Ambedkar was explaining his resignation from the Cabinet of Panditji:

> It is now 4 years, 1 month and 26 days since I was called by the Prime Minister to accept the office of the Law Minister in the Cabinet. The offer came as a great surprise to me. I was in the opposite camp and had already been condemned as unworthy of association when the Interim Government was formed in August 1946. I was left to speculate as to what could have happened to bring about this change in the attitude of the Prime Minister. I had my doubts. I did not know how I could carry on with those who had never been my friends. I had doubts as to whether I could, as a Law Member, maintain the standard of legal knowledge and acumen which had been maintained by those who had preceded me as Law Ministers of the Government of India. But I kept my doubts at rest and accepted the offer of the Prime Minister on the ground that I should not deny my co-operation when it was asked for in the building up of our nation...[42]

---

42 *Dr. Babasaheb Ambedkar, Writings and Speeches,* Vol. XIV, Part II, p. 1318.

In a word, the reluctant expert who eventually yields to the implorings of others so as to help the poor country that needs his talents. Far from a word of gratitude for the fact that, even though he had been heaping scorn at them for a quarter of a century, even though he had been a most ardent member of the British government which had thrown them and kept them in jails for years, the Congress leaders had put all that aside and invited him to join the government, far from there being any word of gratitude, there was not a word even of appreciation, even of a mere acknowledgement at least for their sagacity, if not their magnanimity, in putting so much of the past—of the past that was so recent, of the past that had been so bitter—behind them. The new leaders had implored him to join the government as they had no alternative, so indispensable were the man's talents—that was the implicit refrain.

The diary of Indrani Devi, the widow of Jagjivan Ram, records the exact opposite. In the entry entitled, *'Ambedkar ki sifaarish'*, she records,

> And on this side Ambedkar had started coming over to our house. One day he (Ambedkar) told him to put in a word with Gandhiji to have him (Ambedkar) included in the Cabinet. Before talking to Gandhiji he (Jagjivan Ram) talked to Sardar Patel. Sardar Patel said, do what you think is appropriate. He (Jagjivan Ram) got into quite a quandary—that Ambedkar had always opposed Gandhiji and the Congress, how could he now recommend his case to Gandhiji? Even so, given his large-heartedness, he pleaded with Gandhiji on behalf of Ambedkar, and told him that as he has surrendered in front of you please request Nehruji so that he may be taken into the first Cabinet.[43]

In any event, either as a result of his lobbying or because Pandit Nehru requested him, Ambedkar joined the government.

---

43 Indrani Jagjivan Ram, *Dekhi Suni Beeti Baaten,* Jagjivan Vidya Bhavan, 1995, Vol. II, p. 15.

He broke with Nehru four years later and denounced the Congress and Nehru. He entered into an electoral alliance with the socialists to oppose the Congress in the 1952 elections. His party was wiped out. There were a total of 489 seats in the Lok Sabha. Of these the Congress secured 364, that is, almost three-quarters. Ambedkar's party got no seat in the Parliament, only one seat in the Bombay Assembly, and one in that of Hyderabad.

But presumably the inference to be drawn from this defeat too is the same. 'It was a colossal failure, and Ambedkar fell like a rocket,' writes his admiring biographer, Dhananjay Keer, about the election result. 'It proved once again that there is no gratitude in politics. The nation which had conferred so much glory on him seemed now unwilling to show him gratitude....'[44]

But I anticipate. For the moment we need bear in mind just a few facts.

Throughout the twenty-five years of his public life before the British left India, Ambedkar took positions which were ever so convenient for the British, throughout these twenty-five years he hurled pejoratives at the Congress, in particular Gandhiji. At every turn he put forward formulae and demands which enabled the British to counter the national movement for freedom. The British were fully aware of the use he was to them, and they were anxious to give him a hand so that he could become even more the exclusive leader of the Scheduled Castes. We shall have occasion soon to see what happened at the Round Table Conference in 1931, and what happened in its wake: Gandhiji had to stake his very life to thwart the manoeuvre the British made—in consultation with Ambedkar, and to his great acclaim—to split Hindu society asunder. Gandhiji

---

44 Dhananjay Keer, *Dr. Ambedkar, Life and Mission,* Popular Prakashan, 1990, p. 440.

survived, but he was kept in jail, as were the other Congress leaders. Ambedkar of course was again on his way to England to attend yet another Round Table Conference. And as on the previous occasion, what he said and did was to the full satisfaction of the British rulers. On 28 December 1932, the Secretary of State, Sir Samuel Hoare, was recounting the proceedings for the viceroy. He wrote, 'Ambedkar had behaved very well at the [Round Table] Conference, and I am most anxious to strengthen his hands in every possible way. Coming from a family whose members have almost always been in the [British] Army, he feels intensely that there are no Depressed Class units left. Could you not induce the Commander-in-Chief to give them at least a Company? Ambedkar tells me that the Depressed Class battalion did much better in the Afghan War than most of the other Indian battalions. In any case, I feel sure that at this juncture it would be a really valuable political act to make a move of this kind.'[45]

Next, Ambedkar argued long and vehemently that India must not be given Independence in the foreseeable future. We have already seen some of his urgings in this regard. Consider an example from another sphere. As is well known, apart from the communists, Ambedkar was one of the few politicians who supported the Muslim League demand for Pakistan. One side of his argument was that Muslims cannot stay in a multi-religious society; the other side of his argument was that no one can stay with the Hindus either, by which he always meant 'upper-caste exploiters'. That in brief was the thesis of his book, *Thoughts on Pakistan*. In private he was telling the British something quite different. He had been yearning to be included in the viceroy's administration, and in the mid-1940s it was presumed that, in view of what he had been saying and

45 MSS.EUR.E.240(10), Vol. II.

doing, his induction was just a matter of days. But those were uncertain times and the calculations of the British were changing from day to day: they were at war with Hitler; they knew that opinion within the Congress was divided, some important elements were of the view that Britain should be supported even though they were not prepared to spell out what they would do about India after the war; so they had to keep in mind the possibility of strengthening this section within the Congress. They also knew that inducting a person like Ambedkar would offend the Congress as a whole no end. At the last minute, therefore, the viceroy had called Ambedkar and the other aspirant, M.S. Aney, and told them that he would have to put off the expansion of his Council for the time being. Not only that, in view of what he might have to do to win cooperation of the Congress, the viceroy had had to tell Ambedkar that he could not bind himself or his successor about the future. Recounting his meeting with Ambedkar the viceroy told the Secretary of State on 19 November 1940, in a communication marked *'Private and Personal'*, 'I was at pains to protect my successor and myself so far as he was concerned by making it clear that while if circumstances led me to invite him to work with me again, it would give me personal pleasure to have him as a colleague, I or my successor must be regarded as wholly uncommitted in that matter, and under no obligation of any sort.' The conversation had then turned to the demand for Pakistan. The viceroy noted, 'He [Ambedkar] was quite clear that Muslims proposed to hold to their demand for 50:50 and so gradually lay the foundation of Pakistan, *and he was perfectly content himself, he said, with that state of things, and in favour of the Pakistan idea quite frankly because it meant the British would have to stay in India.* He saw not the least prospect of our overcoming difficulties here by guarantees of any sort and (like most minorities) he has, I suspect, little interest in constitutional progress...'[46]

Eventually of course the British had decided that they would just have to leave. Ambedkar then pleaded with them that they tie the new government by a treaty. Then that they get his organization a place in the new set-up. Then he went and pleaded with Jagjivan Ram, the sort of man on whom he had poured scorn for decades....

But today that very Ambedkar is a Bharat Ratna!

All the facts which have been recounted above were well known fifty years ago. With the passing of the generation that fought for Independence, with the total abandonment of looking up the record, most of all with the rise of casteist politics, they have been erased from public awareness. And that erasure has led to the predictable result: schizophrenia.

To start with, those trading in Ambedkar's name and their apologists have sought to downplay the struggle for independence: the freedom it brought is not 'real', they insist. Exactly as that other group did which teamed up with the British at that crucial hour, 1942—the communists. Indeed, as we shall see in the concluding part of the book, to justify Ambedkar's conduct his followers insist that British rule was better.

Next, they have sought to exaggerate the hardships that Ambedkar had to put up with, to almost rub out the fact, for instance, that at every step—for instance in his education—he received fulsome help from persons belonging to the higher castes; by exaggerating the hardships the apologists seek to explain away Ambedkar's collaborating with the British, his hankering for office: these hardships were the sort that are commonplace in India—one has only to recall the circumstances in which Swami Vivekananda matured,

46 MSS.EUR.F/125/9, p. 428.

one has only to recall the starvation which stared him in the face, the calumny and humiliations he had to fight back; but in the case of one and each of our leaders the hardships became the crucible which steeled their resolve to rid our country of British rule; it is only in Ambedkar's case that his followers and apologists think that those hardships justify his collaborating with the British against the national movement.

And, of course, these persons have made a practice of denouncing and calumnizing Mahatma Gandhi: Gandhiji was the great leader, even more so he was the great symbol of that struggle for freedom; as Ambedkar collaborated with the British to undermine him, as for twenty-five years he heaped on the Mahatma calumnies which the British found so valuable, his apologists abuse and denigrate and belittle the Mahatma. In doing this they work out their own poisons—poisons which, as we shall see, are the inescapable legacy of leaders who have not cast out the thorn of hatred before they come to wield influence. Today the abuse he hurled at Gandhiji provides the precedent: the apologists' case, as Kanshi Ram said recently while explaining the venom his associate Mayawati had spewed at the Mahatma, is, 'We are followers of Babasaheb, we only keep repeating what he used to say.' They are at the same time serving their convenience: they have made Ambedkar's style, so to say, as also the facility with which he allied with those who were out to keep the country subjugated, the rationalization for their own politics.

But the facts lurk in the closet. Lest they spill out and tarnish the icon they need for their politics, lest their politics be shown up for what it is—a trade in the name of the dispossessed—these followers of Ambedkar enforce their brand of history through verbal terrorism, and actual assault.

And intimidation works. Editors and others conclude, 'Better leave bad enough alone.'

2

Where was Ambedkar in 1942? How did he get there?

Our leaders hail the 1942 'Quit India' movement as a giant and decisive stride towards freedom. Every year on 9 August they celebrate its anniversary. They also hail Ambedkar and pay homage to his memory at every turn.

What was Ambedkar doing in 1942?

He was the labour member in the Viceroy's Executive Council—that is, to use current designations, he was the minister in charge of labour in the Cabinet of the British government in India.

How come we never juxtapose the two facts? The answer is simple: in this, as in other matters, facts which run counter to the present fashions, to the present convenience of rulers—and other political groupings—are just erased from public memory. But I anticipate. The facts first.

Ambedkar's appointment as member—that is, minister—of the Viceroy's Council—that is, Cabinet—was announced on 2 July 1942. It was notified on 20 July 1942. (The Congress Working Committee passed the 'Quit India' resolution on 14 July at Wardha, the All-India Congress Committee ratified it on 8 August 1942. The leaders, including Gandhiji were bundled off to jails through raids all over Bombay in the early hours of 9 August.) In a sense the appointment was long overdue.

As we have seen, Ambedkar had for twenty years voiced the exact notions that the British wanted voiced, notions which they found so very useful. He had done so exactly when they most needed him to do so, for instance, at the Round Table Conferences. Ever so often, as we shall see in reviewing the days immediately preceding and following the arrests of Gandhiji and other nationalist leaders in August 1942, he did so not only to their convenience, not only in coordination with them but at their express 'suggestion'.

The coordination had been at its best at the Round Table Conference in 1931. The British had the Aga Khan to proclaim that the Muslims were different from, that their interests were divergent from those of the Hindus, that they stood apart from, and indeed were opposed to the national movement for freedom. The British had selected Ambedkar as the representative of the Depressed Classes. Ambedkar was even more insistent in maintaining that the Scheduled Castes were different from Hindus, that, like the interests of Muslims, their interests were not just different from but were eternally opposed to the interests of Hindus, and that Gandhiji could not speak for them. Given this homework, the Secretary of State could confidently tell the viceroy on 2 October 1931, 'The delegates are much further off with each other than they were last year and I don't believe that there is a least chance of a communal settlement in the Minorities Committee.'[1]

The Conference was soon at a deadlock. Gandhiji requested that the Minorities Committee adjourn so that he might attempt to bring about an agreement among the Indian delegates through informal discussions. Ambedkar held on to his position, including his demand that Scheduled Castes be given separate electorates as the Muslims had been. His attitude was not just one of insistence but of what his

1 MSS.EUR.E.240(1).

admiring biographer calls 'irreverent audacity'. At the sessions and in interviews to the British press, Ambedkar, records his admiring biographer, 'thundered'—against Gandhiji, naturally; his 'vitriolic tone began to rise'—against Gandhiji, naturally; as he 'observed with his caustic ruthlessness'—directed at Gandhiji, naturally; 'Ambedkar's was indeed a ruthless attack on Gandhi'...[2] And so, exactly as the British had hoped and, given their homework, had expected, nothing came of the discussions. Gandhiji announced his 'utter failure'. He was left in no doubt by the end of the Conference that the British would make the decisive move to split Hindu society by instituting separate electorates for the Depressed Classes. He alerted them, he warned them that should they proceed to do so, he would resist the move with his life. The British let him leave England. He had but landed in India, and they threw him into jail. A few months later they announced their 'Communal Award' with its separate electorates for the Depressed Classes. Ambedkar announced his warm support for the award. Gandhiji undertook his famous fast unto death. Ambedkar had to ultimately yield and sign the Poona Accord. Left without their singular champion the British cancelled the announcement. But they continued to hold Gandhiji in prison. And they prepared for yet another Round Table Conference.

Ambedkar's role was the same as it had been the preceding year, and just as helpful to the British. And, the British, as we have seen, were properly appreciative: 'Ambedkar had behaved very well at the [Round Table] Conference,' the Secretary of State informed the viceroy on 28 December 1932, 'and I am most anxious to strengthen his hands in every reasonable way...'[3]

---

2 Dhanajay Keer, *Dr. Ambedkar, Life and Mission,* Popular Prakashan, Bombay, 1990, pp. 171–86.

3 MSS.EUR.E.240(10), Vol. II.

In the ensuing years also the British continued to find him to be more than useful. They saw that at every turn he was straining to take the position that would serve their interests, and meet with their approval. Writing to Sir George Stanley, the governor of Madras, on 24 November 1933, Sir Samuel Hoare remarked, 'During the last two or three years I have seen a great deal of Ambedkar, and, like most of my friends, *I have been impressed by his ability and his manifest desire to support the British influence in India.* He has had a big fight, first of all with Gandhi and secondly with caste Hindus, and on the whole he seems to me to have come out of it well.'[4] As a result they wanted to do both—to reward him, and simultaneously to place him in a position that would ensure that what he said would carry greater weight. Accordingly, over the years the idea of rewarding Ambedkar with a position of influence, in particular a place in the Viceroy's Council cropped up several times in the correspondence between the Secretary of State for India in London and the viceroy in Delhi, between the latter and the governor in Bombay. The appointment had almost come through in 1940, but then, as we saw, had to be aborted at the last minute.

At that time the viceroy had been able to tell both the Secretary of State and later the king that Ambedkar and Aney had both taken the news very well: writing about the plans he had at that stage for expanding his Executive Council, the viceroy reported to the king on 20 February 1941, that he had sent for Ambedkar and Aney, that both of them had accepted his invitation to join the Council, but that he had later had to withdraw the offer. 'Both, I am glad to say, proved entirely reasonable,' the viceroy wrote, 'and each assured me that given the situation that had arisen, he

4 MSS.EUR.E.240(10).

concurred in my view that the plan had better be dropped for the time being...'5

Two months hadn't gone by and the Secretary of State was again pressing arguments upon the viceroy for inducting Ambedkar. In his letter of 13 June 1941 to the viceroy, he observed, 'He is I believe a man of real ability and in some sense represents labour in its most depressed forms. He could be a fourth without I imagine raising the communal issue. It would certainly give news value to your list as well as cheer the untouchables and put Gandhi's nose out of joint.'[6] But the moment didn't come. A few months later when Ambedkar again did not make it to the Council, the frustration burst through. He urged his case to the Secretary of State—the dejection that was manifest flies in the face of the usual claims that Ambedkar was never keen on posts, just as the grounds on which he pleaded for the post were typical—he wanted the post not for himself but so that the Depressed Classes may be represented ! 'I have just had a desperate cable of protest from Ambedkar at his exclusion as the representative of 60 million depressed classes, from your Executive, and suggesting that you might just as well add at least one more,' the Secretary of State informed the viceroy on 6 August, 1941. 'I am leaving it to you to answer him on my behalf, as you know best what to say with the plans you have in view,' the Secretary of State added. 'My inclination would be to let him know that you hope to fit him in the near future. Meanwhile I am quite sure that having added five Indians instead of three to the Executive has made all the difference to the favourable impression the scheme has created here... So far as I am concerned, if you can make a reasonable case for the additional portfolio to pacify Ambedkar, I shouldn't mind very much, and I dare say the Cabinet would swallow it quite cheerfully. But if

5 MSS.EUR.F.125/1, p. 85.

6 MSS.EUR.F.125/20.

you give way to him, you will certainly have the Sikhs on your back with renewed vigour; and I hope you may be able to square Ambedkar with the seat in the offing.'[7] In the event Ambedkar remained on hold.

By early 1942 Ambedkar's induction was again in the air. On 29 January 1942 in a telegram marked *'Immediate'* to the Secretary of State the viceroy notes that meetings of the Congress Working Committee and the AICC have been held. As part of the steps that are to be taken to gear up the government for the challenge that is growing, the viceroy reports that he is thinking of changes in his Council. Ambedkar is a natural for inclusion.[8] The Secretary of State concurs, suggesting at the same time that the portfolios of 'Ambedkar and the Sikh' should be left unspecified for the time being.[9] Three weeks later Linlithgow is telling the Secretary of State, 'As a result of further inquiries I am convinced that Ambedkar is the right and only proper representative of the Depressed Classes'—an assessment which after using him for four more years the British will feel justified in giving up ![10]

The governor's insight

On 29 April 1942, as tension vis-à-vis the Congress mounts, L.S. Amery tells the viceroy, 'I am sure you will do well to bring in Ambedkar.'[11] Events are moving fast. Europe has been at war. The British need Indian support, at the least they have to ensure that India remains calm. Congress leaders have been maintaining that, while the people of India are as resolutely opposed to fascism as anyone,

7 MSS.EUR.F/125/10, p. 144.

8 *Transfer of Power,* Vol. I, pp. 91–92.

9 *Transfer of Power,* Vol. I, pp. 98–99.

10 *Transfer of Power,* Vol. I, p. 211.

11 *Transfer of Power,* Vol. I, p. 868.

India cannot support the war effort unless the British government declares that India will be granted freedom once the war is over. Sir Stafford Cripps has led a mission to India to discuss future constitutional arrangements. The negotiations have broken down.

'As is always the case here,' writes the governor of Bombay Presidency, Sir R. Lumley, in a *Confidential* note to the viceroy, the Marquess of Linlithgow, 'it is not easy to assess precisely the public reactions to the breakdown of negotiations conducted by Sir Stafford Cripps. I am glad to say, however, that I do not notice any deterioration or any bitterness, with the exception which I shall mention later...' He describes what he has learnt about reactions among Congressmen, Muslims, Parsis, etc., and then comes to the exception. It is best to put the account in the governor's own words:

> The exception to which I had referred is Ambedkar. He came to see me to discuss the establishment of the National War Front, and although he has, with enthusiasm, agreed to give it some support, he took the opportunity to let off to me some very bitter steam about the Draft Declaration. He said that he had been as good as told that Congress and the Muslim League were the only bodies which counted, and that if they agreed to the proposals, it would not matter what he or the Depressed Classes thought about them. He professed to be bitterly disillusioned and to feel humiliated. He declared that the proposals went back on the August Declaration, and that, with the example of the Irish Treaty before him, the suggestion that minorities could be safeguarded by means of a treaty was a very poor joke.

Recall that actually Ambedkar had been pressing Cripps on just such a treaty, and that later he was to urge just that kind of a treaty upon Wavell, but that was typical. To proceed with Lumley's account of the discussion with Ambedkar, the governor continued:

> How, he [that is, Ambedkar] asked, could he and his friends be expected to continue their support of Government if they were to be let down in this way? He had thought of resigning from the National Defence Council but had decided to carry on for the time being, but he could not be expected to show any enthusiasm in support of Government. I reasoned with him as best I could, but I fear made little impression upon him.

The governor turned to give the viceroy his reading of what Ambedkar was really after. As events were soon to show, the assessment was perceptive to the dot. The governor wrote:

> This mood of disgruntlement has been noticeable in Ambedkar for a long time—certainly since he was not taken in to the expansion of your Executive Council, as he had hoped. He will, I expect, succeed in obtaining some support for his views amongst his followers in this Province, for he is the only individual amongst them who is capable of thinking for them. *Nevertheless, I feel pretty sure that this disgruntlement is largely a personal matter. As you know, his own financial position has been worrying him for some time. I have reason to believe that he owes money to certain people who have helped him in the past, and that he is unable to pay any of it back, and is even rather rude if they mention the subject. As you know, too, he has been, for some time, anxious to obtain a position in the High Court or elsewhere, in which he could have a chance of providing for his own future. He has given me, for some time, the impression of a man who is no longer really interested in the work he is doing for his own followers, and is anxious to reach a different sphere.*

And the governor pinpointed a central trait of Ambedkar which we find throughout the latter's career. Lumley wrote:

> *He is inclined, unfortunately, to attribute the difficulties of his own position to influences at work against him because he is a member of the Depressed Classes, and from that it is an easy step to the belief that*

> *we do not concern ourselves about him unduly because we do not think it worth-while to secure the support of the Depressed Classes.*

Lumley added his personal recommendation—a mixture of empathy for a person who had strained so hard to be helpful, and a plea in terms of the benefits which were liable to accrue if he were rewarded at that juncture. Lumley concluded his account of the meeting with:

> I would very much like to see something done for him, and I hope that, if a further expansion of your Council is now possible, he will be included—not on personal grounds alone, but so that we may retain the interest of the Depressed Classes. He has been unhelpful about recruitment of Mahars, and does not put his weight behind it overmuch, in spite of the fact that he has long clamoured for Mahars being taken into combatant units. Nevertheless, the recruitment of Mahars continues, but not as well as it would do if he were really keen to help.[12]

The governor had written to the viceroy on 24 April 1942. The viceroy replied in a *Confidential* letter of his own to the governor on 30 April. 'Very many thanks for your letter of 24th April,' he wrote. 'I was greatly interested in your assessment of the reactions in Bombay to the outcome of Cripps' negotiations, and am most grateful for them. *As you know I have Ambedkar very much in mind, and I hope it will be possible for me to do something for him—he has behaved very well so far as I am concerned, and as again you know, had our plans for expansion gone through at an earlier stage he would have been one of those to benefit, and he has the quality and the courage'*—by which, one need be in no doubt, the

12 The *Confidential exchanges* are in the *Transfer of Power* documents, Vol. I, pp. 846–47, 873–74. Lumley's letter is reproduced in *Dr. Babasaheb Ambedkar, Writings and Speeches,* Vol. X, pp. 449–51.

viceroy meant that Ambedkar had the 'courage and quality' to stand on the side of the British, and against the national movement. The viceroy continued, 'I got the impression from various quarters that Cripps possibly treated these minor minorities as we used to call them with insufficient care and that he left on them too definitely the impression that the only people who mattered were Congress and the Muslim League. That may or may not be the case, but in this peculiarly sensitive country, and dealing with men who do hold in their hands to some extent the responsibility for very large masses of people, one cannot, I always feel, be too careful to avoid any suggestion of lack of sympathy or failure to accept the sincerity of those with whom one is dealing'—all this was sanctimonious humbug: the viceroy was doing what he was to do again and again in the next year, that is use every occasion to bad-mouth Cripps; and as for always accepting that the interlocutor was sincere, the way Linlithgow dealt with Gandhiji, the things he wrote about him, the dodges and deceit he deployed against him, some of which we shall encounter as we proceed, give the lie to his little ditty about accepting that the other person is sincere; but at the moment our interest is in what he had to say in response to the governor's recommendation regarding Ambedkar.

The viceroy reassured the governor, and made a forecast about Ambedkar's current bitterness. He said, 'If in the outcome Ambedkar joins my Council I should feel that I had in him a reliable and valuable colleague, and *I have no doubt that any temporary bitterness which he may feel about the way in which he thinks he has been treated will disappear.*' How perceptive that last sentence was, just as how very accurate Lumley's assessment of the man had been—that his overwhelming concern was to get himself a position in the British Government, that *'he has been, for some time, anxious to obtain a position in the High Court or elsewhere, in which he could have a chance of providing for his future,'* that *'he has given me, for some tune, the impression of a man who is no longer interested in the work he is doing for his own followers, and is anxious to reach a different sphere'*—how very accurate these assessments were is evident from the utter loyalty with which Ambedkar stood by the British throughout the four years he was a member of the Viceroy's Council.

Can anyone fail to spot the craven gratitude in the letter that Ambedkar wrote to the viceroy upon hearing that the latter would be demitting office soon? After setting out his usual list of the grievances of the Scheduled Castes in the letter he wrote to Linlithgow on 29 October 1942, Ambedkar concluded:

> *I need not say that I hope the grievances of the Scheduled Castes will be remedied before you go. Believe me, I have read with genuine sorrow that you will be quitting your office in April next. I have no idea who is going to be your successor and what attitude he will adopt towards the Scheduled Castes. In you I have learnt to place great confidence as the benefactor of the Scheduled Castes. You have done the greatest deed towards them by giving them a place in your Executive Council. It is a most revolutionary act for which there can be no parallel in India's history. I have no doubt and no member of the Scheduled Castes has any doubt that if you knew the grievances of the Scheduled Castes you would never hesitate to set them right. It is from this point of view that I say that I am happy to have to seek justice for my people from one who knows that justice is due to them. I know you have the will to do it and that you will not like to leave it to your successor to do what you wish to do, and what you can do. I need hardly say that for this act of justice myself and the 50 millions of the Scheduled Castes will ever remain grateful to you....'*[13]

---

13 *Dr. Babasaheb Ambedkar, Writings and Speeches,* Vol. X, pp. 470–72.

One has only to contrast these fawning words with the venomous words he used to hurl at Gandhiji in season and out, and one is driven to shame. Had Linlithgow not been right when he had surmised, 'If in the outcome Ambedkar joins my Council... I have no doubt that any temporary bitterness which he may feel about the way in which he thinks he has been treated will disappear'? And had the governor of Bombay not been right when he had written that to Ambedkar the test of whether someone or some government was being fair to the Scheduled Castes was whether that person or government was giving to Ambedkar personally what Ambedkar thought he deserved? Was he not right in having guessed that Ambedkar did not care so much for what was done for or happened to his followers as he did for whether he was able to acquire a position that would help him in 'providing for his future'?

Do read the expressions that Ambedkar uses in his letter to the viceroy. 'In you I have learnt to place great confidence as *the benefactor of the Scheduled Castes'*—it is not just that Linlithgow did no more than any other British ruler for the Scheduled Castes—and as we have seen, on the telling of Ambedkar himself the net result of British rule as far as the Scheduled Castes were concerned was that, in spite of what Ambedkar described as the loyal services they had rendered to the British, the Scheduled Castes had remained where they had been; the fact is that Linlithgow did absolutely nothing to alleviate the real problems of the Scheduled Castes; but as he included Ambedkar in his Council, on Ambedkar's telling he was *'the benefactor of the Scheduled Castes'*. 'You have done *the greatest deed* towards them by giving them a place in your Executive Council'—here was a man who had made a profession of retailing allegations about the way these castes had been persecuted and pillaged for thousands of years, and in his reckoning *'the greatest deed'* for them was that the viceroy had given him, Ambedkar, a seat in his Council! No, this was not just 'the greatest deed', on Ambedkar's telling, 'It is *a most revolutionary act for which there can be no parallel in India's history.'* And the touching faith in the viceroy: here was Ambedkar who had been writing tracts after tracts to assert that not only had the Scheduled Castes been exploited for aeons by caste Hindus, their exploitation was of the very essence of Hinduism; but he was ever so confident that between then and April—that is, in just five months—the viceroy would be able to undo this ancient wrong! He had no doubt, no member of the Scheduled Castes had any doubt, Ambedkar said, that the viceroy would remove the injustices to which they had been subjected for centuries, if only the viceroy knew them! What a benefactor of the Scheduled Castes who did not even know the injustices which the objects of his beneficence had been made to suffer for aeons!

And that last sentence: 'I need hardly say that for this act of justice myself and the 50 millions of the Scheduled Castes will ever remain grateful to you...' Yes, Ambedkar did identify with the Scheduled Castes—but was it in the sense that to him *their* interests were *his* interests, or in the sense that to him *his* interests were *their* interests?

But I anticipate. There was still a service that the British were to expect, and demand, and get from their ally before taking him on board.

A command performance

As the summer advanced tension between the Congress and the British grew. The Congress inched towards preparing itself for a nationwide movement. The British began preparing themselves to meet the challenge. On 30 May 1942 L.S. Amery, the Secretary of State for India, sent a telegram to the viceroy marked *'Important, Private and*

Personal'. 'I have telegraphed to you separately about mobilizing press support here for any essential action you may be forced to take in consequence of Gandhi's new campaign. Question occurs to me whether limelight could be somewhat deflected from Congress spokesmen if you could stimulate members of your reconstituted Council, such as C.P. Ramaswami Ayyar and Ambedkar if they are included, to tour and deliver stirring speeches on war effort. By acceptance of your invitation to join Executive members will be pledged to full support of war front. It would certainly be helpful here and in U.S.A. and I should have thought to loyal elements, including army in India, for them to confess publicly their faith in resistance to Japanese menace citing China's example and determination to rouse their countrymen from passive acquiescence to active resistance to the enemy.'

'If any of your Council could be mobilized to undertake such a campaign,' he continued, 'it would be for consideration whether in the course of it they should directly attack Gandhi's ideas of non-violent non-cooperation both with the enemy and with those who are disposed to resist the enemy. If this tactic were adopted an incidental feature of it (which might be given prominence in the U.S.A. and in China which looks to U.S.A. for help) might be to traverse Gandhi's dictum... that though the British must vacate and leave India to chaos it is the Americans that must get out first.'

'In this connection I am now inclined to think that your first instinct in proposing C.P. Ramaswami Ayyar'—another of the sorts of persons whose role we have forgotten today—'for Information portfolio may have been right. His ability and record of spirited resistance to Gandhi's encouragement of Travancore seditionists seem to mark him out for vigorous leadership along these lines....'[14]

---

14 *Transfer of Power,* Vol. II, pp. 150–51.

The Secretary of State reverted to the matter again in yet another telegram the same day marked *'Immediate, Personal'*. 'As we see it present tendency of Press here at any rate is to take possibly superficial view and to regard Gandhi's statements as product of senility. You yourself have, I think most wisely, taken the line that publicity for Gandhi's views is calculated to do him more harm than good at the moment. This is certainly the case in this country and the U.S.A. but I should be grateful for your views as to the desirability of our beginning to prepare public opinion against the possible revelation of Gandhi's real purpose, whatever it may be, and of its effect in India.'

'I quite realize,' Amery continued, 'that it is impossible in the present circumstances to estimate the course of events with any certainty, but I am anxious, as I know you will be, that the public opinion in this country and in the U.S.A. should not be left a moment longer than is prudent under any misapprehension as to the potential dangers of situation and that the ground should be prepared against the necessity of your having to take drastic measures to deal with it. Judicious advance guidance to the Press here and in U.S.A. might well preserve us against ill-informed criticism of 'repressive' measures and enable us to line up the Press fairly....'[15]

The viceroy concurred, and he prepared the governors for mobilizing the loyal elements. By 14 July 1942 the Working Committee had finalized the 'Quit India' resolution. It was released for publication. The resolution showed that while the Congress was not insistent on the Allied forces withdrawing immediately, it was emphatic that British rule must end immediately. The resolution also announced that

15 *Transfer of Power,* Vol. II, pp.151–52.

Gandhiji would lead a nationwide struggle to achieve the objectives of the resolution.

The viceroy sent *'Immediate, Private and Personal'* telegrams to the governor of each province and asked them to get the allies of the British to speak up and denounce Gandhiji and the Congress. Sir A. Hope was asked to secure such statements from prominent non-Brahmins from Madras, Sir J. Herbert was asked to get prominent Muslims to speak up from Bengal, Sir B. Glancy was asked to drum up such statements from the Sikh leaders.

In his *'Secret'* communication to Glancy about discussions in the Executive Council Linlithgow wrote, 'My colleagues, with whom, I need not say, I wholly agree, were also very emphatic as to the importance of propaganda here, at home [that is, in England], in the United States and in China, and I am doing what I can to help along these lines. The suggestion was also made that it was of real importance that we should mobilize as far as possible those individuals and parties throughout the country which did not agree with the Congress resolution or with Gandhi's policy, and endeavour to persuade by such means as we thought proper and expedient to come out in open condemnation of it.'

'Now one of the most important of these elements is the Sikh community,' the viceroy continued. 'I should be most grateful if you would do what you can with Jogendra Singh...and see what can be done to try and get the Sikhs to come out in reasoned criticism and opposition. There is otherwise the grave and obvious risk that the case may go by default, and that the United States and even people at home may think that Gandhi is right in claiming that he is the sole mouthpiece of India and that there is no opposition to his views. Jinnah has already indicated pretty clearly on one or two occasions in the last month his attitude towards Gandhi's propositions. I should like to think that he would do so again, though I have no knowledge what his attitude is likely to be, and for obvious reasons I have no intention of approaching him on the subject. But anything that Sikander [Hayat Khan] could say would, I am certain, be of real value, and I am certain that my publicity people here would see to it that critical comment was transmitted to those quarters likely to be most interested in it.'[16]

But while the viceroy seemed a trifle uncertain whether Jinnah would repeat his views and speak out in public against Gandhiji, while he was hesitant to approach Jinnah to do so, he was neither uncertain whether Ambedkar would agree to speak out and denounce Gandhiji nor had he any hesitation in directing that Ambedkar be asked to do so.

On 16 July 1942 Linlithgow sent an *'Immediate, Private and Personal'* telegram to Roger Lumley, the governor in Bombay. 'I think it is most important in face of Gandhi's agitation to get the various parties and prominent individuals who do not sympathize with his view to come out in public condemnation of it; and anything we can discreetly do to produce that result would, I am sure, be well worthwhile. You may have opportunities of encouraging critical comment in Bombay.' That sort of instruction was sent to governors of other provinces also. The viceroy then turned to a specific matter, and a specific individual.

'I should also be most grateful,' he said in his telegram, 'if you would let Ambedkar know from me for his private and personal information that this matter was discussed yesterday in my Council,'... 'that we agreed that we should postpone final decision until the matter had been before All India Congress Committee on 7th August, and that if the body did ratify Gandhi's resolution and subject to any

---

16 For various communications of this kind, *Transfer of Power,* Vol. II, pp. 395–99, 406–07.

developments that there might be in between we should have to take immediate and drastic action against Congress and its leaders'—do read that again. The viceroy here is not just apprising Ambedkar of a decision of his Council, he is making him aware of the fact that this is what the government will do—that is, 'take immediate and drastic action against Congress and its leaders'. He is doing what the Secretary of State had said would be useful to do. 'By acceptance of your invitation to join Executive members will be pledged to full support of war front,' Amery had counselled. Linlithgow having informed Ambedkar explicitly what government had decided to do and when, Ambedkar cannot but be said to have been fully aware of what he would be joining should he decide to join the government.

'It was also the clear sense of the meeting,' the viceroy wanted the governor to inform Ambedkar, 'that what was possible should be done to encourage either parties or individuals not agreeing with Gandhi's view to make their position clear in public. Otherwise, there is of course great danger of the case going by default in the United States and even at home [that is, in the UK]. If as I trust Ambedkar is in agreement with the general feeling of Council I hope he will do all that he can if opportunity offers in Bombay to swing the Depressed Classes definitely against Congress and to organize such demonstrations or public statements as may be practicable in reasoned condemnation of the line of the main Congress resolution.'[17]

The message was duly and promptly delivered. For in his *'Confidential'* telegram of 17 July 1942 the governor of Bombay informed the viceroy, 'Ambedkar, in conversation, expressed the view that Congress would not receive much support from Labour, and thought that it would receive so little that it might be possible to ignore it'—events just a

17 *Transfer of Power*, Vol. II, pp. 395–96.

month later were to show how off the mark this estimate, as many others of his that we shall encounter, was. 'I have sent him the message contained in your telegram of July the 16th, which arrived after I had seen him. The National War Front, I understand from Griffiths, who happened to be here, is producing a reasoned statement.'[18]

In the event, Ambedkar's appointment was notified on 20 July 1942. The effect of the message from the viceroy and of the announcement of his inclusion in the Viceroy's Council was immediate. On 23 July 1942 by telegram the viceroy was able to inform Amery, the Secretary of State in London, in triumph:

> No. 2169-S. Following from Lumley, dated July 22nd:-Begins. Ambedkar made a strong speech last night declaring civil disobedience at this time 'treachery to India' and 'playing the enemy's game' and urging all Indians as a patriotic duty 'to resist with all the power and resources at their command any attempt on the part of Congress to launch civil disobedience'.
>
> He also announced that before he left for Delhi he would issue a statement explaining the line of policy which the Independent Labour Party and other allied organizations *must* follow. He asked his audience (of his followers) to study that statement and implicitly carry out its instructions. Ends.'

The viceroy added: 'I am asking Puckle to make special arrangements to have this statement when it appears telegraphed to U.K. and U.S.A. and feel sure you will be able to turn it to good use.'[19]

Four days later, just before leaving for Delhi to assume charge Ambedkar gave an interview to *The Times of India.* He characterized Gandhiji's moves as irresponsible and insane. He said that they reflected Gandhi's bankruptcy, and were just an attempt to recover for the Congress the

---

18 *Transfer of Power,* Vol. II, pp. 405–06.

19 *Transfer of Power,* Vol. II, pp. 436–37.

prestige which it had lost in the preceding two years. It would be madness, he told the paper, to weaken law and order when barbarians were at the gates to seize mastery over the country.

What the inspiration and goad had been behind these statements is evident from the report the governor of Bombay sent to the Viceroy during 24–27 August as he surveyed the success which had attended the operation of sweeping Gandhiji and other Congress leaders off to jails on the morning of 9 August. 'Prominent citizens, like Sir Chimanlal Setalvad and Sir Cowasji Jehangir, came out almost at once, after the Wardha meeting with their own highly critical statements of the Congress Resolution,' he reported. 'Dr. Ambedkar responded to your suggestion by a very downright denunciation of Congress on behalf of the Depressed Classes. The National War Front, with commendable courage, issued its own statement....'[20]

Transparent motives

It isn't just that Ambedkar had been doing what they wanted done for so long and that therefore the British wanted to reward him personally. His induction into the Viceroy's Executive Council was part of a larger design. There were two elements to this: to wrest the Scheduled Castes away from Hindu society; and, second, to stuff the Executive Council with reliable henchmen so that decisions of repression and the rest could be announced to have been taken by Indians themselves as much as by the British.

Though their motives had been different, Muslims and Hindus had tried together to heave the British out in 1857. After that, among Muslims it is the collaborationist and capitulationist doctrines of Sir Syed Ahmed which acquired

---

20 *Transfer of Power*, Vol. II, p. 805.

sway. By 1906 this reorientation had proceeded so far that the British could drum up a 'delegation' of Muslims—led by the Aga Khan—to submit to the viceroy a memorandum which the British had themselves drawn up, and which contained that all-important, and for India fatal, demand for separate electorates. This was one of the central devices of the British 'Divide and Rule' policy: to hold out a reward which the group could aspire to only by separating itself from the rest of Indian society.

The same operation had been set afoot among the Sikhs. Ceremonies were introduced in the army which would instil in Sikh recruits the notion that they were not Hindus. Sikh scholars like Kahan Singh of Nabha were taken over to assist in preparing 'histories' which sought to establish that Sikhs had always been not just different from but in essence opposed to the Hindus—it was indeed in the fitness of things that Macauliffe willed the royalties from his 'history' to Kahan Singh. Soon enough the latter's *Hum Hindu Nahin* became the evangelical aide for the British operating in the Punjab as much as for a section of the Sikh leadership. Instructions were given to census officials to ensure that Sikhs were not enumerated as 'Hindus'—'which in fact they are,' the official concerned was constrained to record—in the censuses. The idea that they too should have a separate electorate was insinuated to the Sikhs also.

Such schemes were always in the mind of the British, and they were forwarding proposals to that effect to each other at every turn. In his letter of 10–13 September 1943 Linlithgow forwarded to the Secretary of State a memorandum from the Britasian Colony Committee. The Committee had proposed that the Andaman and Nicobar Islands be reserved for Anglo-Indians, Anglo-Burmese, and Anglo-Malayans. Amery was most interested. 'I confess I was much interested and not a little attracted by the 'Britasian' programme for the resettlement of the Andamans and Nicobars,' he wrote to the viceroy in his letter of 1 October 1943. 'I am by no means sure that something of that sort is not the best way of tackling the problem and making an effective community of them. They would certainly be in a good strategic position and might find employment in a good many directions connected with sea and air transport. Looking back, one can never help regretting that we did not keep Kashmir after the Sikh Wars and use it for the large scale settlement both of old British officers and soldiers and also for Anglo-Indians. If India is to be really capable of holding its own in the future without direct British control from outside, I am not sure that it will not need an increasing infusion of stronger Nordic blood, whether by settlement or intermarriage or otherwise. Possibly, it has been a real mistake of ours in the past not to encourage Indian princes to marry English wives for a succession of generations and so breed a more virile type of native ruler. Perhaps all that may yet come about'—these ruminations just three years before they had to concede Independence to India.[21]

Exactly the same operation—of detaching them from Hindu society—had been going on in regard to tribals: in spite of their objections census officials had been instructed to create a separate group of 'Animists' as distinct from 'Hindus' and to enumerate tribals as belonging to that group.

And there was no ambiguity, neither any circumlocution about motives in all this. 'These aborigines by their mind and conscience offer a surface like clean paper, upon which the missionaries may make a mark,' declaimed Sir Richard Temple, successively the resident at Hyderabad, and the head of the British administration in three provinces

21 *Transfer of Power,* Vol. IV, p. 355. On that last bit about having Indian princes marry English wives and so breed a more virile strain of native rulers, the viceroy wrote one word in the margin: *'Hell!'*

— Central Provinces, Madras, and Bombay; and 'if they (the tribals) are attached, as they rapidly may be, to Christianity, they will form a nucleus round which British power and influence may gather...' The very title of Macauliffe's essay on the Sikhs had been, *The Sikh Religion and its Advantages to the State.*[22]

The Scheduled Castes had of course been the special targets of the missionaries as well as the rulers from the very beginning. By the time of the Simon Commission they too were being enumerated outside the Hindu fold. Separate electorates having worked so very well in pulling Muslims even further away from the national movement, the device was deployed, as we have seen, for the Scheduled Castes also. The design had been foiled by Gandhiji's fast of 1932, but the British had not given up. 'Possibly too,' the Secretary of State writes to the viceroy on 16 January 1943, 'after Gandhi's death it might be worth considering whether the present anomalous electoral arrangements for the Scheduled Castes should not be altered and a direct communal basis substituted, as originally suggested, but revised up to date in accordance with the census figures...'[23]

Ambedkar was the instrument of choice for the British in all these manoeuvres in so far as they related to the Scheduled Castes. The design, motives, steps were as clear as they can be. 'I read Ambedkar's letter and memorandum about the grievances of the Scheduled Castes enclosed in your letter of November 21st,' the Secretary of State, L.S. Amery writes to the viceroy on 16 December 1942. *'It does seem to me as if it would be well worth while giving them a substantial leg-up and assimilating their*

---

22 The steps and elements of these operations are recounted in brief in my *Missionaries in India: Continuities, Changes, Dilemmas,* ASA Publications, New Delhi, 1994.

23 *Transfer of Power,* Vol. III, p. 633.

position increasingly to that of the Muslims. There are, after all, politically very considerable advantages in having two substantial minorities to whom consideration has to be paid, and not to be put in the position of being merely labeled pro-Muslim and anti-Hindu. I realize the practical difficulty of offering a fixed proportion of places to a community which may not be able to produce a sufficient number of educated candidate for the services. Would it not be possible to lay down a proportion to be attained at the end of a given number of years, with a smaller initial proportion, and utilize those years for the development of educational facilities? That would apply to both the civil services and the fighting forces. I am not sure whether, when you or your successor have added one or two more Muslims to the Executive, it might not be worth while adding yet another Untouchable on the basis that after all they are somewhere between a sixth and a seventh of the whole population of India.'[24]

Linlithgow's response is just as telling. In his *'Private and Personal'* communication of 5 January 1943 to Amery, the viceroy writes, 'I have every sympathy for the Depressed Classes, and I am pushing ahead on Ambedkar's memorandum. *I think there is a good deal in the point you make as to the political importance of recognizing so great a minority as the Depressed Classes actually are.* One of the troubles about that is of course that they are so extraordinarily short of personnel of any quality. Ambedkar himself is outstanding. Little Rajah from Madras is not bad but not striking. Siva Raj, whom we have sent to America, has a good deal of edge to him and might come on very well. But there are precious few others whom one has heard of in the community.'[25]

---

24 *Transfer of Power*, Vol. III, p. 390.

25 *Transfer of Power*, Vol. III, p. 456; see also ibid., pp.504–05 for the viceroy's observation that Maxwell in the home department was alive

And in view of what Ambedkar did finally, that is 'convert' to 'Buddhism', it is interesting that something of the same kind was not just presaged but hoped for by the Secretary of State! In the same letter of 16 January 1943, Amery laments, 'The fundamental weakness of the Scheduled Castes is that they are neither one thing nor the other. If they had the courage to turn Christian or Muslim *en bloc* it would be much easier to legislate for them. But so long as they do remain a part of the Hindu system, with no separate religion or basis of organization as such, and continue to regard themselves as Hindus, it does look as if their only chance of betterment lay, not on the political side, but on gradually winning their way socially in the Hindu community.' And then the further lament: 'At present it looks as if, apart from Ambedkar and a handful of others, they have no real notion of what they want to be or of how to organize themselves.'[26]

So, that was one point: apart from rewarding a person who had for so long 'behaved so well', the British were out to 'giving them (the Scheduled Castes) a substantial leg-up and assimilating their position increasingly to that of the Muslims'. There was in addition a more general tactic at work.

Confrontation with the Congress seemed more and more inevitable. It would indeed be useful, the British rulers told each other, to put Indians in the front rank. Ambedkar, with his demonstrated willingness to hurl the harshest possible invective at Gandhiji and the Congress was a natural candidate.

'I do not want to bore you by referring again to non-official Advisers,' the governor of Madras wrote to the viceroy on

---

to this and was already implementing schemes in the same direction as the Secretary of State had suggested.

26 *Transfer of Power,* Vol. III, pp. 633–34.

23 July 1942 about the corresponding proposal in regard to the provinces, 'but this question has again cropped up very acutely in the last few weeks... Many people whom I have seen are not people who could expect or want positions in the Government, but they say the same thing: *mobilize non-Congress opinion, and the best way to do that is to have non-Congress Advisers....* Now that Congress is our avowed enemy, and we are treating them so in the National War Front, *surely it would be wise to get the prominent non-Congress people into the Government which is going to fight Congress.*'[27]

Communication after communication of Linlithgow to Amery shows the same calculation at work. Five days after the governor of Madras wrote the foregoing to him, Linlithgow reports to the Secretary of State about his own plans in the same direction. 'As I write I have almost completed my Council, for Ambedkar, Usman and Srivastava have all joined, and I now await only Jogendra Singh (who is taking over on the 29th) and Sir C. P. Ramaswami Aiyar (who is taking over about the 5th). I should therefore have a full team before the meeting of the A.-I.C.C. on 7th August, and *there may well be some little value in the fact that the important discussions that are now going on about policy towards Congress, and possibly the decision to arrest Gandhi &c., fall to be conducted with a Council entirely non-official save for the Chief and myself, and entirely Indian save for the Chief, myself and Benthall.* Maxwell has been seedy and is likely to be out of action for the best part of a month, and Raisman is of course in London....'[28]

With the day of reckoning just five days away the viceroy reverts to the advantage of humouring along the Indians in his Council so that they become full and inextricable

---

27 *Transfer of Power,* Vol. II, p. 443.

28 *Transfer of Power,* Vol. II, p. 485.

partners to the decisions to arrest Gandhiji and the rest. In his *'Private and Personal'* report to Amery of 3 August 1942, Linlithgow writes of the new members of his Council, 'Old or new, it is very important to ride them as gently as possible, and still more important to avoid leaving behind, in any decisions such as those which one has to take at the present time, any little centres of disaffection or disappointment. They are doing very well so far, but I do not want them to give them a chance of running out on what must be a nasty and most unpopular job, as they might well be tempted to were I to try to ride them on too tight a rein. It is all a business of taking them along with one...'[29]

Three days had not passed and in an *'Immediate, Private and Personal'* telegram to the Secretary of State, Linlithgow returned to the imperative need to keep these frontmen well and conspicuously in the front. The BBC in London had broadcast an item setting out what the attitude of the British government in London was to the forthcoming meeting of the All-India Congress Committee. Members of the Viceroy's Council felt slighted—the item was too truthful! It seemed to imply that the British government in London was laying down on its own how Gandhi, etc., were going to be dealt with. 'I have received very strong protest from my Council against statement made by B.B.C. in their Indian broadcast last night as to the indications given by authoritative circles in England of action that would be taken against A.-I.C.C., &c.,' the viceroy telegraphed.

And what was their anxiety? 'Council have at the moment almost an obsession about their position and extent to which Cripps negotiations have put them in the background, and they are morbidly sensitive of any suggestion that they are being run by His Majesty's Government,' the viceroy explained. 'Their complaint was that

29 *Transfer of Power,* Vol. II, p. 546.

B.B.C. statement would have given impression throughout India that they are not free agents.'

And what was the viceroy's objective and anxiety? The telegram continued: *'Nothing of course is more desirable from our point of view than to keep them full behind us in our present policy and wholly responsible for arrest of Gandhi, &c., if necessary.* And while I think they are unduly touchy, I do hope you will be able to give me something consoling to say to them on this point, and that you will do all you can to shut down any comment of the kind from the B.B.C. I made what play I could with the difficulty of keeping B.B.C. wholly under official control. Position is too delicate here for us to take any chances.'[30]

Two days before the All-India Congress Committee session in Bombay the War Cabinet met in London. Clement Atlee was in the chair. The minutes setting out the conclusions recorded, 'The Secretary of State said that the Viceroy, *who had acted in full accord with his Council,* had adopted an extremely patient attitude, in the hope that the Congress might think better of the course of action they proposed. *His own Council, however had decided that if Congress forced the issue, stern and swift action must be taken.* Evidence was now accumulating that Gandhi and those associated with him meant real mischief...' Notice the use to which the Council was being put—'...the Viceroy, who had throughout acted in full accord with his Council...', the viceroy 'had adopted an extremely patient attitude... His Council, however, had decided that if Congress forced the issue, stern and swift action must be taken...' Recall what the viceroy had told the Secretary of State earlier that day by telegram: 'Nothing of course is more desirable from our point of view than to keep them full behind us in our present policy and wholly responsible

30 *Transfer of Power,* Vol. II, p. 579.

for arrest of Gandhi, &c., if necessary...' And as will be apparent soon, the viceroy had not just been waiting patiently, he had for weeks been drawing up plans worked out to the last detail to swoop down on the Congress leaders. But the British had Indians at hand who for the trappings of office were prepared to be frontmen. Why would they not put these enthusiasts right up in front?

The minutes of the meeting of the War Cabinet adverted to this again: 'In announcing the action taken against the Congress leaders,' it emphasized, 'prominence should be given to the following points:- (a) *This action had the full support of the Members of the Viceroy's Executive Council...*'[31]

In the *'Most Immediate, Most Secret, Personal'* telegram that the Secretary of State sent to Linlithgow past midnight that very day he emphasized, 'As regards publicity Cabinet attach importance to it being emphasized throughout that Congress leaders are not ordinary prisoners but detained as preventive measure. They also consider that once you decide to arrest you should give prominence in publicity to the following points:- (1) *that action taken had full support of members of your Council;* (2) that resolution of Congress Working Committee was only the beginning of far-reaching plan wholly to undermine India's cooperation in war effort. Documentary evidence such as Andhra Committee's circular... should be made public and any other material showing the seriousness of the mischief intended; (3) that our action was taken in the interests of the United Nations as a whole, not merely for the protection of British interests in India.' Notice the emphasis on invoking the members of the Viceroy's Council again. But also keep in mind the point about making out that the resolution of the Congress Working Committee was but the

---

31 *Transfer of Power,* Vol. II, pp. 586–88.

first step of a far-reaching plan: for we shall soon see whom the British fielded to make that charge in the Central Legislative Assembly, and how very closely the person's attack on the Congress voiced the instructions that had come from the British Cabinet.

As news of the arrests reached China, Chiang Kai-shek sent an urgent message to President Roosevelt in Washington requesting the latter to use his good offices with Churchill so that an agreement could be brought about between the British and the Congress—Chiang Kai Shek was genuinely supportive of Indian aspirations and he also felt that the course events had taken would impede the war effort of the Allies.[32] Roosevelt passed the message on 12 August to Churchill who was in Moscow that day. Churchill reacted immediately to nip the initiative in the bud: 'I take it amiss Chiang should seek to make difficulties between us and should interfere in matters about which he has proved himself most ill-informed which affect our sovereign rights,' he told Roosevelt in a *'Secret, Personal'* telegram. *'Decision to intern Gandhi was taken by Executive of twelve, at which only one European was present. These Indians are as good Indian patriots and as able men as any of the Congress leaders. They have shown great courage and it is essential not to weaken their authority...'*[33]

As had been decided, that fact—that the decision had been taken by Indians—became one of the main elements in the propaganda in India also. Gandhiji learnt of it. His comment was precision itself. Writing to the viceroy on 14 August from the Aga Khan's house in Poona where he was detained, Gandhiji began, 'Dear Lord Linlithgow, The Government of India were wrong in precipitating the crisis. The Government Resolution justifying this step is full of distortions and misrepresentations. That you have the

32 His message to Roosevelt is at *Transfer of Power*, Vol. II, p. 672.

33 *Transfer of Power*, Vol. II, p. 687.

approval of your Indian "colleagues" can have no significance, except this, that in India you can always command such services. That co-operation is an additional justification for the demand of withdrawal irrespective of what people and parties may say....'[34]

This pattern continued: Council members like Ambedkar continued to endorse and speak up for what the British wanted done, and the British continued to cite their statements and the fact that these Indians had been associated with taking the decisions, that actually they had been in the forefront of taking the decisions as justification of what was being done.

Amery was appreciation itself. Writing to the viceroy after the Congress leaders were safely in jails he said, 'One of the aspects of your enlarged Executive which has been most helpful, at any rate at our end, has been the way different members have spoken up and stated the case either for the government or against the Congress. Ambedkar has been most effective more than once and so at an earlier stage was Firoz Noon. Even Jogendra was quite useful. *I am sure the more they are encouraged to speak in public or to broadcast and to feel they are defending their own case and the justification for their continuing in office, the better they will get at it themselves, and the greater the cumulative effect both in India and outside. So I hope you will keep them steadily at it.*'[35]

The viceroy did so indeed—humouring them by letting them discuss constitutional questions and the rest. Soon enough he was using the fact of these Indian members having endorsed the decisions to come down on the Congress not just in propaganda addressed to those outside government, he was using it as the handy argument in firming up or countering members themselves who wavered.

---

34 *Transfer of Power,* Vol. II, pp. 702–05.

35 *Transfer of Power,* Vol. III, p. 314.

Recall the hopes which had been put in Sir C.P. Ramaswami Aiyar: 'In this connection I am inclined to think that your first instinct in proposing C.P. Ramaswami Ayyar for the Information portfolio may have been right. His ability and record of spirited resistance to Gandhi's encouragement of Travancore seditionists seem to mark him out for vigorous leadership along these lines...,' the Secretary of State had written in his *'Important, Private and Personal'* telegram on 30 May 1942. And before the storm burst Sir C.P. Ramaswami Aiyar was certainly living up to the Secretary of State's expectations: the Council had met to consider whether, upon being arrested, Gandhiji, etc. should be deported to Aden or some place in Africa, and what ought to be done should Gandhiji embark on a fast—whether he should be released for the duration of the fast and then rearrested, a procedure which was being referred to as the 'cat and mouse treatment'; with less than a day to go before the AICC meeting in Bombay, the viceroy reported in his *'Most Immediate, Personal'* telegram to the Secretary of State, 'I thought it wiser not at this stage to raise the question of cat and mouse treatment, and will keep that till later. But in the course of discussion C.P. Ramaswami Aiyar said in terms (and without provoking any comeback) that in his judgement if Gandhi did fast, he should be left to face the consequences and that it should be made clear that that was not our fault (he added that he thought we should be in a stronger position to carry that policy through if he and the other leaders were interned in India)...'[36] But Sir C.P.'s nerves deserted him the moment the extent of the reaction to the arrests became evident. He started writing letters to the viceroy saying he wanted to leave so that he may go and talk things over with Gandhi, so that he may make the old man see reason.

---

36 *Transfer of Power,* Vol. II, p. 597.

The viceroy told the Secretary of State that he had called Sir C.P. over for a discussion. He had disabused him of the notion that he could have the slightest effect on Gandhi. 'That was my first point,' the viceroy reported. 'I turned now to the point of view of the public and the public interest. Sir C.P. would agree with me that he had joined my Government at a time when it was well known that a collision with Congress was more or less inescapable...' Next, the viceroy told Amery, he put it to Sir C.P. that whatever they might try it would not be possible to erase from the public mind the inference that Sir C.P. had left because he did not agree with the government's action against the Congress. And then the viceroy fielded the Council against Sir C.P.: 'Thirdly,' he wrote recounting his arguments, 'that my Council having decided on a very definite line and having deliberately accepted the Congress challenge, it was now for us to call off non-violence: not for us to ask Gandhi to do so.... Finally, and a very real difficulty which I wished to put in the most friendly way: were Sir C.P. to withdraw from my Council would that not almost certainly mean an early collision with his present colleagues? For their policy had been very clearly and deliberately that we would not approach Gandhi or let anyone else do so.'[37]

As we shall see in detail later, the same sequence and the same device was deployed a few months later—in February 1943—when Gandhiji was going through his twenty-one-day fast and government had definite information that he might die. The viceroy had got the Indians in his Council to endorse the decision that, come what may, they would let Gandhi take the consequences of his decision to fast. This very definitely and in terms included his dying before the fast was concluded. As the days passed members such as

37 *Transfer of Power,* Vol. II, pp. 720–23.

M.S. Aney and J.P. Srivastava began feeling nervous about being parties to the death of Gandhiji—of course Ambedkar felt no qualms on this score, as we shall have occasion to see. These members started urging that instead of having Gandhiji die on their hands, and as he was now so enfeebled that he would not be able to resume political activity of any consequence for quite a while, if ever, the government should release him unconditionally and thereby wash its hands off his death or deterioration.

The viceroy would have none of this, and put the familiar argument to the waverers. 'I have again seen Aney,' he said in his *'Most Immediate'* telegram to the Secretary of State. 'He could only urge that there was little between open offer of release for the purpose and duration of the fast and unconditional release at this stage. I said I saw all the difference in the world. After hours of discussion and by a considerable majority, we had by a Government statement which made it plain that nothing but unconditional release would stop a fast, said that we could not agree to that. We had burnt our boats and could not go back without becoming a laughing stock.' And, as was the wont of Britishers, the viceroy argued in the interest of Indians, indeed in the interest of the Hindus! 'And if the Hindu members generally resigned, they would do irreparable damage not merely to the possibility or idea of a national government, but to the whole practicability of parliamentary government on a democratic basis or constitutional progress for India. I should be very sorry to lose Aney and those who felt with him. But I should be even sorrier for the irretrievable injury Indian constitutional progress would suffer. How would it look if the Hindus collapsed and Jinnah came in on the basis of two or three Hindu officers plus the existing Moslems other than Sultan Ahmed. Aney was badly shaken by all this but is so terrified by fear of responsibility for Gandhi's death that that obliterates all other considerations. Meanwhile I have seen Jogendra, who says he will not resign. Firoz doubts whether these threats will come to anything....'[38]

The next day the viceroy was repeating the point in his *'Immediate, Personal' telegram* to Amery: '...My Hindu colleagues, while very uneasy at thought of what will happen if Gandhi dies, are in a hopelessly weak position logically given fact that our policy was approved by Council after fullest discussion and realize that, and also risk of Jinnah jumping their claim if they run out. I have made it clear to the wobblers that if they feel any doubts they must make up their minds without delay and that I am not prepared to wait....'[39]

Amery sent a minute to the prime minister, Churchill. 'The Gandhi business seems to have gone very satisfactorily so far,' Amery wrote. 'The Viceroy, having allowed his colleagues to have their way over giving Gandhi an opportunity to fast at liberty, was able to persuade them to take the responsibility of seeing it through. It is possible that Aney and some others who were in the minority may still resign. If they do so they will be resigning against the decision of their own Council and showing their unfitness to govern in face of popular hysteria...'[40]

The uses to which Indians were put. The uses for which these Indians made themselves available. As Gandhiji's condition worsened, as the doctors deputed by government informed it that he was not likely to survive the ordeal for much longer, as government remained determined to 'see the thing through'—that is, to let Gandhiji die in consequence of a decision that he had himself taken—as it remained completely unmoved by their appeals, by appeals issued

38 *Transfer of Power,* Vol. III, pp. 654–55.

39 *Transfer of Power,* Vol. III, pp. 656–57.

40 *Transfer of Power,* Vol. III, p. 657.

by leaders from all over the country that at least Gandhiji should be released unconditionally so that he might break or continue his fast as a free man, three members of the Viceroy's Council could take it no longer. H.P. Mody, M.S. Aney and N.R. Sarkar resigned. 'Our resignations from the Governor General's Council have been announced,' they said in a joint statement on 18 February 1943, 'and all we wish to do is to say by way of explanation that certain differences arose on what we regarded as a fundamental issue [the issue of the action to be taken on Mahatma Gandhi's fast], and we felt we could no longer retain our offices...'

The eleventh day into his fast Gandhiji had the gravest crisis. The government's surgeon general reported that he had had a stroke. The surgeon general was even more definite that the end was just hours away. On the 21 February the Bombay government thought it prudent to prepare the country: it issued a communique saying that Mahatma Gandhi was extremely weak, that if the fast was not ended without delay, it might be too late to save his life.

The country was shaken by then.

Not Ambedkar of course. He did not 'wobble' at all. Quite the contrary, he was among the ones who stood by the viceroy—firm that if the old man dies, well he dies.

But confounding all medical opinion, Gandhiji survived. The viceroy in Delhi, the Secretary of State in London, the whole British government proclaimed it as a triumph of the British—the old man has shot his last bolt, and got nothing out of us, they cabled each other. Telegrams flew, letters were dispatched congratulating each other for worsting 'the world's greatest humbug'—Linlithgow's words for Gandhiji, for worsting 'that miserable little old man'—Churchill's words for the Mahatma. They did not forget to compliment each other for those—Ambedkar foremost among them—who had stood by them.

Looking forward to the end of 'the Gandhi business' the Secretary of State wrote to the viceroy on 26 February 1943 in his *'Private and Secret'* communication: 'On the general question of filling up your Council I have already telegraphed and feel very strongly that you should not let yourself be too discouraged by the defection of three of your colleagues over the Gandhi business. After all your Council justified itself outstandingly in August and, even under the peculiarly difficult emotional conditions of the present crisis, only three of your battalions actually deserted the field of battle, while others may have wavered a bit but are still holding their ground. Whatever happens, the credit of those who remained will have increased by their standing fast, while, if Gandhi survives, the quitters will be in an absurd position which will by contrast enhance the credit of those who have stayed'— 'One of the stayers now out with post-fast strain,' wrote the viceroy in the margin.

He wasn't referring to Ambedkar of course.

3

The loyal minister

Ambedkar's appointment as member of the Viceroy's Executive Council was notified on 20 July 1942. He was soon in Delhi and attending sessions of the reconstituted Council. The All-India Congress Committee meeting in Bombay passed the 'Quit India' resolution on 8 August 1942. The resolution had but to be passed and, by a swoop which had been planned and rehearsed meticulously, Congress leaders were swept off to jails. There was a tumultuous reaction—strikes, demonstrations, satyagrahas, violence. Naturally, the British government wanted to make out that there had been little or no reaction. Ambedkar did more than his bit.

Answering questions in the Assembly about the extent of strikes, etc., on 15 September Ambedkar maintained that there had been few. Simultaneously, he stoutly refused to divulge information about them, saying that it would not be in the public interest to do so. 'It is not in the interests of the public to give any information,' he said. 'As I said, I am not prepared to give any information because it is not in the public interest to give any information,' he repeated. 'I have stated that it will not be in public interest to give any information,' he said again...[1]

---

1 See exchanges in the Central Legislative Assembly on 15 September 1942, reproduced in *Dr. Babasabeb Ambedkar, Writings and Speeches,* Vol. X, pp. 553–57.

Three days later the Central Legislative Assembly was in session discussing the situation which had arisen across the country as a consequence of the arrests. The arrests and other acts of government were stoutly defended by the new minister, Ambedkar. Over the preceding two or three years, Ambedkar declared, 'there has been a terrible landslide in the principle of non-violence as has been proclaimed by the Congress.' Indeed, the Congress Working Committee had more than once 'refused to accept the principle of non-violence as a guiding principle of its action', he maintained. In fact, 'right under the very nose of the Congress—Mr. Gandhi,' the Congress was saturated with the spirit of violence, he declared. 'It is not only a fact,' Ambedkar continued, 'that almost all members of the Congress Working Committee—at any rate a great many of them—had ceased to have any faith in non-violence, a great many of them had become indifferent to the principle, but there is enough body of evidence to indicate that inside the Congress there was an attempt being made for a planned campaign of violence.'

'You are making misstatements,' a member protested. 'It is not correct. There is no evidence,' shouted others.

Ambedkar, the new minister, was undeterred. He said that Jayaprakash Narayan had been caught trying to smuggle out some papers through his wife from the Deolali Detention Camp. These papers, declared Ambedkar, proved that 'the Congress was not to be trusted in the lip service which it rendered to the principle of non-violence.' Recall the advice the Secretary of State had been sending, as well as what the War Cabinet had decided in London: '...once you decide to arrest you should give prominence in publicity to the following points:-...(2) that Resolution of the Congress Working Committee was only the beginning of a far-reaching plan wholly to undermine India's cooperation in War effort. Documentary evidence such as the Andhra Committee's circular... should be made public and any other material showing the seriousness of the mischief intended...', and you will see the inspiration for what Ambedkar was proclaiming.

Indeed, Ambedkar went further than duty would have expected even of a minister. Not only were the measures which the government had taken justified, he proclaimed, the very form of government under which India was being held and governed was the very best that anyone could devise! Ambedkar declared, 'If Indians are wanting a government which is democratic, which excludes autocracy, and which by law—not by convention only—imposes upon those who are in charge of the administration a collective responsibility, then my submission to the House is this: that you cannot devise a better form of government than the one we have.' The very fact that under this form of government the viceroy had a veto distinguished it—for the better!—from autocracy: 'in autocracy there is no veto, in responsible government there is veto'!

As Congress leaders rotted in jails, Ambedkar was broadcasting over the radio on behalf of the British government. On 1 January 1943, he declared, 'Labour is not prepared to make a fetish of nationalism.' He put his own meaning on nationalism to knock it aside that much easier: 'If nationalism means the worship of the ancient past—the discarding of everything which is not local in origin and colour—then Labour cannot accept nationalism as its creed. Labour cannot allow the living faith of the dead to become the dead faith of the living. Labour will not allow the ever-expanding spirit of man to be strangled by the hand of the past which has no meaning for the present and no hope for the future; nor will it allow it to be cramped in a narrow jacket of local particularism...'

In ordinary circumstances that would be just vapid grandiloquence: 'Labour cannot allow the living faith of the dead to become the dead faith of the living...' But it was not just that: it was a deliberate caricature of Mahatma Gandhi and a ridiculing of the spirit which had inspired the 'Quit India' resolution. Instead of harping on 'Quit India', Ambedkar declared, the emphasis should have been on 'a New India'. The demand that Independence be declared as a condition for support of the war effort was not understandable, he said. It could have been justified only if there had been 'any sudden conspiracy to rob India of her right to freedom.' 'But there is no evidence of any such conspiracy,' he declared. 'If India's Independence is in the balance,' he said, 'it is because of disunity among Indians. The enemies of India's Independence are Indians and no others,' said Ambedkar from his perch in the council of the British viceroy.

It is superfluous to say: No Englishman could have put it better, for in speeches such as these Ambedkar repeating—word for word—what Englishmen were saying, and wanting others to say.

Ambedkar remained minister right till 1946—he remained not just a loyal, but a pugnacious minister of the British. On issue after issue he was the government's spokesman: on how restrictions placed on labour, on how the reduced dearness allowance were justified in view of the war; on how 'there is a new orientation to the Government's labour policy';[2] on how the arrests of labour leaders were justified as some of them functioned as communists, Congressmen, Hindu Mahasabhaites;[3] on how labour should free itself from the Congress and form a separate party and thereby 'prevent itself from being defrauded in the name of nationalism...'[4]

---

2 For example, *Dr. Babasaheb Ambedkar, Writings and Speeches,* Vol. X, pp. 149–57.

3 *Dr. Babasaheb Ambedkar, Writings and Speeches,* Vol. X, p. 156

4 *Dr. Bahasaheb Ambedkar, Writings and Speeches,* Vol. X, pp. 106–12.

And he stonewalled and covered up what the government found embarrassing. We have to do no more than recall a major scandal of the period to see how doggedly he worked on behalf of the British government he had joined. His attitude and services can be gleaned from the pains he took to cover up for the British government a major scandal of the times.

An example of his services

Barring the communists, few carried out as sustained and virulent a campaign against Mahatma Gandhi and the Independence movement he led than M.N. Roy. As happens in regard to *sub rosa* deals, disputes in Roy's circle resulted in its becoming known that he had been receiving a handsome amount from the British government for this work. Initially, the amount was being paid through the Department for Information and Broadcasting. It was soon channelled through the Department of Labour—that is, the Department of which Ambedkar was in charge.

The scandal was soon in the Legislative Assembly. 'Is the Indian Labour Federation through M.N. Roy being paid Rs 13,000 a month; if so, for what?' asked the members. 'Are the accounts audited?; if so, will the Honourable member lay the statements of account on the table of the House?'

Yes, Ambedkar acknowledged in the Assembly at last on 4 April 1944, the Indian Labour Federation has been receiving Rs 13,000 a month 'for doing propaganda to keep up the morale of industrial labour'. Yes, accounts have been rendered, but 'no useful purpose would be served by placing them on the table.'

'Can the person in charge of the Federation—that is, M.N. Roy—distribute the money to others asking them to do propaganda?' asked the members.

'I have no information as to how the money will be distributed,' replied Ambedkar.

'How is the money shown to have been distributed?' they asked. 'Is that shown by the audit?'

'I have no information,' Ambedkar said, and repeated, 'but the accounts are scrutinized the same way as all other public accounts.'

'Has the Federation made any rules for distributing the amount?' they asked. 'Has it submitted these to government?'

'I have no information on that,' said Ambedkar.

'In that case will you make an enquiry into it?' they asked.

'If the Honourable member will care to put a question, I will make inquiries,' Ambedkar replied.

'Are there any other associations which are getting money like this?' the members asked, nailing the point.

'I must have notice of that question,' replied Ambedkar.

'Has the Honourable member satisfied himself that this is the only organization that will help the government to keep up the morale of labour?' asked the young T.T. Krishnamachari.

'I have no information, I must have notice of that question,' replied Ambedkar.[5]

The pattern was the same from session to session. For the government needed Indians—M.N. Roy, the communists, Ambedkar—to denounce Mahatma Gandhi and the movement he was leading.

Six months later—on 2 November 1944—members were exercised about the matter again. Recall that on the earlier occasion Ambedkar had acknowledged that M.N. Roy's Indian Labour Federation was being paid Rs 13,000 a month. He had also maintained that accounts had been rendered and audited and government were satisfied that the money had been spent for the purposes for

---

5 *Dr. Babasaheb Ambedkar, Writings and Speeches,* Vol. X, pp. 774–76.

which it had been paid. Even that much could not be maintained now.

Ambedkar again acknowledged that Roy was receiving Rs 13,000 a month for 'publication of printed literature, oral propaganda, visual publicity and the disseminating of reassuring news about the war'. About the accounts, he now acknowledged that 'full and regular accounts are not available for the earlier period of the grant', but maintained that government are satisfied that 'this expenditure has achieved the objects for which it was sanctioned.' He said that from 1 June 1944 these accounts would be prepared in the Federation's office by a qualified accountant 'and these will be available to audit in the ordinary way.'

But while 'full and regular accounts are not available,' the objects for which the grant was given have been achieved, Ambedkar insisted. 'May I know,' asked a member, 'if the government are aware that part of this money has been spent on anti-Congress propaganda?'

'They have no information,' replied Ambedkar.[6]

That of course was not true. As we shall see, files of the Home (Political) Department clearly establish that the government was assiduously monitoring Roy's outpourings against Mahatma Gandhi to be certain that it was getting its money's worth. There was much satisfaction at first, for Roy was a forceful polemicist. But soon enough he was being seen as a dwindling asset. He is going to set up another party, the Intelligence Bureau reported, the Radical Democratic Party. It is likely to be another 'party of leaders without a following'. His prose is powerful, but it carries little weight, Richard Tottenham, the powerful additional secretary, Home, recorded on the file, adding the lament, 'If only we could persuade him to write anonymously.' And soon the British had new allies who outdid Roy in the

6 *Dr. Babasaheb Ambedkar, Writings and Speeches,* Vol. X, pp. 779–83.

venom they poured at Gandhi—the Communist Party of India. The communists had come to a secret understanding with the British, their organ, *People's War,* was crammed with denunciations of Gandhiji, Subhash Bose, Jayaprakash Narayan. 'Better and better!' wrote Richard Tottenham on the file as his subordinate put up the latest issue of *People's War* for him to see. 'M.N. Roy will soon have to look to his laurels!' wrote Reginald Maxwell, the Home member, on seeing the issue.[7]

That is what was happening inside government. But naturally, it was not for public consumption. And so, when asked whether part of the money given to M.N. Roy had been used for anti-Congress propaganda, Ambedkar was candour itself: Government 'have no information', he said.

But another thing happened soon enough. From the very beginning members had been demanding to know whether the money was being paid to M.N. Roy personally for him to dispose of as he saw fit or to the Federation for it to disburse according to some rules. Ambedkar had all along insisted that it was being paid to the Federation and not to any individual. But the president of the Federation, Jamnadas Mehta, who was also a member of the Legislative Assembly, issued a public statement that 'it is the blackest lie that the Federation is receiving Rs. 13,000 per month from the government.' 'Who is telling the truth, government or the president of the Federation?' demanded member after member.

'It is not for me to reconcile the two statements,' said Ambedkar while maintaining again that 'from the very beginning the arrangement has been with the Indian Federation of Labour and not with any individual.'

'Is the Honourable member correct or not in having made the statement?' pressed a member.

---

7 An account of these deals and liaisons is given in my *The Only Fatherland: Communists, Quit India, and the Soviet Union,* ASA Publications, Delhi, 1991.

'It is not for me to answer that question,' said Ambedkar.

'May I know who is telling this blackest lie, either the Federation or the Government of India?' asked another member.

'My Honourable friend is free to draw any conclusions that he likes,' replied Ambedkar.[8]

The next day Ambedkar had to acknowledge another embarrassing fact: 'No other labour association has received financial assistance from Government for this purpose,' he said in reply to a written question. Letters had been addressed to both the All-India Trade Union Congress and the Indian Federation of Labour. 'In their reply the All India Trade Union Congress did not ask for any assistance,' said Ambedkar.[9]

Members pressed Ambedkar for answers on the floor of the Assembly again on 7 November, and yet again on 20 November 1944. He continued to stonewall. In December the issue exploded further. By now the president of the Indian Labour Federation, Jamnadas Mehta, MLA, had gone much further. In a statement to United Press he disclosed that he had official correspondence 'showing that the name of the Labour Federation has been used behind the back, over the head and without the knowledge of either its President or its Executive Council and further that Rs. 13,000 per month were obtained by Mr. Roy for himself to be used as he liked.'

Accordingly, on 9 February 1945 the members questioned Ambedkar again on the matter in the Assembly. 'Have you seen this statement?' they asked. 'What have you to say now?' they asked.

'I have nothing to add to the reply I had given,' said Ambedkar.

---

8 *Dr. Babasaheb Ambedkar, Writings and Speeches,* Vol. X, pp. 783–84.

9 *Dr. Babasaheb Ambedkar, Writings and Speeches,* Vol. X, p. 787.

'But I want the Honourable member to reply to my questions,' Lalchand Navalrai, who had been most active in the matter, said, adding, 'I know that the Honourable member is feeling shy over this question because if he makes a statement it would go against his own answers. I submit that the Honourable member should reply to my questions; otherwise there will be an adjournment motion on the subject.'

'It is given to the Federation,' Ambedkar said.

'The Honourable member said the other day that audited copies of accounts will be placed on the table of the House,' another member reminded Ambedkar, and asked, 'Has he done so?'

'They have not been received as yet,' said Ambedkar about a matter which, as we have seen, had been under discussion for months and months.

'Has the Honourable member seen details of this account?' a member asked of Ambedkar—for Ambedkar had been giving certificates in the House to the effect that the money had been properly spent.

'I understand that they are seen by a special officer who has been appointed by government in this behalf,' said Ambedkar.

As he still kept saying that the money had been given not to Roy personally but to the Federation and that it had been properly spent, the then president of the Federation, Jamnadas Mehta, who was present in the House, got up and declared, 'No money has been received by the Federation from the government. The name of the Federation has been used [for receiving the money] behind the back, over the head and without the knowledge of either its Executive Committee or its president. The government have been cheated. It is without the knowledge of the Federation.'

'It is not my information,' is all Ambedkar said by way of reply to this specific disclosure on the floor of the House by none other than the president of the Federation.

'Government have been cheated,' Jamnadas Mehta said again.

Lalchand Navalrai now took over: 'Will the Government take any action now that the Honourable member has been told that government has been cheated?' he asked Ambedkar.

'Government does not believe it has been cheated,' replied Ambedkar.[10]

There were further exchanges in the Assembly on 21 February 1945. As Ambedkar had been insisting that the money had been paid not to Roy but to the Federation, members asked Ambedkar if the money had been credited to the account of the organization?

'I have no knowledge,' he said. 'It is not my business to check the accounts of any organization,' he said.

'You had said the accounts have been audited. Has the auditor's report been received?' a member asked. 'My Honourable friend must put down a specific question on that point,' Ambedkar replied.

'In view of the fact that the Public Accounts Committee for 1942–43 specifically said that no accounts are kept for this money given to Mr Roy,' asked T.S. Avinashlingam Chettiar, 'may I know if the money was given to Mr Roy in his personal name and whether audits were made and what conclusion the auditors came to as to whether the amounts were credited to the organization?'

'I cannot say to whom the money was paid before the new arrangement was made,' replied Ambedkar. 'After the new arrangement was made the money is paid to the person who is known as secretary.'

'Will you give the name of the gentleman? he was asked. 'I shall require notice,' said Ambedkar. That was natural,

10 *Dr. Babasaheb Ambedkar, Writings and Speeches,* Vol. X, pp. 828–31.

for, after all that he had been saying, Ambedkar would have been loath to acknowledge that 'the secretary' of the Federation was none other than the same M.N. Roy!

'In view of the fact that the subsidy to the Labour Federation is not approved by this House, is it the intention of government to discontinue it?' a member asked.

'I do not wish to anticipate the decision,' replied Ambedkar.[11]

On 12 April 1945, the House was seized of the matter again. By then M.N. Roy and Jamnadas Mehta had both published their versions of the affair in booklets.

'Have you seen these contradictory accounts?' Ambedkar was asked. 'Will you get the books and read them?' 'I do not propose to spend my money on purchasing them,' Ambedkar declared. 'If they are sent to me I will read them.'

'If I send the books which I have got with me, will the Honourable member read them?' Lalchand Navalrai pressed.

'If I find time, I will,' said Ambedkar.

Among the three written questions which had occasioned this discussion the second question was: 'Will government please lay a statement of accounts showing how the amount was spent?'

Badri Dutt Pande, who had tabled the questions, therefore asked: 'The Honourable member had said the other day that a statement of the accounts will be placed on the table of the House. When is he going to do that?'

'That does not arise out of this,' declared Ambedkar.

Pande would not let go: 'How did the Honourable member say in reply to my supplementary question that the question does not arise of placing a statement of accounts on the table of the House when it is definitely stated in the

---

11 *Dr. Babasaheb Ambedkar, Writings and Speeches,* Vol. X, pp. 843–45.

question that a statement of accounts should be so laid showing how the amount was spent?,' Pande demanded.

'I have not been able to follow the question,' was Ambedkar's reply.

Pande therefore explained a third time: 'You said just now that the question of laying a statement of the accounts on the table does not arise. But that is a definite part of the question as stated in part (b).'

'I am sorry,' said Ambedkar. 'Such information as I have I will lay on the table of the House.'[12] He did not do that either.

The British never had a high opinion of Roy: 'Opportunist', 'untrustworthy', 'adventurer', 'he and his political intrigues', 'he and his grandiose schemes', 'of no consequence', 'desperate for publicity'—that is how the secret notes on him of the Intelligence Bureau and the Home Department go. However, a friend in need is a friend indeed, and so the monthly grant had been paid. But by now Roy's credibility had been reduced to tatters, the war was drawing to a close, the stonewalling had become more and more of an embarrassment. The grant was accordingly discontinued.

But the full facts were still too inconvenient for the British government, and so, on its behalf, Ambedkar continued to stonewall all discussion. The grant has been discontinued, he told the Assembly on 8 April 1946 in response to persistent questions. 'What was the position between 1945 and its discontinuance?' Diwan Chaman Lal asked. 'I have not got the information but if my Honourable friend will put down a question, I shall answer it,' replied Ambedkar.

'Is it a fact that the accounts were vetted at the time when this grant was discontinued?' Diwan Chaman Lal persisted.

---

12 *Dr. Bahasabeb Ambedkar, Writings and Speeches,* Vol. X, pp. 933–35.

'I must have notice of that,' Ambedkar replied.

Pinning him, Diwan Chaman Lal asked a third time, 'My Honourable friend does not know whether they were vetted after that?' 'I could not tell you,' replied Ambedkar.

'Will the Honourable member look into the matter?,' asked Satya Narain Sinha. 'I have,' said Ambedkar. 'What more can I do?'

Maniben Kara, an associate of Roy in his trade union work, put a question that tells the tale: 'Is it not true that prior to May 1944, the Federation was asked to dispense with submitting of the vouchers and they were asked merely to submit the accounts and also whether the Federation of Labour did not do so according to the instructions of that department?'

Ambedkar's reply: 'I am unable to say. The matter was administered by another department.'

On what the money had been used for, on why the matter had not been placed before the Public Accounts Committee... in every question Ambedkar's replies remained of the same sort.[13] Because the needs of the British government to suppress the facts remained the same.

Three postscripts and one citation are in order.

(1) The entire discussion, as we have seen, revolved around this stream of Rs 13,000 a month. But that was just half the story. When I was gathering material for delivering the M.N. Roy Memorial Lecture in 1983, I discovered that an additional Rs 13,000 had been given to him every month under another guise: as subscription for 1,000 copies of the weekly edition of *Independent India,* the paper of M.N. Roy's Radical Democratic Party, and for 2,000 copies of its daily edition. The files indicate that this information would

---

13 See, for instance, *Dr. Babasaheb Ambedkar, Writings and Speeches,* Vol. X, pp. 1051–55.

have come out in response to a question which K.C. Neogy had asked and which was scheduled to be answered on 21 September 1942. For reasons that are not evident from the files, K.C. Neogy withdrew the question at the last minute. (2) Rs 26,000 a month of the 1940s will amount to around rupees *seven-and-a-half lakhs* a month today. (3) That is quite an amount if we gauge the quality of life it would ensure a couple. Yet it is meagre when one sets it against outlays of governments. That M.N. Roy should have made over his services for it must have confirmed the British in the contemptuous opinion they had of him. That he still remains such a big name in India today speaks of our amnesia.

Ambedkar on his kind, and Panditji on that kind

The role which Ambedkar had played for twenty years and which had culminated in his serving the British as a member of the Viceroy's Council had earned him much opprobrium. He was completely cut off not just from every nationalist leader and group, but even from those of the Harijans. And he was acutely aware of this isolation, of the way he was viewed by his countrymen. A passage in the book which he published at this time to further denounce Gandhiji tells the tale. Much of *What Congress and Gandhi Have Done to the Untouchables* is devoted to explaining, in fact explaining away the fact that in the 1937 elections the Congress won the majority of even the reserved seats and Ambedkar's men and party were dealt a humiliating repudiation. While explaining why this happened, Ambedkar writes with manifest bitterness:

> On the Congress side there were massed all the sinews of war, money and organization. The Non-Congress candidates were without a party chest and had no organization. The Congress boys were the blue boys of the public. They were enemies of British Imperialism,

> out to achieve freedom and independence of the country. Gaol life had invested the Congress candidates with the halo of martyrdom. As a rule no one was selected as a Congress candidate who had not gone to gaol. The Non-Congress candidates were represented by the Congress press—and as I have said there is no other press in India—as the showboys of the British, with no record of service to or sacrifice for the country, agents of British Imperialism, enemies of the country, job hunters, fellows out to sell the interests of the country for a mess of pottage and so on. There was another factor which told in the favour of the Congress candidates and against the Non-Congress candidates. The Congress had boycotted the Montagu-Chelmsford Reforms of 1920 and the Congress candidates had not to answer for any act of commission or omission in regard to the administration of the country. The Non-Congress candidates on the other hand were drawn from those who had worked the Reforms and had to answer for many acts of omission and commission, which is the lot of all those who have the courage to take upon their shoulders the responsibilities of administration...[14]

That refrain so typical of him: that he had joined the British government is proof of his kind having 'the courage to take upon their shoulders the responsibilities of administration', that the people had come to look upon him as a 'showboy of the British, with no record of service to or sacrifice for the country, an agent of British Imperialism,... job hunter,... out to sell the interests of the country for a mess of pottage...' he sees as evidence of the martyrdom he had had to bear in service of the higher objectives he had been pursuing! And that premise which became his hallmark: that while he had collaborated with the British, while he had done everything to thwart the national movement at every turn, while he had for two decades denounced the nationalist leaders, for the people to bear

---

14 B.R. Ambedkar, *What Congress and Gandhi Have Done to the Untouchables*, 1945, see *Dr. Babsaheb Ambedkar, Writings and Speeches*, Vol. IX, p. 149.

any of that in mind while voting, for those nationalist leaders to let that so much as enter their minds when they were selecting personnel for the new government was an abomination, it was proof positive of all three things together—of the high-caste animosities and prejudices of the leaders, of the fact that Indian affairs were still in the grip of the high castes, and of the congenital ingratitude of both, the leaders as well as the people.

Many things can be said about the role of these accomplices of the British government. For the time being what Pandit Nehru remarked about them will do. Writing about the brutal manner in which the government came down on the country in the wake of the 'Quit India' resolution, he wrote:

> Foreign rule over a civilized community suffers from many disadvantages and many ills follow in its train. One of these disadvantages is that it has to rely on the less desirable elements in the population... When there is an actual conflict between the government and the people this tendency to rely on and encourage the undesirable elements in the population becomes even more strongly marked. Many conscientious people of course, through force of circumstances, have to continue to function in the governmental structure, whether they like it or not. But those who come to the top and play the most important roles are chosen for their anti-nationalism, their subservience, their capacity to crush and humiliate their own countrymen. The highest merit is opposition, often the result of personal rivalries and disappointments, to the sentiments and feelings of the great majority of the people. In this turgid and unwholesome atmosphere no idealism or noble sentiment has any place, and the prizes held out are high positions and big salaries. The incompetence or worse failings of the supporters of government have to be tolerated, for the measure of everything is the active support given to that government in crushing its opponents. This leads to the government cohabiting with strange groups and very odd persons. Corruption, cruelty, callousness and a complete disregard of the public welfare flourish and poison the air.

> While much that the government does is bitterly resented, far greater resentment is caused by those Indian supporters of it who become more royalist than the king. The average Indian has a feeling of disgust and nausea at this behaviour and to him such persons are comparable to the men of Vichy or the puppet regimes set up by the German and Japanese governments...
>
> The war afforded a sufficient excuse and was a cover for intense anti-national activities of the government and novel forms of propaganda. Mushroom labour groups were financed to build up 'labour morale' and newspapers containing scurrilous attacks on Gandhi and the Congress were started and subsidized, in spite of the paper shortage which came in the way of other newspapers functioning. Official advertisements, supposed to be connected with the war effort, were also utilized for this purpose. Information centres were opened in foreign countries to carry on continuous propaganda on behalf of the Government of India. Crowds of undistinguished and often unknown individuals were sent on officially organized deputations, especially to the USA, despite the protest of the Central Assembly, to act as propaganda agents and stooges of the British government. Any person holding independent views or critical of government policy had no chance of going abroad; he could neither get a passport nor transport facilities....[15]

Given who had been receiving 'advertisements' and other subsidies, given whose labour union had been propped up and patronized, given who as the loyal minister had done the cover-up, given who had been denouncing nationalism, is there any doubt about the individuals Pandit Nehru had in mind?

---

15 Jawaharlal Nehru, *The Discovery of India,* The Signet Press, Calcutta, 1946, pp. 599–601.

4

The government he joined

By mid-July 1942 the British as well as their allies in India—Ambedkar, M.N. Roy and the rest—had convinced themselves that Gandhiji had tied himself in knots, that he would get little support for the mass programme that seemed to be on the anvil, that in fact his own health had deteriorated to such an extent that there was every prospect of his being out of the way soon, that there were definite signs of his mind having slowed down. These assessments gave great confidence to the British and their allies. They were among the factors which persuaded them that the Congress, and Gandhiji in particular, should be taken head on, that indeed one should 'get one's fist in first'. For this reason even though they had definite information to the effect that Gandhiji would not do anything for a month after the 'Quit India' resolution had been passed by the All India Congress Committee at Bombay on 8 August, they struck in the early hours of 9 August and sent the Congress leaders to prisons. Ambedkar had more than advance information of these assessments as well as these plans. Indeed, as we shall see, he was as energetic a proponent of these repressive measures as any Englishman.

'Will try to get out without too much loss of face'

'Matters as I dictate seem to be working out very much

on the lines one had anticipated,' Linlithgow informed the Secretary of State on 6 July 1942, '—in other words, the lack of any very active response to his [that is, the Mahatma's] blandishments from the country and the absence of any enthusiastic press support look as though they have confirmed him in his view that he would do well to think again about his "Britain get out" slogan. His latest explanation which appears in this week's *Harijan* is not without its humorous side.... he has in fact been so tortuous and so involved in these last five or six weeks that it ought to tell against him to some extent in America and at home; but the difficulty of course is that people's memories are so short and that now-a-days they have so many matters of far greater moment and urgency to occupy them than the collating of the Mahatma's all too frequent explanations of what he is really after...'[1]

The governor of Punjab, Sir B. Glancy, had proposed that stern action be taken against Gandhiji and the *Harijan* for his writings in it. Linlithgow counselled patience on the ground that things were going their way, and that action against *Harijan*, etc., would only give Gandhiji the halo he so desperately needed. 'I feel very great sympathy with your view as to the character of the stuff that appears in the *Harijan*,' he wrote to Glancy on 11 July, 'but I feel equally strongly that this is one of those cases in which it is wise to give the Mahatma a good deal of rope. I gather that he has done himself very great harm indeed, both in America and at home, by the sort of articles he has been putting out, and I am quite certain that we could not by any means in our power have done nearly as much to lower his reputation, or shake the confidence of people outside India in his common sense and realism, as he has managed to do himself through his own publicity. Against that we have, of course,

1 *Transfer of Power;* Vol. II, p. 315.

to set, as I fully recognize, the unfortunate effect of these articles here: and I do not underestimate the importance of their effect. But taking it by and large I think the balance of advantage is still in letting him go ahead, and I have good reason to believe that he has been much disappointed not to have received the advertisement, and also the plausible excuse for action, which the suppression of *Harijan* would have given him.'[2]

The same day as reports came in about discussions among Congress leaders who had started gathering at Wardha, the viceroy was voicing the same confidence and satisfaction in a *'Private and Personal'* message to L.S. Amery, the Secretary of State. 'For the moment, I am, I am bound to say, by no means unduly perturbed,' he wrote. 'I think that the discussions so far reported in the press bring out with remarkable clearness the awkwardness of the position in which Gandhi and his friends find themselves, and Nehru's suggestion that the best way to help China is for us to evacuate India and leave her free, and available as a base of operations for the assistance of China are so absurd that one rubs one's eyes as one reads them. I am inclined to think myself that the old man will play for time and (as so often happened in the past) produce a threatening resolution drafted so as to attract as much attention as possible here, at home and in the United States but also worded so carefully as to leave ample opportunity for Congress to get out without too much loss of face if things look like going badly for it later on.'[3]

Sir H.J. Twynam, the governor of Central Provinces and Berar, who was keeping tabs on the discussions at Wardha sent a *'Secret'* report to the viceroy on 12 July. 'The latest Intelligence report on hand is to the effect that the Congress must take some action and can no longer pursue the "non-

2 *Transfer of Power*, Vol. II, p. 367.

3 *Transfer of Power*, Vol. II, pp. 368–69.

embarrassment" policy,' Twynam reported. But 'A decision in favour of an immediate mass movement seems unlikely and any such movement would, in existing circumstances, probably be impracticable.' The governor was full of reasons for his conclusion: he wrote, 'Apart from the doubts felt by leading Congressmen as to the time being suitable for a mass movement, there can be little doubt that the agricultural population is fully preoccupied with cultivation and with the question of how best to take advantage of the present situation with respect to food-grains. Further, the middle, non-agricultural, classes are not eager to repeat their *satyagraha* martyrdom, especially when jails are congested areas and conspicuous targets, in the event of enemy attack, while families are confronted with difficult problems arising from the shortage of essential commodities and the general rise in the cost of living.'

The governor sketched his forecast on the basis of the various reports he had received: 'It seems likely that Gandhi will be given discretion to strike, as and when he thinks fit, after perhaps he has endeavoured to cover up his traces in respect of his egregious blunders in *Harijan* in connection with "Britain get out" and American aid which, for a moment revealed the real Gandhi with results extremely damaging to Congress in American eyes and even perhaps in the eyes of our own "wild men" at home.' But, as every good civil servant should, the governor hedged himself, adding, 'Nevertheless, it does seem that Gandhi is himself getting desperate now that he sees it is becoming increasingly difficult to achieve his aim of a Congress dominated India...'

But the man has already had to climb down a good deal, Twynam noted, and then there was the assessment of the ally—M.N. Roy: 'As Your Excellency observes, the Mahatma has climbed down considerably lately and indeed M.N. Roy in *Independent India* observes that "he has climbed down to such an extent that his original demand for the withdrawal of the British now becomes an empty formula." The conclusion is therefore inevitable that the demand is just a slogan to whip up enthusiasm for the Congress and a bargaining counter for the British Government.'

This sort of 'assessment', it will repay us to remember, was typical—governors dittoing to the viceroy what they thought was the viceroy's view of the matter; governors, the viceroy and all drawing reinforcement from the views of their collaborators. The pattern, as we shall see, led the government to first underestimate the reaction which the Congress resolution would ignite across the country, and then to justify extreme repression by asserting that this was 'the most serious challenge since 1857'! But we anticipate.

The governor then referred to the other reason for hope, one on which the British, whenever they were in a corner, were hoping to be able to count: the governor reverted to the intelligence reports, and said, 'Your Excellency would have seen reports about Gandhi's health. This is a matter to which I drew attention several months ago and which I have been keeping an eye on since. There have been several references to his inability to function owing to rise in blood pressure, &c. He is now about to complete his 72nd year and I feel that, in the circumstances of his malady, I may at any moment be confronted with the problem regarding the closure of the offices on which we have been in correspondence...'—the governor had been seeking instructions whether flags are to be downed to half-mast, and government offices closed in the event of Gandhiji's death, which he had been forecasting for a while as being imminent.

In the meanwhile there was that other reassurance, namely that the man's mind was not what it used to be: the governor drew attention to the way Gandhiji had taken up the cause of shortages of foodstuffs and the consequential rise in prices. The governor thought this was not just one of those egregious errors that the old man was making with such frequency, it pointed to a pathological deterioration! 'Our local politicians have apparently secured Gandhi's support in making a grievance of this matter,' he wrote. 'This is interesting because it is an indication of how Gandhi's mind seems to be working less efficiently than usual. For the professed protector of the masses to take a narrow view of the problem is surprising. What is the townsman's poison is of course the cultivator's milk and one would have expected Gandhi to rejoice that the agriculturist is at last coming into his own after a succession of many lean years. Not only that, but the ultimate solution of India's problems lies in higher prices of agricultural produce of all kinds. But Gandhi has completely ignored this aspect of the question in order to snatch at a stick with which to beat the Government....'[4] Could it be that the old man knew that the higher prices are being gobbled up by traders in between and the landowners, and are not reaching the tiller and the landless labourer, and that the governor too may not have been oblivious of this reality but had 'completely ignored this aspect of the question in order to snatch at a stick with which to beat' Gandhi?

Before he could dispatch the letter, the governor received the telegram that gave a summary of the resolution which the Congress Working Committee had finalized at Wardha. The governor felt strengthened in the assessment he had sketched earlier. 'This is more or less what was anticipated,' he observed, 'but it is a great deal milder in tone than Gandhi's utterances in *Harijan*... I do not think there is anything in this to give cause for anxiety. The Resolution is to be referred to the A.-I.C.C. for final

---

4 *Transfer of Power,* Vol. II, pp. 371–73.

decision, so that there is time to consider our attitude... The summary seems to indicate that the Resolution has been converted into a bargaining counter, as M.N. Roy suggested, and that Gandhi's splenetic policy and also his policy of neutrality in the War have been defeated. Rajagopalachariar's defection and the lukewarmness of the Muslim members of the Working Committee towards any mass movement have produced a rather amazing change of front as compared with Gandhi's attitude.'[5]

The resolution of the Working Committee had but to be released and the governor of Bombay met Ambedkar to ascertain the latter's assessment of the likely repercussions of the resolution. He found Ambedkar most comforting. Reporting to the viceroy on 17 July, Sir R. Lumley wrote, 'The first reactions to the Congress resolution are not unhealthy, and are certainly more downright than on previous occasions. Sir Chimanlal Setalvad and Sir Cowasji Jehangir came out at once, and spontaneously, with statements expressing strong opposition... Ambedkar, in conversation, expressed the view that Congress would not receive much support from Labour, and thought that it would receive so little general support that it might be possible to ignore it. I have sent him the message contained in your telegram of July the 16th, which arrived after I had met him [the message in which the viceroy had asked Ambedkar to speak up in public against Gandhiji and the Congress line]. The National War Front... is producing a reasoned statement...'[6]

Glancy from Punjab was not as sanguine: 'the situation is becoming increasingly dangerous and.... positive action will soon be unavoidable,' he said in his *'Immediate and Personal'* telegram to the viceroy. Sir T. Stewart, the governor in Bihar, furnished both sorts of assessments:

5 *Transfer of Power,* Vol. II, pp. 371–74.

6 *Transfer of Power,* Vol. II, p. 405.

'Our press is curiously silent on the subject of Gandhi's desire to launch mass Civil Disobedience and in this it reflects the undoubted distaste of the man in the street, be he Congress or non-Congress, for such a programme at the present moment,' and the chief secretary in the province, Godbole, the governor said, 'is inclined to think that it [the mass movement that the Congress was building towards] will be as much of a "flop" as the last,' adding however, 'He [Godbole] is a wise man but Russell and I are inclined to think that he is over-optimistic and that there may be a sufficiency of *proforma* martyrs to embarrass us in regard to jail accommodation.'[7]

But on three things there was unanimity—among the British governors, the viceroy in Delhi, the Secretary of State in London, and of course the accomplices of the government from Bombay to Patna to Madras: one, that Gandhi would give them time—that the Congress would not launch any serious movement till the middle of September or so; second, that the government should seize the advantage that the interval offered and get its punch in first, in particular at 'the villain of the piece', Gandhi; third, that the very first move of government should be a solid, strong blow that incapacitates the Congress, and in particular puts Gandhi out of harm's way for a long time.

The government knew that Gandhiji never launched any movement before giving long notice to the authorities. In the present instance the Working Committee while passing its resolution at Wardha in mid-July had itself declared that the resolution would be put to the All-India Congress Committee, and that the AICC would meet in Bombay during the first week of August. Gandhiji had declared too that he would be writing to the viceroy and would await the reply of the viceroy before deciding on the course of action.

---

7 *Transfer of Power,* Vol. II, pp. 388–90.

Even as he was expressing his satisfaction to the Secretary of State at the way things had gone till then, Linlithgow, as we have seen, told Amery on 11 July, 'I am inclined to think myself that the old man will play for time and (as so often happened in the past) produce a threatening resolution drafted so as to attract as much attention as possible here, at home and in the United States but also worded so carefully as to leave ample opportunity for Congress to get out without too much loss of face if things look like going badly for it later on.'

'But thrice armed he who gets his blow in fust'

The text of the Working Committee's resolution was available on 16 July. It was telegraphed to London by Reuters. The Home Department sent a telegram to the Secretary of State marked *'Important'* that same day giving its preliminary assessment and plans. The telegram also shows the same thing: the government knew that it had time till September, and that it had already come to a decision about what would be the best moment to strike. The Home Department informed the Secretary of State:

> It [the Working Committee resolution] contains objectionable passages; much of it is blatantly hypocritical; and threat of civil disobedience remains. On the other hand, language is more conciliatory than we expected, while appeal to Allied powers and abandonment of non-embarrassment policy has been dropped, although we have reason to believe that these were essential points in Gandhi's original draft. He must have encountered considerable opposition.
>
> After careful consideration we have come to conclusions (a) that resolution, as worded, does not afford good ground for immediate action against Congress at any rate until after it has been ratified by A.-I.C.C...

---

8 *Transfer of Power*, Vol. II, pp. 368–69.

> We are conscious that interval before ratification may give Congress further opportunity for propaganda and maturing their plans, but we shall keep a close censorship on on-going comment, and shall make most of the interval to develop our own counter-propaganda and (? settle) our own plans of action...
>
> Assuming that the resolution is ratified by A.-I.C.C., its terms, if they mean anything, will necessitate a further interval to allow consideration of appeal by His Majesty's Government with the result that Congress will not expect to be in a position to launch civil disobedience much before September. If we are to take up the Congress challenge as we feel we must, it will clearly be desirable to strike before they are ready and the best moment for doing so may well be immediately after ratification by All India Congress Committee....
>
> Meanwhile we are asking Provincial Governments to have their plans in complete readiness by August 7th...[9]

So, they were going to have time. And it was necessary in the view of one and all to get in the first punch, and to make sure that that first punch was itself the knockout blow.

'It is well, I am sure,' wrote Lumley, the governor of Bombay whose advice carried great weight with Linlithgow, to the viceroy on 17 July, 'not to make a precipitate move before the A.-I.C.C. meeting, so that any chance there may be that lack of enthusiasm may cause Gandhi to alter his attitude may have full rein. But once the resolution is ratified, and provided there is no good reason to believe that civil disobedience will not be worked up, I think it will be important to strike before they have time to perfect their plans and stir up feeling. This seems, to me, to be more necessary on account of the difficulties created by the high prices of foodstuffs, which are not likely to be resolved in the near future. I have little doubt that Gandhi will work on that subject as much as possible.'[10]

---

9 *Transfer of Power,* Vol. II, pp. 394–95.

10 *Transfer of Power,* Vol. II, p. 406.

Sir M. Hallett was the governor of the United Provinces. He had had a good deal of experience in dealing with the Congress. He sent a *'Secret'* communication to the viceroy on 21 July. 'I was at one time inclined that we should go for Congress at once, but the arguments the Home Department put forward in a recent telegram showed conclusively that the balance of advantage lay in waiting,' he informed Linlithgow. Press seemed to be favouring the government's view, he noted. There was of course the risk to which the viceroy had drawn attention of the anti-Congress point of view going by default. 'Provided our news agencies are sensible,' Hallett said, echoing the viceroy, '—it often appalls me the amount of power which they wield—I think it will be possible to show that Congress do not represent the country, partly by giving full play to anti-Congress statements, such as the excellent one by Firoz Khan Noon, partly by showing that in spite of Congress, War work is going on well...' He listed the likely waverers, and the uncertainties on the way—the Muslims, the governor said he had learnt from a recent tour, were apprehensive that the government would again enter into negotiations with the Congress, and that the Hindu officers in government were half-hearted in opposing Congress.

'But still under present conditions, most Indians have a respect for the ruling power,' Hallett said, and added, 'provided it does rule and rule effectively. Hence, if we can go for the Congress, at zero hour whenever it may be, I do not anticipate much support for the movement whatever form it may take. I do not think that in the period up till the meeting of the A.-I.C.C. the situation will deteriorate. There is of course a risk, which personally I consider slight, that Congress will increase its influence, but on the other hand their statements may become more and more stupid and that will help us in reconciling British opinion to "repressive measures".' 'I do feel strongly,' the governor concluded, 'that we must get Congress out of the way and I think we can do so. I admit that action against Nehru and Azad is not easy, in view of the anti-Axis statements, but we must go for Gandhi, whatever may happen, and for the Congress organisation and for the Congress press.'[11]

Linlithgow was getting the same sort of advice from the other governors. He had made many inquiries, Sir A. Hope, the governor of Madras wrote to the viceroy on 23 July, 'and the great consensus of opinion is that the Congress are thinking of committing an act of criminal folly... As far as I can make out, there is genuine alarm among the local Congress leaders, outside the extremists, and I do not think that any disobedience movement would have very much support here, although in the Andhra country it would be stronger than in the Tamil... One thing everybody is unanimous about is that if any mass movement does start, it must be squashed at the beginning. The theory of a long rope to hang themselves is not believed in, and certainly not by myself. I feel that a long rope is much more likely to entangle our legs than it will the Congress neck, and I know that this is your view as well...'

'Likewise, as regards the villain of the piece, Gandhi,' Hope wrote, 'he still has great influence among the ignorant masses, and any mention of his name or state of health excites them. If the movement comes to anything, I would suggest arresting him at once and deporting him to Mauritius or Kenya, and prohibit any reference to him in the Press. If he fasts let it not be known; and if he dies announce it six months later.'

Hope expressed the same fear, rather the same additional argument for strong action that the other advisers had been urging: 'One thing the bulk of the non-Congress people fear,' he reported, 'is that strong action will not be taken,

---

11 *Transfer of Power*, Vol. II, pp. 425–26.

and I feel quite confident that, after Congress have shown themselves in their true light, world opinion will agree that strong action must be taken now... I do hope His Majesty's Government do realize the change in the position and will not fall for any apparent weakening in Congress attitude in the next few weeks. They may well feel that they have gone too far, but as you know better than I do, they are an absolutely untrustworthy lot and it will cause immense resentment if we have any further truck with them....'[12]

The governor of United Provinces, Sir M. Hallett followed up his earlier recommendations by another telegram to the viceroy the next day. He drew attention to the report that the director of intelligence had submitted two days earlier, on 22 July. This had said that preparations for the Congress campaign were being made vigourously, leaders were addressing meetings at which instructions were being given verbally, efforts were being made to increase the volunteers force and the Quami Sewa Dal, that the movement was to include 'all known forms of civil disobedience including even cutting telegraph wires'. 'This information appears reliable,' the governor remarked, 'and no doubt you will have corroboration from other sources. It appears probable that A.-I.C.C. meeting will issue ultimatum terminating on September 15th, but ultimatum will obviously conceal and camouflage methods to be adopted. To wait till ultimatum expires before taking action or even for short time after Bombay meeting will be disastrous for delay will give (a) Congress more time for organization, (b) mean that movement will start at more favourable season owing to (i) lull in cultivation activities, (ii) proximity of big religious festivals and (iii) possible intensification of War on Burma front. Delay between publication of resolution and Bombay meeting though giving time to Congress to

12 *Transfer of Potver*, Vol. II, pp. 441–44.

organize has had advantage of obtaining opinions hostile to Congress both in India, Britain and America. No further time needed for this purpose. In fact if we delay to take action after Bombay meeting, there will be usual spate of statements and discussions which will cloud the issue. *Daily Herald* articles and indeed all opinions against Congress policy have been intemperately criticized in Congress press and clearly have not made them reconsider attitude. Delayed action will also dishearten our supporters in India, whose numbers will never be largely increased even by most efficient propaganda campaign but may be decreased if period of uncertainty is prolonged. My Advisers incline to view that action should be taken before Bombay meeting but I think zero hour should be immediately after meeting when assuming resolution is confirmed His Majesty's Government should reiterate their policy and announcement should be made regarding proposed action...'[13]

A week later and with just about a week to go before the Bombay meeting, Sir R. Lumley, the governor of Bombay Presidency emphasized the same points and the need to stick to the same zero hour. In an *'Immediate, Secret'* telegram to the viceroy he recounted that there had been virtually no support to the Congress Resolution outside Congress circles, that on the contrary a number of persons had expressed themselves strongly against the proposed course of action. 'In spite of this considerable opposition,' Lumley noted, 'I have little doubt that Congress will have a large volume of support in Gujarat and appreciable support in Bombay City, and that they count on this turning into serious trouble when Gandhi is arrested, and more so if he fasts. Patel has been in Gujarat organising... If gossip can be believed, Patel is said to have told hearers at

13 *Transfer of Power,* Vol. II, pp. 450–51.

private meetings that they should not be too squeamish about violence this time...'

The governor's conclusion was: 'In general, opposition has developed quite well up to this stage, but Congress leaders have also had a little time to give orders to their followers. It is clear that opposition in India and abroad has had no effect on Patel, except to make him more truculent. Whether it has affected the Nehru-Azad group sufficiently to make a split or postpone(ment) a possibility, I do not know, but my anticipation is that Gandhi means to put maximum pressure on us by fasting. I remain convinced that, unless the Bombay meetings show that Congress does not intend to press its challenge, we must act at once, and make it plain, to all who are waiting to see what Government is going to do, that we shall deal firmly with the challenge.'[14]

The next day, on 1 August, Sir H. Twynam, governor in Central Provinces and Berar, sent his final assessment and recommendation to the viceroy. 'Provincial Congress Committees are getting busy passing resolutions to the effect that they will support Gandhi's threatened movement... As regards the Provincial Congress Committees, I doubt whether their arrangements have proceeded very far. There is still no indication that they have worked up the masses—indeed, all evidence is to the contrary—or have thought out, or organised, any campaign.'

Nevertheless, said the governor, action must be swift and hard. 'Although, therefore, I cannot exaggerate the importance of beheading the movement before it starts, I still think Gandhi's prospects of achieving a mass movement are particularly poor. We must however decapitate the movement the moment it starts. I still have

14 *Transfer of Power*, Vol. II, pp. 511–12.

vivid recollections of the success achieved against the second civil disobedience movement of 1932 when I was personally in charge of the counter-measures in Bengal. That movement was associated with the worst form of the terrorist campaign and yet, by having all our plans ready at zero hour, declaring unlawful all Congress Executive Committees and seizing their premises, the movement was virtually brought under control in three weeks and in many cases it was not even necessary to arrest the personnel of local Congress Committees.'[15]

In London the Secretary of State for India, Amery, had been, if anything, even more enthusiastic about getting in the first blow. He had been goading the viceroy to that effect in telegram after telegram. As the leaders of the Congress gathered in Wardha, the *Hindustan Times* published a report about the likely terms of the resolution they were liable to pass in the ensuing days. Although these terms do not go as far as had been anticipated, Amery told the viceroy in a '*Most Immediate, Private and Personal*' telegram on 13 July, 'that certainly does not affect the fact that the issue of these instructions to the public has been made. It appears to be not repeat not subsidiary measure but essential preparatory action to create number of individual grievances and cases of open conflict & armed suppression on which universal movement will be based justifying appeal to Allied powers. If this is your reading of Gandhi's plan, it would be sheer folly to allow such a challenge to pass on ground that acts of defiance against Government have not yet followed and to leave Gandhi time to work up his campaign.' And Amery invoked the adage he was to invoke again and again: 'Twice armed is he that has his quarrel just but thrice armed he who gets his blow in fust.'[16]

---

15 *Transfer of Power,* Vol. II, pp. 526–28.

16 *Transfer of Power,* Vol. II, pp. 374–75.

The same day he put up a minute to Churchill, the prime minister. He drew attention to the proposed text of the resolution, and remarked:

> The object of the resolution, which is apparently preliminary to a more general resolution telling us to clear out of India, is obviously to create a general atmosphere of disturbance and to provoke cases of open conflict with the authorities so as to poison the atmosphere by the time we have the courage to take action against Congress later on. To my mind, the only course is to act promptly now,
>
> 'Twice armed is he that has his quarrel just;
> But thrice armed he who gets his blow in fust.'
>
> I hope the Cabinet will this afternoon authorize Linlithgow to arrest Gandhi and the Congress Working Committee at once if the resolution is in fact in the terms published in the *Hindustan Times*. We are dealing with men who are now definitely our enemies, inclined to believe in the victory of Japan, and anyhow determined to make the most mischief they can. To appease them or delay in striking at them can only discourage the army and all other loyal elements. I don't think that the effect in America will be serious: anyhow, nothing like as serious as the effect of hesitation and weakness.[17]

Churchill was of course always anxious to get in a blow at Gandhi, and Amery, who knew Churchill well, had put the case in terms that were bound to meet with Churchill's hearty approval.

Amery warmed to the theme again two days later, on 15 July in his *'Private'* communication to the viceroy. 'After all, we are dealing with people who are more and more advancing the claim to be considered as the alternative Government of India,' Amery wrote, 'and ingeniously fortifying that claim step by step. At some point or other we have got to make it quite clear that *we* are the Government of India and that the claim is a

17 *Transfer of Power,* Vol. II, pp. 376–77.

bubble to be pricked. It is of course arguable that the bubble may prick itself by sheer failure of Congress to produce any action. That is what happened over the last *Satyagraha* movement, and if at all it looked likely that the result would be the same this time it might be safe to take the same line. But is it?'

'One thing, I think, is of the first importance,' Amery emphasized, 'and that is that you should make clear either yourself, or through your Council, that there is not the slightest question of our abdicating the functions of Government during the war, or going beyond what was said here on April 28th. I am really sorry that [Sir C.P. Ramaswami] Ayyar will not be available till the beginning of August, for you might have got him at once to punch Congress hard and make it clear that there is not going to be any kind of surrender or negotiation.'[18]

By 24 July there was both, a note of things going their own way as well as renewed determination to scotch the Congress and in particular Gandhiji firmly. 'Gandhi's antics have really been too much this time for the press here and in America,' Amery noted with satisfaction. 'I dare say I may have helped by some frank talks to the lobby Correspondents and the American Press, but I think in the main all the credit should be divided between Gandhi and Nehru! Even the *Daily Herald* and now the official Labour Party have turned against him. Whether all this will have any influence on the old man or on the All-India Committee when it meets, no one can say, but it certainly has justified up to the present your policy of waiting and not taking drastic action prematurely. On the other hand, once you are convinced that he and his clique mean real mischief, the sooner you pounce on them the better.'

Amery, and even more enthusiastically Churchill had been pressing that the moment they were swept off into

18 *Transfer of Power,* Vol. II, p. 391.

custody, Congress leaders, in particular Gandhiji, should be sent off by air to Uganda in East Africa. At first Linlithgow had been a bit doubtful, but he had warmed to the idea by now. 'I am glad,' Amery wrote, 'that as regard the main body you have come round to my view about Uganda. There is not only the dramatic aspect of the act itself, but the fact that they are completely out of reach has something of the same effect as decease. People forget all about them.' The problem had been Gandhiji, as usual: he is the one everyone was most anxious to put beyond reach and out of sight, but the medical assessment was that, his health being what it was, he would not be able to withstand the strain of an air journey. In his case, therefore, the proposal had been modified, with a bit of regret though: 'I am only too sorry,' Amery wrote, 'that Gandhi's health does not allow of his joining U Saw [the Burmese leader] out there. I am tentatively suggesting Aden, which only means a sea voyage, but you may think that also impossible. I quite agree with you that we must not in any way be held directly responsible for his demise, even if we are not prepared to be blackmailed by a threat of fasting to death.'

'I was much interested in Villier's account of his talks with Nehru, which give very much the picture of the man which I have gradually formed myself,' Amery continued, 'that of a man who has spun himself into a cocoon of his own perversion of history and diatribes against the British which blind him to all real facts. The type is not unfamiliar among nationalist intellectuals in other countries—de Valera for instance, though he evidently has some executive ability...'[19]

The viceroy advised patience. He had determined in consultation with the men who were going to deliver the blow, namely the governors, that the blow should be

---

19 *Transfer of Power,* Vol. II, pp. 454–55.

delivered just after the meeting in Bombay which was scheduled for 8 August. And he was preparing the ground systematically. The ban on the Communist Party was lifted. Preparations were made to release communists who were in jails in time for them to attend the meeting of the AICC in Bombay and oppose Gandhiji—leading communists were members of the All-India Congress Committee at that time, and, as I have set out in *The Only Fatherland,*[20] they had already come to a deal with Sir Reginald Maxwell, the Home member and other representatives of the British government. And while under his direction governors were honing plans for the early morning swoop, Linlithgow himself was moving swiftly to ensure exactly what Amery was wishing had happened earlier—that is, he was moving swiftly to induct Indians into his Council, so that the arrests, etc., which were in the works could be shown to have been made with their fullest approval.

And so the steps were finalized. The Home Department summarized these in *'Immediate'* telegrams to the Secretary of State on 24 July and later on 3 August. Leaders of the Congress were to be swept off to jails once the AICC ratified the Working Committee's resolution; once in jail, they were to be completely cutoff from the outside world, and so on. In its telegram of 24 July the Home Department sought the views of the War Cabinet in London about the proposal which had been circulated earlier, and which both Amery in London and the viceroy favoured: 'Main object will be to segregate them all [the Congress leaders] completely from outside contacts,' the Home Department stated, 'and in this connection we should like to know how you would regard proposal that 6 or 8 of the more important members of the Working Committee should be deported to Uganda. We realize that such action might

20 ASA Publications, New Delhi, 1991.

be regarded as extreme but it would have profound effect here and if you approve in principle we should be glad if you could warn governor of Uganda and authorize us to arrange details with him direct...'

The key would lie in the surprise as Gandhi and the Congress, the Home Department noted, would not expect any action till after they had formally launched the movement. 'Banking on probability that Gandhi will expect an interval after ratification before launching movement and may not therefore have circulated his detailed instructions to his followers meanwhile,' the Department cabled, 'we have some hope that this action may prevent move from ever taking shape...'

If Gandhi decides to fast, the Home Department said at this stage, 'cat and mouse' procedure would be adopted—that is, he would be released as soon as his life was in danger to avoid possibility of his dying while a prisoner of government.[21]

The proposal to deport Gandhiji and others went to and fro. By 29 July the commander-in-chief, Eastern Fleet, was informing the First Sea Lord in a *'Rush, Most Secret, Important'* telegram that the viceroy had asked for a warship to be at Bombay by 8 August to convoy the prisoners to Kilindini for Uganda, and that he was planning to use HMS *Manxman* for the purpose.[22] Eventually, the proposal was dropped: while the governors of Punjab, Madras and Central Provinces and Berar were for deportation, the more influential governors —Lumley and Hallett, as well as the governor of Bihar—opposed the move: the leaders could in fact be isolated effectively within India, they said; once they were away it would be that much more difficult to counter rumours that might be put into circulation about them; most important, if Gandhi went

---

21 *Transfer of Power*, Vol. II, pp. 447–50, 534–37.
22 *Transfer of Power*, Vol. II, p. 494.

ahead and commenced a fast and seemed like dying, it would be impossible to 'free' him so that he did not die while in custody of the government. When the proposal was put to the Viceroy's Council, they also opposed it, and the viceroy, who, as we have seen, had decided that having them as a party to the decisions was an essential element in the strategy, decided that in the circumstances the balance of advantage lay in incarcerating the leaders within India.

The proposal of playing 'cat and mouse' with Gandhiji should he decide to fast, as the assessment was he would, also became the subject of anxious exchanges between London, the viceroy and the governors.

The Home Department, as we have seen, had settled on the 'cat and mouse' procedure—that is, to keep Gandhiji imprisoned up to the point that his life was in danger, and at that time to set him 'free' to die outside the custody of government.

Amery didn't approve of such a course, he saw in it a want of resolve. 'What has disturbed me a little is a suggestion, in one of your telegrams I think,' he wrote to the viceroy on 3 August, 'that if Gandhi starts fasting unto death you will let him out. I should have said that this particular form of blackmail is one we should deal with unhesitatingly. The idea that he should get out merely because we are afraid to have him die on our hands, and then promptly get well, or even die surrounded by awed and adoring crowds, does not appeal to me at all. There is, I suppose, the alternative of letting him out when very weak and promptly rearresting him when he gets a little better, but I cannot say that that appeals to me very much, either. After all, he is not going to be detained in prison, but in a comfortable house of his own, the essence of the situation being not hardship but seclusion. If he insists on committing suicide, surely he might as well do it in seclusion and India be informed of the fact afterwards? I should certainly not tolerate the kind of day-to-day bulletins which were issued about the wretched Lord Mayor of Cork years ago.'[23]

This is what the War Cabinet adopted as its decision when it met two days before the 8 August meeting of the All-India Congress Committee in Bombay: the Cabinet minutes recorded, 'The War Cabinet could not agree that the "cat and mouse" procedure should be adopted if Gandhi should hunger-strike while under detention. It should be clearly understood that, once he had been taken under restraint, he must be kept in detention, even though he went on hunger-strike. In view of the difficulties to which his detention in India, while hunger-striking, was likely to give rise, the War Cabinet were strongly of opinion that, as soon as he had been taken under restraint, he should be removed forthwith by sea to some place outside India... Aden was suggested as the first destination. Subsequently he might be transferred to some more suitable place for continued detention—possibly the Sudan... To avoid giving the impression that Gandhi was being selected for special treatment, some dozen or half-dozen of the other leaders who were to be detained should be taken to East Africa by air...'[24] Amery conveyed these conclusions to the viceroy in a *'Most Immediate, Most Secret, Personal'* telegram on 7 August, at 12.05 a.m. '[25]

Indian members of the Viceroy's Council were no less gung-ho about letting Gandhiji die. On the 7 August itself the viceroy had reported to the Secretary of State: 'I thought it wiser not at this stage to raise the question of cat and mouse treatment, and will keep that till later. But in the course of discussion C.P. Ramaswami Aiyar said in terms (and without provoking any comeback) that in his judgement if Gandhi did fast, he should be left to face the consequences and that

---

23 *Transfer of Power,* Vol. II, p. 550.

24 *Transfer of Power,* Vol. II, pp. 586–88.

25 *Transfer of Power,* Vol. II, pp. 595–96.

it should be made clear that that was not our fault (he added that he thought that we should be in a stronger position to carry that policy through if he and the other leaders were interned in India).'[26]

Linlithgow informed the governors of the view which the War Cabinet had taken, and asked them for their reactions to letting Gandhiji die while a prisoner of government. With one exception all the governors thought that would have a very adverse effect, they strongly urged that, should his fast reach a point when his life was endangered, Gandhiji should be released. The same counsel came from the army.[27]

The leaders having been swept off to jails in the early hours on 9 August, the viceroy put the question to his Council on 10 August. After the meeting he informed the Secretary of State of the discussion by telegram. 'Matter was discussed in Council this morning,' his *'Immediate, Private and Personal'* telegram read. 'I gave them no lead and did not disclose your views. I found them almost unanimously in favour of releasing Gandhi from restraint at point at which his fast might become dangerous to life. C.P. was inclined to keep him under restraint even then though Mody on the other hand was in favour of letting him out altogether the moment he started to fast. There are no signs yet I understand from Bombay of any intention on his part to fast, but C.P.'s information is specific that he does intend to do so and to carry things to the end.' Linlithgow emphatically advised that in view of advice from governors and the reactions of his Council, government must be prepared to release Gandhiji in the event he went on a fast and his life were in danger.[28]

The next two letters crossed. In his communication of 11

26 *Transfer of Power,* Vol. II, pp. 596–97.

27 *Transfer of Power,* Vol. II, pp. 632, 635–38.

28 *Transfer of Power,* Vol. II, pp. 646–47.

August Linlithgow thanked Amery warmly for the latter's help in ensuring the fullest support to action that the viceroy had taken, and in getting the War Cabinet to drop the deportation idea. He expressed the hope that it would be possible in the same way to get the Cabinet to abandon their insistence on 'leaving Gandhi to die in prison if he dies on his fast to death'. Amery had already informed him in a postscript to his letter of 8 August, 'Cabinet are deferring to your views as to having G. die on your hands, but clear that he mustn't defeat you. Our best idea so far is to send him to Sevagram as soon as he starts and then draw a cordon round the *ashram* and let no one in or out. Anyhow we await your considered recommendations.'[29]

The matter was considered and reconsidered in the following days. Eventually, the viceroy decided that the plan of releasing Gandhiji when he commenced his fast would not work either 'for reason that the moment he was known to have started a fast there would be an immense concourse of people anxious to dissuade him, to visit him or merely to be spectators and travelling an extensive pilgrimage from all over India; also, it would be most difficult to control the press, which would write up most exciting stories which would have an extremely bad effect on opinion here as well as abroad; while serious problems of public order might arise out of assembling and control of crowds.' Accordingly, Linlithgow and his advisers settled on a modified plan.

He set this out in his *'Immediate, Personal'* telegram to Amery on 29 August: 'What I think would be wise solution is that on Gandhi starting a fast and making it clear that it is a fast to death we should on the assumption that such fast is for the achievement of his inadmissible demands (a) warn him in the name of H.M.G. that we do not propose to

29 *Transfer of Power*, Vol. II, pp. 632, 646.

interfere, that all facilities for medical treatment etc. will be provided but that decision in matter is one which he must take himself: (b) Immediately send Devdas Gandhi, his eldest son, to join him at Aga Khan's Palace: (c) Tell Devdas that we would provide all facilities, doctors, medical or spiritual assistance, food etc. and that he has only to ask for anything he wants; and that also we will put Devdas in charge of arrangements inside Aga Khan's Palace and of Gandhi's health: (d) That there will be no objection to Gandhi seeing a reasonable number of visitors or friends from outside, that we leave selection of names to Devdas but that we expect him to operate that permission in a reasonable sense and to avoid any substantial number of people being let in, and wholly to exclude press: (e) That we shall continue to keep Gandhi under treatment in these conditions until he either abandons his fast or it has a fatal outcome.'[30]

Indians?

We get in these exchanges a preliminary glimpse of the attitude of the British to Gandhiji and others. The ones like Ambedkar who decided to join the government were fully in the know of what the rulers thought of the nationalist leaders and the movement for freedom. Not just that, they knew full well that a confrontation was imminent. They chose to be with the British in that confrontation, rather than be with the national movement. More than that, they knew full well, in the case of persons like Ambedkar they knew in advance what the viceroy and his government intended to do vis-à-vis Gandhiji and others in that confrontation. They joined the government in full awareness of those proposed measures.

---

30 *Transfer of Power,* Vol. II, p. 844.

Recall the message that Linlithgow had sent to the governor in Bombay on 16 July. Ambedkar was not yet a member of the Viceroy's Council, his joining had not even been notified as yet. But the viceroy thought it fit to inform Ambedkar of the course the government had decided to pursue. 'I should also be most grateful,' he told Lumley, 'if you would let Ambedkar know from me for his private and personal information that this matter was discussed yesterday in my Council; that we agreed that we should postpone final decision until matter had been before All-India Congress Committee on 7th August, and that if that body did ratify Gandhi's resolution and subject to any developments that there might be in between we should have to take immediate and drastic action against Congress and its leaders...'[31]

The same day the viceroy gave an account of discussions in the Council to the Secretary of State through his *'Immediate, Personal'* telegram. 'I am quite clear at the same time that the wise course is to have allowed publication of the resolution, to await reactions to it, and pending meeting of the All-India Congress Committee, to complete our preparations and to be ready to strike at once thereafter,' Linlithgow said. 'Issue generally was discussed in my Council today, those present in addition to the chief and myself being Mody, Sultan Ahmed, Aney, Sarkar, Firoz Khan Noon, and Benthall. I was greatly impressed by their unanimity as to necessity for dealing swiftly and sternly with Congress if they force the issue. General estimate was that All-India Congress Committee (though in very many cases with grave misgiving) would ratify resolution of Working Committee, and Council was very insistent on necessity for as much advance propaganda as we could arrange to bring out our side of the case and to stimulate

31 *Transfer of Power*, Vol. II, p. 396.

those elements in this country such as the Muslims, Depressed Classes, &c. who do not accept the Congress principles to make it clear that they do not accept them and also on necessity of putting our case across in the United States and China.'[32]

On 29 July Linlithgow informed Amery, 'We had a good discussion in Council this morning on action against the Congress, and I hope they will stand pretty solid if it comes to the point. Ambedkar, Usman and Srivastava appeared for the first time and made quite useful contributions.'[33]

When the War Cabinet met in London on 6 August to take final stock of the measures to be taken the Secretary of State for India was able, as we have seen, to inform the ministers, 'The Viceroy, who had throughout acted in full accord with his Council, had adopted an extremely patient attitude, in the hope that the Congress might think better of the course of action they proposed. His whole Council, however, had decided that if Congress forced the issue, stern and swift action must be taken...' Accordingly, in recording their conclusions, the Cabinet emphasized, 'In announcing the action taken against the Congress leaders prominence should be given to the following points:- (a) This action had the full support of the Members of the Viceroy's Executive Council...'[34]

The Council was in on details of the operation too. And often the viceroy thought it prudent to defer to them even when his own inclination was to the contrary, and even when the Cabinet in London had decided on a contrary course—for instance, on the question of deporting Gandhiji and others to Uganda, etc.[35]

The viceroy had good reason to be pleased with the

---

32 *Transfer of Power,* Vol. II, pp. 397–98.

33 *Transfer of Power,* Vol. II, p. 489.

34 *Transfer of Power,* Vol. II, pp. 586, 588; also 597.

35 *Transfer of Power,* Vol. II, pp. 596–97.

members he had put in place before coming down on Gandhiji and others. Writing to the Secretary of State two days after the crackdown, Linlithgow observed, 'I think my Council deserve full marks for the way in which they stood up to a most unpopular decision. I had been endeavouring over many days past in individual conversation and also in our regular meetings of Council to lead them in the right direction, though I have scrupulously refrained from taking any decision, even contingent, and have been at pains throughout to emphasize that my mind and theirs must remain open until the crisis came. I was not by any means certain right up to the last that I was going to get a unanimous vote, for certain of my friends were very far from anxious to stand up to this problem. I was quite ready to take the decision myself if it had to be taken, but realizing how great would be the value to Council as an education in responsibility, and equally how great would be the propaganda value outside of a unanimous vote by them, I strained every nerve to secure that result. Mody was extremely miserable. There were in one or two other colleagues signs of doubt. But finally, Council without any dissentient agreed that there was nothing for it in the face of the challenge thrown but to take immediate and drastic action against Gandhi and the Working Committee on the lines with which you are familiar.'[36]

We have seen that Government had every reason to believe that Gandhiji would not start any movement save after a substantial interval, that he would first write to the viceroy, await a reply and so on, and that in spite of this expectation, in fact armed with it the viceroy and his team had decided that the arrests, etc., should be affected immediately after the Bombay meeting. The viceroy narrated to Amery how the discussion on this point had gone

36 *Transfer of Power*, Vol. II, p. 661.

in the Council. 'There was some discussion as to whether it would not be a good thing to wait for the receipt of the letter which Gandhi was alleged in the Press to be sending to me. I pointed out to my colleagues that there was nothing in fact to show that I might expect such a letter beyond rumours in the Press, and C.P. Ramaswami Aiyar was of great assistance here by giving an amusing account of his own epistolary correspondence with the Mahatma at an earlier stage, and the delays and uncertainties and final disappointment which it had involved. As I write there is still no sign of any letter, and we should indeed have been unwise to have waited for one. I do not exclude the possibility that Gandhi may send me something from his place of restraint, and I shall have to consider how to deal with it if he does. But that is a different business, and it will be much easier to handle, now that the decisive step has been taken, than it would have been had we delayed at the end of last week.'[37]

Gandhiji's letter written from detention three days later, on 14 August set out the facts, facts which the viceroy knew full well, and in spite of which, in fact *because* of which Amery, he, their entire team had decided to get in the blow first. 'The Government of India should have waited at least till the time I inaugurated mass action,' Gandhiji wrote. 'I had publicly stated that I fully contemplated sending you a letter before taking concrete action. It was to be an appeal to you for an impartial examination of the Congress case. As you know the Congress has readily filled in every omission that has been discovered in the conception of its demand. So could I have dealt with every difficulty if you had given me the opportunity. The precipitate action of the Government leads one to think that they were afraid that the extreme

---

37 *Transfer of Power,* Vol. II, pp. 661–62.

caution and gradualness with which the Congress was moving towards direct action might make world opinion veer round to the Congress, as it had already begun doing, and expose the hollowness of the grounds for the Government's rejection of the Congress demand. They should surely have waited for an authentic report of my speeches on Friday and on Saturday night after the passing of the resolution by the A.-I.C.C. You would have found in them that I would not hastily begin action. You should have taken advantage of the interval foreshadowed in them, and explored every possibility of satisfying the Congress demand...'[38]

But that is exactly—'taking advantage of the interval foreshadowed in them'—that the viceroy had decided to do long ago. And with him, every member of his Council.

Puffing them up

On the premise that he was performing an educational function which would make things easier for his successor as the then-existent form of government was liable to last a longish time, and of course very alert to the propaganda value of being able to claim that what was being done had the full and unanimous endorsement of the Council members, Linlithgow humoured the members along—allowing them to engage in discussions on subjects which were outside the jurisdiction of the Council, subjects on which he proposed to do nothing and on which therefore discussions in the Council could be no more than college debates. He would modify the text of a statement, he would tell them that he would forward their views to the Secretary of State in London, all the time sharing with the Secretary of State the real reason for giving them this sense of being important!

38 *Transfer of Power,* Vol. II, pp. 702–03.

'I am sorry to have bothered you so much with the text of our resolution,' he wrote to Amery on 11 August when the Congress leaders were safely in jail. 'My heart sank after my first draft, after a couple of hours of round-table discussion, emerged in rags and I was required to produce a modified version at the shortest of notice. But the modified version went down very well, and I think that my colleagues were probably pleased to have had a chance of shooting a few arrows at a target such as this, and of making themselves felt...'[39] He described how members of the Council had resented what they thought was dictation from London, and how important it was to bear in mind that they were liable to work themselves up to feel this way. 'For it is quite essential,' he wrote, 'now that we have a body of this quality and size, to take it with one. The longer they hold together the less risk, I should think, there was of resignations and the more chance of building up a tradition which may be of very considerable value to my successor, and of real assistance to India, if, as seems only too likely, we have to continue with the present form of Council Government for some considerable time'—in five years India would be independent, but in 1942 that event still seemed improbable, a mere possibility that might come about some time in the vague and distant future, that is how it seemed to the British, and most definitely to their associates who had joined their government. No other explanation can account for the sorts of things these latter persons did and said during this period, and none also for the pleas they put forward to the British four years later, for their bewilderment, their near-breakdown, their exasperation in 1945–46 with the British—with the ones in whose boat they had put all their fortune and future. But we anticipate. Linlithgow continued, 'They are of course

---

39 *Transfer of Power,* Vol. II, p. 662.

touchy; they do not quite realize (or will not quite realize) where they stand constitutionally; and they are naturally very anxious to have something to wave before the public as proof of their independence of attitude and the regard in which they are held by His Majesty's Government...'[40]

What the priorities of these persons were, what their concerns were after they had joined the viceroy in hurling Gandhiji and other Congress leaders into jails are well brought out in the *'Immediate, Personal'* telegram which Linlithgow sent to the Secretary of State on 10 August at their urging. 'I have separately reported decision of my Council to deal with situation created by ratification by A.-I.C.C. of Working Committee resolution on lines of which you are aware,' the telegram read. 'That decision was unanimous. Its gravity I need not emphasize. Nor can I overstate its importance to the Members of my Council individually. They are all of them prominent in public life, with long and distinguished records of service to India and to the public. But a decision such as the present must inevitably mean their being pilloried as traitors and reactionaries, and that process has already begun'—in a word the members had consciously and after much deliberation chosen to side with the imperial power, to do in the leaders of the national movement like Gandhiji, to do that which the people saw as betrayal by traitors.

'Those reasons did not deter my colleagues, who saw their duty clear, and once they were satisfied on that they discharged it without hesitation,' the viceroy continued. And now look at what these Indians—Ambedkar and the rest—were anxious about, what it is they wanted to ensure: they did not want to ensure that Gandhiji and others were released soon, not that some sort of agreement would be worked out, *they were nervous that these things might come to pass*!

40 *Transfer of Power*, Vol. II, pp. 663–64.

Linlithgow told the Secretary of State, 'They unanimously desire me to however make clear in the most definite terms possible to His Majesty's Government that (a) they would bitterly resent any early resumption of these negotiations by His Majesty's Government with present leaders of Congress or with any other political party in this country save after full consultation with my Council: (b) that equally they rely on His Majesty's Government to resist any pressure that might be brought upon them by China, the United States or any other of the Allied Nations for a relaxation of the present decision. If circumstances should appear later to call for any revision of policy, that will be a matter on which Government of India will expect to be given an opportunity to express their view to His Majesty's Government.' 'I have told my colleagues,' Linlithgow concluded, 'that I would forward their representation to you and that I felt certain that the Cabinet would treat it with a full appreciation of its significance and with full sympathy for the motives prompting it.'

Here were Indians who had made themselves available to the imperial power, and they were seized by the anxiety of every accomplice, that the principal may just decide that they were dispensable and, when it suited him, strike a deal with the ones they had helped throw into jails. These men, without any base of their own, dependent solely on the prop of alien rulers, were now nervous that, while they had stuck their necks in the noose of betrayal, the imperial power might jettison them and come to terms with the leaders of the national movement they had betrayed. This is the fate that in fact befell them four years later when the British decided that they just could not hold on to India any longer: the extreme discomfiture of members such as Ambedkar comes through in their opportunings to Wavell and others—we are the ones who conquered India for you as your loyal soldiers; in leaving India, in leaving us to deal with the ones whom we had helped you to throw into jails, you are being disregardful of the debt you owe us: that was their refrain.

In an accompanying *'Immediate, Private and Personal'* telegram to Amery, Linlithgow explained that he could hardly exaggerate how strongly the members felt on this score. He said that the way Cripps had gone about his business—dealing with the Congress and the Muslim League as if they were the only entities that mattered—had bitten into these persons deeply, and that therefore it was all the more necessary to assuage their apprehensions. 'They have done so well over this business,' said the viceroy, 'that we must do our utmost to keep them sweet and together, and I trust that you will be able to let me have something suitably soothing in reply to the protest which they unanimously (including Benthall) desire to send to you... I think my colleagues recognize that His Majesty's Government cannot be expected to promise never again to negotiate with the Congress Party. *Truth is that they are deeply exercised about their own position collectively and individually and greatly alarmed lest they may be let down.'* 'I sympathize with them very sincerely,' concluded the viceroy who knew as well as the members the enormity of the steps to which these Indians had agreed to put their names.[41]

A considerate collaborator

The telegrams were scarcely out and a ripple arose: Sir C.P. Ramaswami Aiyar who, as we have seen, had been among the most enthusiastic in putting Gandhiji and the others down with a decisive and pre-emptive sweep, developed cold feet. He went to see the Viceroy on 12 August, and

---

41 *Transfer of Power,* Vol. II, pp. 647–49.

told him that, on reflection, he thought it would be a good idea for him to go and see Gandhiji, and to beg him to call off the Civil Disobedience Movement. The Viceroy immediately informed the Secretary of State of this unexpected development through an *'Immediate, Secret, Private and Personal'* telegram. He told Amery that he was not sure what Sir C.P. was after 'unless it is that he too is beginning to suffer from the strain which this business is putting on the nerves of my Hindu colleagues.' 'Hitherto,' Linlithgow pointed out, 'he has taken exactly the opposite line and been anxious to be stiff.' Linlithgow had sought the reactions of colleagues: 'I have confidentially consulted [A. Ramaswami] Mudaliar and [J.P.] Srivastava. Both are most firmly opposed to any compromise with Gandhi, which, as Mudaliar remarked, would represent an abdication. Srivastava would let him fast to death. I am sure that that would be the attitude of my Muslim colleagues, and almost certainly of Ambedkar; and, while I shall treat C.P.'s request with care and respect, I have no intention of acceding to it. Nor have the least intention of budging myself on this issue, and I [am] proceeding on the basis, which I do not think I need ask you to confirm, that Cabinet will be wholly with me in resisting anything that could be even remotely represented as a climb-down or compromise.' 'We shall no doubt get more of these feelers as time goes on and the strain gets greater. But I am quite prepared in the last resort to see the business through on my own responsibility, if necessary, all the more so as there is nothing in the situation in the country to justify any uneasiness...'[42]

As is well known, C.P. Ramaswami Aiyar eventually did leave, but he made sure to do so as a well-behaved dinner guest leaves, that is in a way that would not inconvenience

---

42 *Transfer of Power*, Vol. II, pp. 668.

the hosts, in this case the British, and certainly not upset them. He called on the viceroy again and again. He sent him letters. The viceroy put the obvious arguments to him: 'You have just about joined the Council; when you did so you knew well that a confrontation was imminent; indeed, you yourself were among the most emphatic that Gandhi and the Congress must be dealt with most sternly; the Council of which you are a part itself decided that there ought to be no compromise with Gandhi; indeed, it is at the urging of you and your colleagues that I wrote to His Majesty's Government in London that the one thing no one here would countenance would be if Government in London entertained any proposal to open negotiations with Gandhi or the Congress; whatever you may say, constructions are bound to be put on your leaving Government, and it will be put out that you have left because you do not approve of the measures which have been taken against the Congress, measures which in fact you have wholeheartedly endorsed; if you go now, you are bound to come in confrontation with your colleagues who have taken these decisions along with you...'

Sir C.P. could not deny any of these things. And yet the typhoon which was sweeping the country in the wake of the arrest of Gandhiji and the others was also no minor thing. He did leave eventually—making out that he was doing so to serve another, and to him higher cause which too was being put in jeopardy by the Congress! Explaining his departure, Sir C.P. declared that the recent statements from Gandhiji and the Congress endangered the prospects of the Indian states, serving which had been his lifelong endeavour, that he was resigning so that he may be free to take on this challenge to the states and their rulers! He was prudent enough to send information to the ruler of Travancore in advance about his decision![43]

---

43 *Transfer of Power*, Vol. II, pp. 668, 720–23, 749–52, 758–61, 763–66, 775, 779–82, 811.

What a relief that statement was to the viceroy: the member had had the grace to go out not to oppose what the British were doing, but to supplement their efforts from another post!

Follow up measures naturally endorsed

The other members didn't do even this much. They held firm. Indeed, as they had endorsed the repression they could not stand anyone, even if he were British who said anything that could be construed to be a criticism of the measures. And having endorsed the main decision to suppress the movement, to render Gandhiji and the other leaders incommunicado and impotent, they had to, and therefore did endorse every consequential follow-up measure, be it the breaking up of strikes or plain lies. An example or two will give the flavour of steps to which these members lent themselves.

As is well known, *The Statesman,* like *The Times of India,* was the voice of Britishers in those days. If ever those running such papers differed from the official line, it was because they thought they had a way which would better safeguard British interests in India than the measures the government was pursuing. The mounting tensions of July 1942 provided one such occasion. On 6 August, and again on 10 August *The Statesman* carried editorials which did not catch the fancy of the viceroy and his Council. The viceroy shot off telegrams to the Secretary of State, along with copies of the editorials and requested him to express the government's displeasure about such pieces to the controllers of the paper. He urged that the controllers should not just warn the [British] editor in Calcutta, but, as warnings were obviously not having the desired effect, they should have the board get the man to proceed on leave immediately and then find someone more suitable.

Drawing the attention of the Secretary of State to the editorial of the paper in its issue of 10 August, that is the day after the Congress leaders had been bundled off to jails, the viceroy said, 'Point is, I fear, approaching at which we may be driven to intervene. I do not know if Catto would feel able to consider instructing Moore confidentially to avoid all editorial reference, whether direct or indirect, to the civil disobedience and Congress situation, since he seems incapable on his own of keeping within the bounds of reasonable comment. Damaging effect on morale and confidence of leaders such as these of which you now have the text—one coming shortly after the other—will be only too obvious to you.'

The Secretary of State took up the matter, and wired back the result: 'In addition to previous efforts Catto cabled Moore very strongly on May 19th and on June 18th to Richardson that unless Moore implicitly obeyed cable of May 19th then they must part company forthwith and after receipt of Richardson's reply in which he said Moore indicated that (there?) might be publicity if forced out, Catto again cabled to Richardson that unless Moore will work in team and accept guidance he must be dropped and indicated this could be done by giving leave of absence on full pay till expiration of contract and regarding publicity he does not quarrel with his associates but if they choose to quarrel with him by encouraging publicity the threat of which is unworthy of Moore this does not worry Catto and would recoil on Moore besides forfeiting Catto's esteem and friendship. In separate cable Catto told Richardson not to cable further about this matter as he had given all guidance possible and that Richardson who is Chairman of *Statesman* Company and Directors must now deal with the matter in regard to which they have Catto's full support and authority.'

Things didn't improve to the satisfaction of the viceroy

and his Council. He lodged another protest with the Secretary of State. The latter took up the matter again, and sent the viceroy a copy of the cable which had been sent to Calcutta as a result. 'I am sure I need not impress upon you and Moore,' the telegram read, 'that you must see *The Statesman* gives Viceroy and his Government fullest support in present emergency. Authority of Government has been challenged and whatever may have been previous expression of political views the present situation is no longer question of politics but of law and order which it is our duty to support to fullest extent. I rely on you both. Leader of 10th very opposite of this spirit... Obvious solution is immediate leave of absence to end his contract.'

The viceroy thanked Amery through an *'Immediate, Private and Personal'* telegram on 12 August. He told Amery that he was letting the governor in Calcutta know what advice had been sent to the personnel in Calcutta, and he told Amery about the feelings of his Council in the matter. They were being even more loyal than the king! And quite naturally so: comment which was critical, specially if it emanated from a Britisher, showed them up in even sharper colours to be the accomplices they were. The viceroy's new cable on the matter read: '....I am most grateful and hope you will thank Catto very warmly for me... I am letting Herbert know position confidentially and asking him to get hold of Richardson and ginger him up for action. It is the more important that something should be done as *The Statesman* leader of the 10th August was raised in my Council today when very strong disposition to take immediate action against Moore and *The Statesman* was manifested. I headed them off that, but much emphasis was laid by various Members on the fact that our gentleness towards Moore was regarded widely as racial discrimination while Benthall indicated that many Europeans would greatly welcome a stronger line with *The Statesman* which was a source of much embarrassment to the extent that it was so widely regarded as representing European opinion when in fact it does not do so.'

The viceroy sent copies of the cables which had been received from London to Sir J. Herbert, the governor of Bengal, and added, 'Between you and me I am quite clear that it is Richardson's weakness that is responsible for a good deal of the trouble, but I cannot see him myself as he is in Calcutta. Could you send for him and confidentially give him gist of Secretary of State's telegram? I personally agree with suggestion at the end of that telegram. We cannot go on like this, for I am under very strong pressure over our forbearance in regard to Moore already...'

Two days later the viceroy was able to report the happy outcome to Amery, and also to claim that it had come about spontaneously without the government having interfered with the freedom of the press! He repeated to the Secretary of State the telegram he had received from the governor of Bengal. The governor had just reported, 'Have discussed with Richardson. Meeting of the Directors of the *Statesman* on August 10th agreed that Moore should be allowed to leave preparatory to retirement on full emoluments, such leave to take effect as soon as conveniently might be able to be arranged...' The viceroy was pleased to add, 'As you will see, action had been taken by Board of the *Statesman* itself following Catto's instructions before I communicated with Herbert. This is very satisfactory'—he didn't of course add that Catto had been spurred to send his instructions by the viceroy's own complaints! 'I would like again to say,' Linlithgow continued, 'how grateful I am to Catto (and to you) for support over a matter which I am satisfied is of great importance as affecting European morale...'[44]

---

44 *Transfer of Power,* Vol. II, pp. 649–50, 670–71, 698.

Consider next another example, one that shows the priorities of government, their duplicity, and the craven concerns of the collaborators. On 28 May 1942 the government raided the offices of the Congress in Allahabad. They recovered documents which contained a record of discussions about what the attitude of the Congress should be to the war, and what course of action it should adopt. The viceroy sent copies of these documents to the Secretary of State in London on 2 June. On the night of 31 July at the meeting of the Viceroy's Council the subject of what use should be made of the documents came up. The viceroy described the discussion in his *'Immediate, Private and Personal'* telegram to the Secretary of State on 1 August:

> We discussed in Council last night question of releasing to Press documents seized from Congress offices in Allahabad on May 28th, copies of which were sent to you in my letter of June 2nd. Those present in addition to Chief and myself were Mudaliar, Mody, Sarker, Firoz, Benthall, Usman, Ambedkar and Srivastava. Council unanimously agreed that these documents should be released to Press. All except Mody (who originally favoured release *after* meeting of A.-I.C.C. but ultimately joined majority) favoured release at earliest possible moment, and we are arranging for publication in morning papers of August 5th.

Two of the Indians present seemed to have had some doubts, but not on behalf of the nationalist movement, nor on the propriety of planting such material. They had a moment of doubt on an entirely different score—namely, whether the papers might not be presenting one nationalist leader—Pandit Nehru as it happens—in an unduly favourable light! As the viceroy explained in his telegram:

> Mudaliar and Ambedkar expressed some doubt as to whether documents might not show Nehru in an unduly favourable light, but general sense of Council (accepted by Mudaliar and

> Ambedkar after discussion) was that telling use could be made for propaganda purposes of contrast between Nehru's attitude as shown in these intimate discussions and his subsequent public attitude and climb down to Gandhi. Benthall stressed damaging effect of evidence that majority of Working Committee were prepared to consider betrayal of India to the enemy. There are sentences in Gandhi's draft and references in Nehru's statement to the fact that draft would be taken as evidence of Gandhi's readiness to surrender to Japan of which telling use could be made, as also damaging references to presence of Americans in India and use of foreign troops. Home Department will be telegraphing to you officially regarding release [to press of seized documents], but I do hope (and am fully confident) that you and your Information Department will be able to give us the same invaluable help on the propaganda side over these documents as you have hitherto. It is clearly of the utmost importance that we should bring out for the benefit of the United States and China readiness of Congress under Gandhi to negotiate with Japan and (in case of America) their critical attitude towards use of foreign troops, &c.

Amery was of course delighted at the discomfiture the publication of these documents would cause the Congress and the assistance they would be to the British. But knowing the steps that were in the works against the Congress, and also how necessary it would be to have ammunition ready at that time to justify arrests of Gandhiji and the other leaders, he counselled holding these documents in reserve till after the Bombay meeting of the AICC—all the more so as, in his assessment, the documents might indeed 'provide a knock-out blow.' Therefore Amery sent a *'Most Immediate, Private and Personal'* telegram to Linlithgow on 3 August. He said:

> While, in view of unanimous decision of your Council, I should in the normal way be most reluctant to suggest any alternative course, I feel I must put to you what seem to me most jmportant considerations pointing to desirability of postponement of

publication unless and until action is taken against Gandhi and the Congress leaders.

He outlined the reasons:

(a) To publish now before opportunity is given to A.-I.C.C. to turn down Working Committee might seem provocative and raise in awkward form question why we held back this information up to the last moment. On the other hand if the A.-I.C.C. endorse Working Committee and you *then* (repeat then) publish that would both illustrate your forbearance up to date and afford extra justification for firm action. It might in fact provide a knock-out blow. I realize that your advisers have been influenced by prospect of publication having effect of creating confusion among number of A.-I.C.C. and so possibly averting their endorsement of A.-I.C.C. As to this I should like you very seriously to consider weight of arguments I have put down above, (b) If contrary to expectation on which we have been working A.-I.C.C. does not endorse Working Committee possibility arises that action may still have to be taken against Gandhi at any rate who may well decide to pursue his policy. In that event material will provide very strong justification for proceeding against him. (c) Finally it must be realized that publication of the material at this stage means a final severance of relations with the Congress leaders implicated.

The Secretary of State requested the Viceroy to send his reactions by *'Most Immediate telegram'*.

The viceroy and his team however moved to ensure publication of the material on the morning of 5 August. It was sent to twelve centres of Reuters. And it was sent in advance to the editor of *The Hindu,* a paper which had always been able in the end to find a way to have its views accord with those that would not offend the British establishment.

Rajaji got wind of what was afoot. He protested to the viceroy, using what he must have thought would be a telling argument—that is, an appeal to the British sense of fair play, to British honour so to say. The viceroy concluded the opposite from what Rajaji had intended—that Rajaji had protested against the plan to publish the material proved to the viceroy that the account of what had transpired at the meeting could not be challenged on the charge of being a forgery, and also that its publication would indeed sow confusion among Congress leaders; therefore, he was even more emboldened to have the material published. He alluded to the development in his communication to the Secretary of State on 3 August. He wrote:

> Meanwhile I have today had an appeal from Rajagopalachari who on hearing (this too a breach of confidence by the editor of *The Hindu* to whom these papers had been sent in confidence for release on the 5th) what was afoot, has sent me a telegram which I repeat separately protesting vigorously against any use being made of them. As I had rather anticipated would be the case he does not suggest, though he was present at the discussions, that the papers are forgeries or that there is no foundation to their content. He concentrates entirely on the point that it is a sad abuse of the proprieties to publish confidential papers of this character. I cannot of course accept that view, any more than I can accept his attempted analogy with Cabinet papers. But the celerity of his reaction and of that of Srinivasan confirms me in my earlier feeling that while publication may have a hardening effect on certain sections of Congress opinion, it ought materially to shake the more responsible elements in that party.

The next day the viceroy reverted to this matter in his *'Immediate'* telegram to the Secretary of State. *'Hindustan Times* of this morning foreshadows publication of these documents,' he said, 'and I do not feel the least doubt that holding up publication would have been impracticable, while politically I think that the harder we hit at this moment the better. You are right in thinking... that what weighed with the Council in deciding on immediate publication was hope of influencing waverers in A.-I.C.C., and anxiety to avoid suggestion that having this important material available we had deliberately held it up till it could no longer strengthen the hands of moderate opinion or influence waverers.' He added, 'I may tell you that I gave Council no lead as to when to publish and their decision was quite spontaneous.'

There was the difficulty of explaining this un-British-like step to the Americans. The government in London, which had had the papers since receiving the viceroy's letter of 2 June and which had been discussing the pros and cons of the timing of publication with the viceroy, pretended that the decision to publish had come as a surprise to it also!

Anthony Eden, then in the Foreign Office, sent a *'Most Immediate and Secret'* telegram to the British representative in Washington, and asked him to convey the following *'Most Secret'* message to President Roosevelt from Clement Atlee:

> My colleagues and I would have wished that you should have known in advance of the Government of India's decision, only communicated to us at the last moment, to publish on 5th August the documents relating to the Congress Party Working Committee's discussions on the Congress Party's resolution of 1st May. These papers with their damaging revelations of the defeatist outlook of the Congress Party leaders and particularly of Gandhi had been in the Government of India's hands for some time but they forbore from disclosing them or from placing any restraint on Congress leaders in the hope that counsels of moderation and specially the opinions expressed in the United States of America might avert any extreme decision. Unfortunately this hope has gradually diminished and after much searching of heart the Government of India decided almost at the last moment on publication which they felt might help to check waverers in the Party by showing up its leaders in their true light...

The representative was asked to convey a message to the Secretary of State in Washington on behalf of Amery, the British Secretary of State for India in London.

Much effort was expended on using these documents to discredit the Congress leaders. Alas, the revelations didn't work the magic which the British rulers had convinced themselves they would. Three days after their publication Amery sent an *'Important, Most Secret'* telegram to Churchill who was on tour in the Middle East. 'On morning of 5th August in order to anticipate meeting of All-India Congress Committee Government of India released text of Gandhi's original draft resolution and discussion in Working Committee thereon at end of April last. This had valuable effect on Press here and in U.S.A. by revealing defeatist tendencies of Congress leaders, but it is doubtful if it has had much effect in discrediting them in India...'[45]

That remained the pattern, from one calculated move to another—the government and its accomplices had every reason to believe that Gandhiji would not launch any movement till the middle of September, that, as was his wont, he would not launch any movement till the last avenue of finding some solution had been explored, yet they swooped down on the Congress leaders and made out that the latter had been on the verge of launching a catastrophic mutiny; the viceroy and even more the accomplices felt that any critical comment would not just inconvenience them, it would show up the accomplices, and so they moved to throttle it; they manufactured 'explanations' for the US administration—the little evasion we have seen is nothing compared to the wholesale distortions in the official handbook which the government put out over the signatures of Richard Tottenham, the additional secretary, Home, to justify its repressive measures. And at every step the Executive Council was not just kept informed, its concurrence was taken. Indeed, as we have seen, often it was even more

---

45 *Transfer of Power*, Vol. II, pp. 516, 539, 543, 554, 556, 608, 6ll, 617.

eager that action be taken than the viceroy himself. Members who continued in the government did so in full knowledge of what was being done to crush the national movement. They saw that there were two sides, and they chose to side with the British.

5

Confronting that 'old rascal', that 'miserable little old man', that 'most successful humbug in the world'

As we saw, the thing that the British were most concerned about was the prospect that Gandhiji might commence a fast the moment he was in detention. Gandhiji did not do so for several months. His associate and secretary for decades, Mahadev Desai, died suddenly on 15 August 1942, within a week of all of them being put in detention. It was a terrible blow to Gandhiji as Mahadev had been more than a son to him. Gandhiji sat through the cremation. He informed the inmates of the Sevagram Ashram by telegram of the death and the cremation, and told them that he would keep the ashes.

He wrote to the viceroy more than once. Nothing came of the letters. On the contrary the government kept putting out distortions accusing Gandhiji of fomenting violence and the rest. Gandhiji protested. To no avail. Nor would the viceroy condescend to explore the possibilities of any solution. His demand was that Gandhiji must dissociate himself from the 'Quit India' resolution, and also furnish assurances for the future course of action that the Congress or he might adopt.

The members of his Council were of course with the viceroy on all this. In fact, as we have seen, their sole anxiety was that the government in London may decide to enter into negotiations with Gandhiji or with some elements in the Congress. This is what they strove to prevent. It is the one thing, they told the viceroy, which would compel them to resign.

The severity of the oppression across the country, the viceroy's replies and the continuing falsehoods which the government was putting out left Gandhiji no alternative. On 29 January he informed the viceroy that he would commence a fast of twenty-one days from the morning of 9 February if he did not receive from government 'soothing balm for my pain'.

The letter from Gandhiji reopened the earlier debate within government: should Gandhi be released for the duration of the fast?. If he was not to be released when he commences the fast, should he be released when he was in imminent danger of dying or should he be allowed to die in detention? Who should be allowed to be present as his condition deteriorated?

'They have, I must say, been very good indeed...'

As will be recalled, the viceroy and his Council had been the embodiment of sternness in July and August. If he decides to fast, he must take the consequences—that was the view, the phrase standing for letting him die. But as the fast was now before them, the Council thought that it would be better to release him when he commenced the fast, and, if he survived, to rearrest him after the twenty-one days were over. The viceroy was still inclined to keep him in detention and, if things came to that, to let him die a prisoner. But he decided that in the confrontation with Gandhiji it was best to have Indians in the front, and so he decided to go along with the decision of the Council. He informed the Secretary of State accordingly, and also sent him the draft of the statement which government would issue at the commencement of the fast. The Secretary of State put the viceroy's telegrams up to the War Cabinet.

Churchill had just got back. The War Cabinet met on the evening of 7 February at 5.30 p.m. In India it was already well into the night—Gandhiji's fast was to begin at 7.30 a.m. on 9 February. The sequence is best described in the words of Amery. In his *'Private'* letter to the Viceroy, Amery reported:

> On Sunday morning Atlee thought that Winston, who was arriving at one o'clock, might be going down to Chequers and would be agreeable to the matter being settled by the Cabinet without him. Not at all! Winston insisted on having a Cabinet himself and launched out on the Gandhi subject at once. At first he continued, as is often his habit, muttering away his dissatisfaction, but giving me the impression that he was going to agree with a shrug of the shoulder. Presently, however, he warmed up and worked himself into one of his states of indignation over India. I made efforts to bring him round to the point that whatever might or might not be the best method of handling so peculiar a situation as the Gandhi one, the issue was not that, but whether you were to override your Council and run the risk of resignations. That point he simply brushed aside by saying that it would not matter if they did all resign: we could carry on just as well without them and this our hour of triumph everywhere in the world was not the time to crawl before a miserable little old man who had always been our enemy. In the face of that mood the Cabinet generally, instead of facing the issue, began looking round for minor points of criticism or uncertainty...

In the event the Cabinet decided to inform the viceroy by cable that it was 'gravely disturbed by the viceroy's proposals', that it could not approve the proposed action. A committee of three was set up to draft a stiff telegram. Amery sent a telegram of his own also. He explained in brief that he had tried during the Cabinet meeting to dissuade the Cabinet from the line they were adopting, that he had urged them to disregard the relative merits of the different courses of action possible, and to concentrate only on the question 'whether at this eleventh hour you can reopen with your colleagues matter already agreed by yourself and so raise directly issue of considered view of Governor-General in Council being overridden from here'. He explained that of course if Linlithgow felt that he could get members of the Council to reverse their decision, well and good. But that if he could not see his way to doing so, 'then say so as briefly and emphatically as you can.' He assured the viceroy, 'You can count on my all-out support of whatever course you may now take.'

In the *'Private'* letter Amery sent that very day he repeated the points to Linlithgow and again assured him of his all-out support 'even if it means my breaking with the Government'. 'I confess I get very fed up at times,' he added, 'with a Cabinet which has no mind of its own and whose members are all terrified of saying anything which would draw Winston's displeasure upon their heads.'[1]

On the same day, 8 February, Churchill sent a telegram of his own also, a *'Most Immediate, Most Secret'* telegram through the War Office and the commander-in-chief. It read:

> Officer decipher. Private for Field Marshal Wavell. Deliver personally to Viceroy for his eye only. From Prime Minister to Viceroy of India. Personal and Private. I earnestly hope you will weigh very carefully the overwhelming opinion of War Cabinet and other Ministers concerned before consenting to a step which is contrary to your own better judgement and that of the Commander-in-Chief on the merits and which I fear would bring our whole government both in India and here at home into ridicule and thus cloud the magnificent work which you have done in these seven anxious years. I ask this as a friend and also because I am convinced that such an episode would be a definite injury to our war policy all over the world which is now moving forward victoriously after so many perils have been surmounted by British resolution. For these larger interests I bear the chief responsibility.[2]

---

1 *Transfer of Power,* Vol. III, pp. 611–13, 618, 632.

2 *Transfer of Power,* Vol. III, p. 619.

Linlithgow reacted immediately. He explained in two *'Most Immediate, Personal'* telegrams to Amery that while his personal opinion was that Gandhi should be allowed to starve himself to death, it would be disastrous to overrule the Council at this late hour and thereby push some members into resigning. This would be disastrous for the whole war effort in the country. He accordingly urged that even if the Cabinet had some reservations about the proposed course, they should leave the matter to him.[3] The viceroy elaborated the point in the letter he sent to Amery the same day, 8 February. He wrote:

> Your account of Winston's attitude towards India, I read with amusement after a Council meeting to approve my draft reply to you this afternoon, about the apprehensions entertained by the Cabinet as to our method of handling Gandhi! I hope you will not have too rough a passage, and that they will not feel they have been bounced. But it really is impossible to expect a Council here, or even the Viceroy—well disciplined as he may be—to hold up action when it has got as far as this and zero is only a few hours off, while points of this type are discussed with London. I made it pretty clear earlier in January that Cabinet must be really prepared to take a chance with me over this and let me go ahead—after all I have to carry at least as heavy a burden as the Cabinet and a very much more direct one. My own attitude has been consistent throughout—I have favoured letting the Mahatma starve himself to death if he wants to. But, save from the Chief, who has been on tour during these last few Councils, I have had no support for that view; and it is quite obvious that while Governors are sharply divided, some important and experienced men, Parliamentary and civil servants alike, are very definitely against it. I have tried to bring out in a telegram I sent you yesterday the extreme importance of our being able to point to a united Council behind whatever policy we do adopt for dealing with Gandhi: for we may

3 *Transfer of Power,* Vol. III, p. 620.

> be quite certain that he is going to give us a great deal of trouble one way or another; that the strain on my colleagues—but of course especially my Hindu colleagues—will be very considerable and that a run out is to be avoided if that is humanly practicable. They have, I must say, been very good indeed, and I am prepared to enter the fray with greater confidence than would have been the case had I not been able to keep them together.

He did not want to make things easy for Gandhi, the viceroy explained, and therefore he had decided to be very direct in his letters to Gandhi. Gandhi's reply, the viceroy told Amery, showed that his own letters had touched Gandhi on the raw, and that 'I anticipate that the tone, or the content, of my letters will inevitably give a certain amount of offence in Hindu circles—it is of course bound to do so in Congress circles.' But there was the countervailing advantage, Linlithgow pointed out: 'But I am ready to take my chance on that, if only because the mere fact that it produces that reaction is in a sense a reassurance to the other elements whom I have mentioned above that I am not out to appease Gandhi, and that I am all for facing up to this sort of problem. Had I been able to have my way and allow him to starve to death if he so desired, that would have been still more the case. But on that point I have been beaten, and the fact that I have been beaten cannot of course be known to the outside world...'[4]

The 'solidarity' is 'considerably shattered'

But the viceroy, his Council, the Cabinet in London had all been reckoning without Gandhiji. While informing Linlithgow of his decision to fast according to capacity for twenty-one days, Gandhiji had told the viceroy that 'Government goaded

---

4 *Transfer of Power*, Vol. III, pp. 637–38.

the people to the point of madness... I cannot interpret in any other manner the repressive measures of the Government of India.' About 60,000 people had been arrested, about 18,000 had been kept in prisons, about 1,630 had been injured in firing, about 940 had been shot and killed outright. On receiving Linlithgow's reply, Gandhiji had told him that 'Your letter, from a satyagrahi's standpoint, is an invitation to fast.'

The government then played what it thought was its master card—they informed Gandhiji that they would release him for the duration of the fast. Gandhiji immediately saw through the game, and wrote back to the viceroy, 'If the temporary release is offered for my convenience, I do not need it. I shall be quite content to take my fast as a detenue or prisoner.' In order to enable the government to consider his reply, he told the viceroy that he would defer commencing his fast by twenty-four hours.

Linlithgow's letter of 8 February had not yet left. He added a long postscript. A lot had happened since he closed the letter, the viceroy wrote. Gandhi's reply had arrived. 'I thought that the best thing to do was to get my Council together immediately,' Linlithgow told Amery on the 9 February, 'and with great difficulty I collected them shivering from their warm beds, and very diversely dressed, for a Council at 12.30 a. m. this morning. Council went on for about three hours. It was incredibly difficult to pin Srivastava to anything. Ambedkar was absent; the Chief was away. The division either way was fifty-fifty—between holding Gandhi, and releasing him if immediate danger; and having cleared the ground to some extent I adjourned till 10.30 this morning. When we resumed Ambedkar was present, and it was quite clear that reflection had had some effect on certain of my other colleagues. I am telegraphing to let you know that in the outcome, after an extremely difficult meeting, subject to clear indications of possible resignations from Mody, Sarker, Aney, Joginder Singh, and conceivably Sultan Ahmed, over the issue of letting Gandhi die in confinement, Council agreed that we could not be blackmailed by Gandhi, and by a majority agreed that if he insisted on going through with his fast he must be left to take his chances.' 'But there was immense pressure to make some small concession,' Linlithgow continued, 'as regards his having his own medical attendants and as regards the visits of friends with the permission of Government (our original suggestion had been "approved by Government", but that proved to have no chance of getting through).' 'I dislike both these concessions,' the viceroy said, 'but I again thought we had done well to get Council unanimously behind so highly important a decision of principle, and I thought it worth making them to a minority. My own feeling was that the position of the Government of India was in fact strengthened by Gandhi's reply. But at the back of it all there remains the fact that there is a percentage that hates the idea of his dying to their discredit, and that most careful handling is essential. And I am very much afraid that the old man (to whom incidentally I give full marks for his reply which was a masterpiece of the usual type!) will force us to face up to that issue. If he does I may have very serious trouble, and a very major issue of policy will arise. But I am in no hurry to consider it...'

The *'Most Immediate'* telegram which the viceroy sent that evening, that is on the 9 February, to Amery brings out the effect Gandhiji's reply had had on the carefully constructed strategems of the governments in Delhi and London, indeed in the case of those who had worked out those strategems in Delhi the effect it had had on the body itself. It also shows where a person like Ambedkar was on letting Gandhiji die at this juncture. The viceroy explained:

> I put to Council in terms issue of (a) releasing Gandhi when in danger of death; (b) holding him. By a majority decision was in favour of holding him now that he had refused our offer to enlarge him for period of fast. Mody, Sultan Ahmed, Aney, Sarker, Jogendra Singh were the minority. Commander-in-Chief was away; otherwise full attendance. Once vote showed them to be in a minority dissenting members indicated that they might have to consider their position. I told them that that must be for them to decide, but that there could be no question of reopening of decision which had been taken by clear majority of Council and that I could not delay going ahead with my instructions to Province(s), &c. (I had earlier emphasized extreme importance of united front by Council, whatever our internal differences of view.) I rather doubt myself, though I may be wrong, if we shall hear much more of this for the moment. But if and when Gandhi is reported to be critically ill and in danger of death, we may then be faced with possibility of resignations on the ground that Government of India are not prepared to set him at liberty unconditionally...

The viceroy added ruefully, 'Solidarity of Council which was exceptionally marked in support of our previous decision had as you will see been considerably shattered by Gandhi's reply.'[5]

The viceroy therefore informed governors of provinces: '...Decision of Council was, by a majority, that in these new circumstances Gandhi, as he did not want to take advantage of our decision, should not be set free if and when he fasts and is in imminent danger. We are however keeping that strictly secret, and I beg that you will do the same.'[6]

An officer visited Gandhiji at 7.30 p.m. on 9 February and conveyed government's decision. Gandhiji went through the communication from the Home Department and remarked that it was clear and self-explanatory, that it did

---

5 *Transfer of Power,* Vol. III, pp. 639–45.

6 *Transfer of Power,* Vol. III, pp. 645–46.

not call for any reply. Therefore, he would begin his fast at 7.30 the next morning. The governor of Bombay reported the exchange by secraphone to the viceroy, '...Irwin [the officer who had gone to deliver the government's reply] comments that the whole atmosphere was pleasant and cordial to a degree, that Gandhi expressed his confidence that he could manage this, and that age increased the prospect of survival. He apparently tends to regard the business as a medical problem and an experiment in endurance.'

'It seems quite clear,' Linlithgow concluded, 'that Gandhi is going ahead with his fast, and apparently in the best of tempers.'[7]

Gandhiji began his fast at 7.30 a.m. on 10 February. The government imposed total censorship on all news about his fast or condition, and of course on any statement which might emanate from him or from anyone who had met him. On 11 February Sushila Nayar, who was attending on Gandhiji, wrote in her dairy, 'Bapu walked to Mahadevbhai's *samadhi* this morning and then had his massage as usual... Bapu has been taking plain water. There is no nausea yet, but he has started feeling weak.'[8]

By that day the solidarity in the Council which the viceroy had tried so hard to maintain, and which he had looked upon as one of his personal achievements was further ruptured. At 1 p.m. on the 11 February Linlithgow sent a *'Most Immediate'* telegram to Amery: 'Aney came to see me this morning,' he reported, 'and told me that he could not remain in office in face of Gandhi's fast.' Aney's argument was novel: he told the viceroy that government had already won its point, that Gandhiji had been so

---

7 *Transfer of Power,* Vol. III, pp. 647–48.

8 Sushila Nayar, *Mahatma Gandhi's Last Imprisonment, The Inside Story,* Har-Anand Publications, New Delhi, 1996, p. 214.; references in this chapter to the 'Diary' refer to this reprint and translation of this Diary.

damaged by what had passed that there was little in the fast, and that therefore government should release him at once and unconditionally. 'He is an old man who might make a mistake,' Aney pleaded, 'and die suddenly.'

The viceroy told Aney that he would hear him at greater length later in the afternoon, in the meanwhile he could not accept the proposal. 'I added,' the viceroy recalled for Amery, 'that if he or any of his friends who felt that they ought to go were unable to persuade us as a Council to reverse our decision, then they ought to go at once. To wait till Gandhi began to sicken would be intolerable.' The viceroy saw Srivastava, and learnt that '(the) most determined efforts are being made by [G.D.] Birla, Purshottamdas etc. to make Hindu Members plus Jogendra plus Ahmed (to) resign.' 'Srivastava is still standing firm,' the viceroy surmised, 'but made it clear that if he was left as the only Hindu in Council his position would be almost impossible.'

The viceroy was quite clear: either these fellows function as the frontmen they were meant to be, or they go and are replaced swiftly. 'I feel sure we must stand firm,' he told Amery, 'and if no non-official Hindu will take the place of those who resign I shall have to put in a few service members.'[9]

Aney called on the viceroy again in the afternoon. 'He could only urge that there was little difference between open offer of release for the purpose and duration of the fast and unconditional release at this stage,' Linlithgow reported in another *'Most Immediate'* telegram to Amery on the evening of 11 February. 'I said I saw all the difference in the world.' As we have seen earlier, the viceroy again put to Aney arguments which he was to direct several times at these waverers in the coming days: 'After hours of

---

9 *Transfer of Power,* Vol. III, pp. 651–52.

discussion and by a considerable majority, we had by a Government statement which made it plain that nothing but unconditional release would stop a fast, said that we could not agree to that,' the Viceroy recounted, 'We had burnt our boats and could not go back without becoming a laughing stock.' He next talked as if the interests of India, and even of Hindus in particular were what he was concerned about: 'And if the Hindu Members generally resigned,' Linlithgow told Aney, 'they would do irreparable damage not merely to the possibility or idea of a national government, but to the whole practicability of parliamentary government on a democratic basis or constitutional progress for India... How would it look if the Hindus collapsed and Jinnah came in on the basis of two three Hindu officers plus the existing Moslems other than Sultan Ahmed.' 'Aney was terribly shaken by all this,' Linlithgow told Amery, 'but is so terrified by fear of responsibility for Gandhi's death that that obliterates all other considerations.'

'Meanwhile I have seen Jogendra,' Linlithgow said, 'who says he will not resign. Firoz [Khan Noon, later prime minister of Pakistan] doubts whether these threats will come to anything. He may be right. But I will make it clear to all concerned, and I have done so very specifically to Aney, that I must have very definite decisions within a couple of days at the outside, and that I cannot wait for them while public feeling rises as Gandhi's fast proceeds.'[10]

The next day saw a distinct change for the worse in Gandhiji's condition. 'Bapu is weaker today,' wrote Sushila Nayar in her diary. 'He is losing weight, about two pounds a day. He had slight nausea but no vomiting. He did not feel strong enough to walk to Mahadevbhai's *samadhi* this morning.'

---

10 *Transfer of Power,* Vol. III, pp. 654–55.

By the evening of that day, the 12 February, Linlithgow was able to give Amery a much more hopeful picture. 'The fast is falling rather flat,' he said in his telegram. 'There has as yet been no adjournment motion on it... There is no sign of any excitement either in the country or locally or with Assembly. I have in the last two days seen the Central Intelligence Officers from all the Provinces. All are perfectly confident of the ability of the Police to hold the position.'

As for the prospect of resignations also things seemed to have been contained. The viceroy reported: 'I saw today Sultan Ahmed, Sarker and Mody. I would judge that there is not much risk of any resignations at any rate unless and until Gandhi's condition becomes critical. Mody says he is most anxious to stay in office, and so I believe are they all, though strain on them may yet prove too great...'

Linlithgow repeated the points he had been putting to the 'wobblers': 'My Hindu colleagues, while uneasy at thought of what will happen if Gandhi dies, are in a hopelessly weak position logically given fact that our policy was approved by Council after fullest discussion and realize that, and also risk of Jinnah jumping their claim if they run out.' 'I have made it clear to the wobblers,' Linlithgow said, 'that if they feel any doubts they must make up their minds without delay and that I am not prepared to wait. I have brought out that policy is either right or wrong: if they dislike it they can go, and they ought to go, now; that the mere fact of Gandhi's physical condition is quite irrelevant; that if they do like the policy they ought to be prepared to stand by it whether he lives or dies...'[11]

So much for the accomplices! Notice two things as we proceed. First, some at least of these persons must have rationalized joining the Viceroy's Council by telling themselves and their associates that by doing so they would

---

11 *Transfer of Power*, Vol. III, pp. 656–57.

be able to influence British policy 'from within'—we can see what weight their opinion carried! Second, do keep on the lookout for the slightest trace in the viceroy's dispatches of any doubts that Ambedkar might have had: he had none whatsoever, and stood completely firm alongside the viceroy and the British government.

Amery summarized for Churchill the 'very satisfactory' way things had proceeded thus far, and apprised him of the untenability of the position of the members who were wobbling. The merit of putting them face-to-face with what the Council had decided earlier, Amery recorded, was that they would be resigning against the decision of the Council of which they had been a part 'and showing their unfitness to govern in face of popular hysteria', they would not be able to claim that they were doing so because of some interference from London. Amery recalled this advantage to Linlithgow also the same day. He had his eye on the propaganda aspect of the matter: as had been ensured in the case of the resignation of Sir C.P. Ramaswami Aiyar earlier, it was vital that if the members did go, they should do so on an issue for which the British could not be blamed: 'The one thing that neither you nor I can afford,' Amery told the viceroy, 'is to have your Executive resign in a body on an issue which would seem to involve either unnecessary arbitrary interference in internal matters from this end, or an overriding of India's interests for the sake of a purely British advantage. So long as interference from here or support from here to your authority is concerned with the good of India or India's part in the war, we can, I am sure, get away with it, even if you have to face resignations. But not otherwise.'[12]

The next day, 13 February, saw a further change in Gandhiji's condition: 'Bapu's nausea has become troublesome,' recorded Sushila Nayar. 'It did not allow him to sleep well last night.'

12 *Transfer of Power,* Vol. III, pp. 657–58.

That very day Churchill sent a *'Most Immediate'* telegram to Linlithgow. He had his own agenda: of puncturing Gandhiji. And his own strategy: given his background and values he could never believe that Gandhiji could be sincere in what he was doing, nor even that Gandhiji was honest enough to be doing what he said he was doing. Churchill's prescription was to demonstrate to the world that Gandhi did not really fast when he said he was fasting! 'I have heard that Gandhi usually has glucose in his water when he is doing his various fasting antics,' he told the viceroy. 'Would it be possible to verify this?,' Churchill inquired, adding, 'There seems to me to be no disposition in America to do otherwise than to ridicule his conduct.'[13]

On the same day, 13 February, to prepare the ground for what might happen, the government published its case for the prosecution—*Congress Responsibility for Disturbances*—in which it held Gandhiji and the Congress responsible for the violence which had occurred in the wake of their arrests on 9 August, and in addition charged that their professions of non-violence were insincere, if not a deliberate falsehood. That very day, General Smuts, who had dealt with Gandhiji in South Africa and who was among the few persons whom the British government had taken care to inform about the fast, declared that to say that Gandhi was a fifth columnist was foolish.

By the fifth day of the fast Gandhiji's condition had deteriorated to such an extent that the surgeon general, Major General Candy, and Colonels Bhandari and Shah who had been monitoring him said in a statement that while Gandhiji's condition could not yet be described as dangerous or critical, 'it is clear that danger is approaching.' Sushila Nayar recorded, 'Nausea and vomiting have made

---

13 *Transfer of Power,* Vol. III, p. 659.

Bapu restless. He is finding it more and more difficult to drink water. He added a few drops of sour lime juice and a little salt and soda bicarb to the water. His reading has been considerably reduced.' General Candy told government that Gandhiji would reach the critical point the following day. The viceroy told Lumley, the governor in Bombay, that 'time has about come for formal intimation about his health to be made to Gandhi by the Surgeon General and (if he agrees) by Gilder.' Linlithgow informed Amery of these exchanges and added, 'Candy is now of the opinion, which Gilder shares, that Gandhi cannot manage to last 21 days...'[14]

In a separate telegram Linlithgow told Amery that 'Position inside Council remains uneasy. Very great pressure is being brought to bear by Hindu elements on Aney, Sarker and Srivastava, while Jogendra Singh, Mody and Ahmed are clearly anxious to be progressive. Latest information is that Aney and Sarker may go if unconditional release is refused and may be followed by certain of the others named, who will be further shaken by latest bulletins... Complete illogicality of Gandhi's position and the risks to the future politics in this country of submitting to his blackmail are entirely obscured in the minds of those mentioned by fear of being held responsible for his death'—notice again, not a trace of any hesitation in Ambedkar; notice also the felicity with which the British viceroy and Amery are always able to detect a principle for their stand, and are always convinced that the Indians who are 'wobbling' are doing so for unworthy reasons: pressure from Hindu elements, inability to stand up to mass hysteria, not having the guts to own their share of responsibility for Gandhiji's death... 'I am myself quite clear,' Linlithgow concluded, 'that we must stand firm against unconditional release.'

---

14 *Transfer of Power,* Vol. III, p. 668.

Linlithgow also responded the same day to the prime minister's query about Gandhiji taking glucose surreptitiously. In a *'Most Immediate, Personal, Most Secret'* telegram he told Churchill:

> This may be the case [that is, Gandhiji may be taking glucose during the fast] but those who have been on attendance on him doubt it, and present Surgeon-General Bombay (a European) says that on a previous fast G. was particularly careful to guard against possibility of glucose being used. I am told that his present medical attendants tried to persuade him to take glucose yesterday and again today, and that he refused absolutely.

'I am delighted,' he told Churchill, 'that American opinion is so sensible and reactions from home equally seem very good. There is a great deal of heat here at the Centre and in political circles, but the country on the whole has taken the news well. Once he begins to go down-hill we may however have more trouble.'

And down hill Gandhiji was certainly going. At the end of an anxious day Sushila Nayar recorded in her diary of 15 February, 'Bapu's nausea, vomiting and restlessness have become more troublesome. He is finding it difficult to drink water even after adding sour lime juice and salt...'

Leaders across the country were stirred to action. Messages and appeals went out. It was decided that about two hundred leaders would meet in Delhi to appeal to the viceroy and the British government in London to take steps that would enable Gandhiji to end his fast. On 15 February Jinnah issued a statement expressing his inability to attend any meeting for the purpose.

The next day, 16 February was worse. Sushila Nayar's entry for 16 February begins: 'Dr. Gajjar arrived from Bombay

---

15 *Transfer of Power*, Vol. III, pp. 668–69.

this morning to examine Bapu's blood and kidney function. Bapu's condition has further deteriorated. He has become so weak that he finds it difficult to hold a glass of water. We transferred him to a special bed used for postoperative patients. It can be wheeled around and the head can be raised, lowered or inclined. His voice has become feeble, but when the doctors visit to see him he smiles and jokes with them.'

The British were full of anticipation and preparation. That day, 16 February, Amery was asking Linlithgow whether the latter had given any fresh guidance to the governors in view of the possibility of Gandhiji's death.[16] That very day the viceroy was informed of the assessment of the surgeon general that 'Gandhi will probably not last longer than a further five days from February 16th, and that the possibility of a sudden collapse cannot be excluded.' Lumley informed the viceroy that in view of this prognosis the decision about releasing Gandhiji could not be delayed long. He said that while all the logic was on the side of government, and while Gandhi had not done anything in the preceding six months which would indicate that he would retrace his steps, 'his death in detention would do great permanent damage to Indian sentiment; and would provide a serious obstacle to eventual settlement.' 'That he will be a nuisance if he is released, is certain,' Lumley conceded. 'But in my view that is likely to be a lesser evil than the long-term reactions which would follow his death in detention.' 'I have not canvassed the views of officials here,' the governor said, 'but those European officers which are known to me, support this opinion completely, and I am probably safe in saying that it is the general view of European officers of the I.C.S. and Police in this Province that it would do irreparable damage to British Indian relations.'[17]

---

16 *Transfer of Power,* Vol. III, p. 669.

17 *Transfer of Power,* Vol. III, p. 671.

The Council was being given the latest information about Gandhiji's deteriorating condition. But no such doubts assailed two members in particular—Ambedkar and Firoz Khan Noon.

Linlithgow remained as unmoved as these Indian members. The day Lumley conveyed the preceding assessment to him over the secraphone, 16 February, Linlithgow sent his periodic '*Private and Personal*' letter to Amery. He had been 'very agreeably surprised by the low temperature in this country' in the face of Gandhi's fast, he told the Secretary of State, and even among Hindus, among whom the general respect for the man probably continued to be as high as ever, there was much private criticism of the wisdom of the Mahatma's fast. He recapitulated the exchanges which he had had with members like Aney, Mody, Sarker and Srivastava. A good deal of pressure was being put on them, Linlithgow said, 'But the fact is that I do not believe that any of these people *want* to resign, and I think they will all hold on as long as they possibly can. They have all told me (except Aney, who I know will regret resigning) that they do not want to go: and Mody,...[personal comment omitted in *Transfer of Power* series], added that he himself felt that the Mahatma's demise would be a real contribution to Indian politics.' 'Yet Mody,' added the viceroy, 'has been for his own political reasons in the forefront of the agitation to let the old man off. This would surprise one were it not that one's experience of this country is now fairly extensive.' The viceroy reiterated his confident forecast: 'If Gandhi, which I hope will not be the case, persists in carrying out the fast and is unable to stand it physically and dies, then I should expect a couple of my colleagues to go (certainly Aney, and possibly Sarker). I rather doubt the remainder moving.'

Linlithgow recalled the deterioration in the Mahatma's condition which the bulletins from Poona had been reporting, adding, 'There is bound to be a progressive deterioration. He is 73 or 74, and though he is being very carefully looked after, there are strains to which no physical frame ought to be exposed at such an age. The bulletins so far issued show that gradual deterioration is beginning. The only thing I am afraid of is, given his arteriosclerosis, which was mentioned in one of the recent bulletins, a sudden heart attack. But he appears to be perfectly obstinate as regards any endeavour to alleviate his condition. He has refused suggestions by Dr. Gilder that he should take glucose, and seems insistent on submitting himself to the full rigour of the game. All we can do in the circumstances is to hope that something may turn up to give him a way out, for he has left himself a loophole by talking of fasting to capacity, though I gather that there is reason now to fear that when he talks of fasting to capacity what he means is the capacity which he estimated himself to have at the moment of beginning his fast, and that if that estimate was a wrong one it would be bad luck so far as Gandhi is concerned but that he would still have to go through with the fast to the full number of days which he had proclaimed himself as intending to endure.'

The viceroy continued to express bewilderment at what Gandhiji's objective could be. Perhaps it was to put pressure on the British to concede something. Could it be that he had calculated that the American government and people would be so moved that they would pressurize the British into making some concession? But surely, by now he should have been disabused of such illusions? The fact that the Muslim League had openly declared that, should government concede anything to Gandhi, it would have to reckon with determined opposition from the League, must be a signal to all, including Gandhi that it wasn't going to be easy for government to concede anything, even if it wanted to do so. And then the fact that public reaction had been 'far from vigorous', as well as the debate in the Assembly the preceding day must have had some influence upon him, the viceroy said, adding, 'If they do not, and if he remains quite set in his determination to fast, I shall be driven to the conclusion that he really does intend to kill himself and get out of his difficulties in that way, for I can see no other explanation.'[18]

What can one say by way of comment, except to add an explanation mark or a sic at the end of observations like that? That Gandhiji was set to kill himself so as to 'get out of his difficulties in that way'!

From London, Amery sent a *'Secret and Private'* communication to Linlithgow. 'Today's telegrams,' he said, 'look as if Gandhi was not very likely to carry on for more than another two or three days without a serious and possibly irremediable collapse. One can only hope that if he does not call off the fast the whole thing may be over quickly and the period of suspense and growing hysteria not be prolonged indefinitely. That may also help with your colleagues, for once the crisis is over one way or the other there can be very little retrospective reason for resignations.'

'Bapu's nausea is a little less today,' begins Sushila Nayar's diary for 17 February, 'but weakness and the difficulty in drinking water have increased. Even under normal conditions Bapu used to be surprised to see one drinking a glassful of water at one go. He could never do it. He has been used to drinking fruit juice or water mixed with honey or lime juice. During the fast he can neither take fruit juice nor honey.

18 *Transfer of Power*, Vol. III, pp. 674–76.

19 *Transfer of Power*, Vol. III, p. 679.

If he is not able to drink water, he will not be able to pull through the 21-day fast. With limited fluids going in, his urine output has gone down considerably which means toxins are accumulating in the body...'

The Bombay government in a communique said, 'Mr. Gandhi had a better day on the whole on Tuesday, but his general condition continues to cause anxiety.'

The communique was less than candid, for the internal assessment in government was that the final crisis was now imminent. The viceroy shot off urgent telegrams to the Secretary of State and the governors, he felt it necessary to break the news formally to the Council, the commander-in-chief contacted the army commanders.

In a *'Most Immediate, Personal'* telegram to Amery, Linlithgow told him, 'Candy's estimate today is that if no change takes place, there might be a collapse consequent on the fast at the end of 5 days (the risk of heart collapse is of course always present). There is no sign as I understand it of any relaxation of Gandhi's determination to proceed with the fast.' He recalled that he had mentioned in one of his earlier telegrams that he had asked Lumley, the governor in Bombay, to see whether Gandhi ought not to be formally informed that he had reached the danger point. 'Lumley informs me that this has now been discussed by Candy with Gilder and Roy [B.C. Roy who had arrived to attend on Gandhiji from Calcutta on the night of 14 February.] The two latter think that more harm than good will be done by such communication. Their reasons are that they would not tell any patient in his condition of a prognosis of this kind; that Dr. Nair [Sushila Nayar] had already told Gandhi that he could not last for 21 days; and that Candy's opinion to the same effect had also been conveyed to Gandhi by the Governor's Secretary. Candy thinks this view not unreasonable especially as in his own opinion there is more danger of death from heart attack than of a slow petering out from starvation. In view of Candy's opinion Lumley thinks the proposal should be dropped, and I have agreed.' 'Argument which weighs with Lumley, force of which I accept,' Linlithgow explained, 'is that if Candy's prognosis that death may result from a sudden heart attack is correct and were to follow immediately or soon after the declaration, we should lay ourselves open to the charge of precipitating the end and would be in a most embarrassing position.'

In a separate *'Most Immediate, Private and Personal'* telegram to the governors of all provinces the viceroy informed them that according to the report of the government doctors who had seen him that night Gandhi's 'general condition is serious, and I understand that Candy's estimate is that collapse might come after about 5 days if there is no change.' He told them to 'treat that as for your most secret and personal information'. The commander-in-chief is informing the army commanders, the viceroy told the governors—'but not (repeat not) of the possible 5-day period'—and asked them to keep in touch with the commanders.

That afternoon Linlithgow had more to report to the Secretary of State. 'Last night's Bombay communique, as you will have seen, reported a further deterioration in Gandhi's health,' he told Amery, 'and I informed my Council (in the light of the full bulletin by Candy) that his condition was by now serious. This has led to a letter this morning from Mody, Aney and Sarker tendering their resignations on the ground that "the majority decision not to release Gandhi unconditionally, even when danger to his life accrued from the fast he had undertaken, is one which we cannot possibly support", and going on to say that "if our differences had been less fundamental, we would have deemed it our duty to submit to the vote of the majority, as, individually, we have done on several occasions".'

The viceroy said that he was going to accept the resignations. 'I have also however informed the three Members that they are bound by their oath of secrecy from which I am not prepared to release them,' Linlithgow added, 'and I am not prepared to agree to any reference to majority or minority decision. I have asked them to redraft their letter in the light of this.'

And the members went back and, like obedient sheep, did so!

The joint statement issued on their behalf was as far from being explicit as they could make it. It said, 'Our resignations from the Governor-General's Council have been announced and all that we desire to do is to say by way of explanation that certain differences arose on what we regarded as a fundamental issue, and we felt that we could no longer retain our offices. We wish to place on record our appreciation of the courtesy and consideration the Viceroy had extended to us throughout the period during which we had the privilege of being associated with him in the Government of the country.' N.R. Sarker issued a somewhat more forthright statement on his own behalf. He said: 'If I decided to lay down my office, it was on an overriding consideration in connection with the latest policy of the Government of India regarding the greatest man of India, who embodies our national aspiration for freedom and stands foremost in the sphere of our progressive social activities, and whose life is ever so vital for bringing about a real and lasting reconciliation between the various communities in India and between India and Great Britain. I will appeal to the British Government to reorient their present policy and take a realistic and helpful attitude in solving the present deadlock.'[20]

On 18 February, there were developments that convinced

---

20 Quoted in Sushila Nayar, *Diary*, p. 222.

all concerned that they were now on the brink of collapse. The doctors' bulletin reported, 'After nine hours of sleep Gandhiji is not feeling fresh. His mind and brain are not alert as usual. Heart is very weak. Condition is causing anxiety. The pathological reports indicate accumulation of fluids and toxins in the body.'

'General Candy is worried,' Sushila Nayar wrote in her diary that day. 'He said to Gandhiji, "You had said that this was a fast to capacity. Your capacity has been exhausted. Why don't you end the fast now?" Bapu explained that fast to capacity did not mean that in the event of danger to life he would give it up. It simply meant that he had not taken a fast unto death. He had estimated his capacity to undertake a 21-day fast. So he must complete it. If God wished him to live, He would save him; if it was His wish to take him away, he would die. If his estimate of his own capacity was wrong, he must pay for it.'

'As the day advanced,' Sushila noted, 'the signs and symptoms of uremia became more pronounced. At night Bapu remarked, "I am not at all feeling well. There is discomfort in the abdomen and the heart region." Looking at the calendar with *"Hei Ram"* inscribed on it, that hung on the wall opposite, he said, "This is my refuge. 'Whatever You do is right. I surrender myself to Your will. Your will, not mine, be done' comes from the depths of my heart."'

The viceroy sent an *'Immediate'* telegram to the governors that day, 18 February, and he repeated it to Amery. 'Gandhi's fast,' it read. 'Your Government will have received Bombay Government's telegram warning them of approach of danger-point, and you will also have had my telegram of February 16th giving the official medical opinion that his condition must be regarded as serious. We cannot tell how things will go but we must be fully prepared for Gandhi's death and must be ready to take common action to deal with the ensuing situation in that event.' Linlithgow informed the governors and Amery that in the event of Gandhiji dying the Bombay government would send all concerned 'a most immediate *en clair* telegram containing the code word "Rubicon".' 'At the same time,' explained the viceroy, 'Bombay Government would arrange to stop all trunk calls and telegrams (except official) from Poona and neighbourhood for two hours after despatch of "Rubicon" telegram. Bare announcement of death will then be given to Press by Bombay Government and we ourselves shall probably issue statement terms of which are under separate consideration.'

It would be unwise to stifle manifestations of national mourning, Linlithgow stressed, and so governments should 'allow as much freedom as possible for reasonable public mourning by whatever means may be customary'. The Bombay government had decided on allowing a public cremation, Linlithgow noted, adding, 'I feel sure that this is the right course.' The problem would be about disposal of the ashes subsequently. He sketched the dilemma: if the ashes were transported by train to distant places like Hardwar or Benares or even Sevagram, and news of their passage spread, 'as it would be bound to do', 'there would be grave danger from crowds *en route,* both at stations, and on the lines, with serious risk of disorder.' 'On the other hand,' noted the viceroy, 'a blank refusal to allow the ashes to be deposited in some sacred place might have even more serious results and if they were not taken to some such place one result would be to create a new centre of pilgrimage in Poona.' He had therefore asked Lumley to explore possibility of transporting them by air to the designated place, Linlithgow said. Reverting to the ashes problem later he said that of course the family would have to be consulted, adding that 'there will be some advantage in not consulting the family in advance about their wishes, since this will give us more justification for delay when the time comes.' He went on to say that nevertheless he thought it most important that possibilities be explored of postponing the removal of the ashes from Poona till things had quietened down, if this could be done without offending religious sentiment, and of conveying the ashes and the party accompanying them by air to the required destination.

The viceroy reverted also to the matter which Twynam had more than once asked him to settle. 'I am clear that, considering Gandhi's position as our prisoner and a declared rebel,' Linlithgow said, 'there can be no question of half-masting flags or sending official messages of condolence to his widow.' But it had been suggested, he noted, that nothing would be lost 'if there were some official recognition of the death of an outstanding personality'—in fact, the government having stood firm, there could be some advantage in now doing something of the sort, closing government offices for a day or half a day, etc.; such a step 'might reduce the resentment resulting from his death in custody and help to keep large numbers of Government Servants steady, while at the same time having a good effect on public opinion and thus possibly reducing risk of disorder...'

An officer was sent by the governor from Bombay to Poona 'to supervise the preparation of arrangements for the funeral and to take responsibility for any immediate decisions which might have to be made.' As the governor noted in his retrospective report to the viceroy, 'Although the eventuality did not arise, plans, so far as they could be made before the event, were ready, and will be useful if the contingency re-occurs...'

Communications such as these show how close in the government's assessment Gandhiji was to dying on

21 *Transfer of Power*, Vol. III, pp. 684–86.

22 *Transfer of Power*, Vol. III, p. 760.

18 February: there is no indication of anything but equanimity among the members who had chosen to continue in the Viceroy's Council even as it contemplated the eventuality. Second, notice the purely pragmatic concerns of the government in the face of the possible death of a man such as Gandhiji. Such were the priorities of the government of which these Indians had chosen to continue as members.

Gandhiji's condition continued to worsen the next day, indeed everyone around could see that it was building up to a terrible crisis. Sushila Nayar recorded in her diary for 19 February, the tenth day of the fast, 'During the night Bapu had excessive salivation and had to spit frequently, with the result that he could not sleep. In the morning he felt a little better and was taking greater interest in his surroundings. Weakness has increased. His hand shakes badly when he holds a glass of water, but he insists on taking water with his own hands. Dr. Roy, Dr. Gilder and I have appealed to the visitors not to strain him with conversation. In the evening his condition worsened. The earache also increased. He said, "I cannot find any peace. Even when I drink water it does not soothe me. I feel heavy in the stomach and there is a sour taste right up to my throat"...'

At 1.05 a.m. that night Linlithgow sent an *'Immediate, Secret, Personal'* telegram to Amery in London. 'Today's communique issued to press on Gandhi's condition shows that the position is now definitely serious. In the event of his death I am asking the Governor of Bombay to telegraph to you code word *'Extra'*. I shall be telegraphing separately as to terms of announcement (which will be as brief as possible and of most objective nature) which will be issued here if the worst unhappily happens.'[23]

Also on the 19 February three hundred leaders of the country – C. Rajagopalachari and others – met in Delhi. They passed a

23 *Transfer of Power,* Vol. III, p. 691.

resolution containing a request to the viceroy that the government take steps to enable Gandhiji to end his fast.

Several things happened on 20 February, the eleventh day of the fast. In the Aga Khan's house there was an important exchange—especially important in view of the insinuation which Churchill had tried to put in circulation that Gandhiji's fasts were a bit of a hoax as he took some glucose during these periods while leading everyone to believe that he was taking nothing.

'Bapu's condition has further deteriorated,' begins Sushila Nayar's entry for the day. 'This morning when General Candy came to see him, Bapu was sleeping... General Candy was of the opinion that we should give intravenous glucose to Bapu. 1 told him Bapu would never agree to it. "Can't we quietly put some glucose in his enema water?" he asked. "We could not possibly cheat Bapu" I told him. He was upset.'

'He is anxious to save Bapu's life by whatever means possible,' Sushila Nayar's entry continues. "It is a doctor's duty to save a patient," he argued. I was startled by this attitude. I whispered to Dr. Gilder that to give glucose solution surreptitiously to Bapu might be dangerous. The shock, when he discovered it, might kill him. Dr. Gilder agreed with me. Dr. B.C. Roy, who arrived a few minutes later, was also firm that nothing should be done surreptitiously. When Bapu awoke, we examined him. General Candy expressed a desire to speak to him alone for a minute. He seemed very upset as I took him in and left him with Bapu. After a few minutes he left Bapu's room by the backdoor.'

'Bapu told us afterwards that after I had left General Candy in his room he walked up and down for a while,' Sushila Nayar's diary continues. 'He was so agitated that he could not speak. Then he came and sat down on a chair near Bapu's bed, got up again and started walking up and down. Ultimately, he gathered up courage and said to Bapu, "Mr. Gandhi I should let you know as a medical man that you have come to the end of your capacity to fast." Bapu listened to him in silence. General Candy could not proceed any further. He was choked with tears. Bapu said to him, "Why do you worry? I am in God's hands. If He wishes to take me away I am ready to go. If He wishes to take more work from me He will keep me alive..."'[24]

That was the news in Poona. In Delhi Linlithgow sent his conclusions, his decisions rather, to the governors on matters which had been the subject of exchanges earlier. 'Gandhi's fast. It is obvious from today's bulletin that Gandhi's condition is increasingly serious, though of course it is impossible to say how much longer he will last. But we must clearly be prepared for a collapse,' the viceroy told the governors. In the light of replies which had been received, Linlithgow said, 'I am clear: (a) that there should be no closure of offices, though Governors will naturally use their wise discretion as to casual leave on or immediately after Gandhi's death, and will probably be disposed to turn a blind eye to unimportant absences without leave... (b) No half-masting or other formal official signs of mourning, (c) As regards processions, meetings, &c, I recognize that circumstances differ in different Provinces, and feel that I can but leave discretion to each Governor to handle his local situation as he thinks best, subject to the interests of security.' He emphasized, 'It is most important to keep proper restraint over the Press.' A certain degree of liberty would inevitably have to be allowed in the days following Gandhi's death for commemorative articles, etc., he said, but the general rules of censorship which he had set out earlier would apply.[25]

By now even the government in London seemed to have realized that when Gandhiji had used the phrase 'fast to

---

24 Sushila Nayar, *Diary*, pp. 226–27.

25 *Transfer of Power*, Vol. III, pp. 704–05.

capacity' it was not to give himself a way out, the import was quite the opposite. Amery wrote to Viscount Simon who was urging this hopeful construction to keep their spirits up. He acknowledged at long last, 'I do not think it is quite correct to say that Gandhi announced that he was not going to fast to death. What he said in his letter to the Viceroy of the 29th January was, "My wish is not to fast unto death, but to survive the ordeal of the feat if God so wills." I should read the phrase "to capacity" to mean that he had modified his usual regimen during a fast to bring a 21-days fast within what he considered his powers; but I doubt if he can be read as meaning that if this proves beyond his powers he will give up the fast rather than die.'[26]

The same day the resolution of the three hundred leaders was summarily turned down. The viceroy did not deign to even acknowledge the plea which had been sent to him. His private secretary sent a reply to Sir Tej Bahadur Sapru! He informed Sapru, 'His Excellency has asked me to say that he has received and considered the resolution adopted by the conference under your chairmanship, of which you were good enough to send him a copy today.' 'The attitude of the Government of India in the matter of Mr. Gandhi's fast is set out clearly and in detail in the communique which they issued on February 10,' he said. And that was that.

The insufferable arrogance of these pups of those days. That a person of Gandhiji's stature should be at death's door, that three hundred leaders of our country should meet and send a request to the viceroy, and that man should not have the courtesy to even respond in his own name, that some minion should send a reply, and that too only to say that all that needed to be said had already been said by government ten days earlier!

---

26 *Transfer of Power*, Vol. III, p. 707.

The twelfth day of the fast, 21 February, was the worst there was to be. It is best to recall it in the entry from Sushila Nayar's diary for the day.

'Bapu has become so weak that he has been trying to drink water from a siphon tube while lying down,' the entry begins. 'He had very little sleep during the night—hardly four and a half hours. There were signs of incipient uraemic coma. Since last evening there has been uraemic smell also. His pulse has become very weak. There has been loss of weight too. Today's bulletin stated, "Uraemic signs are increasing. Further delay in ending the fast will make it difficult to save his life."...'

And then comes the account of what happened that afternoon. Even after the passing of half a century it makes one's blood boil—that a person like Gandhiji should have had to undergo such torture to have the British government reflect on what it was doing to our country, and that even such facts have been so erased from our minds that few today would even know that such was the condition to which he had been pushed, few know the sacrifices that were put in to wrest freedom for us.

Sushila Nayar's diary records: 'At about 4 p.m. Bapu's condition suddenly became grave. I was alone with him in the room. He tried to suck water from the siphon tube. The effort exhausted him. He was hardly able to take a mouthful and lay back exhausted. There was severe nausea. He became extremely restless and started throwing about his hands and feet. His eyeballs turned upwards, his eyelids were half closed. It seemed to me that he was losing consciousness. I put my hand on his pulse and could hardly feel it. My heart beat faster. I wondered "Is Bapu going to pass away in front of me, like Mahadevbhai?" I knew if only he could drink water he would be saved. So I mustered up courage and asked him, "Bapu, has not the time come to add sweet lime juice to your water?" There was no reply for some time. I wondered whether he had heard me. Then there was a slight nod of the head indicating consent. I had already sent for Dr. Gilder. As soon as he arrived, I told him of the development, then rushed out and squeezed out two ounces of fresh sweet lime juice. Mixing it with two ounces of water I slowly poured it into his mouth from the ounce glass. The effect was miraculous. As water quenches the burning embers, his restlessness subsided. He opened his eyes. Just then Ba came into the room. She had been praying outside the room. I wondered if it was the result of her prayer that God had saved Bapu!'

That small band of three or four, alone, cut off from the country. That saint of a man pushed to the edge of death for the sake of our country. The government in full readiness for his death. And we fifty years later completely oblivious of all that—garlanding statues of the very persons who were ensconced in ministerial offices at such a time, who had fully joined up with the British and who watched, unshaken in their equanimity the imminent departure of, to use the phrase of their chief and head, 'that miserable little old man'.

'Candy has informed the Bombay Government,' Linlithgow told Amery, 'that the seizure which affected Gandhi on the 21st of February was the sort of attack which Candy had been expecting all along and is of the opinion that it is impossible to say when there will be a recurrence, possibly with fatal results... "Sweet lime juice" in the bulletin refers to the juice of a sweet lime as opposed to a sour lime. There is no suggestion that any glucose is being taken.'[27]

That is what Linlithgow wrote on 23 February. As Gandhiji did not die, as it began to seem more likely that, in

---

27 *Transfer of Power,* Vol. III, p. 718.

spite of the limit the doctors thought he could manage having been crossed, he would survive, Linlithgow and company reverted to reading fraud and duplicity into what was happening. On 25 February Linlithgow was telling Amery:

> There are in fact signs suggesting that Gandhi's physical crisis on Sunday, the 21st, was deliberately arranged to coincide with the Leaders Conference, and that as soon as it became apparent that we had no intention of giving way, this was communicated to Poona and steps taken to give Gandhi the essential pabulum.[28]

Persons judge others by what they would themselves be doing under those circumstances, the insincere just cannot make themselves believe that others can be acting from any impulse higher than the ones that spur them. In the *'Secret'* note on the fast which the surgeon general submitted on the medical aspects of the fast two days after its conclusion, Major General Candy stated:

> On the 20th, or llth day of the fast, it appeared that the fatal result was at hand. I had a private conversation with him as a patient and informed him that he had reached 'capacity'. I urged him to consider various points. He made no reply, but I think appreciated the position. On the following day the 'crisis' appeared. It should be mentioned that his blood pressure, which in the early days hovered around 200/100, had fallen to 146/92. The crisis was not witnessed by any Government doctor, but was not unexpected and I see no reason to doubt that it actually occurred. It was an attack of a syncopal nature and would be fully explained by a small coronary thrombosis.[29]

But to get back to that fateful day, February 21, when the country nearly lost Gandhiji.

In Delhi the 300 leaders who had been spurned by the

---

28 *Transfer of Power,* Vol. III, p. 728.

29 *Transfer of Power,* Vol. III, p. 770.

viceroy through his private secretary had met again on 20 February. They had resolved that, not having got any hearing here, they should send an appeal to Churchill in London. And so they did on 21 February by telegram.

Unknown to them, that very day Churchill sent another of his telegrams to stiffen the viceroy: '*Immediate.* Following personal and secret from Prime Minister to Viceroy of India (through Field Marshal Wavell),' it read. 'It is a great comfort to me as the Gandhi episode approaches its climax to feel that we can count on your steadfast and unflinching action.'[30]

In the following days, at times it seemed as if the crisis was on its way again; at others the doctors could hope that Gandhiji would survive the twenty-one days. As the hours and days passed and Gandhiji did not die, the viceroy and his colleagues became cocky. All of them convinced themselves that, though there was no proof, Gandhiji must have been administered glucose at some stage! This theory which Churchill had asked them to try and somehow document by now became more or less a fact, one without which Gandhiji's survival, and that his weight did not go on falling as it had in the first half of the fast just could not be explained.[31]

---

30 *Transfer of Power,* Vol. III, p. 711.

31 Though in fairness one must note that the surgeon general always put the point with a tentativeness which the others discarded in the retelling. In his retrospective report on the fast he stated, 'Up to the day of the crisis, Mr. Gandhi took nothing except water, salt and alkalies, and small quantities of sour lime juice which probably totaled at the most 2 or 3 oz. per diem. The rapid change in his condition justified the belief that this statement is correct. At the crisis, he took sweet lime juice in his water, perhaps a few ounces on the 21st February, and on February 22nd, 20 oz., during the day. This was reduced to 12 oz. on February 23rd, and to an average of 9 oz. daily thereafter. It does not seem possible that a man could maintain his weight, much less increase it on such a diet. I am however convinced that if something was added to his diet, he was ignorant of the fact. If anybody added anything, e.g. glucose, I think the

On 24 February, Churchill rejected the request of the 300 leaders who had met in Delhi. He fully endorsed the decision of the government in Delhi to continue to hold Gandhiji as a prisoner.

On 25 February—by now Gandhiji had been without food for sixteen days, his weight was by now no more than 90 lbs.—speaking in the House of Commons, Amery insinuated that the purpose of Gandhiji in undertaking the fast was just to secure his own unconditional release!

That day the scene at the Aga Khan's house was one of renewed anxiety. 'This morning Bapu complained of increased weakness,' Sushila Nayar recorded. 'When General Candy came in the morning he was disappointed to see him and asked, "Why has he reduced the quantity of fruit juice? On Sunday he was in the jaws of death. Does he want to repeat that experience? It is not good to play with death." Dr. Roy remarked, "He himself has said that on Sunday he felt he was going. The choice before him was to add sweet lime juice to his water and live or to embrace death. He chose to live. He said that he did not wish to die. That should not mean that he should continue to stand on the brink of the abyss all the time peering into it."'

---

culprit was Dr. Sushila Nayar...' Candy reverted to this point in concluding his report and to the factor on which Linlithgow had placed so much reliance, namely, that the improvement followed the realization that the government was not going to yield, and would continue to hold Gandhiji as a prisoner. Candy wrote, 'I do not think that the improvement in Mr. Gandhi's condition was due to the declaration by Government that he would not be released, or rather that the improvement was occasioned by this announcement. The improvement began, I think, too late for this. The improvement followed the unexpressed, but shared belief,'that death was near, it may have started with the administration of sweet lime juice, or something may have been added. I strongly suspect that Dr. Nayar took fright, and sacrificed her principles. This will never be known.' [*Transfer of Power,* Vol. III, pp. 770–71.] But in the papers of the period, this supposition became an official 'charge', as she puts it, against Sushila Nayar!

'I tried to explain Bapu's point of view,' Sushila continues. '"The object is not to play with death or to stand over the edge of the abyss. He is merely sticking to his decision, namely, that he would take sweet lime juice merely to make water drinkable: On Sunday when I saw that he could not drink water at all, I asked for his permission to add sweet lime juice to his water and he gave it. He wishes to take the very minimum quantity of fruit juice."'

Sushila Nayar records the ensuing conversation—how General Candy inquired whether Gandhiji alone decided everything concerning himself, how it was permissible for a doctor to tell a lie to save the life of the patient, how he would bring a different ounce measure for Sushila to use while measuring the amount of fruit juice she was to add... And how she would not agree to any of these arguments or dodges as Gandhiji had put all of them on their honour.[32]

On 26 February Linlithgow sent an *'Important, Most Secret'* telegram to Churchill. The telegram gives a glimpse of what these persons really thought of even a person like Gandhiji, and of course of Indians and India. The telegram read:

> I have long known Gandhi as the world's most successful humbug and have not the least doubt that his physical condition and the bulletins reporting it from day to day have been deliberately cooked so as to create the maximum effect on public opinion. The bulletin describing his alleged heart crisis coincided exactly with the meeting of the leaders conference. I have good reason to think, that, though I cannot prove it, that so soon as it became evident that I was prepared to hold him dead or alive, and that there would be no wobbling, word of this was telephoned through from Delhi to Poona, and enough nourishment immediately given him to check the uremia. I have word that Gandhi's doctor in Poona telephoned to Delhi on Wednesday evening, 24th Feb., to tell Gandhi's friends that he was in no

32 Sushila Nayar, *Diary*, pp. 234–36.

danger. There would be no difficulty in his entourage administering glucose or any other food without the knowledge of the Government doctors. Again the wording of the bulletins is much in the hands of Gandhi's own doctors who, if the draft is criticized, immediately claim the right to issue a separate bulletin. The Government doctors think it wise to compromise, and I dare say they are right, because the public here would in those circumstances heed nothing but Gandhi's own bulletin. The degree of nervous tension and hysteria engendered by all this Hindu hocus pocus is beyond belief. I am suggesting slyly to certain American correspondents here that it has not been so much a matter of their heart-strings plucked as of their legs being pulled. I think it will be found that we have won an important victory which will help to discredit a wicked system of blackmail and terror, and I am much obliged to you for your staunch support. If I can discover any firm evidence of fraud I will let you hear but I am not hopeful of this...[33]

That day Churchill, who had been down with pneumonia, sent a *'Personal'* telegram to Field Marshal Smuts. 'I do not think Gandhi has the slightest intention of dying,' he mocked, 'and I imagine he has been eating better meals than I have for the last week. It looks now highly probable that he will see his fast out. What fools we should have been to flinch before all this bluff and sob-stuff. Opinion here has been very steady, and the Viceroy has been very good. Before the fast began we were assured the crisis would be reached on the fourth day. Then on the eleventh day we were all told that if we did not let him out it would be too late and he would never recover. It is now the sixteenth day. As soon as he understood there would be no weakness here he made his arrangements accordingly. You will excuse me, I am sure, if I do not express plainly on paper all my thoughts upon this topic...'[34]

---

33 *Transfer of Power,* Vol. III, p. 737.

34 *Transfer of Power,* Vol. III, p. 738.

'Victory' !

Amery was looking forward to victory! In the *'Private and Secret'* letter he wrote to Linlithgow that day, that is 26 February, he remarked, 'Meanwhile, I have been greatly cheered by your latest telegrams about Gandhi. If he pulls through, as now looks likely, he may have the credit for having exhibited unforeseen powers of physical resistance. But that is all. He would have shot the last bolt in his armoury and failed, and his stock and that of all those who have backed him or developed hysteria on behalf of his release will have gone down proportionately.'[35]

That day's entry in Sushila Nayar's diary was brief, but anxious: 'General Candy again pleaded for increasing the quantity of fruit juice in Bapu's water. I again explained to him why it could not be increased.'

The next day, on 27 February, records Sushila Nayar's diary, 'Bapu's output of urine has decreased during the last two days. General Candy is worried. Dr. Roy recalled a similar crisis last Sunday when the output of urine had dropped for a day or two. He thought Bapu looked weaker and General Candy more anxious...'[36]

Churchill was full of praise and advice the next day. In a *'Personal'* telegram to Linlithgow on 28 February he said, 'It now seems almost certain that the old rascal will emerge all the better from his so-called fast. I highly approve of the spirit of your No. 568-S and the weapon of ridicule, so far as it is compatible with the dignity of the Government of India, should certainly be employed. I shall be saying something on the subject myself in the near future. Your own cool sagacious handling of the matter has given me the greatest confidence and satisfaction.'[37]

---

35 *Transfer of Power,* Vol. III, p. 741.

36 Sushila Nayar, *Diary,* p. 241.

37 *Transfer of Power,* Vol. III, p. 744.

On the last day of the fast Linlithgow was victory itself! 'Looking back over the whole period of the fast,' he wrote in his *'Private and Personal'* letter to Amery on 2 March, 'I feel all the more satisfaction at having been able to stand absolutely firm over this whether I lost my colleagues or not; and though reverence for Gandhi will always reduce the likelihood of Hindu criticism here on what has taken place, there can be no question that he has suffered a major defeat and that the various efforts of his friends and himself to secure his unconditional release or some climbdown on the part of Government have been a complete failure. We have exposed the Light of Asia—Wardha Version—for the fraud it undoubtedly is: blue glass with a tallow candle behind it!! I have sent you an amusing letter from Douglas Young to my Private Secretary written about ten days ago which in terms suggests that what the old man has done is neither more nor less than one of those reducing fasts which people used to do at Champneys, and suggests also that even despite Gandhi's relatively advanced age there is plenty of precedent for people of his age having gone through them successfully. I would not be a bit surprised (indeed I think it more than likely) that the Mahatma has tried to have it both ways, to get the credit of a fast with the possible abandonment of their position by Government together with the physical advantage to his blood pressure, &c. of a course of severe dieting carried over a period which from experience he felt that he was likely to be able to manage....'

Closing the long letter Linlithgow remarked, 'Fast or no fast, I got out for a shoot every weekend, when with my youngest daughter and 4 of my staff, we shot the very big total of 415 snipe in one day and 246 the next. Almost a record, I would suppose.'[38]

---

38 *Transfer of Power,* Vol. III, pp. 746, 750.

How could a man with such values, a man from that sort of a culture at all understand Gandhiji? Is it any surprise that he just could not believe that Gandhiji *did* actually fast, that that glucose he and Churchill were so much after was actually *not* administered? Is it any surprise that he, Churchill and the rest thought that the fast was just a device to secure his release from detention? Is it any surprise that in the fact that Gandhiji survived the ordeal they saw *their* victory?

But that is exactly what these people saw in it. With just hours to go before the end of the fast, Amery wrote in his *'Private and Secret'* communication to the viceroy, *'Vive* Gandhi! That in the most literal sense, namely that he should live at least another 24 hours and break his fast. I think we—and by that I mean specially you—have come remarkably well out of the whole affair. Your handling of your Council on the one hand and your equally resolute handling of the situation *vis-à-vis* the Cabinet here, just made all the difference and prevented what might easily have been a disastrous muddle. As it is, the Government of India comes out the winner and those at any rate who have not resigned will have the credit for their staunchness... As for Gandhi, I suppose he will get a certain measure of credit in India for having survived his fast. Otherwise I think most of the public in India as well as outside will realize that he has used the last weapon and failed...'[39]

At last the day arrived: 3 March. 'Since last night our hearts have been full of gratitude to God,' begins Sushila Nayar's entry for the day.

> ...This morning Swami Anand took away the ashes of Mahadevbhai which had been stored by us.... There was a short prayer before the breaking of the fast, consisting of the first verse of the *Isha Upanishad,* the recitation of the vows to be observed

---

39 *Transfer of Power,* Vol. III, p. 751.

by the *Satyagrahis,* a Hindi hymn with the theme 'The Lord is my refuge', the *Ram Dhun,* a verse from the Koran, and lastly the English hymn 'When I survey the Wondrous Cross.'

After cleaning Bapu's room we brought him in from the verandah... Bapu had decided to start the prayer at 8.50 so that he could break the fast at 9 a.m. Mrs. Naidu suggested that we might wait for General Candy before starting the prayer. So we sang hymns till General Candy came. Dr. Roy recited a poem of Tagore 'Where the mind is without fear and the head is held high.' This was followed by the different items selected for this morning's prayer.

I brought six ounces of orange juice mixed with one ounce of water and handed it to Ba to give to Bapu. I raised the head of his bed to enable him to drink. He spoke in a feeble voice: 'I wish to thank the doctors.' His voice was choked with tears. There was pin-drop silence. After a couple of minutes he continued, 'who have surrounded me with care and affection.' He was again overcome. After he had calmed himself, he continued, 'The triumph is theirs, but the will was God's that I should survive the ordeal. He will show me the next step. You must forgive me for breaking down like this.'

After finishing his speech he took the glass of fruit juice from Ba's hand...[40]

The fast had been a perfect demonstration of the power of a life of truth. The whole Congress leadership was in jail, unable to do anything. The country was floundering, reeling under the repression that the British had unleashed. And here was a 90-lb. man—incarcerated, isolated as the rest. By merely refraining from food he was able to focus the attention of the entire country on what the British had been doing, he was able to 'considerably shatter the unity' of the Viceroy's Council, he was able to teach the people that they were not powerless.

The viceroy and his men were certain that the triumph was not that of the doctors, and of course not that of 'that

40 Sushila Nayar, *Diary,* pp. 244–46.

miserable little old man', but theirs! 'Gandhi has broken his fast,' Linlithgow informed Amery as soon as he got word from Poona and Bombay. 'My best thanks for your firm support and encouragement.'[41]

'Congratulations on your most successful deflation of Gandhi,' responded Amery.[42]

'My dear Linlithgow,' wrote Sir A. Hope, the Governor of Madras, 'First of all, let me congratulate you on the firm stand you took over Gandhi, and the results fully justify your policy. For the first time Gandhi has been debunked, and despite the Press efforts to whip up emotion and mysticism and hints that his survival is miraculous, people generally realize that the fast has been a failure and that Gandhi's bluff has been called...' 'From all I hear, the excitement and emotion was very largely confined to the intelligentsia in the towns,' the governor reported, 'and the villages took little or no interest, which is I think very significant and bears out my previous impression that Congress is rapidly losing ground in the countryside, where the people think much more of food and prices than politics and fasts.'[43]

'I feel that I should like, if I may with respect, to congratulate you on the firm stand taken, in the face of tremendous pressure from so many quarters, against this form of political coercion, as also on being the first Viceroy to defeat Gandhi at his own game,' wrote the governor of Central Provinces and Berar, Sir H. Twynam. 'I think that the most noticeable feature of the reactions to the failure of the fast to produce any concession is astonishment that (a) the Government of India and His Majesty's Government were prepared to face the music if Gandhi had died, and that (b) an "epic fast" had for the first time failed in its effect.

---

41 *Transfer of Power*, Vol. III, p. 753.

42 *Transfer of Power*, Vol. III, p. 754.

43 *Transfer of Power*, Vol. III, pp. 762–63.

Your Excellency is aware how fully I agree that the line taken was the only possible line...'[44]

The viceroy himself was of course conviction itself that Gandhiji had been beaten badly. He was just as convinced that *he* had beaten Gandhiji. 'Let me first say how sorry I am that you should have been so much bothered by the little man,' he wrote to Lumley, the governor in Bombay, 'and how grateful I am to you, and to all your officers, for the trouble you have taken over this difficult situation and for the invaluable help you have given...'

He recounted in detail the various stages through which the whole affair had passed, and the decisions he had taken, and how he had been clear all along that all must stand absolutely firm: 'The developments after that stage are only too familiar to you. I had throughout made it clear in all my discussions in Council that I was in favour, even though I may be in a minority of one, of holding Gandhi until the fast was called off or had a fatal outcome. The pressure on certain of my colleagues became too great, and I lost three of them. There again the moment their resignations were tendered I accepted them and without argument, and I am glad to say I was able to keep the balance (and the majority) of my colleagues, though one or two of them, I dare say, had some rather uncomfortable days... There could be no question in those circumstances in my view as to the balance of advantage, and even had I lost the whole of my Council and had I had to revert to government by officials I would not have hesitated.'

And the viceroy was certain that the victory had been his and that of the government. 'In the event we have come out very well,' he told Lumley. 'We have blunted the weapon of the fast; Congress have suffered (and they know it) a significant defeat; the Muslims, the Scheduled Castes and

---

44 *Transfer of Power,* Vol. III, p. 779.

the Services have been encouraged; the Government has gained a reputation for resolution and firmness of purpose which I fear it may not have enjoyed in the same degree before the fast. After 21 days of fasting neither Gandhi nor the Congress are one whit better off than they were before the fast began save to the extent that they have got back some of the limelight of publicity. Inside the country the reactions have been encouraging. I have been profoundly impressed by the absence of any emotional wave in rural areas. Even in urban areas strong feeling seemed to have been confined to certain very obvious centres. There has been nothing like the tension I can remember in connection even with the Rajkot fast, to say nothing of the Poona fast of ten years ago. Not the least public interest has been shown in the position of the Working Committee, and it has been clearly shown that Congress are without a programme and without a cry, while the wholly unreasonable nature of Gandhi's demands and the difficulty of deciding on which of them he was really taking his stand had not helped him...'[45]

Toady Indians were not lacking in the encomiums they showered on the viceroy. 'The threatened fast of Mr. Gandhi, which we anticipated in August and which he delayed for six months, has now come and gone,' wrote Sir A. Ramaswami Mudaliar, another member of the Viceroy's Council, from London. 'The threat fell flat in America where I was in the earlier stages of the fast and in this country also... I explained in the States and in Canada that no Government would release a prisoner who, as you aptly put it, was trying to blackmail you. I pointed out further that if India was to attain a democratic status at any time, these ideas of "fast unto death" which belonged to the Pre-Christian Era even in Hinduism should not be tolerated. The

45 *Transfer of Power,* Vol. III, pp. 784–90.

Hindu was trying to get away from these archaic ideas and the trouble in Indian politics has been in the last twenty years that Gandhi is trying to put him back into the period of the Dark Ages with its outworn creeds and ancient superstitions. I personally think that the result of the fast will be a considerable deflation of Gandhi's influence and he surely cannot try this weapon once more.'

Mudaliar was only sorry that he had to serve from such a distance! 'I am sorry,' he told the viceroy, 'that my three colleagues resigned: they cannot be too comfortable now in the thought that they did not stand up to the test at a critical period. Perhaps it was a very vain thought but I had the feeling when I heard the news of their resignations that if I had been there I might have prevented the resignations of two of them at least and probably of all three and thereby have been of some help to you.'

And he was unctuousness itself: 'I hope I may be excused,' he drooled concluding his letter, 'for inflicting this long letter on Your Excellency. I need hardly say how much I was concerned during all that period about the heavy responsibility resting with you and the anxious times that you were having and it must be a matter of supreme satisfaction to you that you have come out successful.'[46]

How many times the poor fellow must have drafted and redrafted that letter!

Who won?

The events speak for themselves. The British were gone within four years of triumphs of this sort. Who remembers the Linlithgows today vis-à-vis Gandhiji?

Two points before we proceed. First, as the record makes

46 *Transfer of Power,* Vol. III, p. 791.

obvious, the Council was kept fully informed at every stage. Those who stayed did so in the full knowledge that they were parties to decisions which would in all probability spell the death of Gandhiji. Nor is it just a matter of their having been informed about specific decisions: how could there have been even the slightest doubt about the general character of the regime—after all, it was an imperial government, one that was holding India as a colony—and how could there be the slightest doubt about the rulers themselves?

They made no secret of their objectives, of their determination to keep India, to crush the nationalist movement. Amery had defended Japan's aggression over China in the House of Commons, as Panditji recorded at the time, on the ground that if they condemned what Japan had done in China, they would have to condemn what Britain had done in India and Egypt. And on the top was Churchill. He had waged a determined battle with his colleagues for six years charging them with betraying England by not being resolute enough in holding on to India. At last, having been in Cabinets for two decades, he had broken with the Conservatives because of their pledge to grant Independence to India. Indeed, his absolutely uncompromising insistence that India must remain subjugated was among the principal factors which had dissuaded fellow MPs from paying as much attention to him as they might otherwise have done—even when he started warning them on what the rise of Hitler, what his rearming Germany would spell for the entire civilized world. His views about India, his widely advertised contempt for Gandhiji were known to all. As his admirer, Nirad Chaudhuri, recalls, on the eve of his appointment as Viceroy Churchill had ribbed Reading: Gandhi, whom he had characterized as 'that half-naked *fakir*', 'ought to be laid, bound hand and foot, at the gates of Delhi and then trampled on by an enormous elephant with the new viceroy seated on its back.'[47]

Such declarations of his were on the lips of every nationalist. Writing at the time Panditji recalled, in January 1930 Churchill had declared, 'Sooner or later you will have to crush Gandhi and the Indian Congress and all they stand for.' In December that year he had declared, 'The British nation has no intention whatever of relinquishing control of Indian life and progress... We have no intention of casting away that most truly bright and precious jewel in the crown of the King, which more than all our Dominions and Dependencies constitutes the glory and strength of the British Empire.' He had pooh-poohed all talk of Dominion status and the rest—that sort of talk, he had declared, was just to provide some words and ceremonies to give these fellows some illusions to feed on. 'We have always contemplated it (Dominion Status) as the ultimate goal,' Panditji quoted him as saying, 'but no one has supposed, except in a purely ceremonious sense in the way in which representatives of India attend Conferences during the War, that the principle and policy for India would be carried into effect in any time which it is reasonable or useful for us to foresee.' In December 1931 he had again declared, 'Most of the leading public men—of whom I was one in those days—made speeches—I certainly did—about Dominion Status, but I did not contemplate India having the same constitutional rights and system as Canada in any period which we can foresee... England, apart from her Empire in India, ceases forever to exist as a great power.'[48] Even the modest constitutional advance of the Government of India Act of 1935 was an outrage for Churchill: 'a

---

47 Nirad Chaudhuri, *Thy Hand, Great Anarch,* Chatto and Windus, London, 1987, p. 23.

48 Cf., Jawaharlal Nehru, *The Discovery of India,* The Signet Press, Calcutta, 1946, p. 529.

monstrous monument of sham built by the pygmies,' he had said of it.[49]

Such declarations of Churchill and the rest were on the lips of every schoolboy in India those days. Ambedkar and others who joined up with the British government, who decided to become ministers in it, certainly knew of them.

Second, while, as we have seen, some Indians 'wobbled'—Sir C.P. Ramaswami Aiyar in August 1942, Aney, Sarker and Srivastava in February 1943—two never did: they were Firoz Khan Noon and Ambedkar—the former became the prime minister of Pakistan, the latter is Bharat Ratna!

The months passed, and the concerns of the members of the Viceroy's Council changed with them. They had been anxious to convince the viceroy how they were one with him in wanting Gandhiji and the rest to be put down with the utmost sternness. But as the months passed it became obvious that those cries of *'Triumph'*, of *'Victory'* had been premature: Gandhiji's influence had not diminished, the Congress had not evaporated; the accomplices of British rule were forced to direct their minds to the unthinkable—maybe British Rule over India will end, maybe these very persons we are today keeping in jails will in fact come to power.

By May 1944 Gandhiji had been under detention for twenty months. It had been a terrible time: Mahadev Desai had died, and then Kasturba herself—their last rites had had to be performed within the compound itself, their samadhis, located right there were a constant, physical reminder to Gandhiji of the tragedies this incarceration had brought. His health collapsed suddenly. Linlithgow had left. He had been succeeded by Field Marshal Wavell. Wavell in turn was in Sikkim.

Informed about the collapse of Gandhiji's health, he at

---

49 Cf., R.J. Moore, *Churchill, Cripps, and India*, Oxford, 1979, p. 1.

once wired Amery. 'Sudden deterioration in Gandhi's health has caught me in Sikkim, so have only telegraphic reports to guide me,' he told the Secretary of State. 'Medical opinion and advice from Home Department and from Governors are overwhelming in favour of immediate release. Home Department's interpretation of the Doctors' opinion is that Gandhi is never likely to be an active factor in politics again. Release therefore seems inevitable since we should have no legal justification for detaining him in such condition. Though we shall gain little credit for release if death occurs immediately afterwards we cannot lose anything and therefore sooner release takes place the better. Home Department in fact were in favour of release forthwith without waiting to inform you. I should anticipate serious difficulties and resignations from Executive Council if Gandhi died in custody. Also far better to release before public agitation becomes formidable and we may appear to be yielding to it.'[50]

Amery sent the viceroy's telegram to Churchill and spoke to him. At first Churchill wanted to put off the matter till it had been considered formally by the Cabinet. Eventually, he sent a *'Secret, Most Immediate'* message to Amery: 'I am prepared to agree to Gandhi's release on medical grounds at this time in view of the Viceroy's request. We can always arrest him again if he commits new offences. It is of course understood that there will be no negotiations between him and the Viceroy...'[51]

What was the concern of the members of the Viceroy's Council at this critical moment? They took it ill, for once again Churchill, Amery and the viceroy had not bothered to stage the pretence that the decision had been taken in consultation with them! Wavell felt it prudent to request Amery to make amends. In a *'Private'* telegram to Amery

50 *Transfer of Power,* Vol. IV, pp. 949–50.

51 *Transfer of Power,* Vol. IV, p. 951.

on 10 May 1944 he explained, 'When my decision was taken I was in Sikkim and Council with the exception of Thorne, Chief, Sultan Ahmed and Muhammad Usman were also absent from New Delhi on tour. Sultan Ahmed left on tour on 5th morning. Thorne consulted Chief before telegraphing to me and informed Usman of the decision before it was announced. Council on the 10th, though approving decision taken, felt that fact that they had not been consulted had deprived them of any credit for the release though they had borne the odium of his imprisonment. They referred to your reported statement that you "left the decision to Lord Wavell". It would help if during the next India debate you could find suitable opportunity to say that the decision had the full support of the Council. I was sure of Council support when I took the decision.'[52]

These toadies and their anxieties—to be on the right side first of the British then of the nationalists, their anxiety to have people believe that they were more than puppets!

What they had been parties to

Given the way facts have been erased from public memory, few today know, few would even be able to imagine the ferocity that the government of which these toadies had chosen to be a part had unleashed on the country at that time. Even by official acknowledgement 1,028 persons were killed and 3,200 wounded by police and military firing in the wake of the 1942 resolution. 'These figures are certainly gross underestimates,' Panditji wrote, 'for it has been officially stated that such firing took place on at least 538 occasions, and besides this people were frequently shot at by the police or the

52 *Transfer of Power* Vol. IV. pp. 959–60.

military from moving lorries. It is very difficult to arrive at even an approximately correct figure. Popular estimates place the number of deaths at 25,000, but probably this is an exaggeration. Perhaps 10,000 may be nearer the mark.'

And outright killings were just one device. To continue with Panditji's account: 'The external evidences of rebellion having been crushed, its very roots had to be pulled out, and so the whole apparatus of government was turned in this direction in order to enforce complete submission to British domination. Laws could be produced overnight by the Viceroy's decree or ordinance, but even the formalities of these laws were reduced to a minimum. The decisions of the Federal Court and the High Courts, which were creations and emblems of British authority, were flouted and ignored by the executive, or a new ordinance was issued to override those decisions. Special tribunals (which were subsequently held by the Courts to be illegal) were established functioning without the trammels of the ordinary rules of procedure and evidence, and those sentenced thousands to long terms of imprisonment and many even to death. The police (and specially the Special Armed Constabulary) and the secret service were all-powerful and became the chief organs of the State, and could indulge in any illegalities or brutalities without criticism or hindrance. Corruption grew to giant proportions. Vast numbers of students in schools and colleges were punished in various ways and thousands of young men were flogged. Public activity of all kinds was prohibited unless it was in favour of government.'

'But the greatest sufferers were the simple-hearted, poverty stricken villagers of the rural areas...,' Panditji continued. 'Cases were reported of whole villages being sentenced to flogging to death... Huge sums were imposed on villages as a whole as punitive fines... All the conventions and subterfuges that usually veil the activities of governments were torn aside and only naked force remained as the symbol of power and authority...'[53]

And that repression was just one of the features of this government. It was under this government and at exactly during this period that 'famine' struck Bengal. There was enough food in the country. But getting it to the starving people was not important enough for the alien government. On 29 November 1943 the House of Commons was told that in Calcutta alone 168,000 persons had starved to death. Even the official Famine Inquiry Commission headed by Sir John Woodhead estimated that about *one and a half million* had perished in this man-made famine.

But the viceroy reigned unperturbed in Delhi, his weekend hunts continued, the members of his Council were not deflected from strutting around the country 'dressed in brief authority'.

---

53 Jawaharlal Nehru, *The Discovery of India,* The Signet Press, Calcutta, 1946, pp. 595–96.

The Social Reformer

6

The British stratagem, and its Indian advocate

During the 1857 movement both Hindus and Muslims had fought the British. But as the decades passed Muslims were weaned away to the Sir Syed school of collaboration. The British saw that the main movement against them would come from, that it was arising from within the Hindus. From the late nineteenth century to the time they left, British policy was directed towards dividing the Hindu community, to hacking sections away from it, to propping up groups in other communities who would proclaim that India was not one country, that the movement for freedom from the British did not speak for all Indians.

A key device of this strategy was to proffer a benefit which a group could avail only by asserting its separateness. And among these benefits none was more capable of breaking the people than separate electorates. As is well known, it is in the full knowledge of how separate electorates would wrench the Muslims away from the rest that Lord Minto and his team had a delegation of Muslims submit a demand for separate electorates, and then graciously agreed to concede the demand. The same set of operations was set afoot for the Scheduled Castes. They had been targets of the Christian missionaries and the British administrators for even longer than the Muslims.

The operation took the same form as in the case of Muslims. The notion was put out that they were not a part or Hindu society at all, that they could never be a part of it as to exclude them was of the very essence of Hinduism, that to exclude them and keep them subjugated was an article of faith with every Hindu. Next, the Scheduled Castes having been proclaimed to be a separate group, an inalienably separate group, separate electorates were proffered for them also. This latter manoeuvre reached its apogee at the Round Table Conference in 1931.

The calculation in proffering a benefit like separate electorates was as simple as it was certain to succeed: once a benefit which the target group could secure only by being separate was thrown among them, politics within that group would swirl entirely around that proffered benefit. The moment it was announced that separate electorates, for instance, could become available, those persons would be thrown up within the group who insisted on the separateness of that group, who were constantly frightening the group that its separateness, its 'identity' was in imminent danger of being engulfed by the general community. These leaders would exacerbate such distances as there might be, for to wrest a following each would try to outdo the other in fomenting insecurity in the group, in making more and more extreme demands in the name of that group. As the leaders would be looking for votes, etc., of this group alone, they would not have to spare a thought for the interests of the community as a whole. Quite the contrary, each of the competitors would set out to prove his commitment to this particular group by insisting on measures that manifestly promoted the interests of this group at the cost of the community as a whole.

This was the inevitable sequence—the British had seen it work to the dot in the case of the Muslims. But they did not just stand by passively once they had thrown the benefit in front of the target group. They knew the boost that official recognition gave a person. Accordingly, they consciously and assiduously patronized a particular sort from within the target group—to use the expression which the viceroy and the Secretary of State used in laying out plans in regard to Ambedkar, they did 'everything to strengthen his hands'. The Round Table Conference was a good case in point. The Conference just had to be convened because it was necessary to make a show of taking steps towards constitutional advance. It was also evident that unless the Congress participated in the Conference, it would carry no credibility. But it was just as clear that if the Congress attended and had its way, the British would have to forego more of their power over India than they had any intention of doing.

So the point was to have the Congress attend the Conference, but then hobble it through other groups. The Congress was the organization to thwart, and Gandhiji was the man to thwart. There was little difficulty in doing so.

The Conference had but to begin and participant after participant insisted that he and his group were not party to the national movement for freedom, that what was going on in India was not a national movement at all, that the Congress represented only one element among the people of India.

Gandhiji put his finger on the root of these declamations. Everyone here, he pointed out, was here not because he had been elected by some organization, much less some community. He was here because he had been invited by, selected and nominated by the British government, because the British government had decided that he rather than someone else represented that group or organization. The observation touched Ambedkar to the quick, for he as much as anyone else was saying the things that worked to the British plan.

Having got 'representatives' of every conceivable 'separate element' to the Conference in this way—'representatives' of Indian states, of British commercial interests, of Anglo-Indians, of Parsis, of Sikhs, of Muslims, and of course Ambedkar as representative of the Untouchables—having ensured by the persons they had invited that no agreement would be possible, that Gandhiji would be thwarted at every step, the British at the Round Table Conference could afford to be, and were reasonableness itself: please agree to a scheme among yourselves, they announced; if the various, separate elements are unable to come to an agreement, government will announce an award, they announced; even after the award had been announced, if the separate elements came to an agreement before it had been translated into formal legislation, the government would adopt the alternative they had agreed upon, the government announced. What could be more reasonable? The catch was in the homework the government had already done, it was in the persons whom they had recognized—'anointed' would be the more appropriate word – as 'representative' of the elements which they had decided constituted 'separate' elements in Indian life.

Gandhiji nailed the mischief in the strategy. As is well known, he proposed that informal discussions be held among those who had been invited to the Conference and requested the prime minister to adjourn the formal proceedings of the Conference till these discussions were completed. On 8 October 1931 the Minorities Committee resumed its sessions. Gandhiji was asked to report on the results of the discussions. 'It is with deep sorrow and deeper humiliation that I have to announce utter failure on my part to secure an agreed solution of the communal question through informal conversations among and with the representatives of different groups...,' he began.

'But to say that the conversations have to our utter shame

failed is not to say the whole truth,' he continued. 'Causes of failure were inherent in the composition of the Indian Delegation. We are almost all not elected representatives of the parties or groups whom we are presumed to represent; we are here by nomination of the Government. Nor are those whose presence was absolutely necessary for an agreed solution to be found here. Further, you will allow me to say that this was hardly the time to summon the Minorities Committee. It lacks the sense of reality in that we do not know what it is that we are going to get. If we knew in a definite manner that we were going to get the thing we want, we should hesitate fifty times before we threw it away in a sinful wrangle as it would be if we are told that the getting of it would depend on the ability of the present Delegation to produce an agreed solution of the communal tangle. The solution can be the crown of the *Swaraj* constitution, not its foundation—if only because our differences have hardened, if they have not arisen, by reason of the foreign domination. I have not the shadow of a doubt that the icebag of communal differences will melt under the warmth of the sun of freedom...'

But that is exactly what the British also knew. Hence the insistence—of the British and the accomplices they had set up—that the Congress must first come to an agreement with the various elements the British had anointed, and only then would the British announce the next step to constitutional advance. Soon, this latter phrase was replaced by the point about granting freedom to India—'we are ready to leave,' the British would say, 'it is just that we are unable to do so because the various elements which constitute India are not able to come to an agreement about the form they want the constitution to take after we leave.'

Few did more to help the British in going through the successive steps of this strategy than Ambedkar.

The echo of the British

In the earlier chapter, 'The Freedom Fighter', we have already seen some of the steps by which Ambedkar came to assert conclusions which suited the British.

Whereas Gandhiji and others were fighting to free the country, whereas our leaders from Swami Dayanand and Swami Vivekananda to Sri Aurobindo and the Lokmanya talked in terms of and thought and felt in terms of the Indian people, Ambedkar declared that words such as society, nation and country 'are just amorphous, if not ambiguous, terms. There is no gainsaying that "Nation", though one word, means many classes. Philosophically it may be possible to consider a nation as a unit but sociologically it cannot but be regarded as consisting of many classes and the freedom of the nation if it is to be a reality must vouchsafe the freedom of the different classes comprised in it, particularly those who are treated as the servile classes...'[1]

Second, Ambedkar insisted that within this agglomeration the Untouchables are a separate element, in particular they are not a part of Hindu society, and they are separate from it exactly as Muslims are, or Sikhs, Christians and the rest. Only some paid agents of the Congress among the Untouchables demur at acknowledging this fact, Ambedkar declared: 'The Congress as usual maintains a body of agents from among the Untouchables to shout when need be that the Untouchables are Hindus and that they will die as Hindus,' Ambedkar declared, adding a tautology as proof, 'But even these paid agents will not agree to be counted as Hindus if they are asked to proclaim

1 B.R. Ambedkar, *What Congress and Gandhi Have Done to the Untouchables;* and *Mr. Gandhi and the Emancipation of the Untouchables,* reproduced in *Dr. Babasaheb Ambedkar, Writings and Speeches,* Vol. IX, pp. 201–02.

themselves as Hindus, if Hinduism means belief in caste and Untouchability.'[2]

True, the Hindus and the Untouchables can be said to worship the same deities, Ambedkar could not but acknowledge. But he had a ready answer: that the two do so, he insisted, only makes them followers of the same cult, it does not make them members of the same religion. At best they can be said to belong to similar religions, not to the same religion. The dogmas of the two are different, he said and the observances of the two do not include each other.[3]

Even if the Untouchables are accepted as Hindus, Ambedkar maintained, they cannot be said to be an integral part of Hinduism ! 'Admitting for the sake of argument that they are Hindu by religion,' Ambedkar insisted, 'can it mean anything more than what I have said—namely that they worship the same Gods and Goddesses as the rest of Hindus, they go to the same places of pilgrimage, hold the same supernatural beliefs and regard the same stones, trees, mountains as sacred as the rest of the Hindus do? Is this enough to conclude that the Untouchables and the Hindus are parts of one single community? If that be the logic behind the contention of the Congress then what about the Belgians, Dutch, Norwegians, Swedes, Germans, French, Italians, Slavs, etc.? Are they not all Christians? Do they not all worship the same God? Do they not all accept Jesus as their Saviour? Have they not the same religious beliefs? Obviously there is a complete religious unity between all of them in thought, worship and beliefs. Yet who can dispute that the French, Germans and Italians and the rest are not a single community?' The same held for Whites and Negroes in the USA, he said, they are both Christians but certainly

---

2 *Dr. Babasaheb Ambedkar, Writings and Speeches,* Vol. IX, p. 183.

3 *Dr. Babasaheb Ambedkar, Writings and Speeches,* Vol. IX, pp. 183–84.

not one community. And so also the Christians in India, the Anglo-Indians and the Europeans—all of them follow one religion, but they are not regarded as forming one Christian community. And the Sikhs: there are Mazhabi Sikhs, and there are Ramdasia Sikhs—both sets are Sikhs but they are not one community, Ambedkar said.[4]

Arguments such as these testify to a determination to stick to a thesis than to acuity. For the trick is so obvious. Define 'community' in a particular way, and thereby rule all evidence to the contrary out of court: that is exactly how the British rulers and their allies, the missionaries had been proceeding in regard to the tribals. They defined 'religion' in a particular way, and, in spite of protests of officials in the field, declared that the tribals were not Hindus, that instead they were 'animists'. Indeed, that is how they had been proceeding in regard to Hinduism itself. A 'religion', they told the groups they were targeting for conversions, is one that has *one* God, *one* Prophet and Saviour, *one* Book, *one* Church. Your 'Hinduism' has none of these, come let us give you a proper religion...

It isn't just that the Hindus and the Untouchables have no 'common cycle of participation', Ambedkar maintained. To exclude Untouchables, to keep them down is of the very essence of Hinduism. The Hindu excludes the Untouchable as a matter of faith. He looks upon the latter as an enemy. The enmity between the two is permanent.[5] As the two sets live excluding each other, there is no chance of a harmonious ideology developing, no chance of a common outlook developing which takes account of the interests of all.[6]

---

4 *Dr. Babasaheb Ambedkar, Writings and Speeches,* Vol. IX, pp. 184–85.

5 *Dr. Babasaheb Ambedkar, Writings and Speeches,*Vol. IX, pp. 192–94.

6 *Dr. Babasaheb Ambedkar, Writings and Speeches,*Vol. IX, pp. 193–94.

Here again is politics being father to the argument. All individuals, all neighbours, all relatives, certainly all groups differ not just each from the other, but among themselves too. It is to the convenience of some to base their politics on the differences. They insist on these, they stoke them, they tell the group that its 'identity', its 'essence' consists in those differences, they then frighten the group that that 'identity', that 'essence' is in danger of being swallowed up by the larger community. And on this basis they insist on measures which will perpetuate those differences, which will exacerbate the feelings of 'them versus us' in the group. For the British this was the most fruitful device, it was an adjunct, a particular application of their 'Divide and Rule' policy. In embracing this way of looking at things as their own, persons like Ambedkar and Jinnah became not just accomplices of imperial politics, they became the best of agents, agents who had been so flattered into self-importance that they did not see that they had made the cause of the Imperial rulers their own.

And there was no scope, there was no prospect for bridging the gap between the two groups, Ambedkar insisted. For keeping the Untouchables down was not just a social question, it was not just a matter of faith with the Hindus, it was a political matter—a matter of maintaining another class under one's domination, one's heel. This hegemony the Hindu would never give up. Nor was it just a political matter, of perpetuating power over another, it was a matter of sheer economics, Ambedkar insisted. For the Hindu, Untouchability was a 'gold mine'. The Hindu has no conscience and so it is futile to expect that he would ever agree to jettison Untouchability out of an urge to at last put himself right with God and Man, Ambedkar declared, but even if he were to agree to do so, economic and social advantages of Untouchability would keep him from doing so.

All this was arrant nonsense. It could just as well be argued that keeping so many in isolation and denying them access to skills and learning was the greatest drag on society, that, quite apart from everything else, it was the severest blow that caste Hindus could inflict on their economic interests. And as for doctrine and dogma, reformers like Swami Vivekananda, like Gandhiji, like Narayan Guru had had no difficulty in showing that Untouchability had no sanction in our scriptures, that, on the contrary, the conclusive doctrinal argument against it lay in the central proposition of the scriptures themselves: namely, that all was Brahman, that the same soul inhered in all. There was also the historical fact that whatever might have been the excrescences which had grown around or in the name of Hinduism, the entire and long history of the religion showed that it was uniquely receptive to new ideas, that it was uniquely responsive to reformers, that it was adaptable as no other religion was, and therefore there was no reason to believe that it would not reform itself out of this evil also.

But Ambedkar had already made up his mind. No, Untouchability is of the essence of Hinduism, so it cannot be prised out of it. The religion is adaptable, yes, but that is nothing to look up to, it is nothing to rest one's hopes on. It is no virtue in fact, he declared: 'I am quite aware that there are some protagonists of Hinduism who say that Hinduism is a very adaptable religion,' he said, 'that it can adjust itself to everything and absorb anything. I do not think many people would regard such a capacity in a religion as a virtue to be proud of just as no one would think highly of a child because it has developed the capacity to eat dung, and digest it...' Yes, Hindus can adjust to anything, he scoffed, they produced an *Allahupanishad* to make a place for Akbar's Din-i-Ilahi as the seventh system of Hindu philosophy. Yes, these beef-eating

Brahmins absorbed the non-violence of Buddhism and became a religion of vegetarianism...

What sort of a mind is it that treats a proposition in this way, to which only these things occur as the evidence that needs to be considered in dealing with the proposition that Hinduism is accommodative of reform? But that aside, notice that the abuse of such a person does not abate either way. If the religion sticks to dogma, such a person condemns it—for then no further argument is needed from his point of view: as he has pronounced Untouchability to be of the very essence of the dogma of that religion, now that the religion admittedly sticks by its dogma, it follows that it will never give up on Untouchability, reformers or no reformers. If the religion adapts, if it heeds reformers, the religion is but the child that has learnt to eat dung and digest it. In any case, says Ambedkar, for all its adaptability one thing Hinduism has never given up, and that is Untouchability. And we are back to its being a gold mine for the Hindus, and to economic interests always prevailing in the end over reformers.

Ambedkar had no greater difficulty with any evidence which someone may point to showing that the practice of Untouchability was already eroding. First, there was the Stephen Potter argument—'But not in the South'! Not in the villages, said Ambedkar. And then there was the shift to the non-verifiable: even if the outward manifestations of the practice are getting diluted, Ambedkar declared, the mentality of excluding the Untouchables is not changing, and will not change in any time frame which is worth talking about![7] As good an example of a non-refutable hypothesis as Karl Popper would wish for!

There was with Ambedkar always another step, which we have encountered already, and which was the same as

---

7 *Dr. Babasaheb Ambedkar, Writings and Speeches,* Vol. IX, pp. 194–97.

with Jinnah. If any Muslim dared to not agree with Jinnah's formulations—of Hindus and Muslims being two peoples, of their being two permanently irreconcilable, two permanently hostile peoples—he was doing so only because he was a paid agent of the Congress. Exactly so, if any Harijan did not mouth Ambedkar's formulations—of Hindus and Untouchables being two peoples, of their being two permanently irreconcilable, two permanently hostile peoples—he was doing so only because he was a paid agent of the Congress. Thus, in Ambedkar's reckoning those Untouchables who had joined Gandhiji's work against Untouchability and associated themselves with the Harijan Sevak Sangh 'are just unemployed loafers who are seeking to make politics a source of their livelihood'.[8] Similarly, those untouchables who maintain that Untouchables are Hindus, for instance because they worship the same deities, are just 'paid agents' that the Congress maintains for its convenience.[9]

Fully in the know, but 'Surprised'!

Government had already determined that it would proceed to separate the Scheduled Castes from the rest of Hindu society by decreeing separate electorates. They were accordingly lining up possible allies for what might ensue. On 10 February 1932, in a confidential letter to Sir Frederick Sykes, the governor of Bombay, the viceroy set out what he expected to be accomplished in the province. 'Our aim is of course to detach the people of the Province from the Congress movement, to get them interested in the reforms and to restore normal conditions as soon as possible...,' he wrote. 'In regard to the Muslim question generally we are circulating to the local governments two

8 *Dr. Babasaheb Ambedkar, Writings and Speeches,* Vol. IX, p. 142.
9 *Dr. Babasaheb Ambedkar, Writings and Speeches,* Vol. IX, p. 183.

recent appreciations sent to the Secretary of State, and I can assure you that we are fully alive to the importance of keeping Muslims on the right lines.'[10]

Sykes had of course been pushing this line for some time, and he continued to press it. In the telegram he sent to the viceroy on 11 April Sykes said, 'If we can come down on the minorities side, as I think we should, there is some hope that they will organise on our side.' 'No reconciliation with the Congress is possible,' he continued, and well he might—the government had thrown all the Congress leaders in jail after all. 'The Congress will never be any party to any decision now, and the main thing is to prevent them from interfering. If this is ensured there is not much likelihood of any adverse effect on law and order from a decision in favour of the Muhammadans and other minorities.'[11] Eight days later—on 19 April—he was again telling Wellingdon, 'It is only by helping people to lose faith in the ultimate supremacy of the Congress that we can hope to encourage other parties to organise themselves in such a way as to form a strong effective opposition in the future.'[12] And on 7 June 1932, in his letter to the viceroy, Sykes emphasized, 'I consider that for political purposes the depressed classes should be considered as a community distinct from the Hindus and their representation should be treated as a subtraction from the Hindu vote.' 'I desire to repeat also,' he told the viceroy, 'that there should be no attempt made now to win over the Congress. Any such attempt on our part will inevitably estrange the Muslims and other minorities.'[13]

The calculations and manoeuvres continued. Gandhiji continued in jail.

---

10. MSS.EUR.F.150/4(a).
11. MSS.EUR.F.150/4(a).
12. MSS.EUR.F.150/4(a).
13. MSS.EUR.F.150/4(a).

In pursuit of their policy to split sections of Hindu society away from it, in 1932 the British announced separate electorates for the Depressed Classes also. There was little doubt that this would be as successful in distancing Harijans from the rest of Hindus as it had been in separating Muslims from the rest of Indian society. At the Round Table Conference itself Gandhiji had cautioned the British government that he would resist this attempt to break Hindu society with his life itself.

'I am certain,' Gandhiji had told the Round Table Conference, 'that the question of separate electorates for the "Untouchables" is a modern manufacture of Government.' He had had to accept separate electorates for the religious communities as a necessary evil, he pointed out. But what was the logic for extending this evil to 'Untouchables' also, he asked. 'Separate electorates to the "Untouchables" will ensure them bondage in perpetuity,' Gandhiji pointed out. 'The Mussalmans will never cease to be Mussalmans by having separate electorates. Do you want the "Untouchables" to remain "Untouchables" forever? Well, the separate electorates will perpetuate the stigma. What is needed is destruction of untouchability, and when you have done it, the bar-sinister which has been imposed by an insolent "superior" class upon an "inferior" class will be destroyed. When you have destroyed the bar-sinister, to whom will you give the separate electorates? Look at the history of Europe. Have you got separate electorates for the working classes or women? With adult franchise you give the 'Untouchables' complete security. Even the orthodox would have to approach them for votes...'

As Gandhiji was to tell the inspector general of prisons later when he came to visit him at the Yeravda Jail on the eve of his fast, he had elaborated these points during his conversations with and in private notes to the prime minister. Gandhiji saw that the British were set to pursue their design. Accordingly, he decided that as soon as he got back to India he would begin a campaign to awaken people, especially the Depressed Classes, to the evil inherent in separate electorates. He had but to land and the British arrested him and lodged him in Yeravda Jail.[14]

From the news that trickled to him in jail Gandhiji saw clearly that the British were persevering in their plan to take the next step to divide Indian society. And it was just as clear that they had many an accomplice among Indians who would assist them in advancing the plan. Accordingly, on 11 March 1932 Gandhiji wrote to Sir Samuel Hoare, the Secretary of State in London. He reminded him of the

---

14 Gandhiji recalled this sequence of events in his tetter of 11 March 1932 to the Secretary of State, Sir Samuel Hoare. He wrote, 'You will perhaps recollect that at the end of my speech at the Round Table Conference when the Minorities claim was presented, I had said that I should resist with my life the grant of separate electorates to the Depressed Classes. This was not said in the heat of the moment, nor by way of rhetoric. It was meant to be a serious statement. In pursuance of that statement, I had hoped on my return to India to mobilize public opinion against separate electorates, at any rate for the Depressed Classes. But it was not to be....' He mentioned the same thing to the inspector general of prisons, Lt Colonel E.E. Doyle, when the latter visited him at the Yeravda Jail to assess whether Gandhiji would actually carry out his resolve to fast unto death. In the *Secret* report which he submitted to the governor of the Bombay Presidency, Doyle noted, 'He (that is, Gandhiji) then went on to say that he had intended when he returned to India from England, to arouse, by organised agitation, to political consciousness, the Depressed Classes, who were not politically minded, and who did not understand what separate electorates meant or implied, or what was being decided in their name. But he was lodged in jail within a week of his arrival in India, and the only way he could now 'fight the Award' was to do what he had promised, starve himself to death if need be...' *Report of Inspector General of Prisons, dated 26 August, 1932,* forwarded by the governor of Bombay, F.H. Sykes, to the viceroy, the Earl of Willingdon, in his *Very Secret, Private and Personal* letter on 28 August 1932. At National Archives, Home Department, *Confidential File number 41-/32-Poll. & K.-W.*

resolve he had expressed at the Round Table Conference, specifically on 13 November 1931. He recalled the objections he had advanced to the plan to give separate electorates to the Depressed Classes. 'I am not against their representation in the legislatures,' Gandhiji wrote. 'I should favour everyone of their adults, male or female, being registered as voters, irrespective of educational or property qualifications, and that even though the Franchise test may be stricter for others.' But separate electorates would harm them, as they would harm Hinduism—the Depressed Classes were dependent on so-called caste Hindus, Gandhiji pointed out, and this separation of electorates would tear them away; moreover, it would 'vivisect and disrupt' Hinduism. The question had important political dimensions but, Gandhiji told Hoare, for him the question was primarily a moral and religious one, and that for him the decision to resist this move of the British Government 'is not a method, it is a part of my being. It is a call of conscience which I dare not disobey, even though it may cost whatever reputation for sanity I may possess.'

There was another factor, Gandhiji pointed out—that too was an important one, it too might compel him to take a similar step in the future, but it was not the cause for which he would be fasting at that juncture. 'It is the repression which is going on,' Gandhiji wrote, 'I have no notion when I may receive the shock that would compel the sacrifice.' It would pay us to recall this part of Gandhiji's letter also: for it speaks to what the state of affairs then was, to what the sort of government it was which the accomplices were assisting.

'Repression seems to be crossing what might be called the legitimate limit,' Gandhiji told the Secretary of State from the jail. 'A Government terrorism is spreading through the land. Both English and Indian officials are being brutalized. The latter, high and low, are becoming demoralized by reason of the Government rewarding as meritorious disloyalty to the people and inhuman conduct towards their own kith and kin. The latter are being cowed down. Free speech has been stifled. Goondaism is being practiced in the name of law and order. Women who have come out for public service stand in fear of their honour being insulted.'

'And all this, as it seems to me, is being done in order to crush the spirit of freedom which the Congress represents,' Gandhiji added. 'Repression is not confined to punishing civil breaches to the common law. It goads people to break newly made orders of autocracy designed for the most part to humiliate them.'

'In all these doings as I read them,' Gandhiji said, 'I see no spirit of democracy. Indeed, my recent visit to England has confirmed my opinion that your democracy is a superficial circumscribed thing. In the weightiest matters decisions are taken by individuals or groups, without reference to the Parliament, and these have been ratified by Members having but a vague notion of what they were doing. Such was the case with Egypt, the War of 1914, and such is the case with India. My whole being rebels against the idea that in a system called democratic one man should have the unfettered power of affecting the destiny of an ancient people numbering over three hundred millions, and that his decisions can be enforced by mobilizing the most terrible forces of destruction. To me this is a negation of democracy.'

Gandhiji cautioned Hoare that this system of repression could not but further embitter the already bitter relations between the British and Indian people. He said that while he had till then no undeniable call from within to fast to death against this repression, 'but the events happening outside are alarming enough to agitate my fundamental being.' 'Therefore, in writing to you about the possibility of a fast regarding Depressed Classes,' Gandhiji concluded, 'I felt that I would be untrue to you if I did not tell you also that there was another possibility, not remote of such a fast.'

The British pressed ahead with their plans. The 'representatives' they had chosen to settle the communal question met in Delhi from time to time, and failed to arrive at an agreement. Gandhiji and other leaders continued to be held in prison. The warning he had given at the Round Table Conference, and which he had repeated in his letter to the Secretary of State in March, was of course very much in the government's mind. 'You will remember Gandhi's threat in the event of our deciding for separate electorates for Depressed Classes,' the Secretary of State noted in his *'Private and Personal'* telegram to the viceroy on 22 July 1932. 'No doubt our plan is only half as bad as he was expecting. Nevertheless I imagine it is possible that he will carry his threat out and I think it would be well to make up our minds in advance what to do in this event and I would be glad to know what you and Sykes contemplate and I think that we can enlighten public opinion on issue of separate electorates for Depressed Classes sufficiently to prevent his action having embarrassing consequences outside India if he acts for this reason.'[15]

The files show the viceroy, the governors, the Home Department and the Secretary of State weighing the various ways in which they may handle Gandhiji. And yet when the fast was upon them, and Prime Minister Ramsay MacDonald was replying to the letter of Gandhiji, how did he begin it? 'I have received your letter,' he began, 'with much surprise and let me add with very sincere regret....'—the regret was just as genuine as the surprise was real!

---

15 National Archives, Home Department, *File Number 41-4/32-Poll. & K.-W.*

'Reward, not award'

In any event, the British announced the Communal Award on 17 August 1932. The terms of the award had two manifest purposes: to reward those who had been standing by the British in thwarting the national movement, and to widen the divides in Indian society in such a way and to such an extent that the national movement would be splintered for the indefinite future.

First, the award completely splintered the electorate. There was to be a separate electorate for Muslims of course. There was to be a separate electorate for Europeans. There was to be a separate electorate for Sikhs. There was to be a separate electorate for Anglo-Indians. Seats were to be reserved for Mahrattas. Seats were to be reserved for labour. Seats were to be reserved for commerce and industry. Seats were to be reserved for mining and plantation. Seats were to be reserved for landholders. Seats were to be reserved for universities.

And of course there was to be a separate electorate for the Depressed Classes. Here there was an altogether novel duality, one that was introduced precisely to fend off the charge that the government was dismembering Hindu society. The award provided that Harijans would be part of the general electorate, and also that they would have a separate electorate of their own. In other words they would have two votes each: they would vote in the general electorate to elect one of the candidates in the general constituencies; and in addition they would vote in an electorate of Depressed Classes exclusively to elect candidates from among Depressed Classes alone. The vital device here was the separation of the electorate, for these number of seats which were reserved for these castes was not all that great: of the total 1,600 seats in the provincial legislatures—the award dealt only with the provincial legislatures on the ground, among others, that the extent of representation which was to be given to Indian states was still under consideration—these were only seventy-eight.

We have already noted that this device was a key instrument of the British: it had worked to perfection in the case of Muslims. But it was also the device by which the influence of persons who had been working with the British—Ambedkar the leading light among them—would be solidified over large sections of the population. For their politics was precisely separatist: once the electorate was separated, the group's politics would forever swirl around separateness.

In this case the award sought to reward leaders who had been working with the British, and to push the politics of that group further in the direction of the politics of these leaders. In the case of Muslims, the award went further: it decreed a distribution of seats which, in what would become the prelude to the way the country would be partitioned, handed Punjab and Bengal to them.

'Reward, not award,' said its prophetic critics. The secret reports which the British governors sent to the viceroy about the way the award was being received show that the boon registered well and truly on the Muslim leadership. But the reports also show another thing. In his *Express* and *Secret* letter the chief commissioner of Delhi reported on 22 August, '... Mahomeddans are in reality quite well satisfied, but as a matter of tactics express dissatisfaction on certain points...' The chief commissioner of Ajmer-Merwara reported by telegram the same day, '... Muslim community disposed to regard it as satisfactory.'[16]

Summarizing the reports it had received from various

---

16 Unless indicated otherwise communications between governmental authorities cited in this section are at National Archives, Home Department, *Confidential files Number 31/113/32-Poll., & unprinted K.-W Number 41/4-Poll. & K.-W, of 1932; Number 41-5-32-Poll. & K.-W.*

quarters, the Government of India reported to the Secretary of State by telegram on 22 August itself, '... Muslim reaction to Award cannot altogether be judged from Press, for they are naturally reluctant to declare themselves satisfied. But there seems little doubt that Punjab Muslims are pleased and Bengal Muslims though protesting and to some extent disappointed are likely gradually to realize solid advantages they have gained. Muslims in provinces where Hindus are in majority generally appear satisfied...'

On 23 August, it got further confirmation from the North-West Frontier Province. The government there reported, '... Communal Award generally well received by Muslims.'

On 24 August, the government heard from the Government of the United Provinces to the same effect: 'Muslims generally express satisfaction privately though publicly offering some protest...'

In a separate, handwritten *Top Secret* assessment meant strictly for the viceroy alone, the governor of the United Provinces wrote, '...It is I think clear that we have not got in the Indian press a true reflection of the genuine feelings about the Award. The dissatisfaction expressed by Muslims is unreal. I am told for instance by the friends of Sir Mahomad Iqbal that his protest is only formal; he is really very pleased. Most of the press is Hindu and is bound to express dissatisfaction;... [word unclear] a great part of the Award was discounted in advance. The real objection does not however lie so much in the position given to Muslims in the Punjab etc., as in the feeling that we have by a Machiavellian stroke, and skilful use of our opportunities, so split people up that a wave of national and anti-European feeling will always be broken up...'

The same day, 25 August, the Government of Bengal said in its telegram, '... Statement issued by A.K. Fazl-ul-Haq and thirty prominent Muslims including several members of the Legislative Assembly regard Award as distinct advance and are pleased with it though they demand statutory majority of total Council. Certain Muslims of Congress sympathies but unimportant in Bengal demand joint electorates. General impression of Muslim opinion is that Muslims are satisfied but are determined to continue demand for statutory majority more as an offset to Hindu demands than as demand itself sustainable...' The next day Punjab reported to the same effect.

On 26 August in its telegram to the Secretary of State, the Government of India stated, '... Muslims generally privately well pleased in all provinces though publicly offering some protest as offset to Hindu demands. In Bengal, for instance, they demand statutory majority in whole Council. All-India Muslim Conference at Delhi expresses disappointment at Award being short of Muslim demands in regard to statutory majority in Punjab and Bengal, reduced weightage in some provinces and undue weightage of non-Muslims in Frontier Province...'

The pattern held for other areas just as much. On 31 August the Madras government wrote to say, '... It appears that Muhammadans of this Presidency are in general well satisfied with the Award and that any expressions of discontent which they may have voiced are dictated by considerations of policy rather than by conviction...'

In its demi-official letter the Government of the Central Provinces reported on 5 September 1932, '... The Muhammadans are definitely pleased, though some show of protest is made against what is alledged to be the inadequate representation allowed to them in this province....'

The chief secretary to the Government of the United Provinces wrote on the same day, 5 September to say, '... Muslims generally are well satisfied with the Award, but are afraid that if they express that satisfaction, the result may be that the Hindus will receive the more in those disputes with which the Award itself has not dealt....'

The same day the chief commissioner of Delhi informed government, 'Responsible Muhammadan opinion on the whole, I believe, welcomes the Award, but as the Superintendent of Police, C.I.D., points out Muhammadans will not be prepared to say that they are satisfied as long as they believe that there is a chance of the Award being revised. The Jamiat leaders of course condemn the Award, but for all intents and purposes their views are similar to those of the Congress, as is well known...'

On 9 September, the chief secretary to the Government of Bihar and Orissa wrote to say, '... The Hindu majority are inclined to deplore the recognition of the minority communities, and it is easy for them to go further and accuse His Majesty's Government of deliberately splitting the Indian nation into parts in order to retain power in their own hands and to postpone the arrival of self-government. The Muhammadans are generally satisfied. One meeting of Muhammadans was held at Siwan in which the Award was condemned but no reasons were given and the gentleman who presided subsequently admitted the meeting had been held only on diplomatic grounds...'

On 9 September, the Government of the North-West Frontier Province reiterated the assessment it had sent by telegram earlier and remarked, '... Communal Award has been generally well received by Muhammadan community and such criticism of it as has been made has been with the object of countering charges made by Sikhs and Hindus outside the Province of unfair treatment in representation accorded to their community...'

On 16 September, the reforms commissioner to the Government of Bengal sent a detailed assessment of the reactions to the Communal Award. 'Muhammadan opinion may be described shortly as satisfied,' he wrote from Darjeeling. 'In fact there can be little doubt that in most instances Muhammadans are really more than satisfied, though they may attempt to conceal their satisfaction by attacking the decision on the ground that it has not given them a statutory majority in the whole Council. A number of meetings have been held in Calcutta and in the muffasil to express qualified satisfaction with the Award. In very few instances has complete satisfaction been openly expressed, and it is expected that the Muhammadan community generally will continue to protest against the lack of a statutory majority not because they feel that a statutory majority is really justified, but because they consider that the airing of this grievance will temper the demand of the Hindus for the withdrawal or modification of the Decision...'[17]

On all evidence therefore one target group had seen the reward the government had given it. It had thought it prudent to not let its satisfaction become too public for tactical reasons. And the masters—the British rulers—were ever so understanding of that circumspection.

Gandhiji's perspicacity and foresight

Gandhiji heard news of the award and its terms in jail on 17 August. He slept over it. On 18 August, he wrote to Ramsay MacDonald, the British prime minister, and told him that unless separate electorates for the Depressed Classes were rescinded he would commence a fast unto death at noon on 20 September 1932. Gandhiji recalled the several occasions on which he had cautioned the government that he would have no alternative but to resist its plan to vivisect Hindu society with his life. 'I regret the decision I have taken,' Gandhiji told the prime minister. 'But as a man of

---

17 The letters are at the National Archives, Home Department, *File Number 41-4/32-Poll. & K.-W.*

religion that I hold myself to be, I have no other course left open to me...'

On 26 August, the inspector general of prisons, Bombay, Lt Colonel E.E. Doyle called on Gandhiji. His mission was to assess how determined Gandhiji was to carry out his resolve. He reported that Gandhiji was completely, and with his usual calmness, determined to fast himself to death unless the separate electorate for the Depressed Classes was withdrawn before 20 September. Doyle reported that Gandhiji had told him that 'he had very carefully studied and chosen the words he had used, as he meant every one of them.' Gandhiji recounted to him the various occasions on which he had cautioned the British authorities of what he would have to do if they went ahead with their plan—the statement at the open session of the Round Table Conference, private conversations with the prime minister, private notes to the prime minister, the letter to the Secretary of State.

There was the argument which the British government was peddling—the award had provided separate electorates for the Depressed Classes for twenty years only. The parties could do away with them at the end of that period, that in any case the government had stated in the text of the announcement of the award itself that should the Indian parties come to an agreement about some other plan before the award was made law, the government would adopt that scheme in preference to its own. Neither limb of the argument had anything to it, Gandhiji told the inspector general of prisons. To begin with, by virtue of the award Depressed Classes were cut off from the rest of Hindu society for twenty years. 'Once the legislatures come into being,' Gandhiji asked with his customary perspicacity and foresight, 'who can possibly alter the schism caused?'

Again, the confidential reports which the viceroy and his men were receiving confirmed Gandhiji's apprehensions—

the reports showed that one of the effects of the award was going to be to make any future agreement among Indians that much more difficult, an outcome which of course could not have been very far from the calculations of the British when they announced their award. The reason was manifest: the award would now become the floor; no one would give up what he had got through the award, and, using that as the floor, would demand more. The reforms commissioner with the Government of Bombay reported in a *Confidential* letter on 10 September that Congressmen were opposing the award on the ground, among others, that 'the offer of substituting for the proposed scheme a scheme agreed to by all communities is purely illusory. The communities which may have gained as a result of the Award are not likely to come to an agreement with the other communities.' The reports from Punjab and Bengal contained the reassuring assessments that the positions of the Muslims, etc., were already hardening. In his *Confidential* letter of 14 September the chief secretary to the Government of Punjab reported, 'Muslim opinion in the main has crystallized into a determination to adhere to the Award and to resist any negotiations which might diminish the solid advantages which they consider the Award gives them...' On 16 September the reforms commissioner with the Government of Bengal in another *Confidential* letter reported that 'There are other signs, too, that the Muhammadans mean to safeguard the position they have won. There have been some rumours of Hindu and Muhammadan leaders coming to an agreement on a basis of communal equality, of a "fifty, fifty" basis. These rumours, unsubstantial though they may be, led one Muhammadan paper to characterize Muhammadan leaders who countenanced such proposals as traitors. It appears exceedingly unlikely that the Muhammadans will agree to concede one seat from the quota allocated to them; indeed, there are indications that the Muhammadan leaders are to make every endeavour to secure seats in constituencies which [they] have hitherto regarded as more or less closed to them, e.g., landlord and commercial seats. Attempts are being made, it is said, to found a Muslim chamber of commerce; and it is rumoured that a number of Muslim employees' organizations are about to seek registration under the Trade Unions Act in order that the community may capture at least half of the eight seats allocated to labour in Bengal...'[18]

And there was the other point which Gandhiji had been emphasizing all along, one which the British had been assiduously misrepresenting, it was the lie on which the British and their accomplices had built their entire case. As Doyle reported, Gandhiji told him, 'The Depressed Classes had been given separate electorates, when as a class they did not desire them. A very small minority, the Mahars, under the leadership of Doctor Ambedkar demanded separate electorates, but they were not entitled to speak for the Depressed Classes as a whole, who in the United Provinces, Bengal and elsewhere had definitely declared for Joint Electorates.'

Again, official records show how accurately Gandhiji knew the condition of our people—for the secret notes which the viceroy and his government were receiving from the governors showed exactly the same thing—namely that, far from there being any widespread yearning among the Depressed Classes for separate electorates, there was not even elementary awareness among them about the question, indeed they scarcely knew that an award had been announced ostensibly for their emancipation.

On 23 August, the viceroy told the Secretary of State in a *'Private and Personal'* telegram, 'We recognize that at

---

18 The letters are at the National Archives, Home Department, *File Number 41-4/32-Poll. & K.-W.*

a later stage His Majesty's Government may be forced to make up their minds what in fact the views of the Depressed Classes are, but, in our opinion, they should not take any initiative in the matter...'

A week later, on 30 August the governor of Central Provinces, A.E. Nelson, wrote in a *Confidential* letter to the Viceroy, 'Turning now to the Depressed Classes, the bulk of them are backward and illiterate and are incapable of giving an opinion on the question of joint versus separate electorates. Nor do they understand what is meant by the disruption of Hinduism. Such Depressed Class opinion as there is consists of the opinion of about half a dozen leaders, who are followers of either Dr. Ambedkar or Mr. Rajah. They have no settled convictions as they have transferred their allegiance several times from one to the other of these two gentlemen. It is difficult therefore to ascertain the real feeling of the Depressed Classes on the Communal Award. In the recent debate in the Legislative Council one Depressed Class member spoke against and one in favour of the Award. My information is that the majority of them are pleased with the Award by which they can put up their own nominees and appreciate the value of the double vote conferred upon them. Those who favour joint electorates were caught by the bait of more seats and not by the glamour of the joint nationalist ideal.'

The next day, 31 August, the governor of Bihar and Orissa sent a *Very Secret* assessment to the viceroy. His words could well be taken to be an elaboration of what Gandhiji had been maintaining all along, and what the government had been so assiduously denying. 'It is difficult to prophecy what will be the effect on the Depressed Classes: they are in this Province, entirely unorganized: except in a few *thanas,* where experiments are being made in the preparation of the electoral rolls on the Lothian Plan, the majority are not aware that they are to have any franchise at all, and certainly not that they are offered a separate electorate. This knowledge will only come when the actual roll is under preparation. With persuasion and intimidation from the side of the caste-Hindus they may consent to denunciation of their franchise to avoid responsibility for the Mahatma's death. The truth is that they are not at present in Bihar and Orissa "class conscious", as they are elsewhere in India.' The point came to be referred to again a few days later when the Poona Pact was signed and the viceroy asked the provinces to report what the effect of the pact replacing the government's award was liable to be. In its telegram of 25 September the Government of Bihar and Orissa said, 'Local Government have no material for advising whether terms of settlement only now received are acceptable and so far as the Depressed Classes are concerned there has been no agitation here for separate electorate and their acceptance [of the pact] may be presumed.'

On 16 September the Government of Madras informed the home secretary, M.G. Hallett, through their *Confidential* letter, 'It is difficult at present to say what the rank and file of the Depressed Classes think about the matter. Probably, the majority have not even heard of it as yet and few of them can understand the full implications. The leaders in Madras are adopting a cautious, waiting attitude and are inclined not to take any step until they have heard what Dr. Ambedkar has in mind.' The chief secretary to the Government of Madras in his assessment of 23 September reiterated the same point: 'It must be understood,' he wrote, 'that the majority of the Depressed Classes in this Presidency, being mainly uneducated and unorganized, know little or nothing of the trend of political events, understand little or nothing of what they are told and are generally indifferent to what is going on outside their sphere... Altogether there is a great deal of talk in the air but very little action, and Depressed Class opinion will probably follow the line taken by Ambedkar who commands a great deal of support.'

On 16 September, as we have seen earlier, the reforms commissioner to the Government of Bengal also sent a *Confidential* and detailed assessment. He set out how satisfied the Muslims in reality were with the advantages which had been conferred on them by the award, how, for tactical reasons, they were planning to make pro forma protests regarding the terms, and how their position had hardened after the award so that they were not liable to countenance any agreement which took away any of the additional benefits which the award had conferred on them. Turning to the Depressed Classes he said, 'The Depressed Classes or Scheduled Classes of Bengal are in a somewhat similar position to the Muhammadans. They have complained in public meetings, at which their recognized leaders were present, that the seats allocated to them are disproportionate to their population... The Scheduled Castes have pressed for additional seats mainly to make sure that the ten seats allocated to them in the Decision are guaranteed to them by separate electorates.'[19]

Do these internal and confidential records bear out the assertion of the British at that time, and of course of their collaborators that in decreeing separate electorates for the Scheduled Castes they were responding to a widespread and long-standing demand from the community? Or do they bear out what Gandhiji had told the Round Table Conference—that the demand was just a 'Government manufacture'? Do they not bear out what Gandhiji told the inspector general of prisons as the latter came to ascertain how serious he was in his resolve to carry out his declaration,

19 The letters and telegrams are at the National Archives, Home Department, *File Number 41-4/32-Poll. & K.-W.*; and *File Number 31/113/ 32-Poll. &K.-W.*

namely that the Depressed Classes had been given separate electorates when in fact as a class they had not desired them?

The government's 'indirect publicity'

But all this was twisted around—by the British government, by the British-controlled press, and most vociferously by Ambedkar. The Home Department sent a *Secret* note to all provincial governments. While forwarding it on 27 August 1932, the Department emphasized that 'the Government of India attaches the greatest importance to prompt and vigorous counter propaganda particularly in the districts, emphasizing particularly the point that it is not a question between Gandhi and His Majesty's Government, but between Gandhi and the Depressed Classes.' 'The note is to be used solely for purposes of indirect publicity...,' the government emphasized—that last instruction was to lead to a comic result. The officer receiving it in the most populous province, the United Provinces, read the note, was duly impressed by its call for prompt and vigorous counter-propaganda, but overlooked the caveat that this note was to be 'used solely for purposes of indirect publicity', and issued it straightaway to *The Statesman* and other papers as being an official statement of the government! The note was duly published, and resulted in many an apology to the Central government from the chief secretary down.

The note told the provincial authorities to emphasize that the government had announced the award only because the Indian parties had not been able to come to an agreement, that the announcement of the award had itself indicated that, even though the award had been announced, should all the Indian parties concerned come to an agreement, the government would readily substitute the award by the terms of that agreement. The words in regard to the matter speak for themselves—for they show where the British calculation lay: 'If therefore Mr. Gandhi really decides to make the provisions of the Award regarding the Depressed Classes the occasion for a "hunger-strike", His Majesty's Government will bear no share whatever of the responsibility for the probable outcome of this course of action,' the note asked the provincial authorities to explain. 'The solution of the matter will lie in Indian hands only. Supposing the Depressed Classes, out of sympathy for Mr. Gandhi, or for some other reason, were to decide in agreement with the caste Hindus to forego the system of special constituencies in certain areas which His Majesty's Government are prepared to grant them, the latter would be quite willing to recommend to Parliament the abolition of this particular feature of the Award, provided this did not prejudice the position of other communities under the new constitution. If, however, the Depressed Classes should decide that the disabilities to which they have been subjected in the past necessitate their being afforded temporary protection, under a democratic constitution, by the means afforded by His Majesty's Government, and if Mr. Gandhi should persist in starving himself to death as a protest against this, the responsibility of the consequences will be his alone.' Having patronized, and, to use the words they had used in indicating what they hoped to do for Ambedkar in return for the excellent way in which he had 'behaved' at the Round Table Conference, 'strengthened the hands' of a person like Ambedkar, the British could now put out that this was just a tussle between Gandhi, representing the high-caste Hindus, and the Depressed Classes. Note also how the propaganda was to be phrased: 'Supposing... the Depressed Classes were to decide in agreement with Caste Hindus... If, however, the Depressed Classes should decide that the disabilities to which they have been subjected in the past necessitate...'—when the fact was that all the internal reports to the government themselves were saying that the Depressed Classes had no opinion of their own, that what passed for their opinion was no more than the opinion of the moment of half a dozen leaders, and, as we shall see in a moment, these leaders were bitterly divided on what was the right thing for the Depressed Classes in this regard.

The note told the provincial authorities to emphasize that the Depressed Classes were not being separated from the rest of Hindu society as they would be voting in the general constituencies also. They had been given a separate electorate only because of the hardships to which they had been subjected, the note told the authorities to emphasize. Was this—'the disabilities to which they had been subjected in the past'—the ground on which the delegation had been put together by the British in 1906 so that the demand for separate electorates could be put to the viceroy 'on behalf of the Muslims'? Was this the reason the Sikhs, the Anglo-Indians, the Indian Christians, the Europeans were each being given separate electorates?

In any case, the note told the authorities to explain, the separate electorates for the Depressed Classes had been provided only for twenty years. And this was a necessary safeguard for the Depressed Classes, the note said, 'to ensure that genuine representatives of their interests are returned to the new legislatures.' 'For it would seem obvious,' the note continued, that if the Depressed Classes were only given reserved seats in general electorates in which caste Hindus predominate, 'there would be little likelihood, under existing circumstances, that the majority of the Depressed Class candidates would be other than mere nominees of the caste Hindus.'

'It is surely a matter for astonishment,' the note declared in mock-wonderment, 'that a man like Mr. Gandhi, who unquestionably has the welfare of the down-trodden and oppressed much at heart, should make the introduction of measures designed for their protection the occasion for so drastic and extraordinary a protest.'

Perhaps the only thing we need note is that even fourteen years later when Ambedkar wrote and published his *What Gandhi and the Congress Have Done to the Untouchables*, these were the very points, indeed these were the very words in which he couched his critique—with one exception, of course: he dispensed with British irony and circumlocution. None of the 'a man like Mr. Gandhi, who unquestionably has the welfare of the down-trodden and oppressed much at heart...' To take just one example, the gravamen of Ambedkar's 'analysis' of the elections of 1937, in which the Untouchables themselves trounced Ambedkar's candidates even in the constituencies reserved for the Depressed Classes, is based on one premise alone: namely, that the candidates put up by the Congress, though untouchable by birth, were just surrogates for and stooges of high-caste Hindus.

The British note asked the provincial authorities to emphasize two points in conclusion. A large section of Untouchables, the note said, did not accept Gandhi's view that they would receive fair treatment at the hands of the higher castes in a general electorate. 'Now it is generally accepted in civilized society that the most equitable and wisest method of settling disputes and differences of opinion when they arise is by discussion and argument and an appeal to reason. In this particular instance, however, Mr. Gandhi proposes to convert those who disagree with him to his own way of thinking by the exercise of force. That it will be moral rather than physical force does not render the distinction any the less valid... The essence of Mr. Gandhi's plan clearly is, by a sedulous fostering of popular compassion for him in his suffering, to overwhelm a group of people who have not been able to accept his views regarding a matter which primarily affects them.' 'And the fact cannot be overlooked,' the note slipped in between the sentences about coercing others in a way alien to civilized conduct, 'that Mr. Gandhi himself is not one of the Depressed Classes but a caste Hindu, and it is the Depressed Classes alone who are best entitled to determine where their own interests in this matter lie.'

This was to be the 'indirect publicity'—the Depressed Classes alone are in the best position to decide where their best interests lie in this matter, and Gandhi is a high-caste Hindu—when, as we have seen, governor after governor was reporting that the Depressed Classes in fact had no opinion of their own, that in fact the bulk of them did not even know that an award had been announced and these rival positions were being debated ostensibly in their interest. Again, recall how closely Ambedkar's own arguments and rhetoric followed these very lines.

But publicity was just one of the headaches the government had to deal with. The more important point was: what should be done with Gandhi should he actually start his fast? Should he be released? But what purpose would that serve if, even after being released, he continues his fast? And would the fact that he was now a free man not leave everyone else also free to visit him? Wouldn't the starving Gandhi become a beacon, would the place at which he was starving become a place of pilgrimage for this religious lot? And would he not use his freedom to again whip up the Civil Disobedience movement, and thereby undo all that the government had accomplished with such enormous difficulty? But what if he commences his fast and eventually dies? Would it not be far worse if he were to die as a prisoner of the government in jail rather than if he were to die in his own ashram? But if he were to be released, what would government do if others who were also in detention caught on and started fasting as a good way to get out?

The governors to the viceroy to the Secretary of State to the prime minister... the telegrams flew fast and fevered. In the end the government hit upon what it thought would be a clever via media Gandhi would be shifted to his ashram, the ashram would be cordoned and access limited to those the government permitted. But that plan had to be discarded: the ashram at Ahmedabad would be difficult to cordon off; moving Gandhi to Ahmedabad would become the occasion for vast gatherings on the way; the sentiment for Gandhi in Gujarat is so intense that when news gets out that he is nearing death, or even that he is sinking it would be impossible to regulate the flood of visitors. That plan abandoned, it was thought that the advantages of that course could be ensured just as well by shifting him to a private residence in Poona itself. Tentative houses were inspected in secrecy. The arrangements complete, the government announced that this is what it would be doing: technically, it would release Gandhiji for the duration of the fast, he would be shifted to and asked to stay within a private house and, while persons will be allowed to meet him, access to him would be regulated by government. This was thought to be a very promising compromise between the alternatives. No one could complain that Gandhi had not been allowed access to persons in case he wanted to work out some solution that would stave off his killing himself. If he did deteriorate, it would be in full view of his associates and no one would be able to charge government with having been niggardly in its care. And if he did die, it would be as a free man and not as prisoner of His Majesty's Government. At the same time he would not have the opportunity to revive the Civil Disobedience campaign... There was much satisfaction all round at having hit the golden mean.

As usual, the government had reckoned without Gandhiji.

He shot down their careful calculations and preparations with a single telegram to the private secretary to the viceroy in Simla. He had just read the government announcement with considerable pain, he said. 'To avoid unnecessary trouble and unnecessary public expense also unnecessary worry to myself I would ask Government not to disturb me for I will be unable to conform to any conditions as to movement from place to place or otherwise that may be attached to foreshadowed release.'

The British and Ambedkar in a quandary

Soon after the award was announced, the governments in Bombay and Simla noted that Ambedkar had not reacted. But he was soon in a quandary. The other leaders of the Depressed Classes, in particular M.C. Rajah denounced it roundly. It was an attempt to divide Hindu society, they proclaimed, and in any case what it was giving to the Depressed Classes by way of reserved seats was much, much less than had been recommended under earlier proposals. Ambedkar could not welcome the award too warmly without seeming to have been party to formulating it in the first place. He too came out with a criticism of the award.

He also got in touch with the British government to have a feature or two altered. In particular, he urged that the limit which had been put in the award—namely that its provision of separate electorates would end at the expiry of twenty years—be relaxed. Sir Samuel Hoare, the Secretary of State who was acquainted at first hand with the sterling contribution that Ambedkar had made at the Round Table Conference to hobble Gandhiji, was most anxious to oblige.

Accordingly, in the draft of the reply which the prime minister was to send to Gandhiji a new sentence was slipped in. 'I cannot of course say,' the prime minister was to tell

Gandhiji, 'whether when special constituencies lapse, the Depressed Classes will need any other form of electoral protection and Government's recent declaration does not anticipate the situation which will then arise.'

Forwarding the new draft to the viceroy on 5 September by *Secret* telegram, the Secretary of State told the viceroy, '... Reply is in accordance with draft in which you have concurred with some verbal improvements by the P.M. and others. Sentence in latter part beginning "I cannot say of course whether" has been introduced to cover points raised by Ambedkar as to which I telegraphed to you yesterday.' He was also concerned about another aspect of the line which the viceroy had proposed; the viceroy had told London how his government was making out that the issue really was between the Depressed Classes and Gandhi and not between the British government and Gandhi. To go on doing so would be unwise, Hoare said. 'With reference to end of para 5 of your telegram of August 23rd we should not imply that issue lies between Gandhi and Depressed Classes alone as this would weaken Ambedkar's position which we ought not to do. Therefore it would be well for local authorities to refer to para 4 of Communal Award,' Hoare told the viceroy, 'and to say that the issue which Gandhi now raises does not lie between Gandhi and H.M.G.'

The viceroy had more to worry about than shielding Ambedkar. He sent a strongly worded reply to Hoare the very day, 6 September, that the Secretary of State's telegram reached him. Through a *Private and Personal, Immediate* telegram to Hoare, the viceroy informed him, 'I have consulted my colleagues on suggestion made in your *Private and Personal* telegram of the 5th September 2297 for form of reply to Ambedkar. Intention of His Majesty's Government expressed in paragraph 9 of Communal Award is to our minds entirely clear namely that as stated in paragraph 2 of your telegram depressed classes after twenty years are guaranteed no rights in excess of or different from those of ordinary voters. The reply to Ambedkar which you suggest in para 3 of your telegram is on the other hand inconsistent with your own construction of the Award. We must strongly advise you that any modification of or even any explanatory comment tending to modify the Award will have disastrous results and will lead to threats of non-cooperation far more serious than suggestions in that sense made by Ambedkar to which we attach little weight. We would suggest that the only reply to be given to Ambedkar is to refer him to terms of the Award. We therefore consider that no change need be made in draft reply to Gandhi other than suggested in our telegram No. 595-S of August 27th. We strongly urge early issue of Prime Minister's reply to Gandhi so that whole correspondence may be published with least possible delay...'

On 8 September the Secretary of State informed the viceroy that government in London had agreed not to include that passage to accommodate Ambedkar's recommendation, and told him that the reply to Gandhiji could now issue bearing the date 8 September.

In the letter which now issued after all these anxious consultations between London and India, Ramsay Macdonald, the British prime minister maintained that the unity of Hindus had been provided for in the award by having the Depressed Classes vote in the general electorate also, and that in any case the separate electorate and double vote were just a temporary expedient as they were to lapse after twenty years. He went on to do the predictable thing, that is paste a motive on Gandhiji's decision. He said, 'As I understand your attitude, you propose the extreme course of starving yourself to death not in order to secure that the Depressed Classes should have joint electorates with other Hindus, because that is already provided, nor to maintain unity of Hindus which is also provided, but solely to prevent Depressed Classes, who admittedly suffer from terrible disabilities today, from being able to secure a limited number of representatives of their own choosing to speak on their behalf in Legislatures which will have a dominating influence over their future...'

Gandhiji received the reply by cable on 9 September. He replied at once. 'I have to thank you for your frank and full letter telegraphed and received this day,' he wrote. 'I am sorry, however, that you put upon the contemplated step an interpretation that never crossed my mind. I have claimed to speak on behalf of the very class to sacrifice whose interests you impute to me a desire to fast myself to death. I had hoped that extreme step itself would effectively prevent any such selfish interpretation.' 'Without arguing,' Gandhiji continued,'I affirm that for me this matter is of pure religion. The mere fact of "Depressed" Classes having double votes does not protect them or Hindu society in general from being disrupted. In establishment of a separate electorate at all for "Depressed Classes" I sense the injection of a poison that is calculated to destroy Hinduism and do no good whatsoever to "Depressed Classes".' 'You will please permit me to say,' he told the British prime minister who was suddenly so concerned about the condition of these classes, 'that no matter how sympathetic you may be you cannot come to a correct decision on a matter of such vital and religious importance to parties concerned.' He added—a point which is important in view of the sorts of things that Ambedkar put out against Gandhiji at the time and later—'I should not be against even over-representation of "Depressed" Classes. What I am against is their statutory separation, even in a limited form, from Hindu fold, so long as they choose to belong to it.'

'Do you not realize,' Gandhiji asked the prime minister,

'that if your decision stands and constitution comes into being, you arrest the marvelous growth of work of Hindu reformers who have dedicated themselves to the uplift of their suppressed brethren in every walk of life?'

'I have therefore been compelled reluctantly to adhere to the decision conveyed to you,' Gandhiji said. In view of the insinuation which was implicit in the prime minister's letter, and anticipating with his usual acuteness the propaganda which the British and their megaphones were going to put out, Gandhiji concluded by telling Ramsay MacDonald, 'As your letter may give rise to a misunderstanding, I wish to state that the fact of my having isolated for special treatment the "Depressed" Classes question from other parts of your decision does not in any way mean I approve of or am reconciled to other parts of decision. In my opinion many other parts are open to very grave objection. Only I do not consider them to be any warrant for calling from me such self-immolation as my conscience has prompted to in the matter of "Depressed" Classes.'[20]

M.C. Rajah's reaction

Leaders of the Depressed Classes other than Ambedkar began denouncing the award even more sharply. Speaking in the Central Legislative Assembly on 13 September, M.C. Rajah declared, 'Never in the annals of the history of India has the issue of the Depressed Classes assumed importance as it has today, and for this we of the Depressed Classes must forever be grateful to Mahatma Gandhi. He has told the world, in words which cannot be mistaken, that our regeneration is the fundamental aim of his life...'

He told the Assembly that the correspondence between the British government and Gandhiji showed that the

20 Mahatma Gandhi, *Collected Works*, Vol. LI, pp. 31–32.

former had had enough warning, and that yet they had persisted. As a result it was the Depressed Classes, the very ones in whose name the British had announced their award, that had been put in the worst position. And he nailed the device by which mischief for the future had been built into the announcement. 'The British Government have given their communal decision,' he pointed out. 'They declare that it shall hold good for 20 years in respect of the Depressed Classes, unless there is a unanimous request made before the constitution is framed or ten years after the constitution has worked.' 'I wonder what is meant by a unanimous request,' he asked. 'Has in the political history of any country such literal unanimity ever been attained on any issue? Is the British Government sure that the Britishers are unanimous in giving India a further measure of responsibility? Is even the National Government sure that Conservatives as a whole back its Indian policy? This condition of unanimity is thus a dodge to keep us perpetually divided. I claim that my country is already in favour of common electorates, and I will prove my contention with a few quotations.'

And whom did he proceed to quote? Ambedkar himself! His evidence before the Simon Commission. His statements at the First Round Table Conference at which Ambedkar himself had advocated joint electorates with reserved seats for the Depressed Classes. And the statements of Rao Bahadur Srinivasan.

The Communal Award is going to cut the Depressed Classes off from the governance of the country, Rajah told the Assembly. We want not a few seats 'for voicing our opinion', he said, we want a share in governing our country. As he put the matter, 'The position we took was that under the scheme of government in which Indians would rule, our safety lay not in finding channels for voicing our opinions, but in taking our due share in the governing of the country. Indeed this is my chief attack on the Premier's letter to Mahatma Gandhi. He tells us that he has given separate electorates for twenty years to enable us to get the minimum number of seats to place our views before the Government and legislature of the day. I contend that this privilege we have already enjoyed under the Montford reforms which have enabled us to get representation in numerous local bodies and in legislatures both provincial and central. We are sufficiently organized for that purpose and do not need either special pleading or special succour. In future what we do need as real remedy for our uplift is definite power to elect our representatives from the general constituencies and hold them responsible to us for their actions. I do not know why the Prime Minister calls the scheme of joint electorates with reservation of seats as impracticable. It is already in force in local bodies in Madras and some other provinces and has worked very satisfactorily. I contend, Sir, that the scheme enunciated in the communal decision involves our segregation and makes us politically untouchables. I am surprised at the argument of the Prime Minister that there is no segregation because we can vote for Caste Hindus who will have to solicit our votes. But, Sir, how can we bring about a common ideal of citizenship when Depressed Class representatives are not to solicit votes of higher castes?'

He punctured the sudden protestations of the government to the effect that they were giving separate electorates to the Depressed Classes because the latter would not be able to elect their true representatives so long as they were clubbed together with the Hindus in general. Rajah remarked, 'There is, Sir, another tragic controversy. When we claim special protection from Government for some share in official services which is given by the Government of India to other minorities and backward classes, we are told that we are classed as

Hindus and have no special claim, and when we declare that in the matter of legislative representation we would like to join the general body of Hindus, we are told that we are a separate community. The sufferings which my community has undergone at the hands of Caste Hindus have been acknowledged by Caste Hindus themselves, and I am prepared to admit that there are a large number of reformers among them who are doing everything possible to improve our status and position. I am convinced that there is a change of heart and a change in the angle of vision of Caste Hindus. We, Depressed Classes, feel ourselves as true Hindus as any Caste Hindu can be, and we feel that the moral conscience of the Hindus has been roused to the extent that our salvation lies in bringing about a change from within the main body of Hindu society and not segregating ourselves from them. The course adopted by the Government would certainly arrest the progress of this most laudable movement.'

He turned directly to the argument which the British prime minister had used. 'I must say, Sir, that the Prime Minister's letter in its entire conception and expression has disappointed me,' Rajah declared. 'He argues, for instance, that reservation of seats under joint electorates would not be genuine representation for us. Does the Prime Minister know that the Simon Commission, consisting of seven chosen Britishers, held after a most thorough investigation on the spot that such system would produce genuine representation for us? Even the fear expressed by the Prime Minister is resolved by Mahatma Gandhi, who has said that he is ready to enroll every adult member of the Depressed Class as a voter and impose stricter tests on Caste Hindus.' 'May I ask why the Premier is not prepared to consider this solution?' Rajah inquired.

Rajah concluded by reminding the government that while the separate electorates it had decreed were intended merely to give the Depressed Classes a minimum number of seats, Gandhiji had proposed that they be given over-representation in excess of their share in the population, and that in any case under the pact he, Rajah, had signed with the Hindu Mahasabha leader, Dr Moonje, it had already been agreed that under the joint electorate the Depressed Classes would have seats in proportion to their population. What was so special about what the government are conferring on these classes by their award?

'The crisis that faces us today is very grave,' he warned. 'There hangs in the balance the life of the greatest Indian of our time, and there hangs in the balance the future of millions of down-trodden people of this country. Is the Government going to take the responsibility for killing the one and reducing the other to perpetual servitude?'[21]

'I do not care for these political stunts'

On Gandhiji's request the correspondence which had passed between him, the prime minister and the Secretary of State was released to the press. The country was stunned on learning that Gandhiji had decided to fast unto death on the question.

Not Ambedkar, however. 'I do not care for these political stunts,' he told *The Times of India* in an interview on 14 September. He was defiance, he was truculence personified. 'This threat of Mr. Gandhi,' he said, 'to starve himself to death is not a moral fight but only a political move. I can understand a person trying to negotiate with his political opponent on equal terms by giving him credit for honesty but I will never be moved by these methods.' 'My decision stands,' he told the paper's representative. 'If Mr. Gandhi wants to fight with his life for the interests of the

21 For the text of M.C. Rajah's statement, Pyarelal, *The Epic Fast*, Navjivan, Ahmedabad, 1932, pp. 248–53.

Hindu community, the Depressed Classes will also be forced to fight with their lives to safeguard their interests.'

The correspondent drew Ambedkar's attention to the fact that M.C. Rajah, the other leader of the Untouchables had endorsed the principle of joint electorates with reservations of seats for Depressed Classes. He had said that if this formula were to be accepted the situation could be saved. 'Dr. Ambedkar emphatically said that he would not agree to it,' the paper reported.

The same issue of the paper carried the statement of M.C. Rajah from Simla. He said that those like him who had been disappointed with the turn which events had taken at the Round Table Conference, and who had felt after the Communal Award that 'our cause was lost beyond repair, and that we, who had been made socially untouchable by caste Hindus, were condemned by the British Government to be politically untouchable.' He said that the decision of Gandhiji to starve himself to death on the question had given a world platform to the matter. He reiterated that the solution lay in joint electorates with reservations for the Depressed Classes. He pointed out that Gandhiji's letters showed that he was willing to agree to such an arrangement. There had been no hue and cry against this solution when it had been proposed earlier, Rajah pointed out in an obvious reference to Ambedkar. It was the unholy Minorities Pact—a pact which Ambedkar had signed at the Round Table Conference to set up a joint front against Gandhiji and what he was urging—which had poisoned everything, Rajah declared. He said that everyone should be grateful to Gandhiji for focusing world attention on the matter, and that everyone will pray and contribute to finding the solution which would save Gandhiji's life. 'Let me end with a warning,' he said in an even more obvious reference to Ambedkar, 'that the responsibility on those who may play a mischievous role is great, for they will be playing with the life of the greatest Indian of our time, and the greatest benefactor of the poor and downtrodden classes.' Rajah reiterated the points the next day in telegrams he sent to the leaders of the Depressed Classes all over the country. He stressed that the thing to do was to secure the best terms for the Depressed Classes through joint electorates. One thing had to be admitted, he told his colleagues, namely that, Gandhiji 'has roused to consciousness caste Hindus and has given the greatest impetus to the movement for the uplift of the Depressed Classes, that it is up to the latter not to let such a benefactor die, or at least not to have the responsibility fall on their shoulders.'

Ambedkar was interviewed again by the representative of *The Times of India* on 14 September. He said that he would not be satisfied even if a sufficient number of seats were reserved for the Depressed Classes in the joint electorate. 'I will not be satisfied,' he told the paper, 'because what I want is quality as well as quantity'—this was the same point that the British had asked their provincial authorities to stress, namely that, whatever the number of Depressed Class candidates who might be elected through joint electorates, they would only be nominees and stooges of the caste Hindus.

Ambedkar declined to put forward any proposals of his own on the ground that it was for Gandhiji to come up with proposals. He said the proposals which Gandhiji had mentioned to him in London were 'totally absurd and childish and nobody could consider them.' Everyone by then was proposing a conference where leaders of all sides could meet and weigh different proposals. There is no need for such a conference, Ambedkar declared, because everyone's views are well known. He had no objection to the conference being called, Ambedkar continued, adding, 'I do not know whether I will participate in that conference; I want to know what Mr. Gandhi's proposals are.'

Other Depressed Class leaders were incensed at Ambedkar's attitude, and many spoke up. Ignore his views altogether, declared one. No one has done more for helping lift us up than the Mahatma, said others, his life must be saved at all costs, it is he who can and will persuade caste Hindus to change their attitude. Seize the moment, and secure substantial representation for ourselves in the joint electorate, said still others. *The Times of India* representative in Ahmedabad reported on 15 September, 'The news of Mr. Gandhi's resolve to fast unto death has caused a stir among local Depressed Classes over whom Mr. Gandhi has a strong hold by championing their cause for the last 15 years and founding a labour union for the millhands most of whom are drawn from the Depressed Classes. The men have joined the union in large numbers. Some of the prominent leaders met last night and sent a deputation to Bombay in order to interview Dr. Ambedkar and request him to come to terms with Mr. Gandhi so that he may give up his decision to fast. They have also requested Mr. A.V. Thakkar, Member of the Servants of India Society, who is believed to have some influence over Dr. Ambedkar, to proceed to Bombay in order to interview Dr. Ambedkar with the same purpose...' In Calcutta a meeting of eleven different organizations of the Depressed Classes was held that very day. It passed a resolution disapproving the grant of separate electorates to the Depressed Classes, saying that while these did not secure sufficient representation for the Depressed Classes, they brought about a statutory separation of these classes from the rest of Hindu society—this in turn would disrupt Hindu society on the one hand, and perpetuate the humiliations that were heaped on the Depressed Classes on the other. It appealed to Gandhiji to give up or at least postpone his decision to fast, and to the British government to withdraw this provision of the award and leave the matter entirely to the affected classes to settle among themselves.

As part of the arguments that he was putting forward to work for maximizing the number of seats under a joint electorate, on 16 September Rajah released figures from Simla, where he still was. These showed that in fact in lieu of giving separate electorates, the government's award had reduced the representation of the Depressed Classes woefully. If one went by the terms of the Indian Central Committee, Rajah recounted, out of the total 1,436 seats in the provincial legislatures, the Depressed Classes should have got ninety seats. If one went by the recommendations of the Simon Commission, they should have got 177 seats. If one went by the terms of the Minorities Pact, which had been signed during the Round Table Conference and to which Ambedkar was a signatory, they should have got 237 seats. Against these numbers, the Depressed Classes had been fobbed off in the Communal Award with just 71 seats.[22]

It was a criticism which hit home. A person like Ambedkar—that is, one who was so stridently claiming to speak for the interests of the Depressed Classes—could not explain how an award which gave so little to the Depressed Classes was to be hailed. He could not explain how the fact that these sections had been given separate electorates made up for the much smaller number of seats. He could not explain how these classes should trust a government which had robbed them of the seats to this extent, but be so untrusting of a person like Gandhiji as to be willing to see him starve himself to death.

Government withholds Gandhiji's statement

On 16 September, Gandhiji sent another statement from jail to the Bombay government with the request that it be

22 For the text of the statement, *The Times of India,* 17 September 1932.

released to the press. He reiterated the reasons which had led him to decide on a fast unto death. He again emphasized that his real target was Untouchability itself, that the withdrawal of separate electorates would just be the first step towards this goal. 'Above all,' Gandhiji said in the statement, 'it [the fast] is intended to sting Hindu conscience into right religious action. The contemplated fast is no mere appeal to emotion. By the fast I want to throw the whole of my weight (such as it is) in the scales of justice pure and simple. Therefore, there need be no undue haste or feverish anxiety to save my life...' 'The separate electorate is merely the last straw,' he continued. 'No patched up agreement between caste Hindu leaders and rival "depressed" class leaders will answer the purpose. The agreement to be valid must be real. If the Hindu mass mind is not yet prepared to banish Untouchability root and branch, it must sacrifice me without the slightest hesitation.' 'No compromise which does not ensure the fullest freedom to the "depressed classes" inside the Hindu fold can be an adequate substitute for the contemplated separation,' he made clear. 'Any betrayal of the trust can merely postpone the day of immolation for me and henceforth for those who think with me. The problem before responsible Hindus is to consider whether in the event of social, civic or political persecution of the "depressed classes" they are prepared to face *satyagraha* in the shape of perpetual fast, not by one reformer like me, but an increasing army of reformers whom I believe to exist today in India and who will count their lives of no cost to achieve the liberation of these classes and therethrough [rid] Hinduism of an age-long superstition.' That was his central target, he said now as he had been saying all along. The fast itself of course would have to be withdrawn the moment separate electorates were withdrawn. He again left the door open for the leaders of caste Hindus and the Depressed Classes to work out some solution which did not have this particular feature of separating the Depressed Classes from the rest of Hindu society. 'Since there appears to be a misunderstanding as to the application of my fast,' Gandhiji concluded, 'I may repeat that it is aimed at a statutory separate electorate, in any shape or form, for the "depressed" classes. Immediately that threat is removed once for all, my fast will end.'

He specifically said, 'I hold strong views about reservation of seats, as also about the most proper method of dealing with the whole question. But I consider myself unfit as a prisoner to set forth my proposals. I should however abide by an agreement on the basis of joint electorate that may be arrived at between the responsible leaders of caste Hindus and the "depressed" classes and which has been accepted by mass meetings of all Hindus.'

Could there be any ambiguity? And yet in a moment we shall see how in order to justify his continuing adherence to the British award, Ambedkar insisted that it was not clear whether Gandhiji would accept an agreement based on joint electorates.

Ambedkar was also to put out as his grouse that Gandhiji was not really interested in the welfare of the Depressed Classes. But could there be the slightest doubt about what Gandhiji's real target was in the light of the work that he had been doing for decades on this score, could there be any doubt in view of Gandhiji's statements in this episode either? The goal is the abolition of untouchability, Gandhiji says again and again; it is to be pursued by various means; at the moment, as the British government has used what is our own failing, namely, this evil we have clutched through the ages, as it has used it to adopt what it claims is a solution but which in fact would be ruinous for Hindu society in general and the Untouchables in particular, he is going to fast till the separate electorates are withdrawn or till he dies.

But why did Gandhi make such a song and dance about separate electorates for the Depressed Classes alone, why did he not fast unto death against the same facility being given to Muslims, Sikhs and the rest? Was there no other feature of the Award which was worthy of his concern?, Ambedkar demanded repeatedly. And answered: he did not, that shows that the one thing Gandhi would never tolerate is that the Depressed Classes should be given any substantive power, and that thereby the classes Gandhi represented, namely the Brahmins and Banias should lose their opportunity to go on exploiting these classes. That, as we shall see, was to be Ambedkar's refrain even thirteen years later as he recounted the episode. And yet in this statement as in every other pronouncement of those days Gandhiji was plain as can be. Continuing the statement he said, 'One thing I must make clear. The satisfactory ending to the "depressed" classes question, if it is to come, should in no way mean that I am committed to the acceptance of His Majesty's Government's decision on the other parts of the communal question. I am personally opposed to many other parts of it, which to my mind make the working of any free and democratic constitution well nigh impossible, nor would a satisfactory solution of this question in any way bind me to accept the constitution that may be framed. These are political questions for the National Congress to consider and determine. They are utterly outside my individual capacity. Nor may I as a prisoner air my individual views on these questions. My fast has a narrow application. The "depressed" classes question being predominantly a religious matter, I regard it as specially my own by reason of my life-long concentration on it. It is a sacred personal trust which I may not shirk.'[23]

The statement was sent to the Bombay government on

---

23 Mahatma Gandhi, *Collected Works,* Vol. LI, pp. 62–65.

16 September for being released to the press. The government did not release it till 21 September. By that time the fast had commenced, tensions had built up to feverish levels. Leaders who met Gandhiji in prison to ascertain his views on the 20 and 21 September and learnt of the statement which had been sent a week earlier, and which had clearly specified that the fast was only against the decreeing of separate electorates, which had clearly left the door open for some agreement that did not include this particular feature. Coming out from the jail after meeting Gandhiji the leaders told the press that had this statement been released by the government at the time it had been given to it much of the subsequent misunderstandings would have been avoided. That does seem to put too fine a point on the matter for Gandhiji had been saying the same thing again and again in statement after statement, in particular he had made each of these points crystal clear in the letters he had sent to the British prime minister and the Secretary of State, letters which had all been published—and taken note of, recall Rajah's statement in the Legislative Assembly. The 'misunderstandings' were only in minds which were determined to misrepresent what he was saying.

Suddenly prepared 'to consider everything'

The allies and colleagues of Ambedkar did speak up for his position, but it was evident that the way things were going he was the only one who was standing between Gandhiji and life. There was a sudden 'softening', therefore. 'Ambedkar ready to consider everything, Changed attitude,' headlined *The Times of India* on 17 September. 'Contrary to his earlier uncompromising attitude Dr. B.R. Ambedkar appeared to be in a conciliatory mood...,' reported the paper. 'Speaking of Mr. Gandhi with the prefix 'Mahatma', so unusual with him, he said, 'I am open to conviction. So far as I am concerned, I am willing to consider everything, though I am not willing to allow the rights of the Depressed Classes to be curtailed in any way.' He had received an invitation from Pandit Madan Mohan Malviya to attend a conference on 19 September in Bombay, Ambedkar said, but he had told the organizers, he continued, that it was no use holding a conference in a vacuum, no use holding it till Gandhiji put forward his proposals: 'As soon as Mr. Gandhi's proposals are known, I will give my answer in fifteen minutes.' He had said the same thing to the delegation that had come from Ahmedabad, he told the paper, as well as Mr. Walchand Hirachand with whom he had talked for three hours. As for his own proposals, Ambedkar still would not specify them. He would not say whether joint electorates with reserved seats would be acceptable, he would not say whether anything other than separate electorates would be acceptable to him.

The correspondent tackled him on the point Rajah had raised—namely that it was the Minorities Pact which had ruined the chances of a settlement. Did the fact of Ambedkar having signed the Minorities Pact during the Second Round Table Conference come in the way of his accepting joint electorates, the correspondent asked him. 'He replied emphatically,' wrote the correspondent. 'I do not know why it should have been described as a "pact",' Ambedkar told the paper. 'It had no binding effect on any of the signatories. It was simply a demand which the signatories stated impliedly... I am perfectly free to do anything I like. There is no handicap or fetter of any kind arising out of the "pact". I am as free an agent as I was before the document was signed. My supreme consideration is the interests of the Depressed Classes, whom I represent and nothing else comes in the way.'

A meeting on a 'personal matter', and a statement

On 18 September, the Poona correspondent of *The Times of India* filed a dispatch: 'Dr. Ambedkar in Poona, Interview with Governor.' 'Dr. Ambedkar arrived at Kirkee station at 11.30 a.m. where he was met by Capt. Morrison, A.-D.-C. and taken to Government House,' the paper reported. Dr. Ambedkar was closeted with the governor for over an hour, the paper disclosed. 'My conference with His Excellency today had absolutely nothing to do with Mr. Gandhi or the present situation,' *The Times of India* reported Ambedkar as saying after meeting the governor. 'His Excellency discussed a personal matter with me and I am not at liberty to disclose at present what that was.' 'He categorically denied that the conference was in connection with the Communal Award or with the question of his attitude towards the Round Table Conference,' the paper reported. 'He did not intend visiting Mr. Gandhi in Yeravda or applying for permission to do so. He had no objection to meeting Mr. Gandhi and hearing his views.' The paper quoted Ambedkar as saying, 'I am prepared to consider Mr. Gandhi's proposals when he chooses to make them known and will not adhere rigidly to my present stand if I consider that by departing from it I can secure conditions which will be more advantageous to my people than those granted by the Communal Award.' 'After the interview,' the correspondent's dispatch concluded, 'he paid a short visit to the Depressed Classes Mission and then returned to a hotel near the station to wait for the afternoon train back to Bombay.'

Whatever the purpose of the meeting with the governor, that very day Ambedkar issued a lengthy and minatory statement, that is on the eve of the conference which Pandit Malviya had convened in Bombay, and with just two days to go before Gandhiji was to begin his fast. Mr Gandhi has no difficulty in accepting separate electorates for Muslims and Sikhs and Indian Christians and Anglo-Indians and Europeans, Ambedkar said, it is only when separate electorates are given to the Depressed Classes that his conscience compels him to prevent them from gaining this advantage—a manifest distortion of what Gandhiji had been maintaining, a manifest misrepresentation in view of what Gandhiji had specifically stated in his letters to the prime minister and the Secretary of State. And yet these are the classes that deserve special treatment more than anyone else, said Ambedkar. For howsoever the Hindus may disagree among themselves, Ambedkar declared as usual, they are joined in a standing conspiracy to mercilessly put down any attempt by the Depressed Classes to acquire even a little share in political power. 'This is not the first attempt on the part of the Mahatma to completely dish the Depressed Classes out of political existence,' Ambedkar continued. 'Long before there was the Minorities Pact, the Mahatma tried to enter into an agreement with the Muslims and the Congress. He offered to the Muslims all the fourteen claims which they had put forth on their behalf, and in return asked them to join with him in resisting the claims for social representation made by me on behalf of the Depressed Classes.'

Separate electorates will not separate the Depressed Classes from Hindu society, Ambedkar said. After all, that is the view of Dr. Moonje, 'a much stronger protagonist of the Hindu case and a militant advocate of its interests,' Ambedkar said.

As for the points which Rajah had raised, Ambedkar was scorn itself. 'Mr. Rajah's fulminations have amused me considerably,' he scoffed. 'An intense supporter of separate electorates and the bitterest and most vehement critic of caste Hindu tyranny, now professes faith in the joint electorates and love for the Hindus! How much of that is due to his natural desire to resuscitate himself from the oblivion in which he was cast by his being kept out of the Round Table Conference and how much of it is due to his honest change of faith, I do not propose to discuss'—said Ambedkar, in a way that was typical of him in dealing with an argument, and even more so with a person who did not acknowledge his supremacy. Yes, Rajah is right, the award does not give the Depressed Classes as much as they deserve, Ambedkar conceded, but he has himself been party to the recommendations of the Indian Central Committee which gave scarcely more. As for the award rupturing Hindu society, I do not agree with Rajah, said Ambedkar. Rajah can always refuse to stand from a constituency under the separate electorate; he can instead stand from a general constituency under the joint electorate—thereby he will have the opportunity to preserve the unity of Hindu society and the caste Hindus will have an opportunity to vote for him—again a typical example of the way Ambedkar would deal with another man's point.

He gave what he said was the scheme which Gandhiji had put to him, and the assurances he said Gandhiji was prepared to give on his behalf and that of the Congress. His point in disclosing these details, Ambedkar said, was to disabuse persons who were saying that Gandhiji would accept joint electorates with seats reserved for the Depressed Classes. He could not leave a question which was so important to 'the protection of my people' to the assurances of the Mahatma and the Congress, Ambedkar said. Neither was immortal. 'There have been many Mahatmas in India whose sole objective was to remove Untouchability and to elevate and absorb the Depressed Classes,' Ambedkar said, 'but everyone has failed in his mission. Mahatmas have come and Mahatmas have gone. But the Untouchables have remained Untouchables'—as you read this, do recall the craven faith the same Ambedkar felt towards and expressed to the British viceroy, Lord Linlithgow.

He had enough experience of 'Hindu reformers', Ambedkar said, 'to say that no well-wisher of the Depressed Classes will ever consent to ever allow the uplift of the Depressed Classes to rest upon such treacherous shoulders.' 'Reformers who in moments of crises prefer to sacrifice their principles rather than hurt the feelings of their kindred,' he continued, 'can be of no use to the Depressed Classes.'

As the British note had done, Ambedkar dubbed Gandhiji's proposed fast to be 'coercion', and declared that 'coercion of this sort will not win the Depressed Classes to the Hindu fold if they are determined to get out.' If the Mahatma were but to ask the Depressed Classes what they would prefer—Hinduism or political power—he would find that they would opt for political power. Should the Mahatma persist in his determination to rob the Depressed Classes of the little that they have got as a result of the award, the consequences would be disastrous, Ambedkar said. His fast would be the occasion for 'terrorism by his followers against the Depressed Classes all over the country,' Ambedkar forecast. Already the nationalist press had been distorting what he—that is, Ambedkar—had been saying, he maintained, it had been suppressing his side of the correspondence, it had been indulging in propaganda against his party by publishing exaggerated accounts of meetings and conferences, 'many of which were never held,' Ambedkar charged. 'Silver bullets' had been used to create divisions in the ranks of the Depressed Classes, he charged. There had been clashes too, some of which had ended in violence, he charged.

The conclusion was both an offer to consider what the Mahatma may have to propose, and also a warning. 'Before concluding this statement,' Ambedkar said, 'I desire to assure the public that although I am entitled to regard the matter as closed, I am prepared to consider the proposals of the Mahatma. I however trust that the Mahatma will not drive me to the necessity of making a choice between his life and the rights of my people. For I can never consent to deliver my people bound hand and foot to the Caste Hindus for generations to come.'

A host of things can be said about the statement, and similar ones which Ambedkar was in the habit of issuing. The presumption, arising from the conviction of his own worth which surfaces so often, but also from the confidence that the British authorities would keep his side of the argument up, a confidence that was born of the liaison he was maintaining with those authorities. The insinuation—that Gandhiji was pushing him to handing over *'my'* people 'bound hand and foot to the Caste Hindus for generations to come', etc. But we need bear in mind only one feature: neither in this statement nor in any other one did Ambedkar have any proposal to offer, his demand was that Gandhiji come up with proposals which would be for him to reject or accept! And how could there be any surprise at this stance? For the award which the British had announced had not been a surprise to him, and, as his statements show, it had been to his satisfaction. Such criticisms as he put out were put out pro forma, more to keep up with what Rajah and other leaders of the Depressed Classes were saying than because he found anything definitely wrong with the award. His heart was in separate electorates, and this is exactly what the British had decreed. As we have seen, the thing he was urging the British in private was not any great modification of the award. He was just wanting some formulation so that this particular feature could not be taken to be lapsing even at the end of twenty years.

The conference in Bombay

The conference which Malviyaji had convened began in Bombay on 19 September. There was much fraternizing among the leaders, *The Times of India* reported. Pressmen asked Rajah for his reactions to the statement Ambedkar had issued. 'I have come here to compose differences,' Rajah told them, 'and do not wish to say anything which might have a contrary effect, though I am in a position to reply to all the points made by Dr. Ambedkar.'

'In one instance,' *The Times of India* reported, 'it is said, when Dr. Ambedkar claimed the right of negotiating with Mr. Gandhi alone and no one else, Mr. P. Baloo, the Bombay Depressed Class leader from the opposite camp, reminded Dr. Ambedkar that he had no mandate from the community to speak on their behalf.' 'In the other instance,' the paper continued, 'when Dr. Ambedkar declared that if the caste Hindus mobilized their forces, as they sought to do by the holding of that evening's meetings in the city, he would do the same and mobilize every Depressed Class man, woman and child, Mr. P. Baloo is said to have retorted by saying that Dr. Ambedkar could claim to represent but a single community out of depressed class communities.' Ambedkar said what he had in his statement—that he was willing to save Gandhiji, but not at the cost of the rights of his people. K. Natarajan, the liberal leader and editor of *The Indian Social Reformer,* thereupon pointed out that the only objection Gandhiji had was to the separate electorates. He reminded Ambedkar, the paper reported, that Gandhiji had made it clear in his correspondence with Sir Samuel Hoare that he would not object to the grant of over-representation under a joint electorate to the Depressed Classes. 'Dr. Ambedkar,' said the paper, 'retorted by saying that that was too vague and did not satisfy him.'

That morning

The day, 20 September, came around. The government did not alter the award. Gandhiji awakened around 2.30 a.m. that night. His concerns and mood are best seen by recounting the letters he wrote at that hour: he wrote to Gurudev Rabindranath Tagore, to his critic Srinivasa Sastri of the Servants of India Society, and to Mirabehn.

To the poet he wrote:

September 20, 1932

Dear Gurudev,

This is early morning 3 o'clock of Tuesday. I enter the fiery gate at noon. If you can bless the effort, I want it. You have been to me a true friend because you have been a candid friend often speaking your thoughts aloud. I had looked forward to a firm opinion from you one way or the other. But you have refused to criticize. Though it can now only be during my fast I will yet prize your criticism, if your heart condemns my action. I am not too proud to make an open confession of my blunder, whatever the cost of the confession, if I find myself in error. If your heart approves of the action I want your blessing. It wall sustain me. I hope I have made myself clear.

My love.

M.K. Gandhi

Later, just as he was handing the letter to the superintendent of the jail, he was given a telegram that Tagore had sent him from Santiniketan. Gandhiji added a postscript to the letter. 'Just as I was handing this to the Superintendent, I got your loving and magnificent wire. It will sustain me in the midst of the storm I am about to enter. I am sending you a wire. Thank you.'

Rabindranath Tagore had said in his telegram: 'It is worth sacrificing precious life for the sake of India's unity and her social integrity. Though we cannot anticipate what effect it may have upon our rulers who may not understand its immense importance for our people we feel certain that the supreme appeal of such self-offering to the conscience of our own countrymen will not be in vain. I fervently hope that we will not callously allow such national tragedy to reach its extreme length. Our sorrowing hearts will follow your sublime penance with reverence and love.'

In the telegram that Gandhiji sent in reply, he told Gurudev: 'Have always experienced God's mercy. Very early this morning I wrote seeking your blessing if you could approve action and behold I have it in abundance in your message just received. Thank you.'

As is well known, Gandhiji and Srinivasa Sastri were often at odds. But he too was much in Gandhiji's mind as the Mahatma was preparing himself for what could well be a journey to death. To him Gandhiji wrote:

September 20, 1932

My Dearest Friend and Brother,

This is early morning of Tuesday just a little after 3 o'clock. I have just finished a brief letter to Gurudev.

You have been ever present before me during these days of anguish. I have perhaps read your thought. You know my regard for you. Though we are as poles asunder, or seem to be, in mental outlook at so many points, our hearts are one. Wherever therefore I have been able to agree with you, it has been a matter of pure joy. Perhaps this step of mine has been for you the last straw. Even so I want to have your laceration. For I do not want you to cease to strive with me—I remained in banishment from my eldest brother for, I think, fourteen years. Year after year he sent me curses by registered post. I rejoiced in his curses. His curses were so many sparks of love—I won him. Six months before his death he saw that I was in the right. One of reasons for his wrath was this very question of untouchability. In our case, I do not know who is in error. But I do know that you are as blood-brother to me. At this (may be) last crisis, you must not cease to strive with me. Send me your curses or your blessings. You may open my eyes, where others have failed, if you think I am in error. You know me too well not to know that I have the God-given capacity of owning mistakes, if the conviction comes to me. Do write or wire to me.

I wrote to you a month ago inquiring about your health. I never got a reply. I wonder if you ever got my postcard.

Deep love.

M.K. Gandhi

The third letter was to Mirabehn. She too had been imprisoned, and was lodged in the Arthur Road prison at Bombay. Out of the reverence she bore for Gandhiji, she had applied for permission to see him once before he commenced his fast. The permission had been refused. She had been greatly distressed. Gandhiji had heard of her anguish. To her he wrote:

September 20, 1932

Chi. Mira,

I got up at 2.30 today to write to Gurudev, then to Sastri and then to you. I have your tearing letter. At first I thought I would send it to the Governor. But I rejected the thought as soon as it came. You have chosen to enter the furnace. You must remain in it. My society is no easy job as you have seen all these years. Drink then the poison to the last dregs.

As I wrote that first letter conveying my vow, I thought of you and of Ba. And for a time I became giddy. How would you two bear the thing? But the voice within said, 'If you will enter in, you must give up thought of all attachment.' And the letter went. No anguish will be too terrible to wash out the sin of untouchability. You must therefore rejoice in this suffering and bear it bravely. I know how difficult all this is to do. Yet that is exactly what you have to try to do. Just think and realize that there is no meaning in having the last look. The spirit which you love is always with you. The body through which you learnt to love the spirit is no longer necessary for sustaining that love. It is well that it lasts whilst there is use for it. It is equally well that it perishes when there is no use for it. And since we don't know when it will outlast its use, we conclude that death through whatever cause means that there was no longer any use for it. If it is any comfort, know that Vallabhbhai, Mahadev, Ramdas, Surendra, Devdas, whom I have met are all bearing the thing wonderfully well. Love to your companions. I am glad Kisen is with you. She is a good and brave girl. May God sustain you.

Love.

Bapu[24]

In far away Santiniketan

Far away in Santiniketan, Gurudev Rabindranath Tagore addressed his disciples and associates. The Mahatma's fast is the final, ultimate exposition of non-violence, he said. He began by placing Gandhiji in the context of the great souls who establish their dominion by the power of truth, whose dominion lasts even while they may no longer be present in body. He contrasted the enduring influence of persons such as the Mahatma with the evanescence of their tormentors, and told the assembly that 'those rulers who come from outside remain outside the gate, and directly they are called away from the cloud-topping tower of their foreign possessions the stupendous fabric of unreality vanishes in the void.' 'A shadow is darkening today over India like a shadow cast by an eclipsed sun,' Tagore began. 'The people of a whole country is suffering from a poignant pain of anxiety, the universality of which carries in it a great dignity of consolation. Mahatmaji, who through his life of dedication has made India his own in truth, has commenced his vow of extreme self-sacrifice.'

'Each country has its own inner geography where her spirit dwells,' Gurudev said, 'and where physical force can never conquer even an inch of ground. Those rulers who come from outside remain outside the gate, and directly

24 For the preceding letters, Mahatma Gandhi, *Collected Works*, Vol. LI, pp. 101–03.

they are called away from the cloud-topping tower of their foreign possessions the stupendous fabric of unreality vanishes in the void. But the great soul, who achieves victory through the power of truth, continues his dominion even when he is physically no longer present. And we all know such achievement belongs to Mahatmaji. The fact that he has staked his life for a further and final realization of his hope fills us with awe and makes us think.'

He warned against our habit of reducing even the deepest quest to mere ritual, and then to take that ritual to be the real thing. 'Our leaders have requested us to observe fasting for this day, and there is no harm in it,' he said and warned, 'But there is the risk of some unthinking people putting it in the same category with the fasting that Mahatmaji has begun to observe. Nothing can be more disastrous for us than the utter lessening of the value of a heroic expression of truth by paying it the homage of a mere ceremonial expression of feeling by a people emotionally inclined. The penance which Mahatmaji has taken upon himself is not a ritual but a message to all India and to the world. If we must make that message our own, we should accept it in the right manner through a proper process of realization. The gift of sacrifice has to be received in a spirit of sacrifice.'

He went on to elaborate the great sin that untouchability constituted, how it disabled a large proportion of our own brothers, and also the rest by coarsening and dehumanizing society. This is what Gandhiji had set out to expel, Tagore pointed out. He said, 'Mahatmaji has repeatedly pointed out the danger of those divisions in our country that are permanent insults to humanity, but our attention has not been drawn to the importance of its rectification with the same force as it has been to the importance of Khaddar. The social iniquities upon which all our enemies found their principal support have our time-honoured loyalty, making it difficult for us to uproot them. Against that deep-seated moral weakness in our society Mahatmaji has pronounced his ultimatum, and, though it may be our misfortune to lose him in the battlefield, the fight will be passed to everyone of us to be carried on to the final end. It is the gift of the fight which he is going to offer to us, and if we do not know how to accept it humbly and yet with proud determination, if we cheaply dismiss it with some ceremonials to which we are accustomed and allow the noble life to be wasted with its great meaning missed, then our people will passively roll down the slope of degradation to the blankness of utter futility.'

Tagore turned finally to the incomprehension with which the British had reacted to the Mahatma's resolve, and to the charge that he was taking too extreme a step. The poet said, 'We have observed that the English people are puzzled at the step that Mahatmaji has been compelled to take. They confess that they fail to understand it. I believe that the reason of their failure is mainly owing to the fact that the language of Mahatmaji is fundamentally different from their own. His method of protest is not in accord with the method which they usually follow in cases of grave political crisis. I ask them to remember the terrible days of atrocities that reddened in blood at their door when dismemberment was being forced between Ireland and the rest of Great Britain. Those Englishmen, who imagined it to be disastrous to the integrity of their Empire did not scruple to kill and be killed, even to tear into shreds the decency of civilized codes of honour. The West is accustomed to such violent outbursts in times of desperation and, therefore, such a procedure did not seem strange to them, though to some of them it must have appeared wrong.'

Equally, Gurudev pointed out, 'The dismemberment of a large portion of Hindu society is certainly fatal to its wholeness, and when all our appeals are stubbornly dismissed the reason should not be incomprehensible to other people as to why Mahatmaji is voicing the extreme form of protest on behalf of India. I ask them to imagine what would have happened when the Roman Catholic community of England suffered from a forcible deprivation of its common rights, if some foreign power had come and with efficient benevolence alienated them from the rest of the nation. Very likely the people would like to resort to the method of protest which they consider as honourable in its red fury of violence. In our case the feeling may be similar, though Mahatmaji has made use of its expression which is his own. The message of non-violence, so often expressed by him in words and in deeds, finds today its final exposition in a great language which should be easiest to understand.'[25]

The fast begins

At the Yeravda prison Gandhiji was busy as usual.

There were visitors, among them leaders who had come from Bombay to get his reactions to further formulae which were being tried out. In addition, there was a pile of correspondence to be attended to, there were many telegrams which had to be sent to persons who had been writing and sending him urgent messages from within India and from other parts of the world.

Among the letters he wrote that day was one which was to acquire significance in the coming days. The Depressed Classes leader, P.N. Rajbhoj, had written to Gandhiji seeking his views on the issues which had been thrown up by the government's award and his own fast. The letter had arrived the previous day, and Gandhiji had referred to it

---

25 For the text of Gurudev Tagore's statement, Pyarelal, *The Epic Fast*, Navjivan, Ahmedabad, 1932, pp. 243–47.

during his meeting with the delegation from Bombay. He would reply to it at the earliest opportunity, Gandhiji had told them. Writing as he commenced the fast, Gandhiji told Rajbhoj, 'My fast has reference only to separate electorate. As soon as that is withdrawn the letter of the vow will be satisfied and I would be bound to call off the fast. But a very heavy responsibility will then lie upon me of having a substitute that is infinitely superior to separate electorate.'

Is there any ambiguity in what he was saying? It was exactly what he had been repeating to all who had been meeting him, and to everyone with whom he had been in correspondence about the matter. Yet at the very time in Bombay Ambedkar was maintaining that Gandhiji's purpose and objective was not clear, that it was for Gandhiji to put forward concrete proposals.

Rajbhoj had asked Gandhiji about the formula which leaders like Rajah and others had been favouring, that is joint electorates with statutory reservations for the Depressed Classes. Gandhiji said, 'Looking at the matter in this light [that is, as a person who though a "touchable" by birth was an "untouchable" by choice] I must say that I am not in love with the idea of statutory reservation. Whilst it is not open to the same objection that separate electorate is, I have not a shadow of a doubt that it will prevent the natural growth of the suppressed classes and will remove the incentive to honourable amends from the suppressers. What I am aiming at is a heart understanding between the two, the greatest opportunity of repentance and reparation on the part of the suppressers. I am certain that the moment is ripe for the change of heart among them. I would therefore favour widest possible franchise for the suppressed and establish a convention between the two sections for securing proper election of representatives of the suppressed.' He noted that he had drafted a 'rough tentative scheme' which he had handed to associates and to

Devdas. 'But to me this is not the largest but it is the least part of the reform I want,' he wrote.

'Nothing will satisfy me till the last vestige of untouchability is gone,' he wrote. 'I would therefore insist on a statutory declaration that all public places of worship, wells, schools, etc., should be open to the suppressed precisely on the same terms as the suppressers.' 'This is roughly my idea,' he said. 'If, however, the representatives of suppressed classes will not look at my idea, they are at liberty to have statutory reservation of seats. I should not fast against it but you will not expect me to bless any such scheme. Nor is my blessing essential to its acceptance by the Government. If I get the opportunity, I should certainly try to create public opinion among the suppressed against statutory reservation.'

He told Rajbhoj that if the position he had set out was not clear or not satisfactory, he would be delighted to meet Rajbhoj, Ambedkar and Rajah. 'As you are aware,' he wrote in conclusion alluding to the restrictions under which he had been at the jail till then, 'this has become possible only now.' The letter was made available by Rajah to the press as well as the participants in the conference in Bombay.

There was not the slightest doubt about the immediate issue, there was not the slightest doubt that on the alternative formula—of reservations under joint electorates—while Gandhiji remained opposed to it in principle, he would accept any settlement which the leaders arrived at using this as the basis.

Gandhiji pinpointed his ultimate goal in yet another letter he wrote that day to an associate who had remonstrated with him that his decision to fast was contrary to both reason and dharma. Gandhiji wrote, 'My Step has not been dictated by reason; it was inspired by my inner voice. My reason, however, told me: "Hundreds of persons like you will probably have to die in order to remove the blot of untouchability."

Fasting is a very common practice in Hinduism. I have always loved it. My decision is the cry of my heart. The Prime Minister's decision was only the immediate cause. It provided me with an opportunity to undertake the fast. However, the aim of my fast is not merely to get the decision changed but to bring about the awakening and self-purification which are bound to result from the effort to get the decision changed. In other words this was an opportunity to strike at the very root of untouchability.'[26]

All this was written and felt on the very day that Gandhiji began a journey that could for all he knew end in his death. Could there be any doubt about his commitment to the cause of purging our religion and society of this evil excrescence? But Ambedkar was to read things all together spiteful, even diabolical into these prayerful statements, as we shall soon see.

While the country was in ferment, Pyarelal wrote in his account of the fast, 'Gandhiji after the 13th had passed into a perfect calm and serenity of the spirit.' 'The fateful twentieth of September arrived at last,' Pyarelal wrote of that day. 'He rose early in the small hours of the morning as usual and had his favourite *"Vaishnava Jana"* sung at the morning prayer... He had his usual meal of milk and fruit in the morning. From 6.30 to 8 a.m. he had the Gita recited to him by one of his companions. At 11.30 a.m. he had his last meal of lemon-juice and honey with hot water. The fateful hour approached. The little group prepared themselves for the ordeal by singing a beautiful song sent to Gandhiji by Shrimati Rehanaben, the eldest daughter of Sjt. Abbas Tyabji, the Grand Old Man of Gujarat...

'The jail bell at last struck twelve... Gandhiji's "tussle with God" had commenced.'

---

26 Mahatma Gandhi, *Collected Works*, Vol. LI, pp. 111–12.

Later that day journalists were allowed to go into the prison to meet Gandhiji.

'For the first time in nine months journalists were allowed to see Mr. Gandhi in Yeravda Jail this evening at 5.30 when they were treated to one of the most easily delivered and seriously thoughtful interviews to which it has ever been my fortune to listen,' began the account of *The Times of India* correspondent. 'No journalist could see Mr. Gandhi today and discuss the position with him five hours after he had begun "a fast unto death" without being immensely impressed,' he continued. 'We were ushered into a long narrow room,' he reported, 'surrounded by shelves in which were piled jail-made *durries,* blankets and other articles, the labour of a thousand convicts, and *Swadeshi* to the last thread. There sitting in a chair smiling a welcome was the man upon whom the attention of all India and of the entire Western world, as well as a very large proportion of the Orient has been focused for the last several days.'

'My first question was in regard to the statement I had published earlier that he was indisposed,' the correspondent wrote. 'I was never fitter in my life,' Gandhiji said, 'In fact I have actually been putting on weight. When I was weighed last I was 103 pounds which was a pound more than in the previous week.'

At the very outset Gandhiji expressed surprise that the statement which he had sent to the government on 15 September had still not been released. He went on to reiterate the points which he had been stressing in letters, statements, interviews. 'My fast is only against separate electorates,' he pointed out, 'and not against statutory reservation of seats. To say that I am damaging the cause by uncompromising opposition to statutory reservation of seats is only partly true. Opposed I was, and am even now, but there was never put before me for any acceptance or rejection a scheme for statutory reservation of seats. Therefore, there is no question of my having to decide upon that point. When I developed my own idea about that point, I certainly expressed disappointment, and in my humble opinion, such statutory reservation, short of doing service, may do harm in the sense that it will stop natural evolution. Statutory reservation is like a support to a man. Relying on such support to any extent, he weakens himself.'

Gandhiji pointed out that he was one with, that he was of the 'Depressed Classes', and it was this intimate acquaintance with them which had convinced him 'that if they are ever to rise, it will not be by reservation of seats but will be by strenuous work of Hindu reformers in their midst, and it is because I feel that this separation would have killed all prospect of reform that my whole soul has rebelled against it; and, let me make it plain, that the withdrawal of separate electorates will satisfy the letter of my vow but will never satisfy the spirit behind it, and in my capacity of being a self-chosen Untouchable, I am not going to rest content with a patched-up pact between the "touchables" and the untouchables.'

'What I want, what I am living for, and what I should delight in dying for, is the eradication of untouchability root and branch,' he told the journalists. 'I want, therefore, a living pact whose life-giving effect should be felt not in the distant tomorrow but today, and, therefore, that pact should be sealed by an all-India demonstration of "touchables" and untouchables meeting together, not by way of a theatrical show, but in real brotherly embrace. It is in order to achieve this, the dream of my life for the past fifty years, that I have entered today the fiery gates. The British Government's decision was the last straw. It was a decisive symptom, and with the unerring eye of the physician that I claim to be in such matters, I detected the symptom. Therefore, for me the abolition of separate electorates would be but the beginning of the end, and I would warn all those leaders assembled at Bombay and others against coming to any hasty decision.'

'My life I count of no consequence,' he said. 'One hundred lives given for this noble cause would, in my opinion, be poor penance done by Hindus for the atrocious wrongs they have heaped upon helpless men and women of their own faith. I, therefore, would urge them not to swerve an inch from the path of strictest justice. My fast I want to throw in the scales of justice, and if it wakes up caste Hindus from their slumber, and if they are roused to a sense of their duty, it will have served its purpose. Whereas, if out of blind affection for me, they would somehow or other come to a rough and ready agreement so as to secure the abrogation and then go off to sleep, they will commit a grievous blunder and will have made my life a misery. For, while the abrogation of separate electorates would result in my breaking the fast, it would be living death for me if the vital pact for which I am striving is not arrived at. It would simply mean that, as soon as I called off the fast, I would have to give notice of another in order to achieve the spirit of the vow to the fullest extent.'

Such were the affirmations of the Mahatma just hours into a journey that could lead to death—but for Ambedkar, as we shall see, it was all a stunt, indeed the stunt of an insincere man, that of a dishonest man, a man given to conspiring against the Untouchables.

'In attacking untouchability I have gone to the very root of the matter, and, therefore, it is an issue of transcendental value, far surpassing *Swaraj* in terms of political constitutions,' Gandhiji declared, 'and I would say that such a constitution would be a dead weight if it was not backed by a moral basis, in the shape of the present hope engendered in the breasts of the downtrodden millions that that weight is going to be lifted from their shoulders.' Reverting to the point he had made in his letter to the British prime minister, Gandhiji said, 'It is only because English officials cannot possibly see this living side of the picture that in their ignorance and self-satisfaction they dare to sit as judges upon questions that affect the fundamental being of millions of people, and here I mean both caste Hindus and untouchables, that is, the suppresser and the suppressed; and it was in order to wake up even officialdom from its gross ignorance, if I may make use of such an expression without being guilty of offence, that I felt impelled by a voice from within to offer resistance with the whole of my being.'

He was not out to make a martyr of himself: 'I am as anxious as anyone to live,' he told the correspondents. 'Water has an infinite capacity for prolonging life, and I will take water whenever I feel I require it. You can depend upon me to make a supreme effort to hold myself together so that the Hindu conscience may be quickened as also the British conscience and this agony may end. My cry will rise to the throne of the Almighty God.'[27]

Even this statement Ambedkar twisted and caricatured, and, as we shall see, presented as proof of the fact that Gandhiji's fast was just a put-on, a stunt.

Throughout the next day Gandhiji, in addition to keeping up his usual routine—spinning and the rest—received a number of visitors. Among the visitors were Rajbhoj as well as the delegation from the Bombay conference. 'Agreement tomorrow or never,' remarked G.D. Birla as he came out after discussing possible formulae with Gandhiji, 'he is beginning to show signs of strain,' Birla reported. 'Mr. Gandhi has been removed by the jail authorities from his old quarters to quarters nearer the main entrance so that visitors may be taken to him,' *The Times of India* reported. 'He is seated on a cot, and it is said by those who have seen him that he does not intend to move about more than he can

27 Mahatma Gandhi, *Collected Works*, Vol. LI, pp. 116–20.

help in his effort to conserve his energy.' 'There is no doubt,' the paper continued, 'that he has commenced in dreadful earnest his struggle against death which, according to his own statement, he has no desire to meet. All that passes his lips now is water and of this he partakes at regular intervals. It is understood that for his own sake the Government intend strictly limiting the number of interviews in future in order that he may not be put to unnecessary strain.'

'Visitors to Mr. Gandhi say that the whole business must be complete within seven or eight days at the very outside as it is feared that by the end of ten days Mr. Gandhi will not be in full possession of the faculties of speech and hearing and will be unable to take part in any reasoned discussions,' the paper's correspondent reported. 'It is also feared that after ten days he may become so weak and ill that he may never recover. It is felt that he may live at the most 25 to 30 days. Those who have seen him say that jail conditions are not conducive to keeping him alive for a long time.'

The paper also carried a dispatch from the Associated Press which reported that after the first day of his fast Gandhiji was in good spirits.

And just below it a statement from Ambedkar, which even after all these decades shocks one as to his priorities. 'Nothing to do with Mr. Rajah', ran the headline, 'Dr. Ambedkar's statement'. Mr Gandhi had invited him and Mr Rajah, Ambedkar told the paper, to discuss the proposals which he had submitted to the committee that the Bombay conference had set up.

'I have accepted the invitation,' Ambedkar told the paper, 'but I have made it clear that I will have nothing to do in the way of negotiation with Mr. Rajah and his party, and if Mr. Gandhi wishes to talk with them, he should do so separately. My reason for saying this is that the dispute is really between me and my party on the one hand and Mr.

Gandhi on the other'—exactly what the British note for 'indirect publicity' had said should be emphasized, except that Ambedkar had made the point even more specific. 'Besides,' Ambedkar continued, 'I do wish to mark my emphatic disapproval of the policy of the Congress and the Hindu Mahasabha of creating leaders for the Depressed Class for their own purposes and by their own propaganda and then trying to foist them on the Depressed Classes. In this there is nothing personal against Mr. Rajah. I am starting tonight.'

Within the walls of Yeravda Jail that same day, 21 September, among the visitors who met Gandhiji with their varied ideas for a solution was a delegation on behalf of the Depressed Classes consisting of P.M. Rajbhoj and two associates, S.M. Mate and Limaye. Gandhiji's concerns, his vision, his utter dedication to the cause of uplifting the Untouchables and of eradicating this blot from Hindu society leap up from the record of the conversation. His target was the orthodoxy: in any agreement that came to be signed he wanted a provision by which temples would be opened to all Hindus, he was even in favour of legislation to safeguard the right of all to have access to public places of worship. He told Rajbhoj and the others, 'If I had my way I would insist on temple-entry and the like being included in any pact that may be concluded and I would invite all reformers and untouchables to do so. I am aware that temple-entry is a difficult thing to accomplish in the very limited time that my life can hold out against the fast, but all the parties to the pact should pledge themselves to realize this elementary right of human beings at the earliest opportunity. At the same time I do not want this fast to be used for coercing orthodoxy. The fast is certainly intended to sting even orthodoxy into thinking. But if they cannot get on to this elementary truth about human rights we must have patience. But temples and the like are the property not of orthodoxy but of all Hindus. Therefore this idea of excluding a section of Hindus from the use of public utilities is itself a species of violence, and, therefore, the support of legislation has got to be invoked in order to protect this fundamental right. I recognize, however, that if the majority of the Hindus are against the exercise of this right by the so-called untouchables, mere legislation will be wholly ineffective. But my opinion is that the mind of the majority is for this reform if it comes stealthily. Therefore, reformers should prepare the ground now ceaselessly and vigilantly to convert the passive attitude towards the reform into active approval thereof. This rising tide of opinion in favour of the reform will convince orthodoxy that it is inevitable. The work, therefore, must be free of all violence, even mental.'

Gandhiji reiterated his belief that the first and primary requirement was the missionary work of Hindu reformers, and that what he was really after was social and religious reform of Hindu society. Of course, the immediate task was to ensure that the separation of Depressed Classes from the rest of Hindu society which the separate electorates were going to bring about was prevented, and while he retained serious misgivings about reservations of seats under joint electorates as a solution, if this was what the others agreed to in the circumstances, Gandhiji said, he would go along, though 'with utmost reluctance'.

Gandhiji told the visitors, 'Legislation in a free State always represents the will of the majority. All legislation in advance of general opinion argues bankruptcy of missionary effort. My reliance, therefore, always has been on missionary enterprises. Therefore, for the pact to be a living pact, it is absolutely necessary that it should be a condition precedent to an acceptance of the political part of it, that the caste Hindus party to the pact will not only endorse it but actively move in the matter. My own opinion is quite clear. I would accept any pact that has not a tinge of separate electorate about it. I would, with the utmost reluctance, tolerate reservation of seats under a joint electorate scheme. But I should insist upon what is to me the vital part of the pact, the social and religious reform. And, therefore, whilst if a settlement is arrived at on the joint electorate scheme and separate electorate is withdrawn by the British Government, I will break my fast, I will immediately give notice to the millions of Hindus, who have flocked round me at the innumerable meetings from one end of India to the other, that if within, say, six months the social reform is not demonstrably achieved, the fast will be taken up again. For, if I do not do so I would be guilty of betraying God in whose name I have taken this great fast and the interest of untouchables for whose sake it has been taken.'

What these leaders felt about Ambedkar, how they were convinced that he was playing along with the British, and that the British would begin projecting someone else should Ambedkar agree to some compromise, comes out graphically in the concluding part of the record of the interview of these Depressed Class leaders with Gandhiji. Apparently, the leaders had urged Gandhiji to give up his fast on the ground that, just as Ambedkar was being intransigent at the moment, should even he be brought around to accepting a compromise, the government could just as easily put up some other leader who would then take an equally intransigent position, and Gandhiji would have to go on fasting till death. The record has Gandhiji remarking, 'Sjt. Rajbhoj fears that if Dr. Ambedkar accepts a reasonable compromise, Government may call another leader into being who will declare his opposition, and if that fear is realized there would be eternal opposition by the Government to any pact, and, therefore, my fast must end in my death, and that, therefore, I should give up the fast. Granting that Mr. Rajbhoj's fear is justified I cannot undo a pledge taken with God as witness. We are not able to forecast all future events. We can, therefore, only control our acts, and it is well with us and our cause if we unflinchingly act on the square in spite of the heaviest odds. Our final trust must rest upon the assured victory of truth. Such correct action has without exception confounded the opponents and brought out the intended result, granting of course that the cause is as just as the action is correct. I must not, therefore, on any account, suspend the fast unless its terms are fulfilled.'[28]

By the evening of 21 September, there had been a visible deterioration in Gandhiji's condition. He had been on fast for only thirty-six hours as yet, but clearly he had been drained by the interminable discussions. *The Times of India* reported, 'Intimate friends and associates who were with him in the evening state that they detect a perceptible falling off in Mr. Gandhi's physical condition at the end of thirty six hours fasting. This they attribute to the large demands made on him in the course of the day by numerous interviews involving discussion of a complicated political scheme with persons of varying temperaments. Mr. Gandhi, however, fully kept up his customary regimen sustained only by frequent sips of water. He was able to spin his daily quota of yarn and hold prayers both in the morning and in the evening. It is recalled that he continued these two items of his daily life to the end of his 21 days' fasting in Delhi eight years ago. One who was in attendance on him then states that the first four or five days are the most critical and call for the greatest possible care.'

The next day also the discussions continued—Pyarelal's *The Epic Fast* gives a day-by-day account of these discussions and the formulae that were being weighed. The leaders meeting in Bombay would come up with some

28 Mahatma Gandhi, *Collected Works,* Vol. LI, pp. 125–27.

alternative formulae. They would then travel to Gandhiji to get his reaction. Some hitch would develop. They would travel to Gandhiji so that he might cut through the knot. Ambedkar would insist on some point which the others just could not accept. All would troop to Gandhiji so that he might rule on the matter....

The government was of course not inactive, it was never far from the scene. Among other things, it was ensuring 'indirect publicity'. A typical item in *The Times of India* will repay reading in full. Even after sixty years it speaks volumes: about the lobbies the British were trying to work up, about their efforts to put down those like Rajah who were opposing Ambedkar. In its issue of 23 September *The Times of India's* 'Special Correspondent' in Simla reported as follows:

* * *

Modification of The Communal Award
Condition Needed
Solid Proof of Assent By Depressed Classes
Princes & Mr. Gandhi's Fast
(From Our Special Correspondent)

Simla, September 22. Any agreement reached in Bombay to prevent Mr. Gandhi from starving himself to death will have to be backed up by solid proof that it has the assent of Depressed Classes, at any rate the major portion of them, before it finds acceptance with Government.

Mr. Gandhi's fast is having its repercussions in the most unexpected quarters. It has given much food for thought to several of the Princes now gathered in Simla. Some of them are seriously asking among themselves as to what is there to prevent Mr. Gandhi once he succeeds by a self-imposed fast in driving the Depressed Classes into a particular line of action from practicing this kind of *satyagraha* over some other issue. The fact that Mr. Gandhi's present fast is based on religious consideration rather than on a political issue as such does not affect the argument that one has heard advanced by the Princes.

The more far-seeing among them have pictured the possibility of the fast or Gandhi proclaiming another fast or deciding upon something else equally novel at a future date to mobilize public opinion in order to compel one or more of the States who may join the proposed Federation into a particular course of action.

Princes' Fears

This line of thought is not exactly helpful in persuading the Princes to trust their fortunes at least in part into the hands of those who would have control of the Federal machinery and is in fact calculated to make them recede further and further away from the ideal to which they subscribed after considerable hesitation at the first Round Table Conference. As most people who know anything about the Indian States must be aware several of their age long customs and usages have a religious touch about them. In the temples of some of these States even high Caste Hindus who have crossed the seas, let alone the Depressed Classes, have not the right of worship. Then again in several Hindu States there are numerous State ceremonials in which the Depressed Classes and non-Hindus are not allowed to participate. The caste system is very rigid in most of them. It is as utterly impossible today to persuade the average Marwari of the Rajputana and Central India States to treat a member of the Depressed Class as his brother as it is to ask the Nambudiris of Travancore and Cochin to permit the shadow of an untouchable to fall on them.

Supposing for the sake of argument that one of the Rajputana states like Bikaner and another from the South like Travancore join the Federation, what is there to prevent Mr. Gandhi, once his present move succeeds, to mobilize public opinion in British India against these States to compel their rulers to adopt particular lines of action and to see to it that the moral authority of the Federal Government is thrown in his favour? This is the kind of question which is being quietly debated among the Princes assembled in Simla. Possibly such an attitude of mind is encouraged by those who are not enthusiastic about the Federation scheme. It is equally possible of course, that it represents a pristine fear among the pro-Federationist group. What is significant is its existence.

Muslim Attitude

Then there are the Muslims. The silence that most of them have maintained during the past few days does not mean that they have no point of view to urge. A number of Muslim members of the Central Legislature with whom I have discussed the subject tell me that they are simply waiting to see the outcome of the Hindu leaders' negotiations with Mr. Gandhi. If they reach an agreement within the four corners of the Award the Muslims would then examine it to see if it affected them in any way.

As regards the attitude of the Government of India, the facilities they have given to Mr. Gandhi and to those who desire to see him clearly establish their *bona fides* in the matter.

If Government is convinced that any agreement reached does not upset the Communal Award in any other direction, steps will be taken to secure its 'ratification'.

Mr. Rajah's Somersaults

The latest advices from Bombay and Poona are certainly not couched in optimistic vein and the developments are anxiously watched at Simla. Though Mr. M.C. Rajah has not allowed the caste Hindus to make him a tool in their hands as against Dr. Ambedkar, he is, at the moment, certainly far more popular than Dr. Ambedkar in the Nationalist press. So much play has been made of Dr. Ambedkar's inconsistency in supporting first joint electorates for the Depressed Classes and then swearing by separate electorates that it is only fair to him to bring out the fact that Mr. Rajah has indulged in metamorphosis in precisely the opposite direction. Only in October last year, Mr. Rajah presided at a conference of the Depressed Classes in Madras at which resolutions were passed opining that no constitutional reform without separate electorates would be acceptable to them.

A few weeks later, Mr. Rajah, presiding at the ninth session of the All-India Depressed Classes Conference, held at Gurgaon, Punjab, denounced the Caste Hindus and Mr. Gandhi.

Then came Mr. Rajah's somersault and his pact with Dr. Moonje. Government may well doubt which is the real voice of the Depressed Classes.

* * *

The same day, Rajbhoj strongly criticized the formulae Ambedkar was insisting on. Rajbhoj said that these proposals were no different from separate electorates, and, more important, these demands that Ambedkar was pushing were 'based upon the interests of a small section of the Depressed Classes which he represented and [were] not in the interests of the Depressed Classes as a whole in India.' Speaking from personal knowledge—the correspondence he had had with Gandhiji, the interviews he had had with the Mahatma—Rajbhoj said that while Gandhiji continued to have doubts about joint electorates with reservation of seats for the Depressed Classes, he would accept a settlement which the leaders might reach on this basis. The letter of his fast having been fulfilled by the withdrawal of separate electorates, he would end his fast. Leaders should therefore strive for a solution on this basis.

By 23 September, Gandhiji had tired even more. While 'no alarming symptoms' have developed, the papers reported, 'a feeling of nausea occasionally steals over him. He has difficulty in keeping his eyes open and his voice has grown feeble. He, however, had frequent snatches of sleep during the day, which on the whole, was free from exhausting political discussion for him.'

The government was continuing its 'indirect publicity'. While reporting that should the leaders arrive at some settlement, it would 'receive the immediate and most careful consideration of the Viceroy and his Executive Council', the 'Special Correspondent' of *The Times of India* in Simla reported in terms that gave credence to the apprehension which Rajbhoj had expressed to Gandhiji, namely, that even if Ambedkar were to be brought around, the government could put up some other leader to take an extreme stand. The dispatch from Simla said:

> In the midst of the excitement and emotion produced by Mr. Gandhi's fast some people are apt to lose sight of the fact that any agreement reached in Bombay, if it is to receive official endorsement, must fulfil two important tests. First of all, the agreement must be real in the sense that it must have the full backing of the parties concerned and must be acceptable to the Depressed Classes as

a whole. Secondly, it must fall within the four corners of the Premier's Award.

In regard to the first test, Mr. Rajah and Dr. Ambedkar are not the only spokesmen of the Depressed Classes and Government may require evidence that any arrangement the former may come to with Pandit Malaviya and other Caste Hindu leaders has the support of their communities as a whole, more particularly in the Madras Presidency where the 'Untouchables' are subjected to the worst imaginable treatment.

Late that evening Dr H.D. Gilder examined Gandhiji. He told the press that while Gandhiji had had a fair night, and while his heart action was till then good and his blood pressure was 180 by 100, 'I feel that the margin of safety would soon be passed if unnecessary interviews and the strain of present negotiations that are being carried on in consultation with him are not stopped. Once that margin is passed, even if the fast is broken his life would still be in danger.'

By 24 September, his condition had deteriorated to such an extent that the Government of Bombay informed the viceroy and the Secretary of State in a *Clear Line* wire:

Clear Line. Medical authorities report that Gandhi has now reached stage when two days or so more might see complete collapse both physical and mental and that he is not likely to be able to continue negotiations for much longer. It is just possible that settlement between Caste Hindu and Depressed Class leaders may be reached and agreed to by Gandhi tonight. If reached it will be communicated to Government of India at once. Meanwhile in view of Gandhi's condition we are preparing to move him if necessary to suitable residence near Poona. Gandhi's present intention is to continue fasting until orders on settlement are received from His Majesty's Government but his friends hope to prevail upon him to break his fast pending the receipt of these orders.

At long last the leaders reached agreement on all the points, and the terms were reported to Gandhiji. He signalled his approval. The Poona Pact was signed by Pandit Madan Mohan Malviya, M.R. Jayakar, Sir Tej Bahadur Sapru, Chunilal Mehta, B.R. Ambedkar, M.C. Rajah, Solanki, a lieutenant of Ambedkar, Rajaji, G.D. Birla and twenty others. Rajaji and Ambedkar exchanged the pens with which they had signed the agreement. The text was communicated to the government at once, for every hour mattered.

The Poona Pact

By virtue of this pact the Untouchables were given 148 seats in the legislatures as against the seventy-eight which they had received under the government's award. The more significant change was in the way the legislators belonging to Depressed Classes were to be elected. Under the British scheme these legislators were to be elected by an electorate consisting exclusively of the Depressed Classes: seventy-eight seats had been reserved under this category. Members of these castes were also to have a vote in electing legislators from the general constituencies—that is, they were to have two votes each, one for electing exclusively Depressed Class legislators and another one to elect legislators falling in the general category. The arrangement was to continue for twenty years. By the Poona Pact, the number of seats given to the Depressed Classes was increased to 148. But the basis for electing legislators to them was overturned. The election was to be in two stages. In the first round, Harijans in the reserved constituency were to elect a panel of four candidates; in the second round all voters of the constituency, irrespective of caste, were to elect the person they wanted to be their representative. This arrangement for electing a panel of four in the primary election was to come to an end after ten years 'unless terminated sooner by mutual agreement'. The reservation of seats in the provincial and Central legislatures was to 'continue until determined by mutual agreement between the communities concerned in this settlement.'[29]

Several things about the terms were vital. The electorate which elected the representative would be a common one. The agreement also followed what Gandhiji had maintained all

---

29 The agreement to which the leaders affixed their signatures was as follows:

The following has been arrived at between leaders acting on behalf of the Depressed Classes and of the rest of the Hindu community regarding the representation of the Depressed Classes in the Legislatures and certain other matters affecting their welfare.

1. There shall be seats reserved for the Depressed Classes out of the general electorate seats in the Provincial Legislatures as follows:- Madras: 30; Bombay with Sind:15; Punjab: 8; Bihar and Orissa:18; Central Province: 20; Assam: 7; Bengal: 30; the United Provinces: 20; *Total-148*

These figures are based on the total strength of the Provincial Councils announced in the Prime Minister's decision.

2. Election to these seats shall be by joint electorates subject however to the following procedure: All the members of the Depressed Classes registered in the general electoral roll of a constituency will form an Electoral College which will elect a panel of four candidates belonging to the Depressed Classes for each of such reserved seats by the method of the single vote, and four persons getting the highest number of votes in such primary election shall be the candidates for election by the general electorate.

3. The representation of the Depressed Classes in the Central Legislature shall likewise be on the principle of joint electorates and reserved seats by the method of primary election in the manner provided for in Clause 2 above for their representation in the Provincial Legislatures.

4. In the Central Legislature 18 per centum of the seats allotted to the general electorate for British India in the said Legislature shall be reserved for the Depressed Classes.

5. The system of primary election to a panel of candidates for election to the Central and Provincial Legislatures as hereinbefore mentioned shall come to an end after the first ten years unless terminated sooner by mutual agreement under the provisions of Clause 6 below.

6. The system of representation of Depressed Classes by reserved seats in the Provincial and Central Legislatures as provided for in Clauses 1 and 4 shall continue until determined by mutual agreement between the communities concerned in this settlement.

7. The franchise for the Central and Provincial Legislatures for the Depressed Classes shall be as indicated in the Lothian Committee Report.

along: namely, that he would give any concession whatsoever to thwart the manoeuvre of the British to divide Hindu society permanently. But the most significant gain was an altogether different one: the pact was an agreement arrived at by and among Indians themselves without the British being given a look-in.

Thoughts on the last day

There was now the waiting. Gandhiji's condition was deteriorating by the hour, but he had said that he would not break the fast till the separate electorates were withdrawn. Congratulations started pouring in from all over. Srinivasa Sastri's wire arrived: 'Millions of homes rejoice and bless your superb service performed in your superb style. I confess I trembled in doubt but the result vindicates and establishes you as indisputably the foremost untouchable and "unapproachable".'

The *Free Press* described the scene inside the prison:

> *Poona,* September 11 P.M. (By telephone)
>
> Reports from every person who has been seeing Gandhiji go to show that Gandhiji is growing weaker almost hour by hour. He can only speak in very low whispers—almost too low to be audible.
>
> Whenever there is occasion for him to go to the bathroom, Gandhiji is conveyed on a stretcher but this afternoon he could not even cross over from his cot to the stretcher independently, and had to he assisted.

---

8. There shall be no disabilities attaching to anyone on the ground of his being a member of the Depressed Classes in regard to any elections to local bodies or appointment to the public services. Every endeavour shall be made to secure a fair representation of the Depressed Classes in these respects subject to such educational qualifications as may be laid down for appointment to the public services.

9. In every Province out of the educational grant an adequate sum shall be earmarked for providing educational facilities for the members of the Depressed Classes.

Gandhiji drinks water every half hour, mixed either with soda or with salt. He had given up salt, hut was medically advised to resume taking it.

Spins though weak

In spite of this appalling weakness, Gandhiji insists on doing his daily quota of spinning. He could, however, only spin with very great effort for about 20 minutes this afternoon; and even so, had to be assisted by Sjt. Mahadev Desai. During these 20 minutes Gandhiji had to take rest twice or thrice.

A moving scene

Emotional scenes were witnessed to-day when Mrs. Motilal Nehru came to pay her respects to Gandhiji. Mrs. Motilal Nehru sat by the side of the cot on which Gandhiji lay, and took his arms into hers. Neither spoke a word, and both gazed at each other for several minutes. Mrs. Motilal then burst into tears, and Gandhiji warmly pressed her hand...

Leaders of the caste Hindus met that day, 25 September, in Bombay at the Indian Merchants Chamber Hall to ratify the agreement which had been signed in Poona the previous day. In addition to doing so, they passed a resolution which Gandhiji had drawn up. It read:

This Conference resolves that henceforth, amongst Hindus, no one shall be regarded as an untouchable by reason of his birth and those who have been so regarded hitherto will have the same rights as the other Hindus in regard to the use of public wells, public roads and other public institutions. This right shall have statutory recognition at the first opportunity and shall be one of the earliest acts of the *Swaraj* Parliament, if it shall not have received such recognition before that time.

It is further agreed that it shall be the duty of all Hindu leaders to secure, by every legitimate and peaceful means, an early removal of all social disabilities now imposed by custom upon the so-called untouchable classes including the bar in respect of admission to temples.[30]

---

30 Mahatma Gandhi, *Collected Works,* Vol. LI, p. 139.

Pandit Malviya announced at the conference that a fund of Rs 25 lakhs would be collected for conducting a vigorous campaign against untouchability throughout the country. Ambedkar too spoke at the conference. He expressed his 'sincere thanks on behalf of his party to Mr. Gandhi for bringing about a happy settlement of the Depressed Class problem', reported *The Times of India,* 'and hoped that the caste Hindus would abide by the agreement'. He said 'he believed it was no exaggeration for him to say that no man a few days ago was placed in a greater dilemma than himself,' the paper reported. 'The difficult situation before him was to make a choice between the life of the greatest man in India and the interests of the community which he (Dr. Ambedkar) represented. He was happy to say that it had become possible through the cooperation of his friends to save the life of Mr. Gandhi and at the same time to safeguard the interests of his party. A large part of the credit for this must he said go to Mr. Gandhi. "I was immensely surprised that there was so much in common between Mr. Gandhi and myself. In fact whenever we took our dispute to Mr. Gandhi, I was astounded to see that the man who radically differed from me came to our rescue. I, therefore, say that a very large part of the credit for this agreement must go to him and I am very grateful to him for having extricated me from what might have been a very difficult situation."' 'My only regret,' the paper reported Ambedkar as saying, 'is, why did not Mr. Gandhi take the attitude he took now at the Round Table Conference? If he had shown some consideration and the same attitude as he took now, I think it would not have been necessary for him to undergo the ordeal. I am glad that I am here to support this resolution.'

The viceroy had been in anxious consultation with governors of provinces about what the government should do if the Indian leaders came to an agreement. He had been counselled that there was no option other than for the government in London to cancel the Communal Award, and accept the terms to which the Indians had agreed. The governor of Bombay Presidency in particular had been emphatic: the agreement must be accepted at the earliest possible.

Gandhiji once again made it plain that the British government must accept the agreement unconditionally, that the separate electorates must be withdrawn completely. He also kept emphasizing that the scrapping of the separate electorates would be but a step, that he would not rest till untouchability had been banished. His concerns at that hour are well reflected in the message which he dictated to V.K. Krishna Menon and Ellen Wilkinson who met him on behalf of the India League on 25 September. They had asked him for a message for Great Britain. He said:

> Every day of the fast seems to me conclusive evidence of the hand of God in it. Even I with my boundless faith in God and His mercy was not prepared for this great wave of awakening against untouchability. That some of the great temples should have spontaneously admitted the untouchables without restriction is to me a modern miracle. They have only now admitted God. Hitherto, the images which the custodians, falsely and in their pride, thought had God within were Godless.
>
> The Cabinet decision was to me a timely warning from God that I was asleep when He was knocking at the door and waking me up. The settlement arrived at is to me but the beginning of the work of purification. The agony of the soul is not going to end until every trace of untouchability is gone. I do not want the British Cabinet to come to any hasty decision. I do not want them for saving my life or for appearing to be right with the world to accept it in a niggardly spirit. If they have not realized the true inwardness of the Agreement, they must summarily reject it, but if they have, they will not alter one word or comma of it, but they will implement every condition that is implied in the great settlement which the so-called untouchables and the so-called touchables have arrived at with all their heart and with God as their witness.

> I hope that they and the world will realize that this settlement is, if I may say so in all humility, far superior to the Cabinet decision. There is no pride about it. The Cabinet composed of foreigners, knowing nothing first hand of the Indian conditions or what untouchability could mean, were labouring under a heavy handicap, and even though some Indians had referred this matter to them, they should have declined the responsibility to which they were wholly unequal.
>
> I am not saying this from my penitential bed in any canning spirit or spirit of irritation.
>
> I claim to be a true friend of the British nation and also of the Cabinet, and I would be untrue to them, to myself and to my call, if at this moment I suppressed my relevant opinion. I would like finally to assure Britain that so long as life lasts in me, I shall undergo as many fasts as are necessary in order to purify Hinduism of this unbearable taint. Thank God there is not only one man in this movement but, I believe, there are several thousands who will lay down their lives in order to achieve this reform in its fulness.[31]

Gandhiji also dictated a statement for the press, lest anyone be left in any doubt about what he was aiming at. In the statement he said:

> If the Premier accepts the settlement *in toto* I would be bound to break the fast. The settlement, as far as the political part of it is concerned, merely removes the tremendous obstacle that the Cabinet's decision put in the way of reform. The real part of the settlement is now to come and whilst, if the Premier accepts *in toto* the settlement cabled to him, my fast must end, the real struggle for me only begins. As a matter of fact if the Cabinet had published the correspondence in time I would have been in honour bound to insist on the due fulfilment of the duty that lies on the so-called caste Hindus.
>
> I should be guilty of betrayal of trust if I did not ensure that, but as they had no notice worth the name of my intention to fast, I could not expect them all of a sudden to revolutionize Hindu thought.

---

31 Mahatma Gandhi, *Collected Works,* Vol. LI, pp. 140–41.

They must, therefore, have breathing time for work, and so I have told fellow-workers that if this fast is broken in virtue of the Cabinet's satisfactory answer it would be put in suspension, but sure as fate, it will be taken up again if the part to be performed by the caste Hindus is not well played during the coming months.

The tremendous awakening that has taken place in the country during the five days fills me with hope that orthodoxy will surpass itself and rid Hinduism of the canker of untouchability which is eating into its vitals.[32]

These were the thoughts in his mind in that weakened condition. They were the very ones with which he had begun his fast. They were the ones which had permeated him throughout the fast. Can there be any doubt about his sincerity, about the vision and goal he had set out to realize at the cost of his very life? But we shall see in a moment what Ambedkar made of them.

On the morning of 26 September Dr Gilder and other doctors examined Gandhiji. They said in a statement to the press that while the feeling of nausea which had been troubling Gandhiji and had caused vomiting the previous day had subsided and Gandhiji's blood pressure remained at 185 by 110, 'The disturbing features are that both the acetone and urea content in his urine have increased, the latter to 1.5 per cent.' They added, 'We are definitely of opinion that this portends entry into the danger zone.' Dr Gilder was asked what he and the other doctors had meant by 'the danger zone'. He replied, 'Mahatmaji has no reserve fat and he is living on muscle. This is the stage when an attack of paralysis may intervene any time. We are of opinion that he has entered into that stage that is bringing him nearer his end. There is now danger even if the fast is broken.'

'The whole of the 26th was passed in anxiety and waiting in Yeravda,' Pyarelal wrote. 'The poet who had made a

32 Mahatma Gandhi, *Collected Works*, Vol. LI, pp. 141.

hurried dash to Poona from Calcutta, visited Gandhiji at noon. The meeting was a most touching one. Without a word, he approached Gandhiji's prostrate form and burying his face in the clothes on Gandhiji's breast, remained in that position for several minutes overcome with feeling. He had heard the news that the Cabinet had accepted the Agreement. "I have come floating on the tide of good news. I am so glad that I have come and that I have come in time," he said to Gandhiji as he recovered his voice. Then they talked intimately of several things. The Poet told Gandhiji that so far as the social side of the question of untouchability was concerned he could always be depended upon to do his bit to relieve Gandhiji's burden. He then left his bedside as the strain of conversation was proving too much for Gandhiji.'[33]

Thoughts while breaking the fast

The message from London came eventually. Gandhiji first detected some lacunae in it, but eventually was convinced that the condition he had specified for ending the fast had been met fully. It was decided that he would break the fast at 5.30 that evening. Pyarelal describes the scene in that prison yard:

> The yard was freshly sprinkled over with water. Gandhiji lay on his cot surrounded by the Poet, Shrimati Sarojini Naidu, Shrimati Vasanti Devi, Shrimati Swarup Rani, Shrimati Urmila Devi, Sjt. Ambalal Sarabai and his family, Gandhiji's two companions, Sardar Vallabhbhai Patel and Sjt. Mahadev Desai. Before him were assembled a number of inmates of the Sabarmati Ashram and others, in all about 200 persons. The poet led the prayer by singing a Bengali hymn from *Gitanjali*...

---

33 Pyarelal, *The Epic Fast*, Navjivan, Ahmedabad, 1932, p. 77.

Jeevan jakhan shukaya jaye, karuna-dharaye aisho
Sakal madhuri lukaye jaye, geet-sudharse aisho...

> This was followed by the reciting of some Sanskrit verses by Parchure Shastri, a fellow prisoner from the leper yard of the Yeravda Prison. Then was sung, all joining, Gandhiji's favourite hymn, *Vaishnava Jana.* When it was finished, Shrimati Kasturba handed him the orange juice and Gandhiji broke his fast...[34]

Gandhiji issued a statement for the press. 'The fast undertaken in the name of God was broken in the presence of Gurudev, and Parchure Shastri, the leper prisoner and a learned pandit, seated opposite each other, and in the company of loving and loved ones who had gathered round me,' Gandhiji told the press. 'The breaking was preceded by the Poet singing one of his Bengali hymns, then *mantras* from the Upanishads by Parchure Shastri, and then my favourite hymn, *"Vaishnava Jana".'*

'The hand of God has been visible in the glorious manifestation throughout the length and breadth of India during the past seven days,' he said. He had been sustained by the expressions of support which had poured in from many parts of the world, he said.[35]

Gandhiji as usual was looking ahead and focusing on what had to be done next. He pledged his word to Harijans as he said he would address them from now on: he was pledged to the entire agreement, in particular to carrying forward the processes of reform which the events had sparked off. 'The sacrificial fire, once lit,' Gandhiji said, 'shall not be put out as long as there is the slightest trace of untouchability still left in Hinduism. If it is God's will that it does not end with my life, I have the confidence that there are several

34 Pyarelal, *The Epic Fast,* Navjivan, Ahmedabad, 1932, pp. 79–80, 148–49.
35 Mahatma Gandhi, *Collected Works,* Vol. LI, pp. 143–45.

thousands of earnest reformers who will lay down their lives in order to purify Hinduism of this awful curse.'

What has been agreed to is but a step, he emphasized: 'The settlement is but the beginning of the end. The political part of it, very important though it no doubt is, occupies but a small space in the vast field of reform that has to be tackled by caste Hindus during the coming days, namely, the complete removal of social and religious disabilities under which a large part of the Hindu population has been groaning. I should be guilty of a breach of trust if I did not warn fellow reformers and caste Hindus in general that the breaking of the fast carried with it a sure promise of a resumption of it if this reform is not relentlessly pursued and achieved within a measurable period. I had thought of laying down a period, but I feel that I may not do so without a definite call from within.' It was not long before Ambedkar would pour ridicule and venom on this pledge too.

Gandhiji distributed the credit for the agreement among others. Gandhiji said, 'The settlement arrived at is, so far as I can see, a generous gesture on all sides. It is a meeting of hearts, and my Hindu gratitude is due to Dr. Ambedkar, Rao Bahadur Srinivasan and their party on the one hand and Rao Bahadur M. C. Rajah on the other. They could have taken up an uncompromising and defiant attitude by way of punishment to the so-called caste Hindus for the sins of generations. If they had done so, I at least could not have resented their attitude and my death would have been but a trifling price exacted for the tortures that the outcastes of Hinduism have been going through for unknown generations. But they chose a nobler path and have thus shown that they have followed the precept of forgiveness enjoined by all religions. Let me hope that the caste Hindus will prove themselves worthy of this forgiveness and carry out to the letter ancl spirit every clause of the settlement with all its implications.'[36]

British consolations

The talk in British circles was quite different. True, the old man had been able to substitute an agreement of his own for their plan, but at least the man who had 'won' was Ambedkar—that seemed to be the best construction. The 'Special Correspondent' of *The Times of India* reflected as much in his dispatch of 26 September. 'I understand on excellent authority,' he wrote, 'that it is the unanimous opinion not only of the Government of India but also of the Provincial Governments that under the alternative scheme now agreed upon the Depressed Classes have done amazingly well. Left to themselves no Government in India would have dared to recommend the grant of 148 seats to them in the Provincial Legislatures for fear of provoking a grave agitation among the caste Hindus from one end of the country to the other. It was indeed thought here at one time soon after the commencement of negotiations at Yeravda that Dr. Ambedkar having pitched his demands high and having refused to be browbeaten by Mr. Gandhi's threat to commit suicide would succumb to the pressure exercised by the caste Hindus and their allies in the press and blow like a balloon. The terms which he has succeeded in obtaining will certainly set several of the more orthodox Hindus furiously to think but as their political influence is in inverse proportion to their caste scruples no serious reaction against the Agreement is likely to be felt except perhaps in the Punjab and Bengal where the caste Hindus who have been crying that they have been done down for the benefit of the Muslims are now faced with the necessity of having

36 Mahatma Gandhi, *Collected Works,* Vol. LI, pp. 143–45.

to surrender quite a few of the seats to the Depressed Classes. Under the Communal Award there was no special representation for the Depressed Classes in the Punjab and the Hindus were allotted 43 seats in the general constituencies. The new Agreement lays down that out of these 43 seats, eight must be reserved for the Depressed Classes. Similarly, in Bengal the caste Hindus have to give away from the 80 seats allotted to them no less than 30 as against the maximum of ten provided under the Award....'

There was also the other point: the terms of the Agreement would enable Ambedkar to extend his influence, at any rate in Bombay province. The viceroy had asked the governors to urgently send him their assessment of the likely reactions to, and the consequences of the pact. In his telegram of 25 September, the governor of Bombay noted, '... (2) This morning's medical examination [of Gandhiji] shows no marked change. (3) Gandhi refuses to break fast pending consideration of agreement by the Prime Minister and demands unconditional acceptance. (4) Effect of settlement if accepted would seem probably in this Presidency, where Ambedkar's influence prevails among depressed classes, to upset balance of legislature to detriment of Hindus. By means of secondary election he may be able to ensure that only candidates favourable to him stand for Depressed Class seats, which will number 15 under Supplement as against 10 in Communal Award. In provinces where Rajah's influence might prevail it may have effect adversely to other minorities.' Alas, this hope too was to turn out to have been a gross miscalculation. In the elections which followed in 1937, of the 151 seats assigned to the Scheduled Castes, the Congress secured seventy-eight, and Ambedkar's Independent Labour Party only twelve; in the elections of 1946, of the 151 seats reserved for Scheduled Castes the Congress secured 141, and Ambedkar's party one! But all that lay in the future. At the moment, the thought that the distribution of seats would probably work to the advantage of Ambedkar was something with which the British sought to console themselves.

Gurudev's tribute

On the Indian side the principal reaction was one of relief at the fact that somehow the crisis was over, that Gandhiji had survived. There were misgivings about the number of seats which had been given, this was specially so in the Punjab. But for the moment criticism was hushed by relief. Gurudev Rabindranath Tagore was still in Poona. As Gandhiji's birthday approached, he delivered a speech on 27 September, a speech looking forward to the birthday of the Mahatma, and reflecting on what might have come to pass in its stead. Tagore said:

* * *

> Mahatmaji's birthday appears today before us in an awful majesty of Death which has just left him victorious. It is our great good fortune today that such a man has indeed come to us, and what is still rarer, that we have not repudiated him, as we have so often done with the messengers of Freedom and Truth. His inspiration is actively at work all through India and even beyond its boundaries. It has awakened our consciousness to a truth which goes far beyond the limits of our self-interest. His life itself is a constant call to us to emancipation in service and self-dedication.
>
> Today is the day of our national acknowledgment of Mahatmaji as the great brother, who, in the present age, is the central bond of our brotherhood in our Motherland. I hope we shall be earnestly solemn in our expression of it and never cheapen the meaning of this occasion by merely indulging in emotional pride. Let us be worthy of the call of this age and accept from Mahatmaji's hand the responsibility which he has accepted for himself.
>
> We know that, in the Upanishads, the God who ever dwells in the hearts of all men has been mentioned as Mahatma. The epithet is rightly given to the Man of God whom we are honouring today,

for his dwelling is not within a narrow enclosure of individual consciousness. His dwelling is in the heart of the untold multitude who are born today in India and who are yet to come, and this greatness of his soul, which has power to comprehend other souls, has made possible what never has yet happened in our history, when even masses have been roused to the great fact that India is not merely a geographical entity but is a living truth in which they live and move and have their being.

Today in our determined effort let us join Mahatmaji in his noble task of removing the burden of ages, the burden of disrespect upon the bent back of those who have been stigmatized for the accident of their birth, and the sin of wilful denial, to a large body of our countrymen, of sympathy which is the birth-right of all human beings. We are not only casting off the chain of India's moral enslavement but indicating the path for all humanity. We are challenging the victimization, wherever and in whatever form it may exist, to stand the test of relentless questioning of the conscience which Mahatmaji has brought to bear upon our day.

When Mahatmaji began his penance there were cynics in our own country and abroad who mocked and jeered at him, and yet before our very eyes the wonder has happened. Hard rocks of tradition have been blasted. Irrational prohibitions, cramping our national life, are already showing signs of tottering. Great has been the achievement due to his penance, but it will be a greater glory to him and to us if we can fulfil his vow by fighting to a finish the evils of untouchability, of intolerance, of all that hinders the comradeship of man and man and obstructs our path to freedom and righteousness.

My friends, I appeal to you, do not betray your Great Man and your own humanity by any deviation of your initiative from the pursuit of justice and love towards your fellowmen who have suffered humiliation for ages and remained dumb in a pathetic apathy of resignation, never even blaming Providence and their own cruel destiny. But the angry voice has at last come from the Divine Guide of our history with its warning message that they cut at the root of freedom who, in their unreasoning pride, obstruct the freedom of social communication among their own kindreds.'[37]

---

37 Text in Pyarelal, *The Epic Fast*, Navjivan, Ahmedabad 1932 pp. 92–94.

7

The way to reform

Gandhi now weighs 94 1/2 lbs., the Government of Bombay reported to the Central government in Delhi by telegram on 28 September 1932. It was summarizing the assessment of the medical examination of Gandhiji which it had received through the inspector general of prisons. The urea and acetone content in the urine were still on the higher side, the examination had revealed. His overall condition is satisfactory, the assessment had said, though it is too early to say dogmatically whether the fast has affected his constitution or not.[1]

Gandhiji had by now plunged into the next phase of his work for the banishment of untouchability. His concern was not just about giving some seats in legislatures to the Untouchables, in fact as we have seen he was pushed into doing so only because of the Communal Award. His concern was that they, like every other section of society, be raised. And his prescription for them was the same as it was for every other section: when he addressed the higher-caste Hindus he would reprimand them for what they had made of our religion, of what they had come to practise towards others in the name of that religion; so also with regard to

1 Text of telegram at National Archives, Home Department, *File No. 31/113/32-Poll.*

the lower castes: he emphasized that the way to their rising above their present levels was to purge themselves of the habits, etc., which had crept into them. The way in their case, as in that of every other group, was to make demands on themselves, not demands on others. On the 28th in a note he sent to P.M. Rajbhoj, Gandhiji reverted to this theme. He wrote:

> I have already made my appeal to the caste Hindus as to their duty, but as a self-chosen Harijan I would like to say a word to them also. They have to perform their part during this period of purification. Owing to suppression they have been deprived of ways and means of observing, and the incentive to the observation of, the ordinary laws of cleanliness and the like, but let us hope that a new era has dawned upon us. I hope that Harijans will understand this and in so far as possible they will observe the laws of cleanliness, abstain from intoxicating liquors and drugs and make a mighty effort to get rid of all social evils.[2]

Ambedkar was on the other track already. On the same day, 28 September he addressed a meeting at Worli in Bombay. He claimed victory for himself, and pooh-poohed one of the principal things that had started happening since Gandhiji had announced his intention to fast. Ambedkar said that at the Round Table Conference Mr Gandhi had been strongly opposed to giving anything to the Depressed Classes in the new constitution, but he had now come round. This remarkable turnaround had come about 'due to the fact that they (Mr. Gandhi and his followers) realized that the Depressed Classes were now a force'. 'The speaker continued,' reported *The Times of India,* 'that he had been able to secure for the Depressed Classes a greater degree of representation than had been provided in the Communal Award. Not only had he secured them 148 seats in the various legislatures, but he had also been able to

2 Mahatma Gandhi, *Collected Works,* Vol. LI, p. 149.

secure eight seats for their community in the Punjab.' The Communal Award had dealt only with provincial legislatures; given the way that award had treated the Depressed Classes, said Ambedkar, it is entirely likely that these classes would have been treated in the same niggardly way in regard to the Central legislature. But by the Poona Pact, there also these classes would have 18 per cent representation. The worst part of the Communal Award, Ambedkar said, had been that the reservations provided under it would have come to an end after twenty years, but under the Poona Pact they would continue until caste Hindus and the Depressed Classes came to another agreement.

'Dr. Ambedkar in conclusion sounded a note of warning about temple-entry,' reported the paper. 'A move in this direction had been taken in the city and elsewhere, but they should be careful not to get themselves into the trap. Not that he was against temple-entry but a cry might be raised that since the Depressed Classes were treated as touchables and that untouchability might be removed by allowing them entry into temples, the special representation should be taken away'—a perfect example of Ambedkar's mode of reasoning, a mode that has been internalized by his followers: first he makes a grievance of the fact that caste Hindus do not allow Untouchables to enter the temples; the moment, in response to Gandhiji's fast, the temples are thrown open to the Untouchables, he begins insinuating that it is a trap!

But to continue: *The Times of India* reported him as adding, 'Mere temple-entry would not lift their social status. They should concern themselves more with material interests than spiritual ones; they should strive for bread and not after God. What they should aim at was economic uplift and social equality and adequate representation in government services to safeguard their interests, which had so long been down-trodden. Dr. Ambedkar finally appealed to the audience to organize and consolidate their position and to raise a fund for carrying on their political activities in the future.'

The pact had but to be signed, and the government, squirming at having been thwarted once again by 'the old rascal', moved to shut him off. On 28 September itself a telegram was sent to the governor: '...Government of India on further consideration and in view of inevitable publicity Gandhi is getting at present are of opinion that all restrictions previously in force on correspondence and publicity must be re-imposed at once. Previous rules about interviews should also be re-imposed, but if special appreciations are received not covered by rules they should be referred to Government of India with your opinion and they will be considered on their merits. Gandhi's position should in fact now be that of a State Prisoner as it was before the fast.'

The governor sent his reply by cable the same day: they had themselves been planning to revert to the earlier arrangements, the governor said, it was just that 'In view of Gandhi's condition at conclusion of fast it was deemed advisable not to close down privileges in regard to correspondence and interviews too abruptly;' all interviews with the press had already been stopped, and interviews with relatives and close associates would be allowed only for a day or two more. 'Caste Hindu leaders specially desire to be allowed access to Gandhi to continue campaign for removal of untouchability and Bombay Government are reluctant to place any obstacles in the way,' the telegram said, but added the assurance that the interviews for this purpose would be closely monitored, and 'any sign of linking this with civil disobedience activities will result in complete withdrawal of concessions.'[3]

---

3 National Archives, Home Department, *File No. 31/113/32-Poll. & unprinted K.-W.*

At 12.30 the next morning Major Bhandari conveyed the orders to Gandhiji orally: except G.D. Birla and Mathuradas Vasanji, no visitors, not even for untouchability work; Kasturba to be removed forthwith to the Female Ward..., 'I must confess that I was wholly unprepared for this very sudden and rude reminder that I was but a prisoner whose body was entirely at the mercy of the Government,' Gandhiji wrote to Major Bhandari. 'I would like, however, the Government to know that I am still considered to be convalescent and under orders not even to move from my bed. I had hoped that at least during the convalescent period I would be saved all unnecessary shock to my nerves. However, this need not be a matter of moment to the Government and ought not to worry me overmuch, if at all... But what I cannot understand is this sudden stopping of all visits, even in connection with untouchability work...' The Government could not be unaware of the phenomenal awakening that had taken place in the wake of the fast, he continued, and said that he regarded it as absolutely necessary that he be left completely free to meet whomsoever he wanted to for untouchability work.[4]

Arguments went to and fro. On 1 November, 1932, in his letter to Sir Frederick Sykes, the governor, the viceroy forwarded an argument which fit in well with their objectives. 'There is another side to this too, which was strongly suggested by Fazli Hussain,' the viceroy wrote. 'He holds that the fact of our enabling him [Gandhiji] to be more active on untouchability will probably produce very strong reactions on the part of caste Hindus and will in the end reduce his popularity and influence very considerably.'[5] But that is another story.

Ambedkar and his associates now had their eyes on the Anti-Untouchability League which was being organized in response

---

4 Mahatma Gandhi, *Collected Works,* Vol. LI, pp. 151–52.

5 MSS.EUR.F.150/4(c).

to Gandhiji's insistence that leaders of caste Hindus devote themselves to this work, and for which, in response to his suggestion, Pandit Madan Mohan Malviya, G.D. Birla and others were attempting to raise a fund of Rs 25 lakh. Ambedkar was insistent that the board that was to be set up to direct the work of this association have a number of Depressed Classes persons. Others knew that this was but the first step, for Ambedkar would refuse to recognize anyone who was not his nominee as representing the Depressed Classes.

'We are for the Union Jack'

Predictably, the rupture was soon in the open: Ambedkar and his lieutenants were denouncing the association which those who were setting it up had demurred at handing over to them. *Congress Influence Menace To Depressed Classes,* ran the headline of *The Times of India* on 19 October. *'Warning against uplift work trap',* it continued, *'Dr. P.O. Solanki's grave apprehension: "We are for the Union Jack".'*

The paper reported that Ambedkar had called on Gandhiji at the Yeravda prison and 'expressed very firmly his opinion that there should be a majority of Depressed Class people on these committees [of the proposed Anti-Untouchability League]. He was of opinion that their voice must be predominant and that nothing must be done which might prove unpalatable to them. If the uplift work was to proceed satisfactorily the caste Hindus must assist the Depressed Class people to work out their own salvation and not attempt to uplift them by inducing them to follow the ideals of the caste Hindus in every way....'

'We Are For The Union Jack,' Depressed Classes' Loyalty, ran a heading in the item. 'That there are Congress influences at work which are seriously undermining the very basis of the loyalty of the Depressed Classes to the British Crown is the warning

contained in a statement made by Dr. Solanki, M.L.C., in the course of an interview with our correspondent,' *The Times of India* reported. 'The remarks were made after an interview that Dr. Ambedkar had with Mr. Gandhi at Yeravda Jail when the former wanted a predominant voice for the Depressed Classes in the constitution of the Anti-Untouchability League,' the paper said in its dispatch from Poona.

'Dr. Solanki,' it reported, 'disapproved of any uplift work for the Depressed Classes being carried on with the aid of Congress money. He said that the community stood for the Union Jack and not for the Congress flag.'

The account of the interview is worth reading in full. It ran as follows:

> Dr. Solanki M.L.C., Dr. Ambedkar's trusted lieutenant, was interviewed this morning in regard to the points which were raised by Dr. Ambedkar. In his interview with Mr. Gandhi, he made some important statements on the general position. There was not the slightest doubt, he said, that Mr. Gandhi's fast had awakened the consciences of very many caste Hindus who were quite uninfluenced by politics and who were taking the matter seriously from the point of view taken up by Mr. Gandhi in his original statement to the press in Yeravda Jail.
>
> *Congress influence danger*
>
> On the other hand he feared that there were influences at work which were undermining the very basis of the loyalty of the Depressed Classes to the British Crown. 'Let he who will follow the tri-colour of the Congress, we are for the Union Jack,' he declared.
>
> 'There should be no doubt about that. We are all out for political freedom and national unity, but within the British Empire.'
>
> He then went on to discuss the Anti-Untouchability League and said that he feared very much that the majority of the members on the Committees were distinctly pro-Congress people and Hindu Mahasabhaites.
>
> *Uplift work trap.*
>
> The League proposed spending Rs. 25,00,000 in the next three

years on the uplift of the Depressed Classes. Where was the money to come from? He could only believe that it would come from the same sources as much of the finances of the Congress had come in view of the political colour of those soliciting it. Any uplift work done with this money would have a Congress bias. The Committees would attempt to secure the youthful among the Depressed Classes and train them to their way of thinking solely with the view of solidarity among Hindus, and with a view to establish more firmly the Congress outlook.

If his fears in this direction were well founded, this would lay the axe at the very roots of Depressed Class loyalty to the British Empire. Were the Depressed Classes to allow their loyalty to be bought by the spending of a few lakhs of rupees on the opening of jobs to members of Depressed Classes hitherto sacred to the caste Hindus? The older politically aware members of the community would not be caught in this way, but there was a very grave danger so far as the younger generation was concerned. The only way in which the Caste Hindus could show that they were really sincere would be to allow the Depressed Classes to have the pre-dominant voice in the League Committees and stand by them as brothers with advice and real assistance.[6]

Their eye was on the twenty-five lakh, their anxiety was that some others might claim that they too were doing something to help the Untouchables, their loyalty, as they proclaimed now and were to proclaim repeatedly in the future, was for the Union Jack, and not the national flag or movement.

As for Ambedkar, he was soon on his way to England for the third Round Table Conference. In this also he earned the gratitude of the British no end. On 28 December 1932 the Secretary of State, Sir Samuel Hoare, as we have seen, wrote in his *'Private And Personal'* letter to the viceroy, 'Ambedkar has behaved very well at the Conference, and I am most anxious to strengthen his hands in every reasonable way. Coming from a family whose members have almost

6 *The Times of India*, 19 October 1932.

always been in the Army, he feels intensely the fact that there are no Depressed Class units left. Could you not induce the Commander-in-Chief to give them at least a Company? Ambedkar tells me that the Depressed Class battalion did much better in the Afghan War than most of the other Indian battalions. In any case, I feel sure that at this juncture it would be a really valuable political act to make a move of this kind.'

Was Ambedkar serious even about this demand, about openings in the army for persons from his own sub-caste, the Mahars? Put this plea of Ambedkar to Sir Samuel Hoare alongside the observation of the Governor of Bombay, Roger Lumley. Ambedkar, it will be recalled, had gone to him to express his resentment at the way Cripps had given all the importance to the Congress and the Muslim League, and left leaders like him out of the reckoning. Concluding his plea for doing something for Ambedkar, Lumley wrote:

> I would very much like to see something done for him, and I hope that, if a further expansion of your Council is now possible, he will be included—not on personal grounds alone, but so that we may retain the interest of the Depressed Classes. He has been unhelpful about recruitment of Mahars, and does not put his weight behind it overmuch, in spite of the fact that he has long clamoured for Mahars being taken into combatant units. Nevertheless, the recruitment of Mahars continues, but not as well as it would do if he were really keen to help.[7]

In a word, he was available for assisting in the recruitment of Mahars so long as the British, to recall Lumley's felicitous phrase, helped him 'secure his future'.

Retrospect

Conferences such as the Round Table Conference had ended—

7 *Transfer of Power* documents, Vol. I, pp. 846–47.

to the great satisfaction of the British. Whenever they were compelled to convene such conferences so as to make a show of doing what they could on the constitutional question, they fielded leaders such as Ambedkar. Through these leaders they succeeded in neutralizing Gandhiji.

The principal gain from Gandhiji's fast was that the leaders of the Untouchables came to an agreement with other Indians, and not with the British. Second, the fast gave an unprecedented push to the campaign against untouchability: temples were opened to all Hindus; people all across the country made a sincere effort to rise above the superstition of centuries; an organization came into being to continue the work; the country received a salutary reminder of what Gandhiji's priorities were, that lesson has been a beacon for reformers to this day.

It is also evident that Gandhiji was compelled to agree to what he opposed. Gandhiji had repeatedly opposed reservations of seats even in joint electorates. He had done so at the Round Table Conference also. As we have seen, he continued to be opposed to them even during his fast. But once the British had succeeded in breaking away leaders like Ambedkar with the device of separate electorates Gandhiji had no alternative but to swallow reservations within joint electorates as the lesser evil. That evil was of course to be the beginning: it has spawned what we see today—reservations not just in legislatures, but in services; reservations not just at entry in the services, reservations in promotions too; far from the measure being wound up in twenty years, it has become an evil which has continued to swell every few years. More than any of these specific things, that step has spawned an entire ideology in which jobs are a matter of right, not something for which a person must work and excel. But these are the accretions of a later date, they are the work of leaders who, in this thing as in every other, have made a mockery of what Gandhiji stood for and did.

In any event, Gandhiji had to accept what he had so stoutly opposed, he had to reconcile himself to an arrangement which he still saw as harmful to our society. Once the tension of the fast was over, critics like Sir Chimanlal Setalvad argued that had Gandhiji been half as accommodating at the Round Table Conference as he was in Poona, the country would not have had to concede what it had to in those anxious days. For once Gandhiji had announced his intention to fast, and specially once he had begun his fast, the sole consideration in the minds of all nationalists became to save him somehow. In a trenchant attack on the Poona Pact at the meeting of the Western India Liberal Association in Bombay on 14 October 1932 Sir Chimanlal Setalvad drew attention to this consequence, and pointed to the associated one: once Gandhiji began his fast and the only consideration in everyone's mind became to save him somehow, Setalvad pointed out, the very Ambedkar whose representative capacity Gandhiji had questioned at the Round Table Conference was made into a virtual dictator, and so the latter could afford to be as stubborn as he wanted to be, as unmindful of the opinion of other leaders of Untouchables, not because he commanded a larger following but because a settlement was necessary to save Gandhiji's life and the veto to that settlement lay in Ambedkar's hand. Setalvad recalled that Gandhiji's fast was intended to prevent the separation of the Untouchables from Hindu society. But what were the primary elections now going to do? They would require that the Untouchables be listed on a separate register. Had Gandhiji accepted joint electorates with reservations of seats at the Round Table Conference no separate register would have been necessary, he said.[8]

---

8 *The Times of India,* 15 October 1932.

Clearly, by going ahead and announcing the award with its separate electorates the British had cornered Gandhiji. He must have thought that his warnings would alert them sufficiently so that they would not deploy this particular weapon to divide Hindu society, and thereby further disable the national movement. But, confident of the support of persons like Ambedkar and encouraged by reports about the general lassitude and indifference in the country, they had gone ahead. Gandhiji was now confronted with a fait accompli. His immediate task was to get the British to take back the weapon they had deployed. And there is no doubt that it is only Gandhiji's fast that made them withdraw it. The rest of the country was prostrate as can be. The Civil Disobedience Movement had just about petered out. The leaders were in jail, Gandhiji himself had been in jail for over nine months. Those who were out were afraid of the ordinances which had been promulgated and were being so vigorously enforced. The Viceroy had asked the governors and other high officials to report the reactions to the Communal Award. One official after the other reported that the reaction had been lukewarm, except, as we have seen from the assessments, among Muslims who were very satisfied but had decided as a policy to not be too effusive in public. The condition of those who were opposed to the award, even of those, like the Hindus in Bengal and the Hindus and Sikhs in Punjab whose position had been undermined most visibly, was pathetic, rather it was exactly as it had always been—that is, disabled for all the usual reasons from acting to stem the harm which was being inflicted on them. Two examples will suffice to give a glimpse of how preoccupied and unmindful the people were, and therefore that, had it not been for Gandhiji putting his life on the line, the British would certainly have prevailed and yet another earth-fault in our society would have been widened to fatal proportions.

The preoccupations of our countrymen

In Bengal, as in Punjab, the award deliberately set out to reward the Muslims—it was in this sense the continuance of Curzon's partition of the province, and a foretaste of what was to come in 1947. What did the Hindu leaders of the province do to roll this award back? The *'Confidential'* report which the reforms commissioner of the Government of Bengal sent to the Government of India on 16 September gives us an idea. He wrote:

> Since the issue of the telegram referred to above, much has been written in the local press on the Communal Decision, and a considerable number of meetings have been convened to discuss it, but on the whole it may be said that the publication of the Decision has not been followed by the political activity that might have been expected. This is due to a variety of causes. One is that the majority of the politically-minded population in the country districts have been awaiting guidance from their leaders in Calcutta. Many of these leaders have been fully occupied in a long and arduous session of the Legislative Council, and they have had neither the time nor the energy to apply to intensive propaganda and campaign wok. Another reason is that the Award is looked upon by many as a final decision, against which no appeal is likely to be successful, the prerequisite of such an appeal being complete agreement between the two main communities. A third cause is that many of the more aggressive Hindu politicians are either under control or are at least restrained by the operation of the Ordinances. Moreover, the Decision in itself imposes caution on the Hindu community. It has given marked advantage to Muhammadans as compared with their present position, and the Hindus, though dissatisfied, have had to guard their utterances lest they might be construed as an attack on the Muhammadans. This is probably the reason why Hindu leaders have been more disposed to vent their feelings on the Prime Minister and on the British Government for permitting separate electorates, which they regard as non-national, and to dwell on what

they consider to be the disproportionate share of seats allocated to Europeans and Anglo-Indians than to stress the fact they have been given a relatively inferior position in the future Constitution. There has been, it is true, some recrimination in the press, between the two main communities, but it has been of a minor character.[9]

The position in the other province in which the Hindus were as grievously affected, that is Punjab was, if anything, even worse. The section which felt that it had been harmed the most was the Sikhs. But their politics was such that they just could not get together and act. Two secret dispatches which the Government of Punjab sent to the Government of India depict the condition.

On 14 September, that is, almost a month after the announcement of the Communal Award, the chief secretary of the Punjab government reported to the Government of India as follows:

I am directed to reply to letter no. D.2293/32-Poli., dated the 16th August 1932, in which is requested a further report on the reception given to the Communal Award in this province.

Muslim opinion in the main has been crystallized into a determination to adhere to the Award and to resist any negotiations which might diminish the solid advantages which they consider the Award gives them. They will not at this stage accept joint electorates in any shape or form. They argue that in the present atmosphere of mutual mistrust joint electorates are in themselves dangerous, as, if members of rival communities were to stand for the same seat, there would be danger of communal rioting in every such constituency. They believe further that a Muslim who owed his seat to Hindu votes could not be relied on to further the Muslim cause in the Council.

Hindus other than Hindu agriculturists are gravely dissatisfied. They claim that they have been given 1.10 per cent less votes than

9 Assessment at National Archives, Home Department, *File No. 41-4/ 32-Poll. &K.-W.*

those to which their numerical strength entitles them and that this treatment of a minority is unparalleled and unjust. The phrase 'the poisoned cup of separate electorates' is finding great favour with them. They are not strong enough to make much impression on Punjab politics by themselves, but they are ceaseless in their efforts to secure Sikh co-operation. So far as provincial politics are concerned, they would prefer to have no further advance to a Constitution as foreshadowed in the Award: and in this they are at one with a section of the Sikhs.

The Sikhs on the whole are discontented, but they show signs of breaking up into parties. There is a possibility that the rural Sikhs may combine as agriculturists and break away from communal agitators. Extremist Sikhs led by Tara Singh are anxious to attack Government on this, as on any other, issue, and to convert their community to the adoption of the Congress creed and tactics. This party must however be disappointed at their failure so far to achieve any great results. Their only successful meeting has been one of 8,000 Sikhs, the size of which was due to the fact that the Diwan took place on the occasion of the big cattle fair at Moga in the Ferozepore district. On the other hand, the Sikh Council of Action has failed to persuade members of the Legislative Council to resign their seats, and the meeting planned for September 4th at the house of Raja Narendra Nath in Lahore, which was to be attended by both Sikh and Hindu leaders, had to be abandoned because of refusals to attend: while that held on the 11th has proved infructuous. There are indications that the moderate leaders of the Sikhs whose manifestos, one of which was issued before the Award in the hope of influencing His Majesty's Government, were largely responsible for the initiation of the Sikh agitation, now realize that it is likely to lead to lawlessness unless it is checked, and they are professing anxiety to confine it within constitutional bounds. They know from their experience of the Akali agitation that both those Sikhs who subscribe to the Congress view and also those who are merely unscrupulous agitators would have no hesitation in exploiting the masses for their own ends, *'Sed revocare gradum, hic labor'*—and the line they are likely to adopt is that their quarrel is not with the present Government but with the future constitution and that they are hoping to keep the movement completely within the law, but are preparing the ground for constitutional agitation in every way possible. They advocate sending a representative to the next Round Table Conference with a view to pressing their views before His Majesty's Government. If they fail to secure modification of the Award, their plan is to refuse to work the new Constitution. They claim that at least 44 per cent., and possibly more than 50 per cent., of the Punjab would prefer the present regime to the new Constitution, and they rest their case on the political theory that a change in Constitution cannot be justified unless a substantial majority is in favour of it.[10]

On 23 September the chief secretary of Punjab sent a copy of the report he had received from the deputy commissioner of Amritsar. Dated 19 September, that is one day before the day on which Gandhiji was to commence his fast, it read as follows:

Panthic Day was celebrated on the 17th instant. An attempt was made to hold a Diwan at the Golden Temple at about 7 A.M., and a few people collected. Two or three speakers appeared, but they were late, and the proceedings were postponed to the evening. In the evening the organizers were nervous about the size of the audience, and therefore arranged to hold the Diwan at a place where a daily *katha* of the Guru Granth Sahib is given by the Giyani. The audience at the commencement of the proceedings numbered about one thousand, and, according to the C.I.D. reports, later swelled to about six thousand. My private information is that about two thousand persons were present, and that the organizers will claim in the press that there was a meeting of fifteen thousand. Except for the Akalis who are ordinarily present in the Golden Temple, no member of the audience was wearing a black *pugri* or a black badge. The principal speakers were Bhagat Singh Jamke, Gurbaksh Singh of Delhi and Dalip Singh Doabia. It was noticeable that no well-known Akali addressed the meeting. Bhagat Singh Jamke and Gurbaksh Singh made some objectionable speeches against Government, but Dalip Singh was mainly concerned with statistics, comparisons with other provinces, etc. An objectionable

10 Assessment at National Archives, Home Department, *File no.* 41-47 32-*Poll. &K.-W.*

poem was read by Saran Singh Thande. At the conclusion of the meeting the audience moved to the Akal Takht where a new *khaddar rumal* was placed on the Granth Sahib. The speakers were so nervous about their reception that they had the Guru Granth Sahib opened in the Diwan in order that they might silence interruptions by requesting the audience to remember that they were in the presence of the holy book.

I have so far received no official reports from outlying centres, but I have been privately informed that there were no proceedings of any kind at Guru-ka-Bagh, and that at Baba Bakala a morning Diwan attracted only an audience at about fifty. An evening Diwan was announced, and members of the public were requested to dye their *pugris* in a pan of black dye which was made available at the Gurdwara. No one except the Gurdwara servants seems to have taken action on this suggestion, and the evening Diwan was not held at all.

2. It is obvious that something has gone wrong with the arrangement of the Council of Action. The underlying causes seem to be, first, that the members of the Akali Dal are quarrelling among themselves, and, secondly, that the genuine Akalis dislike the admixture of moderates which was contemplated by Master Tara Singh's original scheme. I have, I think, already reported that a meeting of the organizers of the Sadar Akali Jatha, which was to elect new office-bearers, broke up in confusion. I now learn that there was similar confusion at a meeting of the organizers of Thana Beas which was held over the district border at Bholewal in the Gurdaspur district. At this meeting abuse was freely exchanged, and it was impossible to complete the election. The reasons for the dissension are too intricate for me to enter into here. Broadly speaking it may be said that the Akalis who have obtained office on the various Gurdwara Committees have used or abused their position to appoint their own supporters to minor posts. These appointments, and occasional dismissals for misconduct, have led to quarrels in which there are generally two or more parties. Thus, even from the purely Akali point of view, it seems unlikely at present that a unanimous campaign of any kind can be launched.

3. As regards the position of the Council of Action, the Akalis are disappointed at the failure of the members of the legislatures to resign, and also definitely dislike some of the members. For example in the local Council Bhagat Singh Jamke is regarded as

half-hearted, Sardar Gurdial Singh Salaria, who was appointed president, is much mistrusted, and Dalip Singh Doabia is involved in various intrigues connected with the Patiala State.

The result of the present disagreements is likely to be that on the 25th instant an attempt will be made to prevent the formation of the Khalsa Darbar, and to ensure that the whole of the anti-Government campaign shall be entrusted to the existing Akali Dal organization. I do not know what Master Tara Singh's views on this matter are, but I am told that the local extremists will resent control by any really representative body.

4. Mr. Gandhi's decision to commit suicide has cut across the existing agitation regarding the Communal Award. The Sikhs, on the 17th instant, admitted a Hindu to their Diwan in the evening, and some Sikhs also attended a small Hindu meeting held after the Diwan. Resolutions supporting Mr. Gandhi's demand were passed. The Sikhs are not, I think, really interested in Mr. Gandhi, but they are anxious to secure Hindu support for their own proposals.[11]

A great rock had been hurled at the country, and this is how even the sections which were most affected by it were acting, these are the things with which even the 'fighting arm' of the country was preoccupied. How current the account of Sikh politics sounds! And so it really was Gandhiji alone—alone in that jail, alone facing death under that tree in the jail yard against the British Empire.

Thirteen years later

Ambedkar had signed the pact. In the immediate aftermath, as we have seen, he had first expressed thanks towards Gandhiji, and soon claimed triumph for himself. But the British knew what had happened: the old man, incarcerated and isolated though he was in the jail, had once again seized the initiative from them, their weapon had been blunted, the politics they, and those 'loyal to the Union Jack' had been

---

11 Report at National Archives, Home Department, *File No. 41-4/32-Poll. and K.-W.*

pursuing had been thwarted. And on the contrary a great impetus had been imparted to the efforts to close the earth-fault which had enabled them to deploy this instrument. As the months passed, specially because he could not acquire control over the organization which had been set up to erase the untouchability which he was ostensibly fighting, Ambedkar felt crestfallen, he was furious.

Thirteen years later, Ambedkar, now a member of the British Viceroy's Council and therefore the open associate of the imperial power, was still chaffing at the memory.

Yes, the Poona Pact gave the Untouchables 148 seats instead of the seventy-eight which they had got under the prime minister's award, Ambedkar wrote. But to conclude from this that the pact had given them more than the award is to ignore what the award had in fact given them, Ambedkar declared. The vital things which the award had given them were two: separate electorates and the double vote. The former, Ambedkar maintained, would have meant that the Scheduled Caste persons who were elected would be truly representative of the Untouchables. The double vote would have ensured that no upper caste candidate could ignore the Untouchables. 'The second vote given by the Communal Award was a priceless privilege,' wrote Ambedkar. 'Its value as a political weapon was beyond reckoning... The increase in the number of seats for the Untouchables [under the Poona Pact] is no increase at all and was no recompense for the loss of separate electorate and the double vote...'[12]

That is Ambedkar's judgement at page 90 of the volume. But remember that the key to Ambedkar's fulminations does not lie in the specifics of an issue, in this case the precise provisions of the Poona Pact. It lies in maintaining that Gandhiji can never be in the right. When he is discussing

12 *Dr. Babasaheb Ambedkar, Writings and Speeches*, Vol. IX, p. 90.

the Poona Pact Ambedkar's objective is to show that that determined enemy of the Untouchables, Gandhi, robbed the Untouchables of the boons which the ever-so-sympathetic British government had conferred on them. Later he is establishing the instability of Gandhiji. He argues that Gandhiji was in the habit of sticking to some unimportant point as if it were a matter of principle, and making all sorts of concessions on matters which were actually vital. 'After having gone on a fast unto death,' Ambedkar taunts, 'he signed the Poona Pact. People say that Mr. Gandhi sincerely believed that political safeguards were harmful to the Untouchables. [That itself is a complete caricature of Gandhiji's opposition to separate electorates.] But how could an honest and sincere man who opposed the political demands of the Untouchables, who was prepared to use the Muslims to defeat them, who went on a Fast unto Death, in the end accept the very same demands—*for there is no difference between the Poona Pact and the Communal Award*—when he found that there was no use opposing, as opposition would not succeed? How can an honest and sincere man accept as harmless the demands of the Untouchables which once he regarded as harmful?'[13]

In a word, Gandhiji could never be in the right: he was condemned because by the Poona Pact he took away something which the British Government's Communal Award had given them and which was of inestimable value to the Untouchables; and he was also condemned for abandoning his principles and signing the Poona Pact which was no different from the government's Communal Award!

Contrast this attitude towards whatever Gandhiji did to the way, the fawning way in which Ambedkar read merit and commitment into what the British rulers did. To take just one example, it will repay us to recall the letter Ambedkar wrote to the viceroy, Linlithgow, who had inducted him into

---

13 *Dr. Babasaheb Ambedkar, Writings and Speeches,* Vol. IX, pp. 259–60.

his Council. Ambedkar had learnt that the viceroy was to return to England. He wrote:

> *Believe me, I have read with genuine sorrow that you will be quitting your office in April next. I have no idea who is going to be your successor and what attitude he will adopt towards the Scheduled Castes. In you I have learnt to place great confidence as the benefactor of the Scheduled Castes. You have done the greatest deed towards them by giving them a place in your Executive Council. It is a most revolutionary act for which there can he no parallel in India's history. I have no doubt and no member of the Scheduled Castes has any doubt that if you knew the grievances of the Scheduled Castes you would never hesitate to set them right. It is from this point of view that I say that I am happy to have to seek justice for my people from one who knows that justice is due to them. I know you have the will to do it and that you will not like to leave it to your successor to do what you wish to do, and what you can do. I need hardly say that for this act of justice myself and the 50 millions of the Scheduled Castes will ever remain grateful to you...'*[14]

Notice the trust that Ambedkar reposed in the British viceroy who had given him a post, and the certainty he had and propagated about Gandhiji's insincerity, his dishonesty, his conspiracies. Notice the scorn and worse that Ambedkar poured on the Herculean work that Gandhiji and his associates did to lift the Harijans, and the undying gratitude he felt for the British Viceroy—'...the benefactor of the Scheduled Castes.... the greatest deed towards them... a most revolutionary act for which there can be no parallel in India's history... I need hardly say that for this act of justice myself and the 50 millions of the Scheduled Castes will ever remain grateful to you.' And all this for a mere post! For there is not a whit else that Linlithgow had done for the Scheduled Castes.

---

14 *Dr. Babasaheb Ambedkar, Speeches and Writings*, Vol. X, pp. 470–72.

Gandhiji

Now, for the British the main organization to be thwarted was the Congress, and the one man to be thwarted was Gandhiji. He was the leader of the National Movement, of course, even more so he was the symbol of Indians rediscovering their own tradition, of their acquiring confidence in it. And so he was the main target of Ambedkar's diatribes.

'A worse person could not have been chosen to guide India's destiny,' Ambedkar declared of the Congress decision to send Gandhiji as its representative to the Round Table Conference. 'As a unifying force he is a failure,' said the person who did as much as anyone to thwart Gandhiji's efforts to bring the Indian delegates to agree among themselves rather than hand the decision over to the British. 'Mr. Gandhi presents himself as a man full of humility,' Ambedkar scoffed, but in fact he has spared no opportunity to treat the non-Congress delegates with contempt—and this because of the 'successful compromise' that Mr Gandhi had struck with the British government before coming to the Conference, wrote Ambedkar, the very Ambedkar who was among the ones the British were confident would sing their song! 'From the point of view of knowledge, Mr. Gandhi proved himself to be a very ill-equipped person,' Ambedkar would have us believe. 'On the many constitutional and communal questions 'with which the Conference was confronted, Mr. Gandhi had many platitudes to utter but no views or suggestions of a constructive character to offer. He presented a curious complex of a man who in some cases would threaten to resist in every possible way any compromise on what he regarded as a principle though others regarded it as pure prejudice but in other cases would not mind making the

15 *Dr. Babasaheb Ambedkar, Writings and Speeches,* Vol. IX, pp. 55–56.

worst compromises on issues which appeared to others as matters of fundamental principle on which no compromise should be made.'[15]

Gandhi's attitude at the discussions of the Minorities Committee, Ambedkar wrote, led everyone to believe that 'Mr. Gandhi is the most determined enemy of the Untouchables.' Indeed, Gandhi devoted so much of his time and energy to thwarting the Untouchables, said Ambedkar, 'that it would not be unfair if it was said that the main purpose for which Mr. Gandhi came to the Round Table Conference was to oppose the demands of the Untouchables.'[16] To thwart them Gandhi resorted to 'intrigue', Ambedkar declared, he hatched 'a diabolical plot' through which he tried to inveigh the Muslim delegates into joining him to defeat the demands of the Untouchables—by the latter, of course Ambedkar always means the demands Ambedkar was himself putting forth, demands which Gandhiji had nailed as being 'manufactured by Government'.[17]

As for Gandhiji's fast in the wake of the British Government's announcement of the Communal Award, Ambedkar is scorn itself: '... although Mr. Gandhi declared a fast unto death,' Ambedkar says, 'he did not want to die. He wanted very much to live.'[18] Gandhi is not earnest in his statements, in his programmes about Untouchables, Ambedkar declares, he is not sincere, he is not honest. In fact, he is a conspirator against them. He is an 'open enemy' of the Untouchables, he has put every obstacle in their way. Gandhi would rather that Swaraj perish than that it bring with it political freedom for the Untouchables. Yes, Gandhi declared that he would fast unto death, but the

16 *Dr. Babasaheb Ambedkar, Writings and Speeches,* Vol. IX, p. 70.

17 *Dr. Babasaheb Ambedkar, Writings and Speeches,* Vol. IX, pp. 70–71.

18 *Dr. Babasaheb Ambedkar, Writings and Speeches,* Vol. IX, p. 88.

moment he saw that neither the British government nor the Untouchables would yield, he cowered and pleaded for his life, Ambedkar declared. Here is a representative passage of the kind of things Ambedkar used to write about Gandhiji, things that have now been published and are being sold at subsidized prices by the Education Department of the Government of Maharashtra:

> There was nothing heroic about it [the fast unto death by which Gandhiji sought to get the British government to take back its Communal Award]. It was the opposite of heroic. It was an adventure. It was launched by Mr. Gandhi because he believed that both the Untouchables and the British Government would quake before his threat of fast unto death, and surrender to his demand. Both were prepared to call off his bluff and as a matter of fact did call it off. All his heroism vanished the moment Mr. Gandhi found that he had overdone the trick. The man who had started by saying that he would fast unto death unless the safeguards to the Untouchables were completely withdrawn and the Untouchables reduced to the condition of utter helplessness without rights and without recognition was plaintively pleading 'My life is in your hands, will you save me?' Mr. Gandhi's over-impatience to sign the Poona Pact—though it did not cancel the Prime Minister's Award as he had demanded but only substituted another and a different system of constituent safeguards—is the strongest evidence that the hero had lost his courage and was anxious to save his face and anyhow save his life.
>
> There was nothing noble in the fast. It was a foul and filthy act. The fast was not for the benefit of the Untouchables. It was against them and was the worst form of coercion against a helpless people to give up the constitutional safeguards of which they had become possessed under the Prime Minister's Award and agree to live on the mercy of the Hindus. It was a vile and wicked act. How can the Untouchables regard such a man as honest and sincere?[19]

Gandhism is the doom of the Untouchables, Ambedkar

19 *Dr. Babasaheb Ambedkar, Writings and Speeches,* Vol. IX, p. 259.

proclaimed. It will push them to being primitives. It is a return to nature, to animal life. It is back to nakedness, back to squalor, back to poverty, it is back to ignorance for the vast masses of the people. It calls for pity. Its arguments are as stupid as they are revolting. It is opposed to democracy...[20]

Nothing Gandhiji did could ever be right

If the Congress did not put up Scheduled Caste candidates because they were unlikely to win, Ambedkar would of course be at it—denouncing it for being the instrument of the Brahmin-Bania ruling class, pointing to the smallness of the number of Scheduled Caste persons in its list of candidates. But his denunciation was just as vitriolic when the Congress *did* select Scheduled Caste persons as its candidates, just the reason for the denunciation changed!

The Congress had fielded Scheduled Caste persons as candidates to actually sabotage the independent movement among the Scheduled Castes, he now charged, only to capture a majority so that it could form a government, only so that it could prove Gandhi to have been right when he had claimed that the Congress represented the Untouchables and the Untouchables had trust in it. 'The Congress, therefore, did not hesitate to play a full, mighty and, I may say so, a malevolent part in the election of the Untouchables,' he declared of the 1937 elections, 'by putting up Untouchable candidates on Congress ticket pledged to Congress programme for seats reserved for Untouchables. With financial resources of Congress it made a distinct gain...'[21]—the only way one can understand fulminations of this sort is to see that, by Ambedkar's

20 *Dr. Babasabeb Ambedkar, Writings and Speeches*, Vol. IX, pp. 239–97.

21 *Dr. Babasaheb Ambedkar, Writings and Speeches*, Vol. IX, p. 94.

reckoning, seats being reserved for Untouchables meant that they had been reserved for him, and if someone else put up candidates for those seats, and specially so if these candidates won, he was by definition sabotaging the interests of the Untouchables!

In fact, Ambedkar insisted, there was something even more diabolic in what the Congress had done. Remember that in the passage from page 94 of the book cited above Ambedkar's argument was that the Congress aim in fielding Untouchables as its candidates had been to win as many seats for itself as it could, and by getting the maximum number of Untouchables in legislatures under its banner, to give credence to Gandhiji's claim that the Congress represented the Untouchables and that it is the Congress in which they had faith. The key to each of these goals was for the Congress to win as many seats as possible. For that goal to be attained it was in the interest of the Congress itself to field the very best candidates it could muster. That should be obvious.

But just six pages after charging the Congress with the design of using Untouchables merely as instruments—as devices to win the maximum number of seats and to establish the veracity of Gandhiji's claim—Ambedkar charges the Congress with another 'deep-seated plot', which if true would nullify the first charge!

There was a deep-seated plot, Ambedkar declared, in the criteria the Congress used to select its candidates. It is best to read his own description of this 'deep-seated plot' to see what he could read into anything and everything. He wrote:

> Different classes of qualifications were set down for different classes of candidates. From candidates who came from high caste Hindus as Brahmins and the allied communities those with the highest qualifications were selected. In the case of the Non-Brahmins those with low qualifications were preferred to those with higher qualifications. And in the case of the Untouchables those

> with little or no qualifications were selected in preference to those who had [sic]. I don't say that is true in every case. But the general result was that of the candidates selected by the Congress, the candidates from the Brahmin and allied communities were the most highly educated, candidates from the Non-Brahmins were moderately educated and those from the Untouchables were just about literates.

When the proportion of qualified and educated persons among the Untouchables was so much lower because of centuries of neglect, would that not be the natural result? Recall what the viceroy was writing about the difficulties which the British were facing in this very regard. The Secretary of State had written to the viceroy on 16 December 1942, 'It does seem to me as if it would be well worth while giving them [the Scheduled Castes] a substantial leg-up and assimilating their position increasingly to that of the Muslims. There are, after all, politically very considerable advantages in having two substantial minorities to whom consideration has to be paid, and not to be put in the position of being merely labeled pro-Muslim and anti-Hindu...' He said that he well recognized the practical difficulty of offering to fill a given proportion of seats with persons from a community which may not be able to produce an adequate number of educated candidates for the services. But couldn't something be done? The viceroy had replied, 'I think there is a good deal to the point you make as to the political importance of recognizing so great a minority as the Depressed Classes actually are. One of the troubles about that is of course that they are so extraordinarily short of personnel of any quality. Ambedkar himself is outstanding. Little Rajah from Madras is not bad but not striking. Siva Raj, whom we have sent to America, has a good deal of edge to him and might come on very well. But there are precious few others whom one has heard of in the community.'[22] Was this assessment also the result of some high-caste bias? Ambedkar would never allege that—for the British, in particular the viceroy in question, namely Linlithgow, was, as we have seen 'the benefactor' of the Scheduled Castes who had done a deed unparalleled in history! Wouldn't the persons in Congress who were selecting candidates have been confronted with the same difficulty?

But in their case as usual Ambedkar saw a deep plot. 'This system of selection is very intriguing,' he wrote. 'There seems to be a deep laid game behind it. Anyone who studies it carefully will find that it is designed to allow none but the Brahmins and the allied castes to form the main part of the ministry and to secure for them the support of a docile unintelligent crowd of Non-Brahmins and Untouchables who by their intellectual attainments could never dream of becoming rivals of the minister-folk but would be content to follow the lead for no other consideration except for that of having been raised to the status of members of Legislatures...'[23]

And, having selected unqualified persons to be candidates, Gandhi had turned the predictable trick, ran Ambedkar's argument: now that only unqualified Untouchables were in the Legislatures, Gandhi argued that only those persons must be appointed ministers who had the requisite qualifications. Not only did Gandhi fail to see that a particular type of Untouchable—the one who was barely literate—was in the legislatures only because that is how the Congress had organized the outcome to be, in putting up this bogey of qualifications at the stage of selecting persons for ministerial

22 *Transfer of Power,* Vol. III, pp. 390, 456.

23 *Dr. Bahasaheb Ambedkar, Writings and Speeches,* Vol. IX, pp. 100–01; see also p. 222 where Ambedkar repeats the charge.

posts, Gandhi was only revealing his upper-caste bias—so ran Ambedkar's argument. That Gandhi had put forward this criterion of qualifications, Ambedkar declared, 'only confirms the inner feeling of opposition that lies locked in the heart of Mr. Gandhi'.[24]

Now, just see the logic in all this. The object of the Congress is to win the maximum number of seats in the elections, Ambedkar tells us: given that aim, would it be deliberately selecting the least qualified Untouchables as its candidates? Would that be the way for it to try and maximize the chances of winning the largest number of seats? In any case, what prevented Ambedkar from fielding the better type as his candidates, and winning? As for ministers having the requisite qualifications: once Congress ministries were to be formed, was it not necessary to appoint only qualified persons to the jobs? The claim which had to be countered at the time was the British assertion that Indians were not capable of running governments—was it anything but mere prudence to ensure that only qualified persons entered government in the face of that claim? Ambedkar, however, could see nothing but the conspiracy of his own imagining.

Nor did the 'deep-seated plot' stop at that in Ambedkar's reckoning. 'The second misdeed of the Congress,' Ambedkar declared, 'was to subject the Untouchable Congressmen to the rigours of party discipline. They were completely under the control of the Congress Party Executive. They could not ask a question which it did not like. They could not move a resolution which it did not permit. They could not bring in legislation to which it objected. They could not vote as they chose and could not speak as they felt. They were as dumb driven cattle. One of the objects of obtaining representation in the Legislature

24 *Dr. Bakasaheb Ambedkar, Writings and Speeches,* Vol. IX, p. 100.

for the Untouchables is to enable them to ventilate their grievances and to obtain redress for their wrongs. The Congress successfully and effectively prevented this from happening.'[25]

Assume that everything Ambedkar says about the Scheduled Caste legislators having been stifled by party discipline is true, was it the Scheduled Caste Congressmen alone who were subjected to this party discipline? As that was obviously not the case, was there some equally 'deep-seated plot' in subjecting the others also to party discipline?

Second, recall where Ambedkar was when he wrote this, that is in 1945. He was a member of the Viceroy's Executive Council. And he was there by virtue of being an Untouchable. Was he any less subject to discipline? Was it not true that he 'could not ask a question which it [in his case, the British government] did not like', that he 'could not move a resolution which it did not permit', that he 'could not bring in legislation to which it objected', that he 'could not vote as [he] chose and could not speak what [he] felt'? Now, there can be only two circumstances in which these queries would apply to the Scheduled Caste Congressmen who had come to the legislatures on the Congress ticket and would not apply to Ambedkar who was a minister in the Council of the British viceroy. One that Ambedkar never felt like asking a question which the British did not like, that he never wanted to move a resolution which they did not permit, that he never felt like introducing legislation to which the British objected, that he never wanted to vote in any way contrary to what the British thought was right, that he never felt like saying anything which the British did not feel. The only other explanation can be that in Ambedkar's reckoning the

---

25 *Dr. Babasaheb Ambedkar, Writings and Speeches,* Vol. IX, pp. 101–02.

British, in particular the viceroy whom he served, in fact had the interests of the Untouchables at heart while the Congress, being the instrument of the Brahmin-Bania ruling class, was only out to perpetuate their slavery.

In truth both explanations hold! Ambedkar's views, as we have seen, coincided with those that the British thought appropriate to the occasion, and, as we have also seen, he reposed no trust in Indians, not even in other Scheduled Caste leaders, but he reposed the highest trust in the British.

Either way, Gandhi is wrong as well as dishonest

When Gandhiji returns from South Africa he is plunged into the Champaran Satyagraha, the Rowlatt Act agitation, the satyagraha at Bardoli, the Civil Disobedience and Non-Cooperation movements, and a myriad other issues. Ambedkar's grouse about this period is: Why did Gandhi not launch a movement to open temples to Untouchables? When temple-entry does become a public issue and Gandhiji struggles to open the temples to all, Ambedkar's complaints become the opposite!

Gandhi is doing this only to destroy the separateness of the Untouchables and thereby to deprive them of the very basis of their demands, he declared. Gandhi is taking up the issue only to further his name and fame, Ambedkar declared. Gandhi and his followers are guilty of compelling unwilling Hindus to open their temples, Ambedkar declared, they are lost in the mad pursuit of their objective (of temple-entry) heedless of opposition from persons who have the courage to stand up for their beliefs, Ambedkar declared.

Gandhiji invited Ambedkar to join the movement. Ambedkar predictably spurned the offer. Why should Untouchables waste their energies in trying to enter these places?, he demanded.

In the event a very large number of temples were opened to all. Ambedkar scoffed: only those temples have been thrown open which were dilapidated and deserted, he declared, only those which were being used by dogs and donkeys.

Such is the consistency of Ambedkar—not in wanting an injustice undone, of course, but in spewing venom at Gandhiji! When Gandhiji is busy with other issues Ambedkar is all fire and brimstone: Why is the man not taking up the cause of temple-entry?, he demands. When Gandhiji takes up the matter, the foregoing is what Ambedkar hurls at him.

It is only by wading through the passages that one can form an idea of the malevolence.

'When the owners and trustees of temples were not prepared to throw open their temples to the Untouchables, the Hindus actually started *satyagraha* against them to compel them to fall in line,' Ambedkar complains. 'The *satyagraha* by Mr. Kelappan for securing entry to the Untouchables in the temple at Guruvayur was a part of this agitation. *To force the hands of the trustees of the temples who had the courage to stand against the current* many Hindu legislators came forward, tumbling over one another, with Bills requiring trustees to throw open the temples to the Untouchables if a referendum showed that a majority of the Hindu worshippers voted in favour. There was a spate of such Bills and a race among legislators to take the first place...'[26] In a word, if the leaders do not take up the matter, they are guilty of perpetuating an age-old injustice, and that is but to be expected because they are just the instruments of the Brahmin-Bania ruling class. When these leaders do take up the matter and launch satyagrahas to persuade the trustees, they are guilty of *'compelling'*

26 *Dr. Babasaheb Ambedkar, Writings and Speeches,* Vol. IX, p.107.

trustees, of *'forcing the hands'* of trustees, who, Ambedkar suddenly discovers, are the ones *'who have the courage to stand against the current'*!

Ambedkar said that at one stage Gandhi had been opposed to opening the temples to all. 'His joining the movement for Temple Entry must therefore remain a matter of great surprise,' he declared. 'Why Gandhi took this somersault it is difficult to imagine,' he wrote. Only to insinuate a host of motives—every motive, that is, except the possibility that Gandhiji sincerely believed that our temples should be open to all devotees, that it was unjust, that to keep a devotee from the temple for whom he had veneration was a deep cruelty. 'Was it an honest act of change of heart, due to a conviction that he was in error in opposing the entry of Untouchables in Hindu temples?' Ambedkar asked, with the answer he wanted the reader to infer visible from a mile. 'Was it due to a realization that the political separation between the Hindus and the Untouchables brought about by the Poona Pact might lead to a complete severance of the cultural and religious ties and that it was necessary to counteract the tendency by some such measure as Temple Entry as will bind the two together?,' Ambedkar asked—thereby acknowledging both the things he used to so insistently deny: namely, that there *were* religious and cultural ties between all castes of Hindus including Untouchables, and that the Poona Pact, which had had to be entered into only to thwart the manoeuvre of the British, had opened the prospect of a 'complete severance' of those religious and cultural ties.

'Or was his object in joining the Temple Entry movement to destroy the basis of the claim of the Untouchables for political rights by destroying the barrier between them and the Hindus which makes them separate from the Hindus?' Ambedkar asked with no doubt about the answer he wanted the reader to reach—notice the reasoning: having denounced the barrier which the 'Hindus' had set up so as to keep the Untouchables separate from themselves, suddenly that barrier becomes something that has to be preserved so that the Untouchables can make political demands!

'Or was it because Mr. Gandhi saw before him looming large a possibility of adding to his name and fame and rushed to make the most of it, as is his habit to do?' Ambedkar asked—notice the mindset again: when Gandhiji is busy with other issues and does not take up the cause of temple-entry, Ambedkar declares that he is not doing so because he does not want to forfeit the popularity he has among the Brahmin-Bania ruling class whose instrument he is; when Gandhiji takes up the issue he is declared to be doing so because he sees 'looming large a possibility of adding to his name and fame and rushed to make the most of it, as is his habit to do'. 'The second or the third explanation may be nearer the truth,' Ambedkar concluded—that is, Gandhiji took up the cause of opening temples not because he believed in it but to neutralize the effects of the Poona Pact, and to destroy the separateness of the Untouchables so as to deprive them of a basis of making political demands![27]

Until now Ambedkar's grouse had been that Gandhiji had not taken up the issue of opening up the temples to Untouchables. And now? 'Mr. Gandhi did not mind any opposition,' he charged, 'and was indifferent as to whether it came from the orthodox Hindus or from the Untouchables. He went on *in mad pursuit of* his objective...' On the one hand Ambedkar's charge is that Gandhiji is compelling unwilling trustees to open their temples, that he is forcing the hand of trustees who have the courage to stand against the current. That is on page 107 of the volume. But just eight pages

27 *Dr. Babasaheb Ambedkar, Writings and Speeches,* Vol. IX, pp. 107–08.

later the charge becomes the opposite: namely, that in fact Gandhi has not secured the opening up of any significant temples! 'To put it briefly,' Ambedkar says, 'after a short spurt of activity in the direction of removing untouchability by throwing open temples and wells the Hindu mind returned to its original state. The reports appearing in the "Week to Week" columns of the *Harijan* subsided, became few and far between and ultimately vanished. For myself I am not surprised to find that the Hindu heart was so soon stricken with palsy. For I never believed that there was so much milk of human kindness locked up in the Hindu breast as the "Week to Week" column in the *Harijan* would have the world believe. As a matter of fact a large part of the news that appeared in the "Week to Week" was faked and was nothing but a lying propaganda engineered by Congressmen to deceive the world that the Hindus were determined to fight untouchability. Few temples if any were opened and those that were reported to have been opened most of them were dilapidated and deserted temples which were used by dogs and donkeys.' 'One of the evil effects of the Congress agitation,' said the suddenly solicitous Ambedkar, 'is that it has made the politically minded Hindus a lying squad which will not hesitate to tell any lie if it can help the Congress'[28]—it is not just the sudden concern to keep the Hindus from becoming liars which is so touching but the presumption underlying the regret, namely that, there had been any margin at all for the Congress agitation for temple-entry to make liars out of Hindus: anyone reading Ambedkar would have thought that they had been for centuries congenital liars and that there was no further scope in this regard!

Gandhiji invited Ambedkar to lend support to the temple-entry movement. Ambedkar who had been sniping

---

28 *Dr. Babasaheb Ambedkar, Writings and Speeches,* Vol. IX, pp. 107–08.

at Gandhiji for not having taken up this 'real issue', suddenly declared that this was not the real issue at all, and refused to join or support the movement! Temple-entry is not the real issue, he now declared: the real issue is education and employment; if they have these, the social status of the Untouchables will be higher and then the attitude of the orthodox towards them will automatically change. And then there is the question of self-respect, Ambedkar said. 'Why should an Untouchable beg for admission in a place from which he has been excluded by the arrogance of the Hindus?' he demanded. The key thing was to purge Hinduism of the doctrine of *chaturvarna,* he said, and unless Gandhi ensured this here and now, there was no point in supporting the movement.[29]

Well, it was not worth joining hands with those who were trying to redress this wrong to the Untouchables as, suddenly, it had turned out to be not the real issue. It so happened that elections were soon called. The elections were crucial: if the Congress did not do well in them, the British would get another handle to proclaim that the Congress did not represent the country. To win the elections it was necessary to garner the support of all sections of people. A movement like temple-entry which sought to change the practice and presumptions of a large section of society was necessarily divisive. This was specially so in the south where these prejudices were strong. Keeping the primary objective of Independence in mind, and keeping in mind how vital it was for the attainment of that objective that the Congress do well in the elections, the movement was suspended for the time being. Ambedkar, who had refused to support the movement on the ground that it did not address itself to the real issues, suddenly denounced Gandhiji and the Congress for

---

29 *Dr. Babasaheb Ambedkar, Writings and Speeches,* Vol. IX, pp. 108–13.

abandoning this vital reform, and reproduced the critique of Ranga Iyer to establish that this abandonment was proof positive that Gandhi and the Congress had never been sincere about improving the lot of the Untouchables ![30]

Gandhiji set up the Harijan Sevak Sangh. As is well known, it was through this organization that a large number of persons were spurred and trained to work for Harijan uplift. Over the years it did outstanding work. It became the foremost organization working among them. But predictably Ambedkar had nothing but scorn for it. In fact, that is not quite accurate, he had more than scorn, he had virulent hatred for it.

A huge corpus has been raised by Gandhi for work for Swaraj, he charged, and only a paltry part of it is being spent for Harijan welfare—a typical charge: why was Ambedkar not collecting funds for that kind of work, why was he not spurring the British government of which he was such a useful part to spend more for their uplift? But that was the point about his criticisms: he would not do anything himself, instead he would denounce others for not doing more than they were doing. Gandhiji believed that untouchability was a great stain on Hindu society, that it was the great sin of which the higher-caste Hindus were guilty. His objective therefore was that Hindus from the higher castes must dedicate themselves to this work: they are the ones who must atone for this sin by undertaking this work, he said; their doing so would also have the incidental advantage that it would break the taboo among the higher castes against working among the Harijans. Therefore almost all workers in the Harijan Sevak Sangh, in its governing body, etc., also were higher-caste Hindus. Ambedkar denounced the composition of these bodies for this very reason—Gandhi does not take Untouchables in

30 *Dr. Babasaheb Ambedkar, Writings and Speeches,* Vol. IX, pp. 120–24.

the governing body because of his high-caste prejudices, Ambedkar charged; he does not take them because he does not want Untouchables to have any say on the amount and purposes for which the moneys he has collected in the name of Untouchables should be spent, Ambedkar charged.[31]

As is well known, and as we have seen in the letter Gandhiji wrote to the Depressed Classes leader, Rajbhoj at the end of his fast, Gandhiji's approach to social reform was to change the way of life. He therefore stressed that workers in the Harijan Sevak Sangh must devote themselves to doing constructive work among the Harijans—to awaken them to the rules of hygiene, to spur them to keep their surroundings clean, to motivate them to give up liquor and carrion flesh, to acquire literacy, and the rest. These were the keys to their advancement, Gandhiji taught. And these goals had the incidental advantage that no one among the orthodox could take exception to them; at that time when the primary struggle was for securing the Independence of the country, and when the primary requirement for this struggle was that all sections of society be kept together, and when the primary device of the British was to divide our people, this last virtue of constructive work—that it ensured that what was vital for the upliftment of Harijans would get done and yet no one would be pushed to turning his back on the national movement and joining the British—was a very weighty advantage. But to Ambedkar it was all a ruse, it was a way of not doing the real thing—in this case the real thing being that Gandhi and his Harijan Sevak Sangh must bring about intermarriages and inter-dining among castes.

Gandhi is not working to ensure these, Ambedkar charged, because he does not want to court unpopularity. His sole objective in starting the Harijan Sevak Sangh is

---

31 *Dr. Babascheb Ambedkar, Writings and Speeches,* Vol. IX, pp.126–81.

to destroy the independent movement which the Untouchables have built, Ambedkar charged. Indeed it is to kill the Untouchables themselves with kindness, Ambedkar charged.[32]

Towards other leaders of Harijans

Perhaps there is one thing we should note when we read the things Ambedkar wrote and said about Gandhiji: Ambedkar was just as quick to paste motives on his own colleagues if they did not toe his line. As we have seen, several leaders of the Untouchables were opposed to the intransigence with which Ambedkar was dealing with the question of separate electorates. In particular, they felt that Gandhiji's sincerity and his devotion to lifting the Untouchables could not be questioned. They also emphasized that, whatever the position that Gandhiji might have taken at the Round Table Conference, he was now prepared to ensure 'over-representation' to the Depressed Classes by having seats reserved for them in joint electorates.

Among the Depressed Class leaders who opposed Ambedkar most emphatically, as we have seen, was M.C. Rajah. This is how Ambedkar describes this comrade in his book, *What Congress and Gandhi Have Done to the Untouchables:*

> The only leading member of the Untouchable community was the late Dewan Bahadur Rajah. One cannot help saying that he played a very regrettable part in this business. The Dewan Bahadur was a nominated member of the Central Assembly from 1927. He had nothing to do with the Congress either inside or outside the Assembly. Neither by accident nor by mistake did he appear on the same side as the Congress. Indeed, not only was he a critic of the Congress but its adversary. He was the staunchest friend of the

---

32 *Dr. Babasaheb Ambedkar, Writings and Speeches,* Vol. IX, pp. 140–42.

Government and never hesitated to stand by the Government. He stood for separate electorates for the Untouchables to which the Congress was bitterly opposed. In the crisis of 1932, the Dewan Bahadur suddenly decided to desert the Government and take sides with the Congress. He became the spearhead of the Congress movement for joint electorates and temple-entry. It is impossible to discover a parallel in the conduct of any other public cause. The worst part of the business was that it had none but personal motive behind. The Dewan Bahadur was deeply cut because the Government did not nominate him as a delegate to the Round Table Conference to represent the Untouchables and in his stead nominated Dewan Bahadur R. Srinivasan.

The Government of India had good ground for not nominating him. It was decided that neither the members of the Simon Commission nor the members of the Central Legislative Committee should have a place in the Round Table Conference. The Dewan Bahadur was a member of the Central Legislative Committee and had therefore to be dropped. This was quite a natural explanation. But the wounded pride of Dewan Bahadur Rajah could not let him see it. When the Congress Ministry took office in Madras, when he saw how the Poona Pact was being trampled upon, how his rival was made a Minister and how notwithstanding his services to the Congress he was left out, he bitterly regretted what he did! The fact, however, remains that in the critical year of 1932, Dewan Bahadur Rajah lent his full support to the Congress. He was not only running with the Congress crowd but he took care not to fall out in the race for legislation against untouchability...[33]

Please remember that this is not some British official who is complaining, it is Ambedkar who is doing so—notice the grounds on which he tarnishes his colleague, as well as the motives he reads into his conduct.

All this was excellent as far as the British were concerned. But the next step, the operational conclusion of these assertions was better than excellent. For as the culmination of each of these speeches, essays and books Ambedkar

---

33 *Dr. Babasaheb Ambedkar, Writings and Speeches,* Vol. IX, pp. 113–14.

would declare that for the foregoing 'reasons' the British must *not* concede the demand of the National Movement for Swaraj. For Swaraj would only transfer power into the hands of the Hindus—who, as he had 'shown', were determined to keep the Untouchables in slavery forever. If the British had become too powerless now to resist the demand of Gandhi and his Congress for Independence, they must tie the new state by a treaty which would not just bind it into incorporating certain provisions into the constitution of the new country, but would give the British the right to intervene should the new government not live up to the provisions to which the treaty had bound it.

The method again

The non-party initiative of Sir Tej Bahadur Sapru and others was subjected to the same traits of Ambedkar. The Sapru Committee went out of its way to accommodate him and his views. It as good as waited upon his convenience. In vain. For Ambedkar's method, as far as Indians were concerned, was to stand apart, to heckle and demand, to ask of them that they keep coming up with formulae, and to go on rejecting every proposal they brought up.

As will be recalled, the Sapru Committee was the last serious attempt to devise a constitutional arrangement which would satisfy the Muslim League, and thereby avert the Partition of the country. Ambedkar at first agreed to cooperate fully with the Committee and 'to nominate Scheduled Caste members to the Corrimittee and its subcommittee on Scheduled Castes. After their meeting in Delhi, Tej Bahadur Sapru wrote to him, 'I must express my thanks to you for the sympathy you showed to me at Delhi and for your readiness to help us. I shall be grateful if you will kindly send me the names of the representatives of the Depressed Classes and ask them to agree to membership of my Committee. You may be sure that every latitude will be given to every one for the expression of opinion freely and we shall approach all questions relating to the Depressed Classes and others with every desire to appreciate their point of view and to secure their genuine interest. I hope you will also send me the necessary material showing what exactly should be done for the Depressed Classes.'[34]

Sapru kept waiting for Ambedkar to send the names. After the letter, he sent Ambedkar an express telegram. And then another. Eventually, when he heard from Ambedkar, it wasn't at all what he had expected. Ambedkar backed out casting the usual doubts on the bona fides of the other members who had been taken on board. Ambedkar's letter is worth reading in full:

> I was on tour for the last fortnight. Consequently, did not get your letter and telegram until I reached here yesterday evening. In the meanwhile, I read in the Press the names of those whom you have chosen to be members of your Committee. I am sorry to say, the personnel of the Committee has forced me to take a different view. I must say that some of the members do not inspire any confidence in me. They are persons who have been parties to the communal controversy and are imbued with pre-conceived notions in regard to the question of minority rights. I always understood that your Committee was to be a Committee of pure jurists who would express an opinion on the reasonableness or otherwise of the demands made by various minorities in India. This is what I had bargained for, when I assured you of my co-operation. But I find that your Committee is quite different, both in its composition as well as in its purpose. Under the circumstances, I must decline to nominate members of the Scheduled Castes on the Committee. I am prepared to co-operate if you will reconsider the personnel of your Committee and eliminate from it every active and partisan person, and make it a small body who will do nothing more than report.[35]

---

34 *Constitutional Proposals of the Sapru Committee,* Padma Publications, Bombay, 1946, p. lxxi.

35 *Sapru Committee Report,* pp. Ixxi-lxxii.

Sapru was at pains to explain that he had taken good care to exclude persons who belonged to the Congress, the Muslim League or the Hindu Mahasabha, that he had four retired judges as members, that it would be impossible for him to find persons who had not at some time or the other expressed some kind of opinion, that the point really was whether the persons could not be trusted to approach the question now with a free mind...[36]

Sapru could have saved himself the trouble. What Ambedkar had done was his standard response, the charges he had hurled were his standard arsenal. Recall the way he had dissociated himself from the Harijan Sevak Sangh. And how he was to do so later from Panditji's Cabinet.

The Committee examined Ambedkar's critique of the Poona Pact before recommending that the system of elections which had been agreed to under that pact should be continued—with one modification: namely, that in the primary election no candidate shall be elected unless he secures 20 per cent of the votes polled. Recalling the criticisms that Ambedkar had since hurled at the pact, criticisms which we have reviewed above, in particular his criticism that the pact had taken away the double vote from the Scheduled Castes, the Committee remarked:

> With reference to this criticism we would point out that all these sweeping assertions and arguments now urged *ex post facto* were available to Dr. Ambedkar at the time when he deliberately entered into this Pact at the Yeravda Jail with Mr. Gandhi. He bargained for a price for dropping the double vote and separate electorates which the Prime Minister's Award had given and he obtained, after careful haggling lasting for several hours, nearly double the seats, which he was satisfied was an adequate compensation for what he has lost. We would further point out that there has been only one

36 *Sapru Committee Report*, pp. lxxi-lxxii.

election since the Act of 1935 embodying the provisions of the Poona Pact was enforced and at the election the Poona Pact was acted upon. To generalize against the Poona Pact from one single election is neither fair nor safe. The loss of the double vote in the opinion of Dr. Ambedkar is apparently great or is likely to make Hindu candidates neglectful of, if not hostile to, the interests of the Depressed Classes. We have not been able to find any concrete instances of any such hostility on the part of the 'Caste-Hindus' in the actual working of the legislature or the administration of the various governments.[37]

The Committee pointed out that the method of having all electors vote jointly in the second round to elect the winner—from among the four who had been selected in the primary election by Scheduled Caste voters alone—would work to the advantage of all: it would keep out extremists on both sides. Moreover, the greatest boon would accrue to the Scheduled Castes from the fact that under the scheme of the Committee, and the one to which the Congress had been committed for long there would be universal adult franchise. This would enable the largest expansion in the number of Scheduled Caste voters.[38]

The Committee noted at length the advances that were occurring in the condition of the Scheduled Castes: the way the attitudes of vast numbers towards practices like untouchability and segregation were changing; the ameliorative legislation which had been passed in different provinces. It noted that these changes were occurring because of the work of a number of reformers, in particular because of the work of Gandhiji. 'But apart from this,' the Committee said, 'we may observe that it would be obviously wrong to judge of the whole country or of the general Hindu community by the standards prevailing in

37 *Sapru Committee Report,* p. 223.

38 *Sapru Committee Report,* pp. 222–24.

certain parts of India or in certain sections of the community.'[39] This was exactly the kind of discernment which Ambedkar was not prepared to admit into the discourse for his rhetoric and worked-up anger rested entirely on his insistence that the condition of the Scheduled Castes was what it had been at some time he conjured up, that it could never improve as long as Hinduism continued.

Gandhiji's way and Ambedkar's

The essence of Gandhiji's way to political advance, to social reform was that each group, that each person must make demands not on others but on oneself: recall, for instance, the note Gandhiji sent to the Depressed Class leader, Rajbhoj at the end of his fast. Ambedkar's way, that of the communists, that of our 'activists' today is to make demands on the other, in particular on the government of the day.[40]

Where Gandhiji stressed that the group should eradicate its own shortcomings and the larger things it wanted would follow as a matter of course, Ambedkar poured scorn at this saying that it was worse than useless for the Untouchables to waste their energies in the cultivation of 'private virtues'. There was another, equally far-reaching difference. Gandhiji actually set to work. Ambedkar heckled. Like so many of our 'activists' today, his modus operandi was to proclaim an extreme position, and then pronounce everyone else to be insincere and dishonest on the ground that what they were doing fell short of that extreme position.

There is no point in wasting time and energy cultivating

---

39 *Sapru Committee Report*, pp. 217–22, 225–26.

40 For a brief account of the contrast between the two approaches see 'Gandhiji's way and ours' in my *Individuals, Institutions, Processes*, Viking, 1991, pp. 31–52.

private virtue, Ambedkar declared. What has to be done is to change the environment which breeds the vices, he said.[41] And changing this environment involves two things, he insisted.

First, it requires that 'struggles' be waged which would ensure for the Untouchables their civil rights. These struggles would necessarily entail breaking heads, they will involve 'social disturbance and even bloodshed'. The alternative—he was alluding to the path Gandhiji was urging—Ambedkar scoffed at as being just 'the line of least resistance'. The defect with these alternatives, he said, is that 'they do not *compel* thought, for they do not produce crisis.' One must set up a cadre of workers in the rural areas. They must engage in 'direct action', they must create crises in the countryside. 'The crisis will compel him to think,' Ambedkar said of his demon, the higher-caste Hindu, 'and once he begins to think he will be more ready to change than he is otherwise likely to be...' As Gandhi and his Harijan Sevak Sangh are not prepared to wage such struggles, Ambedkar declared, they are dishonest and insincere when they profess to have the interests of the Untouchables at heart. In fact, their sole objective is to mislead the Untouchables into believing that something is being done for them, it is to wean them away from the ones who are actually prepared to engage in such struggles, and to thereby kill the independent movement among Untouchables.[42]

That this was just talk, that it was just heckling so typical of armchair revolutionaries who do not do anything themselves, and instead, having proclaimed an extreme position pronounce everyone who is actually doing something to be

---

41 *Dr. Babasaheb Ambedkar, Writings and Speeches,* Vol. IX, pp. 134–140.

42 *Dr. Babasaheb Ambedkar, Writings and Speeches,* Vol. IX, pp. 135–36.

doing nothing, will be at once obvious. We have already seen what Ambedkar's reaction was to Gandhiji's request that he join and support the struggle to open temples to all Hindus. Not only did he refuse to participate, as we have seen he denounced that struggle on the ground, among others, that it was seeking to *compel* the trustees who were not prepared to open the temples, who in fact had virtue on their side as they were the ones who had the courage to stand against the prevailing 'fashion'!

The second strand to Ambedkar's approach was to demand 'equality of opportunity' for the Scheduled Castes. But from beginning to end, from the memorandum he circulated at the Round Table Conference[43] to the memorandum he prepared for the Fundamental Rights Subcommittee of the Constituent Assembly—a Memorandum to which we shall soon turn—what he meant by 'equality of opportunity' was just reservations. And reservations. And once again reservations. He maintained that Indian society was completely in the hands of the Brahmin-cum-Bania ruling class; that adult franchise shall only reinforce the grip of this class; that, in addition to the hold the class had over society, it had a complete stranglehold over the apparatus of governance—in particular the civil services, the judiciary and the police. To all this he had one solution: seats must be reserved for the Scheduled Castes in the executive—all branches of it, in the Legislature as well as in the other limbs of the apparatus of governance.

With the experience of the last twenty years we can also see how very wrong he was in the argument he gave for having separate electorates. His case was that unless the Scheduled Castes alone elected Scheduled Caste legislators, the ones who would be elected would just be the nominees of the high-caste Hindus. In fact, it is precisely because we

43 The text of the memorandum is at *Dr. Babasaheb Ambedkar, Writings and Speeches,* Vol. IX, pp. 45–52.

have had joint electorates that every party, every candidate has had to take account of the interests and feelings of the Scheduled Caste voters.

Furthermore, Ambedkar maintained, Scheduled Castes must have separate settlements throughout the country—implicit in this proposal was the demand that they would have the right to run their own affairs in these settlements. One does not have to strain to imagine the kind of cleavages, indeed the permanent separation that such settlements would have entailed, coming as they would on top of separate electorates and a right to jobs on the ground of birth and caste.

In all his writings and speeches till the very departure of the British, to these proposals Ambedkar added one further imperative. The Congress, he declared, is nothing but the instrument of this Brahmin-Bania Raj. Therefore, he said, it will never do the right thing by the Untouchables. Hence, he insisted as we have seen, before they go the British must institute these reservations and separate settlements, or else tie the new government in such a treaty that does not just provide for these, but gives the British the right to intervene should the new government fall short in abiding by these provisions.

The legacy

These propositions of Ambedkar, the vehemence with which he put them forth, the abuse he hurled at Gandhiji and the national movement as part of that vehemence, the motives he pasted on them were of inestimable value to the British.

That he collaborated with the British constitutes a handy rationalization to any 'Dalit' leader who for other reasons wants to avail of the patronage of, say, the foreign missionary groups today.

The abuse, and the pasting of motives too, have become a legacy. Indeed, they are the norm, the model to emulate. They are what prove one's commitment, they are the proof that one has broken free. The journals that are run on the name of 'Dalits' today—with the malicious pasting of motives, with their casteist reductionism, with their abuse—are vivid proof of the legacy. Indeed, the legacy has spread beyond mere language, it now covers behaviour in general. We find all around us today what Ortega Y. Gasset had predicted: mediocrity as the norm, repudiation of standards themselves as elitist, as being nothing but the instruments of the Brahmin-Bania ruling class, civility as nothing but the camouflage of the privileged to hoodwink the gullible poor, vulgarity as a right, intimidation as argument, ignorance as proof. The consequences are before us—in public life, in social life, everywhere. This Ambedkarite reasoning has become the rationale for trampling upon the civil rights—the right to free speech, for instance—of anyone whom these leaders of 'dalits' dub as high caste or as the spokesman or agent of the higher castes.

There is another feature which has had, which invariably has disastrous consequences—both for the particular group whose leader or model weans it on that feature as well as on the larger society of which that group is a part. Recall what Gandhiji's insistence always was. When he was addressing Harijans, he would always counsel them about the things *they* must do: pay attention to bodily hygiene, give up liquor, give up eating carrion meat, keep your houses and surroundings clean, learn to read and write... When he was addressing a crowd of higher caste Hindus, he would scold them for their presumptions vis-à-vis their less fortunate brethren, he would tell them that there was no scriptural sanction for the practices which they had adopted, he would declare that if some scripture sanctioned a thing like untouchability it should just be burnt, he would remonstrate with them to open temples, wells and the like to all classes, he would urge them to take up the task of lifting up the Harijans... In a word, he set out before each group the ways in which *it* was responsible for the state of affairs, he told it what *it* must do to improve its position and thereby the level of society. The way of Ambedkar, the communists etc., was the diametrically opposite one. They dinned into their constituents the belief that *they* had no hand in their condition, that their condition was due to *the other,* indeed to the conspiracies and perfidy of *the other.*

This got them a ready following: ever so many are comforted by the thought, ever so many *want* to hear that they are being held down by the designs and machinations of others; moreover, that others are involved in conspiracies against one liberates one from morality and fairness—that is welcome in itself. But the recoil is soon upon the group. What these leaders and their followers do sets off a powerful reaction, the justifications their leaders have manufactured for adopting means of all sorts become justifications for others also to shed inhibitions. When standards and norms and therefore institutions are destroyed by their assaults, they are left as vulnerable and exposed as everyone else. To the extent that they are weaker and less organized than other sections, that is to the extent that the propaganda of those who incited them to destroy norms and institutions is true, they are even more defenceless than others.

There is in addition another consequence which harms the group, and of course society as much. Recall how Gandhiji taught every group to focus on rectifying its own ways, and how Ambedkar waved this—'the cultivation of private virtue'—aside as worse than a waste of energy: he maintained that by harping on the vices that the Untouchables should purge from among themselves, Gandhi was distracting them from the 'real' task, that is of altering the system. Moreover, by this kind of sermonizing Gandhi was on the one hand perpetuating the existing order, and on the other he was making the Untouchables feel that they themselves were responsible for their condition. This was just the old karma theory dressed up, the reasoning ran, and its function was the same as of that theory, that is to blame the victim and thereby exempt the oppressor.

That all this was the grossest possible caricature of what Gandhiji said and taught goes without saying; one has just to read what he used to tell the higher-caste Hindus to see how he held *them* responsible for the state of affairs, and how stern he was in asking them to change their ways. But I am on the consequence for the group—in the present instance the Untouchables—which is led to believe that their condition is due wholly to what the others are doing, to the conspiracies and congenital perfidy of the others, and that anyone who asks them to attend to changing their own conduct is derailing them into useless activity. For one thing, the very vices which have prevented it from rising in the past remain present and continue to enfeeble it just as much in the future: take the case of temperance; Ambedkar would dismiss Gandhiji's emphasis on having Harijans give up liquor as the obsession of a faddist, as the useless pursuit of private virtue; but one has just to see the toll that drunkenness inflicts upon the Harijans to see that the vice continues to hobble them today.

The other point is that even when some members of the group do rise, when because of the reservations that Ambedkar was so fond of for instance, they do reach positions of authority, their conduct squanders the opportunity. As they have been taught that the counsel to adhere to 'private virtue' is but a conspiracy to divert them, as they have been weaned on the belief that the positions they have reached are their entitlement because of the oppression to which their group has been subjected in the past, they neither aspire to acquire the skills to discharge the responsibilities well nor is their conduct such as befits the positions which they have been accorded. The job is ill-done, and so society is harmed. The conduct of these few is such that it reinforces stereotypes of the group which others have of it, the conduct stokes a reaction. That reaction compounds the conduct: the members of the group do not conclude that they should improve or alter their ways—the expectation that they should do so, they have been taught, is but a device to paste the guilt on them, to divert them from the 'real struggle'. Their remedy therefore is to attribute the strictures about their conduct to the same prejudice and perfidy of the others. And to draw up the wagons: to accuse others of making allegations against them because of their high-caste bias, to knit their 'brothers' in caste networks so as to do in any colleague who happens to point to their conduct.

Mayawati and Kanshi Ram are the natural off-spring of Ambedkar's assertions. The conduct of officers in UP and Bihar who have come in through reservations is the natural consequence. The nemesis cannot but capsize society, and the group along with it.

Two alibis

When they are confronted with such facts, apologists of Ambedkar and those who have made a trade of his name offer two alibis. Ambedkar had one goal in his life and that was the emancipation of the Untouchables, to him working along with the British was of little consequence so long as it helped him help the Untouchables, they say. Second, they explain his collaborating with the British, his intense hatred for Gandhiji and others by pointing to the injustices and humiliations which he had himself suffered as a youth. These are nothing but alibis, but they are dangerous alibis.

As we have seen, even in the eyes of the British what was driving Ambedkar to teaming up with them was not some single-minded devotion to the cause of the Untouchables. It was the hankering for office. Recall what the governor of Bombay, Roger Lumley had written to the viceroy after Ambedkar had called on the governor to express his disgruntlement at the proposals of the Cripps Mission: urging the viceroy to give Ambedkar a position in his Executive Council, Lumley had written:

> ... I feel pretty sure that this disgruntlement is largely a personal matter. As you know, his own financial position has been worrying him for some time. I have reason to believe that he owes money to certain people who have helped him in the past, and that he is unable to pay any of it back, and is even rather rude if they mention the subject. As you know, too, he has been, for some time, anxious to obtain a position in the High Court or elsewhere, in which he could have a chance of providing for his own future. He has given me, for some time, the impression of a man who is no longer really interested in the work he is doing for his own followers, and is anxious to reach a different sphere. He is inclined, unfortunately, to attribute the difficulties of his own position to influences at work against him because he is a member of the Depressed Classes, and from that it is an easy step to the belief that we do not concern ourselves about him unduly because we do not think it worthwhile to secure the support of the Depressed Classes...[44]

It is this anxiety which drove Ambedkar, it is this anxiety which the British put to work.

In any case, even if what drove Ambedkar was a single-minded devotion to the cause of the Untouchables as his apologists would have us believe, manifestly he misjudged the matter completely. For there is next to nothing that he

---

44 *Transfer of Power,* Vol. I, pp. 846–47.

got done from the British for the Untouchables—his own remarks to Wavell and others which have been quoted earlier testify to that: did he not tell them that, in spite of all the services the Scheduled Castes had rendered to them, the British were leaving them in no better condition than the one in which they had been at the time the British took over the country? On the other hand, his speaking up on behalf of the British stratagems, his working to disrupt the unity of the national struggle for freedom was of great assistance to the British. Even if we assume that he was impelled only by his singular concern for the condition of the Untouchables, his career is not an example of what devotion to a cause can accomplish. Rather it is a warning about the way the belief that one is devoted to a cause can mislead one into serving those who are out to keep one's country down.

As we have seen, the alibi just does not hold in the case of Ambedkar because it isn't any overpowering devotion to the cause of the Untouchables which impelled him. But even if it had, his decision to support the British when the main struggle at that time was to free the country from foreign rule is indefensible and constitutes a warning of how 'single issue fundamentalism' ends up impelling even the best of persons into a course of action which, even if it succeeded, would imperil the people at large. Unlike Ambedkar who wanted the British to continue their rule in India, Netaji Subhash Chandra Bose wanted India's freedom above all. As Hitler, and later, Japan were fighting the British, as they were 'the enemy of my enemy' Netaji went to them and sought their help. He invited Hitler to launch campaigns towards India. He collaborated openly with the Japanese forces in their drive towards India. Now, had Hitler and Japan succeeded and with them Netaji's line, India would have been rid of the British—but it would certainly have come under the much more lethal heel of Hitler and Tojo. Even if these powers had not enforced their dominance directly, the indirect impact of their victory would have been terrible: had India won Independence with their help, their ideology, their ways would have been the model for us. In a word, in Ambedkar's case it is not possible to explain the services he rendered to the British by maintaining that he rendered these because he was consumed with the urge to help the Untouchables; but even in the cases of persons who are actually impelled by high motives, unless that devotion is tempered by an awareness of what the singular pursuit of that goal can entail in other spheres, unless it is tempered by an awareness of what consequences the alliances they are entering into for realizing that goal shall entail for the future, unless it is tempered by the realization that the means they use today shall become a licence for certain kinds of behaviour tomorrow, their devotion to the goal shall itself become the cause of much suffering.

The second 'reason' which is given to explain away Ambedkar's collaborating with the British too is no more than an alibi. It too holds a warning. First, the privations or humiliations he suffered were no greater than, they were in fact so much less than, the trials that Ramakrishna Paramhamsa, Swami Vivekananda, Gandhiji, and countless others had to wade through. But even if we assume that Ambedkar suffered such injustices and indignities that they ignited in him a passion to overturn the social system, his life holds an important warning. The lesson is this: unless before the time that people start listening to him the person who has suffered the injustices or indignities has outgrown the bitterness of that moment—the moment Gandhiji is thrown out of the train in South Africa—or phase, his legacy will be destructive: that seed of bitterness in him will become poison in his followers, it will become the justification for evil in his followers. Gandhiji overcame bitterness, the Dalai Lama has overcome bitterness: the legacy of their life and work is love. Ambedkar remained to the end a bitter man: his legacy is the venom of Mayawati, the poison of *Dalit Voice,* just as his joining hands with the British is a rationalization for the current 'Dalit' leaders to subordinate themselves to Church groups.

The great counter-example

'But there is one great service that Ambedkar did to our country, and society. All sorts of persons were after him to get him to convert—along with his followers—to Christianity, to Islam. Had he done so, our country would have been saddled with an enormous difficulty. By choosing to convert eventually to Buddhism, he in a deep sense served India, for he kept himself and thereby his followers within the fold'—this is the ultimate defence which is proffered on his behalf.

Three things should be evident from the outset. First, there is no doubt that had he succumbed to the blandishments of the Christian and Islamic missionaries, our problems would have been greatly exacerbated. It is just as clear that had he converted to Christianity during British rule, his usefulness to the British rulers would have been as good as erased: Ambedkar was of use to them so long as he remained within the Hindu fold, and denounced it; so long as he remained a Hindu and helped counter Gandhiji's claim to speak on behalf of all Indians: Jinnah was there to proclaim that Gandhiji did not speak for Muslims; the British needed a Hindu who would proclaim that Gandhiji did not speak for all Hindus either. Of course, the British were scarcely the ones to put all their cards in the hands of one person—as we saw in reviewing their stratagems when it seemed that an agreement may well be reached by Indians, including Ambedkar—or make it dependent entirely on that person sticking to just one course of action—recall the ruminations of Amery about the advantages that might accrue should Ambedkar get his followers to convert to Christianity or Islam. The third fact to bear in mind is that Ambedkar's conversion to Buddhism was merely a political act: his 'Buddhism' had nothing to do with the teachings and life of the Buddha—there is not the slightest trace of any inner-directed search in Ambedkar, there is not the slightest trace that even an effort has been made to overcome the bitterness or presumption. Indeed, in his writings on the matter he creates a Buddha in his own image!

But there is an even more fundamental point. Conversion to another religion, denunciation of our own religion, of our traditions is not the only way, it is not even an effective way of reforming our society. Ambedkar sowed hatred among groups. He reinforced the shame that the missionaries had sought to instil in us towards our past, our scriptures, our deities. He sowed not just aggressiveness, he sowed abusiveness. Kanshi Ram, Mayawati, Rajashekhar, the Ambedkarites in Maharashtra are his progeny.

Swami Vivekananda had foretold what the consequence of this denunciation and negation, of this 'negative education' would be. 'A negative education, or any training that is based on negation, is worse than death,' he had warned in *The Future of India.* 'The child is taken to school, and the first thing he learns is that his father is a fool, the second thing that his grandfather is a lunatic, the third thing that all his teachers are hypocrites, the fourth that all the sacred books are lies! By the time he is sixteen he is a mass of negation, lifeless and boneless. And the result is that fifty years of such education has not produced one original man in the three Presidencies...'[45] For 'negative education' you just have to substitute words to indicate Ambedkar's

45 Swami Vivekananda, 'The future of India', in *The Complete Works of Swami Vivekananda,* Vol. III, pp. 301–02.

fulminations and works such as his *Riddles of Hinduism,* and as for the products you have to just think of the abusive and negationist Ambedkarites, and the forecast fits to the dot.

The Swami condemned 'every fanatical movement' of 'reform' for the same reason, each of them would leave the same trail of hatred, of self-loathing, of acrimony, he warned, each of them would therefore leave our people and country weakened. He could not, he would not join 'anyone of these condemning societies,' he declared. 'Why condemn?', he asked, and explained:

> There are evils in every society; everybody knows it. Every child of today knows it; he can stand upon a platform and give us a harangue on the awful evils of Hindu society. Every uneducated foreigner who comes here globe-trotting takes a vanishing railway view of India and lectures most learnedly on the awful evils in India. We admit that there are evils. Everybody can show what evil is, but he is the friend of mankind who finds a way out of the difficulty. Like the drowning boy and the philosopher—when the philosopher was lecturing him, the boy cried, 'Take me out of the water first'—so our people cry: 'We have had lectures enough, societies enough, papers enough; where is the man who will lend us a hand to drag us out? Where is the man who really loves us? Where is the man who has sympathy for us?' Ay, that man is wanted. That is where I differ entirely from these reform movements. For a hundred years they have been here. What good has been done except the creation of a most vituperative, a most condemnatory literature? Would to God, it was not here ! They have criticized, condemned, abused the orthodox, until the orthodox have caught their tone and paid them back in their own coin; and the result is the creation of a literature in every vernacular which is the shame of the race, the shame of the country. Is this reform? Is this leading the nation to glory? Whose fault is this?[46]

46 In 'My plan of campaign,' *The Complete Works of Swami Vivekananda,* Vol. III, pp. 214–15. See also, 'A plan of work for India,' *The Complete Works of Swami Vivekananda,* Vol. IV, pp. 371–73.

Swamiji pointed to the other way:

> Did India ever stand in need of reformers? Do you read the history of India? Who was Ramanuja? Who was Shankara? Who was Nanak? Who was Chaitanya? Who was Kabir? Who was Dadu? Who were all these great preachers, one following the other, a galaxy of stars of the first magnitude? Did not Ramanuja feel for the lower classes? Did he not try all his life to admit even the pariah to his community? Did he not try to admit even Mohammedans into his fold? Did not Nanak confer with Hindus and Mohammedans, and try to bring about a new stage of things? They all tried, and their work is still going on. The difference is this. They had not the fanfaronade of the reformers of today; they had no curses on their lips as modern reformers have; their lips pronounced only blessings. They never condemned. They said to the people that the race must always grow. They looked back and said, 'O Hindus, what you have done is good, but, my brothers, let us do better.' They did not say, 'You have been wicked, now let us be good.' They said, 'You have been good, but let us now be better.' That makes a whole world of difference. We must grow according to our nature. Vain is it to attempt the lines of action that foreign societies have engrafted upon us; it is impossible, Glory unto God that it is impossible, that we cannot be twisted and tortured into the shape of other nations.[47]

In a word, denunciation, condemnation, calumnizing the gods and goddesses, pouring ridicule on our scriptures, sowing hatred in the followers is the course Ambedkar adopted. But it was not the only course available. Earlier one of the greatest of reformers of the last hundred and fifty years had adopted the exact opposite course, and thereby accomplished both—he had lifted the lives of millions, and at the same time he had transformed and raised our society. That reformer was from a caste which was not just untouchable but unapproachable—the reformer of course was Narayan Guru, who lived from 1854 to 1928.

---

47 *The Complete Works of Swami Vivekananda*, Vol. III, p. 219.

He did not heckle and spit at our tradition as an outsider. He never made truck with the conquerors and subjugators of India. He attained the highest states of spiritual awareness by immersing himself in the teachings of the Upanishads. He attained those states by practising the austerities and following the methods which our great seers had uncovered. As he attained these states, his entire life became a refutation of the claims of the orthodox as to their superiority, his beatific state became a refutation of the assertions of the orthodox that the esoteric lore was closed to the lower castes. And as he had attained those states, he received universal homage.

He too was upset at the fact that devotees from the lower castes were not being allowed to enter temples. He did not on that account denounce temples. He did not one day shout at others demanding to know why they had not made temple-entry the object of their campaigns, and the next that gaining access to temples was not the real issue. He had his followers construct over a hundred temples—temples with idols of Shiva, of Sharda, a temple with a *jyoti* for an idol, another with a mirror as an idol on which was inscribed *Om Shanti*.

The people of the lower castes, excluded as they were, had fallen prey to lower forms of worship—in which offerings of liquor and flesh were made to the idols. He did not on that count either berate the people or denounce worship, he elevated it—substituting flowers for meat, replacing representations symbolizing the lower passions by deities personifying the higher values and aspirations.

He too was upset by the expensive rituals into which the people had fallen, but he did not on that count denounce the tradition itself. He simplified and ennobled the rituals—and, precisely because he had translated the highest teachings of the tradition into his life, precisely because his life had become a living example of that tradition, his authority to institute the changes was recognized by all, and the reforms were adopted by millions. He asked the lower castes to learn English as well as Sanskrit. He got his followers to set up institutions which would equip the lower castes for modern agriculture and industry.

Whereas Ambedkar taught his followers to hate and confront, Narayan Guru taught that we should never say a harsh word in talking of our own tradition, or even the traditions of others, that only that reform endures which is brought about by example, by persuasion, by taking everyone along. 'Discard superstitions and worship of lower deities with animal sacrifices and other inauspicious rites,' he instructed his preachers. 'Give lectures emphasizing the greatness of the higher modes of worshipping God and the principles of pure Hinduism, the conception of God with and without attributes. Persuade the people to build temples and *mutts* wherever they demand them. But do not run down other religions in malice or in any way likely to cause agitation in the minds of the votaries.' 'To know and to make known; not to argue and win'—that was the motto which the gentle Guru gave to the *Sarva Mat Sammelan* which was held under his auspices. You have just to read Ambedkar's vituperative *Riddles of Hinduism* to see the contrast.

Whereas Ambedkar taught his followers to make demands on others, Narayan Guru taught them to make demands on themselves: just as the Guru persuaded persons of the higher castes to open the temples to devotees of all castes, he strove as hard to ensure that the people of his own caste—the then lowly Ezhavas—stopped their discriminations against the Untouchables, that they too opened *their* temples to devotees from the still lower castes. Instead of pandering to the practices of the lower castes, he preached temperance to castes and tribes whose very mode of living and livelihood revolved around toddy-tapping. He asked his preachers to educate the lower castes to the importance of truth, cleanliness, to instil in them fear of unrighteousness, to instil in them faith in God.

Whereas Ambedkar converted to (his own version of) Buddhism, Narayan Guru consistently taught against conversion, he himself took back into the Hindu fold persons from the lower castes who had gone over to other religions, and his closest disciples who were in a position to testify to his view of the matter taught that there was not an iota of religion in conversions en masse.[48]

The legacy of Narayan Guru is a society elevated, in accord, the lower castes educated and full of dignity and a feeling of self-worth. The legacy of Ambedkar is a bunch screaming at everyone, a bunch always demanding and denouncing, a bunch mired in self-pity and hatred, a society at war with itself. The legacy of Narayan Guru is a country rejuvenated. The legacy of Ambedkar is a country with a deepened sense of shame in its entire past. And thereby further disabled.

---

48 For brief accounts of Narayan Guru's inspiring life, example and teachings see Nataraj Guru, *The Word of the Guru,* Pai and Co., Ernakulam, 1968, and P. Parmeswaran, *Narayan Guru, The Prophet of Renaissance,* Suruchi Sahitya, New Delhi, 1979.

The Manu of Our Times?

8

Wasn't Ambedkar telling the truth?

'Now, Sir, we have inherited a tradition. People always keep on saying to me: "Oh, you are the maker of the Constitution." My answer is I was a hack. What I was asked to do, I did much against my will,' the member said.

P. Sundarayya, the communist leader, fresh from the Telangana struggle—remember this was in 1953—got up: 'Why did you serve your masters then like that?'

Several members were on their feet.

The Chairman: 'Order, order.'

The problem is that because of hatred of the British we have developed some notions about what is democratic and what is not, the member said. We have acquired the notion that to leave some powers to the governor to act in his discretion is undemocratic. 'We have inherited the idea that the Governor must have no power at all, that he must be a rubber stamp,' the member explained. 'If a minister, however scoundrelly he may be, if he puts up a proposal before the Governor, he has to ditto it. That is the kind of conception about democracy which we have developed in this country.'

'But you defended it,' said a member from Rajasthan.

'We lawyers defend many things...,' said the member. Several members rose to protest.

The member went on to say how provisions in regard to

the state executive in the Constitution were defective: that the Governor must be given powers to act in his own discretion, that in particular the governor should be given the power comparable to the power that Section 93 of the Canadian Constitution gave to the Governor General in Canada by which he can examine complaints which he might receive from and on behalf of a section of the population. 'I would like to ask my friend, the Home Member, whether, with the inclusion of section 93 in the Canadian Constitution, he regards the Canadian Constitution to be democratic or undemocratic. What is his answer?'

'My answer is that you had drafted this Constitution,' retorted Dr Kailash Nath Katju.

'You want to accuse me for your blemishes?' the member exclaimed—typically, I might add.

As tempers seemed to be rising, the chairman intervened and remarking, 'He has said that he defended the present Constitution because it was the majority decision,' asked the member to go on.

But the member was soon back to the theme. 'Sir, my friends tell me that I have made the Constitution. But I am quite prepared to say that I shall be the first person to burn it out. I do not want it. It does not suit anybody...'

The member? B.R. Ambedkar, of course.

The Council of States was discussing a bill for the creation of Andhra Pradesh. Ambedkar first reprimanded the government: for twenty years you in the Congress have been saying India should have linguistic provinces and you have already created twenty-three provinces on linguistic lines, and that has not affected the unity of the country in any adverse way; and yet you have dragged your feet in this case. In the next breath, he was saying that the creation of linguistic provinces exposes minorities—in this case linguistic minorities—to the tyranny of the majority. That is why, he said, he was advocating that the constitutional scheme be changed to give the governor the powers to oversee the functioning of the elected governments in this regard.

K.S. Hegde—then a young member from Madras state, later judge of the Supreme Court of India, and later still the Speaker of the Lok Sabha—turned to this speech the next day. He reminded the House, 'Once before I had to ask on the floor of the House whether Dr. Ambedkar continued in the Cabinet for a mere mess of pottage. I would not like to repeat it...' It is astounding to have a person who was put minister in charge of preparing the Constitution disown responsibility in the manner Ambedkar has done and to proclaim that he would burn the Constitution. 'Is he setting a good political precedent?' Hegde asked, adding, 'I am sorry Dr. Ambedkar only abused and got out of the House. If he abuses, he should be prepared to receive the reactions thereof.' 'It came with ill grace from Dr. Ambedkar when he said that his heart was not in the Constitution, that he was merely perpetuating a fraud, to put it in the mildest form.' 'His whole life has been one of a series of contradictions,' Hegde pointed out. 'First he tried to live in communalism and now probably it is too late in the day for him to get himself out of that past. I have nothing but pity for him...'

Even in regard to linguistic provinces, Hegde pointed out Ambedkar's speech had been riddled with contradictions. He had started by chastising the government for not creating linguistic states with dispatch, and then proceeded to warn that the creation of linguistic states would endanger minorities. The reason the creation of a separate Andhra had got held up was something altogether different from what Ambedkar had implied, and it was well known. A committee had been set up, Hegde recalled, to settle how the assets would be divided. 'They went on dividing the stores, land, buildings and everything. Ultimately, they said that unless the city of Madras was included, they were not going to have the Andhra State. Now, who was responsible for the delay? Is it the Andhra leaders or is it the Government of India?' Hegde asked.[1]

I am not on Ambedkar's inconsistencies at the moment, but on his remarks about the authorship of the Constitution: was Ambedkar just palming off responsibility, or was he giving us a glimpse into what his role had actually been in regard to the drafting of the Constitution? That the remarks were not just an off-the-cuff outburst is evident from the fact that he repeated the description to the political scientist and biographer, Michael Brecher during an interview three years later, a few months before his death.[2]

What do the sequences suggest?

Recalling the evolution of the point to which Ambedkar was alluding—whether discretionary powers ought to be vested in the governor—will give us a clue, not just about this particular provision but about the manner in which the Constitution came to be formulated. The provision in question had followed a typical course. The Provincial Constitution Committee—Sardar Patel was the chairman of this Committee—had recommended that while 'for the most part, the Governor will act on advice [of the Council of Ministers], but he is required to act on his discretion in the following matters: (1) the prevention of any grave menace to the peace and tranquillity of the Province or any part thereof...; (2) the summoning and dissolving of the Provincial Legislature...; (3) the superintendence, direction and control of elections...; (4) the appointment of the Chairman and the members of the Provincial Public Service Commission and of the Provincial Auditor-General....' 'It is

---

1 *Proceedings of the Council of States (Rajya Sabha)*, 2 September, 1953, Columns 864–80, and 3 September 1953, Columns 997–1003.

2 Michael Brecher, *Nehru, A Political Biography*, Oxford University Press, 1959, p. 423.

to be noted,' the Committee had added, 'that the Governor, under the proposed Constitution, is to be elected by the people, so that he is not likely to abuse his "discretionary" powers.'

That report had been finalized and submitted to the president of the Constituent Assembly on 27 June 1947. But a fortnight later when Sardar Patel rose to move the report of the Committee for consideration by the Constituent Assembly, he told the Assembly that the report of the Committee 'is not the final draft of the Provincial Constitution'. One by one he reversed the recommendations of the Committee in regard to three of the four items on which according to the report the governor was to exercise his discretion. The only function in regard to which the governor was now envisaged to act on his own was in summoning the legislature.[3]

The Constituent Assembly took up the draft of the relevant Articles for consideration on 31 May and 1 June 1949. The Drafting Committee had suggested two alternative provisions: one providing for a governor who would be directly elected by the people, and the other for a governor who would be appointed by the president. On the latter too there were two possibilities: that the legislature forward a panel of names to the president and the latter appoint one of the persons from the panel; or that the president appoint a person without any panel being put up to him. The draft regarding the powers and functions of the governor, that is Article 143, read: 'There shall be a Council of Ministers with the Chief Minister at the head to aid and advise the Governor in the exercise of his functions except in so far as he is by or under this Constitution

3 For the text of the report of the Provincial Constitution Committee see B. Shiva Rao, *The Framing of India's Constitution, Select Documents,* Vol. II, pp. 656–63; for Sardar Patel's speech moving the Report for consideration by the Assembly, ibid, pp. 664–67.

required to exercise his functions or any of them in his discretion.'

Ambedkar explained, first, that in regard to the method of election or appointment of the governor the Drafting Committee had had no choice but to furnish alternatives for the Constituent Assembly to consider: the Assembly had already accepted the principle that the governor would be elected; as such, Ambedkar explained, 'The Drafting Committee had no choice in the matter at all because according to the directions given to the Drafting Committee it was bound to accept the principle which had been sanctioned by the House itself.' But since then things had proceeded in a different direction, he went on to add: the view now was 'that the Governor is not to have any kind of functions—to use a familiar phraseology, "no functions which he is required to discharge either in his discretion or in his individual judgement". According to the principles of the new Constitution he is required to follow the advice of his Ministry in all matters...' Ambedkar said that the Drafting Committee had made a provision for the alternative of the governor being appointed by the president because 'we felt that the powers of the Governor were so limited, so nominal, his position so ornamental that probably very few would come to stand for election.' He was not bothered by the prospect that there might be a conflict or rivalry between an elected chief minister and an elected governor, Ambedkar said: the chief minister was going to be elected on the basis of the policies and programmes he proposed to implement while the governor was going to be elected on the basis of his personality. He had been persuaded by the other consideration, Ambedkar said: as the Governor was not going to have any substantive functions, how justified would it be to subject the country to the enormous costs of an election for each of these ornamental posts? In fact, said Ambedkar, as 'this functionary is going to be a purely ornamental functionary, how he comes into being, whether by nomination or by some other machinery, is a purely psychological question—what would appeal most to the people—a person nominated or a person in whose nomination the Legislature has in some way participated. Beyond that, it seems to me it has no consequence...'

As that is the position, H.V. Kamath and a number of other members argued, the words in the draft Article 'except in so far as he is by or under this Constitution required to exercise his functions or any of them in his discretion' should be deleted. They tabled an amendment to the draft article for this purpose. Ambedkar and other members of the Drafting Committee now argued the opposite. The words should *not* be deleted, they said, because the Assembly had not yet taken a view on other draft articles of the Constitution which endowed some discretionary powers in the governor. Vesting such powers in an appointed governor is not in any way incompatible with responsible government, Ambedkar said. As under other articles on which the Assembly had yet to take a final view the governor had been assigned functions which he was to discharge in his discretion, 'the House cannot escape from mentioning in some manner that the Governor shall have discretion.'

But does the article relating to the president not require that he must in all matters act in accordance with the advice of the Council of Ministers? Isn't there a difference therefore between articles relating to the President and those relating to the governor, Kamath asked. 'Of course there is,' Ambedkar replied, 'because we do not want to vest the President with any discretionary power. Because the Provincial Governments are required to work in subordination to the Central Government, and therefore in order to see that they do act in subordination to the Central Government the Governor will reserve certain things in order to give the President the opportunity to see that the rules under which the Provincial Governments are supposed to act according to the Constitution or in subordination to the Central Government are observed...'

Clearly, the balance which Ambedkar was indicating on 1 June was very different from the balance he had spelled out on 31 May. B. Shiva Rao speaks to the result: 'It is... worth noting that as the various Articles which conferred these discretionary functions came up for consideration, the Drafting Committee suggested amendments deleting the requirement that the Governor would act in his discretion. As a result, in the Constitution as adopted finally, full ministerial responsibility without any discretionary powers for the Governor was established over the whole field of State administration. The only matter in which the Governor could act independently of his Ministers was in relation to certain tribal areas in Assam where, for a transitional period, the administration was made a Central responsibility and the Governor was to act as the agent of the Central Government. But in spite of this radical change in the content of the powers of the Governor, no change was made in the draft Article 143 and the reference to the Governor exercising certain functions in his discretion still remains. At the revision the Article was renumbered 163.'[4]

Does a sequence such as this speak to the article springing virginal and complete from the mind of one person—Ambedkar in this case—or to some other process? And does the sequence—one day the balance of Ambedkar's argument tilts one way, another day it tilts the other way—not indicate that he was only telling the truth when he told the Rajya Sabha, 'We lawyers defend many things'? And the 'Drafting' Committee: does it lay down what the

---

4 *Constituent Assembly Debates,* Vol. VIII, pp. 467–69, 489–502; and B. Shiva Rao, *The Making of India's Constitution, A Study,* pp. 400–401.

Article shall be, or does it indicate two very dissimilar alternatives and wait upon the Assembly to choose? And the Assembly itself: does it settle the matter unambiguously and finally, or does it for the time being retain words which in fact go contrary to the direction in which its own decision is tending?

Or take another instance. The article relating to the right to property went through several rounds, as we shall see, and was the subject of earnest discussion. It went through many versions: when it came up for consideration at the Premiers' Conference, Ambedkar narrated that the article had caused the Drafting Committee 'a lot of headache', so much so that he suggested that the article be dropped altogether and in its stead an entry be provided in the legislative lists reproducing verbatim the relevant words from the Australian Constitution. Alladi Krishnaswami and others shot down that suggestion on the ground that it would not meet any of the problems which had come up. The drafts and redrafts continued to go to and fro.[5] Eventually, the draft of the article that the Drafting Committee sent up closely followed Section 299 of the Government of India Act, 1935. It provided that no property would be acquired except for a public purpose, and that it would not be acquired without compensation and unless either the amount of compensation was fixed or the principles on which it was to be fixed were set out. When the draft came up for consideration in the Constituent Assembly, Pandit Nehru himself moved an amendment to replace the text wholesale. He told the Assembly that the new text was 'the result of a great deal of consultation', that it reflected a compromise between various approaches.

Two years later, in 1952, the Supreme Court handed down

5 See B. Shiva Rao, *The Making of India's Constitution, Select Documents*, Vol. IV, pp. 697–98, and B. Shiva Rao, *The Making of India's Constitution, A Study*, p. 289.

judgments in which it held that the existence of a public purpose was a prerequisite for the exercise of the power of compulsory acquisition. The government then brought in an amendment to the Constitution which provided, among other things, that 'no such law [aimed at acquiring property] shall be called in question in any court on the ground that the compensation provided by that law is not adequate.' The amendment also provided that where the law did not transfer the property to the state or a corporation owned or controlled by the state 'it shall not be deemed to provide for the compulsory acquisition or requisitioning of property, notwithstanding that it deprives any person of his property.' In a word, there was no longer any need in such cases for either of the two conditions—the existence of a public purpose, or the payment of just compensation. This part of the matter was thus put beyond the reach of courts. Government asserted that the new text was in accord with what the Drafting Committee had intended.

Ambedkar refuted the suggestion. Here is what he told the Rajya Sabha on 19 March 1955: 'Article 31 with which we are dealing now in this Bill is an Article for which I, and the Drafting Committee, can take no responsibility whatsoever. We do not take any responsibility for that. That is not our draft.' He said that at the time this article was being considered 'the Congress Party... was so divided within itself that we did not know what to do, what to put and what not to put.' Ambedkar said that there had been three points of view within the Congress on the question: a section led by Sardar Patel had wanted that the Constitution provide for compensation on the lines of the existing Land Acquisition Act, namely, market price plus 15 per cent; Pandit Nehru wanted that no compensation should be provided for at all; Pandit Pant, who was the chief minister of Uttar Pradesh at the time, had been concerned mainly to safeguard the *zamindari*-abolition legislation he had got through. 'There was thus this tripartite struggle,' Ambedkar told the House, 'and we left it to them to decide in any way they liked. And they merely embodied what their decision was in Article 31. This Article 31, in my judgement, is a very ugly thing, something which I do not like to look at...'[6]

An explanation!

Incidentally, having denounced the article on property as 'a very ugly thing, something which I do not like to look at,' Ambedkar reversed what he had said about the Constitution on the earlier occasion, and remarked, 'If I may say so, and I say it with a certain amount of pride the Constitution which has been given to this country is a wonderful document. It has been said so not by myself, but by many people, many other students of the Constitution. It is the simplest and the easiest. Many, many publishers have written to me asking me to write a commentary on the Constitution, promising a good sum. But I have always told them that to write a commentary on this Constitution is to admit that the Constitution is a bad one and an un-understandable one. It is not so. Anyone who can follow English can understand the Constitution. No commentary is necessary.'

A member from Punjab, Anup Singh, interrupted. 'Last time when you spoke, you said that you would burn the Constitution,' he reminded Ambedkar.

'Do you want a reply to that?' Ambedkar fumed. 'I would give it to you right here.'

'My friend says that the last time I spoke, I said that I wanted to burn the Constitution,' he continued. 'Well, in a

6 *Rajya Sabha Debates*, 19 March 1955, Columns 2450–51.

hurry I did not explain the reason'—there had been no hurry; as we have seen, Ambedkar had spoken at length, he had reverted to that particular point more than once. But to continue, Ambedkar's position now was, 'The reason is this: We built a temple for a god to come in and reside, but before the god could be installed, if the devil had taken possession of it, what else could we do except destroy the temple? We did not intend that it should be occupied by the *Asuras*. We intended it to be occupied by the *Devas*. That is the reason why I said I would rather like to burn it.' That 'explanation' was of course elliptical at best: Ambedkar did not explain who the asuras were and who the devas, nor did he explain how he had again been so wrong in misjudging what would happen—recall how wrong he had been in his forecasts about the elections in 1937, in 1939, in 1946, in 1952. But the 'explanation' was typical of the man—if the Harijan Sevak Sangh is turned over to him, along with the twenty-five lakh that others have collected, then it is an organization for the welfare of Harijans; if it is not turned over to him, it is nothing but yet another instrument of Gandhi and Co. to hoodwink the poor unsuspecting Harijans, and, to boot, another device to undermine the loyalty of the trusting Untouchables to the British Empire. If he won an election, the temple was occupied by devas; as the electorate had wiped him and his party out, the temple was in the hands of asuras. If he was appointed to the Cabinet, Pandit Nehru, Sardar Patel were persons who had been redeemed. Once he had to leave, they were asuras.

B.K.P. Sinha, a member from Bihar, interjected, 'Destroy the devil rather than the temple.'

Ambedkar retorted, true to his view of the rebuffs from the electorate, 'You cannot do it. We have not got the strength. If you will read the *Brahmana*, the *Shatapatha Brahmana*, you will see that the gods have always been defeated by the *Asuras*, and that the *Asuras* had the *Amrit* with them which the gods had to take away in order to survive in the battle. Now, Sir, I am being interrupted...'

Chairman: 'You are being drawn into...'[7]

I am not for the moment on Ambedkar's somersaults. Nor even on which of his assessments of the Constitution is to be taken at face value—that it was so worthless that it ought to be burnt as it served no one's needs, or that, while the Constitution was a 'wonderful document', it ought to be burnt as the structure it had spawned had come to be occupied by devils. I am on what he said about the way the article on property came to be drafted, redrafted and eventually finalized.

Does the sequence he set out speak to one author formulating the text, or to some other, iterative process?

Consider a third example. Few provisions gave rise to as much earnest debate as the 'due process' clause in the Fundamental Rights part of the Constitution. The original drafts—of Sir B.N. Rau, of K.M. Munshi—had provided that no person shall be deprived of his life, liberty or property except by 'due process of law'. This expression, as is well known, had been taken over from what had become the keystone of American judgments on rights of the individual vis-à-vis the state. Through it the courts in the USA had held that the courts would inquire into not just whether the procedures prescribed by law had been adhered to in a formal sense, they would also ensure that the substance of the law under which the state had acted was just. Several persons, including Sir B.N. Rau, drew attention to the fact that this provision had occasioned endless litigation in American courts. They proposed that the words 'due process of law' be replaced by words that would leave greater leeway for the executive, namely 'by procedure established

---

7 *Rajya Sabha Debates,* 19 March 1954, Columns 2451–52.

by law'. (Incidentally, the latter expression too was being taken verbatim from another constitution, in this case the new constitution of Japan.) Others argued that a change of this sort would leave the citizen at the mercy of the executive and the legislature—and in the system that was being adopted, the latter would be in the control of the executive.

Ambedkar's position on the matter swung from one end to the other. When the article came up for consideration in the Constituent Assembly, there was vigorous opposition to the change which had been made. Ambedkar proposed that consideration of the article be postponed for a week so as to give the Drafting Committee more time to come up with a formulation which would harmonize the different concerns that the members were expressing. The Assembly resumed consideration of the draft article on 13 December 1948. Recall what Ambedkar said as he moved the article for the consideration of the Assembly:

> There are two views on this point. One view is this: that the Legislature may be trusted not to make any law which would abrogate the Fundamental Rights of man, so to say, the Fundamental Rights which apply to every individual, and consequently there is no danger arising from the introduction of the phrase 'due process'. Another view is this: that it is not possible to trust the Legislature; the Legislature is likely to err, is likely to be led away by passion, by party prejudice, by party considerations, and the Legislature may make a law which may abrogate what may be regarded as the fundamental principles which safeguard the individual rights of a citizen. We are therefore placed in two difficult positions. One is to give the Judiciary the authority to sit in judgement over the will of the Legislature and to question the law made by the Legislature on the ground that it is not good law, in consonance with fundamental principles. Is that a desirable principle? The second position is that the Legislature ought to be trusted not to make bad laws. It is very difficult to come to any definite conclusion. There are dangers on both sides. For myself I

> cannot altogether omit the possibility of a Legislature packed by partymen making laws which may abrogate or violate what we regard as certain fundamental principles affecting the life and liberty of an individual. At the same time, I do not see how five or six gentlemen sitting in the Federal or Supreme Court examining laws made by the Legislature and by dint of their own individual conscience or their bias or prejudices [can] be trusted to determine which law is good and which law is bad. It is rather a case where a man has to sail between Charybdis and Scylla and I therefore would not say anything. I would leave it to the House to decide in any way it likes.[8]

Are these the words of the author of a document who is informing an Assembly about his creation, or the words of a rapporteur who is asking the Assembly to come to a decision so that he may record it?

A volume can be filled with examples of this kind. The point however will be obvious by now: in speaking as he did in the Rajya Sabha on articles about the powers of the governor or about the right to property was Ambedkar merely passing off responsibility or was he truthfully describing the role that he had actually played? Was he not giving us a glimpse into the way the Constitution was actually framed—by an iterative, collective effort, by the contribution of numerous persons, by numerous accommodations of many, many points of view?

But we should retrace our steps a bit, and first recall what Ambedkar's attitude was to two questions: the question of Indians drafting a Constitution for themselves, and the system of governance which he thought was best suited to the country. Answers to these questions will help put in perspective the claims which are made today on behalf of Ambedkar.

---

8 *Constituent Assembly Debates,* Vol. VII, pp. 1000–01.

9

Ambedkar's Constitution

The demand that Indians must themselves determine the system under which they would be governed had become a part of the freedom movement—in a sense it was the essence of that movement. The Montagu-Chelmsford Reforms, even the Government of India Act of 1935 had been rejected by nationalist opinion on the ground that Indians had not drafted these. At session after session the Congress passed resolutions demanding the setting up of a body, of an assembly of Indians which would draw up a Constitution under which Indians would be governed.

Even the British, specially after they were being pressed by the Second World War, had come gradually to concede the point that a Constituent Assembly should be constituted. In August 1940 the viceroy, Linlithgow, had announced that the government would 'most readily assent to the setting up after the conclusion of the War, with the least possible delay, of a body representative of the principal elements in India's national life in order to devise the framework of the new Constitution and they will lend every aid in their power to hasten decisions on all relevant matters to the utmost degree.' The framing of the new Constitution, the viceroy said, 'should be primarily the responsibility of Indians themselves and should originate from Indian conceptions of the social, economic and political structure of Indian life.' There were of course the riders, riders that kept in the hands of the British the lever by which they had successfully played one section in India against another. Notice that the viceroy's announcement had not promised a body representative of the people of India; it had carefully used the old, well-practised words, 'a body representative of the principal elements in India's national life'—these were the very words by which the British had been putting the Aga Khan, the Muslim League, Ambedkar's group, the British planters, the Anglo-Indians, etc., all at par with the Congress, and then announcing, as they had so successfully done at the Round Table Conferences, that the Indians were not being able to agree on a Constitution. The prospect was all the more certain as in that very announcement the viceroy had added that of course the government would not transfer governance to a system which was opposed by 'large and powerful elements in India's national life'. Even so, the statement was an advance on previous positions of the British government. In 1942 the Cripps Mission declared that on the cessation of hostilities a Constitution-making body would be set up with representatives from both British India and Indian states. They too kept the lever in British hands: Provinces which did not accept the new Constitution would be free to form a Union of their own; and there would be a treaty between the new Constitution-making body and His Majesty's Government to cover all matters arising out of the transfer of power, including the safeguarding of the interests of minorities—a proposal which, as we have seen, Ambedkar urged most dutifully to the very end. On 19 September 1945, the new viceroy, Lord Wavell, announced, 'It is the intention of His Majesty's Government to convene as soon as possible a Constitution-making body...'

As a prelude to elections for the Constituent Assembly, elections were held for the provincial legislatures. As we have seen, Ambedkar's party was totally wiped out. Of the 1,585 seats in the various Assemblies, his Scheduled Castes Federation got only one. The worst of it was that even in the Bombay Presidency, Ambedkar and his party were decimated: of the 175 seats in the Assembly, Ambedkar got none. This meant that there was no way for him to get into the Constituent Assembly from Bombay Presidency. Eventually, he got elected from Bengal—with the help of the Muslim League, says his biographer, probably with the help of British planting interests and 'independents', surmised the Secretary of State, Pethick-Lawrence. But then Bengal was up for partition, and so Ambedkar stood to lose that perch also. To his good fortune, by now the Congress leaders had decided that the past must be put behind the country, and that everyone should be engaged in the new tasks before the country. Accordingly, as we have seen, Dr Rajendra Prasad and Sardar Patel instructed the then chief minister of Bombay, E.G. Kher to ensure that Ambedkar was elected to the Constituent Assembly from Bombay, even if this had to be done by getting some others to withdraw. But I anticipate.

'No need for a Constituent Assembly'

In a word, the nationalists had been demanding a Constitution-making body for decades, and even the British had begun to inch towards the inevitable. Ambedkar on the other hand had all through insisted that India did not need anything approximating a Constituent Assembly—he declared again and again that, even if such an Assembly were to be constituted, it would not be able to accomplish anything at all: in part because Indians just did not have the competence to draw up a Constitution for themselves, and in part because the differences among them were so intractable that the Assembly would never be able to arrive at an agreed scheme.

Ambedkar put forth his arguments succinctly in the presidential address he delivered to his All-India Scheduled Class Federation in Bombay on 6 May 1945.[1]

Earlier a Constitution framed by the British and imposed upon Indians had sufficed, Ambedkar declared, but it would not suffice now.

The reason he gave for this was a curate's egg in itself! In the earlier constitutions, Ambedkar said, it was possible to have a 'breakdown clause', that is a clause—Section 93 in the Government of India Act of 1935—which provided that if constitutional governance broke down in a province, government could still be carried on by being taken over by the Centre. But this could no longer be provided in the new Constitution because the British could not step in and take over the administration if the constitutional machinery failed! [But why couldn't the successor Centre?] Ambedkar concluded:

> Therefore, the new Constitution would have to be one which was formulated by the Indians themselves. Just as a Constitution drawn up by the British and imposed on Indians would no longer do, so also a Constitution drawn up by one powerful section and imposed on others would not do. The new Constitution would have to have the support of all important sections of the country.
>
> It is useless for the British to frame a Constitution for India which they will not remain to enforce. The same result will ensue if the Constitution is imposed by one powerful section or a combination of such sections on other sections. I am, therefore, firmly of opinion that if Indians want Dominion Status, they cannot escape the responsibility of framing their own Constitution. The position is thus inescapable.[2]

---

1 For the text of the Address, *Dr. Babasaheb Ambedkar, Writings and Speeches,* Vol. I, Education Department, Government of Maharashtra, 1979, pp. 357–79.

2 *Dr. Babasaheb Ambedkar, Writings and Speeches,* Vol. I, p. 360.

Surely that would be an argument for convening a Constituent Assembly, but not with Ambedkar. He declared that to conclude from the foregoing that a Constituent Assembly was needed to draw up such a Constitution was wholly misconceived.

Ambedkar gave four reasons for this assertion.

First, he declared, most of the details of what is needed in the new Constitution have already been enacted in the Government of India Act of 1935. To constitute a new Constituent Assembly to do again what has already been done would be both 'absolutely superfluous' and 'an act of supererogation'. 'All that is necessary,' he declared, 'is to delete those sections of the Government of India Act, 1935, which are inconsistent with Dominion Status.' As he put the point:

> I must state that I am wholly opposed to the proposal of a Constituent Assembly. It is absolutely superfluous. I regard it as a most dangerous project, which may involve this country in a Civil War. In the first place, I do not see why a Constituent Assembly is at all necessary. Indians are not in the same position as the Fathers of the American Constitution were, when they framed the Constitution of the United States. They had to evolve ideas, suitable for the Constitution for a free people. They had no constitutional patterns before them to draw upon. This cannot however be the case for Indians. Constitutional ideas and constitutional forms are ready at hand. Again, room for variety is very small. There are not more than two or three constitutional patterns to choose from. Thirdly, there are hardly any big and purely constitutional questions about which there can be said to be much dispute among Indians. It is agreed that the future Indian Constitution should be Federal. It is also more or less settled what subjects should go to the Centre and what to the Provinces. There is no quarrel over the division of Revenues between the Centre and the Provinces, none on Franchise and none on the relation of the Judiciary to the Legislature and the Executive. The only point of dispute, which is outstanding, centres round the question of the residuary powers—whether they should be with the Centre or with the Provinces. But

> that is hardly a matter worth bothering about. Indeed, the provision contained in the present Government of India Act could be adopted as the best compromise.
>
> Having regard to this I cannot see why a Constituent Assembly is necessary to incubate a Constitution. So much of the Constitution of India has already been written out in the Government of India Act, 1935, that it seems to be an act of supererogation to appoint a Constituent Assembly to do the thing over again. All that is necessary is to delete those sections of the Government of India Act, 1935, which are inconsistent with Dominion Status.[3]

Second, he declared that the members of a Constituent Assembly, should it be constituted by Indians, would be liable to be bribed and corrupted and to be made thereby to betray the interests of the people. Again, his words are worth quoting in the original as they give his assessment of fellow Indians:

> There are many other arguments against the plan of a Constituent Assembly. I may mention one, which I confess has influenced me greatly. When I read the history of the Union between Scotland and England, I was shocked at the corruption and bribery that was practiced to win the consent of the Scottish Parliament. The whole of the Scottish Parliament was bought. The chances of corruption and bribery being used in the Indian Constituent Assembly to buy over members to support decisions desired by interested groups are very real. Their effects, I am sure, cannot be overlooked. If this happens, it will not only make mockery of the Constituent Assembly but I feel quite certain that any attempt made to enforce its decisions will result in a Civil War. It is my considered opinion that the proposal of Constituent Assembly is more dangerous than profitable and should not be entertained.[4]

The reader will recall that Ambedkar expressed the same forecast on several occasions—in regard to the other Scheduled Caste leaders in particular.

---

3 *Dr. Babasaheb Ambedkar, Writings and Speeches,* Vol. I, p. 361.

4 *Dr. Babasaheb Ambedkar, Writings and Speeches,* Vol. I, p. 365.

Third, he recounted that Indians had been given several opportunities in the past to devise a Constitution for themselves; and nothing had come of any of these attempts. He said:

> It is not that she had no opportunities to do so. In fact, there have been quite a number. The first opportunity came in 1927, when Lord Birkenhead gave a challenge to Indians asking them to produce a constitution for India. That challenge was taken up. A committee was formed to frame a constitution. A constitution was produced and was known as 'The Nehru Constitution'. It was, however, not accepted by Indians and was buried without remorse. A second opportunity presented itself to Indians in 1930, when they assembled at the Round Table Conference. There again, Indians failed to play their part and write out their own Constitution. A third attempt is the one recently made by the Sapru Committee. The proposals of this committee too have fallen flat.
>
> There is neither enthusiasm nor optimism left to indulge in another attempt. One is pursued by a sense of fatality, which suggests that as every attempt is doomed to failure, none need be made. At the same time I feel that no Indian ought to be so down-hearted or so callous as to let the deadlock sink, as though it was a dead dog, and say that he is prepared to do nothing more than be a mere witness to the political dog-fight that is going on in this country. The failures of the past need not daunt anybody. They do not daunt me. For, I have a feeling that though it is true that all attempts to reach an agreement on the communal question have failed, the failures have been due not so much to any inherent fault of the Indians as they have been due to a wrong approach. I feel confident that my proposals, if considered dispassionately, should be found acceptable. They constitute a new approach and as such I commend them to my countrymen.[5]

Fourth, he said, the real reason on account of which nothing had come of these earlier attempts was that they had failed to provide a solution for the communal problem.

5 *Dr. Babasaheb Ambedkar, Writings and Speeches,* Vol. I, p. 365.

No new Constituent Assembly would be able to provide a solution either. For one thing, the Assemblies that had been envisaged under the Cripps proposals as well as the proposals of the Sapru Committee were not going to be truly representative of the minorities and were therefore not going to command their confidence. The way to get over the communal problem was to accept the scheme—naturally of reservations at all levels and in all spheres—which he was proposing. The way forward was to accept this scheme and not to constitute a Constituent Assembly.

The next day, that is on 7 May 1945, the conference of the Scheduled Castes Federation passed the resolution which Ambedkar had drafted. It vehemently denounced the proposal for a Constituent Assembly which the Sapru Committee had put forward. It opposed the very idea of summoning a Constituent Assembly. And declared that the Assembly which was being sought placed the Scheduled Castes at the mercy of Hindus and Muslims without providing any safeguards for them.[6]

That remained Ambedkar's considered view till the very eve of the formation of the Constituent Assembly. Recall that elections to the provincial Assemblies and the Constituent Assembly were held through 1946, and that the Assembly held its first session on 9 December 1946. Ambedkar had called on the British Cabinet Delegation and the new viceroy, Lord Wavell, on 5 April 1946—that is, seven months after the viceroy had announced the government's decision to convene a Constituent Assembly of Indians so that they may draw up the Constitution for a new India. Wavell recorded a memorandum marked *Secret* about the discussion. Ambedkar told him that the Scheduled Castes had been the earliest source of manpower for the East India Company's army, and that it was because of the

---

6 Mitra's *Annual Register*, 1945, Vol. I, p. 324.

assistance which the Scheduled Castes had rendered them that the British had been able to conquer India, that the Scheduled Castes had been the friends of the British ever since. Ambedkar told the viceroy that 'if India became independent it would be one of the greatest disasters that could happen.'

Ambedkar told the Cabinet Delegation and the viceroy that he had no faith in Indians being able to ensure justice—those in the Assembly who did not belong to the Scheduled Castes were determined to perpetuate the exploitation of the latter; and the members who did belong to the Scheduled castes 'would be bought over to vote against the interests of their communities'. Accordingly, recorded Wavell, 'Dr. Ambedkar said he did not want a Constituent Assembly at all.' Instead he proposed that the tasks which were being contemplated for the Assembly be divided into two groups. The first set were 'constitutional questions properly so called'—relations between the executive and the legislature, composition and functions of the executive, etc. 'To deal with them was beyond the mental capacity of the type of men whom Provincial Assemblies might be expected to send up, and was a job for experts,' Ambedkar told the Britishers. Therefore, Ambedkar said, these questions 'should be referred to a Commission presided over by an eminent constitutional lawyer from Great Britain or the U.S.A. The other members should be two Indian experts and one representative each of the Hindu and Muslim communities...'

The second set of questions were 'communal questions', that is provisions to safeguard the rights of 'Communities', Ambedkar said. On these questions also the ultimate say, Ambedkar maintained, must remain with the British. These questions 'should be referred to a conference of the leaders of different communities', and 'if the conference failed to arrive at an agreed solution, His Majesty's Government would have to make an award. This would no doubt be accepted if it were reasonable...'[7]

This was what Ambedkar was telling the Cabinet Delegation and the viceroy in April 1946!

Even in November 1946—that is, even till just a fortnight before the Constituent Assembly was to begin its first session—there seemed to be every possibility that Ambedkar would do a 'Deliverance Day' again, team up with the Muslim League and boycott the Assembly. In his *Private and Secret* dispatch of 27 November 1946 to the Secretary of State, the viceroy, Lord Wavell, noted, 'The All India Scheduled Castes Federation (Ambedkar's Body) have announced that they will shortly consider whether they should boycott the deliberations of the Constituent Assembly; their present tendency seems to be to do so, and if they do, it would mean that they have moved over to the Muslim League.'[8]

And these views and manoeuvres were as well known to everyone who had been fighting for the country's Independence and who was to soon join the Constituent Assembly as the record of Ambedkar during the preceding quarter-century.

Ambedkar's scheme for the Constitution

The second point to remember is that we do in fact have Ambedkar's scheme for the Constitution by which India ought to be governed. He took pains to set it out in great detail in the same presidential address to the Bombay session of his All-India Scheduled Castes Federation in May 1945, and, as we shall see, later to the Constituent Assembly itself.

---

7 *Transfer of Power,* Vol. VII, pp. 144–47.

8 *Transfer of Power,* Vol. IX, pp. 197–98.

The presidential address was not just an ordinary address, certainly not in the reckoning of Ambedkar himself. Ambedkar was a member of the Viceroy's Executive Council at this time, and he was conscious of speaking while holding what he obviously looked upon as a very important official position. Ordinarily, while addressing a convention of this kind, he would have been expected to speak about the problems facing the Scheduled Castes, he said. But he did not propose to speak on 'so sectarian a subject', he declared at the outset. 'For the moment the responsibility for leading the movement of the Scheduled Castes and facing its day-to-day problems does not lie on my shoulders,' he explained. 'On account of my office I am out of it and I have no desire to take it up. That is one reason why I do not propose to take up a sectarian subject which is related only to the Scheduled castes.'

The second reason, he said, was that 'The Scheduled Castes are often charged as being selfish, interested only in themselves; that they have no constructive suggestions to make for the solution of the country's political problem.' The charge is 'entirely untrue', he said. He believed, Ambedkar said, that this charge should 'be repelled in a positive way by showing that the Scheduled Castes are capable of putting forth constructive proposals for the general political advancement of the country which the country, if it cares to, may consider'.[9]

In a word, this was his considered plan for the structure by which India should be governed.

Attempts at Constitution-making have failed because of the communal problem, Ambedkar explained. And attempts at solving the communal problem have failed because they have just proceeded from method to method as each previous method failed. They have not been based on principles. Ambedkar said:

---

9 *Dr. Babasaheb Ambedkar, Writings and Speeches,* Vol. I, p. 358.

It [the communal problem] has become insoluble because the approach to it is fundamentally wrong. The defect in the present approach is that it proceeds by methods instead of by principles. The principle is that there is no principle. There is only a series of methods. If one method fails another is tried. It is this swing from one method to another which has made the communal problem a jig-saw puzzle. There being no principle there is no guide to tell why a particular method has failed. There being no principle there is no assurance that the new method will succeed.

The attempts at the solution of the Communal Problem are either in the nature of a coward's plan to kow-tow to the bully or of the bully's plan to dictate to the weak. Whenever a community grows powerful and demands certain political advantages, concessions are made to it to win its goodwill. There is no judicial examination of its claim; no judgement on merits. The result is that there are no limits to demands and there are no limits to concessions. A start is made with a demand for separate electorate for a minority. It is granted. It is followed by a demand for a separate electorate for a community irrespective of the fact whether it is a minority or majority. That is granted. A demand is made for separate representation on a population basis. That is granted. This is followed by a demand that the majority rule of another community is intolerable, and therefore without prejudice to its rights to maintain majority rule over other minorities, the majority of the offending community should be reduced to equality. Nothing can be more absurd than this policy of eternal appeasement. It is a policy of limitless demand followed by endless appeasement.

Frankly, I don't blame the community that indulges in this strategy. It indulges in it because it has found that it pays, it pursues it because there are no principles to fix the limits and it believes that more could be legitimately asked and would be easily given. On the other hand, there is a community economically poor, socially degraded, educationally backward and which is exploited, oppressed and tyrannized without shame and without remorse, disowned by society, unowned by Government and which has no security for protection and no guarantee for justice, fair play and equal opportunity. Such a community is told that it can have no safeguards, not because it has no case for safeguards but only because the bully on whom the bill of rights is presented thinks that because the community is not politically organized to have sanctions behind its demand he can successfully bluff.

All this differential treatment is due to the fact that there are no principles, which are accepted as authoritative and binding on those who are parties to the Communal Question. The absence of principles has another deleterious effect. It has made impossible for public opinion to play its part. The public only knows methods and notes that one method has failed, another is being suggested. It does not know why one method has failed and why another is said to be likely to succeed. The result is that the public, instead of being mobilized to force obstinate and recalcitrant parties to see sense and reason, are only witnessing the discussions of Communal Questions wherever they take place as mere shows.[10]

To break out of this bind, Ambedkar said he was proposing a scheme based on two propositions:

(1) That in proceeding to solve the Communal Problem it is essential to define the governing principles which should be invoked for determining the'final solution, and
(2) That whatever the governing principles, they must be applied to all parties equally without fear or favour.[11]

From these propositions Ambedkar derived his scheme for the Constitution of India, the method of governing the country and for solving the communal problem. In essence his solution to the communal problem, and his scheme for the Constitution of India was to reserve seats for caste Hindus, Muslims and Scheduled Castes in equal proportion at all levels and in all branches of the state, and to constitute a structure in which none would dominate the other. The caste Hindus were to sacrifice seats, the Muslims were to

10 *Dr. Babasaheb Ambedkar, Writings and Speeches,* Vol. I, pp. 366–67.
11 *Dr. Babasaheb Ambedkar, Writings and Speeches,* Vol. I, p. 367.

retain what they had in the country taken as a whole and get far more than they had in the provinces in which they were in minority, and the Scheduled Castes were to get the biggest jump. Other communities—the Sikhs, the Indian Christians, the Anglo-Indians—were not to get any share formally in the executive, but conventions were to be set up by which they would get 'a fair share' in the Cabinet. The Scheduled Tribe population was excluded from the calculations altogether.

For the legislature Ambedkar proposed that seats be reserved in both the Central Assembly and the provincial Assemblies, giving tables for each unit. Ambedkar set out the following 'principles' on the basis of which, he said, the legislature should be constituted:

> (1) Majority Rule is untenable in theory and unjustifiable in practice. A majority community may be conceded a relative majority of representation but it can never claim an absolute majority. (I have not framed any scheme of representation for the North-West Frontier Province as the minority is so small that even the principle of relative majority cannot help it.)
> (2) The relative majority of representation given to a majority community in the Legislature should not be so large as to enable the majority to establish its rule with the help of the smallest minorities.
> (3) The distribution of seats should be so made that a combination of the majority and one of the major minorities should not give the combine such a majority as to make them impervious to the interest of the minorities.
> (4) The distribution should be so made that if all the minorities combine they could, without depending on the majority, form a government of their own.
> (5) The weightage taken from the majority should be distributed among the minorities in inverse proportion to their social standing, economic position and educational condition so that a minority which is large and which has a better social, educational and economic standing gets a lesser amount of weightage than a minority

whose numbers are less and whose educational, economic and social position is inferior to that of the others.[12]

The reader will have no difficulty in seeing that the 'solution' which Ambedkar was going to formulate was implicit in these 'principles' so much so that, for all that introductory lecture on the problem having become worse because the solutions were not based on any principles, the 'principles' could be said to have been crafted to yield one and only one 'solution'.

Based on these 'principles' Ambedkar proposed that the Central Assembly, for instance, be constituted by representatives of different communities in the following proportions:

Community	*Percentage of population*	*Percentage of total Seats*
Hindus	54.68	40
Muslims	28.50	32
Scheduled Castes	14.30	20
Indian Christians	1.16	3
Sikhs	1.49	4
Anglo-Indians	0.05	1[13]

To elect members of the Assemblies in these fixed proportions, Ambedkar said, the electorate may be composed by bearing in mind the following 'propositions':

(1) Joint electorate or separate electorate is a matter of machinery for achieving a given purpose. It is not a matter of principle.

(2) The purpose is to enable a minority to select candidates to

12 *Dr. Babasaheb Ambedkar, Writings and Speeches,* Vol. I, pp. 373–74.

13 The tables specifying the allocation of seats in the Central and provincial Assemblies are at *Dr. Babasaheb Ambedkar, Writings and Speeches,* Vol. I, pp. 369–73.

the Legislature who will be real and not nominal representatives of the minority.

(3) While separate electorate gives an absolute guarantee to the minority, that its representatives will be no others except those who enjoy its confidence, a system of joint electorates which will give equal protection to the minorities should not be overlooked.

(4) A four-member constituency, with a right to the minorities to have a double vote and requiring a minimum percentage of minority votes, may be considered as a possible substitute.[14]

As the reader will notice, at least on one point Ambedkar was admitting an aperture for alternatives to be considered: in 1932 he was so adamant on separate electorates that he was prepared to see Gandhiji die rather than dilute that demand. At last he was now urging the 'minorities'—the Scheduled Castes were the foremost among them, he insisted now as always—to consider other alternatives.

But to proceed with Ambedkar's constitutional scheme. From the legislature elected in accordance with those tables of reservations by caste and religion and by an electorate along the foregoing lines, the executive was to be constituted. The nature of the executive should be based on the following 'principles', Ambedkar said:

(1) It must be recognized that in a country like India where there is a perpetual antipathy between the majority and the minorities and on which account the danger of communal discrimination by majority against minorities forms an ever-present menace to the minorities, the Executive power assumes far greater importance than the Legislative power.

(2) In view of (1) above, the system under which a party which has secured a majority at the poll is deemed entitled to form a Government on the presumption that it has the confidence of the majority is untenable in Indian conditions. The majority in India is a communal majority and not a political majority. That being

14 *Dr. Babasaheb Ambedkar, Writings and Speeches,* Vol. I, p. 374.

> the difference, the presumption that arises in England cannot be regarded as a valid presumption in the conditions of India.
> (3) The Executive should cease to be a Committee of the majority party in the Legislature. It should be so constituted that it will have its mandate not only from the majority but also from the minorities in the Legislature.
> (4) The Executive should be non-Parliamentary in the sense that it shall not be removable before the term of the Legislature.
> (5) The Executive should be Parliamentary in the sense that the members of the Executive shall be chosen from the members of the Legislature and shall have the right to sit in the House, speak, vote and answer questions.[15]

From these 'principles' about the structure of the executive, Ambedkar deduced further 'principles' about whose confidence the members of the executive should command. These Ambedkar listed as follows:

> (a) The Prime Minister as the Executive head of the Government should have the confidence of the whole House.
> (b) The person representing a particular minority in the Cabinet should have the confidence of the members of his community in the Legislature.
> (c) A member of the Cabinet shall not be liable to be removed except on impeachment by the House on the ground of corruption or treason.[16]

And from these 'principles' in turn Ambedkar derived the manner in which the posts of prime minister and other ministers ought to be filled. The posts ought to be filled in the following way, Ambedkar said:

> Following these principles, my proposal is that the Prime Minister and the members of the Cabinet from the majority community

---

15 *Dr. Babasaheb Ambedkar, Writings and Speeches,* Vol. I, pp. 368–69.

16 *Dr. Babasaheb Ambedkar, Writings and Speeches,* Vol. I, p. 369.

> should be elected by the whole House by a single transferable vote and that the representatives of the different minorities in the Cabinet should be elected by a single transferable vote of the members of each minority community in the Legislature.[17]

Ambedkar commended this scheme to the Muslims on the ground that it would afford them better protection and that it would advance their interests better than the demand for Pakistan. And he urged the scheme to caste Hindus on the grounds that this is the price which they had to pay in justice for the centuries of exploitation their forbears had indulged in, that this was the only way they could keep India one, and that in any case his scheme would not be affecting their hegemony in spheres other than politics.

To the Muslims he put the matter thus:

> My proposals are for an United India. They are made in the hope that the Muslims will accept them in preference to Pakistan as providing better security than Pakistan does. I am not against Pakistan. I believe it is founded on the principle of self-determination, which it is now too late to question. I am prepared to give them the benefit of the principle, on condition that the Muslims do not deny the benefit of the principles to the Non-Muslim residents of the Area. But I believe, I am entitled to draw the attention of the Muslims to another and a better plan of security. I claim that my plan is better than the plan of Pakistan. Let me state the points which tell in favour of my plan. They are:
>
> (i) Under my proposal the danger of a communal majority which is the basis of Pakistan is removed.
>
> (ii) Under my proposal the weightage at present enjoyed by the Muslims is not disturbed.
>
> (iii) The position of Muslims in the Non-Pakistan Provinces is greatly strengthened by an increase in their representation, which they may not get if Pakistan comes and which will leave them in a more helpless condition than they are in at present.[18]

---

17 *Dr. Babasaheb Ambedkar, Writings and Speeches,* Vol. I, p. 369.

18 *Dr. Babasaheb Ambedkar, Writings and Speeches,* Vol. I, p. 376.

Ambedkar had 'a word to the Hindus' also—it was very different in both, in tone as much as in substance. Ambedkar told the Hindus:

> Much of the difficulty over the Communal Question is due to the insistence of the Hindus that the rule of majority is sacrosanct and that it must be maintained at all costs. The Hindu does not seem to be aware of the fact that there is another rule, which is also operative in fields where important disputes between individuals and nations arise and that rule is a rule of unanimity. If he will take the trouble to examine the position he will realize that such a rule is not a fiction, but it does exist. Let him take the Jury System. In the jury trial the principle is unanimity. The decision is binding upon the judge only if the verdict of the jury is unanimous. Let him take another illustration that of the League of Nations. What was the rule for decisions in the League of Nations? The rule was a rule of unanimity. It is obvious that if the principle of unanimity was accepted by the Hindus as a rule of decision in the Legislature and in the Executive there would be no such thing as a Communal Problem in India.
>
> One may well ask the Hindu that if he is not prepared to concede constitutional safeguards to the minorities, is he prepared to agree to the rule of unanimity? Unfortunately he is not prepared to accept either.
>
> About the rule of majority the Hindu is not prepared to admit any limitations. The majority he wants is an absolute majority. He will not be satisfied with relative majority. He should consider whether his insistence on absolute majority is a fair proposition, which political philosophers can accept. He is not aware that even the Constitution of the United States does not lend support to the absolutist rule of majority rule on which the Hindu has been insisting upon.
>
> Let me illustrate the point from the Constitution of the United States. Take the clause embodying Fundamental Rights. What does that clause mean? It means that matters included in Fundamental Rights are of such supreme concern that a mere majority rule is not enough to interfere with them. Take another illustration, also from the Constitution of the United States. The Constitution says that no

part of the Constitution shall be altered unless the proposition is carried by three-fourths majority and ratified by the States. What does this show? It shows that the United States Constitution recognizes that for certain purposes mere majority rule is not competent.

All these cases are of course familiar to many a Hindu. The pity of it is, he does not read from them the correct lesson. If he did, he would realize that the rule of the majority rule is not as sacrosanct a principle as he thinks it is. The majority rule is not accepted as a principle but is tolerated as a rule. I might also state why it is tolerated. It is tolerated for two reasons: (1) because the majority is always a political majority and (2) because the decision of a political majority accepts and absorbs so much of the point of view of the minority that the minority does not care to rebel against the decision.

In India, the majority is not a political majority. In India the majority is born; it is not made. That is the difference between a communal majority and a political majority. A political majority is not a fixed or a permanent majority. It is a majority which is always made, unmade and remade. A communal majority is a permanent majority fixed in its attitude. One can destroy it, but one cannot transform it. If there is so much objection to a political majority, how very fatal must be the objection to a communal majority?[19]

And then there was the sop, rather an invitation to the Hindus to delude themselves: after all, your real interest is in 'other walks of life', and my scheme will not affect your position in any of those spheres, Ambedkar told the Hindus. He said:

The abandonment of the principle of majority rule in politics cannot affect the Hindus very much in other walks of life. As an element in social life they will remain a majority. They will have the monopoly of trade and business which they enjoy. They will have the monopoly of the property which they have. My proposals do not ask the Hindus to accept the principle of unanimity. My proposals do not ask the Hindus to abandon the principle of

19 *Dr. Babasaheb Ambedkar, Writings and Speeches*, Vol. I, pp. 376–77.

> majority rule. All I am asking them [to do] is to be satisfied with a relative majority. Is it too much for them to concede this?[20]

If they were not going to allow themselves to be taken in by that sleight of hand, Ambedkar had the minatory admonition also, indeed a warning. Ambedkar told the Hindus:

> Without making any such sacrifice the Hindu majority is not justified in representing to the outside world that the minorities are holding up India's Freedom. This false propaganda will not pay. For the minorities are doing nothing of the kind. They are prepared to accept freedom and the dangers in which they [are] likely to be involved, provided they [are] granted satisfactory safeguards. This gesture of the minorities is not to be treated as a matter for which Hindus need not be grateful. It may well be contrasted with what happened in Ireland. Mr. Redmond, the leader of the Irish Nationalists once told Carson, the leader of Ulster, 'Consent to United Ireland. Ask for any safeguard and they shall be granted to you.' He is reported to have turned round and said, 'Damn your safeguards, we don't want to be ruled by you.' The minorities in India have not said that. They are ready to be satisfied with safeguards. I ask the Hindus: Is this not worth a mass? I am sure it is.[21]

In a word, be thankful for the small mercies we are showing you, and lump it.

The scheme reiterated

Now, as I mentioned, this was not some off-the-cuff string of stray thoughts strung together for just some lecture which had to be given. It was Ambedkar's considered scheme for the Constitution of India. This fact will be evident from what followed. By circumstances which have been recounted

20 *Dr. Babasaheb Ambedkar, Writings and Speeches,* Vol. I, pp. 377–78.

21 *Dr. Babasaheb Ambedkar, Writings and Speeches,* Vol. I, p. 378.

above, Ambedkar, having opposed and denounced the proposal for a Constituent Assembly so strenuously, exerted to get himself into the Assembly once the British decided to constitute it none the less. In early 1947 Ambedkar submitted a memorandum to the Constituent Assembly on behalf of the All-India Scheduled Castes Federation. He also published the memorandum in early 1947 as *States and Minorities, What are Their Rights and How to Secure Them in the Constitution of Free India.*[22] The constitutional scheme which the memorandum develops and repeats is more or less the one that Ambedkar had set out in his presidential address of May 1945.

In the presidential address the justification for those patterns of reservations and for that scheme of electing ministers, etc., was that this was the one way the Muslim League could be made to abandon its demand for Pakistan. Even at that time that justification could scarcely stand scrutiny: not even on Ambedkar's writings themselves. Had he not been at pains to show in his book on the demand for Pakistan—a book he had published four years earlier—that a true believer in Islam could not live harmoniously in a multi-religious society? In the intervening four years the position of Jinnah and the Muslim League had hardened tenfold. And yet here was Ambedkar putting his faith in such mechanical formulae. That the scheme was not prompted solely by that justification about keeping the Muslim League from pressing its demand for Pakistan will be evident from the fact that, by the time Ambedkar submitted this memorandum to the Constituent Assembly, Jinnah had made it clear beyond doubt that the Muslim League would not be joining the Constituent Assembly, that it would

22 The memorandum is included in *Dr. Babasaheb Ambedkar, Writings and Speeches,* Vol. I, pp. 381–449. The text is also included in B. Shiva Rao, *The Framing of India's Constitution, Select Documents,* Vol. II, pp. 84–114.

wait for the time a separate Assembly was constituted for an independent Pakistan.

Indeed, Ambedkar had by now received a personal lesson about entertaining hopes of Jinnah. Pandit Nehru had moved the Objectives Resolution on 13 December 1946. The Objectives Resolution was hailed by all: Pandit Nehru was said to have drafted it; it had then been gone over by the Experts Committee which the Congress had constituted. The resolution had gone out of its way to keep the door open for the Muslim League—the powers of the Centre were to be severely circumscribed; trie residuary powers were to be with the federating units, and so on.

But M.R. Jayakar opposed the resolution, saying that it was premature to consider it as the Muslim League had not yet come in, that in case it was passed the chances of the Muslim League coming in would be dashed. Ambedkar seconded him. As the Muslim League had scheduled its session for 20 January 1947, in spite of the misgivings of many members, the Constituent Assembly decided to postpone discussion on the resolution to the third week of January 1947. As the date came round, Jinnah did the predictable thing: he just postponed the session of the Muslim League. Jayakar and Ambedkar were left to explain away the pious hopes they had fed the members of the Constituent Assembly. When the Assembly met again on 20–23 January 1947, Jayakar withdrew his amendment; consideration of the Objectives Resolution and with it the real task of drafting the Constitution commenced.

So, by now it was clear beyond doubt that the Muslim League was not going to join the sessions of the Assembly, that Pakistan was a fact. That Ambedkar none the less again urged the constitutional scheme which he had proposed in May 1945 shows that the scheme had not been formulated to ward off Pakistan. It contained the plan of the structure by which Ambedkar thought India ought to be governed—

after it had become independent and after it had been partitioned.

Ambedkar declared again that the system of parliamentary democracy—with its one-man-one-vote, winner-takes-all, the leader of the majority party forms the government, which in turn consists of persons whom the prime minister chooses—was wholly unsuited to India. In this memorandum to the Fundamental Rights Subcommittee of the Constituent Assembly Ambedkar repeated the arguments which he had listed earlier against the British system. Ambedkar said that the special features of the British parliamentary executive could be taken to be the following:

> (1) It gives a party which has secured a majority in the Legislature the right to form a Government.
> (2) It gives the majority party the right to exclude from Government persons who do not belong to the Party.
> (3) The Government so formed continues in office only so long as it can command a majority in the Legislature. If it ceases to command a majority it is bound to resign either in favour of another Government formed out of the existing Legislature or in favour of a new Government formed out of a newly elected Legislature.[23]

Were this system to be applied to India, Ambedkar argued, it would have the following consequences:

> (1) The British System of Government by a Cabinet of the majority party rests on the premise that the majority is a political majority. In India the majority is a communal majority. No matter what social and political programme it may have the majority will retain its character of being a communal majority. Nothing can alter this fact. Given this fact it is clear that if the British System was copied it would result in permanently vesting Executive power in a communal majority.
> (2) The British System of Government imposes no obligation upon

---

23 *Dr. Babasaheb Ambedkar, Writings and Speeches,* Vol. I, p. 413.

the Majority Party to include in its Cabinet the representatives of Minority Party. If applied to India the consequence will be obvious. It would make the majority community a governing class and the minority community a subject race. It would mean that a communal majority will be free to run the administration according to its own ideas of what is good for the minorities. Such a state of affairs could not be called democracy. It will have to be called imperialism.[24]

'In the light of these consequences,' Ambedkar concluded, 'it is obvious that the introduction of British type of the Executive will be full of menace to the life, liberty and pursuit of happiness of the minorities in general and of the Untouchables in particular.'

Accordingly, India should be governed by the following structure, Ambedkar declared:

(1) That the Executive—Union or State—shall be non-Parliamentary in the sense that it shall not be removable before the term of the Legislature.
(2) Members of the Executive if they are not members of the Legislature shall have the right to sit in the Legislature, speak, vote and answer questions.
(3) The Prime Minister shall be elected by the whole House by single transferable vote.
(4) The representatives of the different minorities in the Cabinet shall be elected by members of each minority community in the Legislature by single transferable vote.
(5) The representatives of the majority community in the Executive shall be elected by the whole House by single transferable vote.
(6) A member of the Cabinet may resign his post in a censure motion or otherwise but shall not be liable to be removed except on impeachment by the House on the ground of corruption or treason.[25]

---

24 *Dr. Babasaheb Ambedkar, Writings and Speeches,* Vol. I, p. 413.
25 *Dr. Babasaheb Ambedkar, Writings and Speeches,* Vol. I, p. 398.

In other words, the nature of the executive was to be the same as Ambedkar had proposed in his presidential address, but with one important difference: ministers could be from outside the legislature. In explaining the proposal Ambedkar said that it was intended to serve the following purposes:

> (i) To prevent the majority from forming a Government without giving any opportunity to the minorities to have a say in the matter.
> (ii) To prevent the majority from having exclusive control over administration and thereby make the tyranny of the minority by the majority possible.
> (iii) To prevent the inclusion by the Majority Party in the Executive [as] representatives of the minorities [of persons] who have no confidence of the minorities.
> (iv) To provide a stable Executive necessary for good and efficient administration.[26]

Ambedkar argued that the system he was proposing, though akin to the system prevalent in the USA, was an improvement over it in that under his proposal ministers, though not members of the legislature, would be able to participate in the proceedings of the legislature. He explained:

> The clause takes the American form of Executives as a model and adapts it to Indian conditions, especially to the requirements of minorities. The form of the Executive suggested in the proposal cannot be objected to on the ground that it is against the principle of responsible government. Indians who are used to the English form of Executive forget that this is not the only form of democratic and responsible Government. The American form of Executive is an equally good type of democratic and responsible form of Government. There is also nothing objectionable in the proposal that a person should not be qualified to become a Minister merely because he is elected to the Legislature. The principle that a

26 *Dr. Babasaheb Ambedkar, Writings and Speeches,* Vol. I, p. 415.

member of the Legislature before he is made a Minister should be chosen by his constituents was fully recognized by the British Constitution for over hundred years. A member of Parliament who was appointed a Minister had to submit himself for election before taking up his appointment. It was only lately given up. There ought therefore to be no objection to it on the ground that the proposals are not compatible with responsible government. The actual proposal is an improved edition of the American form of Government, for the reason that under it members of the Executive can sit in the Legislature and have a right to speak and answer questions.[27]

Much of the memorandum was devoted to spelling out the rights that 'minorities'—in particular the Scheduled Castes—must have. And how the attempt by anyone to curtail them—for instance, the attempt by anyone to subject any Scheduled Caste person to a social boycott—must be construed to be a cognizable offence. These provisions Ambedkar justified by the same sort of arguments and evidence which he had used earlier in books such as *What Gandhi and the Congress Have Done to the Untouchables,* and in his presidential address of May 1945.

Ambedkar repeated his provisions for reservations for the Scheduled Castes—in the legislatures, in the executives, in the services. There were two changes. Though Ambedkar advocated that the Assembly consider giving Scheduled Castes 'weightage'—that is, the Scheduled Castes be given reservations in excess of their share in the population—the articles he proposed were based on their being given reservations in each branch of the state in proportion to their share in the population.

The other change was a stiffening to the pre-September 1932 position. As we saw, in his presidential address Ambedkar had opened an aperture and told the 'minorities' that they should not think that their interests could be

---

27 *Dr. Babasaheb Ambedkar, Writings and Speeches,* Vol. I, p. 415.

safeguarded by separate electorates alone. Since then, as we have seen, Ambedkar's party had been routed in the elections. He therefore reverted to his thesis that the interests of the Scheduled Castes would not be safe in India unless they got separate electorates, and provided in his draft Article that '(a) The system of election introduced in the Poona Pact shall be abolished, (b) In its place, the system of *Separate Electorates* shall be substituted, (c) Franchise shall be adult franchise, (d) The system of voting shall be cumulative.'[28]

These provisions, Ambedkar provided in his draft of the articles, must continue in the first instance for twenty-five years. And even after that period amendments to them, if amendments were ever to be made, must be made in a very special way. Ambedkar specified as follows the procedure that the Constitution must have for amending provisions affecting Scheduled Castes:

> (i) Any proposal for amendment or abrogation shall be initiated in the form of a Resolution in the more Popular Chamber of the Union Legislature.
> (ii) No such Resolution shall be moved -
> (a) unless 25 years have elapsed after the Constitution has come into operation and has been worked; and
> (b) unless six months' notice has been given to the House by the mover of his intention to move such a Resolution.
> (iii) On the passing of such a Resolution, the Legislatures shall be dissolved and a new election held.
> (iv) The original Resolution in the form in which it was passed by the previous Legislatures shall be moved afresh in the same House of the newly elected Union Legislature.
> (v) The Resolution shall not be deemed to have been carried unless it is passed by a majority of two-thirds of the members of the House and also two-thirds of members of the Scheduled Castes who have been returned through separate electorates.[29]

---

28 *Dr. Babasaheb Ambedkar, Writings and Speeches,* Vol. I, p. 401.

29 *Dr. Babasaheb Ambedkar, Writings and Speeches,* Vol. I, p. 404.

Do we find anything like these provisions or this mode of amendment in the Constitution?

In accord with the intellectual fashions of the time, Ambedkar told the Constituent Assembly that political rights would come to naught unless they were accompanied by economic rights. Moreover, he maintained, again in accord with the intellectual presumptions of the time, that these economic rights could only be secured through 'State Socialism'. And this 'State Socialism', he said, could not be secured if it was left to being the subject matter of the ordinary laws of the country. Parliamentary majorities would swing from one party to another, and some party will erase the socialist measures which the previous government had put in place. As he put the argument:

> One essential condition for the success of a planned economy is that it must not be liable to suspension or abandonment. It must be permanent. The question is how this permanence can be secured. Obviously it cannot be secured under the form of Government called Parliamentary Democracy under the system of Parliamentary Democracy, the policy of the Legislature and of the Executive is the policy of the majority for the time being. Under the system of Parliamentary Democracy the majority in one election may be in favour of State Socialism in Industry and in Agriculture. At the next election the majority may be against it. The anti-State Socialism majority will use its Law-making power to undoing the work of the pro-State Socialism majority and the pro-State Socialism majority will use its Law-making power to doing over again what has been undone by their opponents. Those who want the economic structure of society to be modeled on State Socialism must realize that they cannot leave the fulfilment of so fundamental a purpose to the exigencies of ordinary Law which simple majorities—whose political fortunes are never detennined by rational causes—have a right to make and unmake. For these reasons Political Democracy seems to be unsuited for the purpose.[30]

---

30 *Dr. Babasaheb Ambedkar, Writings and Speeches,* Vol. I, p. 411.

Therefore, Ambedkar maintained, 'State Socialism' and its elements must be made a part of the Constitution itself, and for this purpose he proposed the following article:

> The United States of India shall declare as a part of the law of its Constitution -
>
> Protection against Economic Exploitation.
>
> (1) That industries which are key industries or which may be declared to be key industries shall be owned and run by the State;
>
> (2) That industries which are not key industries but which are basic industries shall be owned by the State and shall be run by the State or by Corporations established by the State;
>
> (3) That Insurance shall be a monopoly of the State and that the State shall compel every adult citizen to take out a life insurance policy commensurate with his wages as may be prescribed by the Legislature;
>
> (4) That agriculture shall be State Industry;
>
> (5) That State shall acquire the subsisting rights in such industries, insurance and agricultural land held by private individuals, whether as owners, tenants or mortgagees and pay them compensation in the form of debenture equal to the value of his or her right in the land. Provided that in reckoning the value of land, plant or security no account shall be taken of any rise therein due to emergency, of any potential or unearned value or any value for compulsory acquisition;
>
> (6) The State shall determine how and when the debenture holder shall be entitled to claim cash payment;
>
> (7) The debenture shall be transferable and inheritable property but neither the debenture-holder nor the transferee from the original holder nor his heir shall be entitled to claim the return of the land or interest in any industrial concern acquired by the State or be entitled to deal with it in any way;
>
> (8) The debenture-holder shall be entitled to interest on his debenture at such rate as may be defined by law, to be paid by the State in cash or in kind as the State may deem fit;
>
> (9) Agricultural industry shall be organized on the following basis:
>
> (i) The State shall divide the land acquired into farms of standard size and let out the farms for cultivation to residents of

the villages as tenants (made up of group of families) to cultivate on the following conditions:

(a) The farm shall be cultivated as a collective farm;

(b) The farm shall be cultivated in accordance with rules and directions issued by Government;

(c) The tenants shall share among themselves in the manner prescribed the produce of the farm left after the payment of charges properly leviable on the farm;

(ii) The land shall be let out to villagers without distinction of caste or creed and in such manner that there will be no landlord, no tenant and no landless labourer;

(iii) It shall be the obligation of the State to finance the cultivation of the collective farms by the supply of water, draft animals, implements, manure, seeds, etc.;

(iv) The State shall be entitled —

(a) to levy the following charges on the produce of the farm:

(i) a portion for land revenue;

(ii) a portion to pay the debenture-holders; and

(iii) a portion to pay for the use of capital goods supplied; and

(b) to prescribe penalties against tenants who break the conditions of tenancy or wilfully neglect to make the best use of the means of cultivation offered by the State or otherwise act prejudicially to the scheme of collective farming;

(10) The scheme shall be brought into operation as early as possible but in no case shall the period extend beyond the tenth year from the date of the Constitution coming into operation.[31]

The provision incorporated all the socialist cliches of the period, as well as all the presumptions common to persons who had had no experience in running either an industrial unit or a farm. State ownership of land. Collective farms. A 'modified form of State Socialism' in industry. As if these things are in the habit of getting done just because there is a decree to that effect. As we see, to take just one example, a clause in this scheme specifies that the Constitution 'places squarely on the shoulders of the State the obligation to

---

31 *Dr. Babasaheb Ambedkar, Writings and Speeches,* Vol. I, pp. 396–97.

supply capital necessary for agriculture as well as industry.' And how was this capital to be generated? By the amounts that the state would earn from the fact that insurance had been nationalized, said Ambedkar![32]

The socialist premises were all-pervasive at that time. They got reflected in the Directive Principles part of the Constitution. But to the good fortune of the country, in this regard as in every other regard the Constituent Assembly did not adopt Ambedkar's proposals.

Ambedkar thought particularly highly of his proposals in regard to the constituents of the new United States of India he was proposing, he felt that by virtue of the study he had made of the problem he was specially qualified to suggest what ought to be done on the matter. In the preface to the memorandum he had written:

> Among the many problems the Constituent Assembly has to face, there are two which are admittedly most difficult. One is the problem of the Minorities and the other is the problem of the Indian States. I have been a student of the problem of the Indian States and I hold some very definite and distinct views on the subject. It was my hope that the Constituent Assembly would elect me to the States Committee. Evidently, it has found men of superior caliber for the work. It may also be because I am one of those who are outside the tabernacle and therefore undesirable. I am not sorry to find myself left out. My only regret is that I have lost an opportunity to which I was looking forward for placing my views for the consideration of the Committee.[33]

Accordingly, he was doing 'the next best thing' and including his recommendations on the matter as part of the memorandum on the rights of citizens and minorities, he wrote. With the passage of time the suggestions are not

---

32 *Dr. Babasaheb Ambedkar, Writings and Speeches,* Vol. I, pp. 408–12.

33 *Dr. Babasaheb Ambedkar, Writings and Speeches,* Vol. I, pp. 384–85.

really worth recalling: they involved creating two categories of States—the 'Qualified' and the 'Non-Qualified' States—according to their viability, their ability to defend themselves against aggression, and so on.[34] In the event, the Integration of states proceeded on a different route under the Sardar's firm hand, and over time the distinction between different types of states—the erstwhile Provinces, the Indian princely states and the chief commissioners' units—got erased and recast. The point to note for our present enquiry only is that while Ambedkar did make his recommendations in regard to the organization of states a part of his memorandum to the Constituent Assembly, the Assembly did not incorporate any part of his scheme into the Constitution.

In a word, here was a person who to the very end opposed the idea of constituting a Constituent Assembly to draw up a Constitution for our country, who to the very end was telling the British that granting Independence to India would be 'one of the greatest disasters that could happen', who believed that the sort of Indians who were likely to be elected to the Constituent Assembly did not have the 'mental capacity' to tackle constitutional questions, who *did* frame a scheme for the Constitution but one that finds no reflection whatsoever in the Constitution which was adopted and which we have to this day, who declared again and again that he was *not* the author of the Constitution, that in his view it ought to be burnt, that he had just been 'a hack' doing things he was asked to do much against his will. Yet he is the Father of the Constitution, and if you have any doubt about that, you are a Manuwadi!

---

34 *Dr. Babasaheb Ambedkar, Writings and Speeches,* Vol. I, pp. 389–90, 405–06.

10

The way the Constitution actually evolved

'But was he not the Chairman of the Drafting Committee? And did this Committee not draft the Constitution?'

How mere designations father myths! Yes, Ambedkar was elected chairman of the Drafting Committee but what was this 'Drafting Committee' set up to do?

The Constituent Assembly had been functioning since December 1946. Committees to draft substantive sections of the Constitution began work in January 1947. The 'Drafting Committee' did not come into being till 29 August 1947.

The Constituent Assembly's resolution setting up the Committee declared that it was being set up to *'Scrutinize the Draft of the text of the Constitution prepared by the Constitutional Adviser* giving effect to the decisions taken already in the Assembly and including all matters ancillary thereto or which have to be provided in such a Constitution, and to submit to the Assembly for consideration the text of the Draft Constitution *as revised* by the Committee.' At the very least these terms of reference should alert us to the fact that there already was a draft in existence when this Committee was set up!

And just recall how Ambedkar himself described the role and task of the Drafting Committee. On 4 November 1948 when he rose to present the Draft Constitution to the Constituent Assembly, Ambedkar said, 'The Drafting Committee was in effect charged with the duty of preparing a Constitution in accordance with the decisions of the Constituent Assembly on the reports made by the various committees appointed by it such as the Union Powers Committee, the Union Constitution Committee, the Provincial Constitution Committee and the Advisory Committee on Fundamental Rights, Minorities, Tribal Areas, etc. The Constituent Assembly had also directed that in certain matters the provisions contained in the Government of India Act, 1935, should be followed. Except in points which are referred to in my letter of 21st February, 1948, in which I referred to the departures made and alternatives suggested by the Drafting Committee, I hope the Drafting Committee will be found to have faithfully carried out the directions given to it.'[1] Again, at the least, statements such as these should suggest that various committees had made recommendations on parts of the Constitution which they had been set up to examine, that a draft was in existence, that the draft and the recommendations had then been considered by the Constituent Assembly and decisions on them taken, and that the task of the 'Drafting Committee' was the secretarial task of ensuring that the new Draft incorporated and tallied with the decisions of the Assembly.

Ambedkar maintained no more a year and ten months later on 25 November 1949, when he rose to move that the Constitution as finally settled by the Assembly be adopted. Several members had expressed criticisms of the draft on different grounds. Sir Alladi Krishnaswami Ayyar, T.T. Krishnamachari and other members of the Drafting Committee had given arguments in defence of specific provisions and features of the draft. Making the more

1 *Constituent Assembly Debates,* Vol. VII, p. 31.

general point, Ambedkar said, '...These are the main grounds on which the Constitution is being condemned. I do not say that the principle of parliamentary democracy is the only ideal form of political democracy. I do not say that the principle of no acquisition of private property without compensation is so sacrosanct that there can be no departure from it. I do not say that Fundamental Rights can never be absolute and the limitations set upon them can never be lifted. What I do say is that the principles embodied in the Constitution are the views of the present generation, or, if you think this to be an over-statement, I say they are the views of the members of the Constituent Assembly. *Why blame the Drafting Committee for embodying them in the Constitution?* I say why blame even the members of the Constituent Assembly?...'[2] And he proceeded to quote Jefferson to the effect that in a sense each generation must be considered as a separate nation, with full freedom to reconsider questions for itself. Again, was Ambedkar just passing off responsibility? Or was he stating the truth about the manner in which the Constitution had been framed, in particular was he not right in reminding the members that the 'Drafting Committee' had merely carried out their instructions and recorded their decisions?

Decades of work

Several leaders had devoted and worked for years and years on the kind of system of governance that would be best suited for India. A national convention of leaders had drafted *The Commonwealth of India Bill* in December 1924. The draft bill had been presented at the meeting of the All-India Parties Conference in January 1925, and had been eventually finalized in April that year. In June 1925

---

2 *Constituent Assembly Debates*, Vol. XI, pp. 975–76.

over forty Indian political leaders had commended the bill to the British Parliament. In May 1927 the All-India Congress Committee had passed a resolution at its meeting in Bombay calling upon 'the Working Committee to frame a *Swaraj* Constitution, based on a Declaration of Rights, for India in consultation with elected members of the central and provincial Legislatures and other leaders of political parties.'

At the session in Madras the Congress passed a resolution for framing a Swaraj Constitution. It had considered various drafts which had been submitted to it, the Congress declared, and 'having regard to the general desire of all political parties in the country to unite together in settling a *Swaraj* Constitution,' it authorized the Working Committee to constitute a committee to, in consultation with other organizations, 'draft a *Swaraj* Constitution for India on the basis of a Declaration of Rights, and to place the same for consideration and approval before a special convention to be convened in Delhi not later than March next...'

A few days later the Muslim League had met in Calcutta and authorized its Council to appoint a Subcommittee 'to confer with the Working Committee of the Indian National Congress and such other organizations as the Council may think proper for the purpose of drafting a Constitution for India in which the interest of the Muslim community will be safeguarded...'

The committee had begun work. But some parties and groups had begun arguing that the goal should not be complete Independence, it should be confined to Dominion status. Therefore, as the Motilal Nehru Report was to note subsequently, 'a phrase capable of double-interpretation—"full responsible Government"—was used to avoid a decision on the question of Dominion Status or Independence'. This committee had completed its report. Discussions on it had been scheduled by the All Parties Conference.

But meanwhile, and characteristically, the Council of the Muslim League, which had earlier agreed to participate in consultations on the proposed Constitution, had met and denounced the resolutions of the All Parties Conference, and on that ground it had refused to consider the report of the committee, and to take part in discussions on it.

A new committee had then been appointed with Pandit Motilal Nehru as its chairman. Members had been selected to represent all shades of opinion. Although the Congress had committed itself irrevocably to complete Independence, this committee also desisted from using that expression and instead prepared a Constitution for India as a Dominion. 'On any higher ground [than Dominion status],' the Motilal Nehru report had noted, 'a general agreement was not obtainable....' 'Our deciding as a Committee in favour of such a constitution [for an India having Dominion Status rather than complete Independence] simply means that the maximum degree of agreement was only obtainable on this basis,' the committee had observed. 'It does not mean that any individual Congressman, much less the Congress itself, has given up or toned down the goal of complete Independence.'[3]

In November 1944 the Standing Commjttee of the Non-Party Conference had appointed yet another committee to draw up constitutional proposals for dealing with the communal question. Sir Tej Bahadur Sapru had been designated to head the committee and authorized to appoint members. This committee also had prepared a detailed scheme—of the manner in which the legislature and executive should be constituted, of the Fundamental Rights which would be guaranteed to all citizens, of the special rights

3 On the foregoing, *All Parties Conference, Report of the Committee appointed by the Conference to determine the Principles of the Constitution for India,* AICC, Allahabad, 1928, pp. 17–26.

which would be guaranteed to Scheduled Castes and the minorities, etc.

Over the years several other persons, like the youthful Jawaharlal Nehru who had worked as the secretary of the Motilal Committee, had worked on and thought about specific aspects of the constitutional framework. Even as they criticized the arrangements which the British put in place from time to time—the Montagu-Chelmsford reforms, the Government of India Act of 1935, etc.—the Indian leaders had learnt to work them, they *had* to learn to use them for their struggle. In doing so they had not just acquired familiarity with these arrangements, they had become accustomed to them.

In July 1946 the Congress Working Committee had set up the Congress Experts Committee to prepare materials for the Constituent Assembly. Gandhiji, who, as we know, did not attach that much importance to questions of mere structure, had called K.M. Munshi and told him, 'You should give up whatever you are doing and take up this work. It is very important and you will have to bear your share of the burden.' The Committee had prepared drafts within the parameters of the Cabinet Mission Plan. It had also prepared a draft of what later became the sketch for the famous Objectives Resolution that Pandit Nehru moved in the Constituent Assembly in December 1946.[4]

In a word, when the Constituent Assembly met for the first time in December 1946, it was not beginning work ab initio. Decades and decades of work and reading and scouring of other constitutions, years of immersion in and experience of our own situation and the problems which

---

4 K.M. Munshi has left a brief account of his work in the Committee: cf., *Pilgrimage To Freedom,* Bhartiya Vidya Bhavan, 1967, Vol. I, pp. 104–08. See also B. Shiva Rao, *The Framing of India's Constitution, Select Documents,* Vol. I, pp. 326–43, for the minutes of the meetings and the draft of the Objectives Declaration.

were bedevilling India, years of reflection and deliberation about what could be made to work in India had prepared the ground. The Assembly set up several committees to work out provisions relating to different aspects of the Constitution—a committee to deliberate on Fundamental Rights of citizens, as well as the special safeguards which might be necessary for minorities, another committee to deliberate on the Union Constitution, another one on the Provincial Constitution, one on the division of powers between the Centre and states, and so on.

As early as September 1946, for instance, Sir B.N. Rau had prepared two notes on Fundamental Rights—on whether these should be listed in the future Constitution, and if so what these rights could be; on whether all rights should be justiciable or whether the example of the Irish Constitution should be followed and some non-justiciable rights too should be listed... K.T. Shah had also prepared a comprehensive note which, starting out by listing rights went on to derive many general features of the Constitution which would follow from those rights.

The Advisory Committee on Fundamental Rights, Minorities and Tribal and Excluded Areas was constituted on 24 January 1947. Fifty members were named in the resolution itself, and the president was given the authority to nominate twenty-two more to the committee. Sardar Patel was elected chairman of the committee. In turn, this committee set up five subcommittees. Each subcommittee when it met would have several alternative drafts. It would select one of these as its working document, and proceed to discuss it clause by clause. In the case of the Fundamental Rights Subcommittee, of which Acharya Kripalani was elected chairman, the draft which K.M. Munshi had prepared was picked as the basic document on which the subcommittee would organize its work and discussions. On occasion the committee or the subcommittee would take up a corresponding entry from some other draft. Sir B.N. Rau, the constitutional adviser to the Constituent Assembly, H.V.R. Iyengar, the secretary of the Constituent Assembly, and S.N. Mukherjee, the Assembly's chief draftsman would prepare the revised version of the clause in the light of discussions and decisions. That revised version would be taken up at the next meeting along with the next set of clauses, and would go through further revisions. In this way several clauses went through several revisions.

Once the Union Constitution Committee was constituted—Pandit Nehru was its head—Sir B.N. Rau advised that perhaps it would help members to concretize their proposals if a questionnaire were to be sent out to them which set out the various questions on which they would have to make up their mind. He was asked to draw up the questionnaire. He did so and circulated it on 17 March, 1947. It was not a simple set of questions though: it listed the point and also the provisions which existed regarding that point in constitutions elsewhere. Members were asked to send their proposals by the end of May. The idea was that once their proposals under the different heads were on hand, the constitutional adviser would draw up a draft of the provisions which were to be included regarding the Union. As happens ever so often in India, by the end of May only one member, Sardar Panikkar, had sent in his reactions and tentative answers. Sir B.N. Rau, therefore, drew up an independent memorandum on the Union Constitution.[5] Some other members—for instance Sir Alladi Krishnaswami Ayyar and N. Gopalaswami Ayyangar, K.T. Shah, K.M. Panikkar—also circulated notes for the Committee. Sir B. N. Rau prepared a series of additional notes called *Constitutional Precedents*. These were for all

5 The text of the questionnaire and the memorandum will he found in B. Shiva Rao, *The Framing of India's Constitution, Select Documents*, Vol. II, pp. 433–51, and 470–527.

members of the Assembly. In them Rau set out detailed provisions from other constitutions and indicated the merits and difficulties of adopting a provision along one line rather than another. The *Precedents* covered a truly breathtaking range of constitutions—of the USA, Switzerland, Weimar Germany, Yugoslavia, Turkey, Czechoslovakia, Poland, Ireland, Austria, Belgium, Danzig, Estonia, Lithunia, Liechtenstein, Australia, Canada, South Africa, the USSR, China, Albania, Portugal, Greece, Costa Rica, Bulgaria, Brazil, and others. The questionnaire, the independent memorandum and the *Precedents* became the scaffolding for determining the form that the Constitution of the Union should take.

The same sort of thing happened in regard to the provisions regarding the provinces. The Constituent Assembly set up the Provincial Constitution Committee with Sardar Patel as its head on 30 April 1947. The Committee held its first meeting on 5 May 1947. A questionnaire—really a guide of the terrain ahead—was again prepared by Sir B. N. Rau, and members were asked to send in their proposals by 20 May. Only seven had sent reactions of any kind by the due date. Therefore, as had happened in the case of the provisions dealing with the Union, Sir B.N. Rau prepared another independent memorandum in which he set out possible provisions regarding the units, and circulated it at the end of May. The questionnaire and this memorandum became the working documents for meetings of the Provincial Constitution Committee.[6]

Each of these committees set up subcommittees to formulate, revise, finalize, and sometimes again revise specific provisions from time to time. Often a committee would defer consideration of an issue pending the decision of some other committee on a point which impinged on

---

6 The text of the memorandum will he found in B. Shiva Rao, *The Framing of India's Constitution, Select Documents*, Vol. II, pp. 632–41.

the issue. On occasion a committee would request a joint meeting with another committee, sometimes two committees would set up a joint subcommittee to go into a matter that had relevance to the work of both. On occasion the decision which was taken at the joint meeting was regarded as final as far as the two committees were concerned, sometimes not: thus, for instance, in the minutes of the joint meeting of the two powerful committees—the Union and the Provincial Constitution Committees—held on 11 June 1947, we read, 'It was made clear that the decisions of the Joint Committee, in so far as they were in conflict with the decision taken in either of the two Committees, could only be considered as the recommendations of the Joint Committee to the Committee concerned. It was then open to the Committee concerned to accept or reject the recommendation when making its report to the Constituent Assembly...'[7]

Tentativeness

Tentativeness was quite the hallmark of the reports and recommendations of the committees. The Union Constitution Committee finalized its report on 4 July 1947, only to submit a supplementary report on 13 July 1947, in which it modified some of the recommendations which it had just made. The speech Sardar Patel made on 15 July 1947 in the Constituent Assembly while moving the Report of the Provincial Constitution Committee for consideration is typical. The report had been circulated and had been with the members for a fortnight, he said, adding,

> What I wish to point out in moving this motion is that this report is not the final draft of the Provincial Constitution. According to the

---

7 B. Shiva Rao, *The Framing of India's Constitution, Select Documents,* Vol. II, p. 612.

> instructions given to the Committee, it has settled certain principles of the Provincial Constitution, and therefore, this House need not go into the verbal details or into the exact legal form or constitutional form of these clauses that have been submitted in the memorandum. If the various clauses in the report are, after consideration, adopted, or improved upon, then, it will be the function of the draftsmen or the lawyers who will be entrusted with the work of drafting the Constitution to put them in proper form...
>
> It should also be remembered that this report contains roughly about eighty-five per cent of the draft or eighty-five per cent of the principles of the Provincial Constitution which has to be framed. Because, you will remember that this Hpuse has appointed an Advisory Committee which has to submit its report after the reports of the Minorities Committee and the Tribal and Excluded and Partially Excluded Areas Committee are received. These reports have not yet been received. When they are received, in due course, the Advisory Committee will meet and consider these reports when the question of protection of minorities rights and interests will be taken into account...[8]

Saying that 'some misunderstanding may arise on some of the items mentioned in clause 9,' Sardar Patel, as we have noticed in passing earlier, in effect overturned key recommendations which the committee had formulated. The committee had said in its report that while there would be a Council of Ministers to aid and advise the governor, on four matters he would act on his own discretion. The first of these was 'the prevention of any grave menace to the peace and tranquillity of the Province or any part thereof'. The Sardar said that 'it [what is stated in the report] means that the Governor is probably given powers in the case of a grave menace to the peace and tranquillity of the Province which, I may say, is not exactly the intention of the Committee.' 'The Committee in settling this question, intended to convey,' the Sardar told the Assembly, 'that the Governor shall have only the authority to report to the

8 *Constituent Assembly Debates,* Vol. IV, pp. 577–80.

Union President about the grave situation arising in the Province which would involve a grave menace to the peace of the Province. It was not their intention that this power or authority is to be exercised by the Governor which may perhaps bring a conflict between the ministry and the Governor. The Governor having no control over the services, the authority of administration entirely vests in the Ministry and, therefore, although there was considerable difference of opinion on this question and in view of the prevailing conditions in the country—some thought it would be advisable under the present peculiar unsettled conditions in the country to give some limited powers to the Governor—eventually the Committee came to the conclusion that it would create deadlocks and, therefore, that the proper course would be to limit his powers to the extent of authorizing him to report to the President of the Union. What steps, or what authority the President of the Union exercises would be a matter for the Union Powers Committee to provide in the Union Constitution. But, so far as the Provincial Constitution is concerned, it is agreed that this limited power of reporting only should be given to the Governor.'[9]

The report the Sardar was moving had provided that the governor would act in his discretion on matters relating to 'the superintendence, direction and control of elections'—this recommendation had been made in conformity with an allied recommendation that elections in each unit should be supervised by state Election Commissions which would be appointed by the governor. The Sardar told the House that actually the Fundamental Rights Committee had since recommended that elections ought to be supervised by a national Election Commission appointed by the president, and that the House had already accepted this proposal. Therefore, the Sardar said, the proposal to have the governor

9 *Constituent Assembly Debates*, Vol. IV, p. 579.

act in his discretion regarding the conduct of elections will have to be brought in line with the decision which the House had already taken.[10] The report had also recommended that the governor appoint persons to the Provincial Public Service Commission and to the post of the Provincial Auditor General at his discretion. The Sardar said that these functions also properly fell within the purview of the ministry.

The only things that were left to the discretion of the governor were the power to report to the president in the event of a grave emergency, and the power to summon and dissolve the House...[11]

The point is not about the merit of what was being proposed. And certainly not that the Sardar was on his own overturning the recommendations of the committee whose report he was laying before the House: members of the committee were present in the House, and could have interrupted him right then and there. The points are of a different sort altogether. Notice the tentativeness: no one felt, 'O, this is my proposal, all must accept it; how can I go back on it?...'; the view was: 'This is what we think at the moment would be best for the circumstances in which the country is placed at the moment; but please consider it threadbare.' Notice also the deference shown to decisions which had been taken in some other committee and to the fact that some other committee was going to submit a recommendation on some point and that therefore it would be best to defer coming to a decision on the matter.

Even that is but a stage in the story, so to say. The Sardar placed the report of the committee of which he was the head for consideration. The Constituent Assembly discussed the provisions, and adopted a set of *'Principles of a Model Provincial Constitution'*. Even a cursory glance through

10 *Constituent Assembly Debates,* Vol. IV, p. 579.

11 *Constituent Assembly Debates,* Vol. IV, p. 579.

these *'Principles' tells* us how many changes the provisions were to go through before they took the form we have in the Constitution now.

'1. *Governor:* For each Province,' this document laid down, 'there shall be a Governor to be elected directly by the people on the basis of adult suffrage. 2. *Term of Office:* (1) The Governor shall hold office for a term of four years, except in the event of death, resignation or removal. (2) The Governor may be removed from office for stated misbehaviour by impeachment, the charge to be preferred by the Provincial Legislature... and to be confirmed by the Upper House of the Federal Parliament after investigation by a special committee of that House, the resolution in each case to be supported by no less than two-thirds of the total membership of the House concerned. (3) The Governor shall be eligible for re-election once, but only once.'

The *'Principles'* adopted by the Constituent Assembly also provided for a deputy governor who was to be elected by the provincial legislature on the system of proportional representation by single transferable vote after every general election. Do we find in the Constitution any trace of these provisions *which the Constituent Assembly adopted at this stage?*

Recall what the Sardar had said about the proposals which, though they had been included in the Report of the Provincial Constitution Committee, had been thought better of. Yet the *'Principles'* which the Assembly approved did not winnow out all the items. The memorandum as adopted by the Assembly still envisaged areas in which the governor would act in his discretion, it still envisaged an instrument of instructions which would, among other things, instruct the governor to observe certain norms in constituting the Council of ministers...[12]

---

12 The text of the memorandum which the Constituent Assembly adopted after six days of discussion of the Report of the Provincial

The Report of the Union Constitution Committee followed the same course.

Successive drafts

By August–September 1947 sufficient work had been done for it to be felt that some overall draft should be attempted to take account of what had already been settled and to give further deliberations of the Assembly a direction and focus. Sir B.N. Rau was asked to prepare a draft. By October 1947, with the assistance of the chief draftsman to the Assembly, S.N. Mukherjee, Rau prepared what he called *'The First Draft of the Constitution of India'*. It had 243 articles and thirteen schedules.[13] It incorporated the decisions which the Assembly, had taken till then on the recommendations of the committees it had appointed. Where the matter had not yet been considered, Rau provided possible clauses. As was usual with Rau, his draft was also a guide: in the marginal note to each clause he indicated the corresponding provisions from Constitutions such as those of Ireland, Canada and Australia, and most of all from the document with which the members were most familiar, namely the Government of India Act of 1935. This draft is what became the scaffolding of the Constitution as we know it now.

On 29 August 1947 the Constituent Assembly passed a resolution to constitute a 'Drafting Committee' to *'scrutinize the Draft of the text of the Constitution prepared by the Constitutional Adviser* giving effect to the decisions taken already in the Assembly and including all matters ancillary thereto or which have to be provided in such a Constitution, and to submit to the Assembly for

---

Constitution Committee will be found in B. Shiva Rao, *The Framing of India's Constitution, Select Documents*, Vol. II, pp. 667–74.

13 For the text, B. Shiva Rao, *The Framing of India's Constitution, Select Documents*, Vol. III, pp. 4–197.

consideration the text of the Draft Constitution *as revised* by the Committee.' The Committee had before it the draft of Sir B.N. Rau as well as the comments on it by important members like Sir Alladi Krishnaswami Ayyar, D.P. Khaitan and K.M. Munshi. In addition, it had the report which B.N. Rau had prepared of the discussions he had had with authorities in the UK, Ireland, Canada and the USA on provisions in the Draft.[14]

In keeping with the decision of the leaders to put the past completely behind them, of the seven members who were selected for the Drafting Committee, only one was a Congressman. Ambedkar, who had all along opposed the Congress and denounced the leaders who were now in control, was elected chairman of the Committee. The Drafting Committee went over the constitutional adviser's draft clause by clause from October 1947 to February 1948. The minutes of the Committee—which extend over 200 printed pages of B. Shiva Rao's volumes—testify to the same collective deliberation which we have seen in the work of the substantive committees. Members argue their positions with knowledge and conviction, their sole concern being the interest of the country, clauses are finalized only to be reopened and redrafted,... On 21 February 1948, the Drafting Committee submitted a revised draft to the president. The draft now had 315 articles and 8 schedules.

Apart from being given to all members of the Assembly, the draft was circulated far and wide across the country, and persons and organizations were invited to send their comments on it. The comments were then collated by the constitutional adviser and the secretariat. The constitutional adviser wrote out his observations on all the important suggestions and comments which had come in. Even in

---

14 For the texts of these comments and B.N. Rau's report, B. Shiva Rao, *The Framing of India's Constitution, Select Documents,* Vol. III, pp. 197–234.

summary form, the comments and the constitutional adviser's observations on them cover over 400 printed pages of B. Shiva Rao's volumes.

The Drafting Committee now began evaluating the comments and suggestions in the light of Rau's assessments. The president of the Assembly next constituted a Special Committee to assess the draft as it had emerged from the labours of the Drafting Committee taking into account the comments and suggestions which had been received, the decisions of the Drafting Committee on them as well as the decisions which the Assembly itself had taken.

All through the following months the Assembly continued its deliberations. Various authorities continued to furnish comments. The leaders continued to review the decisions they had taken. The Drafting Committee also met from time to time to incorporate the latest thinking on the questions.

The final draft was presented to the President on 3 November 1949. It was adopted by the Assembly on 26 November 1949.

The Constitution now had 395 articles and 8 schedules. The articles, indeed the entire scheme, had been overhauled in many ways. Several of the articles which had been adopted by the Assembly had been reconsidered and redone. The debates of the Assembly cover twelve volumes and remain models of earnestness and acumen. Ambedkar reminded the Assembly when he rose to move the final motion for adopting the Constitution that approximately 7,635 amendments had been submitted, and of these 2,473 had been actually moved. A scholar records that of the original text, 220 articles had been completely replaced and the wording of another 120 had been materially altered. As we shall see, many provisions were altered in the most basic ways by the interventions of persons whose names few of us would even have heard of since.

That is how the Constitution came to be framed—by the collective, iterative deliberations of a very large number.

Ambedkar was one of these members. In some ways he played an important part. But he was one among a large number. His job was really that of a rapporteur, not that of one who set policy, certainly not that of the creator. To ascribe the Constitution to him, to include the draft in his *Writings and Speeches,* as the set produced by the Maharashtra government does, is, to put it at the least, farcical.

But even this bare sequence does not give us a glimpse of the process as it worked itself out.

11

Who is the author when decisions are by votes?

That the outcome was truly the result of collective debate and deliberation, of persuading others and being persuaded by them, of sticking to one's guns to the end on occasion and at other times agreeing to what the others decided... will become obvious by recalling just one detail: namely that, ever so often the point at issue was settled by a vote. Let us take examples from the deliberations of just the Advisory Committee and two of its subcommittees—those on Fundamental Rights of which Acharya Kripalani was elected the chairman, and on Minorities of which H.C. Mookherjee was elected chairman.

Proposition: Secrecy of Correspondence: Should secrecy of correspondence be included as a Fundamental Right as has been provided in K.M. Munshi's draft? Yes, voted a majority.[1]

Proposition: Freedom of Press: Should a separate provision be made for freedom of the press, or should it be taken to be subsumed under the Fundamental Right to the freedom of speech? No separate provision, decided a majority.[2]

---

1 B. Shiva Rao, *Framing of India's Constitution, Select Documents,* Vol. II, p. 121.

2 B. Shiva Rao, *Framing of India's Constitution, Select Documents,* Vol. II, p. 121.

Proposition: Right of Religious Associations to levy contributions: What about paragraph 20 of Ambedkar's memorandum which provides, 'Religious associations shall be entitled to levy contributions on their members who are willing to pay them if their law of incorporation permits them to do so. No person may be compelled to pay taxes the proceeds of which are specifically appropriated for the use of any religious community of which he is not a member?' Rejected, five votes to three.[3]

Proposition: Diversion of Trust Properties: The draft of Munshi had implied and that of Sir Alladi had specifically provided that properties created and managed by denominations shall not be diverted wholly or in part for purposes other than the ones for which they had been originally created. Ambedkar pointed out that many of the educational trusts which had been set up for 'Hindus' had been set up at a time when the conception of who was a Hindu was circumscribed: such trusts should not be perpetuated through the Constitution. Munshi agreed that this was a valid point and promised to come up with a fresh draft of the clause. Minutes of the next sitting record, 'Mr. Munshi submitted a revised draft on the question of diversion of trust properties. It was decided by a majority of 5 to 3 to drop this matter altogether from the chapter on Fundamental Rights. Mr. Jairamdas Daulatram, Dr. Ambedkar and Mr. Munshi said they would submit minutes of dissent.'[4]

Proposition: Education a Fundamental Right? Should the right to primary education be included as a justiciable right in view of the fact that the state may not have the

---

3 B. Shiva Rao, *Framing of India's Constitution, Select Documents,* Vol. II, pp. 88 and 123.

4 B. Shiva Rao, *Framing of India's Constitution, Select Documents,* Vol. II, pp. 122, 124.

resources to ensure this for everyone? Yes, decided the subcommittee by a majority vote.[5]

Proposition: Military Service, Training? The subcommittee had decided that there must not be any compulsory labour—slavery, bonded labour and the kind: some members had pressed that conscription in the armed forces should also be prohibited. The latter question was reopened, and put to vote. It was decided by a majority of five to three that the Constitution should explicitly prohibit compulsory military service. Ambedkar tried to salvage at least military training as distinct from military service and asked for a separate vote on the proposition that the former should be exempted from the prohibition: unfortunately, this too was lost by five to four.[6]

Proposition: Common Civil Code a Fundamental Right? Should the provision for a Common Civil Code be made a part of the chapter on Fundamental Rights? The matter lies outside the scope of Fundamental Rights, decided the majority. 'The minority,' the minutes note, 'consisted of Mr. Masani, Rajkumari Amrit Kaur, Mrs. Hansa Mehta and Dr. Ambedkar.'[7]

Proposition: Legitimacy and Inheritance: The minutes record, 'Dr. Ambedkar proposed that there should be no difference between legitimate and illegitimate children as far as the law of inheritance was concerned and that some provision to this effect should be inserted. This was negatived by 6 votes against 3.'[8]

Proposition: Remedies for Administrative Discrimination: The minutes record, 'Dr. Ambedkar referred to the last

---

5 B. Shiva Rao, *Framing of India's Constitution, Select Documents,* Vol. II, p. 125.

6 B. Shiva Rao, *Framing of India's Constitution, Select Documents,* Vol. II, pp. 127–28.

7 B. Shiva Rao, *Framing of India's Constitution, Select Documents,* Vol. II, p. 128.

8 B. Shiva Rao, *Framing of India's Constitution, Select Documents,* Vol. II, p. 129.

sentence of the minutes of the meeting held on the 30th March[9] and said that he had hoped to bring forward a draft clause, in consultation with Sir B.N. Rau, in regard to administrative discrimination and remedies to be provided short of an application to the Supreme Court. Unfortunately, in view of Sir B.N. Rau's absence, he had not been able to do so. The Committee decided by a majority that this was a matter which should be first discussed by the Minorities Sub-Committee who may, if necessary, refer it back to the Fundamental Rights Sub-Committee.'[10]

Proposition: Titles: Given the fact that titles during the British period had been given generally to those who had stood by the government and against the national movement, originally the drafts had provided that all titles should be abolished and no titles should be given in the future. But what about military ranks and honours, it was asked, what about academic titles and honours? Sardar Panikkar drew the pertinent distinction: what were being objected to were '*heritable titles*' as these are the ones that create inequalities. The subcommittee on Fundamental Rights, however, chose to stick by the sweeping prohibition and in its report to the Advisory Committee provided:

> 8. No titles except those denoting an office or a profession shall be conferred by the Union.
>
> No citizen of the Union and no person holding any office of profit or trust under the State shall, without the consent of the Union, accept any present, emolument, office or title of any kind from any foreign State.

The matter came up again when the full Advisory Committee met to consider the report of the subcommittee.

---

9 This sentence had read, 'The consideration of para. 3 of Dr. Ambedkar's memorandum was postponed.'

10 B. Shiva Rao, *Framing of India's Constitution, Select Documents,* Vol. II, pp. 135 and 168.

Again there was a spirited discussion. Rajaji proposed that the first paragraph of the clause be deleted. Vigorous discussion ensued. At last Sardar Patel who was presiding said, 'Is it agreed that paragraph 1 may be deleted?' A member, R.K. Sidhwa, felt that was just a way of closing the discussion: he said, 'This matter was discussed in the Fundamental Rights (Sub-) Committee and the sense of the House may be taken.' Accordingly, the Sardar put the point to vote. 'The proposal is that paragraph 1 be deleted,' the Sardar said. 'It is put to the vote. (14 voted against deletion and 10 for deletion.) The clause is retained.' Panikkar then moved an amendment saying that there must not be any heritable titles. The amendment too was put to vote, and carried.[11]

Proposition: Restricting Free Speech: The clause regarding freedom of speech and the provisos to it gave rise to even sharper exchanges. Alladi Krishnaswami Ayyar urged that 'likely to promote class hatred' should be added as one of the grounds on which restrictions may be placed on speech: K.M. Panikkar suggested, 'class or religious hatred', only to change his view in a few moments and say that the reference to 'class hatred' would militate against the whole philosophy of 'socialism': K.M. Munshi wanted the right to be enlarged: Sir Alladi pointed out that what he was proposing was just an incorporation of the restrictions which were already inherent in Section 153 (a) of the Penal Code: Munshi countered by arguing that 'even today sec. 153 (a) is in effect entirely deleted from the Penal Code.' The arguments went to and fro. At last the Sardar said, 'This does not appear to be an easy matter to decide. We can only decide it by vote. So we shall take votes on this now. We shall take communal hatred and class hatred separately. Those who are in favour of Rajaji's amendment will raise

11 B. Shiva Rao, *Framing of India's Constitution, Select Documents,* Vol. II, pp. 172, 227–29.

their hands.' 'The amendment of C. Rajagopalachari was lost,' record the minutes, 'The original clause was retained.' Rajaji remarked, 'I have still a hope in spite of this vote against me that we may be able to induce a reasonable Union to pass a law that communal hatred shall be seditious.' Panikkar said that the suggestion of Ambedkar—that the provision may be made by ordinary law—would meet Rajaji's concern...[12]

Proposition: Secrecy of Correspondence, again: The recommendation of the subcommittee that secrecy of correspondence must be a Fundamental Right came up. Alladi Krishnaswami Ayyar said that he had a 'very strong objection' to the draft clause. It went farther than the Indian Evidence Act—the latter provided protection to correspondence only in special cases. If the clause is retained and there is a conspiracy going on to murder someone, the government would have no right to look into it, he pointed out. Munshi stuck to his draft. The Sardar put the question to vote. The clause was deleted.[13]

Proposition: Religious 'practice': There had been the sharpest possible division on the clause regarding freedom of religion: in addition to *belief* the draft had referred to *'religious practice'* also: Rajkumari Amrit Kaur had said that this would give licence to many to claim protection for many obscurantist practices on the ground that these were religious practices, that it would nullify several progressive laws which had been enacted. Alladi Krishnaswami Ayyar had supported her position in a written note to the subcommittee. The words were not deleted at one stage, they were deleted at the next. The matter came up again at the meeting of the Advisory Committee. Alladi and others

---

12 B. Shiva Rao, *Framing of India's Constitution, Select Documents,* Vol. II, pp. 229–33.

13 B. Shiva Rao, *Framing of India's Constitution, Select Documents,* Vol. II, pp. 233–34.

reiterated their arguments for leaving the words out. Others pressed for their being reintroduced in the clause. Sardar put the matter to vote. The committee voted by a majority of two in favour of the amendment for reinserting the words. Rajaji remarked, 'Having accepted the enlargement of practice of worship we will have to provide against more than one matter, namely first of all, social reforms in the particular community must be permissible with the consent of the Legislature of course. The other thing is conflicts and mutual difficulties. These will have to be provided in a comprehensive clause.' The Sardar said, 'The principle is accepted. You and Dr. Syama Prasad may sit together and draft.'[14]

Proposition: Propagation of Religion: The subcommittee on Fundamental Rights had recommended that the clause on freedom of religion should read, 'All persons are equally entitled to freedom of conscience, to freedom of religious worship and to freedom to profess religion subject to public order, morality or health and to the other provisions of this chapter....' When the draft had gone to the subcommittee on Minorities, they had recommended, first that, for the words 'religious worship', 'religious practice' should be substituted, and that after the words the right should include the right to 'propagate' the religion. K.M. Munshi, Sir Alladi and others pointed out that this could be stretched to include conversion by various means, including force, and that to the extent that merely informing people about the virtues and tenets of the religion was concerned that was already protected by the clause on freedom of speech. The Sardar put the matter to vote. The words 'to propagate' were retained.[15]

---

14 B. Shiva Rao, *Framing of India's Constitution, Select Documents,* Vol. II, pp. 265–67, 290–91.

15 B. Shiva Rao, *Framing of India's Constitution, Select Documents,* Vol. II, pp. 173, 208, 267–68.

Proposition: Kirpans: 'When you are allowed religious practice, why do you want it here?,' Sadar Patel asked Sardar Ujjal Singh about the 'Explanation' which made a special mention of the right of the Sikhs to continue to wear kirpans. But the words 'subject to public order' have been introduced, Ujjal Singh maintained, and so words about the religious practice of the Sikhs ought to be there. Sardar Patel again pointed out, 'Having inserted religious practice, if you say it is *not* a religious practice, then it [a special mention of wearing kirpans] is necessary. The wearing of *kirpans* is recognized as a religious thing.' Rajaji intervened and said, 'Having accommodated in every manner all these fears and apprehensions, we have introduced no doubt the word "practice". This is a major point raised by a large and important community. There is no harm, I think, in our putting it clearly since they have raised this point. Let us say, "The Sikh practice of wearing *kirpans* is recognized herein."' 'We will take a vote on this,' Sardar Patel said. Votes were taken and the clause was retained.[16]

Proposition: Minority Institutions: The drafts of the Subcommittees on Fundamental Rights and on Minorities had provided that all minorities shall have the right to maintain educational and other institutions of their choice, and that these institutions shall be entitled to receive aid from the state on the same terms as other institutions. Rajkumari Amrit Kaur had strenuously opposed the clause on the ground that communal institutions imparting obscurantist teachings would thereby be perpetuated. When the clause came up before the Advisory Committee she again proposed that the clause be deleted. Alladi Krishnaswami Ayyar supported her, Ambedkar too seemed to do so. The matter was put to vote. The majority voted for retaining the clause.[17]

---

16 B. Shiva Rao, *Framing of India's Constitution, Select Documents*, Vol. II, p. 268.

17 B. Shiva Rao, *Framing of India's Constitution, Select Documents*, Vol. II, pp. 280–81.

Proposition: Institutions for Hindus: There was a clause saying that notwithstanding any custom, usage, law, decree, prescription or terms of dedication no Hindu on grounds of caste, birth or denomination shall be kept out of any educational institution which has been set up for the use of the Hindu community or any section thereof. Alladi Krishnaswami Ayyar said, 'If you are going to say, "any section thereof", you are striking at the root of all private benefaction.' Pandit Pant proposed that the clause be deleted. It was deleted.[18]

Proposition: Access to educational institutions: A clause as finalized by the subcommittees provided, 'Equal opportunities of education shall be open to all citizens...' The Sardar said that this had been dropped—'In Bombay, for example,' he said, 'there is the Grant Medical College. It naturally takes boys from Bombay. If this clause is accepted, Bombay may be paying for the education of other people. They have to prevent people coming from outside because they pay for it.' Munshi reminded the committee that the object was not to make a distinction between citizens of that place. But is it [the chapter on justiciable Fundamental Rights] the best place for this?, Sardar Patel inquired. Alladi joined in to forecast that if this was made a justiciable right it would lead to considerable difficulties. The point was put to vote. The majority decided that the clause be deleted.[19]

Proposition: Conversions: Given the great tensions and disturbances which had been occurring because of conversions and reconversions, K.M. Munshi's draft had provided, 'No person under the age of eighteen shall be free to

---

18 B. Shiva Rao, *Framing of India's Constitution, Select Documents,* Vol. II, p. 282.

19 B. Shiva Rao, *Framing of India's Constitution, Select Documents,* Vol. II, pp. 282–83.

change his religious persuasion without the permission of his parent or guardian,' and that 'Conversion from one religion to another brought about by coercion, undue influence or the offering of material inducement is prohibited and punishable by the law of the Union.' The subcommittee on Fundamental Rights had modified the first portion to eliminate the element about permission of the parent or guardian but it had simultaneously introduced an element of ambiguity: as redrafted by the subcommittee this portion now read, 'No person under the age of eighteen shall be made to join or profess any religion other than the one to which he was born or be initiated into any religious order involving a loss of civil status.' The part about conversion by force or inducement too was modified to read, 'Conversion from one religion to another brought about by coercion or undue influence shall not be recognized by law and the exercise of such conversion shall be an offence'—in a word, the offering of material inducements was replaced by the more general but also more ambiguous 'undue influence', and converting persons in these ways was made an offence to be regulated by laws not of the Union necessarily, they could as well be of the units. The Advisory Committee deleted altogether the clause about conversions of persons below the age of eighteen. And in the clause about conversions by coercion or undue influence, it deleted the words that made the carrying out of such conversions an offence. And that is how the clause was sent to the president of the Constituent Assembly by the Committee in its interim report on 23 April 1947. But on 25 August 1947, Sardar Patel sent a supplementary report to the president on behalf of the Committee. In this he remarked, 'It seems to us on further consideration that this clause [about conversion by coercion or undue influence not being recognized by law] enunciates a rather obvious doctrine which it is not necessary to include in the Constitution and we recommend that it be dropped altogether.'[20]

Proposition: Acquisition of Property: The Subcommittee on Fundamental Rights after strenuous discussion provided that 'No property, movable or immovable, of any person or corporation, including any interest in any commercial or industrial undertaking, shall be taken or acquired for *public use* unless the law provides for the payment of *just* compensation for the property taken or acquired and specifies the principles on which and the manner in which the compensation is to be determined.' Pandit Pant argued very sternly against this clause—his apprehension was that it would thwart the zamindari abolition legislation which had been enacted in the United Provinces at the time. He proposed that at the least the words 'public use' should be replaced by the words 'governmental purposes'. There was agitated discussion. Eventually, the point was put to vote in the Advisory Committee. Pandit Pant's proposal was defeated by two votes. Next, the word *'just'* was deleted on the grounds that it would lead to endless litigation and that in any case the decisions of the legislature and the executive on such a matter should not be put to the mercy of a few judges.[21]

After the Subcommittee on Fundamental Rights had drafted its proposals, these were sent to the Subcommittee on Minorities. The task of this Subcommittee was to assess them solely by the impact they were liable to have on the rights and position of the minorities. Dr. H.C. Mookherjee

---

20 B. Shiva Rao, *Framing of India's Constitution, Select Documents,* Vol. II, pp. 76, 174, 291, 305.

21 B. Shiva Rao, *Framing of India's Constitution, Select Documents,* Vol. II, pp. 174, 291.

was the chairman of this Subcommittee. He submitted the report of this group to the chairman of the Advisory Committee on 27 July 1947. The report testifies to the same pattern. At the very outset the report notes:

> The Sub-Committee held prolonged discussions on the various points before them. It was not possible to arrive at unanimous decisions on any point and the voting on many questions was very close. On some points, the voting was equal and the Chairman considered that as the matters were anyhow going to the Advisory Committee, it was pointless for him to exercise a casting vote. On some points, the Sub-Committee came to the conclusion that a decision had best be deferred till the meeting of the full Advisory Committee...[22]

On clause after clause the report of the Subcommittee shows how decisions were arrived at, and how it would be a travesty to identify one person as the author of the recommendations which emerged. It also gives us a glimpse of the all-important point which will come out in sharper focus when we consider provisions on some particular aspect, namely that, the recommendations of such groups were just that—*recommendations* which were sometimes adopted by the parent committee, in this case the Advisory Committee, and sometimes not. The decisions of the Advisory Committee in turn were just its recommendations to the Constituent Assembly which the latter sometimes rejected and sometimes adopted. Often it adopted them at one stage and wholly overturned and replaced them at the next.

The Subcommittee on Minorities decided against separate electorates by a majority of twenty-eight to three. But it also decided twenty-six to three that in principle there should be reservation for recognized minorities. It classified

---

22 B. Shiva Rao, *Framing of India's Constitution, Select Documents*, Vol. II, p. 396.

minorities into three categories: it decided that minorities which constituted less than 1/2 per cent of the population in the Indian Dominion excluding the Indian states—Anglo-Indians, Parsis and plains tribesmen in Assam—should get an extra weightage in determining the number of seats to be reserved for them: simultaneously by nine to four it decided that other minorities should not be given any weightage over and above their share in the population.[23] Does this recommendation find any trace in the Constitution? As will be recalled, in his memorandum Ambedkar had advocated that voting be cumulative: this was put to vote—eight said, 'No,' two said, 'Yes.'[24]

Next, it was proposed that a minority candidate standing for election in a reserved constituency should poll a minimum number of the votes of his community before he could be declared elected. Seven members of the Subcommittee voted for the proposal, seven against. It was therefore decided to leave the matter to the Advisory Committee. Next, notes the report, 'Dr. Ambedkar suggested that candidates of a majority community should, before being declared elected, poll a minimum number of votes from among voters of the minority communities in their constituencies. This was lost by a large majority, only Dr. Ambedkar voting for it.'[25]

As we have seen, Ambedkar and others—for instance, the remaining members of the Muslim League—had advocated that seats in the Cabinet too should be reserved by statute for minorities. The matter was put to vote: eight said, 'No,' seven said, 'Yes.' It was proposed in the alternative that,

---

23 B. Shiva Rao, *Framing of India's Constitution, Select Documents,* Vol. II, pp. 397–98.

24 B. Shiva Rao, *Framing of India's Constitution, Select Documents,* Vol. II, p. 398.

25 B. Shiva Rao, *Framing of India's Constitution, Select Documents,* Vol. II, p. 398.

while the reservations for minorities in the Cabinet need not be made by statute, a provision to the same effect should be made in the instrument of instructions which was to be incorporated as a schedule to the Constitution. 'Yes,' voted twelve, 'No,' said five.[26]

What about reservations in services? Should there be reservations for Scheduled Castes in services? 'Yes,' said sixteen, 'No,' said one. For Muslims? 'Yes,' said nine, 'No,' said seven. For Sikhs? 'Yes,' said six, 'No,' said one. For plains tribals in Assam? 'Yes,' said twelve, 'No,' said one. For Anglo-Indians? 'Yes,' said twelve, 'No,' said three. 'The Parsees and Indian Christians did not ask for reservation in services,' records the report.

But should there be reservations even in posts for which competitive examinations are held? For Scheduled Castes? Eleven for, six against. For Muslims, Sikhs and tribals? Eight against, seven for. 'Anglo-Indians did not want reservations in services of this category,' records the report, 'Parsees and Indian Christians did not want reservations in any services, whether filled by competition or otherwise.' If reservations are to be there, should they be on the basis of the minority's share in the population? Nine said, 'No,' eight said, 'Yes.'[27]

Should there be, as proposed by Ambedkar, an independent officer appointed by the president at the Centre and by governors in the units to report on the working of the safeguards for minorities? 'Yes,' said sixteen, 'No' said two.[28] And so on.

To the reports of both subcommittees individual members appended minutes of dissent. M.R. Masani, Hansa

26 B. Shiva Rao, *Framing of India's Constitution, Select Documents,* Vol. II, p. 397.

27 B. Shiva Rao, *Framing of India's Constitution, Select Documents,* Vol. II, pp. 399–400.

28 B. Shiva Rao, *Framing of India's Constitution, Select Documents,* Vol. II, p. 400.

Mehta, Rajkumari Amrit Kaur, K.M. Munshi himself whose draft had been the working document for the Subcommittee on Fundamental Rights, Jairamdas Daulatram, Ambedkar, Sardar Panikkar, Professor K.T. Shah all submitted notes expressing disagreement with some particular recommendation which the majority of their colleagues on the Subcommittee on Fundamental Rights had settled. These notes of dissent were dutifully appended to the report of the Subcommittee.[29] Similarly, H.J. Khandekar and Amrit Kaur expressed disagreement with the report of the Minorities Subcommittee and its recommendations.[30]

Recall that the recommendations of the Subcommittee on Fundamental Rights had been taken up by the Subcommittee on Minorities to assess them strictly in regard to their likely effect on the interests of minorities. Now the parent Advisory Committee took up the recommendations of the Minorities Subcommittee. The recommendations were again discussed threadbare, members who had not been able to persuade their colleagues in the Subcommittees to their point of view now pressed the arguments before the Advisory Committee, and eventually several of the items had to be settled once again by votes.

Proposition: that there should be separate electorates for elections to legislatures—fifty-four against, three for. *Proposition:* that as a general principle there should be reservation of seats for recognized minorities in legislatures: opposed by Masani who tabled an alternative resolution, 'That the reservation for minorities, whether political or communal, be secured not by reservation of seats but by a system of proportional reservation preferably of cumulative voting in

---

29 The notes of dissent will be found at B. Shiva Rao, *Framing of India's Constitution, Select Documents,* Vol. II, pp. 176–98.

30 B. Shiva Rao, *Framing of India's Constitution, Select Documents,* Vol. II, pp. 400–02.

multi-member constituencies'—original *Proposition* carried, fifty-four to three. *Proposition:* that the reservations shall be for ten years, the position to be reviewed at the end of the period: alternative tabled by R.K. Sidhwa, 'The reservation shall be only for 10 years'—original *Proposition* carried by a large majority...[31]

Sardar Patel, the chairman of the Advisory Committee forwarded its reports to the president on 8 and 25 August 1947. These were discussed by the Constituent Assembly on 27 and 28 of August, and most of the recommendations were adopted. The Assembly reopened the question of reservation for minorities later on, and in May 1949 decided that there would be no reservations for religious minorities, that the only reservations would be for Scheduled Castes and Tribes.

And these are just a few items from the work of just two Subcommittees of just one committee set up by the Constituent Assembly. Other committees proceeded through the same sort of iterations.

When this is how proposals were considered, recommendations finalized, and decisions taken—by discussion, by repeated revisions and reconsideration, by votes—who is to be anointed as the author of the Constitution?

---

31 B. Shiva Rao, *Framing of India's Constitution, Select Documents,* Vol. II, pp. 403–10.

12

The folklore of freedom

We noticed that when the Subcommittee on Fundamental Rights began its work it had before it drafts of K.M. Munshi, Ambedkar and Harnam Singh. It also had notes which Sir B.N. Rau, Alladi Krishnaswami Ayyar, K.T. Shah and others had prepared. It took Munshi's draft as its working document and proceeded to build its recommendations clause by clause. We saw how the formulations proceeded through the Subcommittee, how they went through changes at the hands of the sister Subcommittee on Minorities, how the recommendations of both were then examined and finalized by the parent Advisory Committee. But even that is but a small part of the story: in one direction the drafts which Munshi and others had submitted had a long history of their own stretching decades into the past, in the other the recommendations which emerged from the discussions and rounds of voting in these Subcommittees and the Advisory Committee went through transformations upon transformations in the coming months. It will pay us to take a few steps back to recall what a few documents of the previous decades had concluded on the question, and then to follow the course which the proposals traversed after they left the Advisory Committee.

A committee of 1945

The tabulations of rights which we have been considering were put together in 1946. But in November 1944 the Standing Committee of the Non-Party Conference had set up a committee to examine the communal question from the constitutional angle. Sir Tej Bahadur Sapru was to head it, and appoint members. The committee had appointed four subcommittees including one on Scheduled Castes and one on minorities.[1]

These subcommittees had prepared recommendations regarding Fundamental Rights which they thought ought to be guaranteed to all citizens, as well as special rights and protection which they thought should be guaranteed to the Scheduled Castes and religious minorities.

The committee listed five Fundamental Rights, saying that the detailed formulation of the rights was best left to the body which would be set up to devise the Constitution itself. These rights, which we will immediately recognize when we glance at Part III of the Constitution as we know it, were the following:

(a) the liberties of the individual;
(b) the freedom of Press and association;
(c) equality of rights of citizenship of all nationals irrespective of birth, religion, colour, caste or creed;
(d) full religious toleration, including non-interference in religious beliefs, practices and institutions;
(e) protection to language and culture of all communities.[2]

The committee went somewhat farther in formulating some of these rights, in particular those which would

---

1 The following account is based on *Constitutional Proposals of the Sapru Committee*, Padma Publications, Bombay, December 1945, Reprinted January 1946.

2 *Constitutional Proposals of the Sapru Committee*, op. cit., p. 257.

provide assurance to minorities—after all, the very purpose of the committee was to put together yet another scheme that might dissuade Jinnah from pressing his demand for Pakistan. The first of these were rights to equal opportunities for public employment, to non-discrimination in regard to public employment, and to freedom of worship. But even these could be traced back, and were so traced by the Sapru Committee itself to at least the Proclamation of Queen Victoria, in fact to what the law had been since the Crown had taken over the administration of the country in 1858. Queen Victoria's Proclamation had declared:

> We declare it to be Our Royal Will and Pleasure that none be in any wise favoured, none molested or disquieted by reason of their Religious Faith or Observances; but that all shall alike enjoy the equal and impartial protection of the Law: and We do strictly charge and enjoin all those who may be in authority under Us, that they abstain from all interference with the Religious Belief or Worship of any of Our Subjects, on pain of Our highest Displeasure.
>
> And it is Our further Will that, so far as may be, Our Subjects, of whatever Race or Creed, be freely and impartially admitted to Offices in Our Service, the duties of which they may be qualified, by their education, ability, and integrity, duly to discharge.[3]

And the right regarding equal access to public employment had been incorporated in the laws of the land. Thus Section 298 of the Government of India Act, 1935, had provided that 'No subject of His Majesty domiciled in India shall on grounds only of religion, place of birth, descent, colour or any of them be ineligible for office under the Crown in India.'[4]

The committee had turned next to rights pertaining to religious freedom. It had set up a subcommittee on

---

3 Cited in *Constitutional Proposals of the Sapru Committee,* op. cit., pp. 224–25.

4 *Constitutional Proposals of the Sapru Committee,* op. cit., pp. 224–25.

minorities. That subcommittee had formulated these rights as follows:

> 1. In India there is freedom of religion and conscience.
>
> 2. All inhabitants of India shall have equal right to practise, in public or in private any faith, religion or creed whatsoever, and to assemble for the conduct of religious service in public, in so far as the exercise of these rights does not violate the law or public order and morality and they are exercised with due regard to the religious sentiments of other communities.
>
> 3. All inhabitants shall be entitled to establish, manage and administer at their own expense, religious, charitable and social institutions, schools and other educational establishments and shall have the right to the free use of their own language and script if any and the free exercise of their own religion in such institutions.
>
> Pursuant to this right, they shall be entitled to acquire, own, transfer, hold in trust movable and immovable property subject to the general laws.
>
> 4. All inhabitants shall be free to preach their religion, so far as they do not violate the law of public order and morality or offend the sentiments of other communities.
>
> 5. No inhabitant shall be deprived of his public rights by change of religion.
>
> 6. No citizen shall be subjected to any disability or prejudiced by religion, caste, creed, colour or sex in regard to public employment in any office of power or honour or in the exercise of any trade or calling.

The committee adopted these as its own recommendations, noting that these clauses dealt with what it termed General Fundamental Rights. In addition, it said, there ought to be provisions to assure certain Special Rights. These it listed as follows:

> 1. It shall be the duty of the State to impart education to the children of a minority, of sufficient numerical strength, up to the stage of elementary education, in their own mother tongue and,

where this is not possible, the State shall give adequate aid to such institutions as cater to this need of such minorities.

2. Liberty to establish and change one's place of dwelling is guaranteed in India, subject to public morality and health.

3. Freedom to choose one's occupation as well as to originate enterprises or industries of an agricultural, commercial, industrial or other nature is guaranteed in India. No person may be deprived of this right, save in accordance with and subject to the limits laid down by law.

4. There shall be no discrimination with regard to the continuance or fresh allotments of educational grants-in-aid to denominational institutions. These grants, as far as possible, shall be commensurate with the number of pupils receiving instruction therein.

This provision does not, in any way affect the guarantees given to the Anglo-Indians in this regard in section 83 of the Government of India Act of 1935.

The committee proceeded to list some 'special provisions' for the Sikhs—that their right to *jhatka* meat should not be interfered with, and that no law should be enacted to restrict in any manner or to any extent whatsoever, the manufacture, sale, keeping and wearing of kirpans by them.

On the one hand, the committee's list reflected the demands which were being made in India—those references to jhatka meat and kirpans—and the assurances which it was thought at the time may help dissuade Jinnah from his aim of Pakistan. On the other, the list reflected what the study of other Constitutions of the time had led the committee to conclude would be appropriate for India. The committee drew attention to a pamphlet which it was circulating separately and which had been authored by its joint secretary, K. Santhanam. It recorded, 'In this pamphlet we have collected together the Fundamental Rights incorporated in the Constitutions of the United States of America; the Union of Soviet Socialist Republics, 1936; Swiss Confederation, June 1921; The Irish Free State, 6th December, 1921; The Polish Republic, Law of 17th March

1921; The German Reich, llth August, 1919; Czechoslovakia, 10th September 1919; the Kingdom of Belgium, 7th February, 1931, as revised up to the 15th October, 1921; The Estonian Republic, 15th June, 1920; and the United States of Mexico, 31st January, 1917. We have also given extracts from the Minorities Treaties of the League of Nations..., and also extracts from National States and National Minorities... In addition to this, the constitutional aspect of Fundamental Rights has been discussed at length in an exhaustive note contained in Chapter VI, page 23 of pamphlet No. 3. We desire that it should be treated as a part of this Report.'[5]

Recall that the Subcommittee on Fundamental Rights was to decide that the list of rights should be divided into justiciable Fundamental Rights and the non-justiciable Directive Principles. The Sapru Committee had also recommended a division of rights between justiciable and non-justiciable rights along the lines contained in the Constitution of Ireland.[6]

We today have a Minorities Commission. It is of interest therefore to see that the Sapru Committee had recommended a Minorities Commission to keep watch over the affairs of the minorities. Its words on the matter though are far from what we have made of the Commission. 'We do not think that if the Constitution is worked in the right spirit and if proper relations are established between the Minorities Commission, the Government and the Legislature,' Sapru and his colleagues said, 'there need be any conflict or friction. On the other hand, we very strongly hope that the Minorities Commission will recognize that its primary function is to inform, after enquiry, the Government of the day of the grievances of a particular minority. Its recommendations ought to help and not obstruct the Government in its work...'

---

5 *Constitutional Proposals of the Sapru Committee,* op. cit., pp. 257–58.

6 *Constitutional Proposals of the Sapru Committee,* op.cit., pp. 258–60.

The Committee had recalled that Sir Stafford Cripps in his proposals had envisaged that the rights of the minorities would be guaranteed by a treaty which the new government of India would be required to enter into with the Government of the UK—as we know, Ambedkar had pressed the British to the very last minute for tying the new government in such a treaty. But Sapru and his colleagues had endorsed the view that Sir Reginald Coupland had taken in his *Constitutional Problem of India,* and said, 'Such a Treaty would not accord with the new constitutional status of India, it would be difficult to enforce its terms, and it would not really serve the interests of the Minorities. The real protection of such interests is to be found not in any external authority but only in the law of the land.'

'While, therefore, we recommend that the minorities should receive full and adequate protection in regard to their political, religious, social and economic rights,' the Committee had said, 'we must make an appeal to them that they will regard themselves more and more as integral parts of India. It would indeed be a misfortune if the minorities kept alive memories of the past isolation and unduly emphasized their rights, laying little stress on their duties. A writer of great authority on international law—Dr. W.E. Hall in his *Treatise on International Law*—observes, 'There has been too much stress laid on the rights of minorities in the Peace Treaties and not sufficient to their duties to the States of which they are members; but at the third Assembly of the League of Nations a resolution was passed emphasizing the duty incumbent upon persons belonging to racial, religious or linguistic minorities to cooperate loyally with their fellow-citizens.'[7]

The counsel to the minorities of course sounds alien to our ears after fifty years of secularist bending, but anyone

---

7 *Constitutional Proposals of the Sapru Committee,* op. cit., pp. 262–64.

having glanced at Part III of our Constitution will at once see the lineage in the formulations of the Sapru Committee of the rights listed in the Constitution as we have it today.

A resolution of 1931

But even that was but the latest of such documents. As an example consider the resolution which the Congress passed at its session in Karachi in 1931. Saying that 'In order to end the exploitation of the masses, political freedom must include real economic freedom of the starving millions,' it resolved 'that any Constitution which may be agreed to on its behalf should provide, or enable the *Swaraj* Government to provide, for the following:

1. Fundamental Rights of the people, including:

(i) freedom of association and combination;

(ii) freedom of speech and of the press;

(iii) freedom of conscience and the free profession and practice of religion, subject to public order and morality;

(iv) protection of the culture, language, and scripts of the minorities;

(v) equal rights and obligations of all citizens, without any bar on account of sex;

(vi) no disability to attach to any citizen by reason of his or her religion, caste or creed or sex in regard to public employment, office of power or honour, and in the exercise of any trade or calling;

(vii) equal rights to all citizens in regard to public roads, wells, schools and other places of public resort;

(viii) right to keep and bear arms in accordance with regulations and reservations made in that behalf;

(ix) no person shall be deprived of his liberty nor shall his dwelling or property be entered, sequestered or confiscated, save in accordance with law.

2. Religious neutrality on the part of the State.

3. Adult suffrage.

4. Free primary education.

5. A living wage for industrial workers, limited hours of labour, healthy conditions of work, protection against the economic consequences of old age, sickness and unemployment.
6. Labour to be freed from serfdom or conditions bordering on serfdom.
7. Protection of woman workers, and, specially, adequate provisions for leave during maternity period.
8. Prohibition against employment of children of school-going age in factories.
9. Right of labour to form unions to protect their interests with suitable machinery for settlement of disputes by arbitration.
10. Substantial reduction in agricultural rent or revenue paid by the peasantry and in case of uneconomic holdings exemption from rent for such period as may be necessary, relief being given to small *zamindars* wherever necessary by reason of such reduction.
11. Imposition of a progressive income tax on agricultural incomes above a fixed minimum.
12. A graduated inheritance tax.
13. Military expenditure to be reduced by at least one half of the present scale.
14. Expenditure and salaries in civil departments to be largely reduced. No servant of the State, other than specially employed experts and the like, to be paid above a certain fixed figure which should not ordinarily exceed Rs. 500 per month.
15. Protection of indigenous cloth by exclusion of foreign cloth and foreign yarn from the country.
16. Total prohibition of intoxicating drinks and drugs.
17. No duty on salt manufactured in India.
18. Control over exchange and currency policy so as to help Indian industries and bring relief to the masses.
19. Control by the State of key industries and ownership of mineral resources.
20. Control of usury-direct or indirect.[8]

Item 1 (viii)—that every citizen must have the right to bear arms—would perhaps obscure what items such as

8 For the text of the resolution see Mitra's *Annual Register,* 1931, Vol. I, pp. 277–78.

items 13—that military expenditure must be reduced to half the then prevalent level—14—that the expenditure on salaries of governmental staff should be cut, and that the norm should be a salary of less than Rs. 500—15—that indigenous cloth should be protected—16—total prohibition—and item 17—that there shall be no tax on salt—would ordinarily reveal: that the resolution was moved by none other than Mahatma Gandhi. Notice how closely the items enumerated in item 1 correspond to so many of the provisions of Part III of the Constitution as we know it. And so many of the subsequent items figure in what came to be adopted as Directive Principles of the Constitution. Now, the point is not that, therefore, Gandhiji should be regarded as the author of the Fundamental Rights and Directive Principles parts of the Constitution, but that points such as these were part of the common lore of the times, specifically of the national movement.

A committee of 1928

Step four years further back. As we have noted earlier, at its meetings in Bombay on 15 to 18 May 1927 the All-India Congress Committee had passed a resolution and called upon 'the Working Committee to frame a *Swaraj* Constitution, based on a Declaration of Rights, for India in consultation with elected members of the central and provincial Legislatures and other leaders of political parties'.

The Madras Congress had thereafter passed a resolution on the Swaraj Constitution declaring, 'Having regard to the general desire of all political parties in the country to unite together in settling a *Swaraj* Constitution, and having considered the various drafts submitted to it and the various suggestions received in reply to the Working Committee's circular, this Congress authorizes the Working Committee, which will have the power to co-opt, to confer with similar

Committees to be appointed by other organizations—political, labour, commercial and communal—in the country and to draft a *Swaraj* Constitution for India on the basis of a Declaration of Rights, and to place the same for consideration and approval before a special convention to be convened in Delhi not later than March next...' The Committee submitted its report in March 1928. But by now the Muslim League had executed another one of its somersaults, and boycotted the work of the Committee. The Motilal Nehru Committee had then been constituted. We have seen how the work of this Committee too had been circumscribed.[9]

For our present concern, however, the point to notice is that the Motilal Nehru Committee enumerated nineteen rights. These were as follows:

> (i) All powers of government and all authority, Legislative, Executive and Judicial, are derived from the people and the same shall be exercised in the Commonwealth of India through the organizations established by or under, and in accord with, this Constitution.
> (ii) No person shall be deprived of his liberty nor shall his dwelling or property be entered, sequestered or confiscated, save in accordance with law.
> (iii) Freedom of conscience and the free profession and practice of religion are, subject to public order or morality, hereby guaranteed to every person.
> (iv) The right of free expression of opinion, as well as the right to assemble peaceably and without arms, and to form associations or unions, is hereby guaranteed for purposes not opposed to public order or morality.
> (v) All citizens in the Commonwealth of India have the right to free elementary education without any distinction of caste or

9 On the foregoing, *All Parties Conference, Report of the Committee appointed by the Conference to determine the Principles of the Constitution for India*, General Secretary of the All-India Congress Committee, Allahabad, 1928, pp. 17–26.

creed in the matter of admission into any educational institution, maintained or aided by the State, and such right shall be enforceable as soon as due arrangements shall have been made by competent authority.

(vi) All citizens are equal before the law and possess equal civic rights.

(vii) There shall be no penal law whether substantive or procedural of a discriminative nature.

(viii) No person shall be punished for any act which was not punishable under the law at the time it was committed.

(ix) No corporal punishment or other punishment involving torture of any kind shall be lawful.

(x) Every citizen shall have the right to a writ of *habeas corpus.* Such right may be suspended in case of war or rebellion by an Act of the central Legislature or, if the Legislature is not in session, by the Governor-General in Council, and in such case he shall report the suspension to the Legislature at the earliest possible opportunity for such action as it may deem fit.

(xi) There shall be no state religion for the Commonwealth of India or for any province in the Commonwealth, nor shall the State either directly or indirectly endow any religion or give any preference or impose any disability on account of religious belief or religious status.

(xii) No person attending any school, receiving state aid or other public money shall be compelled to attend the religious instruction that may be given in the school.

(xiii) No person shall by reason of his religion, caste or creed be prejudiced in any way in regard to public employment, office of power or honour and the exercise of any trade or calling.

(xiv) All citizens have an equal right of access to, and use of, public roads, public wells and all other places of public resort.

(xv) Freedom of combination and association for the maintenance and improvement of labour and economic conditions is guaranteed to everyone and of all occupations. All agreements and measures tending to restrict or obstruct such freedom are illegal.

(xvi) No breach of contract of service or abetment thereof shall be made a criminal offence.

(xvii) Parliament shall make suitable laws for the maintenance of health and fitness for work of all citizens, securing of a living wage for every worker, the protection of motherhood, welfare of children, and the economic consequences of old age, infirmity and unemployment.

(xviii) Every citizen shall have the right to keep and bear arms in accordance with regulations made in that behalf.

(xix) Men and women shall have equal rights as citizens.

Note: Notwithstanding anything to the contrary in article IV the Sikhs are entitled to carry *kirpans.*[10]

This Committee was not manufacturing the rights in a vacuum either. It too was building on what had been done earlier—in particular by the provisions of the Irish Constitution and the work of the first, and infructuous committee appointed by the All Parties Conference.

'Canada, Australia and South Africa have no Declaration of Rights in their constitutions but there are various articles to be found in the Constitution of the Irish Free State which may properly be grouped under the general head "Fundamental Rights",' the Motilal Nehru report had noted. 'The reason for this is not far to seek. Ireland is the only country where the conditions obtaining before the Treaty were the nearest approach to those we have in India. The first concern of the people of Ireland was, as indeed it is of the people of India today, to secure Fundamental Rights that have been denied to them. The other Dominions had their rise from earlier British settlements which were supposed to have carried the law of England with them. Ireland was taken and kept under the rule of England against her own will and the acquisition of Dominion Status by her became a matter of Treaty between the two nations. We conceive that the constitutional position in India is very much the same...'[11]

---

10 *All Parties Conference, Report of the Committee appointed by the Conference to determine the Principles of the Constitution for India,* op. cit., pp. 101–03.

11 *All Parties Conference, Report of the Committee appointed by the Conference to determine the Principles of the Constitution for India,* op. cit., p. 89.

Similarly, alluding to the work of the first committee, the Motilal Nehru report had remarked, 'The first Committee of the All Parties Conference went into this question carefully and we have adopted most of their articles...'[12] It had not claimed originality in the rights it was enumerating, on the contrary it had made a point of emphasizing that the rights which it was listing had been enumerated by the preceding committee, and it had noted the additions it was making to some of the articles recommended by that earlier committee.[13] In a word, while we can trace back to the Motilal Nehru Committee's report of 1928 many of the rights we rely on these days, that Committee itself was at pains to stress that it was merely building on the work of others.

A bill of 1925

That was in 1927 and 1928. Going back another four years we find that a National Convention, with Sir Tej Bahadur Sapru as president and Mrs. Annie Besant as general secretary, had prepared a Commonwealth of India Bill in December, 1924. The draft Bill had been presented at the meeting of the All-India Parties Conference in January 1925. It had been eventually finalized at a convention in April that year. In June 1925 over forty Indian political leaders had commended it to the British Parliament.

The Bill had enumerated eight Fundamental Rights as follows:

12 *All Parties Conference, Report of the Committee appointed by the Conference to determine the Principles of the Constitution for India,* op. cit., p. 90.

13 *All Parties Conference, Report of the Committee appointed by the Conference to determine the Principles of the Constitution for India,* op. cit., pp. 90–91.

The 'Fundamental Rights' of the subject are thus defined:-
(a) The liberty of the person is inviolable, and no person shall be deprived of his liberty save in accordance with law and by ordinary Courts of Law, provided, however, that nothing in this Section contained shall be invoked to prohibit, control, or interfere with any act of the civil or military forces of the Commonwealth of India during the existence of a state of war or rebellion. (b) The dwelling on the property of every person is inviolable, and shall not be entered or expropriated or confiscated except in accordance with law. (c) Freedom of conscience and the free profession and practice of religion are, subject to public order or morality, guaranteed to every person. (d) The right of free expression of opinion as well as the right to assemble peaceably and without arms, and to form associations or unions is guaranteed for purposes not opposed to public order or morality. Laws regulating the manner in which the right of forming associations and the right of free assembly may be exercised, shall contain no political, religious, or class distinctions. (e) All persons in the Commonwealth of India have the right to free elementary education, and such right shall be enforceable as soon as due arrangements shall have been made by the competent authority. (f) All persons have an equal right to the use of roads, places of resort dedicated to the public, Courts of Justice and the like, provided they do not disturb public order or disobey any notice issued by a lawful authority. (g) All persons of whatever Nationality, residing within the Commonwealth are equal before the Law and shall be tried for similar effect in Courts of the same order and by Judicial Officer of the same grade and no person shall escape the penalty annexed to any breach of the Law, on account of the nationality, or his caste, or his class, or his occupation. (h) There shall be no sex-disqualification with regard to the franchises, memberships of the Governments, of the Legislatures and of Local Bodies, and all offices, functions and powers shall be open equally to both sexes.[14]

Again, we find successors to almost each of these formulations in the provisions of the Fundamental Rights or Directive Principles parts in the Constitution.

---

14 Mitra's *Annual Register*, 1925, Vol. I, pp. 78–79.

Ambedkar's version of history

That is the background of the provisions, it is manifest, it was known to one and all—the rights, the resolutions and reports set out were the very folklore of the freedom movement. And yet not only is one man the author, that author has his own version of how the provisions came to be.

The Rajya Sabha was debating the Fourth Constitution Amendment Bill. Ambedkar had begun with a familiar denunciation of persons—in particular Pandit Nehru—who had been his colleague till the other day, and his even more familiar denunciation of our past. In that past, only two entities had had Fundamental Rights, he informed the House—the Brahmin and the cow. The Muslims came and took away the rights of these two. But they also did not institute Fundamental Rights: 'What the Muslims did,' Ambedkar said, 'was to give privileges to the Mussalman and no rights to the non-Muslims.' None of the British Acts from 1772 to 1935 had given Fundamental Rights either, he said. 'It is in 1947 or so when *Swaraj* became a fact in this country that this idea of Fundamental Rights emerged,' Ambedkar remarked. 'It is our Constitution which for the first time contains the embodiment of what are called Fundamental Rights. It is a very strange thing that although the foreigners were ruling in this country, namely the British, no one ever agitated for the enactment of the Fundamental Rights. The Congress was in existence from 1886. Let anyone examine the annual resolutions passed by the Congress. They never asked for any Fundamental Rights.'

Gopinath Singh of UP interjected, 'Did you read the Karachi Congress Resolution of 1931?'

'Well,' Ambedkar replied, 'I have no idea of that. They said that they would have Fundamental Rights when they enact a Constitution'—that is not all that they had said, of course, as we have seen the resolution had furnished a list of the rights. But to proceed with Ambedkar's version of history: he continued, 'It is as I say a very strange commentary that no Indian—and the Indians who ran the Congress in the earliest times were intellectual giants: they were not ordinary people, they were most learned, they were wide awake—not one of them to my knowledge asked for any Fundamental Rights'—for what had the Lokmanya suffered six years of solitary confinement, to take just one instance, what had Gandhiji organized the Rowlatt Act satyagraha for except the Fundamental Right to free speech? 'But as soon as *Swaraj* came,' Ambedkar proceeded to maintain, 'there was a demand for Fundamental Rights. It is a matter worth consideration why this happened. Various people would no doubt give various replies, but my reply is very simple. My reply is this—the reason why Indians did not demand Fundamental Rights when the British were here is this. Although the British had their imperialism as one aspect of their rule, there cannot be any doubt that the administration of this country was governed by what is called the rule of justice, equity and good conscience...'—at least he was not advocating the continuation of that imperialism any longer.

'The point is that the British administered this country in a manner in which everybody felt that there was some sense of security,' Ambedkar told the House. 'That is the reason why, in my judgment, nobody in this country clamoured for Fundamental Rights. But as soon as *Swaraj* presented itself, everybody thought—at least many of the minorities thought—that there was the prospect of political authority passing into the hands of a majority, which did not possess what might constitutionally be called constitutional morality. Their official doctrine was inequality of classes. Though there is inequality in every community, or whatever be the word, that inequality is a matter of practice. It is not an official dogma. But with a majority in this country, inequality, as embodied in their *Chaturvarna,* is an official doctrine. Secondly, their caste system is a sword of political and administrative discrimination. The result was that Fundamental Rights became inevitable.'

In contrast to what he had stated so emphatically in the Constituent Assembly, Ambedkar now said, 'What I found—and I know this thing more than probably many do, because I had something to do with it—was that the Congress Party was so jubilant over the Fundamental Rights. They wanted Fundamental Rights, and they thought that Fundamental Rights were so necessary that if the Indian people had a Constitution which did not embody Fundamental Rights, they would appear nude to the world. That was the reason they clamoured for Fundamental Rights...'[15]

In other words, all the struggles and resolutions wiped out with a shrug—'Well, I have no idea about that'; no one demanded Fundamental Rights as the British ruled the country in accordance with 'the rule of justice, equity and good conscience'; if the Fundamental Rights had come to be instituted, it was because, with Swaraj 'presenting itself', the minorities felt that they would be smothered by the majority whose official and unchangeable doctrine was inequality; and the Congress leadership had embraced the provisions only so as not to appear nude before the world!

But I am not on the amnesia that would be natural to a person who had been with the British all those decades during which the others were struggling for precisely those very rights, I am not on his version of his history either. I am only on the texts of those successive reports and resolutions, and the lists they had incorporated of the rights which Indians must have.

---

15 *Rajya Sabha Debates,* 19 March 1954, Columns 2446–50.

And, please remember, the antecedents of the provisions on Fundamental Rights are just one set of examples, the genealogy of other parts of the Constitution—in particular, as we shall see, of the structure itself—can be traced just as easily. That being the case, is one person the author of what the Constitution contains?

13

The subsequent journey

We saw that provisions regarding Fundamental Rights as well as Directive Principles had a long ancestry. All these formulations were well known. They were the stuff of discourse among all who were striving for the country's freedom in those decades. When K.M. Munshi or K.T. Shah, or Ambedkar for that matter sat down to prepare their respective drafts on the question, they were building on the earlier formulations. In any event, as we saw, the draft that K.M. Munshi had prepared became the basic working document for the Subcommittee on Fundamental Rights, and from there for the Subcommittee on Minorities. Every clause of that document was mulled over, various persons made substantial contributions to what was finally accepted. That acceptance was often settled, as we have seen, by votes.

So the document which emerged at each stage was the product of collective deliberation. And at each stage till its final adoption in November 1949 a formulation was but a tentative step.

The Report of the Fundamental Rights Subcommittee provided that 'Slavery... [along with other practices which the clause enumerated, is] hereby prohibited and any contravention of this prohibition shall be an offence.'[1] 'May

1 B. Shiva Rao, *The Framing of India's Constitution, Select Documents,* Vol. II, p. 173.

I suggest that we need not adopt the laws of America as enacted at the time of slavery,' remarked Rajaji when the clause came up before the Advisory Committee. This part of the clause therefore went, and the Committee moved to consider the rest of the provision.[2]

Or consider another example to which reference was made earlier. K.M. Munshi had provided in his enumeration of Fundamental Rights another of the rights about which everyone fighting for freedom had been naturally very particular: 'The right to the secrecy of his correspondence'. The debate on it had been intense: Alladi Krishnaswami had argued that providing a blanket right of this kind would make even the detection of conspiracies to murder impossible. Accordingly, in its report, while it had retained the right, the Subcommittee on Fundamental Rights had added a proviso to the effect, 'Provision may be made by law to regulate the interception or detention of articles and messages in course of transmission by post, telegraph or otherwise on the occurrence of any public emergency or in the interests of public safety or tranquillity.' Alladi Krishnaswami Ayyar reiterated his opposition to the clause in a written comment on the report. 'A clause like this might checkmate the prosecution in establishing any case of conspiracy or abetment in a criminal case and defeat every action for civil conspiracy,' he pointed out, 'the plaintiff being helpless to prove the same by placing before the court the correspondence that passed between the parties, which in all these cases would furnish the most material evidence...' He followed up his comments with a formal note of dissent to the Subcommittee's report. Sardar Panikkar also opposed the provision in the course of his own note of dissent: 'I am of the opinion that this restricts the powers of the Executive machinery unnecessarily,' he

2 B. Shiva Rao, *The Framing of India's Constitution, Select Documents,* Vol. II, p. 255.

wrote, 'and limits the censorship of correspondence and communications to the occurrence of public emergency or in the interests of public safety or tranquillity. I think the administration of criminal law in the country requires a wider provision. For instance, it is impossible to prove conspiracy, bribery and numerous other offences effectively except by the production of correspondence. In fact, the extraordinary facilities open to criminals at the present time by the use of modern methods of communication render the discovery of crime difficult unless certain latitude is allowed to the Executive authorities.' He said he was not against the right which the provision sought to provide, but that the provision required much stricter examination. Notice incidentally, how persons at the time did not shy from stating and standing by positions that our leaders today would be scared to be seen endorsing lest someone charge them with being less than fervent about freedom.

The clause came up for consideration before the Advisory Committee. Sardar Patel was presiding. Ayyar said that he had 'a very strong objection' to the provision, and he recalled his reasons—'If we have this one,' he said, 'then the result will be that if a conspiracy to murder is going on, then the Government will have no right to look into it.' Munshi reacted emphatically, but with some obfuscation: 'The clause is very clear as it stands,' he said. 'It is only after the declaration of a public emergency and not before or in the interest of public safety or public tranquillity. If a conspiracy is going on it is not in the interest of public tranquillity but in the interest of murdering a certain number of people. This clause was copied from the American Constitution. Yet in spite of this the Government can intercept anything.' The Sardar put the clause to vote. The clause was deleted.[3] Who is the author?

3 B. Shiva Rao, *The Framing of India's Constitution, Select Documents,* Vol. II, pp. 75, 139, 158–59, 186–87, 234.

The right to free speech

A volume can be filled with examples of this kind. It would perhaps be more instructive to follow one or two examples at some length than to try and digest a large number in summary form. Let us take up a right with which we are all familiar, namely the right to free speech. As we have seen, this right had been in every list since the Commonwealth of India Bill of 1925. In fact, even before that it was this right which had been the focus of Gandhiji's satyagraha against the Rowlatt Act. It was of course included as the very first right in K.M. Munshi's draft for the Subcommittee on Fundamental Rights. 'Every citizen within the limits of the law of the Union and in accordance therewith,' his draft provided, 'has: (a) the right of free expression of opinion...' The draft made a separate mention of the freedom of the press providing, 'The press shall be free subject to restrictions imposed by the law of the Union as in its opinion may be necessary in the interest of public order and morality.'

Thus two things were specified about the restrictions that might be imposed: the law in regard to them must be a central law, and, in the case of the press, it could seek to restrict the freedom only in the interests of public order and morality.[4] There was vigorous discussion in the subcommittee: some argued that the words 'public order' and 'morality' were vague and could be misused by a determined executive; others argued that, in fact, if restrictions were to be permissible on these grounds alone, even long-standing laws on defamation, etc., would be rendered ultra vires. By the time the clause was finalized by the subcommittee it became:

---

4 B. Shiva Rao, *The Framing of India's Constitution, Select Documents,* Vol. II, p. 75.

> There shall be liberty for the exercise of the following rights subject to public order and morality or to the existence of grave emergency declared to be such by the Government of the Union or the unit concerned whereby the security of the Union or the unit, as the case may be, is threatened:
>
> (a) The right of every citizen to freedom of speech and expression.
>
> The publication or utterance of seditious, obscene, slanderous, libelous or defamatory matter shall be actionable or punishable in accordance with law.[5]

Thus, in addition to public order and morality, the new circumstance of emergency was to govern the exercise of all rights. And the state could also regulate the freedom of speech by laws regarding (i) sedition, (ii) obscenity, (iii) slander, libel and defamation. The clause was again debated intensively when it came before the parent Advisory Committee. But all of it survived, and the Committee made one addition. To the grounds on which the right could be restricted was now added 'blasphemy'.[6] Other freedoms too had provisos which allowed the state to regulate and restrict their exercise.

Sardar Patel rose to move the draft article in the Constituent Assembly on 30 April 1947. Several members had criticized the draft on the charge that what it gave in the main body of the article, it took away in the provisos. There was another, even more basic consideration weighing with the leaders. The new viceroy, Lord Mountbatten, had announced that the British would in any case leave by 30 June 1948. But the Congress was still striving to somehow ensure that power would be handed over to a united India. Everything was being done to assuage Jinnah and the

---

5 B. Shiva Rao, *The Framing of India's Constitution, Select Documents,* Vol. II, p. 172

6 B. Shiva Rao, *The Framing of India's Constitution, Select Documents,* Vol. II, p. 297.

Muslim League. All restrictive clauses in the drafts of the Constitution were being kept in abeyance on the ground that it would be better to include them after discussing their wording with the Muslim League should it eventually join the Assembly. Thus, when he moved the draft article for consideration, Sardar Patel told the Assembly that he was *not* going to move the provisos which gave scope for the state to regulate the exercise of the rights.[7]

Members who had been opposing the provisos naturally felt gratified, though some of them asked for more. Somnath Lahiri, while welcoming the abandonment of the provisos, urged that the expression 'security of the Union' in the draft be replaced by the words 'defence of the Union' on the ground that the former was 'a very vague term and may mean anything'. He also urged that the word 'sedition' be dropped altogether from the Article.[8] Almost a hundred amendments had been proposed, the Sardar had withdrawn the provisos which most of the amendments were aimed at altering. The result was a jumble of amendments and amendments to amendments. 'Sir, I confess I am a little confused,' Pandit Nehru remarked as he rose to intervene. 'I do not know where we stand after all this welter of amendments which have been moved and not moved and withdrawn and not withdrawn. I do not know how other members stand in this matter, but there is utter confusion in my mind as to what is being discussed...'[9]

The discussion continued. Eventually, when the article was adopted it read:

> There shall be liberty for the exercise of the following rights subject to public order and morality and except in a grave emergency declared to be such by the Government of the Union

7 *Constituent Assembly Debates,* Vol. III, pp. 457–58.

8 *Constituent Assembly Debates,* Vol. III, p. 460.

9 *Constituent Assembly Debates,* Vol. III, p. 465.

> or the unit concerned whereby the security of the Union or the unit, as the case may be, is threatened:
>
> (a) The right of every citizen to freedom of speech and expression...
>
> Provision may be made by law to impose such restrictions as may be necessary in the public interest including the protection of minority groups and tribes.[10]

In June it was all over. Jinnah had succeeded. The Congress leaders, in spite of the opposition of Gandhiji, had to accept Mountbatten's plan for the Partition of the country. But even in October 1947 when he drew up the first overall draft of the Constitution, Sir B.N. Rau confined himself to the general restrictions which were indicated in the article as it had been approved by the Assembly. He did not include the heads which had been enumerated in the provisos, and which the Sardar had refrained from moving in the Assembly.

This draft of the constitutional adviser became the working document for the Drafting Committee. As happened in the case of other draft articles, the clause on freedom of speech also was subjected to minute discussion.

The first decision of the Committee was to propose that the proviso in regard to the freedom of speech should be restored. Thus in accordance with its decision on 31 October 1947, the guarantee of the right was to be followed by the original clause, 'Provided that the publication or utterances of seditious, slanderous, libelous or defamatory matter shall be actionable or punishable in accordance with law.'[11] Notice that the reference to 'blasphemous' writings or utterances which had been included in the proviso by the Advisory Committee had now been deleted.

---

10 B. Shiva Rao, *The Framing of India's Constitution, Select Documents,* Vol. II, p. 301.

11 B. Shiva Rao, *The Framing of India's Constitution, Select Documents,* Vol. II, p. 309.

But four days later the Committee agreed to further modify the clause. At the meeting on 4 November 1947 Sir Alladi Krishnaswami Ayyar argued that the proviso as drafted till then would not be enough to save existing laws on libel, slander, defamation or sedition. The Committee agreed that the clause should be redrafted so as to explicitly save existing laws on these matters. Accordingly, the proviso was redrafted to read as follows: 'Nothing in clause (a) of sub-section (1) shall affect the operation of any law relating to libel, slander, defamation or sedition, nor shall prevent the State from making any law with respect thereto.'[12]

Discussions in the Drafting Committee continued, and the clause kept undergoing changes. In the end it read,

> (1) Subject to the other provisions of this Article, all citizens shall have the right—(a) to freedom of speech and expression...(2) Nothing in sub-clause (1) of this Article shall affect the operation of any existing law, or prevent the State from making any law, relating to libel, slander, defamation, sedition or any other matter which offends against decency or morality or undermines the authority or foundation of the State.

Notice the addition at this stage of the new ground, 'or undermines the authority or foundation of the State'. Four provisos to regulate the other rights guaranteed in the article were also reintroduced.[13] And it was in this form that the provision relating to freedom of speech figured in the Draft Constitution as finalized by the Drafting Committee.[14]

The Draft Constitution was circulated far and wide for

---

12 B. Shiva Rao, *The Framing of India's Constitution, Select Documents,* Vol. III, pp. 339–40.

13 B. Shiva Rao, *The Framing of India's Constitution, A Study,* pp. 217–18.

14 B. Shiva Rao, *The Framing of India's Constitution, Select Documents,* Vol. III, p. 522.

comments. The article is 'very clumsily drafted', JP wrote, rights given in the first clause are considerably taken away by the provisos. He urged that the freedom of the press should be recognized separately, and that all provisions qualifying the rights be deleted, except that, where doing so is necessary for protecting aboriginal tribes and backward classes and for preserving public safety and peace, the Union be given the authority to regulate one right—namely the freedom of citizens to sojourn and settle anywhere in the country. Other than this the state must have no right to regulate or abridge the Fundamental Rights which the article was guaranteeing to citizens. The constitutional adviser observed that JP's observations were either asking for what had already been provided or were asking for so much that conceding it would be impractical. On the freedom of the press, he remarked, that the press was already covered by the right to free speech and expression which was being granted to every citizen, more than this the press could not claim.

Pattabhi Sitaramayya and several other members—G. Durgabai, Thakurdas Bhargava, B.V. Keskar, T.T. Krishnamachari, M. Ananthasayanam Ayyangar, K. Santhanam—urged several modifications. In regard to the proviso to the freedom of speech and expression, they proposed that the words 'or undermines the authority or foundation of the State' should be replaced by 'or other matters which undermine the security of the State'—the expression 'authority or foundation of the State' was so wide, they argued, that a determined executive could avail of it to impair even the right to criticize the government of the day.

The Drafting Committee saw merit in this submission, and agreed that the words 'undermines the authority or foundation of the State' should be replaced by the much more restricted 'undermines the security of, or tends to overthrow the State'. The Special Committee which was set up later to consider the comments and the observations of the Drafting Committee and the constitutional adviser on them decided that the proposal to replace the word 'authority' by the word 'security' in the proviso was a valid one, and that this should be done but the rest of the clause should remain.[15]

A fusillade

When the clause came up for consideration in the Constituent Assembly on 1 December 1948, there was a fusillade of opposition. The exceptions provided in regard to freedom of speech got clubbed with the exceptions provided in regard to other rights, and the draft was attacked from various angles. The clause is clumsily drafted, said Damodar Swarup Seth. The rights which it gives are cancelled by the very section, he said. 'Existing laws' are all protected—the law on sedition, the Official Secrets Act; safeguarding against 'undermining the authority or foundation of the State' will give too wide a latitude to the authorities, he pointed out, in fact these features will leave the right 'virtually ineffectual'. 'It is therefore clear that under the Draft Constitution we will not have any greater freedom of the press than we enjoyed under the cursed foreign regime and citizens will have no means of getting a sedition law invalidated, however flagrantly such a law may violate their civil rights,' Seth maintained. The latitude to the state to make laws restricting the rights 'in the interest of the general public' would have the same consequence, he warned.

'In fact, what is given by one right hand seems to be taken away by three or four or five left hands,' K.T. Shah

---

15 B. Shiva Rao, *The Framing of India's Constitution, Select Documents,* Vol. IV, pp. 34, 37–39.

remarked, 'and therefore the Article is rendered nugatory in my opinion.' Sardar Hukum Singh said the provisos 'take away the very soul out of these protective clauses'. H.J. Khandekar as well as other members were just as harsh. Mahboob Ali Baig reminded the Assembly that Sardar Patel had himself made a point in the Assembly itself of not moving these provisos, and that in the discussion which had followed several prominent persons including Pandit Nehru and K.M. Munshi had taken part. And now the very same provisos were being reintroduced.

The members raised objections on several grounds.

First, they maintained, by giving protection to all existing laws the provisos were shielding the very devices which had been the instruments of the British in perpetuating their oppression. The members singled out the law on sedition in particular. This part of the proviso will in fact nullify the provision which had been made in an earlier article, said the members, one which the Assembly had already approved—namely that, a law which violated provisions of the new Constitution would be invalid to the extent of that violation. It provides a blanket protection to the 'lawless laws, the repressive laws'—the criminal law amendments, the press acts, the various security acts, etc.—Mahboob Ali Baig said. Asking, 'If they [the existing laws] are to continue in the same way as before, then where is the change ushered in and so loudly talked of?', Hukum Singh pointed out that by giving approval in advance to all existing laws on sedition, etc., the clause, apart from everything else, would circumscribe the ambit of judicial review also: for the only thing which the judiciary would now have authority to decide would be whether the law related to sedition—if it did, then, by virtue of this clause, the law would be valid in advance. Another member, Bhupinder Singh Mann was as emphatic: 'To apply the existing law in spite of changed conditions really amounts to trifling with the freedom of speech and expression,' he told the House. 'From the very beginning we have stood against the existing laws, but now you are imposing them on us. You want to continue the old order so that there should be no opportunity of a trial, of putting up defence and of an appeal... We do not like this shape of things. If you want to perpetuate all that, then I would like to say that by imposing all these restrictions you are doing a great injustice...' 'What is the situation in India?' Kazi Syed Karimuddin asked. 'Practically there is a state of siege. [Recall that the debate was taking place in December 1948, the country was still coping with the aftermath of Partition and the rest.] There are Goonda Public Safety Act, etc. in all the Provinces in which there is neither appeal, nor any warrant is necessary for arrest, and searches can be made without justification. In spite of this, the Article lays down that the existing laws will be recognized. The unjust laws which do not provide appeals and which do not provide any proper representation will be recognized under Article 13 [subsequently, this was renumbered as Article 19]. There is no doubt that we are living in an emergency period but that does not mean that Article 13 should be in consonance with emergencies...' Ambedkar argued that criticism on this ground was based on a misreading of the article: this article and its provisos had to be read along with the earlier article which provided that any law which was in violation of any provision of this part of the Constitution would to the extent of that violation be invalid. The provisions had to be construed harmoniously.[16]

The second ground of attack could not be answered that easily. Member after member pointed out that under the clause the authority to curtail Fundamental Rights would rest with the legislature which in effect meant the government

---

16 *Constituent Assembly Debates,* Vol. VII, pp. 713, 728, 733, 740–41, 750, 756.

of the day. '... it is said by Dr. Ambedkar in his introductory speech that Fundamental Rights are not absolute,' Mahboob Ali Baig remarked. 'Of course, they are not; they are always subject to the interests of the general public and the safety of the State, but the question is when a certain citizen oversteps the limits so as to endanger the safety of the State, who is to judge? According to me, Sir, and according to well recognized canons, it is not the Executive or the Legislature, but it is the independent Judiciary of the State that has to judge whether a certain citizen has overstepped the limits so as to endanger the safety of the State.' He drew attention to the position in the American Constitution as well as that in Britain, and said, 'It is only in the German Constitution that the Fundamental Rights were subject to the provisions of the law that may be made by the Legislature. That means that the citizens could enjoy only those rights which the Legislature would give them, would permit them to enjoy from time to time. That cuts at the very roots of Fundamental Rights and the Fundamental Rights cease to be fundamental. I dare say, Sir, you know what was the result. Hitler could make his Legislature pass any law...' Hukum Singh pressed the same criticism and said that 'The Honourable Mover [that is, Ambedkar] defended these sub-clauses by remarking that he could quote at least one precedent for each of these restrictions. But it is here that the difference lies, that whereas in those countries it is the Judiciary which regulates the spheres of these freedoms and the extent of the restrictions to be imposed, under Article 13 it is the Legislature that is being empowered with these powers...' We are providing for parliamentary democracy, Mahboob Ali Baig, said which would mean 'rule by a certain political party, by the party Executive or party government'. Is it wise that the power to decide what restrictions on Fundamental Rights are in order should be left with that party by the Constitution itself?

Some members argued in favour of the draft clauses as they stood. T.T. Krishnamachari and others stressed that no rights could be absolute, that even in the US the courts themselves had recognized the validity of several types of restrictions on the exercise of the rights. And the requirement that we operate within limits does not detract from the freedoms, they pointed out: *Kavihin arth akhar bal sancha, Kartal tal gatihin nat nacha,* Algu Rai Shastri recalled, the poet composes to a meter, he is bound by the significance of the words he uses, the dancer moves in accordance with the rhythm. K. Hanumanthaiya said that situations change, that laws had to change with them, that courts could only interpret the laws, they could not legislate; accordingly, someone had to be entrusted with the responsibility of enacting laws, and it was but right that legislatures, which consisted of the true representatives of the people, were being given this authority. T.T. Krishnamachari maintained that the draft struck a golden mean between the rights of the individual and the need to ensure the security of the state and the community, and between the sort of emergency with which the country was confronted at the time and times that would be normal. He too would have preferred the rights to be granted without any qualifying clauses, Seth Govind Das pointed out, 'but if we consider the present national and international situation as also the fact that we have achieved Freedom only recently and our Government too is in infancy, we shall have to admit that it was necessary for the Government to retain the rights it has done after granting these Fundamental Rights. We should see what is happening in our neighbouring country, Burma. We should also keep in view what is happening in another great country of Asia—I mean war-torn China. In view of what is happening in our neighbouring countries and of the situation in our own country, we should consider how necessary it is that the Government should continue to have these powers...'[17]

The House remained uneasy and divided. Some restrictions were necessary, most recognized, but to place the power of deciding what restrictions were legitimate, and of determining the extent to which such restrictions may be imposed in the hands of the legislature and therefore of the executive of the day, most felt was to court danger.

The decisive proposal

The decisive proposal was made by Pandit Thakurdas Bhargava. The House was faced with 'the question of questions', he said: if the rights were to be incorporated without any qualifying restrictions, the State could be endangered; on the other hand, to place the power to regulate them in the Legislatures and the majorities of the day could lead to their being snuffed out. There had to be restrictions, true, but the courts ought to be the final arbiters. Both objectives could be met by providing that restrictions could be imposed but that the restrictions which were imposed had to be *reasonable:* incorporating the prefix *'reasonable'* would restore the jurisdiction of the courts. This suggestion was accepted by all, and that is how, to recall Bhargava's words, the soul of the article on Fundamental Freedoms was restored.[18]

Sedition

While in his original draft to the Subcommittee on Fundamental Rights, K.M. Munshi had included sedition as one of the grounds on which speech and expression could

---

17 *Constituent Assembly Debates,* Vol. VII, pp. 712, 728, 732–33, 735, 750–51, 754–57, 763, 768, 771–72, 776.

18 *Constituent Assembly Debates,* Vol. VII, pp. 735–36, 739.

be restricted, he had long argued that this ground ought to be jettisoned. But the word had survived through all the drafts and redrafts. During the debate in the Constituent Assembly several members objected to the retention of this ground, and recalled how so many patriots—from the Lokmanya down to many who were present in the Assembly itself—had been persecuted on this charge. Seth Govind Das recalled that he belonged to a family which was renowned for its loyalty to the British Empire. 'We had a tradition of being granted titles,' he said. 'My grandfather held the title of Raja and my uncle that of Diwan Bahadur and my father too of Diwan Bahadur. I am very glad that titles will no longer be granted in this country. In spite of belonging to such a family I was prosecuted under Section 124A and that also for an interesting thing. My great-grandfather had been granted a gold waistband inlaid with diamonds. The British Government awarded it to him for helping it in 1857 and the words "In recognition of his services during the Mutiny in 1857" were engraved on it. In the course of my speech during the *satyagraha* movement in 1930, I said that my great-grandfather got this waistband for helping the alien government and that he had committed a sin by doing so, and that I wanted to have engraved on it that the sin committed by my great-grandfather in helping to keep such a government in existence had been expiated by the great-grandson by seeking to uproot it. For this I was prosecuted under Section 124A and sentenced to two years rigorous imprisonment...' K.M. Munshi tabled an amendment urging that 'sedition' be removed from among the grounds on account of which restrictions may be imposed on the freedom of speech and expression. The word was of 'doubtful and varying import', Munshi said. It had been construed so widely that he recalled that even the criticism of a magistrate had been sought to be brought under it, Munshi said. In a democracy criticism of a government had to be distinguished from incitement to undermine the security of the state or order. 'As a matter of fact, the essence of democracy is criticism of government,' Munshi said. 'The party system which necessarily involves an advocacy of the replacement of one government by another is its only bulwark; the advocacy of a different system of government should be welcome because it gives vitality to a democracy.' The gist of the offence which the state had to guard against, he pointed out, was the attempt to overthrow that state, to subvert order itself. This was being provided for. 'Sedition' was thus jettisoned from the clause.[19]

Incidentally, the brief intervention of Munshi in which he moved the amendment to remove sedition from among the grounds also illustrates how so many individuals contributed suggestions even in drafting, etc., suggestions which became matters of consequence. Munshi began by drawing attention to what he called 'a verbal error' in the clause which had been submitted to the Assembly. The clause as it had been sent to the Constituent Assembly provided, 'Nothing in sub-clause (a) of clause (1) of this Article shall affect the operation of any existing law, or prevent the state from making any law relating to libel, etc.' The intention of the draftsman of course was that existing laws *relating to libel, etc.* alone would be protected. But because of the placement of the coma the clause could be construed to mean that while the permission it accorded to new laws the state might make was limited to laws relating to libel, etc., *all* existing laws were saved from challenge on the ground that they infringed freedom of speech and expression. Munshi accordingly suggested that after the words 'shall affect the operation of any existing law' the words 'in so far as it relates to' be added. That was done, and so the

---

19 *Constituent Assembly Debates,* Vol. VII, pp. 730–31.

protection which a determined executive could have claimed for existing laws was circumscribed.[20]

Anyone reading the clause today will recognize that even that was not the end of the matter. As the Constituent Assembly neared the end of its labours, T.T. Krishnamachari, who had by now been inducted into the Drafting Committee, moved an amendment. In fact, when he was called upon to move the amendment he had tabled on behalf of the Drafting Committee, he said that he would *not* move it—for the reason that several members had charged that the amendment was not just filling in a lacuna which had been left in the clause as it had been approved by the Assembly, it tended to widen the scope of powers which the Assembly had given to the state to regulate the freedom of speech and expression. Instead, he said, he would confine himself to filling an important lacuna alone: it was possible that persons may use the freedom of speech to comment on matters which were before the courts and thereby interfere with the course of justice. It was therefore necessary to shield the courts. Accordingly, he proposed that the words 'contempt of court' be added after 'defamation' in the proviso. This was done.[21]

The article deconstructed

Thus when the Constitution was adopted, the article read as follows:

> (1) All citizens shall have the right—(a) to freedom of speech and expression... (2) Nothing in sub-clause (a) of clause (1) shall affect the operation of any existing law in so far as it relates to or prevent the State from making any law relating to libel, slander, defamation, contempt of court or any matter which offends against

---

20 *Constituent Assembly Debates,* Vol. VII, p. 730.

21 *Constituent Assembly Debates,* Vol. X, pp. 394–403.

> decency or morality or which undermines the security of or tends to overthrow the State.

Recall that the original draft which was used as the working document had been prepared by K.M. Munshi. But one cannot for that reason say that Munshi was the author of this provision, for the right that we are considering—that to free speech and expression—had featured in every document relating to rights—the Commonwealth of India Bill of 1925, the Motilal Nehru Report, the Karachi Resolution of the Congress, the Report of the Sapru Committee, and all. Recall next the history of the proviso: it was deleted, then it was reintroduced with several changes; it was part of the draft sent to the Constituent Assembly but then Sardar Patel did not move it. It was reintroduced in the Draft Constitution as finalized by the Drafting Committee...

Even the words as finally adopted bear the stamp of several persons: 'the operation of any existing law' comes from Sir Alladi Krishnaswami Ayyar; 'in so far as it relates to' comes from Munshi's reference to that 'verbal error'; 'contempt of court' comes from the amendment which T.T. Krishnamachari moved at the penultimate hour on behalf of the Drafting Committee; 'sedition' does not figure because of the amendment moved by Munshi; the much less sweeping 'undermines the security of or tends to overthrow the State' figures because of the amendment tabled by Pattabhi Sitaramayya and several others.

And then, the surprise of surprises, there is an inexplicable omission. Recall the intermediate solution which Thakurdas Bhargava had proposed: namely that, the authority given to the state should be confined to imposing *reasonable* restrictions. Ambedkar had accepted the amendment, and everyone had hailed it. And the word 'reasonable' was introduced as a prefix to the word 'restrictions' wherever the latter occurred in the article. But while the word 'restrictions' occurred in the provisos relating to other Fundamental Rights which were enumerated in Article 19(1), it did *not* figure in the proviso relating to free speech. Therefore, the power of the state to impose restrictions on free speech in the interests of the heads which had been enumerated remained untrammelled by the requirement that the restrictions must be reasonable!

Since 1950

Anyone reading the article today will see that even this was not the end of the story. The expression 'reasonable restrictions' occurs in it. The ground 'or tends to overthrow the State' no longer does. Neither do the words 'libel' and 'slander', only 'defamation' survives. On the other hand, three grounds which were not there in the clause as approved by the Constituent Assembly are present: namely, 'friendly relations with foreign states', 'public order', and 'incitement to an offence'. How come?

What happened was this. Within a year of the Constitution being adopted, the Supreme Court handed down two judgments—*Romesh Thapar v. Madras* and *Brij Bhushan v. Delhi*—in which it held that unless the direct and sole objective of the impugned speech or expression was to overthrow the state, it was protected by Article 19. Moreover, for the speech to be actionable it was not sufficient that it endangered public safety or order; its consequences had to be such that the security of the state was menaced. And while committing an offence—murder, rioting and arson—was actionable under the laws, speech inciting others to commit even these heinous offences could not be restricted under the proviso as it had been adopted by the Constituent Assembly. The country had still not got over the after-effects of the Partition, nor of those of the integration of states; the rebellion in Telangana was at hand. The limits which the Supreme Court had prescribed upon the power of the state were thought to be too restrictive. Accordingly, the proviso was altered to incorporate the three additional grounds. The occasion was also used to make good the oversight about the restrictions being only 'reasonable' and to thereby bring the proviso to free speech in line with the provisos to other Fundamental Freedoms. That was in 1951.

But as we shall see upon reading the article in its present form, even this was not the end. In October 1962 the country was administered a devastating shock by China. There was renewed concern about the unity and integrity of the country. Groups had not been wanting in India who had once again chosen to espouse the cause of the adversary, and to question the territorial integrity of the country. Moreover, a number of secessionist movements had reared their heads. The National Integration Council constituted a Committee on National Integration and Regionalism. This Committee recommended, among other things, that Article 19 (2) be amended to include 'the sovereignty and integrity of India' as one of the grounds in the interests of which speech and expression may be restricted. The proviso was accordingly amended in 1963 by the fourteenth amendment to the Constitution.

That is the history of this single clause. But Ambedkar is the author! And if you don't believe that, you are a casteist Manuwadi!

14

Which Ambedkar is the author?

As we have seen, Ambedkar had been an enthusiastic member of the British government in India which had trampled upon the liberties of hundreds of thousands, which had held Gandhiji and thousands of others in jail for years on end. We have also seen that Ambedkar was even more of a 'law and order' man than many Britishers when it came to continuing to hold these leaders of the national movement in prison. But with the British gone, he was all for liberty, he was all for circumscribing the powers of the state vis-à-vis the individual. In his Memorandum to the Subcommittee on Fundamental Rights Ambedkar had provided inter alia that '... nor shall any state deprive any person of life, liberty and property without due process of law'.[1] Notice that he had included 'property' in this clause even as he had in the rest of the memorandum advocated all the cliched programmes of 'Socialism', but then that was just like him. For our present purposes the point of note is his reference to 'due process of law'.

The Subcommittee, as we know, had taken K.M. Munshi's draft as the basic working document. Munshi's wording of the corresponding clause was, for our present purpose, practically identical. He had provided, 'no person

---

1 B. Shiva Rao, *The Framing of India's Constitution, Select Documents,* Vol. II, p. 86.

shall be deprived of his life, liberty or property without due process of law.'[2] Though virtually identical, the drafts of Ambedkar and Munshi were liable to spell in a sense diametrically opposed consequences for the citizen. Ambedkar had provided that the state shall not deprive any person of his life, liberty *and* property save by due process of law. Munshi had provided that the state shall not deprive a person of his life, liberty *or* property save by due process of law. Technically, therefore, if the state took away only one or two of the three without caring for the due process clause, it would be immune to challenge under Ambedkar's provision, but could be hauled up under Munshi's clause. But that slip must have been just an inadvertence on the part of Ambedkar, because by now, with the British gone, Ambedkar was firm on liberty.

When the Subcommittee took up the clause it was pointed out that were the words 'due process of law' to be retained, the courts would acquire the jurisdiction to examine not just the procedural aspects of the law but also the substantive content, and that this could entail, for instance, that 'tenancy legislation which takes away certain rights from landlords and transfers them to tenants without payment of compensation would become invalid except on payment of compensation which the court regards as just'—for the courts could certainly come to the conclusion that though in a formal sense the procedure prescribed had been followed, in substance the legislation was confiscatory and therefore amounted to an infringement and violation of the liberty and property of the landlord. The point was put to vote. Five voted for retaining the clause as Munshi had drafted it, two voted to change it. The clause remained. And that is how it figured in the report of the Subcommittee.[3]

---

2 B. Shiva Rao, *The Framing of India's Constitution, Select Documents,* Vol. II, p. 75.

3 B. Shiva Rao, *The Framing of India's Constitution, Select Documents,* Vol. II, pp. 122, 139.

In his explanatory note to the report of the Subcommittee Sir B.N. Rau noted that the clause had been adopted from Amendment V and Amendment XIV, Section 1 of the US Constitution. He wrote, 'In sending the above "Notes on Clauses", I feel bound to draw attention to the possible effect of certain provisions of the draft.' He pointed out that 40 per cent of the litigation in the US Supreme Court during the preceding half-century had centred round the 'due process' clause. The courts had read varied meanings into the clause over the years, he pointed out, so much so that by now it had come to be said of the clause that 'it means just what the courts say it means. No other definition is possible.' 'Our draft not only borrows this clause...,' he noted, 'but also gives it retrospective effect (... which makes it applicable even to pre-Constitution laws).' He expressed the apprehension that in India too such a provision would lead to 'a vast flood of litigation immediately following upon the Constitution,' and that 'Tenancy laws, laws to regulate money-lending, laws to relieve debt, laws to prescribe minimum wages, laws to prescribe minimum hours of work, etc., will all be liable to be challenged; and not only those which may be enacted in future but also those which have already been enacted.' He cited the way laws in the US which sought to prevent the wholesale takeover of farms by banks and other lenders had been struck down as unconstitutional by the Supreme Court using the 'due process' clause. He acknowledged that such a provision could indeed be a protection against predatory legislation, but also that it could become an impediment to beneficent social legislation. The Irish Constitution had accordingly hedged in the right to private property by providing that the right would be regulated by the principles of social justice and that its exercise would be reconciled with the exigencies of the common good.[4]

---

4 For the text of Sir B.N. Rau's critique, B. Shiva Rao, *The Framing of India's Constitution, Select Documents*, Vol. II, pp. 147–53.

Nevertheless the Subcommittee's report provided, 'No person shall be deprived of his life, liberty or property without due process of law...'[5]

The Sardar's hint is taken up

When this and related clauses came up for consideration in the Advisory Committee, there was a spirited discussion. Several members expressed the apprehensions that Sir B.N. Rau had recorded—that the words had no definite meaning, that they would occasion a flood of litigation. K.M. Munshi doggedly defended the clause as drafted. Rajaji remarked, 'The idea [of the critics] is that these and similar clauses have been taken from countries which made laws at a time when they had no problems whatsoever. What is the good of our copying them?'

Sir Alladi Krishnaswami Ayyar intervened. In fairness to Sir B.N. Rau he must point out what had happened in the Subcommittee, he said. He recalled that the clause had been taken from the American Constitution, that Sir B.N. Rau had drawn pointed attention to its chequered history, to the fact that, while at one stage the clause had been understood to mean that the procedures prescribed had to be adhered to, since then the courts in the US had begun using the clause to examine the substance of the impugned laws also, and to the danger as a consequence that a good deal of beneficent social legislation was liable to be struck down. Sir Alladi said that he too had submitted a note to the same effect to the Subcommittee. But the clause had been retained.

Pandit Pant tried to put a construction on the clause by saying that the Subcommittee had understood the phrase

---

5 B. Shiva Rao, *The Framing of India's Constitution, Select Documents,* Vol. II, p. 173.

'due process' in a procedural sense. Sir Alladi pointed out that such a construction may not bind anyone for long.

Rajaji, Sardar Panikkar and others now joined to express the same apprehensions—laws affecting property, tenancy laws would all be open to challenge. The Sardar hinted at the way out: 'The clause as drafted is all right,' he remarked, 'There is some suspicion about property.'

Pandit Pant asked, 'May I know what the implications are? Will it be open to the Legislature under this to empower the Executive authority to detain a person for, say, six months without any trial being held in any court?' Rajaji replied, 'It will not be possible.' Pandit Pant asked, 'Will it be open under this clause for any Legislature to pass any law that certain property will be acquired for public purposes for ten times its rental value while the market value is 30 times?' Ayyar replied, 'The court may come to the conclusion that it is not due process of law because it is so illusory.' Pant asked, 'Will it be open to the court under this clause to hold that a person who is entitled to eject a tenant at will, will not be entitled to do so hereafter?' Sir Alladi explained, 'It is just possible that the court may come to the conclusion that the legislation is not intra vires!'

'It comes to this,' Pandit Pant concluded, 'the future of this country is to be determined not by the collective wisdom of the representatives of the people, but by the fiats of those alleviated to the Judiciary. If this is the case I strongly oppose it. The words "due process of law" should be altered. The language should be fool-proof so that every judge may be expected to give the same sort of ruling. We should not put in words which give rise to controversies.'

Even though there may be an ordinance allowing the executive to detain a person without trial, the courts may declare such detention to be a violation of 'due process', it was explained, and, on the other hand, even though the legislature may pass a law restricting the rights of landlords the courts may strike it down on the same ground. 'To fetter the discretion of the Legislature will lead to anarchy,' Pandit Pant resumed. 'It will lead to a great deal of trouble. Do you agree that in your province people who are creating all sorts of trouble should be tried in a court before they are prevented from committing mischief which leads to communal disorders? I do not want words to be used here which will create controversy, and which will place the fate of the people of this country on the whims and vagaries of the judges. Your language should be fool-proof. If you intend that there should be no detention, it should be clear.'

Munshi put up a cogent defence: 'Due process only comes to this,' he explained, 'that the legislation which is brought forward is a necessary and proper legislation to secure the end in view and that it is not extravagant with respect to each particular situation.' It is not correct to say that the judges would be putting themselves in the place of the legislature, he said, pointing out that in the American case, of the numerous cases which had gone up, the judges had reversed only 10 to 15 per cent.

Rajaji and Ambedkar questioned him on the point. Endorsing what Pant had said about the need to use expressions which were beyond doubt, Sardar Patel remarked that already and in the Committee itself there were two different interpretations of the law. Pant returned to the charge: 'We are leaving the fate of the country in the hands of lawyers who will be raised to the Bench and they will have to interpret this law,' he warned. He then came to the point which, in addition to the need that there might be to detain persons before they had ignited outrages, had been at the back of his apprehensions. 'In our province we are contemplating the abolition of *zamindaries,*' he remarked, 'and it is just possible that there may be a law to the effect that the bigger *zamindars* may be paid compensation at the rate of ten times their annual value and the smaller ones at forty times. These *zamindars* may go to the court and say that payment must be on the basis of the market rate and the law may hang on for seven years for the Supreme Court to give a decision. We do not want such a thing to happen. If you say that *zamindaries* should not be abolished, that private rights should not be touched, I can understand that. But to put in a law which can be interpreted by different people in different ways is to stop all social progress...'

Sardar Panikkar reverted to the hint which Sardar Patel had floated. The reference to property should be separated from 'life' and 'liberty', he suggested, remarking, 'The court is the guardian of our life and liberty. So far as property is concerned, it must be subjected to legislation...' Everyone, including Munshi, found this to be the best course. Rajaji suggested what could be the 'compromise amendment'. Due process would remain, but it would apply to life and liberty alone, and not to property.

'Then we exclude the word "property" from this clause,' remarked the Sardar. 'The rest of the clause may be passed as it stands.'

Pandit Pant, only one of whose concerns had been the zamindari legislation, exclaimed, 'I do not agree, but I keep quiet.'[6]

And so, in its report to the president of the Constituent Assembly, the Advisory Committee recommended that one of the Fundamental Rights be, 'No person shall be deprived of his life, or liberty without due process of law...'[7] The Constituent Assembly adopted the clause in this form.[8] That was in April–May 1947.

---

6 On these exchanges, B. Shiva Rao, *The Framing of India's Constitution, Select Documents*, Vol. II, pp. 240–47.

7 B. Shiva Rao, *The Framing of India's Constitution, Select Documents*, Vol. II, p. 297, clause 9.

8 B. Shiva Rao, *The Framing of India's Constitution, Select Documents*, Vol. II, p. 301, clause 9.

The American wording replaced by the Japanese and Irish one

One part of the apprehensions of Sir B.N. Rau had been allayed by the deletion of the reference to property from the clause. But 'liberty' was still a word which could be given a very wide and indefinitely comprehensive meaning. Therefore, when he prepared his *First Draft of the Constitution of India,* Sir B.N. Rau qualified the word 'liberty'. In his *Draft* of October 1947 the clause read, 'No person shall be deprived of his life or *personal* liberty without due process of law...'[9]

Soon after he had forwarded his *Draft Constitution* Sir B.N. Rau was asked to proceed on tour to the USA, the UK, Ireland and Canada for exchanging views with authorities there about the provisions which were being contemplated for India. Surprisingly, it was a judge of the US Supreme Court—and one of the most eminent ones at that, Justice Frankfurter—who came down most heavily on the due process clause. Justice Frankfurter told Rau that the power this gave to the judiciary to review executive and legislative action was in the first place undemocratic because it gave a few judges the power to veto legislation enacted by the representatives of the nation, it also threw an unfair burden on the judiciary. Justice Learned Hand went a step further and said that it would be better to have all the Fundamental Rights as moral precepts rather than as 'legal fetters in the Constitution'. Rau reported these views as others to colleagues and leaders back in Delhi.[10]

Both the changes Rau had suggested were now adopted by the Drafting Committee so that in its first *Draft Constitution,* the Drafting Committee rewrote the clause to

---

9 B. Shiva Rao, *The Framing of India's Constitution, Select Documents,* Vol. III, p. 9, clause 16.

10 Rau's tour dispatches are in B. Shiva Rao, *The Framing of India's Constitution, Select Documents,* Vol. III, pp. 217–34; the passage referred to above is at p. 218.

read, 'No person shall be deprived of his life or *personal* liberty *except according to procedure established by law...'* In a footnote to the draft article the Drafting Committee noted that it had thought it best to qualify 'liberty' by 'personal' as it had felt that 'otherwise it might be construed very widely so as to include even the freedoms already dealt with in Article 13.' It noted that it had also substituted 'in accordance with procedure established by law' for 'due process of law' 'as the former is more specific'. In support it cited the corresponding article in the Japanese Constitution from which this wording had been taken—and which read, 'No person shall be deprived of his life or liberty nor shall any other criminal penalty be imposed, except according to *procedure established by law'*—as well as the one from the Constitution of Ireland—which in turn read, 'No citizen shall be deprived of his personal liberty save in accordance with law.'[11]

This version of the article had but to be taken up in the Constituent Assembly that a number of members descended on it as an avalanche. There had been two types of apprehensions, as we have seen. In regard to property the apprehension had been that zamindars and others would be able to use the 'due process' requirement to persuade courts to examine and strike down the substance of laws. In regard to personal liberty the apprehension of persons like Pandit Pant who were responsible for maintaining peace at a time of great turmoil had been that the clause could become an instrument in the hands of antisocial elements who would use it to disable the state from acting against them. The apprehension that vested interests would use the 'due process' requirement to thwart socially progressive legislation had been removed by the reference to property being removed from the draft article. On personal liberty, while

---

11 B. Shiva Rao, *The Framing of India's Constitution, Select Documents,* Vol. III, p. 523, draft Article 15 and corresponding notes.

the view Pandit Pant had expressed was the view of many who were charged with the task of directing administration, members of the Constituent Assembly had the opposite apprehension: they said that if these words are dropped and 'except in accordance with procedure prescribed by law' are substituted for them, the citizen would be left defenceless: in practice the legislature would be in the control of the executive—in a sense, that is why this particular group would have been invited to form the government; the executive would therefore be able to get the legislature to pass whatever law the executive needed; the courts would henceforth be able to do no more than see that the procedure prescribed by law had been adhered to. And which determined executive would not be able to ensure that its officers carried out the arrests, etc., by punctiliously adhering to the procedure?[12]

One after the other, therefore, members strongly advocated that the earlier expression—'due process of law'—be put back in the clause. Munshi pointed out that with the removal of the reference to property there really was no ground for apprehending misuse of the 'due process' requirement. On the other hand, in regard to the two matters that remained in the draft article—life and liberty—it was necessary that a check be provided not just against the executive but also the legislature: the latter could be swayed by emotions and compulsions of the moment, it could be made to pass laws which the executive needed at the moment for its own interests.

Alladi Krishnaswami Ayyar defended the change, and recalled the arguments we have already encountered. 'Due process' was a phrase of 'no definite import', he said. American courts had been reversing the meanings which they had read into it, he said, and drew attention to specific judgments of the US Supreme Court. 'Today, according to

---

12 How prescient these apprehensions were became all too clear during the Emergency imposed by Mrs Indira Gandhi during 1975–77.

Professor Willis,' he recalled, 'the expression means what the Supreme Court says what it means in a particular case.' The power it confers on the judges is also undemocratic, Sir Alladi said, recalling the argument which Justice Frankfurter had pressed on Sir B.N. Rau: 'It is just possible,' he remarked with apparent sarcasm, 'some ardent democrats may have a greater faith in the Judiciary than in the conscious will expressed through the enactment of a popular Legislature. Three gentlemen, or five gentlemen, sitting as a court of law, and after listening to long discourses and arguments of briefed counsel on either side, may appeal to certain democrats more than the expressed wishes of the Legislature or the action of the Executive responsible to the Legislature....' Members wanted the 'due process' requirement to be reinserted because they were very sensitive about persons being detained without trial, Ayyar said, but that was not the meaning the American courts had read into personal liberty. He recalled that in the US the courts had declared the Minimum Wages law to be invalid on the ground that it invaded personal liberty, that on the same analogy social legislation could be put under a great handicap in India. He also echoed the argument that Pandit Pant had urged in the Advisory Committee, namely, the consequences that a requirement like 'due process' could have for the security of the state. Courts are not the only forum in which the arrested person need be given an opportunity to argue for his freedom—he pointed to the Review Board which was already functioning in Madras as an example, the point being that merely because the courts would be confined to inquiring that the procedural requirements had been met did not mean that the citizen would be without the protection of law.[13] The session was adjourned till the next day.

---

13 *Constituent Assembly Debates,* Vol. VII, pp. 842–57; Sir Alladi's defence at pp. 853–55.

The author speaking?

When the Assembly reconvened the next morning, Ambedkar requested the chair to hold over the draft article 'for a little while.'[14] That was on 7 December 1948. The vice-president recalled that when he had called upon Ambedkar to reply 'it was suggested that efforts should be made to arrive at some kind of understanding so that those who had submitted certain amendments might feel satisfied.' He said that he did not know the position which had been reached, and called upon Ambedkar to shed light on what had happened since.

'I must confess that I am somewhat in a difficult position with regard to Article 15 and the amendment which has been moved by my friend Pandit Thakurdas Bhargava...,' Ambedkar began. He recalled that there had been 'two sharp points of view' on the wording. Ambedkar explained what using the 'due process' phrase would entail, and that the question was whether the judiciary should be given authority to examine the substance of a law passed by Parliament in regard to life or personal liberty. Ambedkar, as we have seen earlier, continued:

> There are two views on this point. One view is this: that the Legislature may be trusted not to make any law which would abrogate the Fundamental Rights of man, so to say, the Fundamental Rights which apply to every individual, and consequently, there is no danger arising from the introduction of the phrase 'due process'. Another view is this: that it is not possible to trust the Legislature; the Legislature is likely to err, is likely to be led away by passion, by party prejudice, by party considerations, and the Legislature may make a law which may abrogate what may be regarded as the fundamental principles which safeguard the

---

14 *Constituent Assembly Debates,* Vol. VII, p. 859.

individual rights of a citizen. We are therefore placed in two difficult positions. One is to give the Judiciary the authority to sit in judgement over the will of the Legislature and to question the law made by the Legislature on the ground that it is not good law, in consonance with fundamental principles. Is that a desirable principle? The second position is that the Legislature ought to be trusted not to make bad laws. It is very difficult to come to any definite conclusion. There are dangers on both sides. For myself I cannot altogether omit the possibility of a Legislature packed by party men making laws which may abrogate or violate what we regard as certain fundamental principles affecting the life and liberty of an individual. At the same time, I do not see how five or six gentlemen sitting in the Federal or Supreme Court examining laws made by the Legislature and by dint of their own individual conscience or their bias or their prejudices [can] be trusted to determine which law is good and which law is bad. It is rather a case where a man has to sail between Charybdis and Scylla and I therefore would not say anything. I would leave it to the House to decide in any way it likes.[15]

Is that an author speaking or the member secretary of a body waiting for the body to come to a decision so that the appropriate words may be jotted down?

Pandit Thakurdas's amendment was set aside by the Assembly, and 'in accordance with procedure established by law' remained instead of the original 'due process of law'. Now, who is the author? The Ambedkar who, like K.M. Munshi and others, included 'due process' in his memorandum to the Subcommittee on Fundamental Rights? Or Sir B.N. Rau and Sir Alladi Krishnaswami Ayyar who argued against the expression from the beginning? The Subcommittee on Fundamental Rights and the parent Advisory Committee which nevertheless retained 'due process'? Or Justice Frankfurter who counselled against it? Or the Ambedkar under whose chairmanship the Drafting Committee decided to set aside the expression and replace

15 *Constituent Assembly Debates,* Vol. VII, pp. 999–1001.

it with 'in accordance with procedure established by law'? Or the authors of the Irish and Japanese Constitutions from which the new expression was taken? Or Sir Alladi again—who was the one person who defended the new expression on the floor of the Assembly? Or the Ambedkar who expressed his inability to say anything definite either way, and left the matter to the House? Or the House itself which, being presented two alternatives, chose the one we have?

'Compensation for what was done'

But, as is well known, even that was not the end of the sequence. By now the issue had got entangled with the question of preventive detention. Having seen at first hand during the British rule the use an executive might make of this power, several members wanted no truck with the scope which was being allowed to the legislature to pass any law it deemed fit to authorize preventive detention. The authorities on the other hand had been awakened to the need of such an option, though they were as receptive to the idea as the others that adequate safeguards should be built into the law on the matter.

On 15 September 1949 Ambedkar moved a motion requesting the Assembly to incorporate a new article in the Constitution. 'I know that a large part of the House including myself were greatly dissatisfied with the wording of Article 15,' he now told the Assembly. He said that 'there is no part of our Draft Constitution which has been so violently criticized by the public outside as Article 15.' Explaining the ground for the severe criticism to which the article had been subjected, he said that in effect the article provided that 'all that is necessary is to have a law and the law need not be subject to any conditions or limitations. In other words, it was felt that while this matter was being included in the chapter dealing with Fundamental Rights, we were giving a *carte blanche* to Parliament to make and provide for the arrest of any person under any circumstances as Parliament may deem fit.'

Therefore, he said, 'we are... now... making, if I may say so, compensation for what was done then in passing Article 15. In other words, we are providing for the substance of the law of 'due process' by the introduction of Article 15A.' Ambedkar did not claim originality for the new article either: he said that in fact 'Article 15A merely lifts from the provisions of the Criminal Procedure Code two of the most fundamental principles which every civilized society follows as principles of international justice...'

Thakurdas Bhargava, Bakshi Tek Chand, H.V. Kamath came down as heavily on this new article as they had on Article 15. Bakshi Tek Chand recalled what Ambedkar had himself suggested in his memorandum when 'he was a private member of this House; he had not been installed on the *gaddi* which he is occupying now and which, if I may say so with respect, he is so worthily occupying'; then Ambedkar had 'copied verbatim' the 'due process' clause from the American Constitution—what has made him change his mind, Tek Chand asked. Tek Chand recalled the arguments which K.M. Munshi had so doggedly advanced in favour of sticking to 'due process'—what has made him change his mind, Tek Chand asked. True, the words have been lifted verbatim from the Japanese Constitution, Tek Chand allowed, but that Constitution hedges in these words by several other provisions which have been left out of our draft, he pointed out. The new article 'is nothing but a cloak for denying the liberty of the individual,' Tek Chand said, 'It really comes to nothing.'

The debate continued with one member after another savaging the new draft article. 'Sir, Dr. Ambedkar will please pardon me when I express my fond wish that he and the other members of the Drafting Committee had had the experience of detention in jails before they became members of the Drafting Committee,' said Mahavir Tyagi touching a raw nerve. 'I shall try hereafter to acquire that experience,' Ambedkar replied.

The discussion continued for two days. A large number of amendments had been tabled. Eventually, this new article was adopted, with several changes.[16]

Who is the author? The Ambedkar who commended verbatim the provision of the US Constitution? The Ambedkar who commended verbatim the provision of the Japanese Constitution? The Ambedkar who had second thoughts about what he had piloted through the Constituent Assembly, and suggested a new article as 'compensation'? Or the Ambedkar who was merely arguing the case for the decisions which had been taken collectively by the senior leaders of the Congress?

---

16 *Constituent Assembly Debates,* Vol. IX, pp. 1496–1570.

15

The tug of events

How we forget the tumultuous events which were breaking out all round during the three years in which the Assembly processed the Constitution: the country was partitioned; almost six million were displaced and had to be rehabilitated, almost six lakhs were killed; the country became independent; almost 560 princely states had to be integrated into the rest of the country; Gandhiji was assassinated... It is but natural that these events affected many of the basic conceptions of the Constitution. As the Constituent Assembly neared the end of its labours, members remarked on the changes events had forced upon the Assembly, how these events had deepened the perceptions of the members. They said that the Constitution was all the better for that reason. Referring to the criticism which was common in those days that the Assembly had taken too long in finalizing the Constitution, Pandit Thakurdas Bhargava pointed out, 'No doubt the time of three years taken by the Assembly in preparing the Constitution is a long one but we have made great achievements during this period which I am afraid are not properly assessed by many people. If we had passed the Constitution soon after the Assembly sat in 1946, most of the ills that we had inherited from the British Government as legacy—for example, separate electorates, the existence of 562 states—would have remained embodied in the Constitution...'[1] B. Pattabhi Sitaramayya emphasized the same point. Tracing the history of the demand for having the right to frame our own Constitution, he remarked, 'Finally we came to a stage—all unawares—when this Constituent Assembly of a sort was thrust upon us with its *sections* and *groups* which we fortunately got rid of by paying a very heavy price for it and when we began our deliberations on the 9th December 1946 we were anxious to finish them and some of us had even hoped to finish our deliberations within six months. If we had finished our Constitution in 1946 it would have been a mess, if we had finished it in 1948 it would have been a medley. Fortunately this delay which has occurred has enabled us to see things in their true perspective and it has enabled us to develop administrative changes *pari passu* political developments. Supposing we had finished this before 15th August 1947, what would have been the nature of the Constitution? It would have been quite different. This delay has enabled the legacy which we had inherited from the British to be set right... This delay has also enabled us and our new administrators to piece together the 562 states which were detached and altogether unconnected with one another. Thus it is that while we were developing the Constitution or making efforts in the process of developing this Constitution, we were also taking up administrative measures in order to consolidate this country which we had inherited from the British in a very disorganized condition.'[2]

Following the course of some of the central features of the Constitution will teach us how silly it is to assert that the Constitution sprang out of the head of one person—that in actual fact it evolved as a result of a very large number of persons reflecting upon and absorbing the lessons which events were inflicting upon the country.

1 *Constituent Assembly Debates*, Vol. XI, p. 687.

2 *Constituent Assembly Debates*, Vol. XI, p. 943.

The nature of the Union

Even while the elections for the Constituent Assembly were in progress, the Congress appointed an Experts' Committee in July 1946. It had Panditji as its chairman, and Asaf Ali, K.M. Munshi, N. Gopalaswami Ayyangar, K.T. Shah, D.R. Gadgil, Humayun Kabir and K. Santhanam as its members. Krishna Kripalani was co-opted as a member and convenor. Sardar Patel and Krishna Menon also attended its meetings. It is this group which settled the tasks which the Assembly would take in hand in its initial sittings, and how it would proceed. It also settled some of the committees which the Assembly would constitute to begin preparing parts of the Constitution. Most important, it finalized an 'Objectives Resolution' which the Assembly would adopt at the very outset, a resolution which would set out not just the objectives that the Assembly would strive to accomplish but also a vision for the kind of India it would seek to mould through the Constitution.

Individual members must have contributed to the text. It is said that Panditji put the suggestions together and himself finalized the resolution. The Working Committee of the Congress approved it on the eve of the first session of the Assembly. The Assembly discussed it from 13 to 19 December 1946. But M.R. Jayakar moved a counter-resolution saying that adopting the resolution in the absence of the Muslim League members would fortify their decision to boycott the Assembly. Ambedkar supported him. The leaders decided to defer the adoption of the resolution till after the third week of January as Jinnah had scheduled a meeting of the League for 20 January, and it was hoped that he might still come round. Come the date, and Jinnah postponed his meeting! Therefore, on 20 January 1947 the Assembly resumed the debate on the resolution. After three days of further discussion in which most members hailed the resolution as befitting and eloquent, the Assembly adopted it unanimously on 22 January 1947.

Ambedkar was of course nowhere in the picture at this stage. Equally important, the text of the resolution which the Assembly adopted followed almost to the dot the text which the Congress Experts' Committee had drafted.[3]

Recall that this text was being formulated and finalized during July–November, 1946. The Congress leaders were still striving to ensure Independence for a united India. Every effort was being made not to leave any pretext for Jinnah to buttress his demand for Pakistan on the charge that all sections would not have full security and equality under the new structure. There was also the problem of the princely states. The British were assuring them that paramountcy would devolve as much to them as to the two successor governments, and Jinnah was making overtures to several of them urging them to join the proposed Pakistan rather than India. Thus we find, as one of the foundational objectives in the text prepared by the Congress Experts' Committee as well as the Objectives Resolution as adopted by the Constituent Assembly, the declaration that the territories which join India 'shall possess and retain the status of autonomous units, together with residuary powers, and exercise all powers of and functions of government and administration, save and except such powers as are vested in or assigned to the Union, or as are inherent or implied in the Union or resulting therefrom...'

While moving the Objectives Resolution in the Assembly, Pandit Nehru said that he hoped that in all matters relating

---

3 For the text finalized by the Congress Experts' Committee see B. Shiva Rao, *The Framing of India's Constitution, Select Documents,* Vol. I, pp. 329–331. For the text of the Objectives Resolution adopted by the Constituent Assembly see, *Constituent Assembly Debates,* Vol. I, p. 59.

to the states, they would be dealing with the real representatives of the states. Of course, in regard to matters which related to the rulers the Assembly would be perfectly willing to deal with them also, Pandit Nehru said. He added that he also had the hope that when the Assembly drafted provisions pertaining to the governance of the states, there would be a degree of uniformity—in regard to the degree of freedom which the citizens would enjoy, and also in regard to the machinery of government. 'Nevertheless this is a point to be considered in cooperation and in consultation with the states,' Pandit Nehru said, reflecting the state of affairs at the time. 'I do not wish, and I imagine this Constituent Assembly will not like, to impose anything on the states against their will,' he said. 'If the people of a particular state desire to have a certain form of administration, even though it might be monarchical, it is open to them to have it. The House will remember that even in the British Commonwealth of Nations today, Eire is a Republic and yet in many ways it is a member of the British Commonwealth. So, it is a conceivable thing. What will happen, I do not know, because that is partly for this House and partly for others to decide. There is no incongruity or impossibility about a certain definite form of administration in the states, provided there is complete freedom and responsible government there and the people really are in charge. If monarchical figure-heads are approved by the people of the state, of a particular state, whether I like it or not, I certainly will not like to interfere...'[4]

These considerations, as well as the fluidity of the situation continued throughout the coming months to hover as a cloud over the work of the Assembly and the committees it had set up, and naturally so. When the Advisory

---

4 *Constituent Assembly Debates*, Vol. I, pp. 52–53.

Committee met on 21 April 1947, for instance, to consider the recommendations of the Subcommittee on Fundamental Rights, Sardar Patel asked the members to remember, among other things, 'that we have not yet come to a stage when final decisions have been taken, whether the League will come into the Constituent Assembly or not... Therefore it is necessary to take into account that any clause that may be regarded as involving a major communal issue or communal issues, which may be considered as very important, will not be taken for the time being, because in all major communal issues, according to the document of 16th May [the declaration of the British Government which was taken at this stage to delineate the parameters within which the Constituent Assembly must operate] we have not to decide by a majority of votes, but by agreement. Therefore any decision which we may take should not be such as will give the excuse to anybody to say that we have closed the doors. We have yet to be careful to see that we take no decisions on such questions as may be regarded by people who are not represented here as a hostile act or as an act which will prevent them from coming in...'[5]

Leaders had to bend so far back that the consideration of even such a matter as the right to bear arms had to be deferred. Ambedkar had just pointed out that if such a right were guaranteed, the law to regulate it would have to be a Union law. 'You cannot allow different units to make different laws with regard to the bearing of arms. That would undoubtedly lead to complete anarchy and it would cut at the very root of the security of the Union,' he told the Advisory Committee. 'If one unit with a feeling of disloyalty against the Union as such were to make a law that every member of that unit may possess arms and other units with a

---

5 B. Shiva Rao, *The Framing of India's Constitution, Select Documents,* Vol. II, pp. 213–14.

more peaceable frame of mind were to prevent their citizens from bearing arms, there would be such a great inequality in the position of the different units that it would be a great danger and menace to the stability of the State...' It was at once obvious that such a course would require the enlargement of powers of the Union. Discussion ensued whether the right course would be to wait till the decision of the Muslim League had become clear, or whether the Committee should settle such matters and, if the League did come in later, either discuss the subjects again with it or let it frame constitutions for the areas under its sway. 'At the moment we are at a disadvantage,' Sardar Patel said closing the point. 'There is no harm in keeping this off. We start with propositions which more or less would be agreeable to them. If they come in, we will discuss with them again.'[6]

Six months after he had commended the Objectives Resolution to the Assembly, on 18 July 1947, Pandit Nehru circulated a statement in connection with the report of the Union Powers Committee. In it he said that the points made in the Objectives Resolution and the Preamble which the Assembly had adopted would be incorporated in the final Constitution, adding, 'That Objectives Resolution will have to undergo some modification on account of the political changes resulting from Partition, but the basic principles of the Objectives Resolution will remain.' He informed the members of the Assembly that the resolution had been referred to a subcommittee for making the necessary changes.[7] Among the decisions which was reversed was the idea of vesting residuary powers in the constituent units of the Union.

All this was entirely natural for, on the one hand,

---

6 B. Shiva Rao, *The Framing of India's Constitution, Select Documents,* Vol. II, pp. 237–38.

7 B. Shiva Rao, *The Framing of India's Constitution, Select Documents,* Vol. II, pp. 592–93.

cataclysmic events were taking place, and leaders who were taking the principal decisions in the Assembly also had decisive responsibilities in regard to those events; on the other hand, the work of settling the Constitution under which the new India would be governed also had to proceed apace.

Distribution of powers

Another all-important feature—the distribution of subjects and powers between the Centre and the units—went through the same iterations, it was affected as much by the events which were taking place outside the Assembly.

The Cabinet Mission Plan had limited the functions of the Centre to just three subjects—foreign affairs, defence and communications. The units were to have control over all subjects except those specifically ceded to the Centre. Residuary powers too had been assigned to the units.

Sir B.N. Rau prepared two notes on the subject and circulated them in early September 1946. They set out the subjects which accrued to the Centre as a consequence of foreign affairs, defence and communications. He also set out the relevant provisions in other constitutions.[8]

The Assembly set up the Union Powers Committee in January 1947 with Pandit Jawaharlal Nehru as its chairman. When the Committee commenced work in March, it had before it, in addition to the notes of Sir B.N. Rau, notes from K.M. Munshi and Sir Alladi Krishnaswami Ayyar. Together, the notes dealt with the powers—express, implied,

---

8 For the text of the notes, B. Shiva Rao, *The Framing of India's Constitution, Select Documents,* Vol. II, pp. 687–706. The steps which the committee went through are taken from B. Shiva Rao's introductory remarks to the documents: B. Shiva Rao, *The Framing of India's Constitution, Select Documents,* Vol. II, pp. 687, 728, 743.

resulting—which accrued to the Union as a result of the parameters which the Cabinet Mission had specified, as well as the import and content of each power. In doing so they analysed and adduced judgments of the Privy Council, of the courts of the US, Canada, Australia.[9]

The Union Powers Committee took K.M. Munshi's note and listings as the working document, and considered successively each subject and power listed in the note. 'Defence'—and what would accrue to the Centre as a consequence—generated differences. Sir B.N. Rau was asked to draft a formulation.

A month or so after the Committee had begun work, two representatives of the princely states joined the Committee. The Committee thereupon went over the entire ground again, and set up a subcommittee consisting of K.M. Munshi, N. Gopalaswami Ayyangar and T.T. Krishnamachari to re-examine the items which the Committee had already settled.

Minutes of the meetings show how arguments and inclinations went to and fro on item after item: in the beginning representatives of the princely states were opposed even to a system of uniform federal taxes applicable throughout India on the ground that different areas were at dissimilar stages of development.[10]

The Committee submitted its report to the President of the Assembly on 17 April 1947. It spelt out the powers which accrued to the Centre as a result of its having exclusive responsibility in regard to foreign affairs, defence and communications. N. Gopalaswami Ayyangar, however, submitted a separate note. 'Though for the sake of getting on with the work I signed the Report of the Union Powers

---

9 For the text of the notes, B. Shiva Rao, *The Framing of India's Constitution, Select Documents*, Vol. II, pp. 712–27.

10 For the text of the minutes, B. Shiva Rao, *The Framing of India's Constitution, Select Documents*, Vol. II, pp. 728–42.

Committee yesterday,' the note began, 'I am not altogether satisfied with it. It suffers in places from some loose thinking and certain lack of precision and accuracy. It is true that in a report of this kind, there is no need to insist on absolutely correct drafting, but in view of the personnel of the Committee it was essential to avoid giving room for criticism of what would be spotted as obvious errors.'[11] The Committee has not fully appreciated the distinction between subjects and powers, he wrote; it has omitted to take account of public borrowing, sale proceeds of or income from Union property, and contributions from the units; it 'has omitted to tackle the difficult problem of what matters listed in it should be treated as exclusively Union and what should be treated as common or concurrent'; it has not distinguished between finances for the Union and those raised by the Union: the latter include estate duty, income tax, etc., which are governed by Central laws but the proceeds from which will be shared by the states; and so on. He also opposed the special concession which was being made to the princely states. And he pointed out that the report's portmanteau recommendation that an 'unspecified concurrent list' be included by agreement 'could hardly be justified as it stands'. Harsh words, specially as they came from such a prominent member of the Committee itself.

On 28 April 1947 Gopalaswami Ayyangar himself presented the report to the Assembly on behalf of the Committee. But even as he did so, he informed the House that he was performing 'a merely routine and prosaic duty' of presenting the report, and that he would not be moving the motion to request the House to take the report into consideration. There were several reasons for this, he

11 For the text of the report and the text of Ayyangar's separate note, B. Shiva Rao, *The Framing of India's Constitution, Select Documents,* Vol. II, pp. 743–47 and 747–50 respectively.

explained. The Committee had worked within the parameters prescribed by the Cabinet Mission Plan, he recalled, adding, 'That Plan contains some very unusual features, the unusualness really resulting from the desire to satisfy the wishes of the Muslim League if it ever decided to come in.' 'The coming in of the Muslim League is not yet officially ruled out,' he said, 'there is still a possibility of their coming in, though the probability is perhaps very small. Should this possibility materialize, it would be only just and reasonable that the debate on so important a subject... should be held in a House which contains a full representation of the Muslim League. Whether they will come in or not will be definitely known before the June-July session of the Assembly.' The other reason, he explained, was that while representatives from a few of the princely states had joined, others were yet to do so. Finally, and most important, he said 'there is the question of the present political conversations.' Would the country remain one, would it be partitioned into two or even more parts—the allocation of powers between the Union and the units would naturally be affected by this all-important outcome. He therefore requested the Assembly to accord permission to the Committee to submit a supplementary report after these possibilities had been cleared out of the way.[12]

Soon Partition was announced, and accepted by all. The Committee went over the ground all over again. Pandit Nehru submitted the second report to the president on 5 July 1947. The recommendations were completely different from what they had been in the first report. Panditji set out the reasons in his letter to the president.

With parts of the country seceding to form a separate state, the 16 May Plan on the basis of which the Committee had worked 'is, in many essentials no longer operative',

---

12 *Constituent Assembly Debates,* Vol. III, pp. 380–82.

Panditji recorded. 'In particular we are not now bound by the limitations on the scope of Union Powers.' He recalled what had stood behind the 16 May Plan and, ipso facto, the first report he had forwarded three months earlier: 'The severe limitation on the scope of central authority in the Cabinet Mission's Plan was a compromise accepted by the Assembly much, we think, against its judgement of the administrative needs of the country, in order to accommodate the Muslim League.' 'Now that Partition is a settled fact,' he continued, 'we are unanimously of the view that it would be injurious to the interests of the country to provide for a weak central authority.'

Both the Union Constitution Committee as well as the Union Powers Committee, he informed the president, had since concluded that 'the soundest framework for our Constitution is a federation, with a strong Centre.'

The overwhelming effect of events is evident. As is the continuing influence of the Government of India Act, 1935. Pandit Nehru wrote that the Committee had decided that for distributing powers between the Centre and the units 'the most satisfactory arrangement is to draw up three exhaustive lists on the lines followed in the Government of India Act of 1935, *viz.*, the Federal, the Provincial and the Concurrent.' The lists—which now form Schedule VII of the Constitution—had been prepared accordingly.

Residuary powers were now to be with the Centre. And in that there was another affinity with the 1935 Act. Drafters of the 1935 Act had envisaged two sources of trouble: there could be tugs and pulls between the Centre and the units on which of them had jurisdiction in a particular sphere; second, the larger the sphere which was left undemarcated—that is, the larger the ambit of residuary powers—the greater would be the chances of both, discord and litigation. The solution, as H.M. Seervai noted, which the drafters had alighted upon was to provide an enumeration of powers so exhaustive that it would not matter much who was assigned the residue, and the area over which disputes could arise would be narrowed to the minimum.[13]

In proposing three exhaustive lists the Union Powers Committee consciously followed this lead. 'We think that residuary powers should remain with the Centre,' Panditji now wrote, adding, 'In view however of the exhaustive nature of the three lists drawn up by us, the residuary subjects could only relate to matters which, while they may claim recognition in the future, are not at present identifiable and cannot therefore be included in the lists.'[14]

The result, in regard to the distribution of powers as well as the provisions of the Constitution in general, led H.M. Seervai to exclaim, 'A review of the provisions of the Constitution of India may have impressed the reader, as it has impressed the present writer, with the strange destiny of the Government of India Act, 1935. Little could the framers of that Act have dreamt that in the Constitution of a free India they would find the greatest monument to their drafting skill and constitutional insight.'[15]

Who then is the author? Pandit Nehru and other members of the Union Powers Committee? Events? The draftsmen who put together the Government of India Act of 1935? Or Ambedkar?!

Princely states

Even that was but a stage of course. The Muslim League

---

13 H.M. Seervai, *Constitutional Law of India,* Vol. I, 3rd edition, Tripathi, Bombay, 1983, p. 60.

14 For the text of Pandit Nehru's forwarding letter and the distribution of powers recommended by the Union Powers Committee, B. Shiva Rao, *The Framing of India's Constitution, Select Documents,* Vol. II, pp. 776–95.

15 H.M. Seervai, *Constitutional Law of India,* Vol. I, p. 66.

was out of the way, there was no longer any need to tailor the recommendations in the hope that it would desist from its aim. But the problem of the princely states loomed as large as ever. The British had announced that paramountcy would lapse, and that the princes would be free to join either India or Pakistan. Thus, while in its second report, the Union Powers Committee finalized the distribution of powers between the Centre and the units in regard to the territories covered by 'British India', even this report made a vast distinction between what had been provinces of British India and the princely states. In regard to the latter, the report provided that to the extent its recommendations went beyond the 16 May statement, they should be extended to the princely states only with the consent of the latter. And also that residuary powers 'would vest with them [the princely states] unless they consent to their vesting in the Centre'.

When the states joined the Assembly it was contemplated that they would have their own constitutions devised by their own constituent assemblies. As late as 1949, constituent assemblies were functioning in Mysore, Saurashtra and Travancore-Cochin. Accordingly, the original Draft Constitution finalized by the Drafting Committee contained provisions which placed the princely states on a footing different from the former provinces: draft Articles 224 and 225, for instance, circumscribed the power of Parliament to make laws affecting these states even in regard to subjects in the Union list, and provided that this power 'shall be subject to the terms of any agreement entered into in that behalf by that state or group of states with the Government of India and the limitations contained therein'. There were corresponding limitations on the executive power of the Union, and on the jurisdiction of institutions like the Supreme Court. Draft Article 67 provided that, up to 40 per cent of the total members of the Rajya Sabha, excluding the fifteen nominated members, could be representatives of these states.

By mid-1949 because of the Sardar's monumental work, the integration of these states with the Union was complete. The Sardar rose in the Constituent Assembly on 12 October 1949: he had prepared a speech, he said, but because of the strain that reading it would cause him, he was requesting K.M. Munshi to read it out. An uncharacteristically long and detailed exposition, it was a stirring one.

The Sardar recalled that the British had maintained that with their departure 'Paramountcy' would lapse to the princes, and that they were accordingly free to join India or Pakistan as they wished. 'We agreed to this arrangement in the same manner as we agreed to the Partition of India,' the Sardar noted, 'we accepted it because we had no option to act otherwise.' When the Constituent Assembly began its work, it was contemplated that these states would have their own constitutions prepared by their own constituent assembles, within the framework of the covenants and the Constitution of India, the Sardar explained. Accordingly, provisions had been made in the covenants 'at a time when we were still working under the shadow of the theory, that the assumption, by the Constituent Assembly of India, of the Constitution-making authority in respect of the states would constitute an infringement of the autonomy of the states.' Since then the states had integrated in the country as a result of a 'bloodless revolution,' the Sardar recalled. A series of amendments were therefore being proposed, he said, to place the princely states completely at par with the erstwhile provinces and 'to remove from it (the Constitution) all vestiges of anomalies and disparities which found their way into the new Constitution as a legacy from the past'.[16]

16 *Constituent Assembly Debates,* Vol. X, pp. 161–68.

Now, if we look at the amendments which the Sardar's speech was introducing and commending to the Assembly, they stand in the name of Ambedkar. Is he for that reason the author of those amendments, any more than he is author of the Integration of states?

Governance of states

The Provincial Constitution Committee went through the same cycles of consideration, finalizing, reopening, the Assembly adopting the recommendations, only to overturn them later. Consider provisions in regard to the governor.

When the Provincial Constitution Committee took up the matter on 6 June 1947 members expressed views that ranged across the board. The governor's office should be patterned after that of governors in the USA, urged some: he should be elected directly; he should be the actual head of the executive; ministers should be appointed by him, and they should be responsible to him, not to the legislature. Others proposed the opposite: he should be a nominee and agent of the Centre. A third set urged an intermediate position: the Centre should have wide-ranging powers vis-à-vis the units; and the governor should be the liaison, the link between the Centre and the units... The Committee decided that as the essential point at issue was the kind of constitutional system India should have—Unitary, or Federal with the units ceding some specific powers to the Centre, etc.—the issue should be considered at a joint meeting with the Union Constitution Committee.

The joint meeting was held the next day, and the two committees decided that (i) the governor should be appointed by the unit after an election, and not by the Centre; (ii) he should be chosen by an indirect election: a special electoral college should be chosen on the basis of adult franchise for the purpose. The Provincial Constitution

Committee also decided that he should be removable only by impeachment, and an elaborate procedure for this was spelt out: the charge, which could relate only to stated misbehaviour, to be preferred by the Lower House of the Provincial Legislature and to be tried by the Upper House of the Union Parliament, the resolution in each case to be supported by not less than two-thirds of the total membership of the House concerned.[17]

These provisions were incorporated, with some modifications, by Sir B.N. Rau in the *First Draft of the Constitution of India* which he prepared in October 1947. His *Draft* was further modified in the light of decisions, and the *Draft Constitution* provided that 'The Governor of a state shall be elected by direct vote of all persons who have the right to vote at a general election for the Legislative Assembly of the State.' Unless he was removed or he resigned, the *Draft Constitution* provided, the governor shall hold office for five years. He could be removed by impeachment, but two more hurdles were now built into the procedure. The initial memorandum asking for his impeachment would have to be signed by at least thirty members of the Assembly; the resolution would then be considered by the Assembly, and would have to be passed by not less than two-thirds of the membership of the Assembly; when the charge had been so preferred, it would be sent to the Council of States, that is the Rajya Sabha; the chairman of the Rajya Sabha would then appoint a committee which may consist of or include persons who were not members of the Rajya Sabha, to investigate the charge—the governor would have the right to appear and to be represented at such an investigation; if as a result of the investigation, two-thirds or more of the members of the Rajya Sabha passed a resolution declaring that the charge

---

17 B. Shiva Rao, *The Framing of India's Constitution, Select Documents,* Vol. II, pp. 646–48, 651–52, 657.

against the governor had been sustained, he would stand impeached.

The ground on which he could be impeached also stood altered. As we saw, in the formulations thus far the governor could be impeached on the ground of 'stated misbehaviour'. But the Drafting Committee replaced this with 'violation of the Constitution', and noted that it felt that, as in the case of the president, this should be the only ground on which a governor should be open to impeachment.[18]

The matter continued to be considered and reconsidered, often as a result of decisions that were taken on other parts of the Constitution. By the time the Drafting Committee came to the clauses dealing with the governor, the view had jelled: conflicts and friction could well arise if both the governor and the chief minister were elected entities, specially with the latter being responsible to the legislature in a way that the governor was not. To avoid this eventuality, in the *Draft Constitution* it finalized in February 1948, the Drafting Committee suggested that instead of the governor being directly elected by the people of the unit, the state Assembly should elect a panel of four persons by proportional representation, and the president should choose one of them to be governor.[19]

The *Draft Constitution* was circulated for comments. JP, among others, criticized this alternative also. The Assembly would forward four names, true, he reasoned, but the Union prime minister might advise the president to select one among them who was from the party of the prime minister—even though this person had not received the largest number of votes from the state Assembly. Thus, the

18 *Draft Constitution of India,* clauses 112, 113, 118; B. Shiva Rao, *The Framing of India's Constitution, Select Documents,* Vol. III, pp. 428–30.

19 *Draft Constitution of India,* clause 131; B. Shiva Rao, *The Framing of India's Constitution, Select Documents,* Vol. III, p. 564.

proposal, while trying to reduce the possibilities of a conflict between the state's governor and chief minister, might enhance the chances of a conflict between the Centre and the state. JP proposed that the governor be elected by proportional representation by an electoral college consisting of members of the state legislature and MPs from the state.

The Special Committee which had been set up to evaluate the provisions of the *Draft Constitution* in the light of comments, etc., decided that the post of an elected governor would be 'completely useless', that it may lead to conflicts with the elected chief minister, that the governor may use the occasion of an emergency to override the ministry. It proposed therefore that the governor be appointed directly by the president.[20]

The Drafting Committee reconsidered the matter, but decided to leave it to the Constituent Assembly itself to settle.

That is how the question stood when the Assembly took up the draft article for consideration in May 1949: it had earlier approved *Principles of a Model Provincial Constitution* which provided for a governor directly elected by the people on the basis of adult suffrage; in its *Draft Constitution* of February 1948, the Drafting Committee had provided for the state legislature electing a panel of four on the basis of proportional representation, and the president choosing one of them; the Select Committee had turned its back on all these methods and suggested instead that the governor be directly appointed by the president, and hold office at his pleasure; upon reconsidering the question, the Drafting Committee had decided to leave the draft clause as it was, and to let the Assembly itself decide.

---

20 B. Shiva Rao, *The Framing of India's Constitution, Select Documents,* Vol. IV, pp. 68–70, 409; B. Shiva Rao, *The Framing of India's Constitution, A Study,* pp. 393–94.

A member whom scarcely anyone would recall today, Brajeshwar Prasad, proposed an amendment—the governor should be appointed by the president: no panel, no election, just the president's 'hand and seal'. Brajeshwar Prasad had no time for the clap-trap of federalism and autonomy of which so many members were enamoured; he was out and out for a unitary state—the amendment he tabled was in furtherance of this approach. Prasad envisaged a governor who would be, and be seen by all, including himself, to be the representative of the centre.

Sir Alladi Krishnaswami Ayyar, Pandit Nehru, and even Ambedkar, chairman of the Drafting Committee which had decided not to alter the panel-of-four provision, now expressed vigorous support for Brajeshwar Prasad's amendment.

Sir Alladi Krishnaswami Ayyar pointed out that the governor was going to be 'merely a constitutional head', and that 'the expenses involved in going through the process of elections is out of all proportion to the powers vested in the Governor...' 'There is also the danger of the Governor who has been elected by the people at large getting into a clash with the Premier and the Cabinet responsible to the Legislature which itself has been elected on the basis of universal suffrage. Again, the election itself under modern conditions will have to be fought out on a party ticket. The fact is that even at or during the elections the party will have to rally round a leader who will presumably be the future Premier of the Province. Is the rallying to be round the Governor's name or the Premier's name? In the normal working of the Government also there is danger of a clash between the Ministers and the Governor, whereas the whole basis of the constitutional structure we are erecting depends upon the harmony between the Legislature and the Executive, and between the Executive and the formal head of the Government.'

The central fact to be remembered, Sir Alladi explained, was that 'the Governor is to be a constitutional head, a sagacious counselor and adviser to the Ministry, one who can throw oil over troubled waters.' For this function a person appointed by the president in consultation with the state government—'a person of undoubted ability and position in public life who at the same time has not been mixed up in provincial party struggle or factions'—would be the most appropriate. The fact that the governor would on occasion have to exercise extraordinary powers, Sir Alladi argued, was actually an argument which strengthened the case for having him appointed by the president rather than elected.

Sir Alladi then turned to the panel-of-four proposal which had been included by the Drafting Committee in the *Draft Constitution.*

He had been a member of the Drafting Committee, Sir Alladi Krishnaswami explained. That proposal had actually been advanced—'tentatively', Sir Alladi said—because the Committee felt that there would be difficulties in going through with the decision of the Assembly to elect the governor. 'On a fuller consideration I feel convinced that the panel system is likely to be fraught with great danger,' he said, and pointed to the experience in regard to appointing vice chancellors of universities. 'Supposing three or four people are elected by the Legislature,' he told the Assembly. 'What is the President to do? Is he to give his concurrence to the person who has obtained the largest number of votes or go out of his way and select people who have lesser number of votes?' If he follows the former course, his function would be to merely ditto what the state legislature has decided, and the Assembly would in all likelihood have proceeded on party lines; if he appoints someone other than the one who had obtained the largest number of votes, it was sure to lead to friction, in the state and between the state and the Centre.

Others endorsed the appointment-by-president proposal just as emphatically.

In fact, there was a virtue in having a governor who, as an outsider, was above and away from the parties and politics of the state, Panditji said. The governor's office was going to be a 'purely ornamental' one, Ambedkar said; hence, there was no need to go through elections, etc.[21] And so the scheme in Brajeshwar Prasad's amendment is what we find in the Constitution today.

Who is the author? Sir B.N. Rau whose questionnaire and Model Provincial Constitution laid the groundwork for the work of the Provincial Constitution Committee? Sardar Patel and other members of the Committee? Ambedkar and the Drafting Committee which drafted one proposal but then left the question for the Constituent Assembly? Or the member whose name few would recognize today, Brajeshwar Prasad?

There was another related set of articles which went through the same vicissitudes. Perhaps on the analogy of the vice-president, from the beginning there had been proposals for having in every state a deputy governor in addition to the governor. In its meeting on 8 June 1947 the Provincial Constitution Committee finally decided to reject the proposal. With even the governor having few functions, no one could quite think what the deputy governor would do. The Committee decided that in case there was a vacancy in the office of the governor, it should be filled by the president if it was for a period less than four months, and by a new election for another full term if it was for a longer period.[22]

But the Constituent Assembly decided otherwise. Pandit

---

21 *Constituent Assembly Debates,* Vol. VIII, pp. 424–69. The course the provision took is chronicled in B. Shiva Rao, *The Framing of India's Constitution, A Study,* pp. 391–96.

22 B. Shiva Rao, *The Framing of India's Constitution, Select Documents,* Vol. II, p. 648.

Pant told the Assembly on 16 July 1947 that for the president to have to nominate an officiating governor would be an 'embarrassing duty', and that giving him this power would also 'be somewhat repugnant to the principle of provincial autonomy'. He therefore tabled an amendment providing that every state shall have a deputy governor who would be elected after every general election by the state legislature on the system of proportional representation with single transferable vote.

He said that provisions had already been settled for having at the level of the Union a vice-president elected by the legislature after the general election. His amendment merely sought to provide an office at the level of the units analogous to that of the vice-president at the Centre. That this course had been agreed to by the leaders is evident from the fact that Sardar Patel had told the Assembly while moving the draft clause that, apart from moving the clause, he did not propose to say anything as Pandit Pant had an amendment to move. The Assembly adopted this amendment.[23]

Accordingly, Sir B.N. Rau's *First Draft of the Constitution of India* provided for a deputy governor: 'There shall be a Deputy Governor for every Province,' the *First Draft* said. 'He will be elected by the Provincial Assembly on the system of proportional representation by single transferable vote after every general election. The Deputy Governor will fill a casual vacancy in the office of the Governor for the remainder of the term of office of the Governor and he will also act for the Governor in his absence.'[24]

Although the office had been provided for, no one could still think of any function for the deputy governor to

---

23 *Constituent Assembly Debates,* Vol. IV, pp. 610–15; B. Shiva Rao, *The Framing of India's Constitution, A Study,* p. 389.

24 B. Shiva Rao, *The Framing of India's Constitution, Select Documents,* Vol. II, p. 668.

perform. The only hypothetical function which had survived was to officiate as or assume the office of the governor when the latter was absent or had left office. The Drafting Committee provided a separate article and procedure to deal with this contingency: draft article 120 provided that 'The Legislature of a State may make such provision as it thinks fit for the discharge of the functions of the Governor of the state in any contingency not provided for in this Chapter.'

So, even this function of the potential stepney was taken care of. Yet, in view of the decision that the Constituent Assembly had taken on the matter, the *Draft Constitution* as finalized by the Drafting Committee contained five articles providing for and dealing with the post of a deputy governor. The Committee simultaneously noted that these articles 'should be omitted as the retention of the provisions with regard to the Deputy Governor who will not have any definite functions to perform so long as the Governor is there is hardly necessary in view of the provision contained in Article 120 which empowers the Legislature of the state to make such provisions as it thinks fit for the discharge of the functions of the Governor in any contingency not provided for in this Constitution.' The Committee added that 'as soon as the Constitution comes into force the Legislature may in advance make these provisions.'[25]

By the end, as we know, nothing remained either of the elected governor which the Committee had provided for at this stage, nor of the post of deputy governor.

Communal reservations in legislatures

One of the weapons which had worked most satisfactorily

25 *Draft Constitution,* Part V, Articles 119, 119A, 119B, 119C, 119D; B. Shiva Rao, *The Framing of India's Constitution, Select Documents,* Vol. III, pp. 428–31.

for the British in dividing Indians was to proffer a benefit which members of a group could avail only by insisting on, and establishing their separateness. Separate electorates and reservations were two forms of this weapon. A delegation of Muslims with the Aga Khan at its head had been engineered. It presented a charter of demands to Lord Minto which the British themselves had drawn up, with a separate electorate for Muslims as its centrepiece; the viceroy and later the British government and Parliament had graciously acceded to the demand![26] The device having worked so well for widening the gap between Hindus and Muslims, schemes had been afoot to detach the Scheduled Castes and Tribes in the same way.

As we have seen, Ambedkar became the most vigorous propagandist, putting the demand in terms so extreme and denunciatory that the British would themselves never have felt comfortable using them. That effort, as we have seen, had been defeated by Gandhiji. But at the cost of giving even further rein to the other device—reservations. To defeat the British design, to make the British Cabinet rescind its announcement granting a separate electorate to Harijans also, and to leave just no excuse by which Ambedkar could continue his advocacy of the British device, in the Poona Pact Gandhiji had had to concede reservations for Harijans in legislatures.

By the 1940s the position had worsened. The non-Muslim leadership was drawing up one formula after another, it was diluting its stand on one issue after another so as to satisfy Jinnah and the Muslim League. But nothing had worked: Jinnah had, as he said, forged a pistol, and our leaders had nothing except proposals with which to counter it.

---

26 For a brief recapitulation see my *Missionaries in India: Changes, Continuities, Dilemmas*, ASA, New Delhi, 1995, pp. 196–97, and the references given therein.

In spite of all that had transpired—the Muslim League had stayed away from deliberations of the Assembly and its committees—Muslim members again pressed for separate electorates in the Subcommittee on Minorities. The Subcommittee rejected the demand in July 1947. But only in the Poona Pact mode—that is, by conceding instead that, while the electorate shall be one and joint, there shall be reservations of seats in legislatures 'for different recognized minorities.' As many as twenty-three of the twenty-six members present voted for this clause. It was also decided that the reservations would be for ten years, the position being reconsidered at the end of that period. Minorities were divided into three categories: Anglo-Indians, Parsis and plains tribesmen in Assam—these being minorities which constituted less than ½ per cent in the Indian Dominion, omitting the Indian states; Indian Christians and Sikhs—who constituted less than 1½ per cent; and Muslims and Scheduled Castes—who exceeded 1½ per cent. While some extra weightage was to be given for minorities in the first two categories, in the case of the third category, seats were to be reserved in proportion to their share in the population.[27] This decision was incorporated in the Subcommittee's report.[28] And then in the report of the parent Advisory Committee which Sardar Patel submitted to the president on 8 August 1947.[29] The Constituent Assembly took up the report, and adopted the recommendation granting reservations in seats in Legislatures for religious minorities, with the same categorization and proportions as had been proposed by the Subcommittee on Minority Rights

27 Minutes of the meetings of 23 and 25 July 1947, B. Shiva Rao, *The Framing of India's Constitution, Select Documents,* Vol. II, pp. 392–94.

28 B. Shiva Rao, *The Framing of India's Constitution, Select Documents,* Vol. II, pp. 397–98.

29 See Sardar Patel's forwarding letter and the recommendations of the Committee, B. Shiva Rao, *The Framing of India's Constitution, Select Documents,* Vol. II, pp. 412–14 and 417–18 respectively.

and the Advisory Committee.[30] This was done on 27 and 28 August 1947, within days of the country being partitioned in the name of religion—so powerful was the tug of the past, of the notion that communal reservations were a price one just had to pay to avoid the much greater evil of separate electorates.

In reviewing the *First Draft* of Sir B.N. Rau to bring it in line with recommendations of the committees and the decisions of the Assembly on them, the Drafting Committee decided to add to the new draft articles—Articles 292 to 296 in a separate Part XIV—which it entitled 'Special Provisions Relating to Minorities'. Reservations for religious communities in addition to Scheduled Castes and Tribes, in the Lok Sabha and some of the state Assemblies were the principal feature of these provisions.[31] There were some new twists by now: the Sikhs and Parsis were missing from the list, and draft Article 305 provided that the reservations would lapse after ten years, unless they were extended by a constitutional amendment.

That then was the situation even in February 1948: the Advisory Committee had recommended and the Assembly itself had decided that there shall be reservations in legislatures along communal lines; the Drafting Committee had recorded these decisions in the shape of new draft articles in the *Draft Constitution.*

A number of members—Seth Govind Das, Thakurdas Bhargava, K. Santhanam, M. Ananthasayanam Ayyangar, G. Durgabai, T.T. Krishnamachari, Tajamul Hussain—criticized these provisions, and tabled amendments. They suggested that the articles be deleted altogether, in the alternative that, if reservations were to be made at all, they should be

---

30 B. Shiva Rao, *The Framing of India's Constitution, Select Documents,* Vol. II, pp. 426–28.

31 B. Shiva Rao, *The Framing of India's Constitution, Select Documents,* Vol. II, pp. 477–78, 630–32.

made only for Scheduled Tribes or, at the most, for them and the Scheduled Castes. Some urged that, if reservations are retained, members of communities for whom reservations have been made should not be allowed to stand from general constituencies. Tajamul Hussain and others urged that in any case no reservations should be made for Muslims as a community.[32]

As we know, the first *Draft Constitution* as settled by the Drafting Committee was circulated in February 1948. Because of some unsettled questions in regard to Punjab and West Bengal the Advisory Committee met again on 30 December 1948. By this time the situation had changed, the country had been fully awakened to the consequences of the 'minority-majority' line of the Muslim League. Those who had been opposed to apportioning seats on the basis of religion pressed Sardar Patel that, in spite of the fact that the Constituent Assembly had decided in August 1947 to reserve seats for Muslims, etc., the entire question must be reopened. The minutes of the meeting record:

> 5. Alluding to the motions given notice of by several members seeking to do away with reservation for minorities, the Chairman [Sardar Patel] suggested that the movers should confine their proposals to their own communities, as in the absence of a general agreement it would not be proper to force a minority to give up its right of separate representation. For example, if the Muslims by general agreement among themselves felt that they did not want any reservation, their view should be accepted; but the proposal should come from them and not from a member of any other community.
>
> 6. The Hon'ble Dr. B.R. Ambedkar raised a point of order to the effect that the political safeguards for the minorities having been accepted by the Constituent Assembly of India they were not

32 B. Shiva Rao, *The Framing of India's Constitution, Select Documents,* Vol. IV, pp. 354–62.

> within the reach of the Advisory Committee and that if it was the desire of the Committee to discuss the matter *de novo* the proper procedure was to move amendments to the provisions contained in the *Draft Constitution.* The Chairman ruled that there was no bar to a discussion and that the Committee also could recommend reconsideration of the whole matter. On merits, however, he thought that unless there was general agreement the conclusions already arrived at should not be disturbed.

A general discussion ensued. The Sardar adjourned the meeting announcing that the Committee would meet again at a later date to consider the matter.[33]

The Committee met on 10 and 11 May 1949. Dr H.C. Mookherjee, who was vice-president of the Constituent Assembly, moved a resolution for abolishing all reservations for religions communities. As Sardar Patel wrote to the president on 11 May 1949, this resolution 'found wholehearted support of an overwhelming majority of the members of the Advisory Committee.' The Advisory Committee therefore resolved to recommend to the Constituent Assembly 'that the system of reservation for minorities other than Scheduled Castes in Legislatures be abolished'.

The Sardar recalled that in its original report the Advisory Committee had noted that the minorities were 'by no means unanimous, as to the necessity, in their own interests, of statutory reservation of seats in the Legislatures'. 'Nevertheless, the Committee had recommended reservation of seats,' the Sardar said, quoting the report, '"in order that minorities may not feel apprehensive about the effect of a system of unrestricted joint electorates on the quantum of their representation in the Legislature".'

By the time the Committee met again in December 1948, the situation had changed a great deal and, the Sardar wrote,

---

33 B. Shiva Rao, *The Framing of India's Constitution, Select Documents,* Vol. IV, pp. 597–98.

'Some members of the Committee felt that, conditions having vastly changed since the Advisory Committee made their recommendations in 1947, it was no longer appropriate in the context of free India and of present conditions that there should be reservation of seats for Muslims, Christians, Sikhs or any other religious minority. Although the abolition of separate electorates had removed much of the poison from the body politic, the reservation of seats for religious communities, it was felt, did lead to a certain degree of separatism and was to that extent contrary to the conception of a secular democratic State. Dr. H.C. Mookherjee, Mr. Tajamul Hussain, Shri Lakshmi Kanta Maitra and certain other members gave notices of resolutions seeking to recommend to the Constituent Assembly that there should be no reservation of seats in the Legislatures for any community in India...'

Even so he had deferred a decision, the Sardar explained, as 'I was anxious that the representatives of the minorities on the Committee should have adequate time both to gauge public opinion among their people and to reflect fully on the amendments that had been proposed, so that a change, if effected, would be one sought voluntarily by the minorities themselves and not imposed on them by the majority community.'

Sardar Patel acknowledged that 'the Committee are fully alive to the fact that decisions once reached should not be changed lightly.' 'Conditions have, however, vastly changed since August 1947,' the Sardar continued, 'and the Committee are satisfied that the minorities themselves feel that in their own interests, no less than in the interests of the country as a whole, the statutory reservation of seats for religious minorities should be abolished.'[34]

---

34 B. Shiva Rao, *The Framing of India's Constitution, Select Documents,* Vol. IV, pp. 599–602.

On 25 May 1949, Sardar Patel addressed the Constituent Assembly, and tabled the report of the Advisory Committee. He recalled the considerations on which, in spite of the opposition of members like Dr H.C. Mookherjee and Rajkumari Amrit Kaur, the Advisory Committee had made its original recommendation, and how the Assembly had accepted it 'practically unanimously'. By the time the Committee had met again in December 1948, he told the Assembly, 'the Muslim representatives, some of them, had changed their opinions after full reflection for a long period since the passing of the principles of the Constitution in the August session of 1947. They put forward the plea that all these reservations must disappear and that it was in the interests of the minorities themselves that such reservations in the Legislature must go. It was strongly pressed by the representative from Bihar and supported by other representatives. There was then a little difference of opinion and I was anxious, and so was the Committee, that we should do nothing to take a snatch vote on a question of such vast importance. As the Sikh representatives wanted time to consider their position, we naturally adjourned and met again, during the early part of this month.'

When the Committee had met earlier in the month Dr. Mookherjee had moved the resolution, the Sardar reported, and continued:

> The Committee considering the whole situation came to the conclusion that the time has come when the vast majority of the minority communities have themselves realized after great reflection the evil effects in the past of such reservations on the minorities themselves, and the reservations should be dropped.
>
> In a House of about forty members of the Advisory Committee, there was only one solitary vote against the proposal. So we thought that although these proposals were accepted by this House in August 1947, it was due to us and to the House that we should advise this House to reconsider the position, and put before

> the House a proposal which is consistent with the proclaimed principles of this House for the establishment of a genuine democratic State based purely on nationalistic principles. Therefore, when we found the changed atmosphere, we considered it our duty to come before this House to revise this former decision, which was provisional as has been laid down by this House in several cases. It is under these circumstances that these proposals have been brought before the House.[35]

Now, who is the author? The Ambedkar who in his presidential address and again in his memorandum to the Fundamental Rights Subcommittee strongly advocated communal reservations in legislatures? The Ambedkar who was the chairman of the Drafting Committee which translated the decision of the Constituent Assembly into draft articles in the first *Draft Constitution* and provided for communal reservations? The Ambedkar who in December 1948 opposed reopening the question on the ground that the Assembly had already settled it by its decision of August 1947? Dr H. C. Mookherjee who moved the resolution in the Advisory Committee to abolish such communal reservations? The members of the Advisory Committee who reversed their earlier recommendation? The members of the Constituent Assembly itself who reversed their earlier decision on the matter?...

Or events, and the lessons they were imprinting on the members of the Assembly?

Communal reservations in Cabinets

As we have seen while recalling his presidential address of May 1945, and the memorandum he submitted to the Subcommittee on Fundamental Rights, Ambedkar was not just for communal reservations in legislatures, he wanted

---

35 *Constituent Assembly Debates,* Vol. VIII, pp. 269–72.

communal reservations in Cabinets as well. Not just that: he did not just want a certain proportion of seats in each Cabinet to be reserved for communal minorities; he insisted that the persons from the minorities who were to man these positions must not be selected by the prime minister, they must be elected by only those members of the legislature who belonged to the particular minority; persons from the majority who were to fill the remaining posts too must be elected, but by the whole House: that is, members of communal minorities would have the exclusive right to elect one category of ministers, and they would also have the right to help decide who from the majority shall be appointed ministers!

No one took up his scheme for constituting the Cabinet in the Subcommittee on Fundamental Rights. But Muslim members did press one part of the scheme: there ought to be reservations in the Cabinet on communal lines. In the meeting on 25 July 1947, K.M. Munshi brought the matter to a head, and moved that the Subcommittee recommend that no statutory provision be made for reservation of seats for the minorities in Cabinets. The Subcommittee decided to adopt Munshi's proposal and reject the scheme for communal quotas in the Cabinet, but by the narrowest margin—eight voting for it, and seven against.

As a substitute, Munshi proposed that a 'Convention' should be provided in a schedule to the Constitution along the lines of paragraph VII of the instrument of instructions which had been issued to governors under the Government of India Act of 1935. This paragraph had read:

> VII. In making appointments to his Council of Ministers our Governor shall use his best endeavours to select his Ministers in the following manner, that is to say, to appoint in consultation with the person who in his judgement is most likely to command a stable majority in the Legislature those persons (including so far as practicable members of important minority communities) who will

> best be in a position collectively to command the confidence of the Legislature. In so acting, he shall bear constantly in mind the need for fostering a sense of joint responsibility among his Ministers.

Sir Homy Mody urged that the word 'important' qualifying 'minority communities' be deleted. His suggestion was lost, nine to eight. But the main proposal was endorsed by a large margin: twelve voting for it and five against.[36]

The parent Advisory Committee adopted this proposal, and commended it verbatim to the Assembly.[37] Not just that, in August 1947, the Constituent Assembly itself adopted it.[38]

The first *Draft Constitution* which the Drafting Committee submitted in February 1948 had an Instrument of Instructions for Governors as a schedule—Schedule IV—to the Constitution.[39] Clause 2 of this schedule incorporated verbatim the text of the instructions which had been issued under the 1935 Act, and which had been endorsed by the Subcommittee on Minorities.

On 4 November 1948, while moving the *Draft Constitution* for consideration, Ambedkar did not just refer to the instrument of instructions as Schedule IV of the draft, he told the Assembly that—in addition to the governors—it was proposed to issue such instructions to the president also.[40]

A month and a half later, on 30 December 1948, Ambedkar was speaking on draft Article 61 which dealt with

---

36 B. Shiva Rao, *The Framing of India's Constitution, Select Documents,* Vol. II, pp. 392–93.

37 See Sardar Patel's forwarding letter and the Advisory Committee's report, B. Shiva Rao, *The Framing of India's Constitution, Select Documents,* Vol. II, pp. 415, 418.

38 B. Shiva Rao, *The Framing of India's Constitution, Select Documents,* Vol. II, p. 428.

39 The text of Schedule IV is in B. Shiva Rao, *The Framing of India's Constitution, Select Documents,* Vol. III, p. 650.

40 *Constituent Assembly Debates,* Vol. VII, pp. 31–44, at pp. 41–42.

the Council of Ministers. A member—Mahboob Ali Baig—had moved an amendment which, in essence, advocated a variant of the scheme which Ambedkar himself had championed in his memorandum to the Subcommittee on Fundamental Rights: members of the Council of Ministers, Baig's amendment proposed, must not be appointed by the president on the advice of the prime minister, they ought to be elected by the House of the People on the principle of proportional representation. Ambedkar now opposed this proposal. He said:

> With regard to the second amendment, namely that the Ministers should not be appointed by the President on the advice of the Prime Minister, but should be chosen by proportional representation, I have not been able to understand exactly what is the underlying purpose he [Mahboob Ali Baig] has in mind. So far I was able to follow his arguments, he said the method prescribed in the *Draft Constitution* was undemocratic. Well, I do not understand why it is undemocratic to permit a Prime Minister, who is chosen by the people, to appoint Ministers from a House which is also chosen on adult suffrage, or by people who are chosen on the basis of adult suffrage. I fail to understand why that system is undemocratic. But I suspect that the purpose underlying his amendment is to enable minorities to secure representation in the Cabinet. Now if that is so, I sympathize with the object he has in view, because I realize that a great deal of good administration, so to say, depends upon the fact as to in whose hands the administration vests. If it is controlled by a certain group, there is no doubt about it that the administration will function in the interests of the group represented by that particular body of people in control of administration. Therefore, there is nothing wrong in proposing that the method of choosing the Cabinet should be such that it should permit members of the minority communities to be included in the Cabinet. I do not think that that aim is either unworthy or there is something in it to be ashamed of. But I would like to draw the attention of my friend, Mr. Mahboob Ali Baig, that his purpose would be achieved by an addition which the Drafting Committee proposes to make of a schedule which is called

Schedule III-A. It will be seen that we have in the *Draft Constitution* introduced one schedule called Schedule IV which contains the Instrument of Instructions to the Governor as to how he has to exercise his discretionary powers in the matter of administration. We have analogous to that decided to move an amendment in order to introduce another schedule which also contains a similar Instrument of Instructions to the President. One of the clauses in the proposed Instrument of Instruction will be this:

'In making appointments to his Council of Ministers, the President shall use his best endeavours to select his Ministers in the following manner, that is to say, to appoint a person who has been found by him to be most likely to command a stable majority in Parliament as the Prime Minister, and then to appoint on the advice of the Prime Minister those persons, including so far as practicable, members of minority communities, who will best be in a position collectively to command the confidence of Parliament.'

I think this Instrument of Instructions will serve the purpose, if that is the purpose which Mr. Mahboob Ali Baig has in his mind in moving his amendment. I do not think it is possible to make any statutory provision for the inclusion of members of particular communities in the Cabinet. That, I think, would not be possible, in view of the fact that our Constitution, as proposed, contains the principle of collective responsibility, and there is no use foisting upon the Prime Minister a colleague simply because he happens to be the member of a particular minority community, but who does not agree with the fundamentals of the policy which the Prime Minister and his party have committed themselves to.[41]

The reader would have noticed both points: in arguing against Baig's proposal Ambedkar was now giving the very argument which he had turned down with his usual contempt—recall those interminably repeated assertions about majorities in India not being political but communal majorities; second, Ambedkar was again affirming not just the Instrument

41 *Constituent Assembly Debates*, Vol. VII, pp. 1156–61, at pp. 1157–58.

of Instructions but in addition saying that it was going to be extended to cover the president also.

That was on 30 December 1948. The next day, Ambedkar rose to move an amendment to draft Article 62 so as to incorporate another clause providing:

> (5) (a) In the choice of his Ministers and the exercise of his other functions under this Constitution, the President shall be generally guided by the Instructions set out in Schedule III-A, but the validity of anything done by the President shall not be called in question on the ground that it was done otherwise than in accordance with such Instructions.

Members objected: the second part—barring the courts from examining whether the president had acted in accordance with the instrument of instructions—negates the first part, they argued: it reduces the clause to a mere exhortation. Ambedkar defended the draft clause on the ground that the proper remedy was not to tie the hands of the president or the prime minister by enabling any recalcitrant member to go to the courts but for the legislature to vote out the errant ministry for giving wrong advice, or impeach the president for not adhering to the instrument of instructions.[42] The Assembly amended draft Article 62 and incorporated this additional clause thus giving formal status to the instrument of instructions.

On 11 October 1949 the Constituent Assembly turned to consider these two schedules—Schedule III-A containing instructions for the president, and Schedule IV containing instructions for governors. Members had proposed additions and alterations. T.T. Krishnamachari, speaking on behalf of the Drafting Committee, said that Schedule III-A was *not* being moved for consideration. Brajeshwar Prasad shot up, 'What is the idea? Is it to be held over?'

The president intervened: 'It is not in the *Draft Constitution*,'

---

42 *Constituent Assembly Debates*, Vol. VII, pp. 1184 and 1189.

he said. 'It was given only as an amendment, and when that amendment is not moved, there is no question of amendments to that amendment arising. So Schedule III-A goes, with all its amendments.'

But that could not be said of the Instrument of Instructions for Governors—these had been formally set out in Schedule IV which was very much a part of the *Draft Constitution*. What about that?

T.T. Krishnamachari said, 'Sir, I move that Schedule IV be deleted.'

Several members shot up, 'But how can it be deleted?'

The president asked Ambedkar to explain.

Ambedkar said, 'Mr Krishnamachari will explain.'

TTK said that since the Schedules were drafted it had come to be felt that 'the matter should be left entirely to convention rather than be put into the body of the Constitution...', that 'it is felt to be entirely unnecessary and superfluous to give directions in the Constitution which really should arise out of conventions that grow up from time to time...'

Members were perplexed. 'Sir, I am confused,' said B. Das from Orissa. 'At the fag end of the day a sudden surprise is sprung on us...'

Ambedkar rose to explain the new thinking. First, he said, under the 1935 Act there was an official—the Secretary of State for India—who could ensure that the instructions were carried out by the governors in India: if they did not adhere to the instructions, he had the authority to replace them. The new Constitution did not provide for any such officer. Second, he said, the schedules had been thought of at a time when it was envisaged that a number of discretionary powers would be vested in governors. But the ambit of discretionary powers had since been narrowed down so much that no instructions were now thought to be necessary.[43]

---

43 *Constituent Assembly Debates,* Vol. X, pp. 114–16.

The 'reasons' were of course no better than a lawyer's contrivances. Contrast what Ambedkar was now saying—that the instrument of instructions ought not to be included as there was no officer who had been vested with the authority to ensure that it was adhered to—with what he had said earlier on this very point: that the Legislature is the agency which would ensure that the instructions were adhered to. As for the ambit of discretionary powers, that was but a half-truth: that ambit had indeed been narrowed in the case of the governor as we have seen; but the ambit of such powers in the case of the president was no wider when Ambedkar moved his amendment to formally bind the president to act in accordance with Schedule III-A than it was now.

Which Ambedkar is the author? The Ambedkar who authored the scheme of the 1945 presidential address and his memorandum to the Fundamental Rights Subcommittee—that ministers must be elected by the House, and that too on communal basis? Or the Ambedkar who argued against Mahmood Ali Baig's amendment saying this would be no way to constitute a Cabinet which was collectively responsible to the House? Or the Ambedkar who chaired the Drafting Committee which incorporated a schedule in the *Draft Constitution* containing instructions for governors, the Ambedkar who thereafter moved an amendment to incorporate another schedule extending the instructions to cover the president? Or the Ambedkar who argued in favour of deleting the schedules?

Is Ambedkar speaking as the author of the proposals or as a lawyer arguing a given brief on the principle which he was later to enunciate to the Rajya Sabha, 'We lawyers defend many things?'

Council of Ministers

As we have seen, one of the main objects of the instrument

of instructions was to lay down the principles which the president and governors must follow in constituting their respective Council of Ministers. But there was another, and basic difference in the conception of the Council of Ministers that would be constituted at the Centre and the ones that would be constituted in the states.

To go no farther back than the first *Draft Constitution* as it was settled by the Drafting Committee in February 1948, the draft articles dealing with the Union Council of Ministers—draft Articles 61 and 62—provided inter alia—that 'The Prime Minister shall be appointed by the President and the other ministers shall be appointed by the President *on the advice of the Prime Minister,'* and that *'The Council shall he collectively responsible to the House of the People.'* But in the case of the Council of Ministers in the states, the *Draft Constitution*—in draft Articles 143 and 144—envisaged a very different scheme. It provided, inter alia, that *'The Governor's ministers shall be appointed by him and shall hold office during his pleasure'*— there was no requirement that the governor should appoint the other ministers on the advice of the chief minister; on the contrary, draft Article 144 (6) specified, 'The functions of the Governor under this Article with respect to the appointment and dismissal of ministers shall be exercised by him in his discretion.' Second, there was no provision prescribing that the Council of Ministers would be collectively responsible to the Lower House. There was a third difference also, this one in regard to the functions of the Council of Ministers. In the case of the Council of Ministers at the Centre the *Draft Constitution* provided—in draft Article 61 (1)—'There shall be a Council of Ministers with the Prime Minister at its head to aid and advise the President in the exercise of his functions.' But in the case of the Council of Ministers at the level of the states, the *Draft Constitution* provided— in draft Article 143 (1)—'There shall be a Council of Ministers with the Chief Minister at the head to aid and advise the Governor in the exercise of his functions, *except in so far as he is by or under this Constitution required to exercise his functions or any of them in his discretion.'*

This was an unexplained anomaly, as we have seen: in its report the Provincial Constitution Committee had specified four functions in regard to which the governor must act on his discretion; but when Sardar Patel as the chairman of the Committee had got up to move the report for consideration of the House he had informed the Assembly that upon reconsideration the Committee had concluded that in almost all matters the governor must act on the advice of the Council of Ministers. But the 'Principles of the Provincial Constitution' which the Assembly had approved had for some reason or by some oversight reproduced the earlier formulation. In any case, it is that set of principles which the Drafting Committee had incorporated in the *Draft Constitution.*

The Constituent Assembly took up draft Article 144 for consideration on 1 June 1949. Ambedkar moved far-reaching amendments. He now proposed that the article provide, 'The Chief Minister shall be appointed by the Governor and the other ministers shall be appointed by the Governor *on the advice of the Chief Minister and* the Ministers shall hold office during the pleasure of the Governor.' Second, he proposed that the Article have an additional clause providing, *'The Council shall be collectively responsible to the Legislative Assembly of the State.'* Third, he proposed that clause (6) of the draft article—which had provided that in appointing and dismissing ministers the governor shall act on his discretion—be deleted. These amendments were approved by the Assembly.[44]

---

44 *Constituent Assembly Debates,* Vol. VIII, pp. 503, 507, 521.

What was he the author of—of the original draft article or of these amendments which completely recast the scheme of governance in the states that had been contained in the article?

Even in regard to the wording of the amendments, the text was presaged by others. When the *Draft Constitution* had been circulated for comments, several persons had proposed precisely these changes. T.A. Ramalingam Chettiar had proposed that the draft Article 144 (1) be substituted by, 'The Chief Minister shall be appointed by the Governor and the other ministers shall be appointed by the Governor *on the advice of the Chief Minister.* The ministers shall hold office during the pleasure of the Governor.' Jayaprakash Narayan had proposed that the clause be replaced by 'The Chief Minister shall be appointed by the Governor, and the other ministers shall be appointed by the Governor *on the advice of the Chief Minister.*' He had also proposed that an additional clause be added to the article providing, 'The Council shall be collectively responsible to the Legislature of the state and shall hold office as long as the former commands the confidence of the Legislature.'[45]

Are they the authors or Ambedkar? And are they the authors either? For what were they doing except ask that the scheme which had been adopted for the Centre be the scheme for the states also? So, who is the author—Ambedkar or the person who drafted that scheme for the Centre? But then, was that latter person doing anything more than reproducing in these articles what were the well-known and well-settled principles of the British parliamentary system?

But even that is not an accurate way to portray the sequence, for it suggests that one person acting at one point

---

45 B. Shiva Rao, *The Framing of India's Constitution, Select Documents,* Vol. IV, pp. 78–81.

of time reduced those well-known principles of the parliamentary system into a draft article. That is not what happened in fact. The subject fell within the purview of the Union Constitution Committee headed by Pandit Nehru. This Committee was using as its working document the memorandum prepared by Sir B.N. Rau. In this memorandum Rau had provided, 'There shall be a Council of Ministers with the Prime Minister at the head to aid and advise the President in the exercise of his functions except in so far as he is required by this Constitution to act in his discretion.' Sir B.N. Rau had included a special note to explain and indirectly justify the last few words of the draft clause relating to the exercise by the president of some functions in his discretion. He had also made provision for a Council of State which would be available to assist the president in regard to these functions.[46]

At its meeting on 8 June 1947 the Union Constitution Committee decided that 'the President's power to dissolve the lower chamber of the Federal Legislature should be exercised only on the advice of the Ministers. He should not have the special responsibilities set out in clause 15 of the *Draft Constitution* prepared by the Constitutional Adviser. The members of the Federal Public Service Commission should not be appointed by the President in his discretion.'

The next day the Committee took several decisions which had a bearing on clauses relating to the Council of Ministers. The Committee decided that as it had already been settled that the executive would be of the parliamentary type, there was no further need to deliberate on the type of relations which would subsist between the Council of Ministers and the president. It also decided that 'No special provisions are necessary for the securing of a stable Executive.' Furthermore, that 'No provision should be

46 For the text of the draft article and the note, B. Shiva Rao, *The Framing of India's Constitution, Select Documents,* Vol. II, pp. 476–77.

made in the Constitution regarding the composition of the Executive or the maximum number of ministers.' But Sir Alladi Krishnaswami Ayyar and N. Gopalaswami Ayyangar pressed the point that the Constitution ought to specify at least the minimum elements of a parliamentary executive. The Committee accordingly decided that the Constitution would contain a provision to the following effect, 'The President shall appoint the Prime Minister from among the members of the Federal House of Representatives (the lower chamber of the Central Legislature) and in doing so will ordinarily invite the person who in his judgement is likely to command the largest following in that House to accept the office. The other ministers of the Cabinet will be appointed by the President on the advice of the Prime Minister.'[47]

Panditji presented the report of the Union Constitution Committee to the president on 4 July 1947. The corresponding draft clause in it—clause 10—read, 'There shall be a Council of Ministers with the Prime Minister at the head to aid and advise the President in the exercise of his functions.' The clause had, in accordance with the decision of the Committee, deleted the reference in Sir B.N. Rau's draft to the functions which the president would exercise in his discretion, but, contrary to what had been decided by the Committee in its meeting on 9 June 1947, there was no reference to the effect that the person whom the president would invite to be the prime minister would be the one who was most likely to command the confidence of the House, nor to the fact that the other ministers would be appointed on the advice of the prime minister. And that is the text he moved in the Assembly.[48]

---

47 B. Shiva Rao, *The Framing of India's Constitution, Select Documents,* Vol. II, pp. 555, 556–57. The facts are recounted summarily in B. Shiva Rao, *The Framing of India's Constitution, A Study,* pp. 371–73.

48 *Constituent Assembly Debates,* Vol. IV, pp. 723, 857.

There was prolonged discussion on various aspects of the Union Constitution Committee's report, and several members urged a wide range of proposals, from the presidential system to variants that were close to the method Ambedkar had advocated in his memorandum—Kazi Syed Karimuddin moved an amendment requiring that the prime minister should be elected by the House by single transferable vote, and other ministers should be elected also by the House by proportional representation; Panditji shot this latter proposal down saying, 'I can think of nothing more conducive to creating a feeble ministry than this business of electing them by proportional representation.'[49]

N. Gopalaswami Ayyangar remarked that the clause about the Council of Ministers as it stood in the draft 'does not say anything about the manner in which the Council of Ministers is to be chosen and the responsibility of that Council to the Legislature'. He therefore proposed an amendment to replace the clause by, 'The Prime Minister shall be appointed by the President and the other ministers shall be appointed by the President on the advice of the Prime Minister. The Council shall be collectively responsible to the House of the People.'[50]

Responding to the discussion Panditji said, '... it is perfectly true that the original draft that I placed before the House was not at all clear on various matters. It was not clear because there was no intention of drafting it here. These [the provisions of the report which had been placed before the Assembly] are certain indications for future drafting and some things were obviously taken for granted. It was taken for granted that the Prime Minister would be sent for by the President because he happens to represent the largest party or group in the House; further that the Prime Minister would select his ministers and further that

49 *Constituent Assembly Debates,* Vol. IV, pp. 858–60, 864–65.

50 *Constituent Assembly Debates,* Vol. IV, pp. 860–61.

they would be responsible to the House collectively. All that was taken for granted, but perhaps it is better to put that down clearly and the amendment moved by Sir Gopalaswami Ayyangar puts that down very clearly. Therefore I accept that amendment and I hope the House will also accept it...'[51]

Not the most gracious way to accept a suggestion. In any case, the amendment moved by Ayyangar was adopted. The requirements it lists are the ones we find in the Constitution, and, as we have seen, they also became the basis for altering the corresponding provisions—draft Articles 143 and 144—relating to Councils of Ministers in the states.

Who is the author?

A telltale proviso

Draft Article 144 (1) had a proviso also, and it provides an inkling into the way the Drafting Committee put the *Draft Constitution* together. After the main clause had stated that there shall be a Council of Ministers, etc., the proviso specified, 'Provided that in the states of Bihar, Central Provinces and Berar and Orissa, there shall be a minister in charge of tribal welfare who may in addition be in charge of the welfare of the Scheduled Castes and backward classes or any other work.' When the article was being considered by the Assembly, a member, Rohini Kumar Chaudhuri criticized the proviso on the ground that the purpose was not clear: he asked whether under this proviso only a tribal or Scheduled Caste person could be appointed a minister. The president said, 'There is no question [under the proviso] of representation of Scheduled Castes and backward tribes in the ministry. A minister is to be

51 *Constituent Assembly Debates,* Vol. IV, p. 865.

appointed to look after them; not that he should belong to that tribe or backward community.' Chaudhuri said that tribals and Scheduled Castes had looked upon this proviso as being the provision that would ensure that at least one minister was going to be a tribal or Scheduled Caste person, but, if that was not the case, what was the point of having it?

In the reply he gave to criticisms which had been levelled at the draft article, Ambedkar reverted to the point that Chaudhuri had raised. He explained:

> The reason why this particular clause came to be introduced in the *Draft Constitution* is to be found in the recommendations of the Sub-Committee on tribal people appointed by the Minorities Committee of the Constituent Assembly. In the report made by that Committee, it will be noticed that there is an appendix to it which is called 'Statutory Recommendation'. The proviso which has been introduced in this Article is the verbatim reproduction of the suggestion and the recommendation made by this particular Committee. It is said there that in the provinces of Bihar, Central Provinces and Berar and Orissa, there shall be a separate minister for tribal welfare, provided the minister may hold charge simultaneously of welfare work pertaining to Scheduled Castes and backward classes or any other work. Therefore, the Drafting Committee had no choice except to introduce this proviso because it was contained in that part of the report of the Tribal Committee which was headed 'Statutory Recommendation'. It was the intention of the Committee that this provision should appear in the Constitution itself, that it should not be relegated to any other part of it. That is why this has come from the Drafting Committee and it merely follows the recommendation of the other Committee.[52]

Is that how an author would speak? In speaking as he did, was Ambedkar not giving a true and faithful account of the way the *Draft Constitution* had been put together, of the actual function which the Drafting Committee had

52 *Constituent Assembly Debates*, Vol. VIII, pp. 519–21.

performed—the function of bringing the Draft which Sir B.N. Rau had prepared in line with the recommendations of the committees and the decisions of the Assembly?

And yet that Draft Constitution figures as one of his 'Writings' in Ambedkar's *Writings and Speeches*!

16

Two overarching determinants

A large volume can be filled with examples of the kind which we have been considering. The rights to equality, the right to property, the rights to religious freedom, provisions relating to the superintendence, direction and control of elections, those relating to the Supreme Court and high courts—all of these went through the same process of iterations, of revisions and adoption and reopening and recasting. It will also be obvious by now that what we have today is the result even in regard to a single article, and even in regard to the mere wording of the article, to say nothing of the idea behind the provision, it is the cumulative result of the contribution of many, many persons, so many of whom we would scarcely recognize today. When we scarcely recognize the names of even the legal giants of the period—Sir B.N. Rau, Sir Alladi Krishnaswami Ayyar and others—who would know who Pandit Thakurdas Bhargava was, or H.V. Kamath, to pluck two names which are all over the *Debates*, and yet their contribution to the final outcome was of the first importance.

And these are just the visible persons who contributed. There were so many others who were not members of the Assembly at all, and unlike Sir B.N. Rau were not even in the public eye. Again a chapter can be written about the contribution of these unknowns. I will confine myself to just one example, involving a person who came to hold positions of importance later on, who remained one of the voices of sanity throughout, who came from one of the great patriotic families of India, one whose word all who knew him would trust implicitly, one who lived till the other day so that many readers would have known him personally, but one whom none of us would associate with any contribution to the making of the Constitution.

I have in mind Mr Badr-ud-din Tyabji. He was a young man then, and was appointed deputy secretary in the secretariat of the Constituent Assembly. His was not in any sense a pivotal role. But how even a young man, in a peripheral position contributed to the outcome will be evident from a little episode. It relates to the adoption of our national flag and emblem.

The president of the Constituent Assembly appointed a committee on 23 June 1947 to finalize the flag. Dr Rajendra Prasad was himself the chairman. Maulana Azad, Rajaji, Sarojini Naidu, Sardar Panikkar, K.M. Munshi, B.R. Ambedkar, Frank Anthony, B. Pattabhi Sitaramayya, Hiralal Shastri, Satyanarayan Sinha, Baldev Singh and S.N. Gupta were the members. On record the note which the committee considered was the one by S.D. Kalelkar. The motion for the adoption of the flag which had been chosen stands in the name of Pandit Nehru. Apart from the introductory speech by Panditji, the principal speeches on it were made by Dr Radhakrishnan, Mohammed Saa'dulla and Sarojini Naidu.[1]

So if one goes by the official record one would scout for someone among these persons as being the one to whom we owe the flag. Apart from the fact that the flag had a long history—after all, what was adopted was just the Congress flag with the Ashoka Chakra replacing the

1 B. Shiva Rao, *The Framing of India's Constitution, Select Documents,* Vol. I, pp. 491–509; in particular his introductory note at p. 491.

charkha—the trigger quite obviously lay elsewhere than in the names we encounter in the formal proceedings of the committee and the Assembly. In his delectable memoir, *Memoirs of an Egotist,* Tyabji recalled what transpired on this question and the related one regarding the national symbol. He wrote:

> What fired my imagination most was the design of the national flag and the emblem of India. I wrote an article about it in *The Statesman* in 1951, taking the precaution of first showing it to the Prime Minister. Claims were even then being made by various persons of being the original begetters of the designs of these national symbols. Actually the symbols were finally approved on the basis of the proposals I made to the committee set up for the purpose by the President of the Constituent Assembly, Dr. Rajendra Prasad, and were finally adopted by a resolution drafted by me and passed by the Constituent Assembly.
>
> The design of the national flag—basically the substitution of the *charkha* in the Indian National Congress flag by the Ashokan *dharma chakra*—went through fairly easily, once Mahatma Gandhi saw the impracticability of having a *charkha* so stamped on the flag, that it would look the same from both sides. As it was, on the Congress party flags it looked right only when seen from one side. Looked at from the other side the spindle came before the wheel... The Mahatma had also appreciated the desirability of not using a party symbol, however predominant that party was in the country.
>
> The only point on which I subsequently failed to carry the committee with me was about the colour of the *dharma chakra* on the flag. I had proposed black; this was turned down on the ground that black was inauspicious. It was decided that it should be navy blue, which I think was aesthetically a mistake. Moreover, the navy blue on our flag soon fades and becomes a light blue; and that goes even less with the saffron, white and green of the rest of the flag.
>
> The only other issue raised that I recall was the vehement plea made in the committee by Mr. K.M. Munshi (then an ardent lieutenant of Sardar Patel) for adopting the traditional Hindu saffron flag (the *Bhagwa)* as the national flag. The other members of the committee however stood firm for secularism in this matter.

> Ultimately, it was agreed that the colours of the flag under which the Independence movement had been fought should remain the national colours.
>
> The design of the national emblem took much longer to settle. The committee agreed to let the matter be decided by the Prime Minister and me. After having innumerable designs prepared by a number of artists from all over India (I commissioned them to suggest a crest in which the Ashokan Lion Capital should figure as its central *motif)* and found them unsatisfactory, it dawned on me that all that was really required was to use the Lion Capital itself as the emblem, and eschew any elaboration or embellishment of it. It was a perfect artifact by itself. I put this to the Prime Minister who immediately accepted it. The addition of a scroll with a Sanskrit motif, 'Truth shall prevail,' was an afterthought carried out after I had left the Constituent Assembly Secretariat. I had nothing to do with it; personally I think it rather detracts from the artistic merit of the emblem without adding significantly to its message.'[2]

I am not on Tyabji's assessments of the aesthetics of the national flag and symbol. The point is that the making of the Constitution, like the shaping of the future of our country was in those days a truly national task, it was a national movement, and, as happens in the case of movements, at surcharged moments many, many persons contribute to the outcome, often the casual remark that one gets to put to the right person merely because one happens to be present at a moment at which that vital person is receptive or is exercised about a particular question, makes all the difference to the outcome.

The system which had evolved

Not only did Ambedkar himself not claim authorship of the draft, he did not even claim any great degree of originality for the draft which emerged from these iterations and

---

2 Badr-ud-din Tyabji, *Memoirs of an Egotist,* Vol. I, 1907 to 1956, Roli Books, New Delhi, pp. 172–73.

which he formally tabled. Quite the contrary, he scoffed at those who were looking for originality in the document. Addressing the Assembly on 4 November 1948, while placing the *Draft Constitution* in the Assembly for its consideration, Ambedkar said:

> It is said that there is nothing new in the *Draft Constitution*, that about half of it has been copied from the Government of India Act of 1935 and that the rest of it has been borrowed from the Constitutions of other countries. Very little of it can claim originality. One likes to ask whether there can be anything new in a Constitution framed at this hour in the history of the world. More than a hundred years have rolled over when the first written Constitution was drafted. It has been followed by many countries reducing their Constitutions to writing. What the scope of a Constitution should be has long been settled. Similarly, what should be the fundamentals of a Constitution are recognized all over the world. Given these facts, all Constitutions in their main provisions must look similar. The only new things, if there can be any, in a Constitution framed so late in the day are the variations made to remove the faults and to accommodate it to the needs of the country...

'As to the accusation that the *Draft Constitution* has (re) produced a good part of the provisions of the Government of India Act, 1935,' Ambedkar continued, 'I make no apologies. There is nothing to be ashamed of in borrowing. It involves no plagiarism. Nobody holds any patent rights in the fundamental ideas of a Constitution...'[3]

That this was the position was known to one and all. In the margin of each draft article Sir B.N. Rau had indicated the provisions of other Constitutions on which it was based. As we have seen, provisions of other Constitutions, the judgments of courts in those countries in regard to those provisions, were frequently referred to in the discussions of

3 *Constituent Assembly Debates*, Vol. VII, pp. 37–38.

the committees and the Assembly itself. Often the decision itself would be framed in terms of a reference to the corresponding provision of some foreign Constitution: yes, rights would be divided into justiciable and non-justiciable rights as in the Irish Constitution; 'Sir Alladi Krishnaswami Ayyar proposed a clause,' read the minutes of the meeting of the Subcommittee on Fundamental Rights held on 27 March 1947, 'as in section 44, sub-section 6 of the Irish Constitution, but excluding educational institutions. The insertion of such a clause was accepted.'[4] '*Clause 2:* The Committee decided that paragraph (b) of the proviso to sub-clause (1) of this clause should be re-drafted on the lines of the provisions of impeachment in the Irish Constitution and that sub-clause (2) of this clause should be omitted,' read the minutes of the meeting the Union Constitution Committee held on 30 June 1947...[5] On occasion this borrowing invited sharp responses from even senior members of the Committees: '.... We seem to have proceeded on the basis of what I call the doctrine of the 'the worst precedents', sedulously searched the constitutions of countries and taken from them points whose main claim is their novelty,' Sardar Panikkar wrote in his Minute of Dissent to the Report of the Subcommittee on Fundamental Rights, 'The method of using religious property has been put down as a fundamental right...'[6] 'The idea [behind the criticism which was being voiced about a clause] is that these and similar clauses have been taken from countries which made laws at a time when they had no problems whatsoever,' Rajaji observed during the

---

4 B. Shiva Rao, *The Framing of India's Constitution, Select Documents,* Vol. II, p. 125.

5 B. Shiva Rao, *The Framing of India's Constitution, Select Documents,* Vol. II, p. 562.

6 B. Shiva Rao, *The Framing of India's Constitution, Select Documents,* Vol. II, p. 185.

meeting of the Advisory Committee. 'What is the good of our copying them?' 'May I suggest that we need not adopt laws of America as enacted at the time of slavery....,' Rajaji intervened again during the discussion and proposed that a clause be deleted, and it was deleted...[7]

The overwhelming proportion of provisions were based on the Government of India Act of 1935—and that too was natural: that Act itself built on successive laws under which India had been governed for a hundred years; the administrative structure of the country had grown around these laws, even in combating those laws and provisions it is to that structure which our leaders had grown accustomed, which they had in a sense mastered.

Ambedkar, who had all along been with the British while the rest were fighting to free the country from them, seems actually to have felt a sense of vindication in the fact that, all said and done, the nationalist leaders, who used to rail against the British, in the end had to adopt more or less the system which the British had devised. Recall that Ambedkar formally presented the draft to the Assembly on 21 February 1948. On 28 April that year Ambedkar was the chief guest at a dinner at the Delhi Gymkhana Club. In a starry-eyed account, Alan Campbell-Johnson, the press attache of Lord Mountbatten, recorded in his diary for that day:

> Fay and I dined tonight amid fairy-lights on the lawn of the Delhi Gymkhana Club... The principal guest was Dr. Ambedkar, the Minister of Law, the leader of the untouchables, and a colourful personality in Indian politics over the past twenty years. He is now one of the principal figures associated with the preparation of India's new Constitution, which finally removes the stigma of untouchability from the statute book. As part of his emancipation,

---

7 B. Shiva Rao, *The Framing of India's Constitution, Select Documents,* Vol. II, pp. 240, 255.

> Ambedkar, himself an untouchable, has only recently married a lady doctor who is a Brahmin... Ambedkar himself was in an expansive vein, and gave us a revealing analysis of some of the features of the new Constitution... As evidence of the enduring quality of the 1935 Act, he said that some two hundred and fifty of its clauses had been embodied as they stood into the new Constitution.[8]

On that count, not half but almost four-fifths of the Constitution was from the 1935 Act—for the draft as submitted by the Drafting Committee had 315 Articles.

Nor was it just that by then there had been a history of two hundred years of Constitution making and it was but natural that the framers should seek to build on it. Nor just that the Government of India Act, 1935, had in a sense brought to a culmination the various steps towards constitutional change which had been enacted by the British in response to the situation in India. The system as a whole had got interwoven with our history and governance. K.T. Shah had moved amendments designed to institute a presidential form of governance for the country. After mentioning some of the drawbacks which experience had shown up in that form, Munshi told the Assembly:

> We must not forget that during the last 100 years the Indian public has largely drawn on the traditions of the British Constitutional Law. Most of us, and during the last several generations before us, public men in India, have looked up to the British model as the best. For the last thirty or forty years, some kind of responsibility has been introduced in the governance of this country. Our constitutional traditions have become parliamentary and we have now all our provinces functioning more or less on the British model. As a matter of fact, today the Dominion Government of India is functioning as a full-fledged Parliamentary Government. After this experience why should we go back upon the tradition

---

8 Alan Campbell-Johnson, *Mission With Mountbatten*, 1951, Hamish Hamilton, London, 1985, p. 319.

> that has been built up for over 100 years, and try a novel experiment which was... framed 150 years ago and which has been found wanting even in America? I, therefore, submit that from this point of view that the whole scheme put forward by the various amendments of Professor Shah has not been accepted by the House so far, has not yielded the best possible result elsewhere and is against the tradition which has been built up in India...[9]

During the final debate several members criticized the document which they had assembled to approve on the same ground.[10] Some members alluded to what they

---

9 *Constituent Assembly Debates,* Vol. VII, pp. 984–85.

10 Lakshminarayan Sahu of Orissa declared that the Constitution had 'become a queer and unwholesome amalgam on account of the various provisions which it has borrowed from the Government of India Act and the other constitutions of the world, things that cannot be compounded to form a harmonious whole,' that it had become 'an unnatural product... which under constant changes has almost become shapeless and ludicrous'; Ramnarayan Singh of Bihar declared that in the future people unfamiliar with the way the Constitution was put together 'would say that it was framed not at Delhi but at London,' that it appears to be 'a curious admixture.... "a fantastic mixture of the various constitutions obtaining in the world"'; T. Prakasam, the Andhra Kesari, was as scathing: it is a great document, he said in mock tribute, and Dr. Ambedkar is a great lawyer, a very able man, 'he has shown by the work he has done here, how he would be competent to be a King's Counsel of Great Britain, to be perhaps competent to sit on the Woolsack only; but this is not a Constitution which we, the people of this country wanted... Therefore this Constitution started on the basis of the English Constitution. The Act of 1935 became the basis of this Constitution. We embodied many provisions bodily as it were. They are not of a very extraordinary character, they are not new inventions for the first time by Great Britain. Why should we have been ready to say that we adopt this Constitution of Great Britain of 1935?' Having drawn attention to some of the principles which had underlain governance in ancient India Dr. Raghu Vira remarked, 'But I do not find any such thing in this Constitution,' and he asked, '... if Sir B.N. Rau our Constitutional Adviser could go to Ireland, Switzerland or America to find out how the people of those countries are running their governmental system, could you not find a single person in this who was well read in the political lore of this country who could have told you that this country also has something to contribute, that there was a political

thought was the reason for this patching together of provisions from foreign constitutions, a reason which could not but have cut Ambedkar to the quick. 'When I look into the list of members of the Drafting Committee, and see their names, I must say many of them are very respected names,' K. Hanumanthaiya began. 'Many of them are very able men. But only some of them were in sympathy with the Freedom Movement. Most of them, if I scrutinize the names of members of the Drafting Committee, I find were the people who were not with the Freedom Movement in the sense in which many of our leaders were. They naturally brought their outlook and knowledge of things into the Constitution-making. That was not the kind of psychology or knowledge that the Congress, for instance, or the country needed. I

---

philosophy in this country which had permeated the entire being of the people of this country and which could be used beneficially in preparing a Constitution for India?...' Hukum Singh of Punjab flayed the document on the same ground saying, 'In this Constitution no particular pattern has been followed. A Constitution moulded out of different types will not endure, because it is neither indigenous nor a complete copy of any other single type... It is an enigmatic production, with every part stranger to the other. The English make of Indian frame was already there as the Government of India Act, 1935. We have substituted an American head in the form of a President, replaced the old limbs by an English parliamentary system, poured Australian flexibility in bones and flesh, infused Canadian look of a single Judiciary and added an Irish appendix of Directive Principles and thus brought out a hybrid which we have been pleased to call the Indian Constitution...' Loknath Mishra was as stern: 'I... submit that this Constitution has been framed to please as many as possible but it has been a medley of ideas and ideologies and I think there is no coherent, genuine substance behind it which can hold us on. The reason is simply this. We have been so much imbued with modern ideas—ideas with which we have been spoon-fed for years, that we have forgotten ourselves. Is there nothing genuine in this land which could be a solid foundation for our future Constitution? If you want to go in for a civilization which has not been tested in our land, and which is still on its trial—I think we are going to undo everything real and I do not know what the future will bring us to...' *Constituent Assembly Debates*, Vol. X, pp. 613–14, 639, 696–98, 713, 749, 799.

submit with all humility, they were no doubt very learned in the several laws and rules that were framed before we got our Independence. They were very well versed in case law and code law. But that was not sufficient for hammering out a Constitution for a great country like India and its future...'[11] 'Sir,' B. Das of Orissa said, 'the feeling that has been left in my mind all the time, though the Drafting Committee worked very hard to bring this Constitution to this finish, was that it was a pity that the Constitution did not reflect the spirit of the Congress. How it happened that the Drafting Committee had its majority in non-Congressmen it is not for me to analyze at present, but that feeling persisted in my heart all the time, and I think many of my comrades here will agree with me, that the spirit of the Congress is lacking in this Constitution...'[12]

The criticism was unwarranted. No Constitution is made in a vacuum, ours certainly was not being made in a vacuum. Munshi had been right when, as we have seen, he had emphasized in response to amendments advocating a presidential form of government, that the country had got accustomed to a particular system of governance over the preceding hundred years, and it was natural that the makers of this Constitution should seek to build on it. Others made the same point during the closing sessions in the face of the attack by T. Prakasam and others.[13] Moreover, even where a

---

11 *Constituent Assembly Debates,* Vol. X, p. 616.

12 *Constituent Assembly Debates,* Vol. X, p. 635.

13 N.V. Gadgil said, 'After all, Sir, every Constitution represents the accumulated wisdom of the past and also embodies some elements of experiment in the constitutional sphere. It was not possible.... to write on a clean slate. In the course of the last hundred and fifty years, and more particularly in the course of the last forty years, this country has been accustomed to certain political institutions, and it was not possible to depart violently or substantially from the political trends and tendencies already present in this country...' P.S. Deshmukh picked up this very feature as being one of the strengths of the document: 'One great merit of

provision was borrowed from or had been presaged by some provision in some other Constitution, a host of persons had deliberated long and hard over its suitability to the requirements of India. And the point Ambedkar had made while introducing the draft was a valid one: as written Constitutions were by then being made for two hundred years it was very difficult to conjure up something which had not been envisaged by someone somewhere earlier. So I am not on the criticism which T. Prakasam and others levelled at the Constitution, I am on the limited point of originality: this being the case, persons who had gathered to approve the document having themselves felt misgivings about it having been just cobbled together from bits and pieces picked up from foreign Constitutions, Ambedkar himself having maintained that the overwhelming part of the Constitution had been taken from the 1935 Act, Ambedkar himself not only having disclaimed any originality for the document but maintained that such originality was not even possible that late in the evolution of written Constitutions, to make out, as has become the practice, almost a religious practice in India that the Constitution sprang whole and virginal from the mind of Ambedkar is wholly misconceived.

Congress leadership

One determinant therefore was the heritage of the immediate past. The other, more immediate determinant was the

---

this Constitution I consider,' he said, 'is that the people of this country are not going to have a Constitution very much different from what they are familiar with during the last ten or twelve years. With the exception of responsibility at the Centre it is essentially the Act of 1935. I do not mean this, for the moment at any rate, as a sort of condemnation. I am prepared to regard it as a merit and not a demerit, because the people will not have difficulty in understanding the Constitution...' *Constituent Assembly Debates*, Vol. X, pp. 657–58, 776.

leadership of the Congress, in particular Panditji, Sardar Patel and Dr Rajendra Prasad. The Congress members of the Assembly in general, and the leaders in particular would discuss and settle the matter before the formal meetings. Ambedkar was therefore being truthful when he told the Rajya Sabha that he had carried out decisions of others. During the final sessions several members had spoken to the same effect. Saying that the Constitution was a compromise and 'has all the defects of a compromise', and how it would have been so much better if the draft had been considered by committees, Shiban Lal Saksena told the Assembly:

> Under the procedure adopted, the Drafting Committee could not get the advantage of the free opinion of the whole House and decisions of the Congress Party alone became binding upon it. I personally feel that the Constitution has very much suffered on this account. Out of about 10,000 amendments which appeared on the Order Paper from time to time during the course of the last one year, I think this House had opportunity for discussing hardly a few hundreds. The rest were all guillotined inside the Congress Party and were not moved in this House because the Party did not accept them. Congress Party meetings became meetings of the real Constituent Assembly, and this real Assembly became the mock Assembly where decisions arrived at the Congress party meetings were registered...'[14]

K. Santhanam took the opposite view of the result of prior scrutiny by the Congress, but the fact he testified to was the same. He told the Assembly:

> Finally, the work of the Drafting Committee is, to my mind, beyond all praise. Especially during the last few months they have been so hurried, so much pressed for time that it is remarkable how they did their work. I should also mention that it was not only on the open floor of the House that the Constitution has been

---

14 *Constituent Assembly Debates,* Vol. XI, p. 705.

> scrutinized, but much more severely during the Congress Party meetings. I do not want to mention names, but a group of people in the Party took the greatest pains to scrutinize every clause and every Article and a great deal of improvement was made during those meetings. But for their scrutiny the Constitution would not have been as good as it is...[15]

Mohammed Saa'dulla, a member of the Drafting Committee, responding to the encomiums which were being showered on the Drafting Committee, said, 'Sir, the Drafting Committee was not a free agency. They were handicapped by various methods and circumstances from the very start...' We were merely to dress up the Objectives Resolution, he said, and then there was this House, he said, asking 'How dare any member of the Drafting Committee be so arrogant as to thrust the opinion of seven members against a total number of 308 in this House?' And then there had been the environment, he said, and continued:

> Sir, I remember that many sections of our *Draft Constitution* had to be recast as many as seven times. A draft section is prepared according to the best in each of the members of the Drafting Committee. It is scrutinized by the particular ministerial department of Government. They criticize it and a fresh draft is made to meet their criticisms or requirements. Then it is considered by the biggest bloc, the majority party in the House—I refer to the Congress Parliamentary Party, who alone can give the *imprimatur* of adoption in the House: and sometimes we found that they made their own recommendations which had to be put into proper legal and constitutional shape by the members of the Drafting Committee...[16]

Some members saw in this a reason to lessen their responsibility for the document which they could not bring

15 *Constituent Assembly Debates,* Vol. XI, p. 720.

16 *Constituent Assembly Debates,* Vol. XI, p. 733.

themselves to support fully: declaring that constant changes had left the Constitution 'almost... shapeless and ludicrous', Lakshminarayan Sahu exclaimed, 'I know fully well and I believe that he [Ambedkar] is likely to say in reply that it is not entirely his handiwork. He had to frame the Constitution in accordance with the wishes of the majority party in the country...'; Mahboob Ali Baig thanked Ambedkar warmly saying that he had been the anchor and support of those 'who did not belong to the dominant party which decided questions outside the House beforehand, either confirming or modifying the views of the Drafting Committee—and as it were acted as the final arbiter...', he declared Ambedkar's mastery over constitutional issues to have been 'marvelous, unique, singular and complete', and yet the document was not one that he, Baig, could wholeheartedly endorse for, he told the president, 'But, Sir, unlike you, he [Ambedkar] was not a free agent. So the evils or the defects in the Constitution as it is placed before us today are inherent in the situation in which he was placed and he cannot therefore be personally responsible for them...'[17]

Ambedkar himself was more forthcoming than his followers would find to their taste today. In his closing address to the Assembly he alluded to this all-important role of the Congress—in words which were very different in tone and content from the ones he was to use just a few years later in the Rajya Sabha. Recounting his experience and work in the making of the Constitution he said:

> The task of the Drafting Committee would have been a very difficult one if this Constituent Assembly had been merely a motley crowd, a tessellated pavement without cement, a black stone here and a white stone there in which each member or each group was a law unto itself. There would have been nothing but chaos. This possibility of chaos was reduced to nil by the existence of the

17 *Constituent Assembly Debates*, Vol. XI, p. 742.

> Congress Party inside the Assembly which brought into its proceedings a sense of order and discipline. It is because of the discipline of the Congress Party that the Drafting Committee was able to pilot the Constitution in the Assembly with the sure knowledge as to the fate of each Article and each amendment. The Congress Party is, therefore, entitled to all the credit for the smooth sailing of the *Draft Constitution* in the Assembly.[18]

Now, Ambedkar was not in the inner circle of the Congress which decided the course that articles and amendments were to take, he was not even in the Congress. For long he had been abusing the Congress, and while the Congress leaders had made it a point to induct persons like him into the task of drawing up the Constitution, some of the decades-old wariness must have persisted. The wariness could not but have been sharpened by the flashes of impatience and arrogance that Ambedkar was given to, flashes that on occasion caused offence on the floor of the Assembly to several members and led them to formally protest to the chair.

Thus, on the one hand Ambedkar was not in the inner councils of the Congress, on the other he is here himself telling us how things were decided and how that ensured their smooth passage through the Assembly. But he is the author of the Constitution, and if you don't believe that you are a Manuwadi!

---

18 *Constituent Assembly Debates,* Vol. XI, p. 974.

17

The myth fostered, driven in

Consider a self-evident point. In the proceedings of the Assembly Ambedkar is moving one amendment after another. If he is the one who had written the Constitution, if he is the one who was deciding what it ought to be, how come he was moving all these amendments to what he had himself written? What happened will be obvious; by now the drafts of the Constitution—three in all, the first one by Sir B.N. Rau and then two of the Drafting Committee—were available to members. The third one was circulated all over the country also; comments and suggestions poured in from all quarters; several members wrote to indicate that they would be suggesting amendments—over 7,600 amendments were actually proposed; the constitutional adviser, the key leaders of the Congress, the Drafting Committee and the Special Committee considered these, and came to a view about which of them should be accepted; amendments to the *Draft Constitution* were accordingly prepared; as Ambedkar was the head of the Drafting Committee, these amendments were tabled in his name. That they were tabled in his name or that he formally moved them in the Assembly does not in any sense mean that he authored them, any more than the fact that he moved the original motion that the Assembly take up the *Draft Constitution* for consideration had meant that he had authored that draft. The punctilious Naziruddin Ahmad who was always intervening to correct the punctuation and syntax of the drafts of the articles was again on his feet, even though this was the very last session, a sort of valedictory session, with another amendment about altering an article so as to make it clearer. K. Santhanam interjected to remark that an amendment to that effect had already been proposed—by the Drafting Committee. Naziruddin said in retort:

> The difficulty with these amendments is that most of these amendments have been taken from the amendments of Members. I am of course interested in the correction, but there has been wholesale 'lifting' of amendments of Members and their being passed on as those of the Drafting Committee. I do not grudge them this distinction. This is not the first time this has happened. I have been hinting it all through the second reading stage. They will not openly accept our amendments, but move them as their own.

The president intervened with the softness and skill for which he came to be so loved, 'I do not think the Drafting Committee will grudge any credit to other Members for their amendments.'[1] Such was the position. But this is how the Ambedkar volumes published by the Maharashtra government refer to the question of amendments:

> The discussion on the Articles of the Draft Constitution commenced on 15th November 1948.
>
> *The amendments adopted by the House were those which Dr. Ambedkar had accepted.* These amendments are incorporated here.
>
> *Some of the amendments were not accepted by Dr. Ambedkar initially,* but no detailed explanations were furnished. Some of these amendments are mentioned. But later, during the discussion on each Article, Dr. Ambedkar explained elaborately why he

1 *Constituent Assembly Debates,* Vol. XI, p. 475.

> accepted particular amendments and why the others were not accepted....[2]

In a word, Ambedkar wrote the Constitution. He then sat as a Supreme Court and decided which amendments to accept and which to reject. And that is how we got the Constitution as we have it!

Ambedkar and others on the sequence

Amendments apart, the sequence which the provisions went through was specifically recalled time and again, it was recalled by Ambedkar, by the president, by other participants like K.M. Munshi. And yet the myth.

Here is Ambedkar explaining the sequence as he moves the motion requesting the Assembly to take up the *Draft Constitution* for consideration:

> The Drafting Committee was appointed by a Resolution passed by the Constituent Assembly on August 29, 1947.
>
> The Drafting Committee was in effect charged with *the duty of preparing a Constitution in accordance with the decisions of the Constituent Assembly on the reports prepared by the various Committees appointed by it* such as the Union Powers Committee, the Union Constitution Committee, the Provincial Constitution Committee and the Advisory Committee on Fundamental Rights, Minorities, Tribal Areas, etc. *The Constituent Assembly had also directed that in certain matters the provisions contained in the Government of India Act, 1935, should be followed.* Except in points which are referred to in my letter of the 21st February, 1948, in which I have referred to the departures made and alternatives suggested by the Drafting Committee, I hope the Drafting Committee will be found to have faithfully carried out the directions given to it.[3]

---

2 *Dr. Babasaheb Ambedkar, Writings and Speeches,* Vol. XIII, p. 325.

3 *Constituent Assembly Debates,* Vol. VII, p. 31.

Here is Dr Rajendra Prasad in his final and concluding address recalling the steps which the Constitution that the House was about to adopt had passed:

> The method which the Constituent Assembly adopted in connection with the Constitution was first to lay down its 'terms of reference' as it were in the form of an Objectives Resolution which was moved by Pandit Jawaharlal Nehru in an inspiring speech and which constitutes now the Preamble to our Constitution. It then proceeded to appoint a number of Committees to deal with different aspects of the constitutional problem. Dr. Ambedkar mentioned the names of these Committees. Several of these had as their Chairman either Pandit Nehru or Sardar Patel to whom thus goes the credit for the fundamentals of our Constitution. I have only to add that they worked in a business-like manner and produced reports which were considered by the Assembly and their recommendations were adopted as the basis on which the Draft of the Constitution had to be prepared. This was done by Mr. B.N. Rau, who brought to bear on his task a detailed knowledge of Constitutions of other countries and an extensive knowledge of the conditions of this country as well as his own administrative experience. The Assembly then appointed the Drafting Committee which worked on the original *Draft* prepared by Mr. B.N. Rau and produced the *Draft Constitution* which was considered by the Assembly at great length at the second reading stage. As Dr. Ambedkar pointed out, there were not less than 7,635 amendments of which 2,473 were moved. I am mentioning this only to show that it was not only the members of the Drafting Committee who were giving their close attention to the Constitution, but other members were vigilant and scrutinizing the Draft in all its details. No wonder that we had to consider not only each Article in the Draft, but practically every sentence and sometimes, every word in each Article... In the result the *Draft Constitution* has increased in size, and by the time it has been passed, it has come to have 395 Articles and 8 Schedules, instead of the 243 Articles and 13 Schedules of the original *Draft of Mr* B.N. Rau...[4]

---

4 *Constituent Assembly Debates,* Vol. XI, pp. 986–87.

And here is K.M. Munshi in a retrospective essay explaining the sequence:

> The composition of the Constituent Assembly as also the atmosphere in which the problems were discussed lent themselves to a broad anti-authoritarian outlook. Most of the members of the Constituent Assembly had been fighters for Freedom and lovers of a free democracy. There was complete freedom of discussion for members; and in Dr. Rajendra Prasad we had a President who gave ample opportunity for presenting different points of view. The whip was seldom applied and when applied, more often than not, permission, if sought, was granted to express one's own views.
>
> We had several stages in which the constitutional provisions were discussed. First, we had the Committees which submitted their reports, followed by discussions thereon in the Assembly. Then we had detailed discussion in the Party meeting, followed by a second reading of the draft, clause by clause. Later, the Drafting Committee discussed and revised each clause; then the Congress Party went over each clause, sometimes every word. Lastly, there was the open discussion of the final draft in the Constituent Assembly.
>
> The Chief Ministers of the States who were members of the Constituent Assembly contributed their experience. On occasion, the departments of the Central Government and the States submitted elaborate notes. There was always the encyclopedic knowledge of Sir B.N. Rau at the service of the Assembly. Above all, were Pandit Jawaharlal Nehru's vision of a sovereign democratic India and Sardar Patel's instinctive perception of the sources from which power and stability sprang...[5]

Here then are unambiguous statements of the participants themselves about the steps through which the Constitution passed. The minutes and reports of the committees and subcommittees as well as all the related papers have been lying in the public domain for thirty years, published in four

---

5 K.M. Munshi, 'Sources of the Constitution', in Madan Gopal Gupta, *Aspects of the Indian Constitution,* Central Book Depot, Allahabad, 1956, pp. 75–76.

large volumes of documents covering over 3,300 pages. The debates of the Constituent Assembly have of course been in the public domain for over forty years—they have been published verbatim in twelve volumes. In addition the entire sequence has been most faithfully summarized by a team of scholars headed by B. Shiva Rao, and this recounting has been available for thirty years. And yet the myth, 'Ambedkar wrote the Constitution!'

Four factors

That the myth has come into being and is by now taken as a fact is a tribute first of all to the power of illiteracy in India. You just have to put out a slogan, there is a stampede behind it and it comes to be taken as one of those 'truths that we hold self-evident'. No one looks up anything. Most have not heard anything beyond the assertion that Ambedkar wrote the Constitution, a 'fact' which by now has sunk into their visual cortex because at every turn they see statues of Ambedkar holding the Constitution. The more knowledgeable have heard a bit more. 'But was he not the chairman of the Drafting Committee?,' they ask, as proof of the belief they have internalized. But they never ask, they have never bothered to look up what this so-called 'Drafting Committee' was set up to do.

There is another factor which has fostered the myth. It has become the custom in India to produce even records in partial form. When a book is written on Pandit Nehru, it makes out as if every basic idea as well as a large number of the detailed provisions sprang from his head. When a book is compiled on Dr Rajendra Prasad, it reproduces only those parts of the Constituent Assembly Debates in which he figures, in particular in which members are lauding him for the guidance he has given, the sagacious manner in which he has steered the proceedings. Reading that selection one is led to believe that he was the fulcrum. In the case of Ambedkar of course this method of writing history has been taken to extremes. Not only are only those passages reproduced in which he alone is speaking in the Assembly—and his habit of speaking in the singular, '*I* am afraid, *I* cannot accept that amendment...' helps to spread the myth—from among the speeches of the last session in which everyone was thanking everyone for the contributions he had made, only those portions of the passages in which the member is complimenting Ambedkar are reproduced, and even the adjacent words in which the same member is acknowledging the role of others and thanking them are omitted!

Hagiographers of Ambedkar will recall that in his closing address to the Assembly, the President, Dr Rajendra Prasad, said of Ambedkar and his contribution, 'We could never make a decision which was or could be so right as when we put him on the Drafting Committee and made him its Chairman. He has not only justified his selection but has added lustre to the work which he has done.'[6] That is entirely true, and we can be certain that Dr Rajendra Prasad sincerely meant what he was saying. But the full passage is as follows:

> Before I close I must express my thanks to all the Members of this august Assembly from whom I have received not only courtesy but, if I may say so, also their respect and affection. Sitting in the Chair and watching the proceedings from day to day, I have realized as nobody else could have, with what zeal and devotion the members of the Drafting Committee and especially its Chairman, Dr. Ambedkar, in spite of his indifferent health, have worked. (*Cheers*) We could never make a decision which was or could be so right as when we put him on the Drafting Committee and made him its Chairman. He has not only justified his selection

6 For instance, Dhananjay Keer, *Dr. Ambedkar, Life and Mission,* Popular Prakashan, 1990, pp. 415–16.

but has added lustre to the work which he has done. In this connection it would be invidious to make any distinction as among the other members of the Committee. I know they have all worked with the same zeal and devotion as its Chairman, and they deserve the thanks of the country.

I must convey, if you will permit me, my own thanks as well as the thanks of the House to our Constitutional Adviser, Sir B.N. Rau, who worked honorarily all the time he was here, assisting the Assembly not only with his knowledge and erudition but also enabled the other Members to perform their duties with thoroughness and intelligence by supplying them with the material on which they could work. In this he was assisted by his band of research workers and other members of the staff who worked with zeal and devotion. Tribute has been paid justly to Shri S. N. Mukherjee who has proved of such invaluable help to the Drafting Committee...[7]

The volume in the official collection of the writings and speeches of Ambedkar published by the Maharashtra government which includes the *Draft Constitution* among his writings tells us, 'His colleagues in the Constituent Assembly bestowed on him generous praise and candid approval of his role as the principle [*sic*] architect of our Constitution, and perhaps, Dr. Pattabhi Sitaramayya summed up the sentiments of the Constituent Assembly when he said, "What a steam-roller intellect he brought to bear upon this magnificent task: irresistible, indomitable, unconquerable, leveling down tall palms and short poppies; whatever he felt to be right he stood by, regardless of consequences."'[8] But the full passage is as follows:

When all is said and done, we must realize how much we owe to the half a dozen men that have fashioned this Constitution and given it a shape and form. Our friend, Dr. Ambedkar has gone away, else I should have liked to tell him what a steam-roller

7 *Constituent Assembly Debates,* Vol. XI, pp. 994–95.

8 *Dr. Babasaheb Ambedkar, Writings and Speeches,* Vol. XIII, p. xi.

intellect he brought to bear upon this magnificent task: irresistible, indomitable, unconquerable, leveling down tall palms and short poppies; whatever he felt to be right he stood by, regardless of consequences.

Then there was Sir Alladi, with his oceanic depths of learning, and a whole knowledge of the Constitutional Law of the world on his finger tips. He has made great contributions towards the drawing up of this Constitution. He only has to perfect it all by writing a commentary on it. That was the latest request of Mr. Santhanam and I hope he will fulfill it.

Then we have Mr. Gopalaswami Ayyangar: coy as a maiden and unobtrusive, but rising to the full heights of the necessities of the occasion, combining always the real with the ideal, and bringing a soft and kindly judgement on to a severe issue.

Next you have Mr. Munshi, the like of him we cannot see for his resiliency and receptivity; his wide and varied knowledge, his sharp intellect and ready resourcefulness have been a tremendous aid to us.

Mr. Madhava Rao is not here now. He was a Diwan of Mysore. He had laboured hard in our Committee. He had vast experience from that of an Assistant Commissioner, Mysore, when I was still in my medical studies, until he became Diwan. He too has done his good bit in this work.

Then there is a man, who is almost unnoticed, and whose name has not been mentioned by any of my friends, to whom I would like to refer, the sweet and subdued Sa'adulla, who has brought a rich experience to bear upon the deliberations of this House.

Finally, comes the slim, tall man who sits opposite to me, with his ready and rapier thrusts of repartee and rejoinder, whose (sharp-pointed) intellect always punctures or lacerates the opposition. But he is always able to cover up the injury with his plastic surgery and recuperative powers: and that is Mr. T.T. Krishnamachari.

We have all had the help of these people, but, Sir, the work of all these friends would have been of no use but for the sweetness, the gentleness with which you have turned towards a person when you wanted him to stop in his further speaking: the patience with which you have waited in order to catch his eye—not he to catch your eye—and the very gentle manner in which you have cast the hint that he should now wind up; and when some of us were

> rebellious, disorderly and chaotic, you simply smiled in order to choke this attitude.
>
> It is a great thing I tell you that we have achieved. It is not right to underestimate what we have achieved. Much has been done behind the curtains and but for the discipline and drilling of the majority party in this House, these deliberations would not have come to this happy end...[9]

The remarks of the other members of the Assembly had followed the same pattern—they had been fulsome in expressing their appreciation of the work of Ambedkar, at the same time they had been as grateful and fulsome in acknowledging the contribution of B.N. Rau, S.N. Mukherjee and others. Moreover, at least at that moment, Ambedkar was more generous than his followers are today. This is how he responded to the compliments which had been paid to him and other members of the Drafting Committee:

> As to the compliments which have been showered upon me both by members of the Assembly as well as by my colleagues of the Drafting Committee, I feel so overwhelmed that I cannot find adequate words to express fully my gratitude to them. I came into the Constituent Assembly with no greater aspiration than to safeguard the interests of the Scheduled Castes. I had not the remotest idea that I would be called upon to undertake more responsible functions. I was therefore greatly surprised when the Assembly elected me to the Drafting Committee. I was more than surprised when the Drafting Committee elected me to be its Chairman. There were in the Drafting Committee men bigger, better and more competent than myself such as my friend Sir Alladi Krishnaswami Ayyar. I am grateful to the Constituent Assembly for reposing in me so much trust and confidence and to have chosen me as their instrument and given me this opportunity of serving the country.
>
> The credit that is given to me does not really belong to me. It belongs partly to Sir B.N. Rau, the Constitutional Adviser to the

---

9 *Constituent Assembly Debates,* Vol. XI, pp. 946–47.

> Constituent Assembly who prepared a rough draft of the Constitution for the consideration of the Drafting Committee. A part of the credit must go to the members of the Drafting Committee who, as I have said, have sat for 141 days and without whose ingenuity to devise new formulae and capacity to tolerate and accommodate different points of view, the task of framing the Constitution could not have come to a successful conclusion. Much greater share of the credit must go to Mr. S.N. Mukherjee, the Chief Draftsman of the Constitution. His ability to put the most intricate proposals in the simplest and clearest legal form can rarely be equaled, nor his capacity for hard work. Without his help, this Assembly would have taken many more years to finalize the Constitution. I must not omit to mention members of the staff working under Mr. Mukherjee. For I know how hard they have worked and how long they have toiled sometimes even beyond midnight. I want to thank them all for their cooperation.[10]

But remarks such as these are put by his hagiographers to his large-heartedness, while the remarks of other members about the contribution of Ambedkar are cited as the acknowledgement of truth!

But even these factors—not looking up the record, selective quotations, etc., do not explain the extent to which the myth has spread, and why it has been left unexamined. The real explanations are different. And they are all around us.

As politicians have set out to garner votes through casteist politics and propaganda, they have needed to make an icon of Ambedkar, and so virtues and achievements have been pasted on to him, among them the Constitution.

And the myth has gone unquestioned because of the verbal terrorism, and physical intimidation of those who have set themselves up in this kind of politics.

---

10 *Constituent Assembly Debates,* Vol. X, pp. 973–74.

It was a fine hour

The period between December 1946 when the Constituent Assembly began its work and November 1949 when it adopted the completed Constitution was one of the most turbulent periods in our history. Each person was busy in his allotted task, in particular Panditji and the Sardar had not a moment to spare. Given his close association with the British, given the humiliating defeats which his party had suffered in the 1946 elections, Ambedkar had not expected that he would be called upon to play any significant part in the coming years. But the Congress leaders, prodded no doubt by Gandhiji's large-heartedness, had decided to put the past behind them. As Ambedkar was to say later, when he resigned from Panditji's Cabinet, he was surprised to be invited to join it as the minister for law. Lord Mountbatten too recorded his surprise when he received the names of the new ministers from the prime minister. Ambedkar, as he told the Constituent Assembly in his concluding address, was doubly surprised when he was made the chairman of the Drafting Committee.

He worked diligently, readily abandoning positions he had asserted for two decades. He did a fine job of piloting the clauses which had been settled. Members were full of praise for his contribution. The praise was well merited.

And the fact that he who had opposed the Congress tooth and nail, who had hurled abuse and scorn and misrepresentations at them had been co-opted for the task had the kind of salutary effects which Gandhiji would certainly have anticipated. The Scheduled Caste members of the Constituent Assembly in particular felt proud that one of their own had been given such an important task, they felt proud that he had discharged it with such devotion and skill. After thanking the president for the magnanimous way in which he had conducted the proceedings, V.I. Muniswamy Pillay from Madras told the Assembly:

Sir, as one of the signatories of the epoch-making Poona Pact, you will be happy today that we have opened a new chapter in the history of India by giving equal opportunities to all classes and sections of the people who inhabit India. Sir, Mahatma Gandhi laid the seed for the amelioration of the Depressed Classes and that took shape in a formidable way and today we find ourselves in the company of men who have thought it necessary to afford facilities for the common man in our great country.

Sir, I now proceed to appreciate the great services that have been rendered by the Drafting Committee whose services are so valuable to us; they have not spared days and nights in coming to decisions on important Articles. I must say a word of praise to the calibre and capacity of the Chairman of the Drafting Committee—Dr. B.R. Ambedkar. (*Loud cheers.*) Coming as I do from a community that has produced Dr. Ambedkar, I feel proud that his capacity has now been recognized, not only by the Harijans but by all communities that inhabit India. The Scheduled Castes have produced a great Nandanar a great devotee, a Tirupazanalwar a great Vaishnavite saint, and above all a Tiruvalluvar, the great philosopher whose name and fame is not only known throughout the length and breadth of India but of the whole world.

To that galaxy of great men of Harijans now we have to add Dr. Ambedkar who as a man has been able to show to the world that the Scheduled Castes are no less important but they can rise to heights and give to the world their great services. I know, Sir, that he has served the community of the Harijans and also of India by his great service and sacrifice in preparing a Constitution which will be the order of the day from 26th of January 1950 and I also feel, Sir, [the contribution] of the Chief Draftsman and of the staff that have worked in preparing the Constitution cannot be littled; they equally receive our praise...

The great thing in this Constitution, that is before the House is that the word 'minorities' has been removed. I know, as a matter of fact, it is not the desire of myself or my community to be ever called a minority or Scheduled Castes, we want to merge with the thirty crores of people in this country. But, as Mahatma Gandhi rightly said, it is the change of heart which is required. If the caste Hindus and those people who predominate in this country only show that change of heart, it will be time, Sir, that we ourselves merge into the great community of Indians and I do not want to perpetuate this seclusion forever.

In conclusion, I may, on behalf of the members of the Harijans that are present in this House and of the Harijans outside, assure you and the august Assembly and the Government that we Harijans... [K Hanumanthaiya interjected, 'Do we not represent the Harijans?'] We come under the label Harijans. On behalf of the Harijans, I may assure you and the future Government of India that the Harijans to the last man will uphold the Constitution that has been passed by the Constituent Assembly and work it to the letter and spirit.[11]

S. Nagappa, another Scheduled Caste member from Madras told the Assembly:

From the point of view of the Scheduled Classes, their point was achieved on the day on which Dr. Ambedkar was elected as Chairman of the Drafting Committee. He had been one of the stoutest champions of the cause of the Scheduled Classes. He was elected as the Chairman. Ever since he was elected, the other members of the Scheduled Classes were very reluctant to cooperate; not because they did not want to cooperate, but because they knew Dr. Ambedkar who was a champion of their cause was there to watch and provide such Articles as will be safeguarding the interests of the Scheduled Classes. Well, Sir, this has proved to what heights Dr. Ambedkar, though he is a member of the Scheduled Classes, if an opportunity was given, can rise. He has proved this by his efficiency and the able way in which he has drafted and piloted this Constitution. Now I think this stigma of inefficiency attached to the Scheduled Classes will not be attached hereafter. Only if opportunities are given, they will prove better than anybody else. Now for having played such a great part, on behalf of the Scheduled Classes I congratulate Dr. Ambedkar. It is not the strength of the Scheduled Classes that made him the President of the Drafting Committee but it is the generosity of the majority party and I am very much thankful to them for the same.[12]

---

11 *Constituent Assembly Debates,* Vol. XI, pp. 608–10.

12 *Constituent Assembly Debates,* Vol. XI, p. 754.

There had been a wariness on the other side too, and working together at such a vital national task had dispelled that. Speaking immediately after S. Nagappa, Jaspat Roy Kapoor spoke of the way perceptions had changed:

> Dr. Ambedkar and his colleagues have rightly deserved the praise which has been showered on them by almost every speaker. I had started with a prejudice against Dr. Ambedkar, for I had felt sore many years ago when Mahatma Gandhi was undergoing fast against grant of separate electorates to the Scheduled Castes and I had read in the papers the news that when he had been invited to see Mahatma Gandhi to discuss that question, he once said that for a day or two he was not free because he had to attend to some professional engagements. I felt very sorry then. I do not know how far it is correct. But even if it was so, the great work that he has done during these three years has washed away that particular sin or any other sins which he may have committed. I have developed an admiration and also affection for Dr. Ambedkar for the very useful work and the very patriotic work which he has done. His very first speech in this Assembly had dispelled all my doubts and fears in relation to him and today I can say that I consider him to be one of the best patriots of this country. I have always found him to bring upon the subject a very constructive approach. On many an occasion there seemed to be a deadlock, he came forward with suggestions which resolved those deadlocks. I always found him to rise to the occasion except, unfortunately, on one occasion and that was when he did not agree to give up reservation of seats for the Scheduled Castes. Every other minority gave up the right of reservation of seats, but unfortunately Dr. Ambedkar would not agree to it. I wish he could have also agreed to it and I could have then be in a position today to say that he rose equal to every occasion, but unfortunately I cannot say it today. Be that as it may, the great work he has done except this must be recognized in very grateful terms.
>
> I must also express my gratitude to Shri B.N. Rau, Mr. Mukherjee and his loyal lieutenants...[13]

13 *Constituent Assembly Debates,* Vol. XI, p. 758.

M. Ananthasayanam Ayyangar alluded to the reason which had brought everyone closer:

> All political interests have been represented here. Leaders of all schools of thought are here. Even Dr. Ambedkar, who merely came to watch, has taken a leading part in the framing of this Constitution and he is one of the architects of the Constitution we are now passing. The very person who came to doubt and to criticize has ultimately taken charge of this Constitution and framed it. I congratulate him and I congratulate ourselves for the goodwill shown to him and the manner in which he has reciprocated it. After all, by closer contact we can easily understand one another's viewpoint. So long as we are at a great distance, we make much of the small angularities we have. If this Constitution is worked in the spirit in which it has been framed, I am sure we will be one of the foremost nations in the world.[14]

Ambedkar, as we have seen, responded by telling the House that he was overwhelmed by the praise that had been lavished on him, that he had come into the Assembly with no greater aspiration than to safeguard the interests of the Scheduled Castes, that he had not had the remotest idea that he would be asked to undertake more important tasks, that the credit which had been given to him really belonged to others. And he said:

> Here I could have ended. But my mind is so full of the future of our country that I feel I ought to take this occasion to give expression to some of my reflections thereon. On 26th January 1950, India will be an independent country. (*Cheers.*) What would happen to her Independence? Will she maintain her Independence or will she lose it again? This is the first thought that comes to my mind. It is not that India was never an independent country. The point is that she once lost the Independence she had. Will she lose it a second time? It is this thought which makes me most anxious for the future. What perturbs me greatly is the fact

14 *Constituent Assembly Debates,* Vol. XI, p. 664.

> that not only has India once before lost her Independence, but she lost it by the infidelity and treachery of some of her own people. In the invasion of Sind by Mohammed-bin-Kasim, the military commanders of King Dahar accepted bribes from the agents of Mohammed-bin-Kasim and refused to fight on the side of their King. It was Jaichand who invited Mahommed Ghori to invade India and fight against Prithvi Raj and promised him the help of himself and the Solanki kings. When Shivaji was fighting for the liberation of the Hindus, the other Maratha noblemen and the Rajput kings were fighting the battle on the side of the Moghul Emperors. When the British were trying to destroy the Sikh Rulers, Gulab Singh, their principal commander sat silent and did not help to save the Sikh kingdom. In 1857, when a large part of India had declared a war of Independence against the British, the Sikhs stood and watched the event as silent spectators.
>
> Will history repeat itself? It is this thought which fills me with anxiety. This anxiety is deepened by the realization of the fact that in addition to our old enemies in the form of castes and creeds we are going to have many political parties with diverse and opposing political creeds. Will Indians place the country above their creed or will they place creed above country? I do not know. But this much is certain that if the parties place creed above country, our Independence will be put in jeopardy a second time and probably be lost forever. This eventuality we must all resolutely guard against. We must be determined to defend our Independence with the last drop of our blood.[15]

Cheers had greeted that exhortation.

What a transformation just three years of working with patriots had wrought. Just three years earlier—in April and May 1946—the same Ambedkar had been remonstrating with the viceroy, Lord Wavell, and writing memoranda to A.V. Alexander, a member of the British Cabinet Mission, and telling them to remember that 'British rule in India owes its very existence to the help rendered by the Untouchables. Many Britishers think that India was conquered by the Clives, Hastings,

---

15 *Constituent Assembly Debates,* Vol. XI, pp. 977–78.

Cootes and so on. Nothing can be a greater mistake. India was conquered by an army of Indians and the Indians who formed the army were all Untouchables. British rule in India would have been impossible if the Untouchables had not helped to conquer India. Take the Battle of Plassey which laid the foundation of British rule or the Battle of Kirkee which completed the conquest of India. In both these fateful battles the soldiers who fought for the British were all Untouchables...'[16]

What a change had been wrought. And as a result, Ambedkar's tenure in the Constituent Assembly was indeed a fine hour.

But it didn't last long. Soon Ambedkar's lifelong habits—bitterness, the conviction that he was the only honest and brilliant person, that everyone else was in a conspiracy to keep his worth from being recognized, that everyone *else* was to blame—were back. With them, rancour and accusation and vilification. Those who trade in his name today establish that these traits, and not the labours he put in during the years at the Constituent Assembly, are the legacies which have endured.

---

16 *Dr. Babasabeb Ambedkar, Writings and Speeches,* Vol. X, pp. 492–99.

Invention, Intimidation, Assault

18

'It is painful,' 'It is shameful,' 'It is hateful'

'It was painful to read Arun Shourie's *Is Ambedkar the Manu of our times?,'* writes a reader. After saying that the Congress leaders themselves have showered honours on Ambedkar, and that they had themselves showered him with praise for the pains that he had taken over the Constitution, the reader turns as usual to the conspiracy theory: 'Mr Shourie's column,' he says, 'seems to be part of a larger game, of changing the Constitution.' Many persons have been saying that the Constitution should be changed, several of them—like Mr B.K. Nehru, Mr N.A. Palkhivala—have put forward reasoned proposals for switching to the presidential system, for instance. How would my agreeing or disagreeing with these eminent authorities disprove any of the facts which are on record—in the form of thousands upon thousands of pages of drafts of different parts of the Constitution prepared by Sir B.N. Rau and others, of debates, of the minutes of meetings and decisions taken at them, of Ambedkar's own testimony—about the manner in which the Constitution was put together?

The reader proceeds: 'The camp to which he [that is, me] originally belongs, though was well organized, never participated in the freedom movement. Many of their members were in service of the British government, and after the departure of the Britishers started beating the drums of nationalism. The fact that such people refer to Dr Ambedkar as being "all along with the Britishers" is a mockery of truth and humanity.'

What is the camp to which I am supposed to belong—'originally' or otherwise? But more than that, even if I did belong to some camp, how would that alter the facts about Ambedkar and his opposing the national movement throughout his public carrier right up to and including 1946? How would my being or not being in some camp alter the fact that, having watched him thwart the nationalist proposals at the Round Table Conference, the highest British official dealing with India felt moved to write on 28 December 1932, 'Ambedkar had behaved very well at the Round Table Conference, and I am most anxious to strengthen his hands in every reasonable way'? How does it alter the fact that when the Congress ministries resigned in protest in 1937, Ambedkar joined Jinnah in addressing joint meetings to celebrate 'Deliverance Day'? How does it alter the fact that the Secretary of State was commending Ambedkar to the governor in Madras not just for the ability he detected but because of Ambedkar's 'manifest desire to support the British influence in India'? How does it alter the fact that when the Muslim League started demanding Pakistan formally, Ambedkar gave it his enthusiastic support, simultaneously, as we have seen, telling the viceroy, that he, Ambedkar, was 'in favour of the idea, because it meant that the British will have to stay in India'? And what happens to 'the camp to which he originally belongs' theory when such letters of the viceroy are recalled, not by me as they are in this book, but by Wali Khan, the Pakistani politician and son of Khan Abdul Ghaffar Khan—as they are in his book, *Facts Are Facts*?[1]

---

1 Wali Khan, *Facts are Facts*, Vikas, New Delhi, 1987, pp. 9 and 37.

How does my belonging to this camp or that alter the fact we have seen—namely, that Ambedkar's denunciations of Gandhiji and the Congress in the run-up to the Quit India resolution followed to the dot instructions and suggestions which the viceroy conveyed through the governor in Bombay, Roger Lumley, and which have since been published verbatim by the British as well as the Maharashtra governments? How does it alter the fact that throughout those vital years—1942 to 1946—while the nationalist leaders languished in prison, Ambedkar was such a loyal and enthusiastic minister in the Viceroy's Council? How does it alter the fact that as late as *April 1946* Ambedkar was telling the viceroy, Lord Wavell, that 'if India became independent it would be one of the greatest disasters that could happen'? That he was lobbying hard to ensure that no Constituent Assembly was constituted, telling the viceroy that Indians who were liable to be sent to the Assembly did not have 'the mental capacity' to handle constitutional questions, that instead some Britisher or American should be asked to draw up the Constitution? How does it alter the fact that he was emphatically telling the viceroy that Indians were incapable of ensuring justice—that were such an Assembly to be constituted, those members who did not belong to the Scheduled Castes would have only one aim, and that was to keep the latter down; and those members who did belong to the Scheduled Castes 'would be bought over to vote against the interests of their communities'?

All these facts, as we have seen in detail, are a part of the published record, they were well known fifty years ago—for Ambedkar had never made any secret of whose side he was on. We have seen what happened in the end. The British nonetheless announced that a Constituent Assembly would be constituted. Elections were scheduled. Ambedkar met the British parliamentary delegation, and repeated the same refrain—the Scheduled Castes were the ones which had helped the British conquer India, he reminded them, Independence to India would be a disaster and so on. Lord Pethick-Lawrence gently remonstrated: but we are leaving in any case, he told Ambedkar, wouldn't the interests of the Scheduled Castes be better served if you were to now deal with the Congress leaders rather than putting these points to us...

'Immediately after this interview with the British delegation,' writes his adoring biographer without of course any reference to what Ambedkar had told the delegation, 'Ambedkar returned to Bombay on January 13, 1946, and left for Sholapur... Addressing a public meeting at the place, Ambedkar declared vehemently that if the Scheduled Castes Federation candidates [that is, his candidates] were not returned, he would surrender to the Congress, wear a white cap and work under the Congress.' 'The Provincial elections were held,' the biographer continues. 'It was all over with Ambedkar's Scheduled Castes Federation. His party was utterly routed. Absence of and indifference to the cooperation of caste Hindu votes [that is, of the votes of groups which he had been abusing for a quarter of a century] and lack of organization made Ambedkar eat his words which he had uttered at Sholapur. This was a stunning blow to his prestige as a leader, which drove him to desperation and his bitter mind began to think of drastic methods...'[2]

Even if I had exerted alongside Ambedkar for twenty-five years to fight all who were striving for Independence, how would any of these facts be altered?

'The attempt of the well-known journalist Arun Shourie to lower the stature of such a gigantic personality, the creator of the Constitution of modern India, and the emperor

---

2 Dhananjay Keer, *Dr. Ambedkar, Life and Mission,* Popular Prakashan, Bombay, 1990, p. 378.

of the hearts of crores and crores of Indians, Dr Babasaheb Ambedkar is a hateful attempt,' writes the director of one of the 'Research Centres' founded in the name of Ambedkar. 'In reality, it testifies less to the great Dr Ambedkar and more to the hatred and jealousy which this twentieth-century slave of Manuwadi thinking bears towards the crores and crores of Dalits and poor,' the director continues. 'But he should remember that just as even today, centuries after the death of that blot on humanity, Manu, Manuwad survives, so also Ambedkarwad is alive and shall grow in strength by the day. Only one of the two—Manuwad or Ambedkarwad—is to stay alive. Babasaheb had in any case dug the grave of Manuwad by burning *Manusmriti* in 1927. Now the Dalits and the poor are only completing the task by throwing mud over the grave. The day is not far now when the very name of Manuwad will be erased from this earth. For saving the country, even rabid Manuwadis like Arun Shourie will be compelled to sing the praises of Ambedkarwad. A famous journalist like him should be ashamed of the fact that even today he is saturated with hatred towards such a great personality... To find fault with a person who has been acclaimed in the country as well as abroad is nothing short of treason... I therefore request and warn Arun Shourie to remove the spectacles of hate from his eyes...'

That from the director of a 'Research Centre'. You would have noticed that in all this there is not even an allusion to a single fact, there is not the slightest answer to what Ambedkar had himself said time and again about his *not* having been the author of the Constitution. But omission is not the only feature of such argumentation, there is fabrication.

The director continues: 'And there remains the point about his entering the Constituent Assembly. Manuwadis like Arun Shourie of that time had spared no effort to prevent him from entering the Constituent Assembly. But even then he arrived, triumphing from Bengal.' Ambedkar himself had tried to persuade the British to grant his Scheduled Castes nominees two (later three) seats in the Interim Government on the basis of the fact that he had been able to get elected in indirect elections through the Bengal Assembly. Both Atlee, who was by now prime minister, and Pethick-Lawrence, who was by now Secretary of State for India, pooh-poohed the claim. As we have seen, Pethick-Lawrence informed Atlee that the election had been by proportional representation, and the extent to which Ambedkar had won because of the votes of 'Independents' and Anglo-Indians (that is, sections which had opposed the national movement like him) was not evident. On the assessment of his adoring biographer Ambedkar had got elected from Bengal with the help of the Muslim League.

Those communications to and from Ambedkar too have been published, as of course has the assessment in his biography, but naturally they are of no concern to our director. Quite the contrary, he proceeds to buttress his argument by a truly breathtaking invention. He says, 'To remove him from the Constituent Assembly, those Manuwadis of the time then conspired to give over the Hindu-majority areas of Bengal to the then East Pakistan.' That leaders who had spent their entire lives to win freedom for a united India—for decades and decades when Ambedkar was striving alongside the British to thwart them—would be so frightened of a politician—of one whose party had been so decisively trounced by the Scheduled Castes themselves in the elections—as to partition Bengal and hand it over to Pakistan just to get him out of the Constituent Assembly, how much more fantastic can inventions and fabrications get!

As we have seen, the facts again are the exact opposite, and they too are part of the record. True, Ambedkar stood to lose his seat in the Constituent Assembly as a result of the partition of Bengal. So did Shyama Prasad Mookerjee of the Jan Sangh—did the leaders of the national movement want just as desperately to see Mookerjee out? More important, how did Ambedkar then continue in the Assembly? By the same means as Mookerjee did and several others who had never been part of the Congress. The Congress leaders had gone out of their way to ensure that the Constituent Assembly consisted of all sections of opinion, they had gone to the farthest extent possible to erase all feelings of hurt about the past role of individuals. As we have seen, the Congress had complete mastery over the Assembly: of 296 seats 205 had gone to the Congress, and seventy-three to the Muslim League; but as the latter had boycotted the Assembly, the Congress in effect had 205 of 223 seats. Yet in constituting the seven-member Drafting Committee, the party ensured that only one of the seven members was from the Congress. And it elected as its chairman Ambedkar who had throughout opposed the Congress. It was because of this spirit of reaching out that, as we have seen, when Ambedkar was set to lose his seat in the Assembly, Dr Rajendra Prasad and Sardar Patel were the ones who directed the then chief minister of the Bombay Presidency, B.G. Kher, to ensure that Ambedkar was elected forthwith from Bombay so that he could continue in the Assembly—just as Dr Rajendra Prasad wrote to Dr B.C. Roy, for instance, to ensure that Shyama Prasad Mookerjee and K.C. Neogy were elected from Bengal. These letters too are part of the published record.

But you won't find either the biographers or the directors of Ambedkar institutes referring to them. We have seen that Ambedkar himself had been surprised at this large-heartedness, and for once had expressed gratitude for it: recall what he told the Constituent Assembly in his concluding speech—'As to the compliments which have been showered upon me both by members of the Assembly as well as by my colleagues of the Drafting Committee, I feel so overwhelmed that I cannot find adequate words to express fully my gratitude to them. I came into the Constituent Assembly with no greater aspiration than to safeguard the interests of the Scheduled Castes. I had not the remotest idea that I would be called upon to undertake more responsible functions. I was therefore greatly surprised when the Assembly elected me to the Drafting Committee. I was more than surprised when the Drafting Committee elected me to be its Chairman. There were in the Drafting Committee men bigger, better and more competent than myself such as my friend Sir Alladi Krishnaswami Ayyar. I am grateful to the Constituent Assembly for reposing in me so much trust and confidence and to have chosen me as their instrument and given me this opportunity of serving the country...'

Do these words bear out the sort of invention which his followers put out today, and of which the letter of the director is an example?

Dr Babasaheb Ambedkar could have easily got the post of the president of India if he had supported the Congress party, writes another indignant correspondent. But he resigned from the ministry. From where does this surmise come—that he could easily have become president? Dr Rajendra Prasad had been the president of the Constituent Assembly, he had conducted the affairs with great tact and understanding, he had won the affection and regard of all. The elections had demonstrated—not once but thrice—that rumours of Ambedkar's hold over even the Scheduled Castes were grossly exaggerated. Why would the Congress have given him the presidency of the country easily?

Arun Shourie finds fault with Babasaheb for opposing the national movement, but Bhagat Singh also opposed this movement. Did Bhagat Singh thereupon join the British as minister? It is not the Independence of the country that

Bhagat Singh opposed, as Ambedkar did. Bhagat Singh opposed the notion that the struggle for Independence must be wholly non-violent.

Arun Shourie faults Babasaheb for having joined the Viceroy's Council. But M.S. Aney, Sarker, Joginder Singh, Mody, Sir C.P. Ramaswami were all in the same government also, a correspondent points out. True, as we have noted, they were, and if I were writing a book on them, I would deal with their role in detail. But the articles to which the reader was objecting, and this book deals with Ambedkar. And the reason for writing about him and not about these other sundry figures is simply that he has been made, as they have not the basis of casteist and destructive politics.

'By his article, 'Which Ambedkar is the author?', Arun Shourie has hurt the sentiments of millions of Indians by casting aspersions on Babasaheb Ambedkar,' writes another correspondent. 'I request him to refrain from writing against the SC/STs as they form an integral part of Indian society.' But the article in question had done absolutely nothing but recapitulate the steps through which the right to property, the due process clause etc. had passed, and it had done so by reproducing verbatim what Ambedkar had himself said on these clauses in the Constituent Assembly and in Parliament. Where do sentiments come into the picture? But notice the logic: millions of Indians have convinced themselves that Ambedkar is the author of the Constitution; to state facts to the contrary, even if these are nothing but statements of Ambedkar himself, hurts the sentiments of these millions; ergo, they should not be recalled. Not just that. As the letter indicates, to do so is to write against Scheduled Castes and Scheduled Tribes!

'But these are events of long ago,' writes yet another correspondent. 'What relevance do they have today? It is in bad taste for Shourie to try and tarnish the name of Babasaheb by digging up these outdated facts when millions have accepted Babasaheb as their saviour.' But in what sense are the facts 'outdated'? The very fact that he has been made into an icon makes them relevant. His writings and views continue to be reproduced verbatim in journals—in particular in journals which heap poison on others in the name of Dalits. Indeed, his slanted reading of history, his glorification of the British, his denunciations of Gandhiji and the national movement for freedom are not just reproduced relentlessly today, they are treated as foundations on which further 'scholarship' is to be built. To take just one instance, recall the memorandum Ambedkar had sent to A.V. Alexander of the British Cabinet Mission and what he had told Lord Wavell, the viceroy, just months before the country got its Independence: the Clives, Hastings and Cootes did not capture India, he had told them, we Untouchables conquered it for you. That was said out of pride, and some hurt—the ground for the latter was the old one: we did so much for you, but you are leaving us in the lurch.

Such protestations of fidelity to the imperial power would be an embarrassment for one and all today. But not for the Dalit leadership of today. Far from it they are the precedent to be followed, they are the assertions and statements of the inspired leaders which are to be elaborated and documented. *'British Empire was built with the help of Untouchable soldiers,'* proclaims the journal which is so greatly patronized by our progressive intellectuals, *Dalit Voice.* 'Was there any "India" before the arrival of the Britishers?' the article asks, and answers, 'Historians say that there was nothing like India. The subcontinent was ruled by 542 kings, small and big.' 'It was the British who conquered and built India with the help of an Untouchable army of "Pariahs" of Madras,' it continues in bold type. 'The Pariahs (Untouchables) helped them conquer Burma, Ceylon, Pakistan, and Bangladesh. The British named this empire as "India" in the 19th century.'

'The fact is that the first territory the British East India Company acquired was Madras,' it tells us. 'The British company bosses needed men and women for domestic service as well as to guard their properties and commercial goods. They tried to recruit men and women from the Indian society irrespective of caste and creed but none came forward to serve the Europeans except the Pariahs of Madras...' 'The Untouchables (Pariahs) of Madras,' the journal resumes in bold type, 'shed their sweat and blood to build the British Empire in the world. It was the British who laid the foundation-stone for the present-day progress of India. The other caste people including the Shudras were not willing to join the service under the Europeans...'

'The British had high praise for the Dalit Army for their brave qualities, reliability, sincerity and honesty. Sepoys in large numbers joined the British Army,' it notes with pride. 'The British called this Army the Sappers and Miners of Madras. It was the first regiment in the whole of India...' 'The British people were once boasting that "the sun never sets on the British Empire",' the journal recalls, and reminds us, 'Such a large Empire was built with the help of the Untouchable Army of Madras. For about two centuries other caste men did not join the service under the East India Company.' It recounts the perfidy with which Arcot was captured, but the moral it draws is the exact opposite of what you would expect. It recounts how at the crucial stage Clive's band was in difficulties, and goes on, 'Meanwhile Clive's army within the fort suffered due to shortage of food. Half the English soldiers (100) died. Indian Sepoys of Madras (Untouchables) who loved Clive told him that they would forego their share of cooked rice, which could be distributed to the English soldiers and they (Indian Sepoys) would be satisfied with the watery substance (Kanji) of the cooked rice.'

It proceeds to recall that eventually, after he had received another reinforcement of Sepoys from Madras,

Clive succeeded and soon enough conquered Carnatic. 'The empire-building activity of the British started with Arcot,' proclaims the journal with pride. 'Clive was honoured with golden-sword when he went back to England.'

'This was the second conquest of the British in the South within a short period,' we are told. 'The Company launched its empire-building in North India by conquering Bengal with the help of the Madras Army. They raised an Army in Bengal consisting exclusively of Untouchables of the area. For nearly two centuries the Hindus did not enter the British services under the English or under any other Europeans. The British built their Empire exclusively with the help of Untouchables who loved the British because unlike Hindus they did not observe racism and respected the human rights of Untouchables.'[3]

That is not just elaboration of Ambedkar's protestations, it is the legacy: apart from everything else, look at the inversion—helping the British conquer India becomes the badge of honour, not entering their service to do so becomes the mark of shame ! And all this is being proclaimed not in 1946, as Ambedkar did, but in 1996.

There was nothing wrong in Babasaheb supporting the Partition of the country, writes another correspondent carrying forward the argument of the journal, for in any case the British gave us India, not the Manuwadis. Babasaheb's statement that granting Independence to the country would be the greatest disaster was correct, writes yet another correspondent: the Narasimha Raos, the Sukhrams, the Harshad Mehtas, the Satish Sharmas, the Jayalalithaas have shown that his prediction was correct. All one need say in response is that the fact that such arguments are put forward fifty years after the country has been independent, and that editors feel compelled to publish them bears out all the apprehensions on which this book is based.

But 'arguments' are the smallest part of the arsenal.

3 *Dalit Voice*, 16–30 September 1996, pp. 9–10.

19

Intimidation as argument, assault as proof

It happened so swiftly, in just a few seconds. But it made for headlines in the next morning's papers—four column photographs and all.

Avinash Dharmadhikari had been in the IAS till recently. He had resigned from the service so that he may do more for our society by entering public life. A group devoted to cleaning governance had scheduled a meeting in Pune on 26 February 1996. Mr B.G. Deshmukh, the former Cabinet secretary, was to preside. Avinash was to speak, explaining what had led him to forsake the IAS and indicate what he planned to do in the future. He had pressed me to be present, and give my views on what persons like him who were now outside the administration could do.

It had been a bad day. I had fallen very sick the previous night, and had been tired out further by a lecture at the Symbiosis Management Institute that morning. But there was no way to stay away from the function.

On reaching the venue I was quite surprised—as I always am—at the large number who had gathered. The organizers had scheduled the meeting in an open ground as they had estimated that the gathering would be larger than could be accommodated in any of Pune's halls—and Pune with its long tradition of public lectures has a number of large halls. But the numbers who had turned up were larger than even the organizers had anticipated. Every chair was occupied, many were standing, many-deep on all sides.

But there was no way in which I could speak for long. So Avinash agreed that I would speak first for a few minutes, explain the illness and request leave of the audience.

Mr Deshmukh, Avinash and I had just about sat down on the stage, the compere had just about started asking me to speak that there was some rushing on the left, the side on which I was seated. By the time I turned to look, two or three youngsters had made their way on to the platform. *'Tumhine Babasaheb Ambedkar ke against kutch likha hai?'*—Aren't you the one who has written against Babasaheb Ambedkar?, asked one of them, *'Aapne mera likha hua kuch bhi padha hai kya?'*—Have you read anything I have written?— I asked even as my mind raced, 'Why is this fellow here?' I had not completed the sentence that I saw the other youth positioning a bottle of sorts. A moment later he had splattered me with black paint. And the youth fled. Everyone was taken aback. Naturally, I went up to the mike and told the audience that while, because of illness, I had planned not to speak much, I would now definitely speak. So that I may wash off the paint we would revert to the original programme: Avinash would speak first.

Having washed myself and changed into another shirt, I had my say. And naturally, the audience was even more attentive than it might have been otherwise. The meeting lasted for two-and-a-half hours after the incident.

When I returned to the platform one of the organizers handed me the handbill which associates of the young men had thrown around before running away. I had been smeared on behalf of the Republican Party of India, Pune City, the handbill proclaimed, for defaming Dr Ambedkar.

What had been done was certainly no spontaneous

outburst of rage at what I had written. The assault had a precursor, I was later told. A 'Unity Rally' of the several factions and splinters of the Republican Party and other Dalit organizations had been held in Bombay on 28 January 1996. At this convention a Dalit leader, Jogendra Kawade had denounced me and my articles in vehement terms, he had declared that I was 'betraying the very soil of this country'—Mr Kawade, if you must know, was earlier most in the news when he had founded the Dalit-Muslim Mahasangha in association with, if you please, Haji Mastan, the notorious smuggler.

The handbill said that the action was being taken because of two articles which I had written—but these had been published almost two months earlier, the handbill itself gave the dates. Moreover, the young men just did not seem the kind who read my articles. They had obviously been put up. This was confirmed by what the papers published and what Avinash Dharmadhikari told me the next day: *The Indian Express* reported the next day that later that evening a local leader of the Republican Party, one Avinash Salve had telephoned *The Indian Express* and claimed credit for the performance; it turned out that the person had telephoned another paper earlier in the day and proclaimed that his party men would carry out this deed. In any case, people don't come to public meetings equipped with bottles of paint expecting to be outraged. So, spontaneous outburst at something I might have said or done there and then, it certainly was not.

And what exactly had I written? The articles that had been published till then were based entirely on what Ambedkar himself had written and said. They were based entirely on volumes which have been published at public expense by the Government of Maharashtra in honour of Ambedkar. Does freedom of speech mean that while governments and others shall publish what Ambedkar wrote, the rest of us are not to have the freedom to even quote what they have published? In any case, if something was wrong in what I had written, did the remedy not lie in writing a reasoned and documented reply in the papers?

But that is the one thing such leaders and groups never do. Their speciality is an entirely different one, and they have perfected an entire technology to go with it.

Denunciations at public meetings attended by persons hardly any of whom would have read what the target had written. The smearing of the person with the verbal equivalent of that black paint—with pejoratives, labels and the rest: 'representative of communal and casteist forces', that is the currently fashionable label. The purpose is threefold. First, to scare the person himself, to make him self-conscious of his writing and work—even this works: how often we see our intellectuals say one thing in private and quite the opposite in their writings lest someone brand them 'communal' or afflicted by the 'high-caste bias'. Second, to scare others: this works to an even greater extent—seeing the avalanche that has descended on that one person, a hundred are scared away from saying in public what they acknowledge in private. Third, to scare away one's own followers from the work of that person, to keep them from getting influenced by it, or, to use the politically correct word, from getting contaminated by what the person has written. The greater the difficulty that the leaders have in coming up with facts which would refute what the person has written, the greater their recourse to the label, to the smear, to verbal terrorism so as to scare away their own followers from examining what the person is saying.

Bombardment is an essential element in this labelling and smearing, bombardment of newspapers and their editors. With letters—preferably posted from different places—with phone calls, with visits, and once in a while with demonstration. In this too there are many variants. Most of the letters and phone calls, for instance, are just vituperation. But the sheer volume of them unnerves many: Why take on unnecessary trouble?, most of us conclude, haven't we enough as it is? Even the one who is not going to be scared concludes, 'In any case, the letters show that the articles have hurt the feelings of many persons.' The other variant is to send some pseudo-scholarly 'refutations': papers have on occasion sent me refutations of this sort for comments—in verse X, Sura Y of the Quran it says...declares the article, and in verse Z, Sura A it says...and in verse B, Sura C...The busy editor seldom has time to have the citations examined, and few of us have the sort of background knowledge which will enable one at a glance to make out whether what the fellow is saying has any substance to it. 'There are two sides to the matter,' we conclude, and take the safest course—publish the 'refutations' for now and avoid such subjects in the future. The intimidators' purpose is served.

The bombardment is not always merely literary, the demonstrations are not always confined merely to shouting slogans. Papers in Uttar Pradesh, in Andhra have had their offices attacked, their vans burnt by demonstrators who claimed to have been upset by the columns of mine which the papers had been kind enough to publish. The anger was manifestly not spontaneous: in those cases too the articles which were being made the occasion of the attacks had appeared weeks and weeks earlier.

There is a corresponding technology in regard to public meetings. The commonest of these is to place your men at strategic places in the hall, and at some pre-arranged signal for all of them to start shouting simultaneously. And when others in the audience try to pacify you or when they ask you to take your place and not interrupt the meeting, to start accusing the speaker and the organizers of 'fascism', of being 'anti-democratic', of suppressing opinions which are uncomfortable to them, etc. I have encountered this technique often. A meeting in Vishakhapatnam had been going on in a jam-packed hall for almost two hours; an innocuous question was asked about my views on reservations; I explained briefly why I was opposed to them, and what I thought we should have in their stead; suddenly, half a dozen young men started shouting simultaneously, each insisting that he be allowed to speak immediately, and from the stage... They just would not stop. Even after the meeting was over they trailed me to the waiting car shouting slogans—I was a spokesman of casteist forces, they shouted, five years from now the likes of me would not be allowed to speak anywhere in the country, they shouted. Next day that is what the papers focused on—that representatives of OBCs, etc. had disrupted the meeting.

Some months ago the Andhra Pradesh High Court Bar Association and other bar associations of Hyderabad and Secunderabad asked me to speak on the Supreme Court's judgments on the Uniform Civil Code. I reached the hall a bit before time. The hall was packed. I was introduced to several judges of the high court, several senior advocates and others. As there was still time I was seated by the organizers between a judge of the high court and an advocate wearing the black coat of the profession. We chatted amiably. The advocate, a Muslim gentleman, remarked how he had been reading my articles on Islamic law. He said he did not agree with all that I wrote, but he had no doubts as to the scholarship, the sincerity, etc. Well, the meeting started. I had been speaking for some time, and suddenly this very man stood up and started shouting, 'You are a fraud, you are a fraud, I am saying you are a fraud...' And simultaneously a dozen more started shouting and insisting that they be heard.

And then a thing happened which served the purpose of these persons to the dot. Even though the organizers were appealing to everyone to remain calm, and to remain in their seats, so many in the audience were so upset by what these persons were doing, and as a large proportion of the audience consisted of local advocates they recognised who these persons were and who they were fronting for, that hundreds started shouting these few down. The hall was soon clear of them, and the meeting went on for an hour and a half after the incident. But the shouters had already accomplished two things: thinking that the din might end in a fracas, some of the judges of the high court left; and of course the small disruption made it to the papers the next day. The ringleaders duly rang up the papers to claim credit; their names were thereby in the papers. They turned out to be the son and 'advocate' of the local Muslim leader—a person who, though a formidable fundamentalist in his own right, has been facing rebellion from an erstwhile strongman of his, and is therefore ever on the lookout for 'issues' and headlines.

'Arun Shourie pays for his sins'

The incident in Pune had happened on 26 February 1996. The 1–15 April issue of *Dalit Voice,* the fortnightly magazine much patronized by our progressive intellectuals, carried an article, 'Arun Shourie pays for his sins: Dalits protest Nazi lies.' It was the sort of thing which today passes for 'Dalit literature'.

It was said to be by 'Our Correspondent' but was obviously written by the editor of the magazine, V.T. Rajshekhar. For over a decade now this man has been spreading poison in the name of 'Dalits', and not just poison against individuals—at the height of killings in Punjab he was writing hosannas to Bhindranwale, and my progressive friends used to consider it de rigueur to reproduce and regurgitate the poison. To do so was to be 'authentic', it was to put the country's ear next to 'the mouth of people'. To this day patronizing such stuff is as necessary for, in any case as helpful for establishing one's credentials as wearing Kolhapur chappals, having a four-day stubble, and smoking bidis. Calling such persons to one's seminar is what makes the seminar 'authentic', the gathering at which 'the real voice of the people' has been heard. I need hardly add that perhaps no other section has patronized his kind, and Rajshekhar personally as much as the Christian missionaries.

Here is the full text of the article.

* * *

Bangalore: Finally, the Hindu nazi journalist, Arun Shourie, has been punished by some Ambedkarites of Pune. They applied tar on his face on Feb. 27, 1996 at a public meeting of 'Socialist Brahmins'.

For nearly a decade we have been receiving complaints from Sikhs, Muslims, Christians whom he has been consistently maligning through his writings and speeches. None had the courage to teach him a lesson. Only Ambedkarites had the guts.

As Express editor: But many people do not know the metamorphosis of this Punjabi Brahmin. When he returned from World Bank he became the editor of *Indian Express* at a young age and our boss at the fag end of our career in that daily. He used to like us and support us in our fight against brahminical forces in the Bangalore office of the *Indian Express.* How much he used to admire us and our writings could be proved from the fact that he sent a copy of his first book, *Hinduism - Essence & Consequence* (Vikas 1979). This book was torn to pieces by the upper caste reviewers because in it he criticized the Vaidik vampires and their sacred scriptures. He called it a bundle of contradictions, wordmongering and speculative philosophy. He profusely quoted Upanishads and even denounced brahminism as devoid of ethics.

He questioned the Hindu claim of non-violence, tolerance and such other bullshit.

In fact, we were so shocked on reading this book that we quoted him in the very first book published by the Dalit Sahitya Akademy (*Brahminism - The Curse of India,* 1981). We sent him a copy of our book and he wrote back commending our work. This was the Shourie of the 70s.

If you ask him today he might even deny having written the above-referred book. Because the Shourie of the 90s is an entirely different man.

What brought about this right-about-turn?

Jatwalas upset: When his first book was attacked left and right, torn to pieces and even Vikas forced to withdraw the book, the Punjabi Brahmin quickly realized what upset his *Jatwalas* and what he should do to please them.

The transformation of Arun Shourie from being a bitter critic of brahminism into a blind admirer of brahminism, which automatically made him fan flames of hatred against Sikhs first, then Christians, and then Muslims and finally Dalits, is an interesting story by itself.

Hindu belief system: A Hindu believes what he wants to believe. What he believes need not be a fact. A Hindu is a victim of his belief system.

The young Arun Shourie, fresh from his American education and World Bank background, did not know all this. His love to speak out the *Truth* made him write the famous book, *Hinduism -Essence & Consequence.* He was young and idealistic. He hated injustice. He joined the human rights movement and became vice-president of People's Union for Civil Liberties (PUCL) in Delhi.

His love for justice and truth annoyed his *Jatwalas* and his first book was torn to pieces. He became very 'unpopular' for speaking out the truth.

When he was under all-out attack by the Hindu nazis, we in Bangalore wanted to honour him for writing this book and wrote to him about it but he had no time to come here.

The Punjabi *vaidik* quickly realised that if he had to become 'popular' he must please his *Jatwalas.* The Hindu believes what he wants to believe. He believes that Sikhs, Christians, Muslims are anti-nationais, terrorists, fundamentalists and what not.

Sikh struggle for identity: Just at that time Punjab was hotting up and Sant Bhindranwale was leading the Sikh struggle for identity which the Punjabi Hindus hated. The Punjabi Hindu in Arun Shourie worked and he started selling the idea that Sikhs are anti-national. He went round the country on a speaking spree denouncing Sikhs as anti-national and terrorists and that gave him good publicity in the brahminical toilet papers.

PUCL, however, took strong objection to his spreading the falsehood and he was expelled. From then on he was unstoppable. Today, Arun Shourie is the darling of Hindu nazis because like all Hindus he believes what he wants to believe. His books are selling like hot cakes. He gets awards and rewards. He gets money, name and fame. What more does he want?

Muslim-baiting: In the course of his search for 'popularity', he might have sacrificed *Truth* and sided with injustice. So what? A Hindu believes what he wants to believe. Who bothers about justice and Truth? Ruling upper castes, who trample upon the human rights of the over 85% of the oppressed Indians, are not bothered about justice and *Truth.*

We don't want to go into what he said on Dalits, Babasaheb Ambedkar, Muslims, the Prophet, Christ, Church, Christians, Sikhs and their Gurus. All that he said are available in the pulp. So much for this brahminical belief system which is playing havoc with our society. As it is a separate subject we don't want to deal with it here.

Nature's reply at Pune: Arun Shourie has become a top Hindu nazi leader today—earning in millions like all other Hindu nazis. He was the chief guest at an RSS meeting at Mangalore recently. Medha Patkar, a Maharashtrian Brahmin, was the chief guest, when he was honoured by the Hindu nazi organisation.

Hindu nazis believe that Babri Masjid was a Hindu temple. And that is why they demolished it—later they paid dearly for it. The UP electorate rejected the Hindu nazi party. It was a collective action. The Pune attack on Arun Shourie was an individual action. But both are actions of history.

Lies, crimes on weaker sections can continue for sometime but nature will manufacture its own resistance to lies and injustices. The Pune incident is nature's reply to Arun Shourie's excesses.

But did he realise it? No. *Deccan Herald* (Feb. 28, '96) reports from Pune:

Later, Shourie mounted an attack on the RPI [the Republican Party of India] and said those who talk about Dr. Ambedkar disregard the freedom of expression enshrined in the Constitution. 'What will happen if these people (the miscreants) come to power?' Shourie asked. 'If the act of blackening someone's face can ensure social equality, I am willing to blacken my face everyday,' he said.

Shourie talked about his 'right for free speech and expression' assured in the Constitution. Yes, the Constitution does assure it.

Editor's arrest under TADA: But it depends on who exercised it. If members of the Brahminical Social Order did it nothing will happen to them. Nothing happened to the Nazi Shiv Sena Chief Bal Thackeray when he attacked Muslims and Islam.

But this writer was arrested under TADA in 1986 for our *Dalit Voice* Editorial (Feb. 16, 1986: 'Khalistan Forced on unwilling Sikhs'). This was reproduced by an English weekly, *Dignity*, published from Chandigarh. And this was found objectionable under the TADA. The Chandigarh police came to Bangalore, arrested us, handcuffed us and kept us in Chandigarh jail for 15 days and then quickly released with an apology from the Govt. of India. Why this writer was arrested under TADA?

Why our passport continues to be impounded? Did not the Constitution assure the freedom of press? Yes it did. And still we were arrested under TADA and denied passport.

Similarly, Arun Shourie's face was blackened by the angry Ambedkarites at Pune.

Our people in Karnataka took out *Jatha* to carry the message of Babasaheb to every village but they were violently attacked by the upper castes at Bidar (*DV* Feb. 1, '96, p.3: 'Hindu Nazis attack Dalit *Jatha*').

Centuries of crimes against Dalits: Arun Shourie at Pune loudly protested and quoted the Constitution. But does he know that his *jatwalas* have been kicking, killing, raping, murdering and destroying the little property of Untouchables for centuries? Where was Arun Shourie? What did he do?

We can go on giving hundreds of examples of upper caste crimes against our people but one small incident of Pune is magnified because the obliging brahminical press was there to report it. The same press suppresses the daily crimes on Dalits, Muslims and others. Arun knows it and also wrote about it in his first book.

When Arun Shourie wrote the *Truth* we wanted to honour him but when he wrote untruth our people got angry and humiliated him. We assure him that tomorrow if he does something good, the same Pune Dalits will call him and honour him.

Dalit warning: The daily persecutions of Dalits are continuing in India because the victims of crimes have tolerated such Shouries for too long. The moment they get 'educated' and enlightened by the burning thoughts of Babasaheb, they will blacken or even flatten the face of all the Shouries. That day is only four years away.

This is the warning to Arun Shourie who continues to be a good friend of this writer because we have nothing against him personally.

Remember: Awakened Ambedkarites will refuse to tolerate injustice and untruth. The Shouries are warned.

* * *

The minor point in such writing is the untruth on which it is based. To say nothing of the motives it seeks to paste, here are just a few examples from among the 'facts' on which the article rests its venom.

Never have I said that Sikhs are anti-national; what I wrote about was Bhindranwale, and that what he had come to stand for and the movement he was directing would spell disaster for our country, in particular for the Sikhs; all of that, alas, came to pass; and far from denigrating the Sikhs gurus, my point was that what Bhindranwale was doing was completely contrary to the teaching of the gurus.

Never did I support these 'activists' in anything they were doing against 'Brahminical forces' or forces of any other hue in *The Indian Express;* quite the contrary: on joining *The Indian Express* in 1979 I learnt that persons who were trying to make out that they were fighting 'oppression', etc., in the paper's Bangalore edition were actually the ones who had shot off memoranda to Mrs Gandhi during the Emergency asking her to take over the paper!

Vikas never withdrew my book from the market or anywhere; quite the contrary—they have been so kind as to suggest on several occasions that the book be republished; the reason it has not been republished too has been simple: the book was essentially about the inadequacy of the explanations which our religions give to account for the existence of suffering; but having spent twenty years serving, and loving and being taught by our child, my view of suffering has changed, it has probably deepened—meditation and immersion in the teachings of the Buddha have helped crystallize the experience to which our child awakened us; I do plan to return to the subject—the explanations for suffering—but do not as yet feel up to the task. As for my not acknowledging that I wrote the book, in each of the twelve subsequent books the list 'By the same author' has this particular one at the very top! All this however is of no account to these poisoners: for them the answer is as simple as it is set—if a person says something that accords with what they want to hear, then he is doing so because he is pursuing *Truth;* if he says something contrary, he is seeking popularity in the Brahminical order!

I have never been the vice-president of the People's Union of Civil Liberties.

I have never been expelled from the PUCL.

I never said at Pune, 'If the act of blackening someone's face can ensure social equality, I am willing to blacken my face every day'—Avinash Dharmadhikari, the former IAS official said that, and I felt it was exactly the kind of grandiloquence which gives licence to the bullies.

Though I would have gladly gone for an RSS function, the function for which I went to Mangalore was not of the RSS; it was a function of the Justice K.S. Hegde Foundation; this was the third year since the award was instituted; in the first year it was conferred on Mr Shivram Karanth, in the second on Ms Medha Patkar.

Far from being the 'good friend' of persons such as the editor of this magazine, I believe them to be a curse on public discourse and therefore on our country today.

And so on.

Nor are such untruths without consequence. By them these persons create hate-figures—'anti-Muslim', 'anti-Christian', 'anti-Sikh', 'anti-Dalit'. Few among those to whom such rhetoric is addressed would have read anything that the person in question would have written. But as the canard is repeated again and again, some hothead among them will take it into his head to 'rid the Republic of this troublesome priest'. And these fellows will write another article, 'Arun Shourie pays for his sins'.

Notice too their idea of free speech. The abuse and worse that Ambedkar hurled at Gandhiji for twenty years, why that must be published by the Government of Maharashtra and sold at subsidised prices—as part of the country's tribute to Ambedkar, and because everyone has a right to his opinion. But if you so much as reproduce what the very same volumes record Ambedkar to have written in praise of the British, if you so much as recall what he did as the minister in the Viceroy's Council, why you are being 'anti-Dalit', and it is but right that you should 'pay for your sins'.

Another warning

The very next issue of this magazine, that dated 16–30 April 1996, carried another broadside, *'Warning to Arun Shourie'*. Again, the article is worth reading in full to see the mindset of the ones who have set themselves up in the name of 'Dalits' and also to see the mindset they exert to instil in their followers. Here is the text of the article:

* * *

Enraged Dalits may repeat Pune:
Shourie must stop his nonsense

Our Correspondent

Bangalore: A number of our readers have sent us clippings of *The Asian Age,* (Dec. 29, 1995) titled 'A loyal Minister always covers up a scandal', written by the well publicised 'investigative journalist', Arun Shourie.

The Minister referred to is Babasaheb Ambedkar, who was the Labour Member (minister) in the Viceroy's Executive Council, and the scandal sought to be covered up was the payment of Rs. 13,000 by the Govt. to the noted Marxist leader, M.N. Roy, every month for the purpose of propagating that there was no tumultuous reaction to the arrest of the leaders of the 'Quit India Movement' launched by the Congress on Aug. 9, 1942. The author has sought to prove that Babasaheb took pains to cover up a major scandal for the British Govt. In simple words, the author tries to project Babasaheb as more loyal to British than the Indian cause.

British stooge: The object of this Punjabi Brahmin's article is to paint Babasaheb as a stooge of the British. (*DV* April 1996 p.6: *'Arun Shourie pays for his sins'.)*

Naturally, simpletons among Dalit scholars feel agitated and ask us to rebut the charge.

But we will not rebut Shourie's charges. As experts on *'Hindu Mind'* we are not prepared to fall into the trap laid by Shourie. This is what he has been doing with Muslims, Sikhs and Christians. Attack them, their honoured personalities, their manners and customs and their sacred institutions, their books and beliefs, so that their entire attention is spent on their rebuttal.

Vaidiks know that offence is the best form of defence. Our Pune Ambedkarite brothers also knew this and taught him a good lesson on Feb. 27, '96. Their only single, simple action is more than writing a book rebutting Shourie's bullshit.

That is why we don't want to rebut the charges because we are experts in the art of using the weapons of the enemy against the enemy itself.

We are happy that Shourie has sought to tarnish the name of Babasaheb, the Father of India, because by doing so, he has admitted that the Hindu nazis are now panic-stricken—haunted by

Babasaheb under whose inspiration Dalits have become a mighty force to reckon with.

Nazis roasted alive: Babasaheb's burning thoughts have started roasting the nazis alive and hence the Shouries are shouting and shrieking. Wonderful.

The nazis were initially afraid ot only Muslims. Later the Sikhs started frightening them. Still later the Christians.

Like a mad dog, they have started biting every passer-by. Only lately they have added the Dalits to their list of maligning the original inhabitants of India. And the first direct salvo of this verbal warfare is fired by Arun Shourie against Babasaheb. We are thankful to him for giving this clue of nazi nervousness. We are clubbing the name of Arun Shourie along with the Hindu nazis because we do not consider him a journalist. He does not possess the very first quality of a journalist, i.e. objectivity. A journalist reports impartially, does not twist facts and gives forth right views in an objective manner. He does not trade by projecting the views of one section and suppressing the truth about others. Arun Shourie does the opposite.

We consider Shourie as a propagandist and spokesman of the Hindu nazis. And as such, he has to be loyal to his commanders. Babasaheb has very beautifully said the Brahmins of India have produced any number of 'learned' people but not a single intellectual. Arun Shourie proves this point.

Congress 'Quit India' call: A deep study of the story reveals many things which go against Shourie's very commanders. In the words of our noted Dalit writer, S.K. Biswas, the very Quit India call was hastily given by the Congress out of panic upon Babasaheb's elevation to the position of a Law Member in the Viceroy's Executive Council on July 20, 1942.

'Before this historic and significant incident, there had been, for the last 2,000 years, no Untouchable, no *shudra,* save Muslim slaves, [who] became a member of the governing class. On this all of a sudden, the Hindu governing class launched a volley of vituperative criticism for Ambedkar's accepting the post of Law Member, under the yoke of the foreign ruler, though Lord Satyendra Nath Sinha was the first man to accept such a posting many decades ago.' (*Hindu Raj,* S.K. Biswas, 1996, Dalit - Bahujan

Intellectuals Forum of India, 109/7" Cross, Palace Lower Orchards, Bangalore - 560 003, Rs. 85.)

The Hindus were afraid that an Untouchable of Babasaheb's calibre would snatch the entire show and if the British remained any more in India, more such Babasahebs would be elevated, and therefore they should 'Quit India' before such a tragedy.

Gandhi as a pigmy: Earlier also, when Moulana Hasrat Mohani had moved the *'Swaraj* Resolution' in the 1921 Congress Session, Gandhi had rejected it saying that Indians were not yet mature for independence, and until every villager knows the value of democracy and self-rule, the demand for *swaraj* must be postponed. This was out of the fear that had the British quit then, Moulana Mohamad Ali, who was the leader of all political movements in India in 1921, would have been the Governor-General or Prime Minister of India. In front of Moulana Mohamad Ali not only Gandhi was a new entrant and a pigmy, but also the Congress was a organisation of rich, lazy, pot-bellied despots and retired bureaucrats. And by 1930, when the Congress had grown into a force and completely brahminised, the same resolution was passed. Not a single person asked Gandhi after the resolution, whether every villager in India had become mature enough to value democracy and self rule. (V.T. Rajshekar: *Why Godse Killed Gandhi,* 1984, DSA.)

Thus the 'Quit India' call was actually an attempt to prevent the rise of Untouchables to higher places of power.

The 'Quit India' call was given on Aug. 9, 1942. This was the most shameful and anti-human fascist call ever given in history. Nowhere have a people been asked to go out to any land. So shameful and fascist that many Congress leaders like Rajaji opposed it.

Dalits liked British rule: Where was the need for Babasaheb to ask the British to 'Quit India'? The Dalits have no reason whatsoever to consider the British rule as bad. So also the Shudras.

The great Shudra scholar, Dr. K.V. Puttappa, Poet-Laureate of Karnataka, said, that he would have been picking cowdung had not the British ruled India. Even Gandhi could not declare British rule as bad.

In the 20's when slogans for complete independence were raised, all Indian native rulers were shocked to hear these things against so benevolent a British rule. Gandhi had agreed but counter argued saying 'Benevolent rule is no substitute for self-rule.' In spite of all hate for the British rule, he was compelled to still consider it as 'benevolent rule'.

When the British rule was not considered as bad by other Brahmin rulers, the Shudras and Untouchables also could not call it so. Government schools were opened for them. The Govt. did not discriminate against them. Uniform laws were applied on all, as against the discriminative laws of Manu. Not only Brahmins like Rajaji but all other non-Brahmin leaders like Periyar EVR and Jinnah were not for 'Quit India'. So also Babasaheb.

Brahmins hated British: In fact, the 'Quit India' movement was directed more against Untouchables, Muslims, Sikhs and Shudras than against the British. The protections afforded to these communities under the Govt. of India Act 1935 were telling hard upon the Brahmins. They were afraid of more erosion of their caste privileges if the British continued this policy for longer time to the benefit of other communities.

Therefore, we don't see anything wrong in Babasaheb scuttling the 'Quit India' movement. Rather we are pained at his failure in not destroying this 'movement' in toto.

2. A further study of Shourie's story reveals that though Gandhi was released unconditionally from prison on May 5, 1944, persecution of Babasaheb in the Legislative Assembly by Hindus like T.T. Krishnamachari, Jamnadas Mehta, Lalchand Navalrai, Avinaslingam Chettiar, Badri Dutt Pande, Divan Chimanlal, Satyanarayan Sinha and Maniben Kara continued. Jamnadas Mehta had a special grudge against Babasaheb as the monthly payment was not made to his organisation, Indian Federation of Labour, of which he was the president, but was given to M.N. Roy personally instead of to his Federation, as otherwise Jamnadas Mehta also would have got a share out of it. He was jealous that M.N. Roy had outsmarted him and grabbed the entire money for himself.

3. *Why sympathy for M.N. Roy?:* (1) The irony of the entire story is that Shourie had no accusation against M.N. Roy, who received the money. It is the giver only who is sought to be blamed but not the taker.

4. (2) The money was initially given by the Department of Information and Broadcasting and later through Labour Department. Not a finger was raised against the Information

Dept., and the entire blame was put on Labour Dept. only because Babasaheb was the Labour Member. The conspiracy was only to malign Babasaheb.

5. (3) Questions were raised abruptly without giving any notice. Time and again Babasaheb demanded adequate notice for the question, so that he could call for details from officers and reply. But this was never done. Questions were raised abruptly—only for the purpose of questioning him and grilling him, and never to know the facts.

6. (4) The persecution went on even as late as on April 8, 1946 from Sept. 21, 1942—a period of over four and half years.

7. (5) On Sept. 2, 1946, the Interim Govt. led by Nehru was sworn in of which Babasaheb was not a member. Had he been taken in the Cabinet, or had the Viceroy's Executive Council continued, the torture also would have continued.

Torture chamber: We are thankful to Arun Shourie for digging out these facts, dates, questions and personalities, who all jointly made the Legislative Assembly a torture chamber for Babasaheb.

Bumlicker: One last warning to Shourie. It is his *jatwalas,* any number of them, who were the bumlickers of the British. Only such suckers got British titles like 'Sir', Dewan Bahadur, Rao Bahadur etc. Sir M. Viswesvaraya, Sir C.P. Ramaswamy lyer and most famous Sir Radhakrishnan.

Why Babasaheb did not get the 'Sir' title or any other British royal honour if he had been a sucker or licker? Shourie must stop his nonsense. Or else more Punes will repeat.

This rejoinder of ours should be taken as a model to read between the lines.

* * *

Notice the view of British rule as against the standpoint regarding Gandhiji. Notice the inventions—that Gandhiji opposed the Swaraj resolution of Hasrat Mohani out of the fear that if the British left India at that time Maulana Muhammad Ali of all persons, the very Muhammad Ali who became known in the country because Gandhiji took up the cause of getting him and his brother, Shaukat Ali, released, the very Muhammad

Ali who came to nationwide prominence because Gandhiji took up the cause of the Khilafat and put these two brothers on the stage everywhere, that Gandhiji dreaded Swaraj at the time because he feared that if India became independent at that time this same Muhammad Ali would become Governor General or prime minister! That the Congress leaders passed the Quit India resolution on 8 August 1942 because they got scared by the appointment on 20 July 1942 of Ambedkar to the Viceroy's Council—quite apart from everything else the Congress Working Committee had finalized and released the resolution in mid-July!

And notice that fomenting of the persecution complex: that Ambedkar was questioned in the Assembly about the secret payments to M.N. Roy is presented as 'persecution', indeed as 'torture' by 'Hindus'!

An entire ideology

Intimidation like this is so tempting for the perpetrators only because at any time so very few are doing work of consequence in that field. The maxim of such groups therefore is, 'Thrash one and frighten a hundred.' The answer to that is for a thousand to be doing that kind of work.

At the root of all this is an entire ideology, of condoning, indeed of lauding anything which is done by anyone and everyone who has donned the garb of a leader of the backwards, the Dalits and the Muslims. 'Social Justice' today is nothing but a cover for out-and-out casteist politics. Similarly, 'Dalits' has become the password for, indeed the justification for abuse, for aggression. And such is the condition of our society, in particular of those who control public discourse and of our political leaders, that no one speaks about the poison which is being spread in the name of 'backwards' and 'Dalits'.

It is this ideology which has spawned so many of our

current troubles. An ideology in which, as Ortega Y. Gasset would have said, mediocrity is the norm, in which vulgarity is the right, in which standards are an elitist conspiracy, in which civility and reason are the veneer of the well-to-do, in which intimidation is argument, and assault is proof.

Among the liberals this ideology has become the rationalization for capitulation. And among the leaders of so-called Dalits and OBCs, and of the Muslims it has become the justification for 'direct action'.

Unless this ideology is rolled back the problems that plague us will intensify no end—and paint throwing will be the least of them.

Frequently Cited Texts and Index

Volumes and collections which have been referred to frequently

B.R. Ambedkar, *Dr. Babasaheb Ambedkar, Writings and Speeches,* Volumes 1 to 14, Education Department, Government of Maharashtra, Bombay, 1979–95.

Constituent Assembly Debates, Volumes 1 to 12, Lok Sabha Secretariat, New Delhi, 1985.

Mahatma Gandhi, *Collected Works,* Volumes 1 to 100, Publications Division, Government of India, New Delhi, 1958–93.

Constitutional Relations between Britain and India, The Transfer of Power, Nicholas Mansergh (Editor-in-Chief), Volumes 1 to 12, Her Majesty's Stationery Office, London, 1970–93.

B. Shiva Rao, *The Making of India's Constitution, Select Documents,* Volumes 1 to 4, Indian Institute of Public Administration, New Delhi, 1966–68.

Viceregal Correspondence, Linlithgow Collection, and the *Templewood Collection,* India Office Library and The Public Records Office, London.

National Archives, Government of India, *Home Political Files,* New Delhi.

Note. Throughout the text, unless otherwise indicated, words in italics have been italicized by me, A.S., as have the explanatory words which appear within square parentheses.

Index

Acknowledgements

I am most grateful to the Program for Asian Projects, which is administered by the Magsaysay Foundation and endowed by the Rockefeller Brothers Fund, for their help in completing this study.

To Sita Ram Goel for twice going through the manuscript with a toothcomb.

To my friend and colleague, Sanjay Suri for tracking down several of the documents in the India Office Library and the Public Records Office in London.